Philosophic Classics, Second Edition
Volume V

TWENTIETH-CENTURY PHILOSOPHY

FORREST E. BAIRD, EDITOR
Whitworth College

WALTER KAUFMANN
Late, of Princeton University

Prentice Hall, Upper Saddle River, New Jersey 07458

Library of Congress Cataloging-in-Publication Data

Philosophic classics / Forrest E. Baird, editor.—3rd ed.
    p. cm.
    "Walter Kaufmann, late, of Princeton University."
    Includes bibliographical references.
    Contents: v. 1. Ancient philosophy—v. 2. Medieval philosophy—
v. 3. Modern philosophy—v. 4. Nineteenth-century philosophy. 2nd
ed.—v. 5. Twentiety-century philosophy. 2nd ed.
    ISBN 0–13–021314–4 (v. 1).—ISBN 0–13–021315–2 (v. 2).—ISBN
0–13–021316–0 (v. 3).—ISBN 0–13–021533–3 (v. 4).—ISBN
0–13–021534–1 (v. 5)
    1. Philosophy. I. Baird, Forrest E. II. Kaufmann, Walter
Arnold.
  B21.P39 2000
  100—dc21   98–32332
                                                  CIP

Editor-in-chief: Charlyce Jones-Owen
Acquisitions editor: Karita France
Editorial assistant: Jennifer Ackerman
Production liaison: Fran Russello
Editorial/production supervision:
   Bruce Hobart (Pine Tree Composition)
Prepress and manufacturing buyer:
   Tricia Kenny
Cover director: Jayne Conte
Cover photo: Franz Marc (1880–1916), "The Small Yellow Horses," 1912. Staatgalerie,
   Stuttgart, Germany. Art Resource, NY. © Photograph by Erich Lessing.
Marketing manager: Ilse Wolfe

This book was set in 10/12 Times Roman by Pine Tree Composition, Inc.,
and was printed and bound by R.R. Donnelley & Sons Company.
The cover was printed by Phoenix Color Corp.

Printed in the United States of America

10 9 8 7 6 5 4 3 2 1

ISBN 0-13-021534-1

Prentice-Hall International (UK) Limited, *London*
Prentice-Hall of Australia Pty. Limited, *Sydney*
Prentice-Hall Canada, Inc., *Toronto*
Prentice-Hall Hispanoamericana, S.A., *Mexico*
Prentice-Hall of India Private Limited, *New Dehli*
Prentice-Hall of Japan, Ltd., *Tokyo*
Pearson Education Asia Pte. Ltd., *Singapore*
Editora Prentice-Hall do Brasil, Ltda., *Rio de Janeiro*

This volume is dedicated to my children:
WHITNEY, SYDNEY, and SOREN BAIRD

Contents

Preface

Determining what is a "philosophic classic" becomes more difficult the closer one gets to the present, and I am sure there will be disagreements about particular selections included (or not included) here. In the first place, what counts as "philosophic"? The lines between philosophy, literary criticism, linguistics, sociology, political studies, and other disciplines have become blurred. Are Foucault's writings really philosophy? How about Irigaray? Does a thinker such as Du Bois, who was never called a philosopher in his lifetime, belong in this anthology? If everything is philosophic, then is nothing philosophic? Whereas some may trumpet that we are, indeed, coming to the end of philosophy, this questioning about the nature of philosophy is not a new concept. One of the most important jobs of philosophy over the centuries has been to determine what philosophy is and what it studies. We are presently in a period of redefining the nature and scope of philosophy. Several of the selections included here represent the partial results of this ongoing redefinition.

Second, what counts as a "classic"? One can well imagine an editor at the end of the nineteenth century preparing an anthology of nineteenth-century classics: There would probably be a great deal on F.H. Bradley and nothing on Kierkegaard—a choice no one would even consider today. This anthology of twentieth-century classics is also time-bound and subject to revision. But the philosophers and texts included here are presently seen as classics or as emerging classics. Some, such as the works of Wittgenstein and Heidegger, will undoubtedly continue to be considered "classics" well into the next century. Others, such as the work of Ayer and Moore, are already on the wane—though they still are an important part of the development of twentieth-century Western philosophy.

Commonly twentieth-century philosophers are divided into two groups: Continental thinkers and Anglo-American thinkers. The readings given in this volume represent a balance between these two approaches to philosophy. About half the contributors fall on each side of the great divide. Accordingly, it is possible to trace the development of Continental thought beginning with Husserl and moving through Heidegger, Gadamer, Sartre, de Beauvoir, Merleau-Ponty, Foucault, Derrida, Irigaray, and Habermas. Likewise, one can follow the Anglo-American concerns beginning with Dewey and continuing on through Whitehead, Du Bois, Russell, Moore, Wittgenstein, Ayer, Quine, Austin, Davidson, Rorty, Putnam, and Taylor. (Of course the development of twentieth-century philosophy is hardly that neat and tidy; in recent years the lines have blurred almost beyond recognition.)

For this third edition, I added a brief new selection from an interview with Michel Foucault. I have changed the selections from Heidegger and Irigary. In both cases, I believe these new selections better represent their work. I have also deleted the selection from Rudolf Carnap and instead included A.J. Ayer as a representative of logical positivism. While an argument could be made that Carnap is the more seminal of the two, Ayer's work is more accessible to students. There are dozens of other minor changes throughout the volume including some revisions of the selections from Sartre's *Being and Nothingness*. In choosing texts for this volume, I have tried wherever possible to follow three principles: (1) to use complete works or, where more appropriate, complete sections of works (2) in clear translations (3) of texts central to the thinker's philosophy or widely accepted as part of the "canon." To make the works more accessible to students, most footnotes treating textual matters (variant readings, etc.) have been omitted and all Greek words have been transliterated and put within angle brackets. In addition, each thinker is introduced by a brief essay composed of three sections: (1) biographical (a glimpse of the life), (2) philosophical (a résumé of the philosopher's thought), and (3) bibliographical (suggestions for further reading). The selections given here continue the themes of epistemology and metaphysics/ontology from the nineteenth-century volume. Some important works in social and political philosophy are also included.

Those who use this volume in one-term courses, such as contemporary philosophy, Continental philosophy, or Anglo-American philosophy, will find more material here than can easily fit a normal semester. But this embarrassment of riches gives teachers some choice and, for those who offer the same course year after year, an opportunity to change the menu.

*   *   *

I would like to thank the many people who assisted me in this volume, including the library staff of Whitworth College, especially Hans Bynagle, our library director, who has allowed me to adapt his helpful introduction to twentieth-century philosophy; my colleagues F. Dale Bruner, who made helpful suggestions on all the introductions, and Barbara Filo, who helped make selections for artwork; Crystal L. Downing, Messiah College, who wrote the first drafts for the introductions to Foucault, Derrida, and Rorty; Richard Rorty, University of Virginia, and Hilary Putnam, Harvard University, who read and made suggestions on the introductions to their work; David Carr, Emory University, Stephen Davis, Claremont McKenna College; Gerald V. Kohls, Wayne Pomerleau, and William F. Ryan, Gonzaga University, and Glen Ross, Franklin & Marshall College, who each read some of the introductions and gave helpful advice; Mark Alfino, Tom Jeannot, and Rosemary Volbrecht, all of Gonzaga University, who made suggestions on the selections; my secretary, Michelle Seefried; my production editor, Bruce Hobart, my acquisitions editor, Karita France of Prentice Hall, and my

former acquisitions editors, Angela Stone and Ted Bolen. I would also like to acknowl-
edge the following reviewers: James W. Allard, Montana State University; Robert C.
Bennett, El Centro College; Herbert L. Carson, Ferris State University; Daniel Gra-
ham, Brigham Young University; John Lachs, Vanderbilt University; Helen S. Lang,
Trinity College; Michael Losonsky, Colorado State University; Scott MacDonald, Uni-
versity of Iowa; Terry Pinkard, Georgetown University; Robert Redmond, Virginia
Commonwealth University; Reginald Savage, North Carolina State University;
Stephen Scott, Eastern Washington University; Howard N. Tuttle, University of New
Mexico; Richard J. Van Iten, Iowa State University; Donald Phillip Verene, Emory
University; and Wilhelm S. Wurzer, Duquesne University.

I am especially thankful to my wife, Joy Lynn Fulton Baird, who supported me
in this enterprise.

Finally, I would like to dedicate this last volume to our children, Whitney Jaye
Baird, Sydney Tev Baird, and Soren David Baird. Perhaps someday they or their children will chart new courses for philosophy.

Forrest E. Baird
Professor of Philosophy
Whitworth College
Spokane, WA 99251
email: fbaird@whitworth.edu

INTRODUCTION: A MAP OF
TWENTIETH-CENTURY PHILOSOPHY

by Hans Bynagle

SURVEYING THE PHILOSOPHICAL LANDSCAPE

To appreciate adequately the dynamics of scope and perspective in philosophy it is helpful, even essential, to have at least a basic orientation to the philosophical landscape. For the uninitiated, this can pose some difficulty. Even to get a sense of the major philosophical traditions, to say nothing of countless lesser schools and movements both within and outside the major traditions, is not altogether easy. Familiarizing oneself with the labels that are conventionally attached to them is not difficult, but this is only minimally useful. One needs to be able to place these labels, metaphorically speaking, on at least a rough philosophical map, a map that represents something of the general character of the major philosophical "regions" and how they relate to one another. It is a hard, however, to provide much help in this regard within a brief compass—the compass, for instance, of this introduction. The major philosophical traditions are notoriously difficult to characterize in a nutshell, at least in a way that is meaningful apart from a more detailed antecedent acquaintance with them. Generalizations, especially, are perilous and apt to be misleading.

Fortunately, one can begin to sketch a philosophical map, albeit a *very* rough one, in terms that are largely geographical (a circumstance that makes the metaphor of a "map" somewhat more than just a metaphor). The major divisions of philosophy, while they do not by any means fall neatly along geographical boundaries, do accord to a significant extent with geographical regions, at least in terms of their dominance. So an elementary geographical schema can make a somewhat useful starting point, provided one keeps in mind from the outset that as a philosophical map it is very rudimentary indeed.

THE MAJOR DOMAINS

The most basic division to begin with [is that] between Western and non-Western philosophy. With regard to non-Western, one may think particularly of eastern and southern Asia, highlighting perhaps China and India, which have the most substantial philosophical traditions. Non-Western also takes in parts of western Asia (the Middle East), and certainly includes other parts of the world not usually considered part of "the West" (a term I take to refer chiefly to Europe and the Americas). A case in point

Adapted from Hans Bynagle, *Philosophy: A Guide to the Reference Literature,* 2nd edition (Littleton, CO: Libraries Unlimited, 1997). Reprinted by permission of the author.

would be Africa, insofar as we are thinking of native philosophies. Despite its broader connotation, "non-Western philosophy" has often been used interchangeably with "Eastern philosophy." (The term "Oriental," incidentally, is sometimes used to designate philosophies of Far Eastern Asia only, and sometimes to encompass also philosophies of southern Asia, mainly India, and even those of the Middle East. The broader use seems unwise, since "Oriental" ordinarily brings to mind China and Japan and their near neighbors.)

The line between Western and non-Western philosophy is one that runs through most of the history of philosophy. The next line we need to draw, demarcating major areas within Western philosophy, represents a modern development with roots going back several centuries but dating primarily from the present century. This line serves to divide the philosophical tradition that dominates most of the European continent, known accordingly as Continental philosophy, from the dominant philosophical tradition of England, the United States, and some other countries subject to strong British or American influence (such as Canada and Australia) known as Anglo-American philosophy. This line is perhaps less "clean" even than the previous one, but it does mark a real and well-recognized division.

So far, then, we have demarcated in rough fashion the following philosophical regions: non-Western and Western, and within Western, Continental and Anglo-American. When I wrote the original version of this introduction just over a decade ago, I could add to this philosophical geography, with similarly rough precision, two other major realms. The first was Marxist philosophy, which at the time dominated the Soviet Union and the countries of Eastern Europe. This realm constituted a large and quite active domain, identifiably Western but relatively isolated from both the Continental and Anglo-American domains; extensive contacts between philosophers on either side of the divide, at least, were uncommon. Today, as a result of convulsive political and social changes in the region it once dominated, Marxist philosophy can hardly be said to exist as a distinct domain, at least not in geographical terms.

A second domain that ten years ago seemed important enough to recognize along with the others named so far was labeled Neo-Scholasticism. This philosophy disrupted the tidiness of our mapping scheme, because it overlapped geographically the two regions already labeled Continental and Anglo-American. Neo-Scholasticism—the name derives from Scholasticism, referring to the various philosophical "schools" of the medieval period, from which this tradition takes its primary inspiration—had been for almost a century the reigning though by no means exclusive orientation among Catholic philosophers. It had a sufficiently large following both in Europe and in the Americas (North as well as South) to be ranked among the major extant traditions of Western philosophy. Though Neo-Scholastic philosophy certainly has not suffered the traumatic dislocations experienced by Marxism since 1985, erosions of its status and stature that were already well under way a decade ago have continued to the point where, arguably, it no longer merits recognition at the level of a major philosophical domains.

If the respective fortunes of Marxism and Neo-Scholasticism imply that we need to take erasers to the old map, however, it might be well if our erasures were incomplete, leaving something of the old patterns discernible through the gaps and smudges. Neither domain has vanished entirely by any means—and who knows what their future may yet be? It remains important, accordingly, to know what those realities were. We'll keep Marxism and Neo-Scholasticism, therefore, on our "short list" of the major traditions it's most useful to be aware of, and will say something more about them below.

To sum up, then, we have distinguished five very broad domains that either dominate the philosophical landscape presently or did so until recently: Non-Western, Continental, Anglo-American, Neo-Scholastic, and Marxist.

*   *   *

WESTERN PHILOSOPHIES

The terms "Continental" and "Anglo-American" have been in currency for many years to distinguish the main twentieth-century philosophical traditions of the non-Communist West, yet they are something less than official names for well-defined movements. Until the late 1980s, the term "Continental philosophy" was frequently used as practically synonymous with two related movements, Phenomenology and Existentialism. This is hardly feasible any more. It was always true that the term could be used in a wider sense to encompass other movements that have flourished on the European continent, including an older strain somewhat inadequately labeled Idealism, with roots especially in the eighteenth- and nineteenth-century philosophies of Kant and Hegel, and a more recent movement that goes by the name of Structuralism. An important development in the last ten years, however, has been the meteoric rise to prominence of several newer philosophical positions or orientations originating primarily in Europe, especially in France. Among the labels most commonly associated with them are Poststructuralism, Deconstruction, and Postmodernism. All of these currents have a strongly interdisciplinary character and all tend toward left-of-center political and social positions. They have generated so much interest and discussion not only on their home ground but in the United States, Britain, and other strongholds of Anglo-American philosophy that it becomes necessary to speak of a significant blurring and bridging of the boundary between the Continental and Anglo-American domains during the past decade. It's probably true, as some have observed, that Anglo-American interest in (and certainly enthusiasm for) these newer Continental currents runs much stronger in departments of literature, communication, women's studies, multicultural studies, and others than it does in philosophy departments. If only because of the presence of this wider interest in academe, however, it's harder now than formerly for Anglo-American philosophers simply to ignore Continental philosophy.

CONTINENTAL

I can offer here only the most rudimentary characterizations of a few of the main strands of Continental philosophy already mentioned, beginning with Phenomenology. Founded around the turn of this century by Edmund Husserl, Phenomenology is essentially a philosophical method, one that focuses on careful inspection and description of phenomena or appearances, defined as any object of conscious experience, i.e., that which we are conscious *of*. The inspection and description are supposed to be effected without any presuppositions, and that includes any presuppositions as to whether such objects of consciousness are "real" or correspond to something "external," or as to what their causes or consequences may be. It is believed that by this method the essential structures of experience and its objects can be uncovered. The sorts of experiences and phenomena that Phenomenologists have sought to describe are highly varied, including, for instance, time consciousness, mathematics and logic, perception, experience of the social world, our experience of our own bodies, and moral, aesthetic, and religious experience.

Existentialism, unlike Phenomenology, is not primarily a philosophical method. Neither is it exactly a set of doctrines (at least not any *one* set) but more an outlook or attitude supported by diverse doctrines centered on certain common themes. These themes include the human condition, or the relation of the individual to the world; the human response to that condition (described often in strongly affective and preponderantly negative terms such as "despair," "dread," "anxiety," "guilt," "bad faith," "nausea"); being, especially the difference between the being of persons (which is "existence") and the being of other kinds of things; human freedom; the significance (and unavoidability) of choice and decision in the absence of certainty; and the concreteness and subjectivity of life as lived, over against abstractions and false objectifications.

Existentialism is often thought to be anti-religious (and is, in some of its versions), but there has in fact been a strong current of Christian Existentialism, beginning with the figure often credited with originating Existentialism, the nineteenth-century Danish philosopher Kierkegaard. Existentialism's relationship to Phenomenology is a matter of some controversy, but at least one can say that many of the later Existentialist thinkers, Sartre among them, have employed Phenomenological methods to arrive at or support their specific variations on Existential themes. While Existentialism has been on the wane since the 1960s, it has enjoyed exceptional prominence, even popularity, for a philosophical movement, in part because of its literary expressions by writers such as Sartre, Albert Camus, de Beauvoir, and Marcel.

Structuralism is an interdisciplinary movement united by the principle that social and cultural phenomena, including belief systems and every kind of discourse (literary, political, scientific, etc.), are best understood by analogy with language, itself best understood as a structure of relations among its component parts. Just as in language the crucial determinant of meaning (according to the early structural linguist Ferdinand de Saussure) is neither individual words nor their reference to things outside language but their interrelationships within the linguistic structure, so the crucial element in all social and cultural phenomena is the underlying structure that determines the functions of the various parts. A good deal of Structuralist analysis has been concerned with a kind of unmasking, that is, with revealing political, social, or psychological phenomena as (allegedly) not what they seem or what participants believe them to be but as determined by structures often concealed from view.

This unmasking impulse persists with the group of thinkers sometimes designated Post-structuralists, who both rejected certain presuppositions of Structuralism and added their own more radical ideas about the fundamental role of language in constructing all human perceptions and conceptions of reality. A particular form of this unmasking tendency is Deconstruction, introduced in the work of Jacques Derrida, who is generally counted among Post-structuralists. Any attempt to define Deconstruction must labor in the shadow of Derrida's apparent rejection in advance of all such attempts. Nonetheless, it has seemed fair to many interpreters to characterize it as a form of textual criticism or interpretation whose aim is to unmask and overcome hidden "privileging" that occurs in texts of all kinds. This privileging, for example the privileging of reason, the masculine, the sacred, the literal, or the objective, ect., entails the exclusion, suppression, or marginalization of their opposites—passion, the feminine, the profane, the metaphorical, the subjective, etc.—while at the same time it must presuppose these opposites to sustain or even to make sense of the privileged concept. In this way, it is maintained, texts regularly undermine their own assumptions. As a reading technique uncovering alleged hidden agendas behind the ostensible meaning of a text, Deconstruction takes the further step of denying that the text has a definite meaning. This has become a key thesis for the currents of literary theorizing and criticism that followed in Derrida's wake.

"Postmodernism," finally, has come into vogue as the name for a rather diffuse family of ideas and trends that in significant respects reject, challenge, or aim to supersede "modernity": the convictions, aspirations, and pretensions (as they are now seen to be) of modern Western thought and culture since the Enlightenment. In architecture, where the term first gained currency, it signified the rejection of the highly rationalized, sterile functionalism of modern architecture in favor of an eclecticism that is often playful and, by mixing seemingly incongruous styles, mocks its own seriousness. In philosophy and adjacent disciplines, Postmodernism has come to mean, somewhat analogously, a rejection of the modern mind's confidence in rationality, including, for instance, its pretensions to the attainment of universally valid and objective truth and its confidence in the achievability of progress. As expounded by the French thinker Jean-François Lyotard, it also entailed a profound suspicion and abandonment of what he called "metanarratives," grand narratives or theories purporting to disclose the overall meaning of history and to assign particular events and phenomena, and to deny to others, a place in the grand scheme of things. For Lyotard, such "totalizing" metanarratives, whether offered by religion, Marxism, Darwinism, psychoanalysis, or whatever, need to be deconstructed as coercive and oppressive in their purpose or effect. Certain Anglo-American philosophical strains also meet under the banner of Postmodernism. The American philosopher Richard Rorty, notably, developing themes from Pragmatism and certain quarters of Analytic philosophy and bringing these together with Continental themes, challenged the modern rationalist presumption that philosophy or any branch of knowledge can find secure foundations or achieve genuine representation of reality.

ANGLO-AMERICAN

This provides a handy transition to our closer characterization of Anglo-American philosophy. It is not uncommon to equate Anglo-American philosophy with what is called Analytic or Analytical philosophy, but the term is also used in a broader sense to encompass other movements that have flourished chiefly on British and American soil, for instance Pragmatism, Naturalism, and Process Philosophy. There is much to be said for the wider meaning, which avoids the suggestion that philosophy in England and America is more monolithic than it really is. The equation of Anglo-American with Analytic is also unfortunate from another point of view, in that Analytic philosophy has become the dominant mode of philosophizing in some other areas as well, notably the Scandinavian countries, to say nothing of the inroads it has made in areas where other approaches still dominate the field (the other side of the blurring and bridging of the Continental/Anglo-American boundary), e.g., in Germany. However, given all those qualifications and others, there is no question that Analytic philosophy is the most important philosophical current within the Anglo-American sphere. It is also the one most often contrasted with (and actively opposed to) the Continental movements described above.

What Analytic philosophy is not so easy to say. I believe it is possible to distinguish at least three variants, though they probably represent points on a spectrum rather than discrete alternatives. In the widest and loosest sense, Analytic philosophy is hardly more than a philosophical style, one that takes extreme care with the meanings of words (sometimes with precise definitions of terms and consistency in their use, sometimes with the nuances of ordinary language), that tends to present arguments in meticulous step-by-step fashion (often endeavoring to leave nothing implicit), and that pays close, sometimes minute attention to logical relations (often using logical symbolism or specialized logical terminology to render such relations transparent). In a narrower sense, "Analytic philosophy" designates a philosophical outlook that holds that the primary task or even (in its more extreme version) the only proper task of philosophy—the primary or proper method for attacking philosophical problems—is analysis of one sort or another: of meanings, of concepts, of logical relations, or all of these. We can call this the methodological version. Finally, one may occasionally encounter the term "Analytic philosophy" in contexts where it is reserved for one or more specific doctrines regarding the outcome of correct philosophical analysis. While the Analytic tradition (in either of the two wider senses) owes a great deal to certain specific doctrinal versions—and to major figures who propounded them, such as Bertrand Russell, G.E. Moore, Ludwig Wittgenstein, and J.L. Austin—it would be incorrect to say that Analytic philosophy is the dominant orientation among British and American philosophers if one has in mind this narrowest meaning. In fact, it is not clear that this is true under any but the widest meaning distinguished above.

Common to those who subscribe to the Analytic approach, whether in the broadest sense or a narrower one, is the conviction that to some significant degree, philosophical problems, puzzles, and errors are rooted in language and can be solved or avoided, as the case may be, by a sound understanding of language and careful attention to its workings. This has tended to focus much attention on language and on its close relative, logic, as objects of study for their own sake. (The relationship between language and logic is itself a question subjected to considerable inquiry and debate.) Detractors are apt to point to this concern—they might say this obsession—with language and logic as one aspect of the trivialization of philosophy with which they charge the Analytic movement. Many who are generally loyal or sympathetic to Analytic philosophy may agree that it tended to draw philosophy away from "deep" questions. In any case, the last two to three decades have seen, on the one hand, increased self-searching as to the limitations of the Analytic approach, and on the other, more efforts to apply it to such deeper questions—about the meaning of life, for instance, or the nature of the moral life—in a way that takes them seriously. There has also been more extensive application to "real-life" moral and social issues, so that Analytic approaches and perspectives are well represented in the burgeoning literature of professional ethics, bioethics, and political and social thought.

MARXIST

We turn now to Marxist philosophy, whose recent precipitous decline we have previously noted. Like other aspects of Marxism, such as economics, this philosophy derives its impetus and its fundamental ideas from the writings of Karl Marx and his associate, Friedrich Engels, despite the fact (ironically) that Marx himself considered philosophy an activity proper only to the pre-Communist order. (While this is one notion of Marx that clearly has *not* been taken up in Marxist philosophy, there is some continuity between it and the prevalent hostility in Marxist philosophy toward other philosophical positions, which are regarded as not simply mistaken but as manifestations of class interests and instruments of political struggle.) Marxist philosophy is not easily summarized, but its two central tenants can be readily identified by their conventional labels: dialectical materialism and historical materialism. The former asserts the primacy of matter as the fundamental reality and attempts to state general principles concerning the organization and development of matter. The latter is a theory about history and attempts to state general principles concerning the development of human thought and society in the historical process. Marx's well-known thesis concerning the primacy of economic factors in history is one ingredient of historical materialism. In most Communist countries, Marx's thought was wedded to that of Lenin and known accordingly as Marxism-Leninism.

The crude map with which we began indicated the dominance until recently of Marxist philosophy in the Iron Curtain countries, but it has really been far more widely dispersed than that. Nor has Marxist philosophy been confined to the Communist world. Marxist philosophers were found in many countries, and still are, if considerably fewer in number now, often combining their Marxism with other philosophical orientations. A well-known instance of this is Jean-Paul Sartre's attempt to wed, rather incongruously on the face of it, a somewhat unorthodox Marxism to French Existentialism. An important German movement, the Frankfurt School, associated with the names of Adorno and Habermas (among others) and represented in the United States for a while by Marcus, developed ideas and themes from Marxist without accepting, unless severely qualified, key Marxist dogmas such as historical materialism. Acquaintance with Marxism in the non-Communist West has tended to be more by far way of such exponents working outside than those working inside the Communist sphere.

With the fall of communism and the breakup of the Soviet Union and its East European alliance in the early 1900s, Marxism lost not only its status as the official philosophy of the countries concerned but much of its cultural and ideological influence. Is it dead in this region? It would be premature to say. Defenders of orthodox Marxism still remain in Russia and elsewhere, and may be regaining strength as these countries struggle with their transitions to capitalism. Others are striving to develop compromise positions, combining various strands of Marxist thought with other ideas and orientations, including Eastern-Orthodox Christianity and pre-Communist Russian philosophies as well as Continental and Anglo-American philosophical positions. Still others reject Marxism in toto. In any case, the era when one could simply label this region, "Marxist" on one's philosophical map is over and does not seem about to return, though the future is unknown.

Neo-Scholasticism

We turn, finally, to Neo-Scholasticism. Like the labels connected with other philosophical traditions we have discussed, "Neo-Scholasticism" has a somewhat variable denotation. Not uncommonly, it is used interchangeably with "Neo-Thomism," a term derived from the name St. Thomas Aquinas, a Medieval philosopher whose thought was revived in spirit and to a considerable extent in substance by Catholic thinkers in the mid-nineteenth century, and given quasi-official status in Catholicism by a papal encyclical in 1879. Insofar as Neo-Thomism is the major force within Neo-Scholasticism, the equation is not too far wrong. But in a stricter sense, Neo-Scholastic philosophy harkens back to medieval Christian philosophy more generally, and may draw on and seek to develop the views of other philosophers besides St. Thomas, such as Bonaventure, Duns Scotus, and William of Ockham. Like its medieval ancestor, Neo-Scholasticism, owes a great deal to Aristotle (St. Thomas is often credited with achieving a great synthesis of Aristotelian philosophy and Christian theology) and to other classical philosophers. However, it has also interacted with contemporary currents in both the Anglo-American and Continental spheres, depending to some extent, as one might expect, on the setting in which it is pursued. Neo-Scholasticism largely lost its quasi-official status with the Second Vatican Council of the early 1960s, and its institutional support within Catholicism gradually weakened in the years following. Catholic philosophers now tend to represent a wide range of philosophical positions and orientations. Symptomatic of the trend is the change of title in 1989 of the American Catholic Philosophical Association's journal from *New Scholasticism* to *American Catholic Philosophical Quarterly*.

This concludes our brief overview of the main philosophical traditions that characterize the present and recent philosophical landscape. Dozens, even hundreds of lesser movements within, without, and overlapping the boundaries of these traditions have not been mentioned, let alone described. Nor have I said anything, beyond a bare mention here or there, about historical schools and movements that may have been among the major philosophical alternatives in their time, but have since died out, been absorbed, or reduced to minor outposts on the philosophical landscape.

FEMINIST PHILOSOPHY

This overview is incomplete, nonetheless, without some discussion of feminist philosophy. It would be inaccurate, or at least premature at this point, to place this as a major philosophical tradition alongside the five described above; on the other hand, it is too important a part of the contemporary philosophical scene to go unmentioned here. As a movement or perspective within philosophy, feminist philosophy is broadly concerned with philosophical issues surrounding sexual differences. There is considerable diversity and sometimes disagreement within it, however, regarding the levels at which these issues are important. Some feminist philosophers are centrally concerned with political and social inequalities between men and women and with the philosophical groundwork necessary or helpful for combating those inequalities. Others undertake a more "radical" (i.e., fundamental) critique of traditional philosophy (and other domains of knowledge, such as science) as allegedly dominated by masculine concerns and categories and are concerned to assert the value and legitimacy, and perhaps the superiority, of women's ways of being, knowing, and doing that are different from those of men. These feminist philosophers have proposed distinctively feminist epistemologies, ethics, and metaphysics. Such ground-level concerns overlap with concerns about equality, of course, and often complement them; but the two can also collide— for example, when some who insist on the radical nature of gender differences interpret "equity feminists" as purchasing equality at the price of suppressing those differences (thus maintaining the essential subordination of feminine to masculine).

Feminist philosophy is not independent of the traditions previously described; many who claim the feminist label identify strongly with one another of the Anglo-Amercian, Continental, Marxist, and even Neo-Scholastic traditions. (Whether there is a specifically non-Western form of feminist philosophy I am not sure.) Even when such identification is not strong, or is explicitly rejected, the various groupings and viewpoints identifiable within feminist philosophy—liberal, Marxist, radical, psychoanalytical, existentialist, socialist, postmodern, Christian—clearly differ in the extent to which they draw significant support, inspiration, conceptual frameworks, terminology, ect., from one or several of these traditions.

*   *   *

For secondary works on twentieth-century philosophy, consult the appropriate works from Frederick Copleston's series *A History of Philosophy, Volumes VIII: Bentham to Russell* and *Volume IX: Maine de Brian to Sartre* (New York: Image Doubleday, 1966 and 1974). For specific movements in twentieth-century Western philosophy, see Michael Corrado, *The Analytic Tradition in Philosophy: Background and Issues* (Chicago: American Library Association, 1975); Robert C. Solomon, *From Hegel to Existentialism* (Oxford: Oxford University Press, 1987); Richard Kearney, ed., *Twentieth-Century Continental Philosophy* (London: Routledge, 1994); Giovanna Borradori, *The American Philosopher,* translated by Rosanna Crocitto (Chicago: University of Chicago Press, 1994); D.S. Clarke, *Philosophy's Second Revolution: Early and Recent Analytic Philosophy* (La Salle, IL: Open Court, 1997); and Simon Critchley and William Schroeder, eds., *A Companion to Continental Philosophy* (Oxford: Basil Blackwell, 1997). Robert Audi, ed., *The Cambridge Dictionary of Philosophy* (Cambridge: Cambridge University Press, 1995); Stuart Brown et al., *Biographical Dictionary of Twentieth Century Philosophers* (London: Routledge, 1996); and Hans Bynagle, *Philosophy: A Guide to the Reference Literature,* 2nd edition (Littleton, CO: Libraries Unlimited, 1997) provide helpful reference works.

Philosophers In This Volume

Edmund Husserl
John Dewey
    Alfred North Whitehead
        W.E.B. Du Bois
           Bertrand Russell
           G.E. Moore

                Maurice
                Merleau-Ponty
                A.J. Ayer
                J.L. Austin

Martin Heidegger
Ludwig Wittgenstein

Hans-Georg Gadamer
Jean-Paul Sartre
Simone
de Beauvoir
Willard Van
Orman Quine

Other Important Figures

Henri Bergson
  George Santayana
    Benedetto Croce
      Mahtama Gandhi
      Ernst Cassirern
        Martin Buber
          Jacques Maritain
          José Ortega y Gasset
          Rudolf Carnap

Herbert Marcuse
Gilbert Ryle
    Emmanuel Levinas
    Simone Weil

Brand Blanshard
Susanne Langer

A Sampling of Major Events

Britain taker over India
  American Civil War
      Meiji period in Japan
      Suez Canal opens
        First Impressionist art exhibition in Paris
            Karl Benz produces first retail car
              New Zealand allows women to vote
              Spanish-American War
              Boxer Rebellion in China
              Wright brothers
              invent airplane

| 1860 | 1870 | 1880 | 1890 | 1900 | 1910 |

Donald Davidson
        Michael Foucault
        Hilary Putnam
          Jürgen Habermas
           Jacques Derrida
           Richard Rorty
           Richard Taylor
              Luce Irigaray

Albert Camus
      John Rawls
         Martin Luther King Jr.
          Robert Nozick

        Second World War
          First use of atomic bomb
          First electronic digital computer
          Soviet blockade of Berlin
           Mao Tse-tung gains power in China
         Korean War
            U.S. Supreme Court
            rules against segregation
               Several African countries
               achieve independence
               Vietnam War
First World War
                       Soviet troops invade
   Russian Revolution
                       Czechoslovakia
      Charle sLindbergh flies across the Atlantic
                       First men on the moon
        Hitler becomes Führer
                       Switzerland allows
                        women to vote

1920   1930   1940   1950   1960   1970   1980

EDMUND HUSSERL
1859–1938

Edmund Husserl was born in Prostějov (Prossnitz), Moravia, in what is now the Czech Republic; at that time, it was part of the Austrian Empire. After attending elementary school in Prostějov, Husserl went to *gymnasia* (high schools) in Vienna and Olmütz before enrolling at the University of Leipzig in 1876. For two years, he studied mathematics, physics, and astronomy, attending philosophy lectures only in his spare time. In 1878, he transferred to the Friedrich-Wilhelm University of Berlin, where he continued his study of mathematics (under the renowned Karl Weierstrass) as well as his hobby of philosophy. After three years, he moved to the University of Vienna, where he received a Ph.D. in mathematics in 1883.

Husserl was offered a teaching position in mathematics at Berlin, but he decided to remain in Vienna so that he could continue studying philosophy. He worked with the philosophical psychologist Franz Brentano (1838–1917) during the next two years. Following Brentano's advice, Husserl then moved to the University of Halle, where he published his first book, *Philosophy of Arithmetic* (1891). In 1901, he moved to the University of Göttingen, where he spent the next sixteen years and published a number of important works, including *Ideas: General Introduction to Pure Phenomenology* (1913). His last post was at the University of Freiburg, where he taught until his retirement in 1928. Among his Freiburg associates was Martin Heidegger. Following retirement, Husserl wrote voluminously—though little was published during his lifetime. Toward the end of his life, the Nazis barred him from formal academic activities because of his Jewish ancestry.

After his death in 1938, the Husserl Archive was established in Louvain, Belgium. The Archive has preserved, transcribed, and, over the decades, published

Husserl's shorthand notes as the *Husserliana series.* The Archive has also hosted congresses on, and published essays in, phenomenology.

*   *   *

Franz Brentano, Husserl's teacher, criticized British empiricism for its tendency to present consciousness in terms of ideas or representations. Brentano argued that the key constituent of mental states is intentionality—thought's correlation rather than its immobile state. In order to have consciousness, one must be conscious of something. One cannot just think, one must think *about* something; one cannot just desire, one must have desire *for* something; one cannot just be aware, one must be aware *of* something. In each case, the "something" is the "intentional object" of consciousness. Contrary to Kant, Brentano held that consciousness does not *construct* these objects, it only *points to* them.

The end of the nineteenth century brought two quite different responses to Brentano. The analytic tradition, which tended to dominate English-speaking philosophy, focused almost exclusively on objects of consciousness, ignoring consciousness itself. The phenomenological tradition, dominant on the European continent, examined the nature of consciousness itself.

Husserl is the acknowledged founder of this phenomenological response. Like Descartes, Husserl considered consciousness the main topic for philosophy. In examining the form of this consciousness, Husserl discovered what he called "the natural standpoint":

> I am aware of a world, spread out in space endlessly, and in time becoming and become, without end. I am aware of it, that means, first of all, I discover it immediately, intuitively, I experience it. Through sight, touch, hearing, etc., . . . corporeal things somehow spatially distributed are *for me simply there,* . . . "present," whether or not I pay them special attention by busying myself with them, considering, thinking, feeling, willing.*

This is the world as it is actually lived by an individual. Although we can develop "worlds" of arithmetic or science by our knowledge of things from a particular standpoint, the natural standpoint—the world as actually lived by individuals—is always prior to, and conditioning of, any particular knowledge possible.

Yet according to Husserl, it is possible to get behind this natural standpoint to identify an invariant intentional structure. Husserl developed a method of "bracketing," which he called ⟨*epochē*⟩ (from the Greek word for noncommitment or suspended judgment). For example, I may look with pleasure at a blossoming apple tree. From the natural standpoint, I can see that the tree exists outside of me in space and time and that I am enjoying my psychical state of pleasure. From this standpoint, moreover, there is an assumed relation between me and the apple tree. But Descartes had shown that this perception could be mistaken—I could be hallucinating. As a result, my knowledge of the tree is uncertain. But I can suspend my judgments about the tree and perform an ⟨*epochē*⟩. This "bracketing" moves me from a natural to a phenomenological standpoint,

---

*Edmund Husserl, *Ideas: General Introduction to Pure Phenomenology,* translated by W.R. Boyce Gibson (Atlantic Highlands, NJ: Humanities Press, 1931), Section 2, Chapter 1, ¶27. (Emphasis in original.)

from which I now recognize "a nexus of exotic experiences of perception and pleasure valuation." Of this nexus of intending tree-experiences I *am* certain. By no longer referring to objective existence, by applying the phenomenological ⟨*epochē*⟩ instead, I have arrived at the pure datum of intending experience.

In the latter part of *Ideas* and in several other works, Husserl developed this method further, showing how to use the newly acquired phenomenological data. For example, in examining the experience of time, Husserl found that "lived time" is not the time of clocks and calendars but is always experienced as now. Similarly, in the experience of "lived space" one always finds oneself *here,* and everything else at different degrees of *there.* In his article on "Phenomenology" for the *Encyclopædia Brittanica,* given here (complete), Husserl explained that it is possible to apply the phenomenological method not only to the *objects* of consciousness but to consciousness itself. When we perform such an ⟨*epochē*⟩ on consciousness, we discover an invariant structure: the transcendental ego. "The 'I' and the 'we,' which we apprehend, presuppose the hidden 'I' and 'we' to whom they are 'present.'"

In the selection given here from *The Crisis of European Science and Transcendental Phenomenology* (1936), translated by David Carr, Husserl applies the phenomenological method to the sciences. He begins by explaining the notion of a "life-world" (*Lebenswelt*): the "intuitive surrounding world of life, pregiven as existing for all in common" that is the "realm of original self-evidences." This life-world of subjective experience is and always has been there as the subsoil out of which we develop theories to explain the natural world. Ever since Galileo, science has explained the world by "objectively" mathematizing experience. But, Husserl explains, this mathematized experience is itself an abstraction from the actually experienced world. In order to overcome the vagueness and indeterminacy of ordinary experience to make it quantifiable, the scientist must abstract and interpret the pregiven experience. But such an abstraction and interpretation is not itself "scientific." As David Carr explains,

> The scientist sees himself as overcoming the relativity of our "merely subjective" pictures of the world by finding the *objective* world, the world as it really is. Husserl shows that the scientist can just as easily be seen, by a shift in perspective, as a man who himself has a particular sort of *picture* of the world, and that as such both he and his picture belong *within* the "real" world, which Husserl calls the life-world.*

Husserl's thought continues to be influential. Martin Heidegger used the phenomenological method to develop his ontology, and Jean-Paul Sartre used the method to develop his own "existential" interpretation of consciousness. Maurice Merleau-Ponty refined and further applied the phenomenological method. Husserl has lived on through his followers.

*   *   *

For works on phenomenology in general, see Herbert Speigelberg, *The Phenomenological Movement,* two volumes (The Hague, The Netherlands: Martinus Nijhoff, 1960); Joseph J. Kockelmans, ed., *Phenomenology* (Garden City, NY: An-

---

*David Carr, "Husserl's Problematic Concept of the Life-World," *Husserl: Expositions and Appraisals,* edited by Frederick A. Elliston and Peter McCormick (Notre Dame, IN: University of Notre Dame Press, 1977), p. 207. (Emphasis in original.)

chor Doubleday, 1967); and Christopher Macann, *Four Phenomenological Philosophers: Husserl, Heidegger, Sartre, Merleau-Ponty* (London: Routledge, 1993). For a clear and concise comparison of phenomenology and the analytic tradition, see W.T. Jones, *The Twentieth Century to Wittgenstein and Sartre,* 2nd edition (New York: Harcourt Brace Jovanovich, 1975), Chapters 7 and 8.

Marvin Farber, *The Foundations of Phenomenology* (Albany, NY: SUNY Press, 1943) provides a standard study of Husserl's thought, whereas Joseph J. Kockelmans, *A First Introduction to Husserl's Phenomenology* (Pittsburgh, PA: Duquesne University Press, 1967); David Bell, *Husserl* (New York: Routledge, 1990); and Rudolf Bernet, Iso Kern, and Eduard Marbach, *An Introduction to Husserlian Phenomenology* (Evanston, IL: Northwestern University Press, 1993) provide introductions. Paul Ricoeur, *Husserl: An Analysis of His Phenomenology,* translated by Edward G. Ballard and Lester E. Embree (Evanston, IL: Northwestern University Press, 1967), and Hans-Georg Gadamer, *Philosophical Hermeneutics,* translated by David E. Linge (Berkeley: University of California Press, 1976) have written studies of Husserl as well as important works of philosophy themselves. Among the many studies of particular areas of Husserl's thought, see David Carr, *Phenomenology and the Problem of History: A Study of Husserl's Transcendental Philosophy* (Evanston, IL: Northwestern University Press, 1974); Erazim V. Kohák, *Idea and Experience: Edmund Husserl's Project of Phenomenology in "Ideas I"* (Chicago: University of Chicago Press, 1978); Timothy J. Stapleton, *Husserl and Heidegger: The Question of a Phenomenological Beginning* (Albany, NY: SUNY Press, 1983); and James M. Edie, *Edmund Husserl's Phenomenology: A Critical Commentary* (Bloomington: Indiana University Press, 1987). For collections of essays, see R.O. Elveton, ed., *The Phenomenology of Husserl* (Chicago: Quadrangle Books, 1970); Frederick Elliston and Peter McCormick, eds., *Husserl: Expositions and Appraisals* (Notre Dame, IN: University of Notre Dame Press, 1977)—especially David Carr's article, "Husserl's Problematic Concept of the Life-World"; Robert Sokolowski, ed., *Edmund Husserl and the Phenomenological Tradition* (Washington, DC: Catholic University of America Press, 1988); Barry Smith and David Woodruff Smith, eds., *The Cambridge Companion to Husserl* (Cambridge: Cambridge University Press, 1995); and the *Husserl Studies,* an ongoing journal published by Kluwer Academic Publishers, Hingham, MA.

PHENOMENOLOGY

Phenomenology denotes a new, descriptive, philosophical method, which, since the concluding years of the last century, has established (1) an *a priori* psychological discipline, able to provide the only secure basis on which a strong empirical psychology can be built, and (2) a universal philosophy, which can supply an organum for the methodical revision of all the sciences.

I. PHENOMENOLOGICAL PSYCHOLOGY

Present-day psychology, as the science of the "psychical" in its concrete connection with spatio-temporal reality, regards as its material whatever is present in the world as "ego-istic"; i.e., "living," perceiving, thinking, willing, etc., actual, potential and habitual. And as the psychical is known as a certain stratum of existence, proper to men and beasts, psychology may be considered as a branch of anthropology and zoology. But animal nature is a part of physical reality, and that which is concerned with physical reality is natural science. Is it, then, possible to separate the psychical cleanly enough from the physical to establish a pure psychology parallel to natural science? That a purely psychological investigation is practicable within limits is shown by our obligation to it for our fundamental conceptions of the psychical, and most of those of the psycho-physical.

But before determining the question of an unlimited psychology, we must be sure of the characteristics of psychological experience and the psychical data it provides. We turn naturally to our immediate experiences. But we cannot discover the psychical in any experience, except by a "reflection," or perversion of the ordinary attitude. We are accustomed to concentrate upon the matters, thoughts, and values of the moment, and not upon the psychical "act of experience" in which these are apprehended. This "act" is revealed by a "reflection"; and a reflection can be practised on every experience. Instead of the matters themselves, the values, goals, utilities, etc., we regard the subjective experiences in which these "appear." These "appearances" are phenomena, whose nature is to be a "consciousness-of" their object, real or unreal as it be. Common language catches this sense of "relativity," saying, I was thinking *of* something, I was frightened *of* something, etc. Phenomenological psychology takes its name from the "phenomena," with the psychological aspect of which it is concerned: and the word "intentional" has been borrowed from the scholastic to denote the essential "reference" character of the phenomena. All consciousness is "intentional."

In unreflective consciousness we are "directed" upon objects, we "intend" them, and reflection reveals this to be an immanent process characteristic of all experience, though infinitely varied in form. To be conscious of something is no empty having of that something in consciousness. Each phenomenon has its own intentional structure, which analysis shows to be an ever-widening system of individually intentional and intentionally related components. The perception of a cube, for example, reveals a multiple and synthesized intention: a continuous variety in the "appearance" of the cube, according to differences in the points of view from which it is seen, and corresponding differences in "perspective," and all the difference between the "front side" actually seen at the moment and the "backside" which is not seen, and which remains, therefore, relatively "indeterminate," and yet is supposed equally to be existent. Observation of this "stream" of "appearance-aspects" and of the manner of their synthesis, shows that every phase and interval is already in itself a "consciousness-of" something, yet in such a way that with the constant entry of new phases the total consciousness, at any moment, lacks not synthetic unity, and is, in fact, a consciousness of one and the same object. The intentional structure of the train of a perception must conform to a certain type, if any physical object is to be perceived as there! And if the same object be intuited in other modes, if it be imagined, or remembered, or copied, all its intentional forms recur, though modified in character from what they were in the perception, to correspond to their new modes. The same is true of every kind of psychical experience. Judgment, valuation, pursuit, these also are no empty experiences having in consciousness of judgments, values, goals and means, but are likewise experiences compounded of an intentional stream, each conforming to its own fast type.

Nude Descending a Staircase, Number 2, 1912, by Marcel Duchamp (1887–1968). Duchamp's shattered and reassembled nude figure descending the staircase in robotic rhythm purposely challenges the viewer to derive a personal interpretation of the image—to move beyond the natural standpoint with its judgments concerning spacio-temporal existence. *(Philadelphia Museum of Art: Louise and Walter Arensberg Collection)*

Phenomenological psychology's comprehensive task is the systematic examination of the types and forms of intentional experience, and the reduction of their structures to the prime intentions, learning thus what is the nature of the psychical, and comprehending the being of the soul.

The validity of these investigations will obviously extend beyond the particularity of the psychologist's own soul. For psychical life may be revealed to us not only in self-consciousness but equally in our consciousness of other selves, and this latter source of experience offers us more than a reduplication of what we find in our self-consciousness, for it establishes the differences between "own" and "other" which we experience, and presents us with the characteristics of the "social-life." And hence the further task accrues to psychology of revealing the intentions of which the "social life" consists.

PHENOMENOLOGICAL-PSYCHOLOGICAL AND EIDETIC REDUCTIONS.

The Phenomenological psychology must examine the self's experience of itself and its derivative experience of other selves and of society, but whether, in so doing, it can be free of all psycho-physical admixture, is not yet clear. Can one reach a really pure self-experience and purely psychical data? This difficulty, even since Brentano's discovery of intentionality, as the fundamental character of the psychical, has blinded psychologists to the possibilities of phenomenological psychology. The psychologist finds his self-consciousness mixed everywhere with "external" experience, and non-psychical realities. For what is experienced as external belongs not to the intentional "internal," though our experience of it belongs there as an experience of the external. The phenomenologist, who will only notice phenomena, and know purely his own "life," must practice an ⟨epochē⟩. He must inhibit every ordinary objective "position," and partake in no judgement concerning the objective world. The experience itself will remain what it was, an experience of this house, of this body, of this world in general, in its particular mode. For one cannot describe any intentional experience, even though it be "illusory," a self-contradicting judgment and the like, without describing what in the experience is, as such, the object of consciousness.

Our comprehensive ⟨epochē⟩ puts, as we say, the world between brackets, excludes the world which is simply there! from the subject's field, presenting in its stead the so-and-so-experienced-perceived-remembered-judged-thought-valued-etc., world, as such, the "bracketed" world. Not the world or any part of it appears, but the "sense" of the world. To enjoy phenomenological experience we must retreat from the objects posited in the natural attitude to the multiple modes of their "appearance," to the "bracketed" objects.

The phenomenological reduction to phenomena, to the purely psychical, advances by two steps: (1) systematic and radical ⟨epochē⟩ of every objectifying "position" in an experience, practised both upon the regard of particular objects and upon the entire attitude of mind, and (2) expert recognition, comprehension and description of the manifold "appearances" of what are no longer "objects" but "unities" of "sense." So that the phenomenological description will comprise two parts, description of the "noetic" (⟨neo⟩) or "experiencing" and description of the "noematic" (⟨noema⟩) or the "experienced." Phenomenological experience, is the only experience which may properly be called "internal" and there is no limit to its practice. And as a similar "bracketing" of objective, and description of what then "appears" (⟨"noema"⟩ in ⟨"noesis"⟩), can be performed upon the "life" of another self which we represent to ourselves, the "reductive" method can be extended from one's own self-experience to one's experience of other selves. And, further, that society, which we experience in a common consciousness, may be reduced not only to the intentional fields of the individual consciousness, but also by the means of an inter-subjective reduction, to that which unites these, namely the phenomenological unity of the social life. Thus enlarged, the psychological concept of internal experience reaches its full extent.

But it takes more than the unity of a manifold "intentional life," with its inseparable complement of "sense-unities," to make a "soul." For from the individual life that "ego-subject" cannot be disjoined, which persists as an identical ego or "pole," to the particular intentions, and the "habits" growing out of these. Thus the "inter-subjective," phenomenologically reduced and concretely apprehended, is seen to be a "society" of "persons," who share a conscious life.

Phenomenological psychology can be purged of every empirical and psychophysical element, but, being so purged, it cannot deal with "matters of fact." Any closed field may be considered as regards its "essence," its ⟨eidos⟩, and we may disregard the factual side of our phenomena, and use them as "examples" merely. We shall ignore individual souls and societies, to learn their a priori, their "possible" forms. Our thesis will be "theoretical," observing the invariable through variation, disclosing a typical realm of a priori. There will be no psychical existence whose "style" we shall not know. Psychological phenomenology must rest upon eidetic phenomenology.

The phenomenology of the perception of bodies, for example, will not be an account of actually occurring perceptions, or those which may be expected to occur, but of that invariable "structure," apart from which no perception of a body, single or prolonged, can be conceived. The phenomenological reduction reveals the phenomena of actual internal experience; the eidetic reduction, the essential forms constraining psychical existence.

Men now demand that empirical psychology shall conform to the exactness required by modern natural science. Natural science, which was once a vague, inductive empiric, owes its modern character to the a priori system of forms, nature as it is "conceivable," which its separate disciplines, pure geometry, laws of motion, time, etc., have contributed. The methods of natural science and psychology are quite distinct, but the latter, like the former, can only reach "exactness" by a rationalization of the "essential."

The psycho-physical has an a priori which must be learned by any complete psychology, this a priori is not phenomenological, for it depends no less upon the essence of physical, or more particularly organic nature.

II. TRANSCENDENTAL PHENOMENOLOGY

Transcendental philosophy may be said to have originated in Descartes, and phenomenological psychology in Locke, Berkeley and Hume, although the latter did not grow up primarily as a method or discipline to serve psychology, but to contribute to the solution of the transcendental problematic which Descartes had posed. The theme propounded in the *Meditations* was still dominant in a philosophy which it had initiated. All reality, so it ran, and the whole of the world which we perceive as existent, may be said to exist only as the content of our own representations, judged in our judgments, or, at best, proved by our own knowing. There lay impulse enough to rouse all the legitimate and illegitimate problems of transcendence, which we know. Descartes' "Doubting" first disclosed "transcendental subjectivity," and his "Ego Cogito" was its first conceptual handling. But the Cartesian transcendental "Mens" became the "Human Mind," which Locke undertook to explore; and Locke's exploration turned into a psychology of the internal experience. And since Locke thought his psychology could embrace the transcendental problems, in whose interest he had begun his work, he became the founder of a false psychologistical philosophy which has persisted because men have not analysed their concept of "subjective" into its twofold significance. Once the transcendental problem is fairly stated, the ambiguity of the sense of the "subjective" becomes apparent, and establishes the phenomenological psychology to deal with its one meaning, and the transcendental phenomenology with its other.

Phenomenological psychology has been given the priority in this article, partly because it forms a convenient stepping-stone to the philosophy and partly because it is nearer to the common attitude than is the transcendental. Psychology, both in its eiditic and empirical disciplines, is a "positive" science, promoted in the "natural attitude" with the world before it for the ground of all its themes, while transcendental experience is difficult to realize because it is "supreme" and entirely "unworldly." Phenomenological psychology, although comparatively new, and completely new as far as it uses intentional analysis, can be approached from the gates of any of the positive sciences: and, being once reached, demands only a reemployment, in a more stringent mode, of its formal mechanism of reduction and analysis, to disclose the transcendental phenomena.

But it is not to be doubted that transcendental phenomenology could be developed independently of all psychology. The discovery of the double relativity of consciousness suggests the practice of both reductions. The psychological reduction does not reach beyond the psychical in animal realities, for psychology subserves real existence, and even its eidetic is confined to the possibilities of real worlds. But the transcendental problem will include the entire world and all its sciences, to "doubt" the whole. The world "originates" in us, as Descartes led men to recognize and within us acquires its habitual influence. The general significance of the world, and the definite sense of its particulars, is something of which we are conscious within our perceiving, representing, thinking, valuing life, and therefore something "constituted" in some subjective genesis.

The world and its property, "in and for itself," exists as it exists, whether I, or we, happen, or not, to be conscious of it. But let once this general world, make its "appearance" in consciousness as "the" world. It is thenceforth related to the subjective, and all its existence and the manner of it, assumes a new dimension, becoming "incompletely intelligible," "questionable." Here, then, is the transcendental problem; this "making its appearance," this "being for us" of the world, which can only gain its significance "subjectively," what is it? We may call the world "internal" because it is related to consciousness, but how can this quite "general" world, whose "immanent" being is as shadowy as the consciousness wherein it "exists," contrive to appear before us in a variety of "particular" aspects, which experience assures us are the aspects of an independent, self-existent world? The problem also touches every "ideal" world, the world of pure number, for example, and the world of "truths in themselves." And no existence, or manner of existence, is less wholly intelligible than ourselves. Each by himself, and in society, we, in whose consciousness the world is valid, being men, belong ourselves to the world. Must we, then, refer ourselves to ourselves to gain a worldly sense, a worldly being? Are we both psychologically to be called men, subjects of a psychical life, and yet be transcendental to ourselves and the whole world, being subjects of a transcendental world-constituting life? Psychical subjectivity, the "I" and "we" of everyday intent, may be experienced as it is in itself under the phenomenological-psychological reduction, and being eidetically treated, may establish a phenomenological psychology. But the transcendental subjectivity, which for want of language we can only call again, "I myself," "we ourselves," cannot be found under the attitude of psychological or natural science, being no part at all of the objective world, but that subjective conscious life itself, wherein the world and all its content is made for "us," for "me." We that are, indeed, men, spiritual and bodily, existing in the world, are, therefore, "appearances" unto ourselves, parcel of what "we" have constituted, pieces of the significance "we" have made. The "I" and "we," which we apprehend, presuppose a hidden "I" and "we" to whom they are "present."

To this transcendental subjectivity transcendental experience gives us direct approach. As the psychical experience was purified, so is the transcendental, by a reduction. The transcendental reduction may be regarded as a certain further purification of the psychological interest. The universal is carried to a further stage. Henceforth the "bracketing" includes not the world only but its "souls" as well. The psychologist reduces the ordinarily valid world to a subjectivity of "souls," which are a part of the world which they inhabit. The transcendental phenomenologist reduces the already psychologically purified to the transcendental, that most general, subjectivity, which makes the world and its "souls," and confirms them.

I no longer survey my perception experiences, imagination-experiences, the psychological data which my psychological experience reveals: I learn to survey transcendental experience. I am no longer interested in my own existence. I am interested in the pure intentional life, wherein my psychically real experiences have occurred. This step raises the transcendental problem (the transcendental being defined as the quality of that which is consciousness) to its true level. We have to recognize that relativity to consciousness is not only an actual quality of our world, but, from eidetic necessity, the quality of every conceivable world. We may, in a free fancy, vary our actual world, and transmute it to any other which we can imagine, but we are obliged with the world to vary ourselves also, and ourselves we cannot vary except within the limits prescribed to us by the nature of subjectivity. Change worlds as we may, each must ever be a world such as we could experience, prove upon the evidence of our theories and inhabit with our practice. The transcendental problem is eidetic. My psychological experiences, perceptions, imaginations and the like remain in form and content what they were, but I see them as "structures" now, for I am face to face at last with the ultimate structure of consciousness.

It is obvious that, like every other intelligible problem, the transcendental problem derives the means of its solution from an existence-stratum, which it presupposes and sets beyond the reach of its enquiry. This realm is no other than the bare subjectivity of consciousness in general, while the realm of its investigation remains not less than every sphere which can be called "objective," which considered in its totality, and at its root, is the conscious life. No one, then, can justly propose to solve the transcendental problem by psychology either empirical or eidetic-phenomenological, without *petitio principii* [begging the question], for psychology's "subjectivity" and "consciousness" are not that subjectivity and consciousness, which our philosophy will investigate. The transcendental reduction has supplanted the psychological reduction. In the place of the psychological "I" and "we," the transcendental "I" and "we" are comprehended in the concreteness of transcendental consciousness. But though the transcendental "I" is not my psychological "I," it must not be considered as if it were a second "I," for it is no more separated from my psychological "I" in the conventional sense of separation, than it is joined to it in the conventional sense of being joined.

Transcendental self-experience may, at any moment, merely by a change of attitude, be turned back into psychological self-experience. Passing, thus, from the one to the other attitude, we notice a certain "identity" about the ego. What I saw under the psychological reflection as "my" objectification, I see under the transcendental reflection as self-objectifying, or, as we may also say, as objectified by the transcendental "I." We have only to recognize that what makes the psychological and transcendental spheres of experience parallel is an "identity" in their significance, and that what differentiates them is merely a change of attitude, to realize that the psychological and transcendental phenomenologies will also be parallel. Under the more stringent ⟨*epochē*⟩ the psychological subjectivity is transformed into the transcendental subjectivity, and the psychological inter-subjectivity into the transcendental inter-subjectivity. It is this last which is the concrete, ultimate ground, whence all that transcends consciousness, including all that is real in the world, derives the sense of its existence. For all objective existence is essentially "relative," and owes its nature to a unity of intention, which being established according to transcendental laws, produces consciousness with its habit of belief and its conviction.

PHENOMENOLOGY, THE UNIVERSAL SCIENCE.

Thus, as phenomenology is developed, the Leibnitzian foreshadowing of a universal ontology, the unification of all conceivable *a priori* sciences, is improved, and realized upon the new and non-dogmatic basis of phenomenological method. For phenomenology as the science of all concrete phenomena proper to subjectivity and inter-subjectivity, is *eo ipso* an *a priori* science of all possible existence and existences. Phenomenology is universal in its scope, because there is no *a priori* which does not depend upon its intentional constitution, and derive from this its power of engendering habits in the consciousness that knows it, so that the establishment of any *a priori* must reveal the subjective process by which it is established.

Once the *a priori* disciplines, such as the mathematical sciences, are incorporated within phenomenology, they cannot thereafter be beset by "paradoxes" or disputes concerning principles: and those sciences which have become *a priori* independently of phenomenology, can only hope to set their methods and premises beyond criticism, by founding themselves upon it. For their very claim to be positive, dogmatic sciences bears witness to their dependency, as branches, merely, of that universal, eidetic ontology, which is phenomenology.

The endless task, this exposition of the universum of the *a priori,* by referring all objectives to their transcendental "origin," may be considered as one function in the construction of a universal science of fact, where every department, including the positive, will be settled on its *a priori.* So that our last division of the complete phenomenology is thus: eidetic phenomenology, or the universal ontology, for a first philosophy; and second philosophy as the science of the transcendental inter-subjectivity or universum of fact.

Thus the antique conception of philosophy as the universal science, philosophy in the Platonic, philosophy in the Cartesian, sense, that shall embrace all knowledge, is once more justly restored. All rational problems, and all those problems, which for one reason or another, have come to be known as "philosophical," have their place within phenomenology, finding from the ultimate source of transcendental experience or eidetic intuition, their proper form and the means of their solution. Phenomenology itself learns its proper function of transcendental human "living" from an entire relationship to "self." It can intuite life's absolute norms and learn life's original teleological structure. Phenomenology is not less than man's whole occupation with himself in the service of the universal reason. Revealing life's norms, he does in fact, set free a stream of new consciousness intent upon the infinite idea of entire humanity, humanity in fact and truth.

Metaphysical, teleological, ethical problems, and problems of the history of philosophy, the problem of judgment, all significant problems in general, and the transcendental bonds uniting them, lie within phenomenology's capability.

Phenomenological philosophy is but developing the mainsprings of old Greek philosophy, and the supreme motive of Descartes. These have not died. They split into rationalism and empiricism. They stretch over Kant and German idealism, and reach the present, confused day. They must be reassumed, subjected to methodical and concrete treatment. They can inspire a science without bounds.

Phenomenology demands of phenomenalists that they shall forgo particular closed systems of philosophy, and share decisive work with others toward persistent philosophy.

THE CRISIS OF EUROPEAN SCIENCE AND TRANSCENDENTAL PHENOMENOLOGY (in part)

PART III: THE CLARIFICATION OF THE TRANSCENDENTAL PROBLEM AND THE RELATED FUNCTION OF PSYCHOLOGY

SECTION A: THE WAY INTO PHENOMENOLOGICAL TRANSCENDENTAL PHILOSOPHY BY INQUIRING BACK FROM THE PREGIVEN LIFE-WORLD

*   *   *

§33. THE PROBLEM OF THE "LIFE-WORLD" AS A PARTIAL PROBLEM WITHIN THE GENERAL PROBLEM OF OBJECTIVE SCIENCE.

Briefly reminding ourselves of our earlier discussions, let us recall the fact we have emphasized, namely, that science is a human spiritual accomplishment which presupposes as its point of departure, both historically and for each new student, the intuitive surrounding world of life, pregiven as existing for all in common. Furthermore, it is an accomplishment which, in being practiced and carried forward, continues to presuppose this surrounding world as it is given in its particularity to the scientist. For example, for the physicist it is the world in which he sees his measuring instruments,

Edmund Husserl, *The Crisis of European Science and Transcendental Phenomenology: An Introduction to Phenomenological Philosophy,* Part III, A, §33 and §34, translated by David Carr (Evanston, IL: Northwestern University Press, 1970), pp. 121–135. Copyright © 1970 Northwestern University Press. Reprinted by permission.

hears time-beats, estimates visible magnitudes, etc.—the world in which, furthermore, he knows himself to be included with all his activity and all his theoretical ideas.

When science poses and answers questions, these are from the start, and hence from then on, questions resting upon the ground of, and addressed to, the elements of this pregiven world in which science and every other life-praxis is engaged. In this life-praxis, knowledge, as prescientific knowledge, plays a constant role, together with its goals, which are in general satisfactorily achieved in the sense which is intended and in each case usually in order to make practical life possible. But a new civilization (philo-sophical, scientific civilization), rising up in Greece, saw fit to recast the idea of "knowledge" and "truth" in natural existence and to ascribe to the newly formed idea of "objective truth" a higher dignity, that of a norm for all knowledge. In relation to this, finally, arises the idea of a universal science encompassing all possible knowledge in its infinity, the bold guiding idea of the modern period. If we have made this clear to ourselves, then obviously an explicit elucidation of the objective validity and of the whole task of science requires that we first inquire back into the pregiven world. It is pregiven to us all quite naturally, as persons within the horizon of our fellow men, i.e., in every actual connection with others, as "the" world common to us all. Thus it is, as we have explained in detail, the constant ground of validity, an ever available source of what is taken for granted, to which we, whether as practical men or as scientists, lay claim as a matter of course.

Now if this pregiven world is to become a subject of investigation in its own right, so that we can arrive, of course, at scientifically defensible assertions, this re-quires special care in preparatory reflections. It is not easy to achieve clarity about what kind of peculiar scientific and hence universal tasks are to be posed under the title "life-world" and about whether something philosophically significant will arise here. Even the first attempt to understand the peculiar ontic sense of the life-world, which can be taken now as a narrower, now as a broader one, causes difficulties.

The manner in which we here come to the life-world as a subject for scientific in-vestigation makes this subject appear an ancillary and partial one within the full sub-ject of objective science in general. The latter has become generally, that is, in all its particular forms (the particular positive sciences), incomprehensible as regards the possibility of its objective accomplishment. If science becomes a problem in this way, then we must withdraw from the operation of it and take up a standpoint above it, sur-veying in generality its theories and results in the systematic context of predicative thoughts and statements, and on the other side we must also survey the life of acts practiced by working scientists, working with one another—their setting of goals, their termination in a given goal, and the terminating self-evidence. And what also comes under consideration here is precisely the scientists' repeated recourse, in different gen-eral manners, to the life-world with its ever available intuited data; to this we can im-mediately add the scientists' statements, in each case simply adapted to this world, statements made purely descriptively in the same prescientific manner of judging which is proper to the "occasional" statements of practical, everyday life. Thus the problem of the life-world, or rather of the manner in which it functions and must func-tion for scientists, is only a partial subject within the above-designated whole of objec-tive science (namely, in the service of its full grounding).

It is clear, however, that prior to the general question of its function for a self-evident grounding of the objective sciences there is good reason to ask about the life-world's own and constant ontic meaning for the human beings who live in it. These human beings do not always have scientific interests, and even scientists are not al-ways involved in scientific work; also, as history teaches us, there was not always in the world a civilization that lived habitually with long-established scientific interests. The life-world was always there for mankind before science, then, just as it continues its manner of being in the epoch of science. Thus one can put forward by itself the problem of the manner of being of the life-world; one can place oneself completely upon the ground of this straightforwardly intuited world, putting out of play all objective-scientific opinions and cognitions, in order to consider generally what kind of "scientific" tasks, i.e., tasks to be resolved with universal validity, arise in respect to this world's own manner of being. Might this not yield a vast theme for study? Is it not the case that, in the end, through what first appears as a special subject in the theory of science, that "third dimension" is opening up, immediately destined in advance to engulf the whole subject matter of objective science (as well as all other subject matters on the "plane")? At first this must appear peculiar and unbelievable. Many paradoxes will arise; yet they will be resolved. What imposes itself here and must be considered before everything else is the correct comprehension of the essence of the life-world and the method of a "scientific" treatment appropriate to it, from which "objective" scientific treatment, however, is excluded.

§34. EXPOSITION OF THE PROBLEM OF A SCIENCE OF THE LIFE-WORLD.

a. The Difference Between Objective Science and Science in General.

Is not the life-world as such what we know best, what is always taken for granted in all human life, always familiar to us in its typology through experience? Are not all its horizons of the unknown simply horizons of what is just incompletely known, i.e., known in advance in respect of its most general typology? For prescientific life, of course, this type of acquaintance suffices, as does its manner of converting the unknown into the known, gaining "occasional" knowledge on the basis of experience (verifying itself internally and thereby excluding illusion) and induction. This suffices for everyday praxis. If, now, something more can be and is to be accomplished, if a "scientific" knowledge is supposed to come about, what can be meant other than what objective science has in view and does anyway? Is scientific knowledge as such not "objective" knowledge, aimed at a knowledge substratum which is valid for everyone with unconditioned generality? And yet, paradoxically, we uphold our assertion and require that one not let the handed-down concept of objective science be substituted, because of the century-old tradition in which we have all been raised, for the concept of science in general.

The title "life-world" makes possible and demands perhaps various different, though essentially interrelated, scientific undertakings; and perhaps it is part of genuine and full scientific discipline that we must treat these all together, though following their essential order of founding, rather than treating, say, just the one, the objective-logical one (this particular accomplishment within the life-world) by itself, leaving the others completely out of scientific consideration. There has never been a scientific inquiry into the way in which the life-world constantly functions as subsoil, into how its manifold prelogical validities act as grounds for the logical ones, for theoretical truths. And perhaps the scientific discipline which this life-world as such, in its universality, requires is a peculiar one, one which is precisely not objective and logical but which, as the ultimately grounding one, is not inferior but superior in value. But how is this completely different sort of scientific discipline, for which the objective sort has always been substituted up to now, to be realized? The idea of objective truth is predetermined in its whole meaning by the contrast with the idea of the truth in pre- and extra-scientific life. This latter truth has its ultimate and deepest source of verification in experience which is "pure" in the sense designated above, in all its modes of perception, memory, etc. These words, however, must be understood actually as prescientific life understands them; thus one must not inject into them, from current objective science, any psychophysical, psychological interpretation. And above all—to dispose of an important point right away—one must not go straight back to the supposedly immediately given "sense-data," as if *they* were immediately characteristic of the purely intuitive data of the life-world. What is actually first is the "merely subjective-relative" intuition of prescientific world-life. For us, to be sure, this "merely" has, as an old inheritance, the disdainful coloring of the ⟨*doxa*⟩. In prescientific life itself, of course, it has nothing of this; there it is a realm of good verification and, based on this, of well-verified predicative cognitions and of truths which are just as secure as is necessary for the practical projects of life that determine their sense. The disdain with which everything "merely subjective and relative" is treated by those scientists who pursue the modern ideal of objectivity changes nothing of its own manner of being, just as it does not change the fact that the scientist himself must be satisfied with this realm whenever he has recourse, as he avoidably must have recourse, to it.

b. The Use of Subjective-Relative Experiences for the Objective Sciences, and the Science of Them.

The sciences build upon the life-world as taken for granted in that they make use of whatever in it happens to be necessary for their particular ends. But to use the life-world in this way is not to know it scientifically in its own manner of being. For example, Einstein uses the Michelson experiments and the corroboration of them by other researchers, with apparatus copied from Michelson's, with everything required in the way of scales of measurement, coincidences established, etc. There is no doubt that everything that enters in here—the persons, the apparatus, the room in the institute, etc.—can itself become a subject of investigation in the usual sense of objective inquiry, that of the positive sciences. But Einstein could make no use whatever of a theoretical psychological-psychophysical construction of the objective being of Mr. Michelson; rather, he made use of the human being who was accessible to him, as to everyone else in the prescientific world, as an object of straightforward experience, the human being whose existence, with this vitality, in these activities and creations within the common life-world, is always the presupposition for all of Einstein's objective scientific lines of inquiry, projects, and accomplishments pertaining to Michelson's experiments. It is, of course, the one world of experience, common to all, that Einstein and every other researcher knows he is in as a human being, even throughout all his activity of research. [But] precisely this world and everything that happens in it, used as needed for scientific and other ends, bears, on the other hand, for every natural scientist in his thematic orientation toward its "objective truth," the stamp "merely subjective and relative." The contrast to this determines, as we said, the sense of the "objective" task. This "subjective-relative" is supposed to be "overcome"; one can and should correlate with it a hypothetical being-in-itself, a substrate for logical-mathematical "truths-in-themselves" that one can approximate through ever newer and better hypothetical approaches, always justifying them through experiential verification. This is the one side. But while the natural scientist is thus interested in the objective and is involved in his activity, the subjective-relative is on the other hand still functioning for him, not as something irrelevant that must be passed through but as that which ultimately grounds the theoretical-logical ontic validity for all objective verification, i.e., as the source of self-evidence, the source of verification. The visible measuring scales, scale-markings, etc., are used as actually existing things, not as illusions; thus that which actually exists in the life-world, as something valid, is a premise.

c. Is the Subjective-Relative an Object for Psychology?

Now the question of the manner of being of this subjective sphere, or the question of the science which is to deal with it in its own universe of being, is normally disposed of by the natural scientist by referring to psychology. But again one must not allow the intrusion of what exists in the sense of objective science when it is a question of what exists in the life-world. For what has always gone under the name of psychology, at any rate since the founding of modern objectivism regarding knowledge of the world, naturally has the meaning of an "objective" science of the subjective, no matter which of the attempted historical psychologies we may choose. Now in our subsequent reflections the problem of making possible an objective psychology will have to become the object of more detailed discussions. But first we must grasp clearly the contrast between objectivity and the subjectivity of the life-world as a contrast which determines the fundamental sense of objective-scientific discipline itself, and we must secure this contrast against the great temptations to misconstrue it.

d. The Life-World as Universe of What Is Intuitable in Principle; the "Objective-True" World as in Principle Nonintuitable "Logical" Substruction.

Whatever may be the chances for realizing, or the capacity for realizing, the idea of objective science in respect to the mental world (i.e., not only in respect to nature), this idea of objectivity dominates the whole universitas of the positive sciences in the modern period, and in the general usage it dominates the meaning of the word "science." This already involves a naturalism insofar as this concept is taken from Galilean natural science, such that the scientifically "true," the objective, world is always thought of in advance as nature, in an expanded sense of the word. The contrast between the subjectivity of the life-world and the "objective," the "true" world, lies in the fact that the latter is a theoretical-logical substruction, the substruction of something that is in principle not perceivable, in principle not experienceable in its own proper being, whereas the subjective, in the life-world, is distinguished in all respects precisely by its being actually experienceable.*

The life-world is a realm of original self-evidences. That which is self-evidently given is, in perception, experienced as "the thing itself," in immediate presence, or, in

---

*In life the verification of being, terminating in experience, yields a full conviction. Even when it is inductive, the inductive anticipation is of a possible experienceability which is ultimately decisive. Inductions can be verified by other inductions, working together. Because of their anticipations of experienceability, and because every direct perception itself includes inductive moments (anticipation of the sides of the object which are not yet experienced), everything is contained in the broader concept of "experience" or "induction."

memory, remembered as the thing itself; and every other manner of intuition is a pre-sentification of the thing itself. Every mediate cognition belonging in this sphere—broadly speaking, every manner of induction—has the sense of an induction of something intuitable, something possibly perceivable as the thing itself or rememberable as having-been-perceived, etc. All conceivable verification leads back to these modes of self-evidence because the "thing itself" (in the particular mode) lies in these intuitions themselves as that which is actually, intersubjectively experienceable and verifiable and is not a substruction of thought; whereas such a substruction, insofar as it makes a claim to truth, can have actual truth only by being related back to such self-evidences.

It is of course itself a highly important task, for the scientific opening-up of the life-world, to bring to recognition the primal validity of these self-evidences and indeed their higher dignity in the grounding of knowledge compared to that of the objective-logical self-evidences. One must fully clarify, i.e., bring to ultimate self-evidence, how all the self-evidence of objective-logical accomplishments, through which objective theory (thus mathematical and natural-scientific theory) is grounded in respect of form and content, has its hidden sources of grounding in the ultimately accomplishing life, the life in which the self-evident givenness of the life-world forever has, has attained, and attains anew its prescientific ontic meaning. From objective-logical self-evidence (mathematical "insight," natural-scientific, positive-scientific "insight," as it is being accomplished by the inquiring and grounding mathematician, etc.), the path leads back, here, to the primal self-evidence in which the life-world is ever pregiven.

One may at first find strange and even questionable what has been simply asserted here, but the general features of the contrast among levels of self-evidence are unmistakable. The empiricist talk of natural scientists often, if not for the most part, gives the impression that the natural sciences are based on the experience of objective nature. But it is not in this sense true that these sciences are experiential sciences, that they follow experience in principle, that they all begin with experiences, that is, all their inductions must finally be verified through experiences; rather, this is true only in that other sense whereby experience [yields] a self-evidence taking place purely in the life-world and as such is the source of self-evidence for what is objectively established in the sciences, the latter never themselves being experiences of the objective. The objective is precisely never experienceable as itself; and scientists themselves, by the way, consider it in this way whenever they interpret it as something metaphysically transcendent, in contrast to their confusing empiricist talk. The experienceability of something objective is no different from that of an infinitely distant geometrical construct and in general no different from that of all infinite "ideas," including, for example, the infinity of the number series. Naturally, "rendering ideas intuitive" in the manner of mathematical or natural-scientific "models" is hardly intuition of the objective itself but rather a matter of life-world intuitions which are suited to make easier the conception of the objective ideals in question. Many [such] conceptual intermediaries are often involved, [especially since] the conception itself does not always occur so immediately, cannot always be made so self-evident in its way, as is the case in conceiving of geometrical straight lines on the basis of the life-world self-evidence of straight table-edges and the like.

As can be seen, a great deal of effort is involved here in order to secure even the presuppositions for a proper inquiry, i.e., in order first to free ourselves from the constant misconstructions which mislead us all because of the scholastic dominance of objective-scientific ways of thinking.

e. The Objective Sciences as Subjective Constructs—Those of a Particular Praxis, Namely, the Theoretical-Logical, Which Itself Belongs to the Full Concreteness of the Life-World.

If the contrast [under discussion] has been purified, we must now do justice to the essential interrelatedness [of the elements contrasted]: objective theory in its logical sense (taken universally: science as the totality of predicative theory, of the system of statements meant "logically" as "propositions in themselves," "truths in themselves," and in this sense logically joined) is rooted, grounded in the life-world, in the original self-evidences belonging to it. Thanks to this rootedness objective science has a constant reference of meaning to the world in which we always live, even as scientists and also in the total community of scientists—a reference, that is, to the general life-world. But at the same time, as an accomplishment of scientific persons, as individuals and as joined in the community of scientific activity, objective science itself belongs to the life-world. Its theories, the logical constructs, are of course not things in the life-world like stones, houses, or trees. They are logical wholes and logical parts made up of ultimate logical elements. To speak with Bolzano, they are "representations-in-themselves" ["*Vorstellungen an sich*"] "propositions in themselves," inferences and proofs "in themselves," ideal unities of signification whose logical ideality is determined by their ⟨*telos*⟩, "truth in itself."

But this or any other ideality does not change in the least the fact that these are human formations, essentially related to human actualities and potentialities, and thus belong to this concrete unity of the life-world, whose concreteness thus extends farther than that of "things." Exactly the same thing is true, correlative to this, of scientific activities—those of experiencing, those of arriving at logical formations "on the basis of" experience—activities through which these formations appear in original form and original modes of variation in the individual scientists and in the community of scientists: the original status of the proposition or demonstration dealt with by all.

But here we enter an uncomfortable situation. If we have made our contrast with all necessary care, then we have two different things: life-world and objective-scientific world, though of course [they are] related to each other. The knowledge of the objective-scientific world is "grounded" in the self-evidence of the life-world. The latter is pregiven to the scientific worker, or the working community, as ground; yet, as they build upon this, what is built is something new, something different. If we cease being immersed in our scientific thinking, we become aware that we scientists are, after all, human beings and as such are among the components of the life-world which always exists for us, ever pregiven; and thus all of science is pulled, along with us, into the—merely "subjective-relative"—life-world. And what becomes of the objective world itself? What happens to the hypothesis of being-in-itself, related first to the "things" of the life-world, the "objects," the "real" bodies, real animals, plants, and also human beings within the "space-time" of the life-world—all these concepts being understood, now, not from the point of view of the objective sciences but as they are in prescientific life?

Is it not the case that this hypothesis, which in spite of the ideality of scientific theories has direct validity for the scientific subjects (the scientists as human beings), is but *one* among the many practical hypotheses and projects which make up the life of human beings in this life-world—which is at all times consciously pregiven to them as available? Do not all goals, whether they are "practical" in some other, extrascientific sense or are practical under the title of "theory," belong *eo ipso* to the unity of the life-world, if only we take the latter in its complete and full concreteness?

On the other hand, we have seen also that the propositions the theories, the whole edifice of doctrine in the objective sciences are structures attained through certain activities of scientists bound together in their collaborative work—or, to speak more exactly, attained through a continued building-up of activities, the later of which always presuppose the results of the earlier. And we see further that all these theoretical results have the character of validities for the life-world, adding themselves as such to its own composition and belonging to it even before that as a horizon of possible accomplishments for developing science. The concrete life-world, then, is the grounding soil [*der grundende Boden*] of the "scientifically true" world and at the same time encompasses it in its own universal concreteness. How is this to be understood? How are we to do justice systematically—that is, with appropriate scientific discipline—to the all-encompassing, so paradoxically demanding, manner of being of the life-world?

We are posing questions whose clarifying answers are by no means obvious. The contrast and the inseparable union [we have been exploring] draw us into a reflection which entangles us in more and more troublesome difficulties. The paradoxical interrelationships of the "objectively true world" and the "life-world" make enigmatic the manner of being of both. Thus [the idea of a] true world in any sense, and within it our own being, becomes an enigma in respect to the sense of this being. In our attempts to attain clarity we shall suddenly become aware, in the face of emerging paradoxes, that all of our philosophizing up to now has been without a ground. How can we now truly become philosophers?

We cannot escape the force of this motivation. It is impossible for us to evade the issue here through a preoccupation with aporia and argumentation nourished by Kant or Hegel, Aristotle or Thomas.

f. The Problem of the Life-World Not as a Partial Problem But Rather as a Universal Problem for Philosophy.

Of course, it is a new sort of scientific discipline that is required for the solution of the enigmas which now disquiet us: it is not mathematical, nor logical at all in the historical sense; it cannot already have before it, as an available norm, a finished mathematics, logic, or logistic, since these are themselves objective sciences in the sense which is presently problematical and, as included in the problem, cannot be presuppositions used as premises. At first, as long as one only makes contrasts, is only concerned with oppositions, it could appear that nothing more than or different from objective science is needed, just as everyday practical life undertakes its rational reflections, both particular and general, without needing a science for them. It just is this way, a fact familiar to all, unthinkingly accepted rather than being formulated as a fundamental fact and thought through as a subject for thinking in its own right—namely, that there are two sorts of truth: on the one side, everyday practical situational truths, relative, to be sure, but, as we have already emphasized, exactly what praxis, in its particular projects, seeks and needs; on the other side there are scientific truths, and their grounding leads back precisely to the situational truths, but in such a way that scientific method does not suffer thereby in respect to its own meaning, since it wants to use and must use precisely these truths.

Thus it could appear—if one allows oneself to be carried along by the thoughtless naïveté of life even in the transition from the extralogical to the logical, to the objective-scientific praxis of thinking—that a separate investigation under the title "life-world" is an intellectualistic enterprise born of a mania, peculiar to modern life, to theorize everything. But, on the other hand, it has at least become apparent that we cannot let the matter end with this naïveté, that paradoxical enigmas announce themselves here: merely subjective relativity is supposedly overcome by objective-logical theory, yet the latter belongs, as the theoretical praxis of human beings, to the merely subjective and relative and at the same time must have its premises, its sources of self-evidence, in the subjective and relative. From here on this much is certain: that all problems of truth and of being, all methods, hypotheses, and results conceivable for these problems—whether for worlds of experience or for metaphysical higher worlds—can attain their ultimate clarity, their evident sense or the evidence of their nonsense, only through this supposed intellectualistic hypertrophy. This will then include, certainly, all ultimate questions of legitimate sense and of nonsense in the busy routine of the "resurrected metaphysics" that has become so vocal and so bewitching of late.

Through this last series of considerations the magnitude, the universal and independent significance, of the problem of the life-world has become intelligible to us in an anticipatory insight. In comparison with this the problem of the "objectively true" world or that of objective-logical science—no matter how pressing it may repeatedly become, and properly so—appears now as a problem of secondary and more specialized interest. Though the peculiar accomplishment of our modern objective science may still not be understood, nothing changes the fact that it is a validity for the life-world, arising out of particular activities, and that it belongs itself to the concreteness of the life-world. Thus in any case, for the sake of clarifying this and all other acquisitions of human activity, the concrete life-world must first be taken into consideration; and it must be considered in terms of the truly concrete universality whereby it embraces, both directly and in the manner of horizons, all the built-up levels of validity acquired by men for the world of their common life and whereby it has the totality of these levels related in the end to a world-nucleus to be distilled by abstraction, namely, the world of straightforward intersubjective experiences. To be sure, we do not yet know how the life-world is to become an independent, totally self-sufficient subject of investigation, how it is supposed to make possible scientific statements—which as such, after all must have their own "objectivity," even if it is in a manner different from that of our sciences, i.e., a necessary validity to be appropriated purely methodically, which we and everyone can verify precisely through this method. We are absolute beginners here, and have nothing in the way of a logic designed to provide norms; we can do nothing but reflect, engross ourselves in the still not unfolded sense of our task, and thus secure, with the utmost care, freedom from prejudice, keeping our undertaking free of alien interferences (and we have already made several important contributions to this); and this, as in the case of every new undertaking, must supply us with our method. The clarification of the sense of the task is, indeed, the self-evidence of the goal *qua* goal; and to this self-evidence belongs essentially the self-evidence of the possible "ways" to it. The intricacy and difficulty of the preliminary reflections which are still before us will justify themselves, not only because of the magnitude of the goal, but also because of the essential strangeness and precariousness of the ideas which will necessarily become involved.

Thus what appeared to be merely a problem of the fundamental basis of the objective sciences or a partial problem within the universal problem of objective science has indeed (just as we announced in advance that it would) proven to be the genuine and most universal problem. It can also be put this way: the problem first appears as the question of the relation between objective-scientific thinking and intuition; it concerns, on the one hand, then, logical thinking as the thinking of logical thoughts, e.g., the physicist's thinking of physical theory, or purely mathematical thinking, in which mathematics has its place as a system of doctrine, as a theory. And, on the other hand, we have intuiting and the intuited, in the life-world prior to theory. Here arises the ineradicable illusion of a pure thinking which, unconcerned in its purity about intuition, already has its self-evident truth, even truth about the world—the illusion which makes the sense and the possibility, the "scope," of objective science questionable. Here one concentrates on the separateness of intuiting and thinking and generally interprets the nature of the "theory of knowledge" as theory of science, carried out in respect to two correlative sides* (whereby science is always understood in terms of the only concept of science available, that of objective science). But as soon as the empty and vague notion of intuition—instead of being something negligible and insignificant compared to the supremely significant logical sphere in which one supposedly already has genuine truth—has become the problem of the life-world, as soon as the magnitude and difficulty of this investigation take on enormous proportions as one seriously penetrates it, there occurs the great transformation of the "theory of knowledge" and the theory of science whereby, in the end, science as a problem and as an accomplishment loses its self-sufficiency and becomes a mere partial problem.

What we have said also naturally applies to logic, as the *a priori* theory of norms for everything "logical"—in the overarching sense of what is logical, according to which logic is a logic of strict objectivity, of objective-logical truths. No one ever thinks about the predications and truths which precede science, about the "logic" which provides norms within this sphere of relativity, or about the possibility, even in the case of these logical structures conforming purely descriptively to the lifeworld, of inquiring into the system of principles that give them their norms *a priori*. As a matter of course, traditional objective logic is substituted as the *a priori* norm even for this subjective-relative sphere of truth.

*I.e., the subjective and the objective.

JOHN DEWEY
1859–1952

Charles Sanders Peirce, William James, and John Dewey were the great American pragmatists. The youngest of the three, John Dewey, was born and raised in Burlington, Vermont. His father, Archibald Dewey, was a successful grocer. Dewey's mother, Lucina Artemisia Rich Dewey, was deeply involved in philanthropic work, through which Dewey and his brother came into contact with the poor. The New England traditions of hard work, modesty, and honesty and the American belief in democracy combined with his family's concern for social justice to create Dewey's unique *persona*.

Following an adequate but unexceptional career in the local schools, Dewey attended the University of Vermont, after which he taught classics, algebra, and science at a high school in Pennsylvania. After two years of teaching, he returned to Burlington to continue his studies in philosophy. Encouraged by his former philosophy professor and by the editor of a philosophy journal, he borrowed five hundred dollars and enrolled in graduate school at the newly formed Johns Hopkins University. Peirce was one of his teachers, though at the time Dewey was more influenced by the Hegelian idealism of G.S. Morris.

After completing his dissertation on Kant's psychology and receiving a Ph.D. in 1884, Dewey joined the faculty of the University of Michigan. During his ten years there, Dewey began to move in more practical directions. For example, he began working with the education department on issues in teacher training, and he wrote books on psychology, including *Psychology* (1887) and *The Psychology of Number and Its Application to Methods of Teaching Arithmetic* (1895). At Michigan, Dewey met and married one of his students, Alice Chipman, and together they had five children and adopted a sixth.

In 1894, Dewey moved to the University of Chicago to become the head of the Department of Philosophy, Psychology, and Pedagogy—his three major interests by this time. In this position, he set up a laboratory school, the "Dewey School," in which his theories of education and teacher training were tested and refined. The school was student-centered and emphasized learning by doing—rather than by rote memory—and it profoundly effected American education. Dewey's most influential books, *School and Society* (1900) and *The Child and the Curriculum* (1902), came out of his work at the laboratory school. In Chicago, Dewey was also involved in a number of social causes, including Jane Addams's Hull House, where he worked with those affected by urbanization.

In 1904, Dewey became embroiled in a dispute with the administration of the University of Chicago over the appointment of Alice Dewey as principal of the Dewey School. The Deweys left Chicago and John Dewey, by now acknowledged as one of the leading educators in the country, accepted a position at Columbia University, where, for the next twenty-five years, he taught and wrote, and from which he traveled extensively. He lectured on education in Japan, China, and the Soviet Union. Throughout his Columbia period and even after his retirement in 1929, Dewey continued his involvement with social issues. He was a founder of the American Civil Liberties Union and the American Association of University Professors. Dewey also wrote prolifically (the bibliography of his works is over 150 pages long) in philosophy and education and on a variety of social issues.

*   *   *

Whereas Husserl called for a return to the disinterested rationality of the Greeks, Dewey called all such spectator knowledge disastrous. Whereas Husserl condemned "naturalism," Dewey called on philosophers to adapt the method of the natural sciences to resolve practical problems, particularly the problem of human values. In fact, Dewey saw his philosophy, which he called "instrumentalism," as a bridge between science and ethics.

According to Dewey, genuine inquiry begins with an "indeterminate situation"—with confusion or perplexity. Articulating the nature of the problem is the first stage of inquiry: "To see that a situation requires inquiry is the initial step in inquiry." Next, one creates hypotheses to resolve the difficulty. These hypothetical solutions are then clarified and refined still further by reasoning and clarifying meanings. These stages of hypothesis-creation and meaning-clarification will use concepts or "instruments" (hence the name "instrumentalism") as their tools. Finally, one is ready for the final stage of testing the reasoned solution. If successful, the inquiry will result in "a cleared-up, unified, resolved situation at the close." In such a cleared-up situation, the original elements of the problem will be converted into a "unified whole."

The knowledge gained by a successful inquiry is expressed in propositions that are "warrantedly assertible." Dewey purposely avoided the word "true" in order to eliminate the false notion of "truth" as a metaphysical absolute. He used the word "truth" only to refer to those "processes of change so directed that they achieve an intended consummation."

Dewey's minimalist definition of truth flies in the face of the Western philosophy inherited from the Greeks, which is one long search for a larger truth. In *Quest for Certainty* (1929), for example, Dewey explains that "man has a fundamental urge to seek security"; and it is this "insecurity [that] generates the quest for certainty." The Greeks sought to overcome this insecurity by exalting pure intellect over practical issues. Knowledge became the office by which one "uncovers the antecedently real"—a conception that endured long after the Greeks.

In "Construction of the Good" from *Quest for Certainty,* reprinted here (complete), Dewey explains how this Greek conception of knowledge and certainty led to a bifurcation between science and values, and he offers instead a way to reintegrate the two realities. After reviewing Western philosophy's decline, Dewey presents his main thesis concerning values:

> *Judgments about values are judgments about the conditions and the results of experienced objects; judgments about that which should regulate the formation of our desires, affections and enjoyments.*

By making values a type of judgment—"value judgments"—Dewey puts values back into philosophy. The instrumental method used successfully in science can be used with values as well. Such value-inquiry begins with a problem—what ought I to do?—and then uses the instruments of concepts to lead to solutions— to value judgments. Such a value inquiry would require understanding the nature of an experienced object in order to know if that object will naturally and repeatedly yield satisfaction, that is, if it is capable of being valued. But like all judgments in science, value judgments too will never be final. Just as initial judgments about physical objects may later prove deceptive, so also our initial enjoyment of an object may later be regretted. This view removes values from the domain of absolute truth, on the one hand, but it also removes them from the subjective realm of mere emotion.

*   *   *

For general works on pragmatism (which include sections on Dewey and place his thought in a wider context), see H.S. Thayer, "Pragmatism," in *A Critical History of Western Philosophy,* edited by D.J. O'Connor (New York: The Free Press, 1964); Amelie O. Rorty, ed., *Pragmatic Philosophy* (New York: Anchor Doubleday, 1966); H.S. Thayer, *Meaning and Action: A Critical History of Pragmatism,* 2nd edition (Indianapolis, IN: Bobbs-Merrill, 1981); Charles Moore, *The Pragmatic Movement in America* (New York: George Braziller, 1970); Israel Scheffler, *Four Pragmatists: A Critical Introduction to Peirce, James, Mead, and Dewey* (New York: Humanities Press, 1974); John E. Smith, *Purpose and Thought: The Meaning of Pragmatism* (New Haven, CT: Yale University Press, 1978); and Richard Rorty, *The Consequences of Pragmatism* (Minneapolis: University of Minnesota Press, 1982).

A good place to begin the study of Dewey is Sidney Hook, *John Dewey: An Intellectual Portrait* (Westport, CT: Greenwood Press, 1971). Other general introductions include George R. Geiger, *John Dewey in Perspective* (New York: Oxford University Press, 1958), which emphasizes Dewey's aesthetics; Richard Bernstein, *John Dewey* (New York: Washington Square Press, 1966); and J.E. Tiles, *Dewey* (New York: Routledge, 1988). For a highly critical examination of Dewey's philosophy, see W.T. Feldman, *The Philosophy of John Dewey: A Critical Analysis* (1934; reprinted New York: Greenwood Press, 1968). For collections of essays, see Sidney Hook, ed., *John Dewey: Philosopher of Science and Freedom* (New York: Barnes & Noble, 1950); Paul A. Schlipp, ed., *The Philoso-*

phy of John Dewey, 2nd edition (New York: Tudor, 1951); C.W. Hendel, ed., *John Dewey and the Experimental Spirit in Philosophy* (New York: Bobbs-Merrill, 1959); and Sidney Morganbesser, ed., *Dewey & His Critics: Essays from "The Journal of Philosophy"* (Indianapolis, IN: Hackett, 1977).

THE QUEST FOR CERTAINTY (in part)

CHAPTER 10: THE CONSTRUCTION OF GOOD

We saw at the outset of our discussion that insecurity generates the quest for certainty. Consequences issue from every experience, and they are the source of our interest in what is present. Absence of arts of regulation diverted the search for security into irrelevant modes of practice, into rite and cult; thought was devoted to discovery of omens rather than of signs of what is to occur. Gradually there was differentiation of two realms, one higher, consisting of the powers which determine human destiny in all important affairs. With this religion was concerned. The other consisted of the prosaic matters in which man relied upon his own skill and his matter-of-fact insight. Philosophy inherited the idea of this division. Meanwhile in Greece many of the arts had attained a state of development which raised them above a merely routine state; there were intimations of measure, order and regularity in materials dealt with which give intimations of underlying rationality. Because of the growth of mathematics, there arose also the ideal of a purely rational knowledge, intrinsically solid and worthy and the means by which the intimations of rationality within changing phenomena could be comprehended within science. For the intellectual class the stay and consolation, the warrant of certainty, provided by religion was henceforth found in intellectual demonstration of the reality of the objects of an ideal realm.

With the expansion of Christianity, ethico-religious traits came to dominate the purely rational ones. The ultimate authoritative standards for regulation of the dispositions and purposes of the human will were fused with those which satisfied the demands for necessary and universal truth. The authority of ultimate Being was, moreover, represented on earth by the Church; that which in its nature transcended intellect was made known by a revelation of which the Church was the interpreter and guardian. The system endured for centuries. While it endured, it provided an integration of belief and conduct for the western world. Unity of thought and practice extended down to every detail of the management of life; efficacy of its operation did not depend upon thought. It was guaranteed by the most powerful and authoritative of all social institutions.

Its seemingly solid foundation was, however, undermined by the conclusions of modern science. They effected, both in themselves and even more in the new interests and activities they generated, a breach between what man is concerned with here and now and the faith concerning ultimate reality which, in determining his ultimate and eternal destiny, had previously given regulation to his present life. The problem of restoring integration and cooperation between man's beliefs about the world in which he lives and his beliefs about the values and purposes that should direct his conduct is the deepest problem of modern life. It is the problem of any philosophy that is not isolated from that life.

The attention which has been given to the fact that in its experimental procedure science has surrendered the separation between knowing and doing has its source in the fact that there is now provided within a limited, specialized and technical field the possibility and earnest, as far as theory is concerned, of effecting the needed integration in the wider field of collective human experience. Philosophy is called upon to be the theory of the practice, through ideas sufficiently definite to be operative in experimental endeavor, by which the integration may be made secure in actual experience. Its central problem is the relation that exists between the beliefs about the nature of things due to natural science to beliefs about values—using that word to designate whatever is taken to have rightful authority in the direction of conduct. A philosophy which should take up this problem is struck first of all by the fact that beliefs about values are pretty much in the position in which beliefs about nature were before the scientific revolution. There is either a basic distrust of the capacity of experience to develop its own regulative standards, and an appeal to what philosophers call eternal values, in order to ensure regulation of belief and action; or there is acceptance of enjoyments actually experienced irrespective of the method or operation by which they are brought into existence. Complete bifurcation between rationalistic method and an empirical method has its final and most deeply human significance in the ways in which good and bad are thought of and acted for and upon.

As far as technical philosophy reflects this situation, there is division of theories of values into two kinds. On the one hand, goods and evils, in every region of life, as they are concretely experienced, are regarded as characteristic of an inferior order of Being—intrinsically inferior. Just because they are things of human experience, their worth must be estimated by reference to standards and ideals derived from ultimate reality. Their defects and perversion are attributed to the same fact; they are to be corrected and controlled through adoption of methods of conduct derived from loyalty to the requirements of Supreme Being. This philosophic formulation gets actuality and force from the fact that it is a rendering of the beliefs of men in general as far as they have come under the influence of institutional religion. Just as rational conceptions were once superimposed upon observed and temporal phenomena, so eternal values are superimposed upon experienced goods. In one case as in the other, the alternative is supposed to be confusion and lawlessness. Philosophers suppose these eternal values are known by reason; the mass of persons that they are divinely revealed.

Nevertheless, with the expansion of secular interests, temporal values have enormously multiplied; they absorb more and more attention and energy. The sense of transcendent values has become enfeebled; instead of permeating all things in life, it is more and more restricted to special times and acts. The authority of the church to declare and impose divine will and purpose has narrowed. Whatever men say and profess, their tendency in the presence of actual evils is to resort to natural and empirical means to remedy them. But in formal belief, the old doctrine of the inherently disturbed and unworthy character of the goods and standards of ordinary experience persists. This divergence between what men do and what they nominally profess is closely connected with the confusions and conflicts of modern thought.

It is not meant to assert that no attempts have been made to replace the older theory regarding the authority of immutable and transcendent values by conceptions more congruous with the practices of daily life. The contrary is the case. The utilitarian theory, to take one instance, has had great power. The idealistic school is the only one in contemporary philosophies, with the exception of one form of neo-realism, that makes much of the notion of a reality which is all one with ultimate moral and religious values. But this school is also the one most concerned with the conservation of "spiritual" life. Equally significant is the fact that empirical theories retain the notion that thought and judgment are concerned with values that are experienced independently of them. For these theories, emotional satisfactions occupy the same place that sensations hold in traditional empiricism. Values are constituted by liking and enjoyment; to be enjoyed and to be a value are two names for one and the same fact. Since science has extruded values from its objects, these empirical theories do everything possible to emphasize their purely subjective character of value. A psychological theory of desire and liking is supposed to cover the whole ground of the theory of values; in it, immediate feeling is the counterpart of immediate sensation.

I shall not object to this empirical theory as far as it connects the theory of values with concrete experiences of desire and satisfaction. The idea that there is such a connection is the only way known to me by which the pallid remoteness of the rationalistic theory, and the only too glaring presence of the institutional theory of transcendental values can be escaped. The objection is that the theory in question holds down value to objects *antecedently* enjoyed, apart from reference to the method by which they come into existence; it takes enjoyments which are causal because unregulated by intelligent operations to be values in and of themselves. Operational thinking needs to be applied to the judgment of values just as it has now finally been applied in conceptions of physical objects. Experimental empiricism in the field of ideas of good and bad is demanded to meet the conditions of the present situation.

The scientific revolution came about when material of direct and uncontrolled experience was taken as problematic; as supplying material to be transformed by reflective operations into known objects. The contrast between experienced and known objects was found to be a temporal one; namely, one between empirical subject-matters which were had or "given" prior to the acts of experimental variation and redisposition and those which succeeded these acts and issued from them. The notion of an act whether of sense or thought which supplied a valid measure of thought in immediate knowledge was discredited. Consequences of operations became the important thing. The suggestion almost imperatively follows that escape from the defects of transcendental absolutism is not to be had by setting up as values enjoyments that happen anyhow, but in defining value by enjoyments which are the consequences of intelligent action. Without the intervention of thought, enjoyments are not values but problematic goods, becoming values when they re-issue in a changed form from intelligent behavior. The fundamental trouble with the current empirical theory of values is that it merely formulates and justifies the socially prevailing habit of regarding enjoyments as they are actually experienced as values in and of themselves. It completely side-steps the question of regulation of these enjoyments. This issue involves nothing less than the problem of the directed reconstruction of economic, political and religious institutions.

There was seemingly a paradox involved in the notion that if we turned our backs upon the immediately perceived qualities of things, we should be enabled to form valid conceptions of objects, and that these conceptions could be used to bring about a more secure and more significant experience of them. But the method terminated in disclosing the connections or interactions upon which perceived objects, viewed as events, depend. Formal analogy suggests that we regard our direct and original experience of things liked and enjoyed as only *possibilities* of values to be achieved; that enjoyment becomes a value when we discover the relations upon which its presence depends. Such a causal and operational definition gives only a conception of a value, not a value itself. But the utilization of the conception in action results in an object having secure and significant value.

The formal statement may be given concrete content by pointing to the difference between the enjoyed and the enjoyable, the desired and the desirable, the satis*fy-ing* and the satis*factory*. To say that something is enjoyed is to make a statement about a fact, something already in existence; it is not to judge the value of that fact. There is no difference between such a proposition and one which says that something is sweet or sour, red or black. It is just correct or incorrect and that is the end of the matter. But to call an object a value is to assert that it satisfies or fulfills certain conditions. Function and status in meeting conditions is a different matter from bare existence. The fact that something is desired only raises the *question* of its desirability; it does not settle it. Only a child in the degree of his immaturity thinks to settle the question of desirability by reiterated proclamation: "I want it, I want it, I want it." What is objected to in the current empirical theory of values is not connection of them with desire and enjoyment but failure to distinguish between enjoyments of radically different sorts. There are many common expressions in which the difference of the two kinds is clearly recognized. Take for example the difference between the ideas of "satisfying" and "satisfactory." To say that something satisfies is to report something as an isolated finality. To assert that it is satis*factory* is to define it in its connections and interactions. The fact that it pleases or is immediately congenial poses a problem to judgment. How shall the satisfaction be rated? Is it a value or is it not? Is it something to be prized and cherished, *to be* enjoyed? Not stern moralists alone but everyday experience informs us that finding satisfaction in a thing may be a warning, a summons to be on the lookout for consequences. To declare something satis*factory* is to assert that it meets specifiable conditions. It is, in effect, a judgment that the thing "will do." It involves a prediction; it contemplates a future in which the thing will continue to serve; it *will* do. It asserts a consequence the thing will actively institute; it will *do*. That it is satisfying is the content of a proposition of fact; that it is satisfactory is a judgment, an estimate, an appraisal. It denotes an attitude *to be* taken, that of striving to perpetuate and to make secure.

It is worth notice that besides the instances given, there are many other recognitions in ordinary speech of the distinction. The endings "able," "worthy" and "ful" are cases in point. Noted and notable, noteworthy; remarked and remarkable; advised and advisable; wondered at and wonderful; pleasing and beautiful; loved and lovable; blamed and blameable, blameworthy; objected to and objectionable; esteemed and estimable; admired and admirable; shamed and shameful; honored and honorable; approved and approvable, worthy of approbation, etc. The multiplication of words adds nothing to the force of the distinction. But it aids in conveying a sense of the fundamental character of the distinction; of the difference between mere report of an already existent fact and judgment as to the importance and need of bringing a fact into existence; or, if it is already there, of sustaining it in existence. The latter is a genuine practical judgment, and marks the only type of judgment that has to do with the direction of action. Whether or no we reserve the term "value" for the latter (as seems to me proper) is a minor matter; that the distinction be acknowledged as the key to understanding the relation of values to the direction of conduct is the important thing.

This element of direction by an idea of value applies to science as well as anywhere else. For in every scientific undertaking, there is passed a constant succession of estimates; such as "it is worth treating these facts as data or evidence; it is advisable to try this experiment; to make that observation; to entertain such and such a hypothesis; to perform this calculation," etc.

The word "taste" has perhaps got too completely associated with arbitrary liking to express the nature of judgments of value. But if the word be used in the sense of an appreciation at once cultivated and active, one may say that the formation of taste is the chief matter wherever values enter in, whether intellectual, esthetic or moral. Relatively immediate judgments, which we call tact or to which we give the name of intuition, do not precede reflective inquiry, but are the funded products of much thoughtful experience. Expertness of taste is at once the result and the reward of constant exercise of thinking. Instead of there being no disputing about tastes, they are the one thing worth disputing about, if by "dispute" is signified discussion involving reflective inquiry. Taste, if we use the word in its best sense, is the outcome of experience brought cumulatively to bear on the intelligent appreciation of the real worth of likings and enjoyments. There is nothing in which a person so completely reveals himself as in the things which he judges enjoyable and desirable. Such judgments are the sole alternative to the domination of belief by impulse, chance, blind habit and self-interest. The formation of a cultivated and effectively operative good judgment or taste with respect to what is esthetically admirable, intellectually acceptable and morally approvable is the supreme task set to human beings by the incidents of experience.

Propositions about what is or has been liked are of instrumental value in reaching judgments of value, in as far as the conditions and consequences of the thing liked are thought about. In themselves they make no claims; they put forth no demand upon subsequent attitudes and acts; they profess no authority to direct. If one likes a thing he likes it; that *is* a point about which there can be no dispute:—although it is not so easy to state just *what* is liked as is frequently assumed. A judgment about what is *to be* desired and enjoyed is, on the other hand, a claim on future action; it possesses *de jure* and not merely *de facto* quality. It is a matter of frequent experience that likings and enjoyments are of all kinds, and that many are such as reflective judgments condemn. By way of self-justification and "rationalization," an enjoyment creates a tendency to assert that the thing enjoyed is a value. This assertion of validity adds authority to the fact. It is a decision that the object has a right to exist and hence a claim upon action to further its existence.

The analogy between the status of the theory of values and the theory of ideas about natural objects before the rise of experimental inquiry may be carried further. The sensationalistic theory of the origin and test of thought evoked, by way of reaction, the transcendental theory of *a priori* ideas. For it failed utterly to account for objective connection, order and regularity in objects observed. Similarly, any doctrine that identifies the mere fact of being liked with the value of the object liked so fails to give direction to conduct when direction is needed that it automatically calls forth the assertion that there are values eternally in Being that are the standards of all judgments and the obligatory ends of all action. Without the introduction of operational thinking, we oscillate between a theory that, in order to save the objectivity of judgments of values, isolates them from experience and nature, and a theory that, in order to save their concrete and human significance, reduces them to mere statements about our own feelings.

Not even the most devoted adherents of the notion that enjoyment and value are equivalent facts would venture to assert that because we have once liked a thing we should go on liking it; they are compelled to introduce the idea that *some* tastes are to be cultivated. Logically, there is no ground for introducing the idea of cultivation; liking is liking, and one is as good as another. If enjoyments *are* values, the judgment of value cannot regulate the form which liking takes; it cannot regulate its own conditions. Desire and purpose, and hence action, are left without guidance, although the question of regulation of their formation is the supreme problem of practical life. Values (to sum up) may be connected inherently with liking, and yet not with every liking but only with those that judgment has approved, after examination of the relation upon which the object liked depends. A casual liking is one that happens without knowledge of how it occurs nor to what effect. The difference between it and one which is sought because of a judgment that it is worth having and is to be striven for, makes just the difference between enjoyments which are accidental and enjoyments that have value and hence a claim upon our attitude and conduct.

In any case, the alternative rationalistic theory does not afford the guidance for the sake of which eternal and immutable norms are appealed to. The scientist finds no help in determining the probable truth of some proposed theory by comparing it with a standard of absolute truth and immutable being. He has to rely upon definite operations undertaken under definite conditions—upon method. We can hardly imagine an architect getting aid in the construction of a building from an ideal at large, though we can understand his framing an ideal on the basis of knowledge of actual conditions and needs. Nor does the ideal of perfect beauty in antecedent Being give direction to a painter in producing a particular work of art. In morals, absolute perfection does not seem to be more than a generalized hypostatization of the recognition that there is a good to be sought, an obligation to be met—both being concrete matters. Nor is the defect in this respect merely negative. An examination of history would reveal, I am confident, that these general and remote schemes of value actually obtain a content definite enough and near enough to concrete situations as to afford guidance in action only by consecrating some institution or dogma already having social currency. Concreteness is gained, but it is by protecting from inquiry some accepted standard which perhaps is outworn and in need of criticism.

When theories of values do not afford intellectual assistance in framing ideas and beliefs about values that are adequate to direct action, the gap must be filled by other means. If intelligent method is lacking, prejudice, the pressure of immediate circumstance, self-interest and class-interest, traditional customs, institutions of accidental historic origin, are not lacking, and they tend to take the place of intelligence. Thus we are led to our main proposition: *Judgments about values are judgments about the conditions and the results of experienced objects; judgments about that which should regulate the formation of our desires, affections and enjoyments.* For whatever decides their formation will determine the main course of our conduct, personal and social.

If it sounds strange to hear that we should frame our judgments as to what has value by considering the connections in existence of what we like and enjoy, the reply is not far to seek. As long as we do not engage in this inquiry enjoyments (values if we choose to apply that term) are casual; they are given by "nature," not constructed by art. Like natural objects in their qualitative existence, they at most only supply material for elaboration in rational discourse. A *feeling* of good or excellence is as far removed from goodness in fact as a feeling that objects are intellectually thus and so is removed from their being actually so. To recognize that the truth of natural objects can be reached only by the greatest care in selecting and arranging directed operations, and then to suppose that values can be truly determined by the mere fact of liking seems to leave us in an incredible position. All the serious perplexities of life come back to the genuine difficulty of forming a judgment as to the values of the situation; they come back to a conflict of goods. Only dogmatism can suppose that serious moral conflict is between something clearly bad and something known to be good, and that uncertainty lies wholly in the will of the one choosing. Most conflicts of importance are conflicts between things which are or have been satisfying, not between good and evil. And to suppose that we can make a hierarchical table of values at large once for all, a kind of catalogue in which they are arranged in an order of ascending or descending worth, is to indulge in a gloss on our inability to frame intelligent judgments in the concrete. Or else it is to dignify customary choice and prejudice by a title of honor.

The alternative to definition, classification and systematization of satisfactions just as they happen to occur is judgment of them by means of the relations under which they occur. If we know the conditions under which the act of liking, of desire and enjoyment, takes place, we are in a position to know what are the consequences of that act. The difference between the desired and the desirable, admired and the admirable, becomes effective at just this point. Consider the difference between the proposition "That thing has been eaten," and the judgment "That thing is edible." The former statement involves no knowledge of any relation except the one stated; while we are able to judge of the edibility of anything only when we have a knowledge of its interactions with other things sufficient to enable us to foresee its probable effects when it is taken into the organism and produces effects there.

To assume that anything can be known in isolation from its connections with other things is to identify knowing with merely having some object before perception or in feeling, and is thus to lose the key to the traits that distinguish an object as known. It is futile, even silly, to suppose that some quality that is directly present constitutes the whole of the thing presenting the quality. It does not do so when the quality is that of being hot or fluid or heavy, and it does not when the quality is that of giving pleasure, or being enjoyed. Such qualities are, once more, effects, ends in the sense of closing termini of processes involving causal connections. They are something to be investigated, challenges to inquiry and judgment. The more connections and interactions we ascertain, the more we *know* the object in question. Thinking is search for these connections. Heat experienced as a consequence of directed operations has a meaning quite different from the heat that is casually experienced without knowledge of how it came about. The same is true of enjoyments. Enjoyments that issue from conduct directed by insight into relations have a meaning and a validity due to the way in which they are experienced. Such enjoyments are not repented of; they generate no after-taste of bitterness. Even in the midst of direct enjoyment, there is a sense of validity, of authorization, which intensifies the enjoyment. There is solicitude for perpetuation of the *object* having value which is radically different from mere anxiety to perpetuate the *feeling* of enjoyment.

Such statements as we have been making are, therefore, far from implying that there are values apart from things actually enjoyed as good. To find a thing *enjoyable* is, so to say, a *plus* enjoyment. We saw that it was foolish to treat the scientific object as a rival to or substitute for the perceived object, since the former is intermediate between uncertain and settled situations and those experienced under conditions of greater control. In the same way, judgment of the value of an object to be experienced is instrumental to appreciation of it when it is realized. But the notion that every object that happens to satisfy has an equal claim with every other to be a value is like supposing that every object of perception has the same cognitive force as every other. There is no knowledge without perception; but objects perceived are *known* only when they are determined as consequences of connective operations. There is no value except where there is satisfaction, but there have to be certain conditions fulfilled to transform a satisfaction into a value.

The time will come when it will be found passing strange that we of this age should take such pains to control by every means at command the formation of ideas of physical things, even those most remote from human concern, and yet are content with haphazard beliefs about the qualities of objects that regulate our deepest interests; that we are scrupulous as to methods of forming ideas of natural objects, and either dogmatic or else driven by immediate conditions in framing those about values. There is, by implication, if not explicitly, a prevalent notion that values are already well known and that all which is lacking is the will to cultivate them in the order of their worth. In fact the most profound lack is not the will to act upon goods already known but the will to know what they are.

It is not a dream that it is possible to exercise some degree of regulation of the occurrence of enjoyments which are of value. Realization of the possibility is exemplified, for example, in the technologies and arts of industrial life—that is, up to a definite limit. Men desired heat, light, and speed of transit and of communication beyond what nature provides of itself. These things have been attained not by lauding the enjoyment of these things and preaching their desirability, but by study of the conditions of their manifestation. Knowledge of relations having been obtained, ability to produce followed, and enjoyment ensued as a matter of course. It is, however, an old story that enjoyment of these things as goods is no warrant of their bringing only good in their train. As Plato was given to pointing out, the physician may know to heal and the orator to persuade, but the ulterior knowledge of whether it is better for a man to be healed or to be persuaded to the orator's opinion remains unsettled. Here there appears the split between what are traditionally and conventionally called the values of the baser arts and the higher values of the truly personal and humane arts.

With respect to the former, there is no assumption that they can be had and enjoyed without definite operative knowledge. With respect to them it is also clear that the degree in which we value them is measurable by the pains taken to control the conditions of their occurrence. With respect to the latter, it is assumed that no one who is honest can be in doubt what they are; that by revelation, or conscience, or the instruction of others, or immediate feeling, they are clear beyond question. And instead of action in their behalf being taken to be a measure of the extent in which things are values to us, it is assumed that the difficulty is to persuade men to act upon what they already know to be good. Knowledge of conditions and consequences is regarded as wholly indifferent to judging what is of serious value, though it is useful in a prudential way in trying to actualize it. In consequence, the existence of values that are by common consent of a secondary and technical sort are under a fair degree of control, while those denominated supreme and imperative are subject to all the winds of impulse, custom and arbitrary authority.

This distinction between higher and lower types of value is itself something to be looked into. Why should there be a sharp division made between some goods as physical and material and others as ideal and "spiritual"? The question touches the whole dualism of the material and the ideal at its root. To denominate anything "matter" or "material" is not in truth to disparage it. It is, if the designation is correctly applied, a way of indicating that the thing in question is a condition or means of the existence of something else. And disparagement of effective means is practically synonymous with disregard of the things that are termed, in eulogistic fashion, ideal and spiritual. For the latter terms if they have any concrete application at all signify something which is a desirable consummation of conditions, a cherished fulfillment of means. The sharp separation between material and ideal good thus deprives the latter of the underpinning of effective support while it opens the way for treating things which should be employed as means as ends in themselves. For since men cannot after all live without some measure of possession of such matters as health and wealth, the latter things will be viewed as values and ends in isolation unless they are treated as integral constituents of the goods that are deemed supreme and final.

The relations that determine the occurrence of what human beings experience, especially when social connections are taken into account, are indefinitely wider and more complex than those that determine the events termed physical; the latter are the outcome of definite selective operations. This is the reason why we know something about remote objects like the stars better than we know significantly characteristic things about our own bodies and minds. We forget the infinite number of things we do not know about the stars, or rather that what we call a star is itself the product of the elimination, enforced and deliberate, of most of the traits that belong to an actual existence. The amount of knowledge we possess about stars would not seem very great or very important if it were carried over to human beings and exhausted our knowledge of them. It is inevitable that genuine knowledge of man and society should lag far behind physical knowledge.

But this difference is not a ground for making a sharp division between the two, nor does it account for the fact that we make so little use of the experimental method of forming our ideas and beliefs about the concerns of man in his characteristic social relations. For this separation religions and philosophies must admit some responsibility. They have erected a distinction between a narrower scope of relations and a wider and fuller one into a difference of kind, naming one kind material, and the other mental and moral. They have charged themselves gratuitously with the office of diffusing belief in the necessity of the division, and with instilling contempt for the material as something inferior in kind in its intrinsic nature and worth. Formal philosophies undergo evaporation of their technical solid contents; in a thinner and more viable form they find their way into the minds of those who know nothing of their original forms. When these diffuse and, so to say, airy emanations recrystallize in the popular mind they form a hard deposit of opinion that alters slowly and with great difficulty.

What difference would it actually make in the arts of conduct, personal and social, if the experimental theory were adopted not as a mere theory, but as a part of the working equipment of habitual attitudes on the part of everyone? It would be impossible, even were time given, to answer the question in adequate detail, just as men could not foretell in advance the consequences for knowledge of adopting the experimental method. It is the nature of the method that it has to be tried. But there are generic lines of difference which, within the limits of time at disposal, may be sketched.

Change from forming ideas and judgments of value on the basis of conformity to antecedent objects, to constructing enjoyable objects directed by knowledge of consequences, is a change from looking to the past to looking to the future. I do not for a moment suppose that the experiences of the past, personal and social, are of no importance. For without them we should not be able to frame any ideas whatever of the conditions under which objects are enjoyed nor any estimate of the consequences of esteeming and liking them. But past experiences are significant in giving us intellectual instrumentalities of judging just these points. They are tools, not finalities. Reflection upon what we have liked and have enjoyed is a necessity. But it tells us nothing about the *value* of these things until enjoyments are themselves reflectively controlled, or, until, as they now recalled, we form the best judgment possible about what led us to like this sort of thing and what has issued from the fact that we liked it.

We are not, then, to get away from enjoyments experienced in the past and from recall of them, but from the notion that they are the arbiters of things to be further enjoyed. At present, the arbiter is found in the past, although there are many ways of interpreting what in the past is authoritative. Nominally, the most influential conception doubtless is that of a revelation once had or a perfect life once lived. Reliance upon precedent, upon institutions created in the past, especially in law, upon rules of morals that have come to us through unexamined customs, upon uncriticized tradition, are other forms of dependence. It is not for a moment suggested that we can get away from customs and established institutions. A mere break would doubtless result simply in chaos. But there is no danger of such a break. Mankind is too inertly conservative both by constitution and by education to give the idea of this danger actuality. What there is genuine danger of is that the force of new conditions will produce disruption externally and mechanically: this is an ever present danger. The prospect is increased, not mitigated, by that conservatism which insists upon the adequacy of old standards to meet new conditions. What is needed is intelligent examination of the consequences that are actually effected by inherited institutions and customs, in order that there may be intelligent consideration of the ways in which they are to be intentionally modified in behalf of generation of different consequences.

This is the significant meaning of transfer of experimental method from the technical field of physical experience to the wider field of human life. We trust the method in forming our beliefs about things not directly connected with human life. In effect, we distrust it in moral, political and economic affairs. In the fine arts, there are many signs of a change. In the past, such a change has often been an omen and precursor of changes in other human attitudes. But, generally speaking, the idea of actively adopting experimental method in social affairs, in the matters deemed of most enduring and ultimate worth, strikes most persons as a surrender of all standards and regulative authority. But in principle, experimental method does not signify random and aimless action; it implies direction by ideas and knowledge. The question at issue is a practical one. Are there in existence the ideas and the knowledge that permit experimental method to be effectively used in social interests and affairs?

Where will regulation come from if we surrender familiar and traditionally prized values as our directive standards? Very largely from the findings of the natural sciences. For one of the effects of the separation drawn between knowledge and action is to deprive scientific knowledge of its proper service as a guide of conduct—except once more in those technological fields which have been degraded to an inferior rank. Of course, the complexity of the conditions upon which objects of human and liberal value depend is a great obstacle, and it would be too optimistic to say that we have as yet enough knowledge of the scientific type to enable us to regulate our judgments of value very extensively. But we have more knowledge than we try to put to use, and until we try more systematically we shall not know what are the important gaps in our sciences judged from the point of view of their moral and humane use.

For moralists usually draw a sharp line between the field of the natural sciences and the conduct that is regarded as moral. But a moral that frames its judgments of value on the basis of consequences must depend in a most intimate manner upon the conclusions of science. For the knowledge of the relations between changes which enable us to connect things as antecedents and consequences is science. The narrow scope which moralists often give to morals, their isolation of some conduct as virtuous and vicious from other large ranges of conduct, those having to do with health and vigor, business, education, with all the affairs in which desires and affection are implicated, is perpetuated by this habit of exclusion of the subject-matter of natural science from a rôle in formation of moral standards and ideals. The same attitude operates in the other direction to keep natural science a technical specialty, and it works unconsciously to encourage its use exclusively in regions where it can be turned to personal and class advantage, as in war and trade.

Another great difference to be made by carrying the experimental habit into all matter of practice is that it cuts the roots of what is often called subjectivism, but which is better termed egoism. The subjective attitude is much more widespread than would be inferred from the philosophies which have that label attached. It is as rampant in realistic philosophies as in any others, sometimes even more so, although disguised from those who hold these philosophies under the cover of reverence of and enjoyment of ultimate values. For the implication of placing the standard of thought and knowledge in antecedent existence is that our thought makes no difference in what is significantly real. It then affects only our own attitude toward it.

This constant throwing of emphasis back upon a change made in ourselves instead of one made in the world in which we live seems to me the essence of what is objectionable in "subjectivism." Its taint hangs about even Platonic realism with its insistent evangelical dwelling upon the change made within the mind by contemplation of the realm of essence, and its depreciation of action as transient and all but sordid—a concession to the necessities of organic existence. All the theories which put conversion "of the eye of the soul" in the place of a conversion of natural and social objects that modifies goods actually experienced, [are] a retreat and escape from existence— and this retraction into self is, once more, the heart of subjective egoisms. The typical example is perhaps the other-worldliness found in religions whose chief concern is with the salvation of the personal soul. But other-worldliness is found as well in estheticism and in all seclusion within ivory towers.

It is not in the least implied that change in personal attitudes, in the disposition of the "subject," is not of great importance. Such change, on the contrary, is involved in any attempt to modify the conditions of the environment. But there is a radical difference between a change in the self that is cultivated and valued as an end, and one that is a means to alteration, through action, of objective conditions. The Aristotelian-medieval conviction that highest bliss is found in contemplative possession of ultimate Being presents an ideal attractive to some types of mind; it sets forth a refined sort of enjoyment. It is a doctrine congenial to minds that despair of the effort involved in creation of a better world of daily experience. It is, apart from theological attachments, a doctrine sure to recur when social conditions are so troubled as to make actual endeavor seem hopeless. But the subjectivism so externally marked in modern thought as compared with ancient is either a development of the old doctrine under new conditions or is of merely technical import. The medieval version of the doctrine at least had the active support of a great social institution by means of which man could be brought into the state of mind that prepared him for ultimate enjoyment of eternal Being. It had a certain solidity and depth which is lacking in modern theories that would attain the result by merely emotional or speculative procedures, or by any means not demanding a change in objective existence so as to render objects of value more empirically secure.

The nature in detail of the revolution that would be wrought by carrying into the region of values the principle now embodied in scientific practice cannot be told; to attempt it would violate the fundamental idea that we know only after we have acted and in consequences of the outcome of action. But it would surely effect a transfer of attention and energy from the subjective to the objective. Men would think of themselves as agents not as ends; ends would be found in experienced enjoyment of the fruits of a transforming activity. In as far as the subjectivity of modern thought represents a discovery of the part played by personal responses, organic and acquired, in the causal production of the qualities and values of objects, it marks the possibility of a decisive gain. It puts us in possession of some of the conditions that control the occurrence of experienced objects, and thereby it supplies us with an instrument of regulation. There is something querulous in the sweeping denial that things as experienced, as perceived and enjoyed, in any way depend upon interaction with human selves. The error of doctrines that have exploited the part played by personal and subjective reactions in determining what is perceived and enjoyed lies either in exaggerating this factor of constitution into the sole condition—as happens in subjective idealism—or else in treating it as a finality instead of, as with all knowledge, an instrument in direction of further action.

A third significant change that would issue from carrying over experimental method from physics to man concerns the import of standards, principles, rules. With the transfer, these, and all tenets and creeds about good and goods, would be recognized to be hypotheses. Instead of being rigidly fixed, they would be treated as intellectual instruments to be tested and confirmed—and altered—through consequences effected by acting upon them. They would lose all pretence of finality—the ulterior source of dogmatism. It is both astonishing and depressing that so much of the energy of mankind has gone into fighting for (with weapons of the flesh as well as of the spirit) the truth of creeds, religious, moral and political, as distinct from what has gone into efforts to try creeds by putting them to the test of acting upon them. The change would do away with the intolerance and fanaticism that attend the notion that beliefs and judgments are capable of inherent truth and authority; inherent in the sense of being independent of what they lead to when used as directive principles. The transformation does not imply merely that men are responsible for acting upon what they profess to believe; that is an old doctrine. It goes much further. Any belief as such is tentative, hypothetical; it is not just to be acted upon, but is to be *framed* with reference to its office as a guide to action. Consequently, it should be the last thing in the world to be picked up casually and then clung to rigidly. When it is apprehended as a tool and only a tool, an instrumentality of direction, the same scrupulous attention will go to its formation as now goes into the making of instruments of precision in technical fields. Men, instead of being proud of accepting and asserting beliefs and "principles" on the ground of loyalty, will be as ashamed of that procedure as they would now be to confess their assent to a scientific theory out of reverence for Newton or Helmholz or whomever, without regard to evidence.

If one stops to consider the matter, is there not something strange in the fact that men should consider loyalty to "laws," principles, standards, ideals to be an inherent virtue, accounted unto them for righteousness? It is as if they were making up for some secret sense of weakness by rigidity and intensity of insistent attachment. A moral law, like a law in physics, is not something to swear by and stick to at all hazards; it is a formula of the way to respond when specified conditions present themselves. Its soundness and pertinence are tested by what happens when it is acted upon. Its claim or authority rests finally upon the imperativeness of the situation that has to be dealt with, not upon its own intrinsic nature—as any tool achieves dignity in the measure of needs served by it. The idea that adherence to standards external to experienced objects is the only alternative to confusion and lawlessness was once held in science. But knowledge became steadily progressive when it was abandoned, and clues and tests found within concrete acts and objects were employed. The test of consequences is more exacting than that afforded by fixed general rules. In addition, it secures constant development, for when new acts are tried new results are experienced, while the lauded immutability of eternal ideals and norms is in itself a denial of the possibility of development and improvement.

The various modifications that would result from adoption in social and humane subjects of the experimental way of thinking are perhaps summed up in saying that it would place *method and means* upon the level of importance that has, in the past, been imputed exclusively to ends. Means have been regarded as menial, and the useful as the servile. Means have been treated as poor relations to be endured, but not inherently welcome. The very meaning of the word "ideals" is significant of the divorce which has obtained between means and ends. "Ideals" are thought to be remote and inaccessible of attainment; they are too high and fine to be sullied by realization. They serve vaguely to arouse "aspiration," but they do not evoke and direct strivings for embodiment in actual existence. They hover in an indefinite way over the actual scene; they are expiring ghosts of a once significant kingdom of divine reality whose rule penetrated to every detail of life.

It is impossible to form a just estimate of the paralysis of effort that has been produced by indifference to means. Logically, it is truistic that lack of consideration for means signifies that so-called ends are not taken seriously. It is as if one professed devotion to painting pictures conjoined with contempt for canvas, brush and paints; or love of music on condition that no instruments, whether the voice or something external, be used to make sounds. The good workman in the arts is known by his respect for his tools and by his interest in perfecting his technique. The glorification in the arts of ends at the expense of means would be taken to be a sign of complete insincerity or even insanity. Ends separated from means are either sentimental indulgences or if they happen to exist are merely accidental. The ineffectiveness in action of "ideals" is due precisely to the supposition that means and ends are not on exactly the same level with respect to the attention and care they demand.

It is, however, much easier to point out the formal contradiction implied in ideals that are professed without equal regard for the instruments and techniques of their realization, than it is to appreciate the concrete ways in which belief in their separation has found its way into life and borne corrupt and poisonous fruits. The separation marks the form in which the traditional divorce of theory and practice has expressed itself in actual life. It accounts for the relative impotency of arts concerned with enduring human welfare. Sentimental attachment and subjective eulogy take the place of action. For there is no art without tools and instrumental agencies. But it also explains the fact that in actual behavior, energies devoted to matters nominally thought to be inferior, material and sordid, engross attention and interest. After a polite and pious deference has been paid to "ideals," men feel free to devote themselves to matters which are more immediate and pressing.

It is usual to condemn the amount of attention paid by people in general to material ease, comfort, wealth, and success gained by competition, on the ground that they give to mere means the attention that ought to be given to ends, or that they have taken for ends things which in reality are only means. Criticisms of the place which economic interest and action occupy in present life are full of complaints that men allow lower aims to usurp the place that belongs to higher and ideal values. The final source of the trouble is, however, that moral and spiritual "leaders" have propagated the notion that ideal ends may be cultivated in isolation from "material" means, as if means and material were not synonymous. While they condemn men for giving to means the thought and energy that ought to go to ends, the condemnation should go to them. For they have not taught their followers to think of material and economic activities as *really* means. They have been unwilling to frame their conception of the values that should be regulative of human conduct on the basis of the actual conditions and operations by which alone values can be actualized.

Practical needs are imminent; with the mass of mankind they are imperative. Moreover, speaking generally, men are formed to act rather than to theorize. Since the ideal ends are so remotely and accidentally connected with immediate and urgent conditions that need attention, after lip service is given to them, men naturally devote themselves to the latter. If a bird in the hand is worth two in a neighboring bush, an actuality in hand is worth, for the direction of conduct, many ideals that are so remote as to be invisible and inaccessible. Men hoist the banner of the ideal, and then march in the direction that concrete conditions suggest and reward.

Deliberate insincerity and hypocrisy are rare. But the notion that action and sentiment are inherently unified in the constitution of human nature has nothing to justify it. Integration is something to be achieved. Division of attitudes and responses, compartmentalizing of interests, is easily acquired. It goes deep just because the acquisition is unconscious, a matter of habitual adaptation to conditions. Theory separated from concrete doing and making is empty and futile; practice then becomes an immediate seizure of opportunities and enjoyments which conditions afford without the direction which theory—knowledge and ideas—has power to supply. The problem of the relation of theory and practice is not a problem of theory alone; it is that, but it is also the most practical problem of life. For it is the question of how intelligence may inform action, and how action may bear the fruit of increased insight into meaning: a clear view of the values that are worth while and of the means by which they are to be made secure in experienced objects. Construction of ideals in general and their sentimental glorification are easy; the responsibilities both of studious thought and of action are shirked. Persons having the advantage of positions of leisure and who find pleasure in abstract theorizing—a most delightful indulgence to those to whom it appeals—have a large measure of liability for a cultivated diffusion of ideals and aims that are separated from the conditions which are the means of actualization. Then other persons who find themselves in positions of social power and authority readily claim to be the bearers and defenders of ideal ends in church and state. They then use the prestige and authority their representative capacity as guardians of the highest ends confers on them to cover actions taken in behalf of the harshest and narrowest of material ends.

The present state of industrial life seems to give a fair index of the existing separation of means and ends. Isolation of economics from ideal ends, whether of morals or of organized social life, was proclaimed by Aristotle. Certain things, he said, are conditions of a worthy life, personal and social, but are not constituents of it. The economic life of man, concerned with satisfaction of wants, is of this nature. Men have wants and they must be satisfied. But they are only prerequisites of a good life, not intrinsic elements in it. Most philosophers have not been so frank nor perhaps so logical. But upon the whole, economics has been treated as on a lower level than either morals or politics. Yet the life which men, women and children actually lead, the opportunities open to them, the values they are capable of enjoying, their education, their share in all the things of art and science, are mainly determined by economic conditions. Hence we can hardly expect a moral system which ignores economic conditions to be other than remote and empty.

Industrial life is correspondingly brutalized by failure to equate it as the means by which social and cultural values are realized. That the economic life, thus exiled from the pale of higher values, takes revenge by declaring that it is the only social reality, and by means of the doctrine of materialistic determination of institutions and conduct in all fields, denies to deliberate morals and politics any share of causal regulation, is not surprising.

When economists were told that their subject-matter was merely material, they naturally thought they could be "scientific" only by excluding all reference to distinctively human values. Material wants, efforts to satisfy them, even the scientifically regulated technologies highly developed in industrial activity, are then taken to form a complete and closed field. If any reference to social ends and values is introduced it is by way of an external addition, mainly hortatory. That economic life largely determines the conditions under which mankind has access to concrete values may be recognized or it may not be. In either case, the notion that it is the means to be utilized in order to secure significant values as the common and shared possession of mankind is alien and inoperative. To many persons, the idea that the ends professed by morals are impotent save as they are connected with the working machinery of economic life seems like deflowering the purity of moral values and obligations.

The social and moral effects of the separation of theory and practice have been merely hinted at. They are so manifold and so pervasive that an adequate consideration of them would involve nothing less than a survey of the whole field of morals, economics and politics. It cannot be justly stated that these effects are in fact direct consequences of the quest for certainty by thought and knowledge isolated from action. For, as we have seen, this quest was itself a reflex product of actual conditions. But it may be truly asserted that this quest, undertaken in religion and philosophy, has had results which have reinforced the conditions which originally brought it about. Moreover, search for safety and consolation amid the perils of life by means other than intelligent action, by feeling and thought alone, began when actual means of control were lacking, when arts were undeveloped. It had then a relative historic justification that is now lacking. The primary problem for thinking which lays claim to be philosophic in its breadth and depth is to assist in bringing about a reconstruction of all beliefs rooted in a basic separation of knowledge and action; to develop a system of operative ideas congruous with present knowledge and with present facilities of control over natural events and energies.

We have noted more than once how modern philosophy has been absorbed in the problem of affecting an adjustment between the conclusions of natural science and the beliefs and values that have authority in the direction of life. The genuine and poignant issue does not reside where philosophers for the most part have placed it. It does not consist in accommodation to each other of two realms, one physical and the other ideal and spiritual, nor in the reconciliation of the "categories" of theoretical and practical reason. It is found in that isolation of executive means and ideal interests which has grown up under the influence of the separation of theory and practice. For this, by nature, involves the separation of the material and the spiritual. Its solution, therefore, can be found only in action wherein the phenomena of material and economic life are equated with the purposes that command the loyalties of affection and purpose, and in which ends and ideals are framed in terms of the possibilities of actually experienced situations. But while the solution cannot be found in "thought" alone, it can be furthered by thinking which is operative—which frames and defines ideas in terms of what may be done, and which uses the conclusions of science as instrumentalities. William James was well within the bounds of moderation when he said that looking forward instead of backward, looking to what the world and life might become instead of to what they have been, is an alteration in the "seat of authority."

It was incidentally remarked earlier in our discussion that the serious defect in the current empirical philosophy of values, the one which identifies them with things actually enjoyed irrespective of the conditions upon which they depend, is that it formulates and in so far consecrates the conditions of our present social experience. Throughout these chapters, primary attention has perforce been given to the methods and statements of philosophic theories. But these statements are technical and specialized in formulation only. In origin, content and import they are reflections of some condition or some phase of concrete human experience. Just as the theory of the separation of theory and practice has a practical origin and a momentous practical consequence, so the empirical theory that values are identical with whatever men actually enjoy, no matter how or what, formulates an aspect, and an undesirable one, of the present social situation.

For while our discussion has given more attention to the other type of philosophical doctrine, that which holds that regulative and authoritative standards are found in transcendent eternal values, it has not passed in silence over the fact that actually the greater part of the activities of the greater number of human beings is spent in effort to seize upon and hold onto such enjoyments as the actual scene permits. Their energies and their enjoyments are controlled in fact, but they are controlled by external conditions rather than by intelligent judgment and endeavor. If philosophies have any influence over the thoughts and acts of men, it is a serious matter that the most widely held empirical theory should in effect justify this state of things by identifying values with the objects of any interest as such. As long as the only theories of value placed before us for intellectual assent alternate between sending us to a realm of eternal and fixed values and sending us to enjoyments such as actually obtain, the formulation, even as only a theory, of an experimental empiricism which finds values to be identical with goods that are the fruit of intelligently directed activity has its measure of practical significance.

ALFRED NORTH WHITEHEAD
1861–1947

Alfred North Whitehead was born on February 15, 1861, in Ramsgate, Kent, near Canterbury in southern England. His father, who had been headmaster of the village private school, was ordained in the Church of England just before Whitehead's birth. As the pastor's son in a small town, Whitehead experienced a childhood blessed with close-knit relationships, powerful characters, and a strong sense of community. The boy also imbibed a sense of history. Near his home, St. Augustine, the missionary, had converted the Saxon King Ethelbert to Christianity. Whitehead also enjoyed visits to nearby Canterbury Cathedral and knew the spot where in A.D. 1170 Thomas à Becket had been murdered. When Whitehead later reflected on his environment, he wrote, "It shows how historical tradition is handed down by the direct experience of physical surroundings."*

As a boy, Whitehead was educated at home by his father. At age fourteen, he went away to one of England's oldest schools, in Sherborne, Dorsetshire. Once again, Whitehead was surrounded by history. Referring to the then current young-earth interpretation of the Bible, Whitehead asserted,

> We had plenty of evidence that things had been going on for a long time. It never entered into anybody's mind to regard six thousand years seriously as the age of mankind—not because we took up with revolutionary ideas, but because our continuity with nature was a patent, visible fact.**

*Alfred North Whitehead, *Essays in Science and Philosophy* (New York: Philosophical Library, 1947), p. 5.
***Ibid.*, p. 32.

Following a classical education at Sherborne, Whitehead received a scholarship to study mathematics at Trinity College, Cambridge. Though he focused on mathematics, never attending lectures outside his field, Whitehead learned philosophy through informal conversations with faculty and friends. By his graduation in 1884, Whitehead had memorized whole sections of Kant's *Critique of Pure Reason.*

For the next twenty-five years, Whitehead taught mathematics at Cambridge. Whitehead's career there was both personally satisfying and professionally successful. In 1890, Whitehead married Evelyn Willoughby Wade, and together they had four children. That same year, Bertrand Russell enrolled at Trinity and began his lifelong friendship with Whitehead. Following the publication of Whitehead's first book, *A Treatise on Universal Algebra,* in 1898, he and Russell began collaborating on the *Principia Mathematica.* Published between 1910 and 1913, this monumental work attempted to show how the principles of arithmetic are extensions of the principles of logic.

In 1910, Whitehead abruptly left Cambridge and moved to London. Without a teaching position, Whitehead at first washed bottles at the University of London. But within a year, he was teaching at the university, and in 1914 he became professor of applied mathematics at the university's Imperial College of Science and Technology. He later became dean of the faculty of science and president of the senate of the University of London.

Whitehead continued his work in mathematics but was increasingly attracted to the philosophy of science. In his London period, he also published several books, including *An Introduction to Mathematics* (1911), *The Organization of Thought* (1917), *The Concept of Nature* (1920), and *The Principle of Relativity* (1922).

In 1924, at the age of sixty-three, Whitehead was invited to join the philosophy department at Harvard University. Though the offer was originally for five years, the university wanted Whitehead to teach as long as he was able. For the next thirteen years, Whitehead thrived at Harvard. With his wife Evelyn, he held a weekly open house for students, providing both hot chocolate and warm conversation. Whitehead offered one of the first team-taught classes in the United States with his colleague W.E. Hocking. It was during this Harvard period that Whitehead produced his most influential books, *Science and the Modern World* (1925), *Religion in the Making* (1926), *Adventure of Ideas* (1933), *Modes of Thought* (1935), and, especially, *Process and Reality* (1929).

By his death in 1947, Whitehead was widely known and read by philosophers and theologians. Analytic philosophers hailed him as co-author of the groundbreaking *Principia Mathematica,* a work that was celebrated by W.V.O. Quine as "one of the great intellectual monuments of all time." Theologians and philosophers still pay tribute to his contributions to process thought.

*   *   *

Ever since the Pre-Socratic Parmenides rejected Heraclitus's flux, Western philosophy has been dominated by a philosophy of substance. Whitehead sought to replace substance with process or organism, to replace static descriptions with dynamic ones. According to Whitehead, only a process philosophy of organism can account for the creativity, diversity, and interdependence of immediate experience.

In *Process and Reality,* Whitehead developed this alternative philosophy most fully. Unfortunately, the book is notoriously difficult to understand, using a special vocabulary to surmount the substantive language of traditional philosophy. Our selection is taken from a compendium of the work, ably edited by Donald W. Sherburne.

We can begin with Whitehead's notion of an *actual entity.* Whereas the universe is diverse, Whitehead explains that "it lies in the nature of things that the many enter into complex unity." The unity that results from a moment of unification (what Whitehead calls "concrescence") is an *actual entity.* These actual entities "are the final real things of which the world is made up." This means that there are nothing but actual entities: Even God is an actual entity. Further, these actual entities are really complex and interdependent drops of experience.

Actual entities relate to one another by means of *prehending* (grasping) or *feeling* (sympathizing). By either of these processes, an actual entity can incorporate data from another entity. In bringing together the feelings of separate entities from the past into a unity of feeling in the present, the actual entity reaches "satisfaction." At this point, the actual entity perishes and becomes a datum for new instances of concrescence.

This process of becoming and ceasing to be has three "formative elements": potentiality, creativity, and God. *Potentiality,* for Whitehead, involves a Platonic conception of eternal objects. But these eternal objects are not "things" in the sense of having existence in the temporal world. Rather, they represent the potential for all actual entities, present and future. *Creativity,* according to Whitehead, is the "principle of novelty" by which actual entities are combined.

The final formative element, *God,* has two natures. God's *primordial nature* is a nontemporal entity that eternally values the timeless realm of eternal objects. God's *consequent nature* is "the physical prehension by God of the actualities of the evolving universe," which prehension preserves as the actual entities of the temporal world. God integrates the physical feelings of God's consequent nature with the conceptual feelings of God's primordial nature, thereby relating all entities on a grand scale. Put in simpler terms, Whitehead divides the traditional concepts of the goodness of God and the power of God, which had been united since St. Augustine.

*   *   *

For general studies of Whitehead, see Victor Lowe, *Understanding Whitehead* (Baltimore, MD: The Johns Hopkins Press, 1962); Nathaniel Lawrence, *Alfred North Whitehead: A Primer of his Philosophy* (New York: Twayne, 1974); and Paul Grimley Kuntz, *Alfred North Whitehead* (Boston: Twayne, 1984). Edward Pols, *Whitehead's Metaphysics: A Critical Examination of "Process and Reality"* (Carbondale: Southern Illinois Press, 1967) and Elizabeth M. Kraus, *The Metaphysics of Experience: A Companion to Whitehead's "Process and Reality"* (New York: Fordham University Press, 1979) are guides to Whitehead's *magnum opus.* Among the many books exploring process metaphysics are John W. Lango, *Whitehead's Ontology* (Albany, NY: SUNY Press, 1972); Stephen David Ross, *Perspective in Whitehead's Metaphysics* (Albany, NY: SUNY Press, 1983); Lewis S. Ford, *The Emergence of Whitehead's Metaphysics* (Albany, NY: SUNY Press, 1984); Thomas E. Hosinski, *Stubborn Fact and Creative Advance: An Introduction to the Metaphysics of Alfred North Whitehead* (Lanham, MD: Rowman &

Littlefield, 1993); and Nicholas Rescher, *Process Metaphysics: An Introduction to Process Philosophy* (Albany, NY: SUNY Press, 1996). John B. Cobb Jr. and David Ray Griffin, *Process Theology: An Introductory Exposition* (Philadelphia: Westminster Press, 1976); Laurence F. Wilmot, *Whitehead and God: Prolegomena to Theological Reconstruction* (Waterloo, ONT: Wilfrid Laurier University Press, 1979); and Stephen T. Franklin, *Speaking from the Depths* (Grand Rapids, MI: Eerdmans, 1990) study Whitehead's philosophy of religion. Finally, for collections of essays, see Paul Arthur Schilpp, ed., *The Philosophy of Alfred North Whitehead* (New York: Tudor/The Library of Living Philosophers, 1941); George L. Kline, ed., *Alfred North Whitehead: Essays on his Philosophy* (Englewood Cliffs, NJ: Prentice Hall, 1963); and Charles Hartshorne, ed., *Whitehead's Philosophy: Selected Essays, 1935–1970* (Lincoln: University of Nebraska Press, 1972).

PROCESS AND REALITY (selections)

CHAPTER 1: THE ACTUAL ENTITY*

I. THE ACTUAL ENTITY

The positive doctrine of these lectures is concerned with the becoming, the being, and the relatedness of 'actual entities.' 'Actual entities'—also termed 'actual occasions'—are the final real things of which the world is made up. There is no going behind actual entities to find anything more real. They differ among themselves: God is an actual entity, and so is the most trivial puff of existence in far-off empty space.

The presumption that there is only one genus of actual entities constitutes an ideal of cosmological theory to which the philosophy of organism endeavours to conform. The description of the generic character of an actual entity should include God, as well as the lowliest actual occasion, though there is a specific difference between the nature of God and that of any occasion. But, though there are gradations of importance, and diversities of function, yet in the principles which actuality exemplifies all are on the same level. The final facts are, all alike, actual entities; and these actual entities are drops of experience, complex and interdependent.

[In his first *Meditation*], Descartes uses the phrase *res vera* in the same sense as that in which I have used the term 'actual.' It means 'existence' in the fullest sense of that term, beyond which there is no other. Descartes, indeed, would ascribe to God 'existence' in a generically different sense. In the philosophy of organism, as here developed, God's existence is not generically different from that of other actual entities, except that he is 'primordial' in a sense to be gradually explained.

*[The section divisions and all comments in footnotes are Sherburne's.]

Alfred North Whitehead, *Process and Reality* (New York: Macmillan, 1929) as condensed in *A Key to Whitehead's "Process and Reality,"* edited by Donald W. Sherburne (New York: Macmillan, 1966), pp. 7–35.

'Concrescence' is the name for the process in which the universe of many things acquires an individual unity in a determinate relegation of each item of the 'many' to its subordination in the constitution of the novel 'one.' An actual occasion is nothing but the unity to be ascribed to a particular instance of concrescence. This concrescence is thus nothing else than the 'real internal constitution' of the actual occasion in question. The process itself is the constitution of the actual entity; in Locke's phrase, it is the 'real internal constitution' of the actual entity.

This is a theory of monads; but it differs from Leibniz's in that his monads change. In the organic theory, they merely *become*. Each monadic creature is a mode of the process of 'feeling' the world, of housing the world in one unit of complex feeling, in every way determinate. Such a unit is an 'actual occasion'; it is the ultimate creature derivative from the creative process.

Each actual entity is conceived as an act of experience arising out of data. The objectifications of other actual occasions form the given data from which an actual occasion originates. Each actual entity is a throb of experience including the actual world within its scope. It is a process of 'feeling' the many data, so as to absorb them into the unity of one individual 'satisfaction.' Here 'feeling' is the term used for the basic generic operation of passing from the objectivity of the data to the subjectivity of the actual entity in question. Feelings are variously specialized operations, effecting a transition into subjectivity. They replace the 'neutral stuff' of certain realistic philosophers. An actual entity is a process, and is not describable in terms of the morphology of a 'stuff.'

This word 'feeling' is a mere technical term; but it has been chosen to suggest that functioning through which the concrescent actuality appropriates the datum so as to make it its own. A feeling appropriates elements of the universe, which in themselves are other than the subject, and absorbs these elements into the real internal constitution of its subject by synthesizing them in the unity of an emotional pattern expressive of its own subjectivity. Feelings are 'vectors'; for they feel what is *there* and transform it into what is *here*. We thus say that an actual occasion is a concrescence effected by a process of feelings.

The philosophy of organism is a cell-theory of actuality. The cell is exhibited as appropriating, for the foundation of its own existence, the various elements of the universe out of which it arises. Each process of appropriation of a particular element is termed a prehension. I have adopted the term 'prehension' to express the activity whereby an actual entity effects its own concretion of other things. In Cartesian language, the essence of an actual entity consists solely in the fact that it is a prehending thing (i.e., a substance whose whole essence or nature is to prehend).

There are two species of prehensions, the 'positive species' and the 'negative species.' A 'feeling' belongs to the positive species of 'prehensions.' An actual entity has a perfectly definite bond with each item in the universe. This determinate bond is its prehension of that item. A negative prehension is the definite exclusion of that item from positive contribution to the subject's own real internal constitution. A positive prehension is the definite inclusion of that item into positive contribution to the subject's own real internal constitution. This positive inclusion is called its 'feeling' of that item. All actual entities in the actual world, relatively to a given actual entity as 'subject,' are necessarily 'felt' by that subject, though in general vaguely.

A feeling cannot be abstracted from the actual entity entertaining it. This actual entity is termed the 'subject' of the feeling. It is in virtue of its subject that the feeling is one thing. If we abstract the subject from the feeling we are left with many things. Thus a feeling is one aspect of its own subject.

II. PREHENSIONS

The first analysis of an actual entity, into its most concrete elements, discloses it to be a concrescence of prehensions, which have originated in its process of becoming. All further analysis is an analysis of prehensions. Every prehension consists of three factors: (a) the 'subject' which is prehending, namely, the actual entity in which that prehension is a concrete element; (b) the 'datum' which is prehended; (c) the 'subjective form' which is how that subject prehends that datum.

1. DATUM

A 'simple physical feeling' entertained in one subject is a feeling for which the initial datum is another single actual entity, and the objective datum is another feeling entertained by the latter actual entity.

Figure 1. A Simple Physical Feeling
Here a diagram will help the reader visualize the relationships described. An actual entity has been seen to be constituted by its feelings, or prehensions. Hence each actual entity will be portrayed as a pie cut into pieces—the pie is the sum of its pieces as the actual entity is the sum of its prehensions. In Figure 1, B is the concreascing, subject actual entity, the entity in the process of becoming. A is an actual entity in the immediate past of B, which is being prehended by B. X is one of B's prehensions, the prehension that "reaches out" to include A in B, the "vector" (from the Latin, vectus, past participle of veho, to carry—used in mathematics to denote a line having a fixed direction in space) that bears the A-ness of A into B. M, N, and O are prehensions constitutive of A. N is the particular prehension in A selected by B to represent A, to objectify A, in B's concrescence. All the other prehensions in A are negatively prehended by B; Y and Z represent negative prehensions that eliminate certain aspects of A's constitution from relevance to B's feelings. Letters inserted in the following text correlate Whitehead's descriptive phrases with the labels of Figure 1.

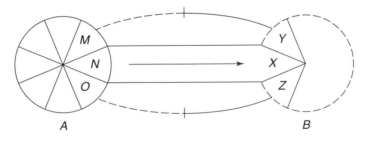

Thus in a simple physical feeling *[X]* there are two actual entities concerned. One of them *[B]* is the subject of that feeling, and the other *[A]* is the initial datum of the feeling. A second feeling *[N]* is also concerned, namely, the objective datum of the simple physical feeling. This second feeling *[N]* is the 'objectification' of its subject *[A]* for the subject *[B]* of the simple physical feeling *[X]*. The initial datum *[A]* is objectified as being the subject of the feeling *[N]* which is the objective datum: the objectification is the 'perspective' of the initial datum. The prehension *[N]* in one subject *[A]* becomes the objective datum for the prehension *[X]* in a later subject *[B]*, thus objectifying the earlier subject *[A]* for the later subject *[B]*. Objectification relegates into irrelevance, or into a subordinate relevance, the full constitution of the objectified entity. Some real component in the objectified entity assumes the role of being how that particular entity is a datum in the experience of the subject.

A feeling *[X]* is the appropriation of some elements in the universe to be components in the real internal constitution of its subject *[B]*. The elements are the initial data; they are what the feeling feels. But they are felt under an abstraction. The process of the feeling involves negative prehensions *[Y,Z]* which effect elimination. There is a transition from the initial data to the objective datum effected by the elimination. The objective datum is the perspective of the initial datum. Thus the initial data *[A]* are felt under a 'perspective' which is the objective datum *[N]* of the feeling *[X]*.

In virtue of this elimination *[Y,Z]* the components of the objective datum *[N]* have become 'objects' intervening in the constitution of the subject *[B]* of the feeling *[X]*. In the phraseology of mathematical physics a feeling has a 'vector' character. A feeling *[X]* is the agency by which other things *[A]* are built into the constitution of its *[X's]* one subject in process of concrescence *[B]*.

A simple physical feeling is an act of causation. The actual entity which is the initial datum *[A]* is the 'cause,' the simple physical feeling *[X]* is the 'effect,' and the subject entertaining the simple physical feeling *[B]* is the actual entity 'conditioned' by the effect. This 'conditioned' actual entity *[B]* will also be called the 'effect.' All complex causal action can be reduced to a complex of such primary components. Therefore simple physical feelings will also be called 'causal' feelings [or feelings of causal efficacy]. The 'power' of one actual entity on the other is simply how the former is objectified in the constitution of the other.

A simple physical feeling has the dual character of being the cause's feeling reenacted for the effect as subject. By reason of this duplicity in a simple feeling there is a vector character which transfers the cause into the effect. It is a feeling from the cause which acquires the subjectivity of the new effect without loss of its original subjectivity in the cause. Simple physical feelings embody the reproductive character of nature, and also the objective immortality of the past. In virtue of these feelings time is the conformation of the immediate present to the past. Such feelings are conformal feelings.

2. SUBJECTIVE FORM

A feeling—i.e., a positive prehension—is essentially a transition effecting a concrescence. Its complex constitution is analysable into five factors which express what that transition consists of, and effects. The factors are: (i) the 'subject' which feels, (ii) the 'initial data' which are to be felt, (iii) the 'elimination' in virtue of negative prehensions, (iv) the 'objective datum' which is felt, (v) the 'subjective form' which is *how* that subject feels that objective datum. An actual entity, on its subjective side, is nothing else than what the universe is for it, including its own reactions. The reactions are the subjective forms of the feelings. There are many species of subjective forms, such as emotions, valuations, purposes, adversions, aversions, consciousness, etc.

The essential novelty of a feeling attaches to its subjective form. The initial data, and even the objective datum, may have served other feelings with other subjects. But the subjective form is the immediate novelty; it is how *that* subject is feeling that objective datum. There is no tearing this subjective form from the novelty of this concrescence. It is enveloped in the immediacy of its immediate present. The subjective form is the ingression of novel form peculiar to the new particular fact, and with its peculiar mode of fusion with the objective datum. In the becoming, it meets the 'data' which are selected from the actual world.

A feeling can be genetically described in terms of its process of origination, with its negative prehensions whereby its many initial data become its complex objective datum. In this process the subjective form originates, and carries into the feeling the way in which the feeling feels. The way in which the feeling feels expresses how the feeling came into being. It expresses the purpose which urged it forward, and the obstacles which it encountered, and the indeterminations which were dissolved by the originative decisions of the subject.

Physical feelings are always derived from some antecedent experient. Occasion *B* prehends occasion *A* as an antecedent subject experiencing a sensum with [a subjective form of] emotional intensity. *B*'s subjective form of emotion is conformed to *A*'s subjective form. Thus there is a vector transmission of emotional feeling of a sensum from *A* to *B*. In this way *B* feels the sensum as derived from *A* and feels it with an emotional form also derived from *A*. This is the most primitive form of the feeling of causal efficacy. In physics it is the transmission of a form of energy.

Apart from inhibitions or additions, weakenings or intensifications, due to the history of its production, the subjective form of a physical feeling *[X]* is re-enaction of the subjective form of the feeling felt *[N]*. The subjective form, amid its own original elements, always involves reproduction of the pattern of the objective datum. Thus the cause passes on its feeling to be reproduced by the new subject as its own, and yet as inseparable from the cause. There is a flow of feeling. But the re-enaction is not perfect. The feeling is always novel in reference to its data; since its subjective form, though it must always have reproductive reference to the data, is not wholly determined by them.

The cause *[A]* is objectively in the constitution of the effect *[B]*, in virtue of being the feeler of the feeling *[N]* reproduced in the effect [as *X*] with partial equivalence of subjective form. The reason why the cause *[A]* is [merely] objectively in the effect, is that the cause's feeling *[N]* cannot, as a feeling, be abstracted from its subject *[A]* which is the cause.

III. SATISFACTION, SUPERJECT, AND OBJECTIVE IMMORTALITY*

An actual entity is a process in the course of which many operations with incomplete subjective unity terminate in a completed unity of operation, termed the 'satisfaction.' The actual entity terminates its becoming in one complex feeling involving a com-

---

*[A cluster of three notions—"satisfaction," "superject," and "objective immortality"—elucidates the completion of the process constitutive of the actual entity. An actual entity initiates its process by prehending many other datum occasions in its causal past. Then occur the complexities of concrescence during which the many initial single feelings of the world are integrated into one complex feeling of that occasion's actual world. This final, complex, integrated feeling is the satisfaction of that occasion. The satisfaction closes up, completes, concludes the actual entity. The satisfaction of an actual entity determines its character as superject—i.e., the character it has as objectively immortal, its character as an object encountered as initial datum by succeeding actual entities.]

pletely determinate bond with every item in the universe, the bond being either a positive or a negative prehension. This termination is the 'satisfaction' of the actual entity.

The process of the concrescence is a progressive integration of feelings controlled by their subjective forms. In this synthesis, feelings of an earlier phase sink into
the components of some more complex feeling of a later phase. Thus each phase adds
its element of novelty, until the final phase in which the one complex 'satisfaction' is
reached. This process of the integration of feeling proceeds until the concrete unity of
feeling is obtained. In this concrete unity all indetermination as to the realization of
possibilities has been eliminated. The many entities of the universe, including those
originating in the concrescence itself, find their respective roles in this final unity. The
'satisfaction' is the culmination of the concrescence into a completely determinate
matter of fact.

The attainment of a peculiar definiteness is the final cause which animates a particular process; and its attainment halts its process, so that by transcendence it passes
into its objective immortality as a new objective condition added to the riches of definiteness attainable. It enjoys an objective immortality in the future beyond itself.

The peculiarity of an actual entity is that it can be considered both 'objectively'
and 'formally.' The 'formal' aspect is functional so far as that actual entity is concerned: by this it is meant that the process involved is immanent in it. The 'formal' reality of the actuality in question belongs to its process of concrescence and not to its
'satisfaction.' The 'objective' aspect is morphological so far as that actual entity is
concerned: by this it is meant that the process involved is transcendent relatively to it,
so that the essence of its satisfaction is *sentiri*. The objective consideration is pragmatic. It is the consideration of the actual entity in respect to its consequences.

The terminal unity of operation, here called the 'satisfaction,' embodies what the
actual entity is beyond itself. In Locke's phraseology, the 'powers' of the actual entity
are discovered in the analysis of the satisfaction. It is the actual entity as a definite, determinate, settled fact, stubborn and with unavoidable consequences. Its own process,
which is its own internal existence, has evaporated, worn out and satisfied; but its effects are all to be described in terms of its 'satisfaction.' The 'effects' of an actual entity are its interventions in concrescent processes other than its own. Any entity, thus
intervening in processes transcending itself, is said to be functioning as an 'object.' It
is the one general metaphysical character of all entities of all sorts, that they function
as objects. It is this metaphysical character which constitutes the solidarity of the universe.

An actual entity is to be conceived both as a subject presiding over its own immediacy of becoming, and a superject which is the atomic creature exercising its function of objective immortality. It has become a 'being'; and it belongs to the nature of
every 'being' that it is a potential for every 'becoming.' To be actual must mean that
all actual things are alike objects, enjoying objective immortality in fashioning creative
actions; and that all actual things are subjects, each prehending the universe from
which it arises.

It is fundamental to the metaphysical doctrine of the philosophy of organism,
that the notion of an actual entity as the unchanging subject of change is completely
abandoned. An actual entity is at once the subject experiencing and the superject of its
experiences. It is subject-superject, and neither half of this description can for a moment be lost sight of. The term 'subject' will be mostly employed when the actual entity is considered in respect to its own real internal constitution. But 'subject' is always
to be construed as an abbreviation of 'subject-superject.'

The term 'subject' has been retained because in this sense it is familiar in philosophy. But it is misleading. The philosophies of substance presuppose a subject which then encounters a datum, and then reacts to the datum. The philosophy of organism presupposes a datum which is met with feelings, and progressively attains the unity of a subject. But with this doctrine, 'superject' would be a better term than 'subject.' The subject-superject is the purpose of the process originating the feelings. The feelings are inseparable from the end at which they aim; and this end is the feeler. The feelings aim at the feeler, as their final cause. The feelings are what they are in order that their subject may be what it is. Then transcendently, since the subject is what it is in virtue of its feelings, it is only by means of its feelings that the subject objectively conditions the creativity transcendent beyond itself. In our own relatively high grade of human existence, this doctrine of feelings and their subject is best illustrated by our notion of moral responsibility. The subject is responsible for being what it is in virtue of its feelings. It is also derivatively responsible for the consequences of its existence because they flow from its feelings.

If the subject-predicate form of statement be taken to be metaphysically ultimate, it is then impossible to express this doctrine of feelings and their superject. It is better to say that the feelings aim at their subject, than to say that they *are aimed at* their subject. For the latter mode of expression removes the subject from the scope of the feeling and assigns it to an external agency. Thus the feeling would be wrongly abstracted from its own final cause. This final cause is an inherent element in the feeling, constituting the unity of that feeling. An actual entity feels as it does feel in order to be the actual entity which it is. In this way an actual entity satisfies Spinoza's notion of substance: it is *causa sui*.

An 'actual entity' is a *res vera* in the Cartesian sense of that term; it is a Cartesian 'substance,' and not an Aristotelian 'primary substance.' But Descartes retained in his metaphysical doctrine the Aristotelian dominance of the category of 'quality' over that of 'relatedness.' In these lectures 'relatedness' is dominant over 'quality.' All relatedness has its foundation in the relatedness of actualities; and such relatedness is wholly concerned with the appropriation of the dead by the living—that is to say, with 'objective immortality' whereby what is divested of its own living immediacy becomes a real component in other living immediacies of becoming. This is the doctrine that the creative advance of the world is the becoming, the perishing, and the objective immortalities of those things which jointly constitute *stubborn fact* [i.e., actual entities].

This doctrine of organism is the attempt to describe the world as a process of generation of individual actual entities, each with its own absolute self-attainment. This concrete finality of the individual is nothing else than a decision referent beyond itself. The 'perpetual perishing' of individual absoluteness is thus foredoomed. But the 'perishing' of absoluteness is the attainment of 'objective immortality.'

The notion of 'satisfaction' is the notion of the 'entity as concrete' abstracted from the 'process of concrescence'; it is the outcome separated from the process, thereby losing the actuality of the atomic entity, which is both process and outcome. 'Satisfaction' provides the individual element in the composition of the actual entity— that element which has led to the definition of substance as 'requiring nothing but itself in order to exist.' But the 'satisfaction' is the 'superject' rather than the 'substance' or the 'subject.' It closes up the entity; and yet is the superject adding its character to the creativity whereby there is a becoming of entities superseding the one in question. This satisfaction is the attainment of something individual to the entity in question. It cannot be construed as a component contributing to its own concrescence; it is the ultimate fact, individual to the entity.

IV. The Ontological Principle*

Every condition to which the process of becoming conforms in any particular instance, has its reason *either* in the character of some actual entity in the actual world of that concrescence, *or* in the character of the subject which is in process of concrescence. This is the 'ontological principle.' This ontological principle means that actual entities are the only *reasons;* so that to search for a *reason* is to search for one or more actual entities.

The 'ontological principle' broadens and extends a general principle laid down by John Locke in his *Essay* (Bk. II, Ch. XXIII, Sect. 7), when he asserts that 'power' is 'a great part of our complex ideas of substances.' The notion of 'substance' is transformed into that of 'actual entity'; and the notion of 'power' is transformed into the principle that the reasons for things are always to be found in the composite nature of definite actual entities—in the nature of God for reasons of the highest absoluteness, and in the nature of definite temporal actual entities for reasons which refer to a particular environment. The ontological principle can be summarized as: no actual entity, then no reason.

The actual world is built up of actual occasions; and by the ontological principle whatever things there are in any sense of 'existence,' are derived by abstraction from actual occasions. Apart from the experiences of subjects there is nothing, nothing, nothing, bare nothingness. The most general term 'thing'—or, equivalently, 'entity'—means nothing else than to be one of the 'many' which find their niches in each instance of concrescence. Each instance of concrescence *is itself* the novel individual 'thing' in question. There are not 'the concrescence' *and* the 'novel thing': when we analyse the novel thing we find nothing but the concrescence. 'Actuality' means nothing else than this ultimate entry into the concrete, in abstraction from which there is mere nonentity. In other words, abstraction from the notion of 'entry into the concrete' is a self-contradictory notion, since it asks us to conceive a thing as not a thing.

Descartes does not explicitly frame the definition of actuality in terms of the ontological principle, that actual occasions form the ground from which all other types of existence are derivative and abstracted; but he practically formulates an equivalent in subject predicate phraseology, when he writes: "For this reason, when we perceive any attribute, we therefore conclude that some existing thing or substance to which it may be attributed, is necessarily present" (*Principles of Philosophy,* Part I, 52). For Descartes the word 'substance' is the equivalent of my phrase 'actual occasion.' I refrain from the term 'substance,' for one reason because it suggests the subject-predicate notion; and for another reason because Descartes and Locke permit their substances to undergo adventures of changing qualifications, and thereby create difficulties.

For rationalistic thought, the notion of 'givenness' carries with it a reference beyond the mere data in question. It refers to a 'decision' whereby what is 'given' is separated off from what for that occasion is 'not given.' This element of 'givenness' in things implies some activity procuring limitation. The word 'decision' does not here imply conscious judgment, though in some 'decisions' consciousness will be a factor. The word is used in its root sense of a 'cutting off.' The ontological principle declares that every decision is referable to one or more actual entities, because in separation from actual entities there is nothing, merely nonentity—'The rest is silence.'

The ontological principle asserts the relativity of decision; whereby every decision expresses the relation of the actual thing, *for which* a decision is made, to an actual thing *by which* that decision is made. But 'decision' cannot be construed as a casual adjunct of

*[The importance of the concept of an actual entity is emphasized by what Whitehead terms "the ontological principle."]

an actual entity. It constitutes the very meaning of actuality. An actual entity arises from decisions *for* it, and by its very existence provides decisions *for* other actual entities which supersede it. Thus the ontological principle is the first stage in constituting a theory embracing the notions of 'actual entity,' 'givenness,' and 'process.' Just as 'potentiality for process' is the meaning of the more general term 'entity,' or 'thing'; so 'decision' is the additional meaning imported by the word 'actual' into the phrase 'actual entity.' 'Actuality' is the decision amid 'potentiality.' It represents stubborn fact which cannot be evaded. The real internal constitution of an actual entity progressively constitutes a decision conditioning the creativity which transcends that actuality.

CHAPTER TWO: THE FORMATIVE ELEMENTS

I. ETERNAL OBJECTS*

By stating my belief that the train of thought in these lectures is Platonic, I mean that if we had to render Plato's general point of view with the least changes made necessary by the intervening two thousand years of human experience in social organization, in aesthetic attainments, in science, and in religion, we should have to set about the construction of a philosophy of organism. In such a philosophy the actualities constituting the process of the world are conceived as exemplifying the ingression (or 'participation') of other things which constitute the potentialities of definiteness for any actual existence. The things which are temporal [actual entities] arise by their participation in the things which are eternal [eternal objects].

But these lectures are not an exegesis of Plato's writings; the entities in question are not necessarily restricted to those which he would recognize as 'forms.' Also the term 'idea' has a subjective suggestion in modern philosophy, which is very misleading for my present purposes; and in any case it has been used in many senses and has become ambiguous. The term 'essence,' as used by the Critical Realists, also suggests their use of it, which diverges from what I intend. Accordingly, by way of employing a term devoid of misleading suggestions, I use the phrase 'eternal object.' If the term 'eternal objects' is disliked, the term 'potentials' would be suitable. The eternal objects are the pure potentials of the universe; and the actual entities differ from each other in their realization of potentials. Any entity whose conceptual recognition does not involve a necessary reference to any definite actual entities of the temporal world is called an 'eternal object.'

An eternal object is always a potentiality for actual entities; but in itself, as conceptually felt, it is neutral as to the fact of its physical ingression in any particular actual entity of the temporal world. 'Potentiality' is the correlative of 'givenness.' The meaning of 'givenness' is that what is 'given' might not have been 'given'; and that what *is not* 'given' *might have been* 'given.' It is evident that 'givenness' and 'poten-

*[In the last few sentences of Chapter One reference was made by Whitehead to "potentiality" and to "creativity." These terms refer to two of the three formative elements, namely, eternal objects and creativity. The third formative element is God. The status of each of these formative elements, and the relationships holding among them, will be clarified gradually. It is from their mutual interaction that the universe of actual entities emerges—hence the appropriateness of Whitehead's designation, "formative" elements. To understand the functioning of the formative elements is to understand more clearly the nature of the actual entities they "form." The first formative element to be considered is the element of pure potentiality in the universe, the eternal objects.]

tiality' are both meaningless apart from a multiplicity of potential entities. These potentialities are the 'eternal objects.' Apart from 'potentiality' and 'givenness,' there can be no nexus of actual things in process of supersession by novel actual things. The alternative is a static monistic universe, without unrealized potentialities; since 'potentiality' is then a meaningless term.

The functioning of an eternal object in the self-creation of an actual entity is the 'ingression' of the eternal object in the actual entity. An eternal object can be described only in terms of its potentiality for 'ingression' into the becoming of actual entities; and its analysis only discloses other eternal objects. It is a pure potential. The term 'ingression' refers to the particular mode in which the potentiality of an eternal object is realized in a particular actual entity, contributing to the definiteness of that actual entity.

Actual occasions in their 'formal' constitutions are devoid of all indetermination. Potentiality has passed into realization. They are complete and determinate matter of fact, devoid of all indecision. But eternal objects involve in their own natures indecision. They are, like all entities, potentials for the process of becoming. Their ingression expresses the *definiteness* of the actuality in question. But their own natures do not in themselves disclose in what actual entities this potentiality of ingression is realized.

An eternal object in abstraction from any one particular actual entity is a potentiality for ingression into actual entities. In its ingression into any one actual entity, either as relevant or as irrelevant, it retains its potentiality of indefinite diversity of modes of ingression, a potential indetermination rendered determinate in this instance. The definite ingression into a particular actual entity is not to be conceived as the sheer evocation of that eternal object from 'not-being' into 'being'; it is the evocation of determination out of indetermination. Potentiality becomes reality; and yet retains its message of alternatives which the actual entity has avoided. In the constitution of an actual entity:—whatever component is red, might have been green; and whatever component is loved, might have been coldly esteemed.

Prehensions of actual entities—i.e., prehensions whose data involve actual entities—are termed 'physical prehensions'; and prehensions of eternal objects are termed 'conceptual prehensions' [or 'conceptual feelings']. In the technical phraseology of these lectures, a conceptual feeling is a feeling whose 'datum' is an eternal object. Analogously a negative prehension is termed 'conceptual,' when its datum is an eternal object.

A conceptual feeling is feeling an eternal object in the primary metaphysical character of being an 'object,' that is to say, feeling its *capacity* for being a realized determinant of process. Immanence and transcendence are the characteristics of an object: as a realized determinant it is immanent; as a capacity for determination it is transcendent; in both rôles it is relevant to something not itself. There is no character belonging to the actual apart from its exclusive determination by selected eternal objects. The definiteness of the actual arises from the exclusiveness of eternal objects in their function as determinants. If the actual entity be *this,* then by the nature of the case it is not *that* or *that.* The fact of incompatible alternatives is the ultimate fact in virtue of which there is definite character. A conceptual feeling is the feeling of an eternal object in respect to its general capacity as a determinant of character, including thereby its capacity of exclusiveness.

An actual entity in the actual world of a subject *must* enter into the concrescence of that subject by *some* simple causal feeling, however vague, trivial, and submerged. Negative prehensions may eliminate its distinctive importance. But in some way, by some trace of causal feeling, the remote actual entity is prehended positively. In the case of an eternal object, there is no such necessity. In any given concrescence, it may be included positively by means of a conceptual feeling; but it may be excluded by a negative prehension. The actualities *have* to be felt, while the pure potentials can be dismissed. So far as concerns their functionings as objects, this is the great distinction between an actual entity and an eternal object. The one is stubborn matter of fact; and the other never loses its 'accent' of potentiality.*

The potentiality for being an element in a real concrescence of many entities into one actuality, is the one general metaphysical character attaching to all entities, actual and non-actual [i.e., to actual entities and eternal objects]. Every item in its universe is involved in each concrescence. In other words, it belongs to the nature of a 'being' that it is a potential for every 'becoming.' This is the 'principle of relativity.' It asserts that the notion of an 'entity' means 'an element contributory to the process of becoming.'

The principle of universal relativity directly traverses Aristotle's dictum, '[A substance] is not present in a subject.' On the contrary, according to this principle an actual entity is present in other actual entities. In fact if we allow for degrees of relevance, and for negligible relevance, we must say that every actual entity is present in every other actual entity. The philosophy of organism is mainly devoted to the task of making clear the notion of 'being present in another entity.' This phrase is here borrowed from Aristotle: it is not a fortunate phrase, and in subsequent discussion it will be replaced by the term 'objectification.' The functioning of one actual entity in the self-creation of another actual entity is the 'objectification' of the former for the latter actual entity. The Aristotelian phrase suggests the crude notion that one actual entity is added to another *simpliciter*. This is not what is meant. One rôle of the eternal objects is that they are those elements which express how any one actual entity is constituted by its synthesis of other actual entities.

The organic philosophy does not hold that the 'particular existents' [i.e., actual entities] are prehended apart from universals [i.e., eternal objects]; on the contrary, it holds that they are prehended by the mediation of universals. In other words, each actuality is prehended by means of some element of its own definiteness. Eternal objects determine *how* the world of actual entities enters into the constitution of each one of its members via its feelings. The eternal objects function by introducing the multiplicity of actual entities as constitutive of the actual entity in question. For the philosophy of organism, the primary data are always actual entities absorbed into feeling in virtue of certain universals shared alike by the objectified actuality and the experient subject.

A simple physical feeling enjoys a characteristic which has been variously described as 're-enaction,' 'reproduction,' and 'conformation.' This characteristic can be more accurately explained in terms of the eternal objects involved. There are eternal objects determinant of the definiteness of the objective datum which is the 'cause,' and eternal objects determinant of the definiteness of the subjective form belonging to the 'effect.' When there is re-enaction there is one eternal object with two-way functioning, namely, as partial determinant of the objective datum, and as partial determinant of the subjective form. In this two-way rôle, the eternal object is functioning relationally between the initial data on the one hand and the concrescent subject on the other. In the conformal feelings the *how* of feeling reproduces what is felt. Some conformation is necessary as a basis of vector transition, whereby the past is synthesized with the present. The one eternal object in its two-way function, as a determinant of the datum and as a determinant of the subjective form, is thus relational. In this sense the solidarity of the universe is based on the relational functioning of eternal objects.

---

*[This initial account of the doctrine of eternal objects can now be used to make a very important point. Chapter One made it clear that every concrescing actual entity involves other actual entities in its process of becoming—i.e., other actual entities serve as data for concrescing subjects. A prehension is a vector in that it bears along what is there, transforming it into what is here. Eternal objects play a crucial role in effecting this transformation. To understand this role is to understand a Whiteheadian principle as basic as the "ontological principle"—namely, the "principle of relativity."]

II. God*

The scope of the ontological principle is not exhausted by the corollary that 'decision' must be referable to an actual entity. Everything must be somewhere; and here 'somewhere' means 'some actual entity.' It is a contradiction in terms to assume that some explanatory fact can float into the actual world out of nonentity. Nonentity is nothingness. Every explanatory fact refers to the decision and to the efficacy of an actual thing. Accordingly the general potentiality of the universe must be somewhere; since it retains its proximate relevance to actual entities for which it is unrealized. This 'somewhere' is the non-temporal actual entity.

The things which are temporal [actual occasions] arise by their participation in the things which are eternal [eternal objects]. The two sets are mediated by a thing which combines the actuality of what is temporal with the timelessness of what is potential. This final entity is the divine element in the world, by which the barren inefficient disjunction of abstract potentialities obtains primordially the efficient conjunction of ideal realization. By this recognition of the divine element the general Aristotelian principle is maintained that, apart from things that are actual, there is nothing—nothing either in fact or in efficacy.

The endeavor to understand eternal objects in complete abstraction from the actual world results in reducing them to mere undifferentiated nonentities. Accordingly the differentiated relevance of eternal objects to each instance of the creative process requires their conceptual realization in the primordial nature of God. The general relationships of eternal objects to each other, relationships of diversity and of pattern, are their relationships in God's conceptual realization. Apart from this realization, there is mere isolation indistinguishable from nonentity.

In what sense can unrealized abstract form be relevant? What is its basis of relevance? 'Relevance' must express some real fact of togetherness among forms. The ontological principle can be expressed as: All real togetherness is togetherness in the formal constitution of an actuality. So if there be a relevance of what in the temporal world is unrealized, the relevance must express a fact of togetherness in the formal constitution of a non-temporal actuality. But by the principle of relativity there can only be one non-derivative actuality, unbounded by its prehensions of an actual world. Unfettered conceptual valuation, 'infinite' in Spinoza's sense of that term, is only possible once in the universe; since that creative act is objectively immortal as an inescapable condition characterizing creative action. Such a primordial superject of creativity achieves, in its unity of satisfaction, the complete conceptual valuation of all eternal objects. This is the ultimate, basic adjustment of the togetherness of eternal objects on which creative order depends. It is the conceptual adjustment of all appetites in the form of aversions and adversions. It constitutes the meaning of relevance. Its status as an actual efficient fact is recognized by terming it the 'primordial nature of God.'

The primordial created fact is the unconditioned conceptual valuation of the entire multiplicity of eternal objects. This is the 'primordial nature' of God. He is the unconditioned actuality of conceptual feeling at the base of things; so that, by reason of this primordial actuality, there is an order in the relevance of eternal objects to the process of creation. He is the actual entity in virtue of which the *entire* multiplicity of eternal objects obtains its graded relevance to each stage of concrescence. Apart from

---

*[The second formative element to be considered is God. The simplest way to introduce the Whiteheadian concept of God is to apply the ontological principle to the notion of a realm of eternal objects. The result reveals much about the second formative element, and also reveals its relationship to the first formative element.]

God, there could be no relevant novelty. His unity of conceptual operations is a free creative act, untramelled by reference to any particular course of things. It is deflected neither by love, nor by hatred, for what in fact comes to pass. The *particularities* of the actual world presuppose *it;* while *it* merely presupposes the *general* metaphysical character of creative advance, of which it is the primordial exemplification. The primordial nature of God is the acquirement by creativity of a primordial character.

This ideal realization of potentialities in a primordial actual entity constitutes the metaphysical stability whereby the actual process exemplifies general principles of metaphysics, and attains the ends proper to specific types of emergent order. By reason of the actuality of this primordial valuation of pure potentials, each eternal object has a definite, effective relevance to each concrescent process. Apart from such orderings, there would be a complete disjunction of eternal objects unrealized in the temporal world. Novelty would be meaningless, and inconceivable. By reason of this complete valuation, the objectification of God in each derivate actual entity results in a graduation of the relevance of eternal objects to the concrescent phases of that derivate occasion. There will be additional ground of relevance for select eternal objects by reason of their ingression into derivate actual entities belonging to the actual world of the concrescent occasion in question. But whether or no this be the case, there is always the definite relevance derived from God. Thus possibility which transcends realized temporal matter of fact has a real relevance to the creative advance. Apart from God, eternal objects unrealized in the actual world would be relatively non-existent for the concrescence in question. For effective relevance requires agency of comparison, and agency belongs exclusively to actual occasions. This divine ordering is itself matter of fact, thereby conditioning creativity. It is here termed 'God'; because the contemplation of our natures, as enjoying real feelings derived from the timeless source of all order, acquires that 'subjective form' of refreshment and companionship at which religions aim.

1. GOD AND SUBJECTIVE AIM*

This doctrine of the inherence of the subject in the process of its production requires that in the primary phase of the subjective process there be a conceptual feeling of subjective aim. The immediacy of the concrescent subject is constituted by its living aim at its own self-constitution. The initial stage of its aim is an endowment which the subject inherits from the inevitable ordering of things, conceptually realized in the nature of God. Each temporal entity derives from God its basic conceptual aim, relevant to its actual world, yet with indeterminations awaiting its own decisions. Thus the initial stage of the aim is rooted in the nature of God, and its completion depends on the self-causation of the subject superject.

God is the principle of concretion; namely, he is that actual entity from which each temporal concrescence receives that initial aim from which its self-causation starts. That aim determines the initial gradations of relevance of eternal objects for conceptual feeling;

*[The purpose of this section on God is to understand his functioning as a formative element. And now that certain general remarks about God have been made, his role as formative element can be indicated more precisely. To understand God as formative element is to understand the part played by his primordial nature in the formation of the subjective aim of each and every actual occasion in the temporal world. Subjective aim must not be confused with subjective form. Subjective form is how a feeling is felt by the concrescing subject of that feeling. Subjective aim concerns the direction to be taken by the concrescing subject in the process that constitutes the very being of that subject. The subject does not exist prior to its concrescence, it comes into being with its concrescence, it is its concrescence—its being is its becoming. Every concrescence, which is causa sui, faces the question of what sort of entity it will make itself. The subjective aim, derived from God, is a lure (to be more or less completely followed) toward that way of becoming which is most in line with God's own aim of creating intensity of harmonious feeling in the world.]

and constitutes the autonomous subject in its primary phase of feelings with its initial conceptual valuations, and with its initial physical purposes. Thus the transition of the creativity from an actual world to the correlate novel concrescence is conditioned by the relevance of God's all-embracing conceptual valuations to the particular possibilities of transmission from the actual world, and by its relevance to the various possibilities of initial subjective form available for the initial feelings. If we prefer the phraseology, we can say that God and the actual world jointly constitute the character of the creativity for the initial phase of the novel concrescence. The subject, thus constituted, is the autonomous master of its own concrescence into subject-superject. It passes from a subjective aim in concrescence into a superject with objective immortality. At any stage it is subject-superject.

2. COHERENCE OF THE CONCEPT "GOD"*

God is not to be treated as an exception to all metaphysical principles, invoked to save their collapse. He is their chief exemplification. The presumption that there is only one genus of actual entities constitutes an ideal of cosmological theory to which the philosophy of organism endeavours to conform. The description of the generic character of an actual entity should include God, as well as the lowliest actual occasion, though there is a specific difference between the nature of God and that of any occasion.

An actual entity has a threefold character. (i) It has the character 'given' for it by the past; the 'objectifications' of the actual entities in the actual world, relative to a definite actual entity, constitute the efficient causes out of which *that* actual entity arises. (ii) It has the subjective character aimed at in its process of concrescence; the 'subjective aim' at 'satisfaction' constitutes the final cause, or lure, whereby there is determinate concrescence. (iii) It has the superjective character, which is the pragmatic value of its specific satisfaction qualifying the transcendent creativity; that attained 'satisfaction' remains as an element in the content of creative purpose.

In the case of the primordial actual entity, which is God, there is no past. Thus the ideal realization of conceptual feeling takes the precedence. There is still, however, the same threefold character: (i) The 'primordial nature' of God is the concrescence of an unity of conceptual feelings, including among their data all eternal objects. The concrescence is directed by the subjective aim, that the subjective forms of the feelings shall be such as to constitute the eternal objects into relevant lures of feeling severally appropriate for all realizable basic conditions. (ii) The 'consequent nature' of God is the physical prehension by God of the actualities of the evolving universe. His primordial nature directs such perspectives of objectification so that each novel actuality in the temporal world contributes such elements as it can to a realization in God free from inhibitions of intensity by reason of discordance. (iii) The 'superjective' nature of God is the character of the pragmatic value of his specific satisfaction qualifying the transcendent creativity in the various temporal instances.

It is to be noted that every actual entity, including God, is something individual for its own sake; and thereby transcends the rest of actuality. And also it is to be noted that

---

*[It might appear that the concept of God is an ad hoc creation that, although it serves to link actuality and potentiality, is not itself correlated with other basic principles of the system. Such unrelatedness of basic principles results in incoherence. Whitehead is aware that the charge of incoherence might be brought against him, and in the following passages he argues that he has not introduced a mere *deus ex machina* unrelated to the other elements of his philosophy. The second and third aspects of the threefold character of God introduced in these passages, namely, his consequent nature and his superjective nature, may not be clearly understood by the reader. This is of no concern at the moment . . . It is enough at present to sense that they constitute evidence for Whitehead's claim that God is neither unrelated to nor an exception to the principles of the system.]

every actual entity, including God, is a creature transcended by the creativity which it qualifies. A temporal occasion in respect to the second element of its character, and God in respect to the first element of his character satisfy Spinoza's definition of substance, that it is *causa sui*. To be *causa sui* means that the process of concrescence is its own reason for the decision in respect to the qualitative clothing of feelings. It is finally responsible for the decision by which any lure for feeling is admitted to efficiency. The freedom inherent in the universe is constituted by this element of self-causation.

3. SUMMARY AND TRANSITION
TO CREATIVITY

God is the organ of novelty, aiming at intensification. He is the lure for feeling, the eternal urge of desire. The primary element in the 'lure for feeling' is the subject's prehension of the primordial nature of God. His particular relevance to each creative act as it arises from its own conditioned standpoint in the world, constitutes him the initial 'object of desire' establishing the initial phase of each subjective aim. Apart from the intervention of God, there could be nothing new in the world, and no order in the world. The course of creation would be a dead level of ineffectiveness, with all balance and intensity progressively excluded by the cross currents of incompatibility. The novel feelings derived from God are the foundations of progress.

This is the conception of God, according to which he is considered as the outcome of creativity, as the foundation of order, and as the goad towards novelty. 'Order' and 'novelty' are but the instruments of his subjective aim which is the intensification of 'formal immediacy.' Thus God's purpose in the creative advance is the evocation of intensities. This function of God is analogous to the remorseless working of things in Greek and in Buddhist thought. The initial aim is the best for that *impasse*. But if the best be bad, then the ruthlessness of God can be personified as *Atè*, the goddess of mischief. The chaff is burnt. What is inexorable in God, is valuation as an aim towards 'order'; and 'order' means 'society permissive of actualities with patterned intensity of feeling arising from adjusted contrasts.'

God can be termed the creator of each temporal actual entity. But the phrase is apt to be misleading by its suggestion that the ultimate creativity of the universe is to be ascribed to God's volition. The true metaphysical position is that God is the aboriginal instance of this creativity, and is therefore the aboriginal condition which qualifies its action. Viewed as primordial, he is the unlimited conceptual realization of the absolute wealth of potentiality. In this aspect, he is not *before* all creation, but *with* all creation. It is the function of actuality to characterize the creativity, and God is the eternal primordial character. But of course, there is no meaning to 'creativity' apart from its 'creatures,' and no meaning to 'God' apart from the creativity and the 'temporal creatures,' and no meaning to the temporal creatures apart from 'creativity' and 'God.'

III. CREATIVITY*

In all philosophic theory there is an ultimate which is actual in virtue of its accidents. It is only then capable of characterization through its accidental embodiments, and apart

---

*[The third formative element is creativity. The concluding paragraph of the preceding section cryptically adumbrates the relationship between God and creativity. A more careful account of this elusive but crucial concept, creativity, is now required.]

from these accidents is devoid of actuality. In the philosophy of organism this ultimate is termed 'creativity'; and God is its primordial, non-temporal accident. The creativity is not an external agency with its own ulterior purposes. In monistic philosophies, Spinoza's or absolute idealism, this ultimate is God, who is also equivalently termed 'The Absolute.' In such monistic schemes, the ultimate is illegitimately allowed a final, 'eminent reality,' beyond that ascribed to any of its accidents.

Creativity is another rendering of the Aristotelian 'matter,' and of the modern 'neutral stuff.' But it is divested of the notion of passive receptivity, either of 'form,' or of external relations; it is the pure notion of the activity conditioned by the objective immortality of the actual world—a world which is never the same twice, though always with the stable element of divine ordering. Creativity is without a character of its own in exactly the same sense in which the Aristotelian 'matter' is without a character of its own. It is that ultimate notion of the highest generality at the base of actuality. It cannot be characterized, because all characters are more special than itself. But creativity is always found under conditions, and described as conditioned. The non-temporal act of all-inclusive unfettered valuation [i.e., God] is at once a creature of creativity and a condition for creativity. It shares this double character with all creatures.

An actual entity feels as it does feel in order to be the actual entity which it is. In this way an actual entity satisfies Spinoza's notion of substance: it is *causa sui*. All actual entities share with God this characteristic of self-causation. For this reason every actual entity also shares with God the characteristic of transcending all other actual entities, including God. The universe is thus a creative advance into novelty. The alternative to this doctrine is a static morphological universe.*

'Creativity,' 'many,' 'one' are the ultimate notions involved in the meaning of the synonymous terms 'thing,' 'being,' 'entity.' The term 'many' presupposes the term 'one,' and the term 'one' presupposes the term 'many.' The term 'one' stands for the singularity of an entity. The term 'many' conveys the notion of 'disjunctive diversity'; this notion is an essential element in the concept of 'being.' There are many 'beings' in disjunctive diversity.

'Creativity' is [i] the principle of *novelty*. An actual occasion is a novel entity diverse from any entity in the 'many' which it unifies. Thus 'creativity' introduces novelty into the content of the many, which are the universe disjunctively. The creative action is the universe always becoming one in a particular unity of self-experience, and thereby adding to the multiplicity which is the universe as many.

'Creativity' is [ii] that ultimate principle by which the many, which are the universe disjunctively, become the one actual occasion, which is the universe conjunctively. It lies in the nature of things that the many enter into complex unity. In their natures, entities are disjunctively 'many' in process of passage into conjunctive unity. The fundamental inescapable fact is the creativity in virtue of which there can be no 'many things' which are not subordinated in a concrete unity. Thus a set of all actual occasions is by the nature of things a standpoint for another concrescence which elicits a concrete unity from those many actual occasions. It is inherent in the constitution of

*[Two considerations of prime importance emerge from this initial statement. In the first place, creativity is not to be conceived as an "external agency with its own ulterior purposes"—i.e., it must not violate the ontological principle but must be explicable by an appeal to actual entities. Second, creativity is the concept that must account for the perpetual "creative advance into novelty" that is the cornerstone of Whitehead's process philosophy. The account of creativity in *PR* is terse to the point of obscurity. Whitehead's basic statements on the topic will now be presented, followed by an interpretive commentary (in footnote).]

the immediate, present actuality that a future will supersede it. The creativity in virtue of which any relatively complete actual world is, by the nature of things, the datum for a new concrescence, is termed 'transition.'

Thus the 'production of novel togetherness' is the ultimate notion embodied in the term 'concrescence.' The ultimate metaphysical principle is the advance from disjunction to conjunction, creating a novel entity other than the entities given in disjunction. The world expands through recurrent unifications of itself, each, by the addition of itself, automatically recreating the multiplicity anew. The novel entity is at once the togetherness of the 'many' which it finds, and also it is one among the disjunctive 'many' which it leaves; it is a novel entity, disjunctively among the many entities which it synthesizes. The many become one, and are increased by one.

Nature is never complete. It is always passing beyond itself. This is the creative advance of nature. The 'creative advance' is the application of this ultimate principle of creativity to each novel situation which it originates. The creative process is rhythmic: it swings from the publicity of many things to the individual privacy; and it swings back from the private individual to the publicity of the objectified individual. The former swing is dominated by the final cause which is the ideal; and the latter swing is dominated by the efficient cause which is actual. The oneness of the universe, and the oneness of each element in the universe, repeat themselves to the crack of doom in the creative advance from creature to creature.*

*[The basic principle underlying these tightly packed sentences is enunciated twice by Whitehead: "It lies in the nature of things that the many enter into complex unity," and again, "The fundamental inescapable fact is the creativity in virtue of which there can be no 'many things' which are not subordinated in a concrete unity." In short, the universe abhors a "many" and moves, via the unity of a fresh concrescence, to overcome a "many." The thrust of the system is immediately evident when it is seen, however, that creativity is also "the principle of novelty." This means that the new unity that "subordinates" a "many" is itself a novel entity disjunctively diverse from everything else in the universe, so that in "subordinating" a "many" it itself in effect creates another "many" requiring "subordination." In short, to assuage the abhorrent situation is to recreate that very same abhorrent condition.

In this perpetual sequence is contained the basic rhythm of process. In *Modes of Thought* (p. 120) Whitehead writes: "There is a rhythm of process whereby creation produces natural pulsation, each pulsation forming a natural unit of historic fact." The natural units of historic fact are the actual entities and the rhythm is the alternation between "one" and "many" that repeats itself "to the crack of doom in the creative advance from creature to creature."

In this account of creativity there has been no repudiation of the ontological principle. Each individual among the "many" and each "one" that emerges are all alike actual occasions, whereas "creativity" is only the "universal of universals characterizing ultimate matter of fact" (*PR*, p. 31), the ultimate principle descriptive of the nature of actual entities. As the ultimate principle descriptive of the one-many relationship inhering in the coming-to-be of actual entities, creativity points up the fact that actual entities are not independent of and separate from one another. There is a perpetual advance to fresh actual occasions precisely because the actual entities are not wholly independent, but rather are linked in the creative process resulting from the one-many relationship that binds them together. This doctrine of creativity is therefore the natural outcome of two principles introduced in Chapter One that also emphasize the interdependence of actual entities, namely, the Principle of Relativity and the principle that every actual entity is superject as well as subject.]

W.E.B. Du Bois
1868–1963

William Edward Burghardt Du Bois was born and raised in Great Barrington, Massachusetts. His mother, Mary Burghardt, was descended from a West African slave. His father, Alfred Du Bois, came from a long line of French Huguenots (Protestants). As W.E.B. Du Bois himself later put it, he was born "with a flood of Negro blood, a strain of French, a bit of Dutch, but thank God! no Anglo-Saxon."

The town of Great Barrington had a small African American population and a rather informal color line. The only people explicitly oppressed on the basis of race were Irish immigrants. But, as Du Bois explains in our reading, there was also a deeper, more implicit, kind of racism. Du Bois came to see himself as part of a "problem": the "problem of the Negro." He understood that he was different from others in school and that he was "shut out from their world by a vast veil."

Du Bois's initial response was to excel at whatever he did, to make himself exhibit A in putting the lie to racial inferiority. While still in high school, Du Bois became a correspondent for the *New York Globe,* a black newspaper. He excelled academically and, following graduation, several local churches collected money to send him to college. In 1885, Du Bois enrolled at Fisk University, an all-black school in Nashville, Tennessee.

Following graduation from Fisk, Du Bois received a Harvard scholarship for a second bachelor's degree in philosophy. Studying with William James and George Santayana, Du Bois developed a Hegelian philosophy that made sense of the black experience. Du Bois went on to receive an M.A. at Harvard in 1892.

Following travel in Europe, Du Bois taught Greek and Latin at Wilberforce University, a black institution in Xenia, Ohio. At the same time, he completed his doctorate in sociology, becoming the first African American to receive a

61

Ph.D. from Harvard. His dissertation, *The Suppression of the African Slave Trade to the United States of America, 1638–1870* (1896), was published as the first in the Harvard Historical Studies Series.

In 1896, Du Bois married Nina Gomer, and together they had two children. That same year, Du Bois accepted a position at the University of Pennsylvania. He was commissioned to produce the first systematic study of blacks, *The Philadelphia Negro,* which was published in 1899. Interviewing over five thousand people for this study, Du Bois came to the conclusion that hard work, persistence, and patience in seeking reforms were the keys to improving the lot of African Americans in Philadelphia.

Following the study's completion, Du Bois was called to Atlanta University, where he taught for the next thirteen years. In Atlanta, Du Bois's social and political philosophies changed radically. The political climate in the late-1800s grew increasingly antagonistic toward blacks as the remnants of Reconstruction disappeared and *Plessey* v. *Ferguson* (1896) legalized "separate but equal" segregation. Du Bois himself suffered numerous indignities as he traveled in the South. He was especially repelled by the lynching of a black farm laborer in 1899 and by the antiblack Atlanta riots of 1906.

During this period, Du Bois challenged Booker T. Washington, president of Tuskegee Institute and African American leader. Washington advocated that his people accept a posture of submissiveness and modest aspiration, claiming, "It is at the bottom of life we must begin and not at the top."* In his earlier days, Du Bois might have agreed, but he was no longer willing to wait patiently at the bottom. Instead, Du Bois argued that blacks must assert themselves, particularly the "Talented Tenth" in the African American community, who would "be leaders of thought and missionaries of culture among their people."**

At Atlanta University, Du Bois began putting his ideas into political action. He was the secretary of the first Pan-African Conference in 1900 and helped organize the First Universal Races Congress in 1911 (both in London). In 1905, he was a founder of the Niagara Movement, which led in 1910 to the founding of the National Association for the Advancement of Colored People (NAACP). During this period Du Bois, made a number of sociological studies of blacks in the South. He also published his most famous book, *The Souls of Black Folks: Essays and Sketches* (1903).

With the founding of the NAACP in 1910, Du Bois left teaching to become editor of the organization's monthly organ, *The Crisis.* Du Bois's move from social scientist to political activist was now complete. For the next twenty-four years, Du Bois wrote, edited, organized, and labored tirelessly for racial equality.

In 1926, Du Bois accepted an invitation to the Soviet Union and returned full of praise for the new "Socialist Republic." He was now convinced that African Americans could find liberation in socialism. As his views moved further and further left, his relations with the NAACP were strained. Du Bois now regarded the NAACP's ideal of integration as not only unattainable but as even undesirable. When he publicly supported "nondiscriminatory segregation," he was forced to resign his position with the NAACP. He returned to teaching at Atlanta University, where he remained until retiring in 1943.

---

*Quoted in Julius Lester, ed., *The Seventh Son: The Thought and Writings of W.E.B. Du Bois,* two volumes. (New York: Random House, 1971), vol. 1, p. 42.
  ***Ibid.*, p. 44.

Du Bois spent a busy "retirement" in political activism. For four years, he returned to the NAACP as director of the department of special research. Among his many other activities in retirement, he was a consultant to the founding of the United Nations, co-chair of the Fifth Pan-African Congress, vice-chair of the Council of African Affairs, and chair of the Peace Information Center. At the age of eighty-seven, he even ran for senator of New York on the Progressive Party ticket.

In the late-1940s and early-1950s, Du Bois became even more enthusiastic about the USSR and The People's Republic of China. In 1951, as the Cold War warmed up, Du Bois was indicted as an "unregistered agent" of the Soviet Union. Though acquitted of all charges, Du Bois was embittered with life in the United States, and for the rest of the 1950s he traveled extensively in Eastern Europe and China. In 1959, Du Bois received the Lenin Peace Prize, and in 1961 he officially joined the Communist Party of the United States. Du Bois left the United States for good in 1961, becoming a citizen of the African state of Ghana. There he died at the age of ninety-five. Following a state funeral led by Ghana's president Kwame Nkrumah, Du Bois was buried in Accra, Ghana.

*   *   *

To understand Du Bois's philosophy, one must begin with the Hegelianism that runs through his work. Hegel had argued that the "the study of world history . . . represents the rationally necessary course of the World Spirit."* All human history is a dialectical process whereby the World Spirit becomes conscious of itself as free. Whenever a thesis of freedom is asserted, it is opposed by an antithesis. These are then both overcome by a synthesis that incorporates the best of both. In particular, Hegel held that the World Spirit that is coming to a consciousness of freedom is always the spirit of specific world-historical *peoples,* not individuals. Hegel traced the development of this World Spirit through six historical peoples: Chinese, Indians, Egyptians, Greeks, Romans, and Germans.

Du Bois accepted Hegelian history and applied it to the experience of African Americans. In our reading from *The Souls of Black Folks,* Du Bois refers to Hegel's six historical peoples and adds,

> The Negro is a sort of seventh son, born with a veil, and gifted with second-sight in this American world,—a world which yields him no true self-consciousness, but only lets him see himself through the revelation of the other world.

According to Du Bois, "Black folk's" consciousness of freedom is newer and richer than that of any previous world-historical people because of slavery. As one writer explains,

> Out of slavery and out of the later striving of black folk for whiteness in an oppressive white world came a rising sense of black soul. Thus it was that white thesis bred black antithesis, which took the best of white culture and moved it upward toward a new synthesis.**

---

*Hegel, *Reason in History: A General Introduction to the Philosophy of History,* see Forrest E. Baird and Walter Kaufmann, *Nineteenth-Century Philosophy* (New York: Prentice Hall, 2000), p. 54.
**Joel Williamson, *The Crucible of Race* (New York: Oxford University Press, 1984), p. 405.

While using Hegelian notions, Du Bois noticed something unique about the self-consciousness of black folk. As a "problem," as an "other," black folk develop a kind of "double-consciousness." Black folk have the "sense of always looking at one's self through the eyes of others." This "twoness," this consciousness of "two souls, two thoughts, two unreconciled strivings; two warring ideals in one dark body," means that black folk must uniquely struggle to find true self-consciousness and self-identity.

Although in some ways Du Bois is more activist than philosopher, his thought has been enormously influential. His identification of a "black soul" provided a theoretical base for African American studies. His identification of a unique black culture gave blacks both dignity and an alternative to the assimilationist tendencies of integrationists. His discovery of double-consciousness and his notion of the "other" anticipated some recent debates in Continental philosophy.

*   *   *

A good place to begin studying Du Bois is Julius Lester, ed., *The Seventh Son: The Thought and Writings of W.E.B. Du Bois,* two volumes. (New York: Random House, 1971). For biographies of Du Bois, see Jack B. Moore, *W.E.B. Du Bois* (Boston: Twayne, 1981); Manning Marable, *W.E.B. Du Bois: Black Radical Democrat* (Boston: Twayne, 1986); David L. Lewis, *W.E.B. Du Bois: Biography of a Race, 1868–1919* (New York: Henry Holt, 1993); and Du Bois's own autobiographies, *Dusk of Dawn* (New York: Harcourt, Brace, 1940) and *The Autobiography of W.E.B. Du Bois,* edited by Herbert Aptheker (New York: International, 1968). Studies of Du Bois's social and political involvements include Francis L. Broderick, *W.E.B. Du Bois: Negro Leader in a Time of Crisis* (Stanford, CA: Stanford University Press, 1959); Elliot Rudwick, *W.E.B. Du Bois: Voice of the Black Protest Movement* (1960; reprinted Urbana: University of Illinois Press, 1982); Rayford W. Logan, ed., *W.E.B. Du Bois: A Profile* (New York: Hill and Wang, 1971); and Cary D. Wintz, *African-American Political Thought, 1890–1930: Washington, Du Bois, Garvey, and Randolph* (Armonk, NY: Sharpe, 1996). For a more philosophical treatment of Du Bois, see Joel Williamson, *The Crucible of Race* (New York: Oxford University Press, 1984) and Bernard W. Bell, Emily R. Grosholz, and James B. Stewart, eds., *W.E.B. Du Bois on Race and Culture: Critiques and Extrapolations* (London: Routledge, 1996).

THE SOULS OF BLACK FOLKS (in part)

CHAPTER 1: OF OUR SPIRITUAL STRIVINGS

O water, voice of my heart, crying in the sand,
    All night long crying with a mournful cry,
As I lie and listen, and cannot understand
        The voice of my heart in my side or the voice of the sea,

O water, crying for rest, is it I, is it I?
  All night long the water is crying to me.

Unresting water, there shall never be rest
  Till the last moon droop and the last tide fail,
And the fire of the end begin to burn in the west;
    And the heart shall be weary and wonder and cry like the sea,
  All life long crying without avail,
    As the water all night long is crying to me.

—*Arthur Symons*

Between me and the other world there is ever an unasked question: unasked by some through feelings of delicacy; by others through the difficulty of rightly framing it. All, nevertheless, flutter round it. They approach me in a half-hesitant sort of way, eye me curiously or compassionately, and then, instead of saying directly, How does it feel to be a problem? they say, I know an excellent colored man in my town; or, I fought at Mechanicsville; or, Do not these Southern outrages make your blood boil? At these I smile, or am interested, or reduce the boiling to a simmer, as the occasion may require. To the real question, How does it feel to be a problem? I answer seldom a word.

And yet, being a problem is a strange experience,—peculiar even for one who has never been anything else, save perhaps in babyhood and in Europe. It is in the early days of rollicking boyhood that the revelation first bursts upon one, all in a day, as it were. I

W.E.B. Du Bois (on the left) and his high school graduating class, Great Barrington, Massachusetts, 1884. *(W.E.B. Du Bois Library)*

remember well when the shadow swept across me. I was a little thing, away up in the hills of New England, where the dark Housatonic winds between Hoosac and Taghkanic to the sea. In a wee wooden schoolhouse, something put it into the boys' and girls' heads to buy gorgeous visiting-cards—ten cents a package—and exchange. The exchange was merry, till one girl, a tall newcomer, refused my card,—refused it peremptorily, with a glance. Then it dawned upon me with a certain suddenness that I was different from the others; or like, mayhap, in heart and life and longing, but shut out from their world by a vast veil. I had thereafter no desire to tear down that veil, to creep through; I held all beyond it in common contempt, and lived above it in a region of blue sky and great wandering shadows. That sky was bluest when I could beat my mates at examination-time, or beat them at a foot-race, or even beat their stringy heads. Alas, with the years all this fine contempt began to fade; for the worlds I longed for, and all their dazzling opportunities, were theirs, not mine. But they should not keep these prizes, I said; some, all, I would wrest from them. Just how I would do it I could never decide: by reading law, by healing the sick, by telling the wonderful tales that swam in my head,—some way. With other black boys the strife was not so fiercely sunny: their youth shrunk into tasteless sycophancy, or into silent hatred of the pale world about them and mocking distrust of everything white; or wasted itself in a bitter cry, Why did God make me an outcast and a stranger in mine own house? The shades of the prison-house closed round about us all: walls strait and stubborn to the whitest, but relentlessly narrow, tall, and unscalable to sons of night who must plod darkly on in resignation, or beat unavailing palms against the stone, or steadily, half hopelessly, watch the streak of blue above.

After the Egyptian and Indian, the Greek and Roman, the Teuton and Mongolian, the Negro is a sort of seventh son, born with a veil, and gifted with second-sight in this American world,—a world which yields him no true self-consciousness, but only lets him see himself through the revelation of the other world. It is a peculiar sensation, this double-consciousness, this sense of always looking at one's self through the eyes of others, of measuring one's soul by the tape of a world that looks on in amused contempt and pity. One ever feels his twoness,—an American, a Negro; two souls, two thoughts, two unreconciled strivings; two warring ideals in one dark body, whose dogged strength alone keeps it from being torn asunder.

The history of the American Negro is the history of this strife,—this longing to attain self-conscious manhood, to merge his double self into a better and truer self. In this merging he wishes neither of the older selves to be lost. He would not Africanize America, for America has too much to teach the world and Africa. He would not bleach his Negro soul in a flood of white Americanism, for he knows that Negro blood has a message for the world. He simply wishes to make it possible for a man to be both a Negro and an American, without being cursed and spit upon by his fellows, without having the doors of Opportunity closed roughly in his face.

This, then, is the end of his striving: to be a co-worker in the kingdom of culture, to escape both death and isolation, to husband and use his best powers and his latent genius. These powers of body and mind have in the past been strangely wasted, dispersed, or forgotten. The shadow of a mighty Negro past flits through the tale of Ethiopia the Shadowy and of Egypt the Sphinx. Throughout history, the powers of single black men flash here and there like falling stars, and die sometimes before the world has rightly gauged their brightness. Here in America, in the few days since Emancipation, the black man's turning hither and thither in hesitant and doubtful striving has often made his very strength to lose effectiveness, to seem like absence of power, like weakness. And yet it is not weakness,—it is the contradiction of double aims. The double-aimed struggle of the black artisan—on the one hand to escape white contempt for a nation of mere hewers of wood and drawers of water, and on the other hand to plough and nail and dig for a poverty-stricken horde—could only result in making him a poor craftsman, for he had but half a heart in either cause. By the poverty and ignorance of his people, the Negro minister or doctor was tempted toward quackery and demagogy; and by the criticism of the other world, toward ideals that made him ashamed of his lowly tasks. The would-be black savant was confronted by the paradox that the knowledge his people needed was a twice-told tale to his white neighbors, while the knowledge which would teach the white world was Greek to his own flesh and blood. The innate love of harmony and beauty that set the ruder souls of his people a-dancing and a-singing raised but confusion and doubt in the soul of the black artist; for the beauty revealed to him was the soul-beauty of a race which his larger audience despised, and he could not articulate the message of another people. This waste of double aims, this seeking to satisfy two unreconciled ideals, has wrought sad havoc with the courage and faith and deeds of ten thousand thousand people,—has sent them often wooing false gods and invoking false means of salvation, and at times has even seemed about to make them ashamed of themselves.

Away back in the days of bondage they thought to see in one divine event the end of all doubt and disappointment; few men ever worshipped Freedom with half such unquestioning faith as did the American Negro for two centuries. To him, so far as he thought and dreamed, slavery was indeed the sum of all villainies, the cause of all sorrow, the root of all prejudice; Emancipation was the key to a promised land of sweeter beauty than ever stretched before the eyes of wearied Israelites, In song and exhortation swelled one refrain—Liberty; in his tears and curses the God he implored had Freedom in his right hand. At last it came,—suddenly, fearfully, like a dream. With one wild carnival of blood and passion came the message in his own plaintive cadences:—

"Shout, O children!
Shout, you're free!
For God has bought your liberty!"

Years have passed away since then,—ten, twenty, forty; forty years of national life, forty years of renewal and development, and yet the swarthy spectre sits in its accustomed seat at the Nation's feast. In vain do we cry to this our vastest social problem:—

"Take any shape but that, and my firm nerves
Shall never tremble!"

The Nation has not yet found peace from its sins; the freedman has not yet found in freedom his promised land. Whatever of good may have come in these years of change, the shadow of a deep disappointment rests upon the Negro people,—a disappointment all the more bitter because the unattained ideal was unbounded save by the simple ignorance of a lowly people.

The first decade was merely a prolongation of the vain search for freedom, the boon that seemed ever barely to elude their grasp,—like a tantalizing will-o'-the-wisp, maddening and misleading the headless host. The holocaust of war, the terrors of the Ku Klux Klan, the lies of carpet-baggers, the disorganization of industry, and the contradictory advice of friends and foes, left the bewildered serf with no new watchword beyond the old cry for freedom. As the time flew, however, he began to grasp a new idea. The ideal of liberty demanded for its attainment powerful means, and these the Fifteenth Amendment gave him. The ballot, which before he had looked upon as a visible sign of freedom, he now regarded as the chief means of gaining and perfecting the liberty with which war had partially endowed him. And why not? Had not votes made war and emancipated millions? Had not votes enfranchised the freedmen? Was anything impossible to a power that had done all this? A million black men started with renewed zeal to vote themselves into the kingdom. So the decade flew away, the revolution of 1876 came, and left the half-free serf weary, wondering, but still inspired. Slowly but steadily, in the following years, a new vision began gradually to replace the dream of political power,—a powerful movement, the rise of another ideal to guide the unguided, another pillar of fire by night after a clouded day. It was the ideal of "book-learning"; the curiosity, born of compulsory ignorance, to know and test the power of the cabalistic letters of the white man, the longing to know. Here at last seemed to have been discovered the mountain path to Canaan; longer than the highway of Emancipation and law, steep and rugged, but straight, leading to heights high enough to overlook life.

Up the new path the advance guard toiled, slowly, heavily, doggedly; only those who have watched and guided the faltering feet, the misty minds, the dull understandings, of the dark pupils of these schools know how faithfully, how piteously, this people strove to learn. It was weary work. The cold statistician wrote down the inches of progress here and there, noted also where here and there a foot had slipped or some one had fallen. To the tired climbers, the horizon was ever dark, the mists were often cold, the Canaan was always dim and far away. If, however, the vistas disclosed as yet no goal, no resting-place, little but flattery and criticism, the journey at least gave leisure for reflection and self-examination; it changed the child of Emancipation to the youth with dawning self-consciousness, self-realization, self-respect. In those sombre forests of his striving his own soul rose before him, and he saw himself,—darkly as through a veil; and yet he saw in himself some faint revelation of his power, of his mission. He began to have a dim feeling that, to attain his place in the world, he must be himself, and not another. For the first time he sought to analyze the burden he bore upon his back, that dead-weight of social degradation partially masked behind a half-named Negro problem. He felt his poverty; without a cent, without a home, without land, tools, or savings, he had entered into competition with rich, landed, skilled neighbors. To be a poor man is hard, but to be a poor race in a land of dollars is the very bottom of hardships. He felt the weight of his ignorance,—not simply of letters, but of life, of business, of the humanities; the accumulated sloth and shirking and awkwardness of decades and centuries shackled his hands and feet. Nor was his burden all poverty and ignorance. The red stain of bastardy, which two centuries of systematic legal defilement of Negro women had stamped upon his race, meant not only the loss of ancient African chastity, but also the hereditary weight of a mass of corruption from white adulterers, threatening almost the obliteration of the Negro home.

A people thus handicapped ought not to be asked to race with the world, but rather allowed to give all its time and thought to its own social problems. But alas! while sociologists gleefully count his bastards and his prostitutes, the very soul of the toiling, sweating black man is darkened by the shadow of a vast despair. Men call the shadow prejudice, and learnedly explain it as the natural defence of culture against barbarism, learning against ignorance, purity against crime, the "higher" against the "lower" races. To which the Negro cries Amen! and swears that to so much of this strange prejudice as is founded on just homage to civilization, culture, righteousness, and progress, he humbly bows and meekly does obeisance. But before that nameless prejudice that leaps beyond all this he stands helpless, dismayed, and well-nigh speechless; before that personal disrespect and mockery, the ridicule and systematic humiliation, the distortion of fact and wanton license of fancy, the cynical ignoring of the better and the boisterous welcoming of the worse, the all-pervading desire to inculcate disdain for everything black, from Toussaint to the devil,—before this there rises a sickening despair that would disarm and discourage any nation save that black host to whom "discouragement" is an unwritten word.

But the facing of so vast a prejudice could not but bring the inevitable self-questioning, self-disparagement, and lowering of ideals which ever accompany repression and breed in an atmosphere of contempt and hate. Whisperings and portents came borne upon the four winds: Lo! we are diseased and dying, cried the dark hosts; we cannot write, our voting is vain; what need of education, since we must always cook and serve? And the Nation echoed and enforced this self-criticism, saying: Be content to be servants, and nothing more; what need of higher culture for half-men? Away with the black man's ballot, by force or fraud,—and behold the suicide of a race! Nevertheless, out of the evil came something of good,—the more careful adjustment of education to real life, the clearer perception of the Negroes' social responsibilities, and the sobering realization of the meaning of progress.

So dawned the time of *Sturm und Drang:* storm and stress to-day rocks our little boat on the mad waters of the world-sea; there is within and without the sound of conflict, the burning of body and rending of soul; inspiration strives with doubt, and faith with vain questionings. The bright ideals of the past,—physical freedom, political power, the training of brains and the training of hands,—all these in turn have waxed and waned, until even the last grows dim and overcast. Are they all wrong,—all false? No, not that, but each alone was over-simple and incomplete,—the dreams of a credulous race-childhood, or the fond imaginings of the other world which does not know and does not want to know our power. To be really true, all these ideals must be melted and welded into one. The training of the schools we need to-day more than ever,—the training of deft hands, quick eyes and ears, and above all the broader, deeper, higher culture of gifted minds and pure hearts. The power of the ballot we need in sheer self-defence,—else what shall save us from a second slavery? Freedom, too, the long-sought, we still seek,—the freedom of life and limb, the freedom to work and think, the freedom to love and aspire. Work, culture, liberty,—all these we need, not singly but together, not successively but together, each growing and aiding each, and all striving toward that vaster ideal that swims before the Negro people, the ideal of human brotherhood, gained through the unifying ideal of Race; the ideal of fostering and developing the traits and talents of the Negro, not in opposition to or contempt for other races, but rather in large conformity to the greater ideals of the American Republic, in order that some day on American soil two world-races may give each to each those characteristics both so sadly lack. We the darker ones come even now not altogether empty-handed: there are to-day no truer exponents of the pure human spirit of the Declaration of Independence than the American Negroes; there is no true American music but the wild sweet melodies of the Negro slave; the American fairy tales and folk-lore are Indian and African; and, all in all, we black men seem the sole oasis of simple faith and reverence in a dusty desert of dollars and smartness. Will America be poorer if she replace her brutal dyspeptic blundering with lighthearted but determined Negro humility? or her coarse and cruel wit with loving jovial good-humor? or her vulgar music with the soul of the Sorrow Songs?

Merely a concrete test of the underlying principles of the great republic is the Negro Problem, and the spiritual striving of the freedmen's sons is the travail of souls whose burden is almost beyond the measure of their strength, but who bear it in the name of an historic race, in the name of this the land of their fathers' fathers, and in the name of human opportunity.

BERTRAND RUSSELL
1872–1970

Bertrand Arthur William Russell was born into a prestigious family in Trelleck, Wales. His parents, Lord and Lady Amberley, were close friends with John Stuart Mill, and Russell's grandfather, Lord John Russell, had been prime minister to Queen Victoria. Both of Russell's parents died by the time he was three, and so, with his brother, he was sent to live with his grandparents, Lord and Lady Russell. When his grandfather died a few years later, his grandmother took responsibility for his education. Unlike most privileged English boys, Russell did not attend a boarding school—Lady Russell did not approve of them. Instead, she arranged for a series of Swiss and German governesses, followed by English tutors, to educate her grandsons. Although Russell thus enjoyed virtually every privilege, he later reported that his adolescent life seemed so bleak that he would have committed suicide had he not been "restrained by the desire to know more mathematics."

In 1890, Russell entered Cambridge University, where he was finally able to study his beloved mathematics on his own. His years at the university were the happiest of his life. He quickly established himself as one of the brightest students, and he formed several close friendships, including a lifelong one with G.E. Moore (1873–1958). Following graduation, Russell served briefly with the British ambassador to France before moving to Berlin to study economics and political theory. In 1895, Russell was elected a fellow of Trinity College, Cambridge, and worked extensively on the foundations of mathematics. He published *Principles of Mathematics* (1903) and, together with Alfred North Whitehead, the epoch-making *Principia Mathematica* (1910–1913). During this time, Russell also made the first of three unsuccessful runs for Parliament.

Russell was appointed lecturer in philosophy at Cambridge in 1910—a position he held until 1916, when he was dismissed for his opposition to the continued fighting of World War I. He also spent six months in jail for alleging that U.S. troops were used for strikebreaking in America. He was reinstated in his Cambridge position in 1919 but soon resigned and never again assumed permanent teaching duties. During his years as a lecturer, Russell also produced some of his most important works of philosophy and logic, including *The Problems of Philosophy* (1912), *Our Knowledge of the External World* (1914), and *Introduction to Mathematical Philosophy* (written while in prison and published in 1919).

In his post-teaching period, Russell wrote and lectured widely—often taking controversial positions on social and political issues. For example, he alienated many of his socialist friends when, after a visit to the Soviet Union in 1920, he published his observations in *The Theory and Practice of Bolshevism:*

> [Russia is] one vast prison in which the jailors were cruel bigots. When I found my friends applauding these men as liberators and regarding the regime that they were creating as a paradise, I wondered . . . whether it was my friends or I that were mad.

His book *Marriage and Morals* (1929) caused a stir by minimizing the seriousness of extramarital affairs and by advocating informal trial marriages. His works on religion, *What I Believe* (1925), *Religion and Science* (1935), and *Why I Am Not a Christian* (1957), made Russell's atheism explicit. Russell also tried his hand at practical social reform. With his second wife Dora, he started a school in 1927 to implement the educational theories of his books *On Education: Especially Early Childhood* (1926) and *Education and the Social Order* (1932).

In 1938, Russell accepted a visiting professorship at the University of Chicago and later at the University of California at Los Angeles. He declined a permanent offer from UCLA in order to accept an invitation from the College of the City of New York; however, before he could begin teaching a judge ruled him unfit, claiming, among other things, that Russell's appointment would constitute "a chair of indecency." Russell mocked the decision on the title page of his *An Inquiry into Meaning and Truth,* published the next year, by listing his many honors and then adding "Judicially pronounced unworthy to be Professor of Philosophy at the College of the City of New York (1940)." To that long list of honors, he would be able to add the Nobel Prize for literature in 1950.

In his later years, Russell continued to write on a variety of topics—and to get into trouble with authorities. At age eighty-nine, he served another jail sentence—this time for his part in a nuclear-disarmament rally in London. By the time of his death, in 1970, Russell was acknowledged as the leading British philosopher of the century.

*   *   *

It is difficult to summarize Russell's thought, partly because he developed and abandoned several philosophical theories during his long lifetime. Philosopher C.D. Broad once commented, "As we all know, Mr. Russell produces a different system of philosophy every few years." Even though the specifics of Russell's philosophic enterprise evolved, reflecting his fertile and inventive mind, at least two basic assumptions remained within his mature philosophy.

First, Russell believed philosophy should be scientific and analytical. As he wrote in "Logical Atomism" (1924):

> Although . . . comprehensive construction is part of the business of philosophy, I do not believe it is the most important part. The most important part, to my mind, consists in criticizing and clarifying notions which are apt to be regarded as fundamental and accepted uncritically. As instances I might mention: mind, matter, consciousness, knowledge, experience, causality, will, time. I believe all these notions to be inexact and approximate, essentially infected with vagueness, incapable of forming part of any exact science.

Second, in "criticizing and clarifying notions," Russell was committed to the principle of parsimony known as "Ockham's Razor" (after the medieval thinker, William of Ockham). Ockham's injunction asserted that "entities are not to be multiplied beyond necessity," meaning one should always seek the simplest explanation. Russell's version of this principle, articulated in several of his works, states that "Whenever possible, substitute constructions out of known entities for inferences to unknown entities."

In the selection from *The Problems of Philosophy* reprinted here, Russell wields this razor in an analysis of the common objects of our sensory perception and our language about such objects. Russell points out that sense-data are the only "known entities" actually given in experience:

> What the senses *immediately* tell us is not the truth about the object as it is apart from us, but only the truth about certain sense-data which, so far as we can see, depend upon the relations between us and the object. (Emphasis in original.)

Rather than inferring some "unknown entity" (such as "being" or "substance") as the cause of our sense-data, we can consider a given object to be the class or collection of all sense-data we normally associate with that object. Our knowledge of physical objects is not direct but is gained by "acquaintance" with the sense-data that make up the appearance of an object.

The language used to make propositions about such objects also depends on acquaintance. To use language in a meaningful manner, "the meaning we attach to our words must be something with which we are acquainted" either in terms of a thing or a description. Using Russell's example, a statement about Julius Caesar can be meaningful because, although we have no acquaintance with the "thing" (i.e., we have not met Caesar), we do have in mind some description of Caesar.

Our second selection, "Mysticism and Logic," given here complete, represents Russell at his nontechnical best. In the essay, Russell defines mysticism as "little more than a certain intensity and depth of feeling in regard to what is believed about the universe." He goes on to argue that mysticism is mistaken in its understanding of knowledge, unity, time, and the nature of evil. Despite his scathing attack on mystical beliefs, Russell finds "an element of wisdom" in the mystical attitude and claims that all the greatest philosophers have felt a need for mysticism.

The two selections given here include some of Russell's major themes and give some sense of his style, but his contributions to philosophy go beyond what has been included. His work in mathematics and logic changed both of those disciplines; his theory of logical atomism represented an important step in the philosophy of language; his theories of descriptions and of types helped clear up a number of logical puzzles; and in addition there are his writings on education, sociology, politics, and religion. In short, Russell touched on virtually all areas of human existence, and even those who differ with his conclusions cannot help but be impressed with the breadth and depth of his thought.

*   *   *

For biographical information, see Ronald William Clark, *The Life of Bertrand Russell* (New York: Knopf, 1976); Katharine Tait, *My Father, Bertrand Russell* (Bristol, UK: Thoemmes, 1996); or Russell's autobiography, *The Autobiography of Bertrand Russell* (Boston: Little, Brown, 1967). A.J. Ayer, *Russell and Moore: The Analytic Heritage* (Cambridge, MA: Harvard University Press, 1971) puts Russell's thought in the context of analytic philosophy, whereas J. Watling, *Bertrand Russell* (New York: British Book Center, 1971); A.J. Ayer, *Bertrand Russell* (Chicago: University of Chicago Press, 1988); and John Slater, *Bertrand Russell* (Bristol, Gloucester: Thoemmes, 1994) provide general introductions. Studies on specific areas of Russell's thought include Lillian Woodworth Aiken, *Bertrand Russell's Philosophy of Morals* (New York: Humanities Press, 1963); Robert J. Clack, *Bertrand Russell's Philosophy of Language* (The Hague, The Netherlands: Martinus Nijhoff, 1969); and Elizabeth R. Eames, *Bertrand Russell's Theory of Knowledge* (New York: George Braziller, 1969). For collections of essays, see Paul A. Schilpp, ed., *The Philosophy of Bertrand Russell* (New York: Tudor, 1951)—part of the Library of Living Philosophers; Ralph Schoenman, ed., *Bertrand Russell: Philosopher of the Century* (Boston: Little, Brown, 1967); E.D. Klemke, ed., *Essays on Bertrand Russell* (Urbana: University of Illinois Press, 1970); D.F. Pears, ed., *Bertrand Russell* (Garden City, NY: Anchor Doubleday, 1972); A.D. Irvine and G.A. Wedeking, eds., *Russell and Analytic Philosophy* (Toronto:University of Toronto Press, 1993); Ray Monk and Anthony Palmer, eds., *Bertrand Russell and the Origins of Analytical Philosophy* (Bristol, UK: Thoemmes, 1996).

THE PROBLEMS OF PHILOSOPHY
(in part)

CHAPTER 1: APPEARANCE AND REALITY

Is there any knowledge in the world which is so certain that no reasonable man could doubt it? This question, which at first sight might not seem difficult, is really one of the most difficult that can be asked. When we have realized the obstacles in the way of a straightforward and confident answer, we shall be well launched on the study of philosophy—for philosophy is merely the attempt to answer such ultimate questions, not carelessly and dogmatically, as we do in ordinary life and even in the sciences, but crit-

Bertrand Russell, *The Problems of Philosophy* (Oxford: Oxford University Press, 1912). Reprinted by permission of Oxford University Press.

ically, after exploring all that makes such questions puzzling, and after realizing all the vagueness and confusion that underlie our ordinary ideas.

In daily life, we assume as certain many things which, on a closer scrutiny, are found to be so full of apparent contradictions that only a great amount of thought enables us to know what it is that we really may believe. In the search for certainty, it is natural to begin with our present experiences, and in some sense, no doubt, knowledge is to be derived from them. But any statement as to what it is that our immediate experiences make us know is very likely to be wrong. It seems to me that I am now sitting in a chair, at a table of a certain shape, on which I see sheets of paper with writing or print. By turning my head I see out of the window buildings and clouds and the sun. I believe that the sun is about ninety-three million miles from the earth; that it is a hot globe many times bigger than the earth; that, owing to the earth's rotation, it rises every morning, and will continue to do so for an indefinite time in the future. I believe that, if any other normal person comes into my room, he will see the same chairs and tables and books and papers as I see, and that the table which I see is the same as the table which I feel pressing against my arm. All this seems to be so evident as to be hardly worth stating, except in answer to a man who doubts whether I know anything. Yet all this may be reasonably doubted, and all of it requires much careful discussion before we can be sure that we have stated it in a form that is wholly true.

To make our difficulties plain, let us concentrate attention on the table. To the eye it is oblong, brown, and shiny, to the touch it is smooth and cool and hard; when I tap it, it gives out a wooden sound. Any one else who sees and feels and hears the table will agree with this description, so that it might seem as if no difficulty would arise; but as soon as we try to be more precise our troubles begin. Although I believe that the table is "really" of the same colour all over, the parts that reflect the light look much brighter than the other parts, and some parts look white because of reflected light. I know that, if I move, the parts that reflect the light will be different, so that the apparent distribution of colours on the table will change. It follows that if several people are looking at the table at the same moment, no two of them will see exactly the same distribution of colours, because no two can see it from exactly the same point of view, and any change in the point of view makes some change in the way the light is reflected.

For most practical purposes these differences are unimportant, but to the painter they are all-important: the painter has to unlearn the habit of thinking that things seem to have the colour which common sense says they "really" have, and to learn the habit of seeing things as they appear. Here we have already the beginning of one of the distinctions that cause most trouble in philosophy—the distinction between "appearance" and "reality," between what things seem to be and what they are. The painter wants to know what things seem to be, the practical man and the philosopher want to know what they are; but the philosopher's wish to know this is stronger than the practical man's, and is more troubled by knowledge as to the difficulties of answering the question.

To return to the table. It is evident from what we have found, that there is no colour which preeminently appears to be *the* colour of the table, or even of any one particular part of the table—it appears to be of different colours from different points of view, and there is no reason for regarding some of these as more really its colour than others. And we know that even from a given point of view the colour will seem different by artificial light, or to a colour-blind man, or to a man wearing blue spectacles, while in the dark there will be no colour at all, though to touch and hearing the table will be unchanged. This colour is not something which is inherent in the table, but something depending upon the table and the spectator and the way the light falls on the table. When, in ordinary life, we speak of *the* colour of the table, we only mean the sort of colour which it will seem to have to a normal spectator from an ordinary point of view under usual conditions of light. But the other colours which appear under other conditions have just as good a right to be considered real; and therefore, to avoid favouritism, we are compelled to deny that, in itself, the table has any one particular colour.

The same thing applies to the texture. With the naked eye one can see the grain, but otherwise the table looks smooth and even. If we looked at it through a microscope, we should see roughnesses and hills and valleys, and all sorts of differences that are imperceptible to the naked eye. Which of these is the "real" table? We are naturally tempted to say that what we see through the microscope is more real, but that in turn would be changed by a still more powerful microscope. If, then, we cannot trust what we see with the naked eye, why should we trust what we see through a microscope? Thus, again, the confidence in our senses with which we began deserts us.

The *shape* of the table is no better. We are all in the habit of judging as to the "real" shapes of things, and we do this so unreflectingly that we come to think we actually see the real shapes. But, in fact, as we all have to learn if we try to draw, a given thing looks different in shape from every different point of view. If our table is "really" rectangular, it will look, from almost all points of view, as if it had two acute angles and two obtuse angles. If opposite sides are parallel, they will look as if they converged to a point away from the spectator; if they are of equal length, they will look as if the nearer side were longer. All these things are not commonly noticed in looking at a table, because experience has taught us to construct the "real" shape from the apparent shape, and the "real" shape is what interests us as practical men. But the "real" shape is not what we see, it is something inferred from what we see. And what we see is constantly changing in shape as we move about the room; so that here again the senses seem not to give us the truth about the table itself, but only about the appearance of the table.

Similar difficulties arise when we consider the sense of touch. It is true that the table always gives us a sensation of hardness, and we feel that it resists pressure. But the sensation we obtain depends upon how hard we press the table and also upon what part of the body we press with; thus the various sensations due to various pressures or various parts of the body cannot be supposed to reveal *directly* any definite property of the table, but at most to be *signs* of some property which perhaps *causes* all the sensations, but is not actually apparent in any of them. And the same applies still more obviously to the sounds which can be elicited by rapping the table.

Thus it becomes evident that the real table, if there is one, is not the same as what we immediately experience by sight or touch or hearing. The real table, if there is one, is not *immediately* known to us all, but must be an inference from what is immediately known. Hence, two very difficult questions at once arise; namely, (1) Is there a real table at all? (2) If so, what sort of object can it be?

It will help us in considering these questions to have a few simple terms of which the meaning is definite and clear. Let us give the name of "sense-data" to the things that are immediately known in sensation: such things as colours, sounds, smells, hardnesses, roughnesses, and so on. We shall give the name "sensation" to the experience of being immediately aware of these things. Thus, whenever we see a colour, we have a sensation of the colour, but the colour itself is a sense-datum, not a sensation. The colour is that *of* which we are immediately aware, and the awareness itself is the sensation. It is plain that if we are to know anything about the table, it must be by means of the sense-data—brown colour, oblong shape, smoothness, etc.—which we associate with the table; but, for the reasons which have been given, we cannot say that the table *is* the sense-data, or even that the sense-data are directly properties of the table. Thus a problem arises as to the relation of the sense-data to the real table, supposing there is such a thing.

The real table, if it exists, we will call a "physical object." Thus we have to consider the relation of sense-data to physical objects. The collection of all physical objects is called "matter." Thus our two questions may be re-stated as follows: (1) Is there any such thing as matter? (2) If so, what is its nature?

The philosopher who first brought prominently forward the reasons for regarding the immediate objects of our senses as not existing independently of us was Bishop Berkeley (1685–1753). His *Three Dialogues between Hylas and Philonous, in Opposition to Sceptics and Atheists,* undertake to prove that there is no such thing as matter at all, and that the world consists of nothing but minds and their ideas. Hylas has hitherto believed in matter, but he is no match for Philonous, who mercilessly drives him into contradictions and paradoxes, and makes his own denial of matter seem, in the end, as if it were almost common sense. The arguments employed are of very different value: some are important and sound, others are confused or quibbling. But Berkeley retains the merit of having shown that the existence of matter is capable of being denied without absurdity, and that if there are any things that exist independently of us they cannot be the immediate objects of our sensations.

There are two different questions involved when we ask whether matter exists, and it is important to keep them clear. We commonly mean by "matter" something which is opposed to "mind," something which we think of as occupying space and as radically incapable of any sort of thought or consciousness. It is chiefly in this sense that Berkeley denies matter; that is to say, he does not deny that the sense-data which we commonly take as signs of the existence of the table are really signs of the existence *of* something independent of us, but he does deny that this something is, non-mental, that it is neither mind nor ideas entertained by some mind. He admits that there must be something which continues to exist when we go out of the room or shut our eyes, and that what we call seeing the table does really give us reason for believing in something which persists even when we are not seeing it. But he thinks that this something cannot be radically different in nature from what we see, and cannot be independent of seeing altogether, though it must be independent of *our* seeing. He is thus led to regard the "real" table as an idea in the mind of God. Such an idea has the required permanence and independence of ourselves, without being—as matter would otherwise be—something quite unknowable, in the sense that we can only infer it, and can never be directly and immediately aware of it.

Other philosophers since Berkeley have also held that, although the table does not depend for its existence upon being seen by me, it does depend upon being seen (or otherwise apprehended in sensation) by *some* mind—not necessarily the mind of God, but more often the whole collective mind of the universe. This they hold, as Berkeley does, chiefly because they think there can be nothing real—or at any rate nothing known to be real—except minds and their thoughts and feelings. We might state the argument by which they support their view in some such way as this: "Whatever can be thought of is an idea in the mind of the person thinking of it; therefore nothing can be thought of except ideas in minds; therefore anything else is inconceivable, and what is inconceivable cannot exist."

Such an argument, in my opinion, is fallacious; and of course those who advance it do not put it so shortly or so crudely. But whether valid or not, the argument has been very widely advanced in one form or another; and very many philosophers, perhaps a majority, have held that there is nothing real except minds and their ideas. Such philosophers are called "idealists." When they come to explaining matter, they either say, like Berkeley, that matter is really nothing but a collection of ideas, or they say, like Leibniz (1646–1716), that what appears as matter is really a collection of more or less rudimentary minds.

But these philosophers, though they deny matter as opposed to mind, nevertheless, in another sense, admit matter. It will be remembered that we asked two questions; namely, (1) Is there a real table at all? (2) If so, what sort of object can it be? Now both Berkeley and Leibniz admit that there is a real table, but Berkeley says it is certain ideas in the mind of God, and Leibniz says it is a colony of souls. Thus both of them answer our first question in the affirmative, and only diverge from the views of ordinary mortals in their answer to our second question. In fact, almost all philosophers seem to be agreed that there is a real table: they almost all agree that, however much our sense-data—colour, shape, smoothness, etc.—may depend upon us, yet their oc- currence is a sign of something existing independently of us, something differing, per- haps, completely from our sense-data, and yet to be regarded as causing those sense- data whenever we are in a suitable relation to the real table.

Now obviously this point in which the philosophers are agreed—the view that there *is* a real table, whatever its nature may be—is vitally important, and it will be worth while to consider what reasons there are for accepting this view before we go on to the further question as to the nature of the real table. Our next chapter, therefore, will be concerned with the reasons for supposing that there is a real table at all.

Before we go farther it will be well to consider for a moment what it is that we have discovered so far. It has appeared that, if we take any common object of the sort that is sup- posed to be known by the senses, what the senses *immediately* tell us is not the truth about the object as it is apart from us, but only the truth about certain sense-data which, so far as we can see, depend upon the relations between us and the object. Thus what we directly see and feel is merely "appearance," which we believe to be a sign of some "reality" be- hind. But if the reality is not what appears, have we any means of knowing whether there is any reality at all? And if so, have we any means of finding out what it is like?

Such questions are bewildering, and it is difficult to know that even the strangest hypotheses may not be true. Thus our familiar table, which has roused but the slightest thoughts in us hitherto, has become a problem full of surprising possibilities. The one thing we know about it is that it is not what it seems. Beyond this modest result, so far, we have the most complete liberty of conjecture. Leibniz tells us it is a community of souls; Berkeley tells us it is an idea in the mind of God; sober science, scarcely less wonderful, tells us it is a vast collection of electric charges in violent motion.

Among these surprising possibilities, doubt suggests that perhaps there is no table at all. Philosophy, if it cannot *answer* so many questions as we could wish, has at least the power of *asking* questions which increase the interest of the world, and show the strangeness and wonder lying just below the surface even in the commonest things of daily life.

*   *   *

CHAPTER 5: KNOWLEDGE BY ACQUAINTANCE AND KNOWLEDGE BY DESCRIPTION

In the preceding chapter [on "Idealism"] we saw that there are two sorts of knowledge: knowledge of things, and knowledge of truths. In this chapter we shall be concerned exclusively with knowledge of things, of which in turn we shall have to distinguish two kinds. Knowledge of things, when it is of the kind we call knowledge by *acquain-*

tance, is essentially simpler than any knowledge of truths, and logically independent of knowledge of truths, though it would be rash to assume that human beings ever, in fact, have acquaintance with things without at the same time knowing some truth about them. Knowledge of things by *description,* on the contrary, always involves, as we shall find in the course of the present chapter, some knowledge of truths as its source and ground. But first of all we must make clear what we mean by "acquaintance" and what we mean by "description."

We shall say that we have *acquaintance* with anything of which we are directly aware, without the intermediary of any process of inference or any knowledge of truths. Thus in the presence of my table I am acquainted with the sense-data that make up the appearance of my table—its colour, shape, hardness, smoothness, etc.; all these are things of which I am immediately conscious when I am seeing and touching my table. The particular shade of colour that I am seeing may have many things said about it—I may say that it is brown, that it is rather dark, and so on. But such statements, though they make me know truths *about* the colour, do not make me know the colour itself any better than I did before: so far as concerns knowledge of the colour itself, as opposed to knowledge of truths about it, I know the colour perfectly and completely when I see it, and no further knowledge of it itself is even theoretically possible. Thus the sense-data which make up the appearance of my table are things with which I have acquaintance, things immediately known to me just as they are.

My knowledge of the table as a physical object, on the contrary, is not direct knowledge. Such as it is, it is obtained through acquaintance with the sense-data that make up the appearance of the table. We have seen that it is possible, without absurdity, to doubt whether there is a table at all, whereas it is not possible to doubt the sense-data. My knowledge of the table is of the kind which we shall call "knowledge by description." The table is "the physical object which causes such-and-such sense-data." This *describes* the table by means of the sense-data. In order to know anything at all about the table, we must know truths connecting it with things with which we have acquaintance: we must know that "such-and-such sense-data are caused by a physical object." There is no state of mind in which we are directly aware of the table; all our knowledge of the table is really knowledge of *truths,* and the actual thing which is the table is not, strictly speaking, known to us at all. We know a description, and we know that there is just one object to which this description applies, though the object itself is not directly known to us. In such a case, we say that our knowledge of the object is knowledge by description.

All our knowledge, both knowledge of things and knowledge of truths, rests upon acquaintance as its foundation. It is therefore important to consider what kinds of things there are with which we have acquaintance.

Sense-data, as we have already seen, are among the things with which we are acquainted; in fact, they supply the most obvious and striking example of knowledge by acquaintance. But if they were the sole example, our knowledge would be very much more restricted than it is. We should only know what is now present to our senses: we could not know anything about the past—not even that there was a past—nor could we know any truths about our sense-data, for all knowledge of truths, as we shall show, demands acquaintance with things which are of an essentially different character from sense-data, the things which are sometimes called "abstract ideas," but which we shall call "universals." We have therefore to consider acquaintance with other things besides sense-data if we are to obtain any tolerably adequate analysis of our knowledge.

The first extension beyond sense-data to be considered is acquaintance by memory. It is obvious that we often remember what we have seen or heard or had otherwise present to our senses, and that in such cases we are still immediately aware of what we remember, in spite of the fact that it appears as past and not as present. This immediate knowledge by memory is the source of all our knowledge concerning the past: without it, there could be no knowledge of the past by inference, since we should never know that there was anything past to be inferred.

The next extension to be considered is acquaintance by *introspection*. We are not only aware of things, but we are often aware of being aware of them. When I see the sun, I am often aware of my seeing the sun; thus "my seeing the sun" is an object with which I have acquaintance. When I desire food, I may be aware of my desire for food; thus "my desiring food" is an object with which I am acquainted. Similarly we may be aware of our feeling pleasure or pain, and generally of the events which happen in our minds. This kind of acquaintance, which may be called self-consciousness, is the source of all our knowledge of mental things. It is obvious that it is only what goes on in our own minds that can be thus known immediately. What goes on in the minds of others is known to us through our perception of their bodies, that is, through the sense-data in us which are associated with their bodies. But for our acquaintance with the contents of our own minds, we should be unable to imagine the minds of others, and therefore we could never arrive at the knowledge that they have minds. It seems natural to suppose that self-consciousness is one of the things that distinguish men from animals: animals, we may suppose, though they have acquaintance with sense-data, never become aware of this acquaintance. I do not mean that they *doubt* whether they exist, but that they have never become conscious of the fact that they have sensations and feelings, nor therefore of the fact that they, the subjects of their sensations and feelings, exist.

We have spoken of acquaintance with the contents of our minds as *self-consciousness*, but it is not, of course, consciousness of our *self*: it is consciousness of particular thoughts and feelings. The question whether we are also acquainted with our bare selves, as opposed to particular thoughts and feelings, is a very difficult one, upon which it would be rash to speak positively. When we try to look into ourselves we always seem to come upon some particular thought or feeling, and not upon the "I" which has the thought or feeling. Nevertheless there are some reasons for thinking that we are acquainted with the "I," though the acquaintance is hard to disentangle from other things. To make clear what sort of reason there is, let us consider for a moment what our acquaintance with particular thoughts really involves.

When I am acquainted with "my seeing the sun," it seems plain that I am acquainted with two different things in relation to each other. On the one hand there is the sense-datum which represents the sun to me, on the other hand there is that which sees this sense-datum. All acquaintance, such as my acquaintance with the sense-datum which represents the sun, seems obviously a relation between the person acquainted and the object with which the person is acquainted. When a case of acquaintance is one with which I can be acquainted (as I am acquainted with my acquaintance with the sense-datum representing the sun), it is plain that the person acquainted is myself. Thus, when I am acquainted with my seeing the sun, the whole fact with which I am acquainted is "Self-acquainted-with-sense-datum."

Further, we know the truth "I am acquainted with this sense-datum." It is hard to see how we could know this truth, or even understand what is meant by it, unless we were acquainted with something which we call "I." It does not seem necessary to suppose that we are acquainted with a more or less permanent person, the same today as yesterday, but it does seem as though we must be acquainted with that thing, whatever its nature, which sees the sun and has acquaintance with sense-data. Thus, in some sense it would seem we must be acquainted with our Selves as opposed to our particular experiences. But the question is difficult, and complicated arguments can be adduced on either side. Hence, although acquaintance with ourselves seems *probably* to occur, it is not wise to assert that it undoubtedly does occur.

We may therefore sum up as follows what has been said concerning acquaintance with things that exist. We have acquaintance in sensation with the data of the outer senses, and in introspection with the data of what may be called the inner sense— thoughts, feelings, desires, etc.; we have acquaintance in memory with things which have been data either of the outer senses or of the inner sense. Further, it is probable, though not certain, that we have acquaintance with Self, as that which is aware of things or has desires towards things.

In addition to our acquaintance with particular existing things, we also have acquaintance with what we shall call universals, that is to say, general ideas, such as *whiteness, diversity, brotherhood,* and so on. Every complete sentence must contain at least one word which stands for a universal, since all verbs have a meaning which is universal. . . . It is only necessary [at this point] to guard against the supposition that whatever we can be acquainted with must be something particular and existent. Awareness of universals is called conceiving, and a universal of which we are aware is called a *concept.*

It will be seen that among the objects with which we are acquainted are not included physical objects (as opposed to sense-data), nor other people's minds. These things are known to us by what I call "knowledge by description," which we must now consider.

By a "description" I mean any phrase of the form "a so-and-so" or "the so-and-so." A phrase of the form "a so-and-so" I shall call an "ambiguous" description; a phrase of the form "the so-and-so" (in the singular) I shall call a "definite" description. Thus "a man" is an ambiguous description, and "the man with the iron mask" is a definite description. There are various problems connected with ambiguous descriptions, but I pass them by, since they do not directly concern the matter we are discussing, which is the nature of our knowledge concerning objects in cases where we know that there is an object answering to a definite description, though we are not *acquainted* with any such object. This is a matter which is concerned exclusively with *definite* descriptions. I shall therefore, in the sequel, speak simply of "descriptions" when I mean "definite descriptions." Thus a description will mean any phrase of the form "the so-and-so" in the singular.

We shall say that an object is "known by description" when we know that it is "the so-and-so," i.e. when we know that there is one object, and no more, having a certain property; and it will generally be implied that we do not have knowledge of the same object by acquaintance. We know that the man with the iron mask existed, and many propositions are known about him; but we do not know who he was. We know that the candidate who gets the most votes will be elected, and in this case we are very likely also acquainted (in the only sense in which one can be acquainted with some one else) with the man who is, in fact, the candidate who will get the most votes; but we do not know which of the candidates he is, i.e. we do not know any proposition of the form "A is the candidate who will get most votes" where A is one of the candidates by name. We shall say that we have "merely descriptive knowledge" of the so-and-so when, although we know that the so-and-so exists, and although we may possibly be acquainted with the object which is, in fact, the so-and-so, yet we do not know any proposition "*a* is the so-and-so," where *a* is something with which we are acquainted.

When we say "the so-and-so exists," we mean that there is just one object which is the so-and-so. The proposition "a is the so-and-so" means that *a* has the property so-and-so, and nothing else has. "Mr. A. is the Unionist candidate for this constituency" means "Mr. A. is a Unionist candidate for this constituency, and no one else is." "The Unionist candidate for this constituency exists" means "some one is a Unionist candidate for this constituency, and no one else is." Thus, when we are acquainted with an object which is the so-and-so, we know that the so-and-so exists; but we may know that the so-and-so exists when we are not acquainted with any object which we know to be the so-and-so, and even when we are not acquainted with any object which, in fact, is the so-and-so.

Common words, even proper names, are usually really descriptions. That is to say, the thought in the mind of a person using a proper name correctly can generally only be expressed explicitly if we replace the proper name by a description. Moreover, the description required to express the thought will vary for different people, or for the same person at different times. The only thing constant (so long as the name is rightly used) is the object to which the name applies. But so long as this remains constant, the particular description involved usually makes no difference to the truth or falsehood of the proposition in which the name appears.

Let us take some illustrations. Suppose some statement made about Bismarck. Assuming that there is such a thing as direct acquaintance with oneself, Bismarck himself might have used his name directly to designate the particular person with whom he was acquainted. In this case, if he made a judgement about himself, he himself might be a constituent of the judgement. Here the proper name has the direct use which it always wishes to have, as simply standing for a certain object, and not for a description of the object. But if a person who knew Bismarck made a judgement about him, the case is different. What this person was acquainted with were certain sense-data which he connected (rightly, we will suppose) with Bismarck's body. His body, as a physical object, and still more his mind, were only known as the body and the mind connected with these sense-data. That is, they were known by description. It is, of course, very much a matter of chance which characteristics of a man's appearance will come into a friend's mind when he thinks of him; thus the description actually in the friend's mind is accidental. The essential point is that he knows that the various descriptions all apply to the same entity, in spite of not being acquainted with the entity in question.

When we, who did not know Bismarck, make a judgement about him, the description in our minds will probably be some more or less vague mass of historical knowledge—far more, in most cases, than is required to identify him. But, for the sake of illustration, let us assume that we think of him as "the first Chancellor of the German Empire." Here all the words are abstract except "German." The word "German" will, again, have different meanings for different people. To some it will recall travels in Germany, to some the look of Germany on the map, and so on. But if we are to obtain a description which we know to be applicable, we shall be compelled, at some point, to bring in a reference to a particular with which we are acquainted. Such reference is involved in any mention of past, present, and future (as opposed to definite dates), or of here and there, or of what others have told us. Thus it would seem that, in some way or other, a description known to be applicable to a particular must involve some reference to a particular with which we are acquainted, if our knowledge about the thing described is not to be merely what follows *logically* from the description. For example, "the most long-lived of men" is a description involving only universals, which must apply to some man, but we can make no judgements concerning this man which involve knowledge about him beyond what the description gives. If, however, we say, "The first Chancellor of the German Empire was an astute diplomatist," we can only be assured of the truth of our judgement in virtue of something with which we are acquainted—usually a testimony heard or read. Apart from the information we convey to others, apart from the fact about the actual Bismarck, which gives importance to our judgement, the thought we really have contains the one or more particulars involved, and otherwise consists wholly of concepts.

All names of places—London, England, Europe, the Earth, the Solar System—similarly involve, when used, descriptions which start from some one or more particulars with which we are acquainted. I suspect that even the Universe, as considered by metaphysics, involves such a connexion with particulars. In logic, on the contrary, where we are concerned not merely with what does exist, but with whatever might or could exist or be, no reference to actual particulars is involved.

It would seem that, when we make a statement about something only known by description, we often *intend* to make our statement, not in the form involving the description, but about the actual thing described. That is to say, when we say anything about Bismarck, we should like, if we could, to make the judgement which Bismarck alone can make, namely, the judgement of which he himself is a constituent. In this we are necessarily defeated, since the actual Bismarck is unknown to us. But we know that there is an object B, called Bismarck, and that B was an astute diplomatist. We can thus *describe* the proposition we should like to affirm, namely, "B was an astute diplomatist," where B is the object which was Bismarck. If we are describing Bismarck as "the first Chancellor of the German Empire," the proposition we should like to affirm may be described as "the proposition asserting, concerning the actual object which was the first Chancellor of the German Empire, that this object was an astute diplomatist." What enables us to communicate in spite of the varying descriptions we employ is that we know there is a true proposition concerning the actual Bismarck, and that however we may vary the description (so long as the description is correct) the proposition described is still the same. This proposition, which is described and is known to be true, is what interests us; but we are not acquainted with the proposition itself, and do not know it, though we know it is true.

It will be seen that there are various stages in the removal from acquaintance with particulars: there is Bismarck to people who knew him; Bismarck to those who only know of him through history; the man with the iron mask; the longest-lived of men. These are progressively further removed from acquaintance with particulars; the first comes as near to acquaintance as is possible in regard to another person; in the second, we shall still be said to know "who Bismarck was"; in the third, we do not know who was the man with the iron mask, though we can know many propositions about him which are not logically deducible from the fact that he wore an iron mask; in the fourth, finally, we know nothing beyond what is logically deducible from the definition of the man. There is a similar hierarchy in the region of universals. Many universals, like many particulars, are only known to us by description. But here, as in the case of particulars, knowledge concerning what is known by description is ultimately reducible to knowledge concerning what is known by acquaintance.

The fundamental principle in the analysis of prepositions containing descriptions is this: *Every proposition which we can understand must be composed wholly of constituents with which we are acquainted.*

We shall not at this stage attempt to answer all the objections which may be urged against this fundamental principle. For the present, we shall merely point out that, in some way or other, it must be possible to meet these objections, for it is scarcely conceivable that we can make a judgement or entertain a supposition without knowing what it is that we are judging or supposing about. We must attach *some* meaning to the words we use, if we are to speak significantly and not utter mere noise; and the meaning we attach to our words must be something with which we are acquainted. Thus when, for example, we make a statement about Julius Caesar, it is plain that Julius Caesar himself is not before our minds, since we are not acquainted with him. We have in mind some *description* of Julius Caesar: "the man who was assassinated on the Ides of March," "the founder of the Roman Empire," or, perhaps, merely "the man whose name was *Julius Caesar*." (In this last description, *Julius Caesar* is a noise or shape with which we are acquainted.) Thus our statement does not mean quite what it seems to mean, but means something involving, instead of Julius Caesar, some description of him which is composed wholly of particulars and universals with which we are acquainted.

The chief importance of knowledge by description is that it enables us to pass beyond the limits of our private experience. In spite of the fact that we can only know truths which are wholly composed of terms which we have experienced in acquaintance, we can yet have knowledge by description of things which we have never experienced. In view of the very narrow range of our immediate experience, this result is vital, and until it is understood, much of our knowledge must remain mysterious and therefore doubtful.

* * *

CHAPTER 15: THE VALUE OF PHILOSOPHY

Having now come to the end of our brief and very incomplete review of the problems of philosophy, it will be well to consider, in conclusion, what is the value of philosophy and why it ought to be studied. It is the more necessary to consider this question, in view of the fact that many men, under the influence of science or of practical affairs, are inclined to doubt whether philosophy is anything better than innocent but useless trifling, hair-splitting distinctions, and controversies on matters concerning which knowledge is impossible.

This view of philosophy appears to result, partly from a wrong conception of the ends of life, partly from a wrong conception of the kind of goods which philosophy strives to achieve. Physical science, through the medium of inventions, is useful to innumerable people who are wholly ignorant of it, thus the study of physical science is to be recommended, not only, or primarily, because of the effect on the student, but rather because of the effect on mankind in general. Thus utility does not belong to philosophy. If the study of philosophy has any value at all for others than students of philosophy, it must be only indirectly, through its effects upon the lives of those who study it. It is in these effects, therefore, if anywhere, that the value of philosophy must be primarily sought.

But further, if we are not to fail in our endeavour to determine the value of philosophy, we must first free our minds from the prejudices of what are wrongly called "practical" men. The "practical" man, as this word is often used, is one who recognizes only material needs, who realizes that men must have food for the body, but is oblivious of the necessity of providing food for the mind. If all men were well off, if poverty and disease had been reduced to their lowest possible point, there would still remain much to be done to produce a valuable society; and even in the existing world the goods of the mind are at least as important as the goods of the body. It is exclusively among the goods of the mind that the value of philosophy is to be found; and only those who are not indifferent to these goods can be persuaded that the study of philosophy is not a waste of time.

Philosophy, like all other studies, aims primarily at knowledge. The knowledge it aims at is the kind of knowledge which gives unity and system to the body of sciences, and the kind which results from a critical examination of the grounds of our convictions, prejudices, and beliefs. But it cannot be maintained that philosophy has had any very great measure of success in its attempts to provide definite answers to its questions. If you ask a mathematician, a mineralogist, a historian, or any other man of learning, what definite body of truths has been ascertained by his science, his answer will last as long as you are willing to listen. But if you put the same question to a philosopher, he will, if he is candid, have to confess that his study has not achieved positive results such as have been achieved by other sciences. It is true that this is partly accounted for by the fact that, as soon as definite knowledge concerning any subject becomes possible, this subject ceases to be called philosophy, and now becomes a separate science. The whole study of the heavens, which now belongs to astronomy, was once included in philosophy; Newton's great work was called "the mathematical principles of natural philosophy." Similarly, the study of the human mind, which was a part of philosophy, has now been separated from philosophy and has become the science of psychology. Thus, to a great extent, the uncertainty of philosophy is more apparent than real: those questions which are already capable of definite answers are placed in the sciences, while those only to which, at present, no definite answer can be given, remain to form the residue which is called philosophy.

This is, however, only a part of the truth concerning the uncertainty of philosophy. There are many questions—and among them those that are of the profoundest interest to our spiritual life—which, so far as we can see, must remain insoluble to the human intellect unless its powers become of quite a different order from what they are now. Has the universe any unity of plan or purpose, or is it a fortuitous concourse of atoms? Is consciousness a permanent part of the universe, giving hope of indefinite growth in wisdom, or is it a transitory accident on a small planet on which life must ultimately become impossible? Are good and evil of importance to the universe or only to man? Such questions are asked by philosophy, and variously answered by various philosophers. But it would seem that, whether answers be otherwise discoverable or not, the answers suggested by philosophy are none of them demonstrably true. Yet, however slight may be the hope of discovering an answer, it is part of the business of philosophy to continue the consideration of such questions, to make us aware of their importance, to examine all the approaches to them, and to keep alive that speculative interest in the universe which is apt to be killed by confining ourselves to definitely ascertainable knowledge.

Many philosophers, it is true, have held that philosophy could establish the truth of certain answers to such fundamental questions. They have supposed that what is of most importance in religious beliefs could be proved by strict demonstration to be true. In order to judge of such attempts, it is necessary to take a survey of human knowledge, and to form an opinion as to its methods and its limitations. On such a subject it would be unwise to pronounce dogmatically; but if the investigations of our previous chapters have not led us astray, we shall be compelled to renounce the hope of finding philosophical proofs of religious beliefs. We cannot, therefore, include as part of the value of philosophy any definite set of answers to such questions. Hence, once more, the value of philosophy must not depend upon any supposed body of definitely ascertainable knowledge to be acquired by those who study it.

The value of philosophy is, in fact, to be sought largely in its very uncertainty. The man who has not tincture of philosophy goes through life imprisoned in the prejudices derived from common sense, from the habitual beliefs of his age or his nation, and from convictions which have grown up in his mind without the co-operation or consent of his deliberate reason. To such a man the world tends to become definite, finite, obvious; common objects rouse no questions, and unfamiliar possibilities are contemptuously rejected. As soon as we begin to philosophize, on the contrary, we find, as we saw in our opening chapters, that even the most everyday things lead to problems to which only very incomplete answers can be given. Philosophy, though unable to tell us with certainty what is the true answer to the doubts which it raises, is able to suggest many possibilities which enlarge our thoughts and free them from the tyranny of custom. Thus, while diminishing our feeling of certainty as to what things are, it greatly increases our knowledge as to what they may be; it removes the somewhat arrogant dogmatism of those who have never travelled into the region of liberating doubt, and it keeps alive our sense of wonder by showing familiar things in an unfamiliar aspect.

Apart from its utility in showing unsuspected possibilities, philosophy has a value—perhaps its chief value—through the greatness of the objects which it contemplates, and the freedom from narrow and personal aims resulting from this contemplation. The life of the instinctive man is shut up within the circle of his private interests: family and friends may be included, but the outer world is not regarded except as it may help or hinder what comes within the circle of instinctive wishes. In such a life there is something feverish and confined, in comparison with which the philosophic life is calm and free. The private world of instinctive interests is a small one, set in the midst of a great and powerful world which must, sooner or later, lay our private world in ruins. Unless we can so enlarge our interests as to include the whole outer world, we remain like a garrison in a beleaguered fortress, knowing that the enemy prevents escape and that ultimate surrender is inevitable. In such a life there is no peace, but a constant strife between the insistence of desire and the powerlessness of will. In one way or another, if our life is to be great and free, we must escape this prison and this strife.

One way of escape is by philosophic contemplation. Philosophic contemplation does not, in its widest survey, divide the universe into two hostile camps—friends and foes, helpful and hostile, good and bad—it views the whole impartially. Philosophic contemplation, when it is unalloyed, does not aim at proving that the rest of the universe is akin to man. All acquisition of knowledge is an enlargement of the Self, but this enlargement is best attained when it is not directly sought. It is obtained when the desire for knowledge is alone operative, by a study which does not wish in advance that its objects should have this or that character, but adapts the Self to the characters which it finds in its objects. This enlargement of Self is not obtained when, taking the Self as it is, we try to show that the world is so similar to this Self that knowledge of it is possible without any admission of what seems alien. The desire to prove this is a form of self-assertion and, like all self-assertion, it is an obstacle to the growth of Self which it desires, and of which the Self knows that it is capable. Self-assertion, in philosophic speculation as elsewhere, views the world as a means to its own ends; thus it makes the world of less account than Self, and the Self sets bounds to the greatness of its goods. In contemplation, on the contrary, we start from the not-Self, and through its greatness the boundaries of Self are enlarged; through the infinity of the universe the mind which contemplates it achieves some share in infinity.

For this reason greatness of soul is not fostered by those philosophies which assimilate the universe to Man. Knowledge is a form of union of Self and not-Self; like all union, it is impaired by dominion, and therefore by any attempt to force the universe into conformity with what we find in ourselves. There is a widespread philosophical tendency towards the view which tells us that Man is the measure of all things, that truth is man-made, that space and time and the world of universals are properties of the mind, and that, if there be anything not created by the mind, it is unknowable and of no account for us. This view, if our previous discussions were correct, is untrue; but in addition to being untrue, it has the effect of robbing philosophic contemplation of all that gives it value, since it fetters contemplation to Self. What it calls knowledge is not a union with the not-Self, but a set of prejudices, habits, and desires, making an impenetrable veil between us and the world beyond. The man who finds pleasure in such a theory of knowledge is like the man who never leaves the domestic circle for fear his word might not be law.

The true philosophic contemplation, on the contrary, finds its satisfaction in every enlargement of the not-Self, in everything that magnifies the objects contemplated, and thereby the subject contemplating. Everything, in contemplation, that is personal or private, everything that depends upon habit, self-interest, or desire, distorts the object, and hence impairs the union which the intellect seeks. By thus making a barrier between subject and object, such personal and private things become a prison to the intellect. The free intellect will see as God might see, without a *here* and *now*, without hopes and fears, without the trammels of customary beliefs and traditional prejudices, calmly, dispassionately, in the sole and exclusive desire of knowledge—knowledge as impersonal, as purely contemplative, as it is possible for man to attain. Hence also the free intellect will value more the abstract and universal knowledge into which the accidents of private history do not enter, than the knowledge brought by the senses, and dependent, as such knowledge must be, upon an exclusive and personal point of view and a body whose sense-organs distort as much as they reveal.

The mind which has become accustomed to the freedom and impartiality of philosophic contemplation will preserve something of the same freedom and impartiality in the world of action and emotion. It will view its purposes and desires as parts of the whole, with the absence of insistence that results from seeing them as infinitesimal fragments in a world of which all the rest is unaffected by any one man's deeds. The impartiality which, in contemplation, is the unalloyed desire for truth, is the very same quality of mind which, in action, is justice, and in emotion is that universal love which can be given to all, and not only to those who are judged useful or admirable. Thus contemplation enlarges not only the objects of our thoughts, but also the objects of our actions and our affections: it makes us citizens of the universe, not only of one walled city at war with all the rest. In this citizenship of the universe consists man's true freedom, and his liberation from the thraldom of narrow hopes and fears.

Thus, to sum up our discussion of the value of philosophy; philosophy is to be studied, not for the sake of any definite answers to its questions, since no definite answers can, as a rule, be known to be true, but rather for the sake of the questions themselves; because these questions enlarge our conception of what is possible, enrich our intellectual imagination and diminish the dogmatic assurance which closes the mind against speculation; but above all because, through the greatness of the universe which philosophy contemplates, the mind also is rendered great, and becomes capable of that union with the universe which constitutes its highest good.

MYSTICISM AND LOGIC

Metaphysics, or the attempt to conceive the world as a whole by means of thought, has been developed, from the first, by the union and conflict of two very different human impulses, the one urging men towards mysticism, the other urging them towards science. Some men have achieved greatness through one of these impulses alone, others through the other alone: in Hume, for example, the scientific impulse reigns quite unchecked, while in Blake a strong hostility to science co-exists with profound mystic insight. But the greatest men who have been philosophers have felt the need both of science and of mysticism: the attempt to harmonise the two was what made their life, and what always must, for all its arduous uncertainty, make philosophy, to some minds, a greater thing than either science or religion.

Before attempting an explicit characterisation of the scientific and the mystical impulses, I will illustrate them by examples from two philosophers whose greatness lies in the very intimate blending which they achieved. The two philosophers I mean are Heraclitus and Plato.

Heraclitus, as every one knows, was a believer in universal flux: time builds and destroys all things. From the few fragments that remain, it is not easy to discover how he arrived at his opinions, but there are some sayings that strongly suggest scientific observation as the source.

"The things that can be seen, heard, and learned," he says, "are what I prize the most." This is the language of the empiricist, to whom observation is the sole guarantee of truth. "The sun is new every day," is another fragment; and this opinion, in spite of its paradoxical character, is obviously inspired by scientific reflection, and no doubt seemed to him to obviate the difficulty of understanding how the sun can work its way underground from west to east during the night. Actual observation must also have suggested to him his central doctrine, that Fire is the one permanent substance, of which all visible things are passing phases. In combustion we see things change utterly, while their flame and heat rise up into the air and vanish.

"This world, which is the same for all," he says, "no one of gods or men has made; but it was ever, is now, and ever shall be, an ever-living Fire, with measures kindling, and measures going out."

"The transformations of Fire are, first of all, sea; and half of the sea is earth, half whirlwind."

This theory, though no longer one which science can accept, is nevertheless scientific in spirit. Science, too, might have inspired the famous saying to which Plato alludes: "You cannot step twice into the same rivers; for fresh waters are ever flowing in upon you." But we find also another statement among the extant fragments: "We step and do not step into the same rivers; we are and are not."

The comparison of this statement, which is mystical, with the one quoted by Plato, which is scientific, shows how intimately the two tendencies are blended in the system of Heraclitus. Mysticism is, in essence, little more than a certain intensity and depth of feeling in regard to what is believed about the universe; and this kind of feeling leads Heraclitus, on the basis of his science, to strangely poignant sayings concerning life and the world, such as:

"Time is a child playing draughts, the kingly power is a child's."

It is poetic imagination, not science, which presents Time as despotic lord of the world, with all the irresponsible frivolity of a child. It is mysticism, too, which leads Heraclitus to assert the identity of opposites: "Good and ill are one," he says; and again: "To God all things are fair and good and right, but men hold some things wrong and some right."

Much of mysticism underlies the ethics of Heraclitus. It is true that a scientific determinism alone might have inspired the statement: "Man's character is his fate"; but only a mystic would have said:

"Every beast is driven to the pasture with blows"; and again:

"It is hard to fight with one's heart's desire. Whatever it wishes to get, it purchases at the cost of soul"; and again:

"Wisdom is one thing. It is to know the thought by which all things are steered through all things."

Examples might be multiplied, but those that have been given are enough to show the character of the man: the facts of science, as they appeared to him, fed the flame in his soul, and in its light he saw into the depths of the world by the reflection of his own dancing swiftly penetrating fire. In such a nature we see the true union of the mystic and the man of science—the highest eminence, as I think, that it is possible to achieve in the world of thought.

In Plato, the same twofold impulse exists, though the mystic impulse is distinctly the stronger of the two, and secures ultimate victory whenever the conflict is sharp. His description of the cave is the classical statement of belief in a knowledge and reality truer and more real than that of the senses:

> Imagine a number of men living in an underground cavernous chamber, with an entrance open to the light, extending along the entire length of the cavern, in which they have been confined, from their childhood, with their legs and necks so shackled that they are obliged to sit still and look straight forwards, because their chains render it impossible for them to turn their heads round: and imagine a bright fire burning some way off, above and behind them, and an elevated roadway passing between the fire and the prisoners, with a low wall built along it, like the screens which conjurors put up in front of their audience, and above which they exhibit their wonders.
>
> I have it, he replied.
>
> Also figure to yourself a number of persons walking behind this wall, and carrying with them statues of men, and images of other animals, wrought in wood and stone and all kinds of materials, together with various other articles, which overtop the wall; and, as you might expect, let some of the passers-by be talking, and others silent.
>
> You are describing a strange scene, and strange prisoners.
>
> They resemble us, I replied.
>
> Now consider what would happen if the course of nature brought them a release from their fetters, and a remedy for their foolishness, in the following manner. Let us suppose that one of them has been released, and compelled suddenly to stand up, and turn his neck round and walk with open eyes towards the light; and let us suppose that he goes through all these actions with pain, and that the dazzling splendour renders him incapable of discerning those objects of which he used formerly to see the shadows. What answer should you expect him to make, if some one were to tell him that in those days he was watching foolish phantoms, but that now he is somewhat nearer to reality, and is turned towards things more real, and sees more correctly; above all, if he were to point out to him the several objects that are passing by, and question him, and compel him to answer what they are? Should you not expect him to be puzzled, and to regard his old visions as truer than the objects now forced upon his notice?

Yes, much truer. . . .

Hence, I suppose, habit will be necessary to enable him to perceive objects in that upper world. At first he will be most successful in distinguishing shadows; then he will discern the reflections of men and other things in water, and afterwards the realities; and after this he will raise his eyes to encounter the light of the moon and stars, finding it less difficult to study the heavenly bodies and the heaven itself by night, than the sun and the sun's light by day.

Doubtless.

Last of all, I imagine, he will be able to observe and contemplate the nature of the sun, not as it *appears* in water or on alien ground, but as it is in itself in its own territory.

Of course.

His next step will be to draw the conclusion, that the sun is the author of the seasons and the years, and the guardian of all things in the visible world, and in a manner the cause of all those things which he and his companions used to see.

Obviously, this will be his next step. . . .

Now this imaginary case, my dear Glaucon, you must apply in all its parts to our former statements, by comparing the region which the eye reveals, to the prison house, and the light of the fire therein to the power of the sun: and if, by the upward ascent and the contemplation of the upper world, you understand the mounting of the soul into the intellectual region, you will hit the tendency of my own surmises, since you desire to be told what they are; though, indeed, God only knows whether they are correct. But, be that as it may, the view which I take of the subject is to the following effect. In the world of knowledge, the essential Form of Good is the limit of our enquiries, and can barely be perceived; but, when perceived, we cannot help concluding that it is in every case the source of all that is bright and beautiful,—in the visible world giving birth to light and its master, and in the intellectual world dispensing, immediately and with full authority, truth and reason;—and that whosoever would act wisely, either in private or in public, must set this Form of Good before his eyes. [*Republic,* 514 ff., translated by Davies and Vaughan]

But in this passage, as throughout most of Plato's teaching, there is an identification of the good with the truly real, which became embodied in the philosophical tradition, and is still largely operative in our own day. In thus allowing a legislative function to the good, Plato produced a divorce between philosophy and science, from which, in my opinion, both have suffered ever since and are still suffering. The man of science, whatever his hopes may be, must lay them aside while he studies nature; and the philosopher, if he is to achieve truth must do the same. Ethical considerations can only legitimately appear when the truth has been ascertained: they can and should appear as determining our feeling towards the truth, and our manner of ordering our lives in view of the truth, but not as themselves dictating what the truth is to be.

There are passages in Plato—among those which illustrate the scientific side of his mind—where he seems clearly aware of this. The most noteworthy is the one in which Socrates, as a young man, is explaining the theory of ideas to Parmenides.

After Socrates has explained that there is an idea of the good, but not of such things as hair and mud and dirt, Parmenides advises him "not to despise even the meanest things," and this advice shows the genuine scientific temper. It is with this impartial temper that the mystic's apparent insight into a higher reality and a hidden good has to be combined if philosophy is to realise its greatest possibilities. And it is failure in this respect that has made so much of idealistic philosophy thin, lifeless, and insubstantial. It is only in marriage with the world that our ideals can bear fruit: divorced from it, they remain barren. But marriage with the world is not to be achieved by an ideal which shrinks from fact, or demands in advance that the world shall conform to its desires.

Parmenides himself is the source of a peculiarly interesting strain of mysticism which pervades Plato's thought—the mysticism which may be called "logical" because it is embodied in theories on logic. This form of mysticism, which appears, so far as the West is concerned, to have originated with Parmenides, dominates the reasonings of all the great mystical metaphysicians from his day to that of Hegel and his modern disciples. Reality, he says, is uncreated, indestructible, unchanging, indivisible; it is "immovable in the bonds of mighty chains, without beginning and without end; since coming into being and passing away have been driven afar, and true belief has cast them away." The fundamental principle of his inquiry is stated in a sentence which would not be out of place in Hegel: "Thou canst not know what is not—that is impossible—nor utter it; for it is the same thing that can be thought and that can be." And again: "It needs must be that what can be thought and spoken of is; for it is possible for it to be, and it is not possible for what is nothing to be." The impossibility of change follows from this principle; for what is past can be spoken of, and therefore, by the principle, still is.

Mystical philosophy, in all ages and in all parts of the world, is characterised by certain beliefs which are illustrated by the doctrines we have been considering.

There is, first, the belief in insight as against discursive analytic knowledge: the belief in a way of wisdom, sudden, penetrating, coercive, which is contrasted with the slow and fallible study of outward appearance by a science relying wholly upon the senses. All who are capable of absorption in an inward passion must have experienced at times the strange feeling of unreality in common objects, the loss of contact with daily things, in which the solidity of the outer world is lost, and the soul seems, in utter loneliness, to bring forth, out of its own depths, the mad dance of fantastic phantoms which have hitherto appeared as independently real and living. This is the negative side of the mystic's initiation: the doubt concerning common knowledge, preparing the way for the reception of what seems a higher wisdom. Many men to whom this negative experience is familiar do not pass beyond it, but for the mystic it is merely the gateway to an ampler world.

The mystic insight begins with the sense of a mystery unveiled, of a hidden wisdom now suddenly become certain beyond the possibility of a doubt. The sense of certainty and revelation comes earlier than any definite belief. The definite beliefs at which mystics arrive are the result of reflection upon the inarticulate experience gained in the moment of insight. Often, beliefs which have no real connection with this moment become subsequently attracted into the central nucleus; thus in addition to the convictions which all mystics share, we find, in many of them, other convictions of a more local and temporary character, which no doubt become amalgamated with what was essentially mystical in virtue of their subjective certainty. We may ignore such inessential accretions, and confine ourselves to the beliefs which all mystics share.

The first and most direct outcome of the moment of illumination is belief in the possibility of a way of knowledge which may be called revelation or insight or intuition, as contrasted with sense, reason, and analysis, which are regarded as blind guides leading to the morass of illusion. Closely connected with this belief is the conception of a Reality behind the world of appearance and utterly different from it. This Reality is regarded with an admiration often amounting to worship; it is felt to be always and everywhere close at hand, thinly veiled by the shows of sense, ready, for the receptive mind, to shine in its glory even through the apparent folly and wickedness of Man. The poet, the artist, and the lover are seekers after that glory: the haunting beauty that they pursue is the faint reflection of its sun. But the mystic lives in the full light of the vision: what others dimly seek he knows, with a knowledge beside which all other knowledge is ignorance.

The second characteristic of mysticism is its belief in unity, and its refusal to admit opposition or division anywhere. We found Heraclitus saying "good and ill are one"; and again he says, "the way up and the way down is one and the same." The same attitude appears in the simultaneous assertion of contradictory propositions, such as: "We step and do not step into the same rivers; we are and are not." The assertion of Parmenides, that reality is one and indivisible, comes from the same impulse towards unity. In Plato, this impulse is less prominent, being held in check by his theory of ideas; but it reappears, so far as his logic permits, in the doctrine of the primacy of the Good.

A third mark of almost all mystical metaphysics is the denial of the reality of Time. This is an outcome of the denial of division; if all is one, the distinction of past and future must be illusory. We have seen this doctrine prominent in Parmenides; and among moderns it is fundamental in the systems of Spinoza and Hegel.

The last of the doctrines of mysticism which we have to consider is its belief that all evil is mere appearance, an illusion produced by the divisions and oppositions of the analytic intellect. Mysticism does not maintain that such things as cruelty, for example, are good, but it denies that they are real: they belong to that lower world of phantoms from which we are to be liberated by the insight of the vision. Sometimes— for example in Hegel, and at least verbally in Spinoza—not only evil, but good also, is regarded as illusory, though nevertheless the emotional attitude towards what is held to be Reality is such as would naturally be associated with the belief that Reality is good. What is, in all cases, ethically characteristic of mysticism is absence of indignation or protest, acceptance with joy, disbelief in the ultimate truth of the division into two hostile camps, the good and the bad. This attitude is a direct outcome of the nature of the mystical experience: with its sense of unity is associated a feeling of infinite peace. Indeed it may be suspected that the feeling of peace produces, as feelings do in dreams, the whole system of associated beliefs which make up the body of mystic doctrine. But this is a difficult question, and one on which it cannot be hoped that mankind will reach agreement.

Four questions thus arise in considering the truth or falsehood of mysticism, namely:

    I. Are there two ways of knowing, which may be called respectively reason and intuition? And if so, is either to be preferred to the other?
    II. Is all plurality and division illusory?
    III. Is time unreal?
    IV. What kind of reality belongs to good and evil?

On all four of these questions, while fully developed mysticism seems to me mistaken, I yet believe that, by sufficient restraint, there is an element of wisdom to be learned from the mystical way of feeling, which does not seem to be attainable in any other manner. If this is the truth, mysticism is to be commended as an attitude towards life, not as a creed about the world. The metaphysical creed, I shall maintain, is a mistaken outcome of the emotion, although this emotion, as colouring and informing all other thoughts and feelings, is the inspirer of whatever is best in Man. Even the cautious and patient investigation of truth by science, which seems the very antithesis of the mystic's swift certainty, may be fostered and nourished by that very spirit of reverence in which mysticism lives and moves.

I. REASON AND INTUITION*

Of the reality or unreality of the mystic's world I know nothing. I have no wish to deny it, nor even to declare that the insight which reveals it is not a genuine insight.

What I do wish to maintain—and it is here that the scientific attitude becomes imperative—is that insight, untested and unsupported, is an insufficient guarantee of truth, in spite of the fact that much of the most important truth is first suggested by its means. It is common to speak of an opposition between instinct and reason; in the eighteenth century, the opposition was drawn in favour of reason, but under the influence of Rousseau and the romantic movement instinct was given the preference, first by those who rebelled against artificial forms of government and thought, and then, as the purely rationalistic defence of traditional theology became increasingly difficult, by all who felt in science a menace to creeds which they associated with a spiritual outlook on life and the world. Bergson, under the name of "intuition," has raised instinct to the position of sole arbiter of metaphysical truth. But in fact the opposition of instinct and reason is mainly illusory. Instinct, intuition, or insight is what first leads to the beliefs which subsequent reason confirms or confutes; but the confirmation, where it is possible, consists, in the last analysis, of agreement with other beliefs no less instinctive. Reason is a harmonising, controlling force rather than a creative one. Even in the most purely logical realm, it is insight that first arrives at what is new.

Where instinct and reason do sometimes conflict is in regard to single beliefs, held instinctively, and held with such determination that no degree of inconsistency with other beliefs leads to their abandonment. Instinct, like all human faculties, is liable to error. Those in whom reason is weak are often unwilling to admit this as regards themselves, though all admit it in regard to others. Where instinct is least liable to error is in practical matters as to which right judgment is a help to survival: friendship and hostility in others, for instance, are often felt with extraordinary discrimination through very careful disguises. But even in such matters a wrong impression may be given by reserve or flattery; and in matters less directly practical, such as philosophy deals with, very strong instinctive beliefs are sometimes wholly mistaken, as we may come to know through their perceived inconsistency with other equally strong beliefs. It is such considerations that necessitate the harmonising mediation of reason, which tests our beliefs by their mutual compatibility, and examines, in doubtful cases, the possible sources of error on the one side and on the other. In this there is no opposition to instinct as a whole, but only to blind reliance upon some one interesting aspect of instinct to the exclusion of other more commonplace but not less trustworthy aspects. It is such one-sidedness, not instinct itself, that reason aims at correcting.

These more or less trite maxims may be illustrated by application to Bergson's advocacy of "intuition" as against "intellect." There are, he says, "two profoundly different ways of knowing a thing. The first implies that we move round the object: the second that we enter into it. The first depends on the point of view at which we are placed and on the symbols by which we express ourselves. The second neither depends on a point of view nor relies on any symbol. The first kind of knowledge may be said

---

*This section, and also one or two pages in later sections, have been printed in a course of Lowell lectures *On Our Knowledge of the External World,* published by the Open Court Publishing Company. But I have left them here, as this is the context for which they were originally written. [Russell's note.]

to stop at the *relative;* the second, in those cases where it is possible, to attain the *absolute.*" The second of these, which is intuition, is, he says, "the kind of *intellectual sympathy* by which one places oneself within an object in order to coincide with what is unique in it and therefore inexpressible." In illustration, he mentions self-knowledge: "there is one reality, at least, which we all seize from within, by intuition and not by simple analysis. It is our own personality in its flowing through time—our self which endures." The rest of Bergson's philosophy consists in reporting, through the imperfect medium of words, the knowledge gained by intuition, and the consequent complete condemnation of all the pretended knowledge derived from science and common sense.

This procedure, since it takes sides in a conflict of instinctive beliefs, stands in need of justification by proving the greater trustworthiness of the beliefs on one side than of those on the other. Bergson attempts this justification in two ways, first by explaining that intellect is a purely practical faculty to secure biological success, secondly by mentioning remarkable feats of instinct in animals and by pointing out characteristics of the world which, though intuition can apprehend them, are baffling to intellect as he interprets it.

Of Bergson's theory that intellect is a purely practical faculty, developed in the struggle for survival, and not a source of true beliefs, we may say, first, that it is only through intellect that we know of the struggle for survival and of the biological ancestry of man: if the intellect is misleading, the whole of this merely inferred history is presumably untrue. If, on the other hand, we agree with him in thinking that evolution took place as Darwin believed, then it is not only intellect, but all our faculties, that have been developed under the stress of practical utility. Intuition is seen at its best where it is directly useful, for example in regard to other people's characters and dispositions. Bergson apparently holds that capacity, for this kind of knowledge is less explicable by the struggle for existence than, for example, capacity for pure mathematics. Yet the savage deceived by false friendship is likely to pay for his mistake with his life; whereas even in the most civilised societies men are not put to death for mathematical incompetence. All the most striking of his instances of intuition in animals have a very direct survival value. The fact is, of course, that both intuition and intellect have been developed because they are useful, and that, speaking broadly, they are useful when they give truth and become harmful when they give falsehood. Intellect, in civilised man, like artistic capacity, has occasionally been developed beyond the point where it is useful to the individual; intuition, on the other hand, seems on the whole to diminish as civilisation increases. It is greater, as a rule, in children than in adults, in the uneducated than in the educated. Probably in dogs it exceeds anything to be found in human beings. But those who see in these facts a recommendation of intuition ought to return to running wild in the woods, dyeing themselves with woad and living on hips and haws.*

Let us next examine whether intuition possesses any such infallibility as Bergson claims for it. The best instance of it, according to him, is our acquaintance with ourselves; yet self-knowledge is proverbially rare and difficult. Most men, for example, have in their nature meannesses, vanities, and envies of which they are quite unconscious, though even their best friends can perceive them without any difficulty. It is true that intuition has a convincingness which is lacking to intellect: while it is present, it is almost impossible to doubt its truth. But if it should appear, on examination, to be

*[A "woad" is an herbal dye; "hips" are the fruits of a rose bush; and "haws" are hawthorn berries.]

at least as fallible as intellect, its greater subjective certainty becomes a demerit, making it only the more irresistibly deceptive. Apart from self-knowledge, one of the most notable examples of intuition is the knowledge people believe themselves to possess of those with whom they are in love: the wall between different personalities seems to become transparent, and people think they see into another soul as into their own. Yet deception in such cases is constantly practised with success; and even where there is no intentional deception, experience gradually proves, as a rule, that the supposed insight was illusory, and that the slower more groping methods of the intellect are in the long run more reliable.

Bergson maintains that intellect can only deal with things in so far as they resemble what has been experienced in the past, while intuition has the power of apprehending the uniqueness and novelty that always belong to each fresh moment. That there is something unique and new at every moment, is certainly true; it is also true that this cannot be fully expressed by means of intellectual concepts. Only direct acquaintance can give knowledge of what is unique and new. But direct acquaintance of this kind is given fully in sensation, and does not require, so far as I can see, any special faculty of intuition for its apprehension. It is neither intellect nor intuition, but sensation, that supplies new data; but when the data are new in any remarkable manner, intellect is much more capable of dealing with them than intuition would be. The hen with a brood of ducklings no doubt has intuition which seems to place her inside them, and not merely to know them analytically; but when the ducklings take to the water, the whole apparent intuition is seen to be illusory, and the hen is left helpless on the shore. Intuition, in fact, is an aspect and development of instinct, and, like all instinct, is admirable in those customary surroundings which have moulded the habits of the animal in question, but totally incompetent as soon as the surroundings are changed in a way which demands some non-habitual mode of action.

The theoretical understanding of the world, which is the aim of philosophy, is not a matter of great practical importance to animals, or to savages, or even to most civilised men. It is hardly to be supposed, therefore, that the rapid, rough and ready methods of instinct or intuition will find in this field a favourable ground for their application. It is the older kinds of activity, which bring out our kinship with remote generations of animal and semi-human ancestors, that show intuition at its best. In such matters as self-preservation and love, intuition will act sometimes (though not always) with a swiftness and precision which are astonishing to the critical intellect. But philosophy is not one of the pursuits which illustrate our affinity with the past: it is a highly refined, highly civilised pursuit, demanding, for its success, a certain liberation from the life of instinct, and even, at times, a certain aloofness from all mundane hopes and fears. It is not in philosophy, therefore, that we can hope to see intuition at its best. On the contrary, since the true objects of philosophy, and the habit of thought demanded for their apprehension, are strange, unusual, and remote, it is here, more almost than anywhere else, that intellect proves superior to intuition, and that quick unanalysed convictions are least deserving of uncritical acceptance.

In advocating the scientific restraint and balance, as against the self-assertion of a confident reliance upon intuition, we are only urging, in the sphere of knowledge, that largeness of contemplation, that impersonal disinterestedness, and that freedom from practical preoccupations which have been inculcated by all the great religions of the world. Thus our conclusion, however it may conflict with the explicit beliefs of many mystics, is, in essence, not contrary to the spirit which inspires those beliefs, but rather the outcome of this very spirit as applied in the realm of thought.

II. UNITY AND PLURALITY

One of the most convincing aspects of the mystic illumination is the apparent revelation of the oneness of all things, giving rise to pantheism in religion and to monism in philosophy. An elaborate logic, beginning with Parmenides, and culminating in Hegel and his followers, has been gradually developed, to prove that the universe is one indivisible Whole, and that what seem to be its parts, if considered as substantial and self existing, are mere illusion. The conception of a Reality quite other than the world of appearance, a reality one, indivisible, and unchanging, was introduced into Western philosophy by Parmenides, not, nominally at least, for mystical or religious reasons, but on the basis of a logical argument as to the impossibility of not-being, and most subsequent metaphysical systems are the outcome of this fundamental idea.

The logic used in defence of mysticism seems to be faulty as logic, and open to technical criticisms, which I have explained elsewhere. I shall not here repeat these criticisms, since they are lengthy and difficult, but shall instead attempt an analysis of the state of mind from which mystical logic has arisen.

Belief in a reality quite different from what appears to the senses arises with irresistible force in certain moods, which are the source of most mysticism, and of most metaphysics. While such a mood is dominant, the need of logic is not felt, and accordingly the more thoroughgoing mystics do not employ logic, but appeal directly to the immediate deliverance of their insight. But such fully developed mysticism is rare in the West. When the intensity of emotional conviction subsides, a man who is in the habit of reasoning will search for logical grounds in favour of the belief which he finds in himself. But since the belief already exists, he will be very hospitable to any ground that suggests itself. The paradoxes apparently proved by his logic are really the paradoxes of mysticism, and are the goal which he feels his logic must reach if it is to be in accordance with insight. The resulting logic has rendered most philosophers incapable of giving any account of the world of science and daily life. If they had been anxious to give such an account, they would probably have discovered the errors of their logic; but most of them were less anxious to understand the world of science and daily life than to convict it of unreality in the interests of a super-sensible "real" world.

It is in this way that logic has been pursued by those of the great philosophers who were mystics. But since they usually took for granted the supposed insight of the mystic emotion, their logical doctrines were presented with a certain dryness, and were believed by their disciples to be quite independent of the sudden illumination from which they sprang. Nevertheless their origin clung to them, and they remained—to borrow a useful word from Mr. Santayana—"malicious" in regard to the world of science and common sense. It is only so that we can account for the complacency with which philosophers have accepted the inconsistency of their doctrines with all the common and scientific facts which seem best established and most worthy of belief.

The logic of mysticism shows, as is natural, the defects which are inherent in anything malicious. The impulse to logic, not felt while the mystic mood is dominant, reasserts itself as the mood fades, but with a desire to retain the vanishing insight, or at least to prove that it was insight, and that what seems to contradict it is illusion. The logic which thus arises is not quite disinterested or candid, and is inspired by a certain hatred of the daily world to which it is to be applied. Such an attitude naturally does not tend to the best results. Everyone knows that to read an author simply in order to refute him is not the way to understand him; and to read the book of Nature with a conviction that it is all illusion is just as unlikely to lead to understanding. If our logic is to find the common world intelligible, it must not be hostile, but must be inspired by a genuine acceptance such as is not usually to be found among metaphysicians.

III. TIME

The unreality of time is a cardinal doctrine of many metaphysical systems, often nominally based, as already by Parmenides, upon logical arguments, but originally derived, at any rate in the founders of new systems, from the certainty which is born in the moment of mystic insight. As a Persian Sufi poet says:

> Past and future are what veil God from our sight.
> Burn up both of them with fire! How long
> Wilt thou be partitioned by these segments as a reed?

The belief that what is ultimately real must be immutable is a very common one: it gave rise to the metaphysical notion of substance, and finds, even now, a wholly illegitimate satisfaction in such scientific doctrines as the conservation of energy and mass.

It is difficult to disentangle the truth and the error in this view. The arguments for the contention that time is unreal and that the world of sense is illusory must, I think, be regarded as fallacious. Nevertheless there is some sense—easier to feel than to state—in which time is an unimportant and superficial characteristic of reality. Past and future must be acknowledged to be as real as the present, and a certain emancipation from slavery to time is essential to philosophic thought. The importance of time is rather practical than theoretical, rather in relation to our desires than in relation to truth. A truer image of the world, I think, is obtained by picturing things as entering into the stream of time from an eternal world outside, than from a view which regards time as the devouring tyrant of all that is. Both in thought and in feeling, even though time be real, to realise the unimportance of time is the gate of wisdom.

That this is the case may be seen at once by asking ourselves why our feelings towards the past are so different from our feelings towards the future. The reason for this difference is wholly practical: our wishes can affect the future but not the past, the future is to some extent subject to our power, while the past is unalterably fixed. But every future will some day be past: if we see the past truly now, it must, when it was still future, have been just what we now see it to be, and what is now future must be just what we shall see it to be when it has become past. The felt difference of quality between past and future, therefore, is not an intrinsic difference, but only a difference in relation to us: to impartial contemplation, it ceases to exist. And impartiality of contemplation is, in the intellectual sphere, that very same virtue of disinterestedness which, in the sphere of action, appears as justice and unselfishness. Whoever wishes to see the world truly, to rise in thought above the tyranny of practical desires, must learn to overcome the difference of attitude towards past and future, and to survey the whole stream of time in one comprehensive vision.

The kind of way in which, as it seems to me, time ought not to enter into our theoretic philosophical thought, may be illustrated by the philosophy which has become associated with the idea of evolution, and which is exemplified by Nietzsche, pragmatism, and Bergson. This philosophy, on the basis of the development which has led from the lowest forms of life up to man, sees in *progress* the fundamental law of the universe, and thus admits the difference between *earlier* and *later* into the very citadel of its contemplative outlook. With its past and future history of the world, conjectural as it is, I do not wish to quarrel. But I think that, in the intoxication of a quick success, much that is required for a true understanding of the universe has been forgotten. Something of Hellenism, something, too, of Oriental resignation, must be combined with its hurrying Western self-assertion before it can emerge from the ardour of youth into the mature wisdom of manhood. In spite of its appeals to science, the true scientific philosophy, I think, is something more arduous and more aloof, appealing to less mundane hopes, and requiring a severer discipline for its successful practice.

Darwin's *Origin of Species* persuaded the world that the difference between different species of animals and plants is not the fixed immutable difference that it appears to be. The doctrine of natural kinds, which had rendered classification easy and definite, which was enshrined in the Aristotelian tradition, and protected by its supposed necessity for orthodox dogma, was suddenly swept away for ever out of the biological world. The difference between man and the lower animals, which to our human conceit appears enormous, was shown to be a gradual achievement, involving intermediate beings who could not with certainty be placed either within or without the human family. The sun and the planets had already been shown by Laplace to be very probably derived from a primitive more or less undifferentiated nebula. Thus the old fixed landmarks became wavering and indistinct, and all sharp outlines were blurred. Things and species lost their boundaries, and none could say where they began or where they ended.

But if human conceit was staggered for a moment by its kinship with the ape, it soon found a way to reassert itself, and that way is the "philosophy" of evolution. A process which led from the amoeba to Man appeared to the philosophers to be obviously a progress—though whether the amoeba would agree with this opinion is not known. Hence the cycle of changes which science had shown to be the probable history of the past was welcomed as revealing a law of development towards good in the universe—an evolution or unfolding of an idea slowly embodying itself in the actual. But such a view, though it might satisfy Spencer and those whom we may call Hegelian evolutionists, could not be accepted as adequate by the more whole-hearted votaries of change. An ideal to which the world continuously approaches is, to these minds, too dead and static to be inspiring. Not only the aspiration, but the ideal too, must change and develop with the course of evolution: there must be no fixed goal, but a continual fashioning of fresh needs by the impulse which is life and which alone gives unity to the process.

Life, in this philosophy, is a continuous stream, in which all divisions are artificial and unreal. Separate things, beginnings and endings, are mere convenient fictions: there is only smooth unbroken transition. The beliefs of to-day may count as true to-day, if they carry us along the stream; but tomorrow they will be false, and must be replaced by new beliefs to meet the new situation. All our thinking consists of convenient fictions, imaginary congealings of the stream: reality flows on in spite of all our fictions, and though it can be lived, it cannot be conceived in thought. Somehow, without explicit statement, the assurance is slipped in that the future, though we cannot foresee it, will be better than the past or the present: the reader is like the child which expects a sweet because it has been told to open its mouth and shut its eyes. Logic, mathematics, physics disappear in this philosophy, because they are too "static"; what is real is no impulse and movement towards a goal which, like the rainbow, recedes as we advance, and makes every place different when it reaches it from what it appeared to be at a distance.

I do not propose to enter upon a technical examination of this philosophy. I wish only to maintain that the motives and interests which inspire it are so exclusively practical, and the problems with which it deals are so special, that it can hardly be regarded as touching any of the questions that, to my mind, constitute genuine philosophy.

The predominant interest of evolutionism is in the question of human destiny, or at least of the destiny of Life. It is more interested in morality and happiness than in knowledge for its own sake. It must be admitted that the same may be said of many other philosophies, and that a desire for the kind of knowledge which philosophy can give is very rare. But if philosophy is to attain truth, it is necessary first and foremost that philosophers should acquire the disinterested intellectual curiosity which characterises the genuine man of science. Knowledge concerning the future—which is the kind of knowledge that must be sought if we are to know about human destiny—is possible within certain narrow limits. It is impossible to say how much the limits may be enlarged with the progress of science. But what is evident is that any proposition about the future belongs by its subject-matter to some particular science, and is to be ascertained, if at all, by the methods of that science. Philosophy is not a short cut to the same kind of results as those of the other sciences: if it is to be a genuine study, it must have a province of its own, and aim at results which the other sciences can neither prove nor disprove.

Evolutionism, in basing itself upon the notion of *progress,* which is change from the worse to the better, allows the notion of time, as it seems to me, to become its tyrant rather than its servant, and thereby loses that impartiality of contemplation which is the source of all that is best in philosophic thought and feeling. Metaphysicians, as we saw, have frequently denied altogether the reality of time. I do not wish to do this; I wish only to preserve the mental outlook which inspired the denial, the attitude which, in thought, regards the past as having the same reality as the present and the same importance as the future. "In so far," says Spinoza,* "as the mind conceives a thing according to the dictate of reason, it will be equally affected whether the idea is that of a future, past, or present thing." It is this "conceiving according to the dictate of reason" that I find lacking in the philosophy which is based on evolution.

IV. GOOD AND EVIL

Mysticism maintains that all evil is illusory, and sometimes maintains the same view as regards good, but more often holds that all Reality is good. Both views are to be found in Heraclitus: "Good and ill are one," he says, but again, "To God all things are fair and good and right, but men hold some things wrong and some right." A similar twofold position is to be found in Spinoza, but he uses the word "perfection" when he means to speak of the good that is not merely human. "By reality and perfection I mean the same thing," he says; but elsewhere we find the definition: "By good I shall mean that which we certainly know to be useful to us." Thus perfection belongs to Reality in its own nature, but goodness is relative to ourselves and our needs, and disap-

*Quotations here are all from Spinoza's *Ethics.*

pears in an impartial survey. Some such distinction, I think, is necessary in order to understand the ethical outlook of mysticism: there is a lower mundane kind of good and evil, which divides the world of appearance into what seem to be conflicting parts; but there is also a higher, mystical kind of good, which belongs to Reality and is not opposed by any correlative kind of evil.

It is difficult to give a logically tenable account of this position without recognising that good and evil are subjective, that what is good is merely that towards which we have one kind of feeling, and what is evil is merely that towards which we have another kind of feeling. In our active life, where we have to exercise choice, and to prefer this to that of two possible acts, it is necessary to have a distinction of good and evil, or at least of better and worse. But this distinction, like everything pertaining to action, belongs to what mysticism regards as the world of illusion, if only because it is essentially concerned with time. In our contemplative life, where action is not called for, it is possible to be impartial, and to overcome the ethical dualism which action requires. So long as we remain *merely* impartial, we may be content to say that both the good and the evil of action are illusions. But if, as we must do if we have the mystic vision, we find the whole world worthy of love and worship, if we see

> The earth, and every common sight . . .
> Apparell'd in celestial light,

we shall say that there is a higher good than that of action, and that this higher good belongs to the whole world as it is in reality. In this way the twofold attitude and the apparent vacillation of mysticism are explained and justified.

The possibility of this universal love and joy in all that exists is of supreme importance for the conduct and happiness of life, and gives inestimable value to the mystic emotion, apart from any creeds which may be built upon it. But if we are not to be led into false beliefs, it is necessary to realise exactly what the mystic emotion reveals. It reveals a possibility of human nature—a possibility of a nobler, happier, freer life than any that can be otherwise achieved. But it does not reveal anything about the non-human, or about the nature of the universe in general. Good and bad, and even the higher good that mysticism finds everywhere, are the reflections of our own emotions on other things, not part of the substance of things as they are in themselves. And therefore an impartial contemplation, freed from all preoccupation with Self, will not judge things good or bad, although it is very easily combined with that feeling of universal love which leads the mystic to say that the whole world is good.

The philosophy of evolution, through the notion of progress, is bound up with the ethical dualism of the worse and the better, and is thus shut out, not only from the kind of survey which discards good and evil altogether from its view, but also from the mystical belief in the goodness of everything. In this way the distinction of good and evil, like time, becomes a tyrant in this philosophy, and introduces into thought the restless selectiveness of action. Good and evil, like time, are, it would seem, not general or fundamental in the world of thought, but late and highly specialised members of the intellectual hierarchy.

Although, as we saw, mysticism can be interpreted so as to agree with the view that good and evil are not intellectually fundamental, it must be admitted that here we are no longer in verbal agreement with most of the great philosophers and religious teachers of the past. I believe, however, that the elimination of ethical considerations from philosophy is both scientifically necessary and—though this may seem a paradox—an ethical advance. Both these contentions must be briefly defended.

The hope of satisfaction to our more human desires—the hope of demonstrating that the world has this or that desirable ethical characteristic—is not one which, so far as I can see, a scientific philosophy can do anything whatever to satisfy. The difference between a good world and a bad one is a difference in the particular characteristics of the particular things that exist in these worlds: it is not a sufficiently abstract difference to come within the province of philosophy. Love and hate, for example, are ethical opposites, but to philosophy they are closely analogous attitudes towards objects. The general form and structure of those attitudes towards objects which constitute mental phenomena is a problem for philosophy, but the difference between love and hate is not a difference of form or structure, and therefore belongs rather to the special science of psychology than to philosophy. Thus the ethical interests which have often inspired philosophers must remain in the background: some kind of ethical interest may inspire the whole study, but none must obtrude in the detail or be expected in the special results which are sought.

If this view seems at first sight disappointing, we may remind ourselves that a similar change has been found necessary in all the other sciences. The physicist or chemist is not now required to prove the ethical importance of his ions or atoms; the biologist is not expected to prove the utility of the plants or animals which he dissects. In pre-scientific ages this was not the case. Astronomy, for example, was studied because men believed in astrology: it was thought that the movements of the planets had the most direct and important bearing upon the lives of human beings. Presumably, when this belief decayed and the disinterested study of astronomy began, many who had found astrology absorbingly interesting decided that astronomy had too little human interest to be worthy of study. Physics, as it appears in Plato's *Timaeus* for example, is full of ethical notions: it is an essential part of its purpose to show that the earth is worthy of admiration. The modern physicist, on the contrary, though he has no wish to deny that the earth is admirable, is not concerned, as physicist, with its ethical attributes: he is merely concerned to find out facts, not to consider whether they are good or bad. In psychology, the scientific attitude is even more recent and more difficult than in the physical sciences: it is natural to consider that human nature is either good or bad, and to suppose that the difference between good and bad, so all-important in practice, must be important in theory also. It is only during the last century that an ethically neutral psychology has grown up; and here too, ethical neutrality has been essential to scientific success.

In philosophy, hitherto, ethical neutrality has been seldom sought and hardly ever achieved. Men have remembered their wishes, and have judged philosophies in relation to their wishes. Driven from the particular sciences, the belief that the notions of good and evil must afford a key to the understanding of the world has sought a refuge in philosophy. But even from this last refuge, if philosophy is not to remain a set of pleasing dreams, this belief must be driven forth. It is a commonplace that happiness is not best achieved by those who seek it directly; and it would seem that the same is true of the good. In thought, at any rate, those who forget good and evil and seek only to know the facts are more likely to achieve good than those who view the world through the distorting medium of their own desires.

We are thus brought back to our seeming paradox, that a philosophy which does not seek to impose upon the world its own conceptions of good and evil is not only more likely to achieve truth, but is also the outcome of a higher ethical standpoint than one which, like evolutionism and most traditional systems, is perpetually appraising the universe and seeking to find in it an embodiment of present ideals. In religion, and in every deeply serious view of the world and of human destiny, there is an element of submission, a realisation of the limits of human power, which is somewhat lacking in the modern world, with its quick material successes and its insolent belief in the boundless possibilities of progress. "He that loveth his life shall lose it"; and there is danger lest, through a too confident love of life, life itself should lose much of what gives it its highest worth. The submission which religion inculcates in action is essentially the same in spirit as that which science teaches in thought; and the ethical neutrality by which its victories have been achieved is the outcome of that submission.

The good which it concerns us to remember is the good which it lies in our power to create—the good in our own lives and in our attitude towards the world. Insistence on belief in an external realisation of the good is a form of self-assertion, which, while it cannot secure the external good which it desires, can seriously impair the inward good which lies within our power, and destroy that reverence towards fact which constitutes both what is valuable in humility and what is fruitful in the scientific temper.

Human beings cannot, of course, wholly transcend human nature; something subjective, if only the interest that determines the direction of our attention, must remain in all our thought. But scientific philosophy comes nearer to objectivity than any other human pursuit, and gives us, therefore, the closest constant and the most intimate relation with the outer world that it is possible to achieve. To the primitive mind, everything is either friendly or hostile; but experience has shown that friendliness and hostility are not the conceptions by which the world is to be understood. Scientific philosophy thus represents, though as yet only in a nascent condition, a higher form of thought than any pre-scientific belief or imagination, and, like every approach to self-transcendence, it brings with it a rich reward in increase of scope and breadth and comprehension. Evolutionism, in spite of its appeals to particular scientific facts, fails to be a truly scientific philosophy because of its slavery to time, its ethical preoccupations, and its predominant interest in our mundane concerns and destiny. A truly scientific philosophy will be more humble, more piecemeal, more arduous, offering less glitter of outward mirage to flatter fallacious hopes, but more indifferent to fate, and more capable of accepting the world without the tyrannous imposition of our human and temporary demands.

G.E. MOORE
1873–1958

George Edward Moore was born in 1873 in an affluent middle-class suburb of London. His father was a medical doctor and his mother a descendent of prominent Quaker merchants. Like his seven siblings, Moore received his early education at home from his father. When he was eight, Moore entered Dulwich College, a highly regarded day school within walking distance of his home. While there, Moore underwent a Christian conversion, becoming what he would later call an "ultra-evangelical." For two years he distributed tracts, attended Christian meetings, and studied the Bible. Gradually, however, his religious fervor waned, due in large part to his oldest brother's influence. By the time of his graduation in 1892, he had become "a complete Agnostic," remaining wary of religious enthusiasm for the rest of his life.

Following graduation from Dulwich, Moore entered Trinity College, Cambridge, to study classics. Here Moore met his lifelong friend Bertrand Russell. Partly as a result of his contact with Russell, Moore changed the focus of his studies from classics to philosophy. He was particularly interested in ethics, and he wrote a thesis on the notion of the self in Kant's ethical works. On the basis of this treatise, Moore was elected to a six-year fellowship at Trinity. During this time, he published his first book, *Principia Ethica* (1903).

By the time his fellowship ended in 1904, both of Moore's parents had died, leaving him and his siblings with a considerable inheritance. Moore found it unnecessary to work, and he spent the next seven years in private study. He first moved to Edinburgh to share a house with a friend, but then he joined two of his sisters in a suburb of London. Moore wrote a bit, including the book *Ethics* (1912), and worked his way through such difficult works as Russell's *Principles of Mathematics*.

In 1911, Moore returned to Cambridge as a lecturer in Moral Science. The next twenty-eight years were a time of both personal and professional success for Moore. Moore's lectures were attended by outstanding students, such as Ludwig Wittgenstein and F.P. Ramsey. In 1916, Moore married one of his students, Dorothy Ely, and together they had two sons, Nicholas and Timothy. In 1921, Moore was named editor of the philosophy journal *Mind.* And in 1925, Moore succeeded his own teacher, James Ward, as professor of philosophy at Cambridge. Moore also continued to write extensively, primarily in the form of journal articles.

Following mandatory retirement in 1939, Moore was succeeded as professor of philosophy by his former student Wittgenstein. Moore accepted offers to lecture at a number of American colleges, and he and his wife spent World War II in New York, California, and New Jersey. Moore returned to England in 1944 and received the Order of Merit in 1951. (Reportedly, when given the award, Moore was shocked to find that King George VI had never heard of Wittgenstein.) Moore died quietly in 1958 at the age of eighty-five.

Though Moore did not produce much in terms of the quantity of his writing, the quality of his careful work and his clear and direct style of writing have enormously influenced English philosophical thought. His colleague, C.D. Broad, described him as "a man of simple tastes and character, absolutely devoid of all [affectation], pose, and flummery."*

*   *   *

It is hard to imagine that a person who had lived through two world wars could say "I do not think that the world or the sciences would ever have suggested to me any philosophical problems." But as Moore himself admits, his philosophical interests were generally stimulated by "things which other philosophers have said about the world or the sciences."** Specifically, Moore was interested in discovering what other philosophers *meant* by what they affirmed, and he wanted to know what reasons they had for their affirmations.

When Moore started at Cambridge in 1892, British philosophy was dominated by the work of Hegel. F.H. Bradley at Oxford and J.E. McTaggart at Cambridge both advocated a neo-Hegelian idealism that Moore found problematic. In his famous paper "The Refutation of Idealism" (1903), reprinted here (complete), Moore raises questions about the idealist claim that the universe is "spiritual," specifically George Berkeley's claim that "*esse is percipi*" ("to be is to be perceived"). Moore claims that whatever might be the "exact meaning" of this claim, "it is certainly meant to assert (1) that the universe is very different indeed from what it seems, and (2) that it has quite a large number of properties which it does not seem to have." After extensively exploring possible meanings of Berkeley's thesis, Moore concludes that "in all the senses ever given to [Berkeley's claim], it is false." It is important to note that Moore does *not* conclude anything about "whether Reality is or is not spiritual." Rather, his conclusions merely

---

*C.D. Broad, Obituary in *The Manchester Guardian,* October 25, 1958, as quoted in G.E. Moore, *Philosophical Papers* (London: Allen & Unwin, 1959), p. 12.

**G.E. Moore, "Autobiography," in Paul Arthur Schilpp, ed., *The Philosophy of G.E. Moore* (La Salle, IL: Open Court, 1942), p. 14.

Trinity College, Cambridge University. Bertrand Russell, G.E. Moore, and Ludwig Wittgenstein all attended, and later taught at, this prestigious institution. *(Culver Pictures, Inc.)*

assert that no sufficient reasons for doubting the existence of material things has been given and that if we persist in doubting their existence anyway, we cannot avoid absolute skepticism.

Moore was neither interested in developing an overall metaphysical scheme nor in discovering the "truth." Instead, he saw his job as a philosopher to be the analysis of meaning. In arguing for analysis over metaphysics and truth, Moore was one of the initiators of the "linguistic turn" in Anglo-American philosophy. Russell, Wittgenstein, Rudolf Carnap, Gilbert Ryle, A.J. Ayer, and J.L. Austin, among many others, all accepted the spirit, if not the exact content, of Moore's philosophy.

*   *   *

For further study, A.R. White, "G.E. Moore," in *A Critical History of Western Philosophy,* edited by D.J. O'Connor (New York: The Free Press, 1964) provides an excellent short introduction to Moore's thought, whereas A.R. White, *G.E. Moore: A Critical Exposition* (New York: Humanities Press, 1969) and Thomas Baldwin, *G.E. Moore* (London: Routledge, 1990) provide general book-length studies of Moore's thought. Paul Levy, *G.E. Moore and the Cambridge Apostles* (New York: Holt, Rinehart and Winston, 1980) and Tom Regan, *Bloomsbury's Prophet: G.E. Moore and the Development of His Moral Philosophy* (Philadelphia: Temple University Press, 1986) examine Moore's ideas in their historical context. E.D. Klemke, *The Epistemology of G.E. Moore* (Evanston, IL: Northwestern University Press, 1969); Shukla Sarker, *The Epistemology and Ethics of G.E. Moore: A Critical Evaluation* (New York: Humanities Press, 1981); David O'Connor, *The Metaphysics of G.E. Moore* (Dordrecht, The Netherlands: D. Reidel, 1982); Robert Peter Sylvester, *The Moral Philosophy of G.E. Moore* (Philadelphia: Temple University Press, 1990); and William H. Shaw, *Moore on Right and Wrong: The Normative Ethics of G.E. Moore*

(Dordrecht, The Netherlands: Kluwer, 1995) provide studies of specific areas of Moore's thought. For comparisons of Moore with other thinkers in this volume, see A.J. Ayer, *Russell and Moore: The Analytical Heritage* (Cambridge, MA: Harvard University Press, 1971) and Avrum Stroll, *Moore and Wittgenstein on Certainty* (Oxford: Oxford University Press, 1994). Finally, Paul Arthur Schilpp, ed., *The Philosophy of G.E. Moore* (LaSalle, IL: Open Court, 1942) provides an autobiography of Moore, essays on Moore's ideas, and his reply to the essays.

THE REFUTATION OF IDEALISM

Modern Idealism, if it asserts any general conclusion about the universe at all, asserts that it is *spiritual.* There are two points about this assertion to which I wish to call attention. These points are that, whatever be its exact meaning, it is certainly meant to assert (1) that the universe is very different indeed from what it seems, and (2) that it has quite a large number of properties which it does not seem to have. Chairs and tables and mountains *seem* to be very different from us; but, when the whole universe is declared to be spiritual, it is certainly meant to assert that they are far more like us than we think. The idealist means to assert that they are *in some sense* neither lifeless nor unconscious, as they certainly seem to be; and I do not think his language is so grossly deceptive, but that we may assume him to believe that they really are very different indeed from what they seem. And secondly when he declares that they are *spiritual,* he means to include in that term quite a large number of different properties. When the whole universe is declared to be spiritual, it is meant not only that it is in some sense *conscious,* but that it has what we recognise in ourselves as the *higher* forms of consciousness. That it is intelligent; that it is purposeful; that it is not mechanical; all these different things are commonly asserted of it. In general, it may be said, this phrase "reality is spiritual" excites and expresses the belief that the *whole* universe possesses *all the qualities* the possession of which is held to make us so superior to things which seem to be inanimate: at least, if it does not possess exactly those which we possess, it possesses not one only, but several others, which, by the same ethical standard, would be judged equal to or better than our own. When we say it is *spiritual* we mean to say that it has quite a number of excellent qualities, different from any which we commonly attribute either to stars or planets or to cups and saucers.

Now why I mention these two points is that when engaged in the intricacies of philosophic discussion, we are apt to overlook the vastness of the difference between this idealistic view and the ordinary view of the world, and to overlook the number of *different* propositions which the idealist must prove. It is, I think, owing to the vastness of this difference and owing to the number of different excellences which Idealists attribute to the universe, that it seems such an interesting and important question whether Idealism be true or not. But, when we begin to argue about it, I think we are apt to forget what a vast number of arguments this interesting question must involve: we are apt

G.E. Moore, "The Refutation of Idealism" (1903) from *Philosophical Studies* (London: Routledge & Kegan Paul, 1970). Reprinted by permission of Routledge and Kegan Paul.

to assume, that if one or two points be made on either side, the whole case is won. I say this lest it should be thought that any of the arguments which will be advanced in this paper would be sufficient to disprove, or any refutation of them sufficient to prove, the truly interesting and important proposition that reality is spiritual. For my own part I wish it to be clearly understood that I do not suppose that anything I shall say has the smallest tendency to prove that reality is not spiritual: I do not believe it possible to re-fute a single one of the many important propositions contained in the assertion that it is so. Reality may be spiritual, for all I know; and I devoutly hope it is. But I take "Ideal-ism" to be a wide term and to include not only this interesting conclusion but a number of arguments which are supposed to be, if not sufficient, at least *necessary,* to prove it. Indeed I take it that modern Idealists are chiefly distinguished by certain arguments which they have in common. That reality is spiritual has, I believe, been the tenet of many theologians; and yet, for believing that alone, they should hardly be called Ideal-ists. There are besides, I believe, many persons, not improperly called Idealists, who hold certain characteristic propositions, without venturing to think them quite suffi-cient to prove so grand a conclusion. It is, therefore, only with Idealistic *arguments* that I am concerned; and if any Idealist holds that *no* argument is necessary to prove that reality is spiritual, I shall certainly not have refuted him. I shall, however, attack at least one argument, which, to the best of my belief, is considered necessary to their po-sition by all Idealists. And I wish to point out a certain advantage which this procedure gives me—an advantage which justifies the assertion that, if my arguments are sound, they will have refuted Idealism. If I can refute a single proposition which is a necessary and essential step in all Idealistic arguments, then, no matter how good the rest of these arguments may be, I shall have proved that Idealists have *no reason whatever* for their conclusion.

Suppose we have a chain of argument which takes the form: Since A is B, and B is C, and C is D, it follows A is D. In such an argument though "B is C" and "C is D" may both be perfectly true, yet if "A is B" be false, we have no more reason for assert-ing A is D than if all three were false. It does not, indeed, follow that A is D is false; nor does it follow that no other arguments would prove it to be true. But it does follow that, so far as this argument goes, it is the barest supposition, without the least bit of evidence. I propose to attack a proposition which seems to me to stand in this relation to the conclusion "Reality is spiritual." I do not propose to dispute that "Reality is spir-itual;" I do not deny that there may be reasons for thinking that it is: but I do propose to show that one reason upon which, to the best of my judgment, all other arguments ever used by Idealists depend is *false.* These other arguments may, for all I shall say, be em-inently ingenious and true; they are very many and various, and different Idealists use the most different arguments to prove the same most important conclusions. Some of these *may* be sufficient to prove that B is C and C is D; but if, as I shall try to show, their "A is B" is false the conclusion A is D remains a pleasant supposition. I do not deny that to suggest pleasant and plausible suppositions may be the proper function of philosophy: but I am assuming that the name Idealism can only be properly applied where there is a certain amount of argument, intended to be cogent.

The subject of this paper is, therefore, quite uninteresting. Even if I prove my point, I shall have proved nothing about the Universe in general. Upon the important question whether Reality is or is not spiritual my argument will not have the remotest bearing. I shall only attempt to arrive at the truth about a matter, which is in itself quite trivial and insignificant, and from which, so far as I can see and certainly so far as I shall say, no conclusions can be drawn about any of the subjects about which we most want to know. The only importance I can claim for the subject I shall investigate is that it seems to me to be a matter upon which not Idealists only, but all philosophers and psychologists also, have been in error, and from their erroneous view of which they have inferred (validly or invalidly) their most striking and interesting conclusions. And that it has even this importance I cannot hope to prove. If it has this importance, it will indeed follow that all the most striking results of philosophy—Sensationalism, Agnosticism and Idealism alike—have, for all that has hitherto been urged in their favour, no more foundation than the supposition that a chimera lives in the moon. It will follow that, unless new reasons never urged hitherto can be found, all the most important philosophic doctrines have as little claim to assent as the most superstitious beliefs of the lowest savages. Upon the question what we have *reason* to believe in the most interesting matters, I do therefore think that my results will have an important bearing; but I cannot too clearly insist that upon the question whether these beliefs are true they will have none whatever.

The trivial proposition which I propose to dispute is this: that *esse* is *percipi.* This is a very ambiguous proposition, but, in some sense or other, it has been very widely held. That it is, in some sense, essential to Idealism, I must for the present merely assume. What I propose to show is that, in all the senses ever given to it, it is false.

But, first of all, it may be useful to point out briefly in what relation I conceive it to stand to Idealistic arguments. That wherever you can truly predicate *esse* you can truly predicate *percipi,* in some sense or other, is, I take it, a necessary step in all arguments, properly to be called Idealistic, and, what is more, in all arguments hitherto offered for the Idealistic conclusion. If *esse* is *percipi,* this is at once equivalent to saying that whatever is, is experienced; and this, again, is equivalent, in a sense, to saying that whatever is, is something mental. But this is not the sense in which the Idealist *conclusion* must maintain that Reality is *mental.* The Idealist *conclusion* is that *esse* is *percipere;* and hence, whether *esse* be *percipi* or not, a further and different discussion is needed to show whether or not it is also *percipere.* And again, even if *esse* be *percipere,* we need a vast quantity of further argument to show that what has *esse* has also those higher mental qualities which are denoted by spiritual. This is why I said that the question I should discuss, namely, whether or not *esse* is *percipi,* must be utterly insufficient either to prove or to disprove that reality is spiritual. But, on the other hand, I believe that every argument ever used to show that reality is spiritual has inferred this (validly or invalidly) from "*esse* is *percipere*" as one of its premisses; and that this again has never been pretended to be proved except by use of the premiss that *esse* is *percipi.* The type of argument used for the latter purpose is familiar enough. It is said that since whatever is, is experienced, and since some things are which are not experienced by the individual, these must at least form part of some experience. Or again that, since an object necessarily implies a subject, and since the whole world must be an object, we must conceive it to belong to some subject or subjects, in the same sense in which whatever is the object of our experience belongs to us. Or again, that, since thought enters into the essence of all reality, we must conceive behind it, in it, or as its essence, a spirit akin to ours, who think: that "spirit greets spirit" in its object. Into the validity of these inferences I do not propose to enter: they obviously require a great deal of discussion. I only desire to point out that, however correct they may be, yet if *esse* is not *percipi,* they leave us as far from a proof that reality is spiritual, as if they were all false too.

But now: Is *esse percipi?* There are three very ambiguous terms in this proposition, and I must begin by distinguishing the different things that may be meant by some of them.

And first with regard to *percipi*. This term need not trouble us long at present. It was, perhaps, originally used to mean "sensation" only; but I am not going to be so unfair to modern Idealists—the only Idealists to whom the term should now be applied without qualification—as to hold that, if they say *esse* is *percipi,* they mean by *percipi* sensation only. On the contrary I quite agree with them that, if *esse* be *percipi* at all, *percipi* must be understood to include not sensation only, but that other type of mental fact, which is called "thought"; and, whether *esse* be *percipi* or not, I consider it to be the main service of the philosophic school, to which modern Idealists belong, that they have insisted on distinguishing "sensation" and "thought" and on emphasising the importance of the latter. Against Sensationalism and Empiricism they have maintained the true view. But the distinction between sensation and thought need not detain us here. For, in whatever respects they differ, they have at least this in common, that they are both forms of consciousness or, to use a term that seems to be more in fashion just now, they are both ways of experiencing. Accordingly, whatever *esse* is *percipi* may mean, it does *at least* assert that whatever is, is *experienced.* And since what I wish to maintain is, that even this is untrue, the question whether it be experienced by way of sensation or thought or both is for my purpose quite irrelevant. If it be not experienced at all, it cannot be either an object of thought or an object of sense. It is only if being involves "experience" that the question, whether it involves sensation or thought or both, becomes important. I beg, therefore, that *percipi* may be understood, in what follows, to refer merely to what is *common* to sensation and thought. A very recent article states the meaning of *esse* is *percipi* with all desirable clearness in so far as *percipi* is concerned. "I will undertake to show," says Mr. Taylor, "that what makes [any piece of fact] real can be nothing but its presence as an inseparable aspect of a *sentient experience.*"* I am glad to think that Mr. Taylor has been in time to supply me with so definite a statement that this is the ultimate premiss of Idealism. My paper will at least refute Mr. Taylor's Idealism, if it refutes anything at all: for I shall undertake to show that what makes a thing real cannot possibly be its presence as an inseparable aspect of a sentient experience.

But Mr. Taylor's statement though clear, I think, with regard to the meaning of *percipi* is highly ambiguous in other respects. I will leave it for the present to consider the next ambiguity in the statement: *Esse* is *percipi*. What does the copula mean? What can be meant by saying that *esse* is *percipi*? There are just three meanings, one or other of which such a statement must have, if it is to be true; and of these there is only one which it can have, if it is to be important. (1) The statement may be meant to assert that the word "*esse*" is used to signify nothing either more or less than the word "*percipi*": that the two words are precise synonyms: that they are merely different names for one and the same thing: that what is meant by *esse* is absolutely identical with what is meant by *percipi*. I think I need not prove that the principle *esse* is *percipi* is not thus intended merely to define a word; nor yet that, if it were, it would be an extremely bad definition. But if it does not mean this, only two alternatives remain. The second is (2) that what is meant by *esse,* though not absolutely identical with what is meant by *percipi,* yet *includes* the latter as a *part* of its meaning. If this were the meaning of "*esse* is *percipi*," then to say that a thing was real would not be the same thing as to say that it was experienced. That it was *real* would mean that it was experienced and *something else besides:* "being experienced" would be *analytically essential* to reality, but would not be the whole meaning of the term. From the fact that a thing was real we

International Journal of Ethics, October, 1902.

should be able to infer, by the law of contradiction, that it was experienced; since the latter would be *part* of what is meant by the former. But, on the other hand, from the fact a thing was experienced we should *not* be able to infer that it was real; since it would not follow from the fact that it had one of the attributes essential to reality, that it *also* had the other or others. Now, if we understand *esse* is *percipi* in this second sense, we must distinguish *three* different things which it asserts. First of all, it gives a definition of the word "reality," asserting that word stands for a complex whole, of which what is meant by "*percipi*" forms a part. And secondly it asserts that "being experienced" forms a part of a certain whole. Both these propositions may be true, and at all events I do not wish to dispute them. I do not, indeed, think that the word "reality" is commonly used to include "*percipi*": but I do not wish to argue about the meaning of words. And that many things which are experienced are also something else—that to be experienced forms part of certain wholes, is, of course, indisputable. But what I wish to point out is, that neither of these propositions is of any importance, unless we add to them a *third*. That "real" is a convenient name for a union of attributes which *sometimes* occurs, it could not be worth any one's while to assert: no inferences of any importance could be drawn from such an assertion. Our principle could only mean that when a thing happens to have *percipi* as well as the other qualities included under *esse,* it has *percipi:* and we should never be able to *infer* that it was experienced, except from a proposition which already asserted that it was both experienced and something else. Accordingly, if the assertion that *percipi* forms part of the whole meant by reality is to have any importance, it must mean that the whole is organic, at least in this sense, that the other constituent or constituents of it *cannot* occur without *percipi*, even if *percipi* can occur without them. Let us call these other constituents *x*. The proposition that *esse* includes *percipi,* and that therefore from *esse percipi* can be inferred, can only be important if it is meant to assert that *percipi* can be inferred from *x*. The only importance of the question whether the whole *esse* includes the part *percipi* rests therefore on the question whether the part *x* is necessarily connected with the part *percipi*. And this is (3) the third possible meaning of the assertion *esse* is *percipi:* and, as we now see, the only important one. *Esse* is *percipi* asserts that wherever you have *x* you also have *percipi* that whatever has the property *x* also has the property that it is experienced. And this being so, it will be convenient if, for the future, I may be allowed to use the term "*esse*" to denote *x alone.* I do not wish thereby to beg the question whether what we commonly mean by the word "real" does or does not include *percipi* as well as *x*. I am quite content that my definition of "*esse*" to denote *x,* should be regarded merely as an arbitrary verbal definition. Whether it is so or not, the only question of interest is whether from *x percipi* can be inferred, and I should prefer to be able to express this in the form: can *percipi* be inferred from *esse*? Only let it be understood that when I say *esse,* that term will not for the future *include percipi:* it denotes only that *x,* which Idealists, perhaps rightly include along with *percipi* under *their* term *esse.* That there is such an *x* they must admit on pain of making the proposition an absolute tautology; and that from this *x percipi* can be inferred they must admit, on pain of making it a perfectly barren analytic proposition. Whether *x* alone should or should not be called *esse* is not worth a dispute: what is worth dispute is whether *percipi* is necessarily connected with *x*.

   We have therefore discovered the ambiguity of the copula in *esse* is *percipi*, so far as to see that this principle asserts two distinct terms to be so related, that whatever has the one, which I call *esse*, has also the property that it is experienced. It asserts a necessary connexion between *esse* on the one hand and *percipi* on the other; these two words denoting each a distinct term, and *esse* denoting a term in which that denoted by *percipi* is not included. We have, then in *esse* is *percipi,* a *necessary synthetic* proposition which I have undertaken to refute. And I may say at once that, understood as such, it cannot be refuted. If the Idealist chooses to assert that it is merely a self-evident truth, I have only to say that it does not appear to me to be so. But I believe that no Idealist ever has maintained it to be so. Although this—that two distinct terms are necessarily related—is the only sense which "*esse* is *percipi*" can have if it is to be true and important, it *can* have another sense, if it is to be an important falsehood. I believe that Idealists all hold this important falsehood. They do not perceive that *esse* is *percipi* must, if true, be *merely* a self-evident synthetic truth: they either identify with it or give as a reason for it another proposition which must be false because it is self-contradictory. Unless they did so, they would have to admit that it was a perfectly unfounded assumption; and if they recognised that it was *unfounded,* I do not think they would maintain its truth to be evident. *Esse* is *percipi,* in the sense I have found for it, *may* indeed be true; I cannot refute it: but if this sense were clearly apprehended, no one, I think, would believe that it was true.

Idealists, we have seen, must assert that whatever is experienced, is *necessarily* so. And this doctrine they commonly express by saying that "the object of experience is inconceivable apart from the subject." I have hitherto been concerned with pointing out what meaning this assertion must have, if it is to be an important truth. I now propose to show that it may have an important meaning, which must be false, because it is self-contradictory.

It is a well-known fact in the history of philosophy that *necessary* truths in general, but especially those of which it is said that the opposite is inconceivable, have been commonly supposed to be *analytic,* in the sense that the proposition denying them was self-contradictory. It was in this way, commonly supposed, before Kant, that many truths could be proved by the law of contradiction alone. This is, therefore, a mistake which it is plainly easy for the best philosophers to make. Even since Kant many have continued to assert it; but I am aware that among those Idealists, who most properly deserve the name, it has become more fashionable to assert that truths are *both* analytic and synthetic. Now with many of their reasons for asserting this I am not concerned: it is possible that in some connexions the assertion may bear a useful and true sense. But if we understand "analytic" in the sense just defined, namely, what is proved by the law of contradiction *alone,* it is plain that, if "synthetic" means what is *not* proved by this alone, no truth can be both analytic and synthetic. Now it seems to me that those who do maintain truths to be both, do nevertheless maintain that they are so in this as well as in other senses. It is, indeed, extremely unlikely that so *essen*tial a part of the historical meaning of "analytic" and "synthetic" should have been entirely discarded, especially since we find no express recognition that it is discarded. In that case it is fair to suppose that modern Idealists have been influenced by the view that certain truths can be proved by the law of contradiction alone. I admit they also expressly declare that they can *not:* but this is by no means sufficient to prove that they do not also think they are; since it is very easy to hold two mutually contradictory opinions. What I suggest then is that Idealists hold the particular doctrine in question, concerning the relation of subject and object in experience, because they think it is an analytic truth in this restricted sense that it is proved by the law of contradiction alone.

I am suggesting that the Idealist maintains that object and subject are necessarily connected, mainly because he fails to see that they are *distinct,* that they are *two,* at all. When he thinks of "yellow" and when he thinks of the "sensation of yellow," he fails to see that there is anything whatever in the latter which is not in the former. This being so, to deny that yellow can ever *be* apart from the sensation of yellow is merely to deny that yellow can ever be other than it is; since yellow and the sensation of yellow are absolutely identical. To assert that yellow is necessarily an object of experience is to assert that yellow is necessarily yellow—a purely identical proposition, and therefore proved by the law of contradiction alone. Of course, the proposition also implies that experience is, after all, something distinct from yellow—else there would be no reason for insisting that yellow is a sensation: and that the argument thus both affirms and denies that yellow and sensation of yellow are distinct, is what sufficiently refutes it. But this contradiction can easily be overlooked, because though we are convinced, in other connexions, that "experience" does mean something and something most important, yet we are never distinctly aware *what* it means, and thus in every particular case we do not notice its presence. The facts present themselves as a kind of antinomy: (1) Experience *is* something unique and different from anything else; (2) Experience of green is entirely indistinguishable from green; two propositions which cannot both be true. Idealists, holding both, can only take refuge in arguing from the one in some connexions and from the other in others.

But I am well aware that there are many Idealists who would repel it as an utterly unfounded charge that they fail to distinguish between a sensation or idea and what I will call its object. And there are, I admit, many who not only imply, as we all do, that green is distinct from the sensation of green, but expressly insist upon the distinction as an important part of their system. They would perhaps only assert that the two form an inseparable unity. But I wish to point out that many, who use this phrase, and who do admit the distinction, are not thereby absolved from the charge that they deny it. For there is a certain doctrine, very prevalent among philosophers nowadays, which by a very simple reduction may be seen to assert that two distinct things both are and are not distinct. A distinction is asserted; but it is *also* asserted that the things distinguished form an "organic unity." But, forming such a unity, it is held, each would not be what it is *apart from its relation to the other.* Hence to consider either by itself is to make an *illegitimate abstraction.* The recognition that there are "organic unities" and "illegitimate abstractions" in this sense is regarded as one of the chief conquests of modern philosophy. But what is the sense attached to these terms? An abstraction is illegitimate, when and only when we attempt to assert of a *part*—of something abstracted— that which is true only of the *whole* to which it belongs: and it may perhaps be useful to point out that this should not be done. But the application actually made of this principle, and what perhaps would be expressly acknowledged as its meaning, is something much the reverse of useful. The principle is used to assert that certain abstractions are *in all cases* illegitimate; that whenever you try to assert *anything whatever* of that which is *part* of an organic whole, what you assert can only be true of the whole. And this principle, so far from being a useful truth, is necessarily false. For if the whole can, nay *must,* be substituted for the part in all propositions and for all purposes, this can only be because the whole is absolutely identical with the part. When, therefore, we are told that green and the sensation of green are certainly distinct but yet are not separable, or that it is an illegitimate abstraction to consider the one apart from the other, what these provisos are used to assert is, that though the two things are distinct yet you not only can but must treat them as if they were not. Many philosophers, therefore, when they admit a distinction, yet (following the lead of Hegel) boldly assert their right, in a slightly more obscure form of words, *also* to deny it. The principle of organic unities, like that of combined analysis and synthesis, is mainly used to defend the practice of holding *both* of two contradictory propositions, wherever this may seem convenient. In this, as in other matters, Hegel's main service to philosophy has consisted in giving a name to and erecting into a principle, a type of fallacy to which experience had shown philosophers, along with the rest of mankind, to be addicted. No wonder that he has followers and admirers.

I have shown then, so far, that when the Idealist asserts the important principle "*Esse* is *percipi*" he must, if it is to be true, mean by this that: Whatever is experienced also must be experienced. And I have also shown that he may identify with, or give as a reason for, this proposition, one which must be false, because it is self-contradictory. But at this point I propose to make a complete break in my argument. "*Esse* is *percipi*," we have seen, asserts of two terms, as distinct from one another as "green" and "sweet," that whatever has the one has also the other: it asserts that "being" and "being experienced" are necessarily connected: that whatever *is* is *also* experienced. And this, I admit cannot be directly refuted. But I believe it to be false; and I have asserted that anybody who saw that "*esse* and *percipi*" were as distinct as "green" and "sweet" would be no more ready to believe that whatever is is also experienced, than to believe that whatever is green is also sweet. I have asserted that no one would believe that "*esse* is *percipi*" if they saw how different *esse* is from *percipi:* but *this* I shall not try to prove. I have asserted that all who do believe that "*esse* is *percipi*" identify with it or take as a reason for it a self-contradictory proposition: but this I shall not try to prove. I shall only try to show that certain propositions which I assert to be believed, are false. That they are believed, and that without this belief "*esse* is *percipi*" would not be believed either, I must leave without a proof.

I pass, then, from the uninteresting question Is "*esse percipi*?" to the still more uninteresting and apparently irrelevant question "What is a sensation or idea?"

We all know that the sensation of blue differs from that of green. But it is plain that if both are *sensations* they also have some point in common. What is it that they have in common? And how is this common element related to the points in which they differ?

I will call the common element "consciousness" without yet attempting to say what the thing I so call *is*. We have then in every sensation two distinct terms, (1) "consciousness," in respect of which all sensations are alike; and (2) something else, in respect of which one sensation differs from another. It will be convenient if I may be allowed to call this second term the "object" of a sensation: this also without yet attempting to say what I mean by the word.

We have then in every sensation two distinct elements, one which I call consciousness, and another which I call the object of consciousness. This must be so if the sensation of blue and the sensation of green, though different in one respect, are alike in another: blue is one object of sensation and green is another, and consciousness, which both sensations have in common, is different from either.

But, further, sometimes the sensation of blue exists in my mind and sometimes it does not; and knowing, as we now do, that the sensation of blue includes two different elements, namely consciousness and blue, the question arises whether, when the sensation of blue exists, it is the consciousness which exists, or the blue which exists, or both. And one point at least is plain: namely that these three alternatives are all different from one another. So that, if any one tells us that to say "Blue exists" is the *same* thing as to say that "Both blue and consciousness exist," he makes a mistake and a self-contradictory mistake.

But another point is also plain, namely, that when the sensation exists, the consciousness, at least, certainly does exist; for when I say that the sensations of blue and of green both exist, I certainly mean that what is common to both and in virtue of which both are called sensations, exists in each case. The only alternative left, then, is that either both exist or the consciousness exists alone. If, therefore, any one tell us that the existence of blue is the same thing as the existence of the sensation of blue he makes a mistake and a self-contradictory mistake, for he asserts *either* that blue is the same thing as blue together with consciousness, or that it is the same thing as consciousness alone.

Accordingly to identify either "blue" or any other of what I have called "*objects*" of sensation, with the corresponding sensation is in every case, a self-contradictory error. It is to identify a part either with the whole of which it is a part or else with the other part of the same whole. If we are told that the assertion "Blue exists" is *meaningless* unless we mean by it that "The sensation of blue exists," we are told what is certainly false and self-contradictory. If we are told that the existence of blue is inconceivable apart from the existence of the sensation, the speaker *probably* means to convey to us, by this ambiguous expression, what is a self-contradictory error. For we can and must conceive the existence of blue as something quite distinct from the existence of the sensation. We can and must conceive that blue might exist and yet the sensation of blue not exist. For my own part I not only conceive this, but conceive it to be true. Either therefore this terrific assertion of inconceivability means what is false and self-contradictory or else it means only that *as a matter of fact* blue never can exist unless the sensation of it exists also.

And at this point I need not conceal my opinion that no philosopher has ever yet succeeded in avoiding this self-contradictory error: that the most striking results both of Idealism and of Agnosticism are only obtained by identifying blue with the sensation of blue: that *esse* is held to be *percipi*, solely because *what is experienced* is held to be identical with *the experience of it*. That Berkeley and Mill committed this error will, perhaps, be granted: that modern Idealists make it will, I hope, appear more probable later. But that my opinion is plausible, I will now offer two pieces of evidence. The first is that language offers us no means of referring to such objects as "blue" and "green" and "sweet," except by calling them sensations: it is an obvious violation of language to call them "things" or "objects" or "terms." And similarly we have no natural means of referring to such objects as "causality" or "likeness" or "identity," except by calling them "ideas" or "notions" or "conceptions." But it is hardly likely that if philosophers had clearly distinguished in the past between a sensation or idea and what I have called its object, there should have been no separate name for the latter. They have always used the same name for these two different "things" (if I may call them so): and hence there is some probability that they have supposed these "things" *not* to be two and different, but one and the same. And, secondly, there is a very good reason why they should have supposed so, in the fact that when we refer to introspection and try to discover what the sensation of blue is, it is very easy to suppose that we have before us only a single term. The term "blue" is easy enough to distinguish, but the other element which I have called "consciousness"—that which sensation of blue has in common with sensation of green—is extremely difficult to fix. That many people fail to distinguish it at all is sufficiently shown by the fact that there are materialists. And, in general, that which makes the sensation of blue a mental fact seems to escape us: it seems, if I may use a metaphor, to be transparent—we look through it and see nothing but the blue; we may be convinced that there is *something* but *what* it is no philosopher, I think, has yet clearly recognised.

But this was a digression. The point I had established so far was that in every sensation or idea we must distinguish two elements, (1) the "object," or that in which one differs from another; and (2) "consciousness," or that which all have in common— that which makes them sensations or mental facts. This being so, it followed that when a sensation or idea exists, we have to choose between the alternatives that either object alone, or consciousness alone, or both, exist; and I showed that of these alternatives one, namely that the object only exists, is excluded by the fact that what we mean to assert is certainly the existence of a mental fact. There remains the question: Do both exist? Or does the consciousness alone? And to this question one answer has hitherto been given universally: That both exist.

This answer follows from the analysis hitherto accepted of the relation of what I have called "object" to "consciousness" in any sensation or idea. It is held that what I call the object is merely the "content" of a sensation or idea. It is held that in each case we can distinguish two elements and two only, (1) the fact that there is feeling or experience, and (2) *what* is felt or experienced; the sensation or idea, it is said, forms a whole, in which we must distinguish two "inseparable aspects," "content" and "existence." I shall try to show that this analysis is false; and for that purpose I must ask what may seem an extraordinary question: namely what is meant by saying that one thing is "content" of another? It is not usual to ask this question; the term is used as if everybody must understand it. But since I am going to maintain that "blue" is *not* the content of the sensation of blue, and what is more important, that, even if it were this analysis would leave out the most important element in the sensation of blue, it is necessary that I should try to explain precisely what it is that I shall deny.

What then is meant by saying that one thing is the "content" of another? First of all I wish to point out that "blue" is rightly and properly said to be part of the content of a blue flower. If, therefore, we also assert that it is part of the content of the sensation of blue, we assert that it has to the other parts (if any) of this whole the same relation which it has to the other parts of a blue flower—and we assert only this: we cannot mean to assert that it has to the sensation of any relation which it does not have to the blue flower. And we have seen that the sensation of blue contains at least one other element beside blue—namely, what I call "consciousness," which makes it a sensation. So far then as we assert that blue is the content of the sensation, we assert that it has to this "consciousness" the same relation which it has to the other parts of a blue flower: we do assert this, and we assert no more than this. Into the question what exactly the relation is between blue and a blue flower in virtue of which we call the former part of its "content" I do not propose to enter. It is sufficient for my purpose to point out that it is the general relation most commonly meant when we talk of a thing and its qualities; and that this relation is such that to say the thing exists implies that the qualities also exist. The *content* of the thing is *what* we assert to exist, when we assert *that* the thing exists.

When, therefore, blue is said to be part of the content of the "sensation of blue," the latter is treated as if it were a whole constituted in exactly the same way as any other "thing." The "sensation of blue," on this view, differs from a blue bead or a blue beard, in exactly the same way in which the two latter differ from one another: the blue bead differs from the blue beard, in that while the former contains glass, the latter contains hair; and the "sensation of blue" differs from both in that, instead of glass or hair, it contains consciousness. The relation of the blue to the consciousness is conceived to be exactly the same as that of the blue to the glass or hair: it is in all three cases the quality of a *thing*.

But I said just now that the sensation of blue was analysed into "content" and "existence," and that blue was said to be *the* content of the idea of blue. There is an ambiguity in this and a possible error, which I must note in passing. The term "content" may be used in two senses. If we use "content" as equivalent to what Mr. Bradley calls the "*what*"—if we mean by it the *whole* of what is said to exist, when the thing is said to exist, then blue is certainly not *the* content of the sensation of blue: part of the *content* of the sensation is, in this sense of the term, that other element which I have called consciousness. The analysis of this sensation into the "content" "blue," on the one hand, and mere existence on the other, is therefore certainly false; in it we have again the self-contradictory identification of "Blue exists" with "The sensation of blue exists." But there is another sense in which "blue" might properly be said to be the content of the sensation—namely, the sense in which "content," like <*eidos*> is opposed to "substance" or "matter." For the element "consciousness," being common to all sensations, may be and certainly is regarded as in some sense their "substance," and by the "content" of each is only meant that in respect of which one differs from another. In this sense then "blue" might be said to be *the* content of the sensation; but, in that case, the analysis into "content" and "existence" is, at least, misleading, since under "existence" must be included "*what* exists" in the sensation other than blue.

We have it, then, as a universally received opinion that blue is related to the sensation or idea of blue, as its *content,* and that this view, if it is to be true, must mean that blue is part of *what* is said to exist when we say that the sensation exists. To say that the sensation exists is to say both that blue exists and that "consciousness," whether we call it the substance of which blue is *the* content or call it another part of the content, exists too. Any sensation or idea is a "*thing,*" and what I have called its object is the quality of this thing. Such a "thing" is what we think of when we think of a *mental image.* A mental image is conceived as if it were related to that of which it is the image (if there be any such thing) in exactly the same way as the image in a looking-glass is related to that of which it is the reflection; in both cases there is identity of content, and the image in the looking-glass differs from that in the mind solely in respect of the fact that in the one case the other constituent of the image is "glass" and in the other case it is consciousness. If the image is of blue, it is not conceived that this "content" has any relation to the consciousness but what it has to the glass: it is conceived *merely* to be its *content.* And owing to the fact that sensations and ideas are all considered to be *wholes* of this description—things in the mind—the question: What do we know? is considered to be identical with the question: What reason have we for supposing that there are things outside the mind *corresponding* to these that are inside it?

What I wish to point out is (1) that we have no reason for supposing that there are such things as mental images at all—for supposing that blue is part of the content of the sensation of blue, and (2) that even if there are mental images, no mental image and no sensation or idea is *merely* a thing of this kind: that "blue," even if it is part of the content of the image or sensation or idea of blue, is always *also* related to it in quite another way, and that this other relation, omitted in the traditional analysis, is the *only* one which makes the sensation of blue a mental fact at all.

The true analysis of a sensation or idea is as follows. The element that is common to them all, and which I have called "consciousness," really *is* consciousness. A sensation is, in reality, a case of "knowing" or "being aware of" or "experiencing" something. When we know that the sensation of blue exists, the fact we know is that there exists an awareness of blue. And this awareness is not merely, as we have hitherto seen it must be, itself something distinct and unique, utterly different from blue: it also has a perfectly distinct and unique relation to blue, a relation which is *not* that of thing or substance to content, nor of one part of content to another part of content. This relation is just that which we mean in every case by "knowing." To have in your mind "knowledge" of blue, is *not* to have in your mind a "thing" or "image" of which blue is the content. To be aware of the sensation of blue is *not* to be aware of a mental image—of a "thing," of which "blue" and some other element are constituent parts in the same sense in which blue and glass are constituents of a blue bead. It is to be aware of an awareness of blue; awareness being used, in both cases, in exactly the same sense. This element, we have seen, is certainly neglected by the "content" theory: that theory entirely fails to express the fact that there is, in the sensation of blue, this unique relation between blue and the other constituent. And what I contend is that this omission is *not* mere negligence of expression, but is due to the fact that though philosophers have recognised that *something* distinct is meant by consciousness, they have never yet had a clear conception of *what* that something is. They have not been able to hold *it* and *blue* before their minds and to compare them, in the same way in which they can compare *blue* and *green*. And this for the reason I gave above: namely that the moment we try to fix our attention upon consciousness and to see *what,* distinctly, it is, it seems to vanish: it seems as if we had before us a mere emptiness. When we try to introspect the sensation of blue, all we can see is the blue: the other element is as if it were diaphanous. Yet it can be distinguished if we look attentively enough, and if we know that there is something to look for. My main object in this paragraph has been to try to make the reader *see* it; but I fear I shall have succeeded very ill.

It being the case, then, that the sensation of blue includes in its analysis, beside blue, *both* a unique element "awareness" *and* a unique relation of this element to blue, I can make plain what I meant by asserting, as two distinct propositions, (1) that blue is probably not part of the content of the sensation at all, and (2) that, even it were, the sensation would nevertheless not be the sensation *of* blue, if blue had only this relation to it. The first hypothesis may now be expressed by saying that, if it were true, then, when the sensation of blue exists, there exists a *blue awareness:* offence may be taken at the expression, but yet it expresses just what should be and is meant by saying that blue is, in this case, a *content* of consciousness or experience. Whether or not, when I have the sensation of blue, my consciousness or awareness is thus blue, my introspection does not enable me to decide with certainty: I only see no reason for thinking that it is. But whether it is or not, the point is unimportant, for introspection *does* enable me to decide that something else is also true: namely that I am aware *of* blue, and by this I mean, that my awareness has to blue a quite different and distinct relation. It is possible, I admit, that my awareness is blue *as well* as being *of* blue: but what I am quite sure of is that it is *of* blue; that it has to blue the simple and unique relation the existence of which alone justifies us in distinguishing knowledge of a thing from the thing known, indeed in distinguishing mind from matter. And this result I may express by saying that what is called the *content* of a sensation is in very truth what I originally called it—the sensation's *object.*

But, if all this be true, what follows?

Idealists admit that some things really exist of which they are not aware: there are some things, they hold, which are not inseparable aspects of *their* experience, even if they be inseparable aspects of some experience. They further hold that some of the things of which they are sometimes aware do really exist, even when they are not aware of them: they hold for instance that they are sometimes aware of other Minds, which continue to exist even when they are not aware of them. They are, therefore, sometimes aware of something which is *not* an inseparable aspect of their own experience. They *do know some* things which are *not* a mere part or content of their experience. And what my analysis of sensation has been designed to show is, that whenever I have a mere sensation or idea, the fact is that I am then aware of something which is equally and in the same sense *not* an inseparable aspect of my experience. The awareness which I have maintained to be included in sensation is the very same unique fact which constitutes every kind of knowledge: "blue" is as much an object, and as little a mere content, of my experience, when I experience it, as the most exalted and independent real thing of which I am ever aware. There is, therefore, no question of how we are to "get outside the circle of our own ideas and sensations." Merely to have a sensation is already to *be* outside that circle. It is to know something which is as truly and really *not* a part of my experience, as anything which I can ever know.

Now I think I am not mistaken in asserting that the reason why Idealists suppose that everything which is must be an inseparable aspect of some experience, is that they suppose some things, at least, to be inseparable aspects of *their* experience. And there is certainly nothing which they are so firmly convinced to be an inseparable aspect of their experience as what they call the *content* of their ideas and sensations. If, therefore, this turns out in every case, whether it be also the content or not, to be at least *not* an inseparable aspect of the experience of it, it will be readily admitted that nothing else which we experience ever is such an inseparable aspect. But if we never experience anything but what is *not* an inseparable aspect of *that* experience, how can we infer that anything whatever, let alone *everything,* is an inseparable aspect of *any* experience? How utterly unfounded is the assumption that "*esse* is *percipi*" appears in the clearest light.

But further I think it may be seen that if the object of an Idealist's sensation were, as he supposes, *not* the object but merely the content of that sensation, if, that is to say, it really were an inseparable aspect of his experience, each Idealist could never be aware either of himself or of any other real thing. For the relation of a sensation to its object is certainly the same as that of any other instance of experience to its object; and this, I think, is generally admitted even by Idealists: they state as readily that *what* is judged or thought or perceived is the *content* of that judgment or thought or perception, as that blue is the content of the sensation of blue. But, if so, then when any Idealist thinks he is *aware* of himself or of any one else, this cannot really be the case. The fact is, on his own theory, that himself and that other person are in reality mere *contents* of an awareness, which is aware *of* nothing whatever. All that can be said is that there is an awareness in him, *with* a certain content: it can never be true that there is in him a consciousness *of* anything. And similarly he is never aware either of the fact that he exists or that reality is spiritual. The real fact, which he describes in those terms, is that his existence and the spirituality of reality are *contents* of an awareness, which is aware of nothing—certainly not, then, of it own content.

And further if everything, of which he thinks he is aware, is in reality merely a content of his own experience he has certainly no *reason* for holding that anything does exist except himself: it will, of course, be possible that other persons do exist; solipsism will not be necessarily true; but he cannot possibly infer from anything he holds that it is not true. That he himself exists will of course follow from his premiss that many things are contents of *his* experience. But since everything, of which he thinks himself aware, is in reality merely an inseparable aspect of that awareness; this premiss allows no inference that any of these contents far less any other consciousness, exists at all except as an inseparable aspect of his awareness, that is, as part of himself.

Such, and not those which he takes to follow from it, are the consequences which *do* follow from the Idealist's supposition that the object of an experience is in reality merely a content or inseparable aspect of that experience. If, on the other hand, we clearly recognise the nature of that peculiar relation which I have called "awareness of anything"; if we see that *this* is involved equally in the analysis of *every* experience — from the merest sensation to the most developed perception or reflexion, and that *this* is in fact the only essential element in an experience—the only thing that is both common and peculiar to all experiences—the only thing which gives us reason to call any fact mental; if, further, we recognise that this awareness is and must be in all cases of such a nature that its object, when we are aware of it, is precisely what it would be, if we were not aware: then it becomes plain that the existence of a table in space is related to my experience of *it* in precisely the same way as the existence of my own experience is related to my experience of *that*. Of both we are merely aware: if we are aware that the one exists, we are aware in precisely the same sense that the other exists; and if it is true that my experience can exist, even when I do not happen to be aware of its existence, we have exactly the same reason for supposing that the table can do so also. When, therefore, Berkeley, supposed that the only thing of which I am directly aware is my own sensations and ideas, he supposed what was false; and when Kant supposed that the objectivity of things in space *consisted* in the fact that they were "Vorstellungen" having to one another different relations from those which the same "Vorstellungen" have to one another in subjective experience, he supposed what was equally false. I am as directly aware of the existence of material things in space as of my own sensations; and *what* I am aware of with regard to each is exactly the same—namely that in one case the material thing, and in the other case my sensation does really exist. The question requiring to be asked about material things is thus not: What reason have we for supposing that anything exists *corresponding* to our sensations? but: What reason have we for supposing that material things do *not* exist, since *their* existence has precisely the same evidence as that of our sensations? That either exist *may* be false; but if it is a reason for doubting the existence of matter, that it is an inseparable aspect of our experience, the same reasoning will prove conclusively that our experience does not exist either, since that must also be an inseparable aspect of our experience of *it*. The only *reasonable* alternative to the admission that matter exists *as well as* spirit, is absolute Scepticism—that, as likely as not *nothing* exists at all. All other suppositions—the Agnostic's, that something, at all events, does exist, as much as the Idealist's, that spirit does—are, if we have no reason for believing in matter, as baseless as the grossest superstitions.

MARTIN HEIDEGGER
1889–1976

Martin Heidegger was born and died in the small German town of Messkirch in the Black Forest region of Baden-Württemberg. His father was the caretaker of the local Catholic church. Heidegger was reared as a Catholic and attended local secondary schools, where he was particularly interested in the ancient Greeks and the classics; this classical heritage remained the bedrock of his intellectual life. As a teenager in a Jesuit seminary, he was captivated by Franz Brentano's work on Aristotle's understanding of "Being." He made the study of Being his life's work and never wavered from that goal.

After a brief period as a Jesuit novice, Heidegger studied philosophy at the University of Freiburg. Excused from World War I for health reasons, he finished his studies in 1916 with a thesis on the medieval thinker John Duns Scotus. For the next seven years, he taught at the university, the last three years as the assistant to Edmund Husserl. During this period of time, Heidegger apprenticed himself to Husserl's phenomenological method, using it on his own special study of Being. In 1923, Heidegger moved to the University of Marburg where, in 1927, he published *Being and Time*, which proved to be his *magnum opus*. This work was dedicated to his teacher and friend Husserl. When Husserl retired in 1928, Heidegger assumed Husserl's chair of philosophy at the University of Freiburg.

What followed is one of the most controversial episodes in recent philosophy. When the Nazis came to power in 1933, the rector of the University of Freiburg was ousted and Heidegger was elected to replace him. In the course of his inaugural lecture as rector, Heidegger made the following remarks:

"Academic Freedom," celebrated so often, is banished from the German university;
. . . this freedom was not genuine because it was only negative. . . . The concept of
freedom [for] the German student is now brought back to its truth. From this truth
the bond and service of the German student will unfold in [the] future.*

Later that same year Heidegger wrote in the student newspaper:

Doctrine and "ideas" shall no longer govern your existence. The Führer himself,
and only he, is the current and future reality of Germany, and his word is your law.
Learn to know ever more deeply within you: "From now on every matter demands
determination and every action demands responsibility."
   Heil Hitler!
   MARTIN HEIDEGGER**

Critics claim that Heidegger had always been sympathetic to the Nazi cause
and that he apparently disowned his teacher Husserl (who was Jewish). As late
as 1953, Heidegger affirmed the "inner truth and greatness" of the Nazi movement. He once said that philosophy could be done properly only in either the
German or the Greek language and that among the moderns, the Germans alone,
as a people placed by history between the barbarians of America to the west and
Russia to the east, could save Western thought.

Heidegger's supporters point to his refusal to endorse the firing of two anti-
Nazi deans, which led to his resignation as rector within a year. Furthermore, say
some, it is unfair to judge Heidegger's early support for the Nazis from a
post–Second World War point of view. Heidegger in 1933 could not be expected
to know the unspeakable horrors of 1939 to 1945. Finally, supporters ask
philosophers especially to avoid the *argumentum ad hominem:* Even if Heidegger were partially compromised, that is not sufficient reason to dismiss a whole
body of thought.

Whatever the truth in this debate, Allied occupation powers considered the
evidence of Nazi collaboration sufficient to bar Heidegger from teaching between 1945 and 1951. Hence, after the war, Heidegger spent much of his time in
his simple hut at Todtnauberg in the Black Forest. He retired permanently from
teaching in 1959. Late in life he visited Greece and France but lived his final
years largely in quiet seclusion.

*   *   *

In his major work, *Being and Time (Sein und Zeit),* Heidegger announced the interest that would dominate his writings throughout his life: "The question of the
meaning of Being." According to Heidegger, the Pre-Socratics had understood
Being, but subsequent Western thinkers had forgotten Being itself by focusing
too intently on individual beings. As a result, contemporary metaphysics no
longer recalled the seminal question of Being.

   **Die Selbstbehauptung der Deutschen Universität (The Self-Affirmation of the German Univer-
sity, 1933)* as quoted in Walter Kaufmann, *Discovering the Mind, Volume II: Nietzsche, Heidegger,
and Buber* (New York: McGraw-Hill, 1980), p. 221.
   **Freiburger Studentenzeitung, November 3, 1933, p. 1, quoted in Martin Heidegger, *German
Existentialism,* translated with an introduction by Dagobert D. Runes (New York: Philosophical Library, 1965), pp. 27–28.

Nazi Party Congress at Nuremberg, 1934 (Hitler is standing in the center). The lives of an entire generation of philosophers were directly influenced by Hitler's rise to power in 1934. Husserl died as an outcast because of his Jewish ancestry; Heidegger was an early Nazi sympathizer (though there is a great deal of debate about his later feelings toward and involvement with the party); Sartre was a German prisoner-of-war and together with Merleau-Ponty was later a member of the resistance; Wittgenstein volunteered as a hospital orderly in England; and Quine, Austin, and Davidson served in the Allied war effort. *(National Archive)*

In order to gain some understanding of Being, Heidegger suggests we examine the one being with which we are intimately acquainted: the human being. The phenomenological method (Husserl), which "unconceals" the data of experience by allowing these data to "show themselves," provides the way to such an examination. Using this method to examine the self, one discovers one's self as a "being-in-the-world" or *Dasein* ("being-there").

Dasein is different from other realities. First, "in its very Being, that Being is an issue for it"; that is, *Dasein* is aware of Being. Second, the kind of Being of which *Dasein* is aware is called "existence." Human existence is not to be grasped the way one understands the existence of rocks or planets, but in the special ways of anticipation of, and decision for, possibilities. As the self confronts its choices, it especially recognizes that with death, "being-in-the-world" eventually becomes "no-longer-being-there." This awareness of *Dasein* as "being-toward-death" is filled with *Angst* (dread). Borrowing Kierkegaard's analysis of dread, Heidegger says that the self can try to avoid this *Angst* by losing the "I" in the "they"—that is, by ignoring its individuality and becoming part of the crowd. But a "they" existence is "inauthentic" and removed from Being. Instead, authentic being—"being-toward-death"—can reveal to *Dasein* a "freedom" that releases it from the "Illusions of the 'they'" and allows it to embrace Angst.

In our first selection, Chapter 1 of *An Introduction to Metaphysics* (1953), given here in the Ralph Manheim translation, Heidegger puts the question of Being in stark terms: "Why is there anything at all, rather than nothing?" This might seem an odd question to us, but it is odd (asserts Heidegger) only because we have lost our original amazement in the very presence of Being itself. Following a lengthy discussion of this issue, Heidegger asks the further question, "How is it with being?" Not well at all, he concludes. Heidegger argues that modern "technological frenzy" has led us to the brink of disaster because it induces the awful forgetfulness of Being. But Heidegger does not end with pessimism. It is possible, he concludes,

> to recapture, to repeat, the beginning of our historical spiritual existence, in order to transform it into a new beginning . . . to restore man's historical being-there (*Dasein*) . . . to the domain of being, which it was originally incumbent on man to open up for himself.

Our second selection, "Building Dwelling Thinking,"* translated by Albert Hofstadter, gives an example of this recovery of Being. According to Heidegger, "It is language that tells us about the nature of a thing. . . ." So by analyzing language it is possible to uncover Being. Applying this insight, Heidegger examines words for "building" and "dwelling" and concludes that

1. Building is really dwelling.
2. Dwelling is the manner in which mortals are on the earth.
3. Building as dwelling unfolds into the building that cultivates growing things and the building that erects buildings.

In fact, according to Heidegger, dwelling is "*the basic character* of Being in keeping with which mortals exist." Accordingly he goes on to explain in some detail what it means to talk of "building" and what it is to say that we "dwell." He concludes that while we may talk about housing shortages, the real issue is that we must learn what it is to dwell at all.

Heidegger has had more than his share of critics. Analytic philosophers have particularly criticized his use of language. One such philosopher concluded that "Heidegger's account of human life, where it is not vacuous, is transparently false."** However, despite the criticisms of his life and thought, Heidegger has profoundly affected philosophy—especially in the field he originated: philosophical hermeneutics. Further, his insights have been developed in psychoanalysis and literary theory and in phenomenology and theology, and they continue to shape contemporary views.

*   *   *

---

*Note the lack of commas in the title to emphasize the essential connectedness of these three concepts.

**Alasdair MacIntyre, "Existentialism," in D.J. O'Connor, *A Critical History of Western Philosophy* (New York: The Free Press, 1964), p. 518.

General introductions to Heidegger's thought include Marjorie Grene, *Martin Heidegger* (New York: Hillary House, 1957); W.J. Richardson, *Heidegger: Through Phenomenology to Thought* (New York: Humanities Press, 1963); J.A. Kockelman, *Heidegger: A First Introduction to His Philosophy,* translated by T. Schrynemakers (Pittsburgh, PA: Duquesne University Press, 1965); J.L. Mehta, *Martin Heidegger: The Way and the Vision* (Honolulu: University Press of Hawaii, 1976); George Steiner, *Martin Heidegger* (New York: Viking Press, 1978); Michael Inwood, *Heidegger* (Oxford: Oxford University Press, 1997); and Herman Philipse, *Heidegger's Philosophy of Being: A Critical Interpretation* (Princeton: Princeton University Press, 1999). For criticism of Heidegger's thought, see Walter Kaufmann, *Discovering the Mind, Volume II: Nietzsche, Heidegger, and Buber* (New York: McGraw-Hill, 1980); Hans-Georg Gadamer, *Heidegger's Ways,* translated by John W. Stanley (Albany, NY: SUNY Press, 1994); and Joanna Hodge, *Heidegger and Ethics* (Oxford: Routledge, 1995). Michael Gelven, *A Commentary on Heidegger's "Being and Time"* (New York: Harper & Row, 1970); E.F. Kaelin, *Heidegger's "Being and Time": A Reading for Readers* (Tallahassee: University Presses of Florida, 1988); and Stephen Mulhall, *Heidegger and Being and Time* (Oxford: Routledge, 1996) provide guides to Heidegger's major work. For comparative studies, see Arne Naess, *Four Modern Philosophers: Carnap, Wittgenstein, Heidegger, Sartre,* translated by Alastair Hannay (Chicago: University of Chicago Press, 1968); Timothy J. Stapleton, *Husserl and Heidegger* (Albany, NY: SUNY Press, 1983); Allan Megill, *Prophets of Extremity: Nietzsche, Heidegger, Foucault, Derrida* (Berkeley: University of California Press, 1985); and Ron L. Cooper, *Heidegger and Whitehead: A Phenomenological Examination into the Intelligibility of Experience* (Athens: Ohio University Press, 1993). Collections of essays include Thomas Sheehan, ed., *Heidegger: The Man and the Thinker* (Chicago: Precedent, 1981); Hubert L. Dreyfus and Harrison Hall, eds., *Heidegger: A Critical Reader* (Oxford: Basil Blackwell, 1992); John Sallis, ed., *Reading Heidegger* (Bloomington: Indiana University Press, 1993); Charles Guignon, ed., *The Cambridge Companion to Heidegger* (Cambridge: Cambridge University Press, 1993); and the multivolume Christopher Macann, ed., *Martin Heidegger: Critical Assessments* (Oxford: Routledge, 1993). For advanced studies on Heidegger, see titles in the series "Northwestern University Studies in Phenomenology & Existential Philosophy."

Finally, out of the large number of recent books on the controversy surrounding Heidegger's Nazi ties, one may consult Victor Farías, *Heidegger and Nazism,* edited by Joseph Margolis and Tom Rockmore (Philadelphia: Temple University Press, 1989); Joseph Margolis and Tom Rockmore, eds., *The Heidegger Case* (Philadelphia: Temple University Press, 1992); Tom Rockmore, *On Heidegger's Nazism and Philosophy* (Berkeley: University of California Press, 1992); Heinrich Wiegrand Petzet, *Encounters and Dialogues with Martin Heidegger 1929–1976,* translated by Parvis Emad and Kenneth Malz (Chicago: University of Chicago Press, 1993); Richard Wolin, ed., *The Heidegger Controversy* (Cambridge, MA: MIT Press, 1993); Leslie Paul Thiele, *Timely Meditations: Martin Heidegger and Postmodern Politics* (Princeton, NJ: Princeton University Press, 1995); Berel Lang, *Heidegger's Silence* (Ithaca, NY: Cornell University Press, 1996); and Julian Young, *Heidegger, Philosophy, and Nazism* (Cambridge: Cambridge University Press, 1997).

AN INTRODUCTION TO METAPHYSICS
(in part)

CHAPTER 1: THE FUNDAMENTAL QUESTION
OF METAPHYSICS

Why are there essents* rather than nothing? That is the question. Clearly it is no ordinary question. "Why are there essents, why is there anything at all, rather than nothing?"—obviously this is the first of all questions, though not in a chronological sense. Individuals and peoples ask a good many questions in the course of their historical passage through time. They examine, explore, and test a good many things before they run into the question "Why are there essents rather than nothing?" Many men never encounter this question, if by encounter we mean not merely to hear and read about it as an interrogative formulation but to ask the question, that is, to bring it about, to raise it, to feel its inevitability.

And yet each of us is grazed at least once, perhaps more than once, by the hidden power of this question, even if he is not aware of what is happening to him. The question looms in moments of great despair, when things tend to lose all their weight and all meaning becomes obscured. Perhaps it will strike but once like a muffled bell that rings into our life and gradually dies away. It is present in moments of rejoicing, when all the things around us are transfigured and seem to be there for the first time, as if it might be easier to think they are not than to understand that they are and are as they are. The question is upon us in boredom, when we are equally removed from despair and joy, and everything about us seems so hopelessly commonplace that we no longer care whether anything is or is not—and with this the question "Why are there essents rather than nothing?" is evoked in a particular form.

But this question may be asked expressly, or, unrecognized as a question, it may merely pass through our lives like a brief gust of wind; it may press hard upon us, or, under one pretext or another, we may thrust it away from us and silence it. In any case it is never the question that we ask first in point of time.

But it is the first question in another sense—in regard to rank. This may be clarified in three ways. The question "Why are there essents rather than nothing?" is first in rank for us first because it is the most far reaching, second because it is the deepest, and finally because it is the most fundamental of all questions.

It is the widest of all questions. It confines itself to no particular essent of whatever kind. The question takes in everything, and this means not only everything that is present in the broadest sense but also everything that ever was or will be. The range of this question finds its limit only in nothing, in that which simply is not and never was. Everything that is not nothing is covered by this question, and ultimately even nothing itself; not because it is *something*, since after all we speak of it, but because it is nothing. Our question reaches out so far that we can never go further. We do not inquire into this and that, or into each essent in turn, but from the very outset into the essent as

*Essents" = "existents," "things that are."

Martin Heidegger, *An Introduction to Metaphysics,* translated by Ralph Manheim, Chapter 1 (New Haven, CT: Yale University Press, 1959), pp. 1–51. Reprinted by permission.

a whole, or, as we say for reasons to be discussed below: into the essent as such in its entirety.

This broadest of questions is also the deepest: Why are there essents . . . ? Why, that is to say, on what ground? from what source does the essent derive? on what ground does it stand? The question is not concerned with particulars, with what essents are and of what nature at any time, here and there, with how they can be changed, what they can be used for, and so on. The question aims at the ground of what is insofar as it is. To seek the ground is to try to get to the bottom; what is put in question is thus related to the ground. However, since the question is a question, it remains to be seen whether the grounds arrived at is really a ground, that is, whether it provides a foundation; whether it is a primal ground [Ur-grund]; or whether it fails to provide a foundation and is an abyss [Ab-grund]; or whether the ground is neither one nor the other but presents only a perhaps necessary appearance of foundation—in other words, it is a non-ground [Ungrund]. Be that as it may, the ground in question must account for the being of the essent as such. This question "why" does not look for causes that are of the same kind and on the same level as the essent itself. This "why" does not move on any one plane but penetrates to the "underlying" ["zu-grunde" liegend] realms and indeed to the very last of them, to the limit; turning away from the surface, from all shallowness, it strives toward the depths; this broadest of all questions is also the deepest.

Finally, this broadest and deepest question is also the most fundamental. What do we mean by this? If we take the question in its full scope, namely the essent as such in its entirety, it readily follows that in asking this question we keep our distance from every particular and individual essent, from every this and that. For we mean the essent as a whole, without any special preference. Still, it is noteworthy that in this questioning one kind of essent persists in coming to the fore, namely the men who ask the question. But the question should not concern itself with any particular essent. In the spirit of its unrestricted scope, all essents are of equal value. An elephant in an Indian jungle "is" just as much as some chemical combustion process at work on the planet Mars, and so on.

Accordingly, if our question "Why are there essents rather than nothing?" is taken in its fullest sense, we must avoid singling out any special, particular essent, including man. For what indeed is man? Consider the earth within the endless darkness of space in the universe. By way of comparison it is a tiny grain of sand; between it and the next grain of its own size there extends a mile or more of emptiness; on the surface of this grain of sand there lives a crawling, bewildered swarm of supposedly intelligent animals, who for a moment have discovered knowledge.* And what is the temporal extension of a human life amid all the millions of years? Scarcely a move of the second hand, a breath. Within the essent as a whole there is no legitimate ground for singling out this essent which is called mankind and to which we ourselves happen to belong

But whenever the essent as a whole enters into this question, a privileged, unique relation arises between it and the act of questioning. For through this questioning the essent as a whole is for the first time opened up as such with a view to its possible ground, and in the act of questioning it is kept open. In relation to the essent as such in its entirety the asking of the question is not just any occurrence within the realm of the essent, like the falling of raindrops for example. The question "why" may be said to confront the essent as a whole, to break out of it, though never completely. But that is exactly why the act of questioning is privileged. Because it confronts the essent as a

*Cf. Nietzsche, Über Wahreit und Lüge im aussermoralischen Sinne. 1873 Nachlass.

whole, but does not break loose from it, the content of the question reacts upon the questioning itself. Why the why? What is the ground of this question "why" which presumes to ask after the ground of the essent as a whole? Is the ground asked for in this why not merely a foreground—which would imply that the sought-for ground is again an essent? Does not the "first" question nevertheless come first in view of the intrinsic rank of the question of being and its modulations?

To be sure, the things in the world, the essents, are in no way affected by our asking of the question "Why are there essents rather than nothing?" Whether we ask it or not, the planets move in their orbits, the sap of life flows through plant and animal.

But *if* this question is asked and if the act of questioning is really carried out, the content and the object of the question react inevitably on the act of questioning. Accordingly this questioning is not just any occurrence but a privileged happening that we call an event.

This question and all the questions immediately rooted in it, the questions in which this one question unfolds—this question "why" is incommensurable with any other. It encounters the search for its own why. At first sight the question "Why the why?" looks like a frivolous repetition ad infinitum of the same interrogative formulation, like an empty and unwarranted brooding over words. Yes, beyond a doubt, that is how it looks. The question is only whether we wish to be taken in by this superficial look and so regard the whole matter as settled, or whether we are capable of finding a significant event in this recoil of the question "why" upon itself.

But if we decline to be taken in by surface appearances we shall see that this question "why," this question as to the essents as such in its entirety, goes beyond any mere playing with words, provided we possess sufficient intellectual energy to make the question actually recoil into its "why"—for it will not do so of its own accord. In so doing we find out that this privileged question "why" has its ground in a leap through which man thrusts away all the previous security, whether real or imagined, of his life. The question is asked only in this leap; it is the leap; without it there is no asking. What "leap" means here will be elucidated later. Our questioning is not yet the leap; for this it must undergo a transformation; it still stands perplexed in the face of the essent. Here it may suffice to say that the leap in this questioning opens up its own source—with this leap the question arrives at its own ground. We call such a leap, which opens up its own source, the original source or origin *[Ur-sprung]*, the findings of one's own ground. It is because the question "Why are there essents rather than nothing?" breaks open the ground for all authentic questions and is thus at the origin *[Ur-sprung]* of them all that we must recognize it as the most fundamental of all questions.

It is the most fundamental of questions because it is the broadest and deepest, and conversely.

In this threefold sense the question is the first in rank—first, that is, in the order of questioning within the domain which this first question opens, defining its scope and thus founding it. Our question is the *question* of all authentic questions, i.e. of all self-questioning questions, and whether consciously or not it is necessarily implicit in every question. No questioning and accordingly no single scientific "problem" can be fully intelligible if it does not include, i.e. ask, the question of all questions. Let us be clear about this from the start: it can never be objectively determined whether anyone, whether we, really ask this question, that is whether we make the leap, or never get beyond a verbal formula. In a historical setting that does not recognize questioning as a fundamental human force, the question immediately loses its rank.

Anyone for whom the Bible is divine revelation and truth has the answer to the question "Why are there essents rather than nothing?" even before it is asked: everything that is, except God himself, has been created by Him. God himself, the increate creator, "is." One who holds to such faith can in a way participate in the asking of our question, but he cannot really question without ceasing to be a believer and taking all the consequences of such a step. He will only be able to act "as if" . . . On the other hand a faith that does not perpetually expose itself to the possibility of unfaith is no faith but merely a convenience: the believer simply makes up his mind to adhere to the traditional doctrine. This is neither faith nor questioning, but the indifference of those who can busy themselves with everything, sometimes even displaying a keen interest in faith as well as questioning.

What we have said about security in faith as one position in regard to the truth does not imply that the biblical "In the beginning God created heaven and earth" is an answer to our question. Quite aside from whether these words from the Bible are true or false for faith, they can supply no answer to our question because they are in no way related to it. Indeed, they cannot even be brought into relation with our question. From the standpoint of faith our question is "foolishness."

Philosophy is this very foolishness. A "Christian philosophy" is a round square and a misunderstanding. There is, to be sure, a thinking and questioning elaboration of the world of Christian experience, i.e. of faith. That is theology. Only epochs which no longer fully believe in the true greatness of the task of theology arrive at the disastrous notion that philosophy can help to provide a refurbished theology if not a substitute for theology, which will satisfy the needs and tastes of the time. For the original Christian faith philosophy is foolishness. To philosophize is to ask "Why are there essents rather than nothing?" Really to ask the question signifies: a daring attempt to fathom this unfathomable question by disclosing what it summons us to ask, to push our questioning to the very end. Where such an attempt occurs there is philosophy.

It would not serve our purpose to begin our discussion with a detailed report on philosophy. But there are a few things that all must know who wish to concern themselves with philosophy. They can be briefly stated.

All essential philosophical questioning is necessarily untimely. This is so because philosophy is always projected far in advance of its time, or because it connects the present with its antecedent, with what *initially* was. Philosophy always remains a knowledge which not only cannot be adjusted to a given epoch but on the contrary imposes its measure upon its epoch.

Philosophy is essentially untimely because it is one of those few things that can never find an immediate echo in the present. When such an echo seems to occur, when a philosophy becomes fashionable, either it is no real philosophy or it has been misinterpreted and misused for ephemeral and extraneous purposes.

Accordingly, philosophy cannot be directly learned like manual and technical skills; it cannot be directly applied, or judged by its usefulness in the manner of economic or other professional knowledge.

But what is useless can still be a force, perhaps the only real force that has no immediate echo in everyday life can be intimately bound up with a nation's profound historical development, and can even anticipate it. What is untimely will have its own times. This is true of philosophy. Consequently there is no way of determining once and for all what the task of philosophy is, and accordingly what must be expected of it. Every stage and every beginning of its development bears within it its own law. All that can be said is what philosophy cannot be and cannot accomplish.

A question has been stated: "Why are there essents rather than nothing?" We have claimed first place for this question and explained in what sense it is regarded as first.

We have not even begun to ask the question itself, but have digressed into a discussion about it. Such a digression is indispensable. For this question has nothing in common with our habitual concerns. There is no way of familiarizing ourselves with this question by a gradual transition from the things to which we are accustomed. Hence it must, as it were, be singled out in advance, presented. Yet in introducing the question and speaking of it, we must not postpone, let alone forget, the questioning itself.

Here then let us conclude our preliminary remarks.

Every essential form of spiritual life is marked by ambiguity. The less commensurate it is with other forms, the more it is misinterpreted.

Philosophy is one of the few autonomous creative possibilities and at times necessities of man's historical being-there.* The current misinterpretations of philosophy, all of which have some truth about them, are legion. Here we shall mention only two, which are important because of the light they throw on the present and future situation of philosophy. The first misinterpretation asks too much of philosophy. The second distorts its function.

Roughly speaking, philosophy always aims at the first and last grounds of the essent, with particular emphasis on man himself and on the meaning and goals of human being-there. This might suggest that philosophy can and must provide a foundation on which a nation will build its historical life and culture. But this is beyond the power of philosophy. As a rule such excessive demands take the form of a belittling of philosophy. It is said, for example: Because metaphysics did nothing to pave the way for the revolution it should be rejected. This is no cleverer than saying that because the carpenter's bench is useless for flying it should be abolished. Philosophy can never *directly* supply the energies and create the opportunities and methods that bring about a historical change; for one thing, because philosophy is always the concern of the few. Which few? The creators, those who initiate profound transformations. It spreads only indirectly, by devious paths that can never be laid out in advance, until at last, at some future date, it sinks to the level of a commonplace; but by then it has long been forgotten as original philosophy.

What philosophy essentially can and must be is this: a thinking that breaks the paths and opens the perspectives of the knowledge that sets the norms and hierarchies, of the knowledge in which and by which a people fulfills itself historically and culturally, the knowledge that kindles and necessitates all inquiries and thereby threatens all values.

The second misinterpretation involves a distortion of the function of philosophy. Even if philosophy can provide no foundation for a culture, the argument goes, it is nevertheless a cultural force, whether because it gives us an over-all, systematic view of what is, supplying a useful chart by which we may find our way amid the various possible things and realms of things, or because it relieves the sciences of their work by reflecting on their premises, basic concepts, and principles. Philosophy is expected to promote and even to accelerate—to make easier as it were—the practical and technical business of culture.

---

*[The word *Dasein* is ordinarily translated as "existence." It is used in "normal," popular discourse. But Heidegger breaks it into its components *Da*, "there" and *Sein*, "being," and puts his own definition on it. In general he means man's conscious, historical existence in the world, which is always projected into a there beyond its here. The German word *Dasein* has often been carried over into translations; the English strikes me as preferable]

But—it is in the very nature of philosophy never to make things easier but only more difficult. And this not merely because its language strikes the everyday understanding as strange if not insane. Rather, it is the authentic function of philosophy to challenge historical being there and hence, in the last analysis, being pure and simple. It restores to things, to the essents, their weight (being). How so? Because the challenge is one of the essential prerequisites for the birth of all greatness, and in speaking of greatness we are referring primarily to the works and destinies of nations. We can speak of historical destiny only where an authentic knowledge of things dominates man's being-there. And it is philosophy that opens up the paths and perspectives of such knowledge.

The misinterpretations with which philosophy is perpetually beset are promoted most of all by people of our kind, that is, by professors of philosophy. It is our customary business—which may be said to be justified and even useful—to transmit a certain knowledge of the philosophy of the past, as part of a general education. Many people suppose that this is philosophy itself, whereas at best it is the technique of philosophy.

In correcting these two misinterpretations I cannot hope to give you at one stroke a clear conception of philosophy. But I do hope that you will be on your guard when the most current judgments and even supposed observations assail you unawares. Such judgments are often disarming, precisely because they seem so natural. You hear remarks such as "Philosophy leads to nothing," "You can't do anything with philosophy," and readily imagine that they confirm an experience of your own. There is no denying the soundness of these two phrases, particularly common among scientists and teachers of science. Any attempt to refute them by proving that after all it does "lead to something" merely strengthens the prevailing misinterpretation to the effect that the everyday standards by which we judge bicycles or sulphur baths are applicable to philosophy.

It is absolutely correct and proper to say that "You can't do anything with philosophy." It is only wrong to suppose that this is the last word on philosophy. For the rejoinder imposes itself: granted that we cannot do anything with philosophy, might not philosophy, if we concern ourselves with it, do something *with* us? So much for what philosophy is not.

At the outset we stated a question: "Why are there essents rather than nothing?" We have maintained that to ask this question is to philosophize. When in our thinking we open our minds to this question, we first of all cease to dwell in any of the familiar realms. We set aside everything that is on the order of the day. Our question goes beyond the familiar and the things that have their place in everyday life. Nietzsche once said (*Werke* 7, 269): "A philosopher is a man who never ceases to experience, see, hear, suspect, hope, and dream extraordinary things , , ,"

To philosophize is to inquire into the extra-ordinary. But because, as we have just suggested, this questioning recoils upon itself, not only what is asked after is extra-ordinary but also the asking itself. In other words: this questioning does not lie along the way so that we bump into it one day unexpectedly. Nor is it part of everyday life: there is no requirement or regulation that forces us into it; it gratifies no urgent or prevailing need. The questioning itself is "out of order." It is entirely voluntary, based wholly and uniquely on the mystery of freedom, on what we have called the leap. The same Nietzsche said: "Philosophy . . . is a voluntary living amid ice and mountain heights" (*Werke*, 15, 2). To philosophize, we may now say, is an extra-ordinary inquiry into the extra-ordinary.

In the age of the earliest and crucial unfolding of Western philosophy among the Greeks, who first raised the authentic question of the essent as such in its entirety, the essent was called ⟨*physis*⟩. This basic Greek word for the essent is customarily translated as "nature." This derives from the Latin translation, *natura,* which properly means "to be born," "birth." But with this Latin translation the original meaning of the Greek word ⟨*physis*⟩ is thrust aside, the actual philosophical force of the Greek word is destroyed. This is true not only of the Latin translation of *this* word but of all other Roman translations of the Greek philosophical language. What happened in this translation from the Greek into the Latin is not accidental and harmless; it marks the first stage in the process by which we cut ourselves off and alienated ourselves from the original essence of Greek philosophy. The Roman translation was later taken over by Christianity and the Christian Middle Ages. And the Christian Middle Ages were prolonged in modern philosophy, which, moving in the conceptual world of the Middle Ages, coined those representations and terms by means of which we still try to understand the beginnings of Western philosophy. These beginnings are regarded as something that present-day philosophers have supposedly transcended and long since left behind them.

But now let us skip over this whole process of deformation and decay and attempt to regain the unimpaired strength of language and words; for words and language are not wrappings in which things are packed for the commerce of those who write and speak. It is in words and language that things first come into being and are. For this reason the misuse of language in idle talk, in slogans and phrases, destroys our authentic relation to things. What does the word ⟨*physis*⟩ denote? It denotes self-blossoming emergence (e.g. the blossoming of a rose), opening up, unfolding, that which manifests itself in such unfolding and perseveres and endures in it; in short, the realm of things that emerge and linger on. According to the dictionary ⟨*phyein*⟩ means to grow or make to grow. But what does growing mean? Does it imply only to increase quantitatively, to become more and larger?

⟨*Physis*⟩ as emergence can be observed everywhere, e.g. in celestial phenomena (the rising of the sun), in the rolling of the sea, in the growth of plants, in the coming forth of man and animal from the womb. But ⟨*physis*⟩, the realm of that which arises, is not synonymous with these phenomena, which today we regard as part of "nature." This opening up and inward-jutting-beyond-itself [*in-sich-aus-sich-hinausstehen*] must not be taken as a process among other processes that we observe in the realm of the essent. ⟨*Physis*⟩ is being itself, by virtue of which essents become and remain observable.

The Greeks did not learn what ⟨*physis*⟩ is through natural phenomena, but the other way around: it was through a fundamental poetic and intellectual experience of being that they discovered what they had to call ⟨*physis*⟩. It was this discovery that enabled them to gain a glimpse into nature in the restricted sense. Hence ⟨*physis*⟩ originally encompassed heaven as well as earth, the stone as well as the plant, the animal as well as man, and it encompassed human history as a work of men and the gods; and ultimately and first of all, it meant the gods themselves as subordinated to destiny. ⟨*Physis*⟩ means the power that emerges and the enduring realm under its sway. This power of emerging and enduring includes "becoming" as well as "being" in the restricted sense of inert duration. ⟨*Physis*⟩ is the process of a-rising, of emerging from the hidden, whereby the hidden is first made to stand.

But if, as is usually done, ⟨*physis*⟩ is taken not in the original sense of the power to emerge and endure, but in the later and present signification of nature; and if moreover the motion of material things, of the atoms and electrons, of what modern physics investigates as ⟨*physis*⟩, is taken to be the fundamental manifestation of nature, then the first philosophy of the Greeks becomes a nature philosophy, in which all things are held to be of a material nature. In this case the beginning of Greek philosophy, as is perfectly proper for a beginning according to the common-sense view, gives the impression of what we, once again in Latin, designate as primitive. Thus the Greeks become essentially a higher type of Hottentot, whom modern science has left far behind. Disregarding the lesser absurdities involved in this view of the beginning of Western philosophy as something primitive, we need only say this: those who put forward such an interpretation forget that what is under discussion is philosophy, one of man's few great achievements. But what is great can only begin great. Its beginning is in fact the greatest thing of all. A small beginning belongs only to the small, whose dubious greatness it is to diminish all things; small are the beginnings of decay, though it may later become great in the sense of the enormity of total annihilation.

The great begins great, maintains itself only through the free recurrence of greatness within it, and if it is great ends also in greatness. So it is with the philosophy of the Greeks. It ended in greatness with Aristotle. Only prosaic common sense and the little man imagine that the great must endure forever, and equate this duration with eternity.

The Greeks called the essent as a whole ⟨physis⟩. But it should be said in passing that even within Greek philosophy a narrowing of the word set in forthwith, although the original meaning did not vanish from the experience, knowledge, and orientation of Greek philosophy. Knowledge of its original meaning still lives on in Aristotle, when he speaks of the grounds of the essent as such (see *Metaphysics,* I, 1003a27).

But this narrowing of ⟨physis⟩ in the direction of "physics" did not occur in the way that we imagine today. We oppose the psychic, the animated, the living, to the "physical." But for the Greeks all this belonged to ⟨physis⟩ and continued to do so even after Aristotle. They contrasted it with what they called ⟨thesis⟩, thesis, ordinance, or ⟨nomos⟩, law, rule in the sense of ⟨ethos⟩. This, however, denotes not mere norms but mores, based on freely accepted obligations and traditions; it is that which concerns free behavior and attitudes, the shaping of man's historical being, the ⟨ethos⟩ which under the influence of morality was later degraded to the ethical.

The meaning of ⟨physis⟩ is further restricted by contrast with ⟨technē⟩—which denotes neither art nor technology but a knowledge, the ability to plan and organize freely, to master institutions (cf. Plato's *Phaedrus*). ⟨Technē⟩ is creating, building in the sense of a deliberate producing. (It would require a special study to explain what is essentially the same in ⟨physis⟩ and ⟨technē⟩.) The physical was opposed to the historical, a domain which for the Greeks was part of the originally broader concept of ⟨physis⟩. But this has nothing whatever to do with a naturalistic interpretation of history. The realm of being as such and as a whole is ⟨physis⟩—i.e. its essence and character are defined as that which emerges and endures. It is experienced primarily through what in a way imposes itself most immediately on our attention, and this was the later, narrower sense of ⟨physis⟩: ⟨ta physei onta, ta physika⟩, nature. If the question concerning ⟨physis⟩ in general was asked at all, i.e. if it was asked: What is the realm of being as such? it was primarily ⟨ta physei onta⟩ that gave the point of departure. Yet from the very outset the question could not dwell in this or that realm of nature, inanimate bodies, plants, animals, but had to reach out beyond ⟨ta physika⟩.

In Greek, "beyond something" is expressed by the word ⟨meta⟩. Philosophical inquiry into the realm of being as such is ⟨meta ta physika⟩; this inquiry goes beyond the essent, it is metaphysics. Here it is not important to follow the genesis and history of this term in detail.

Accordingly, the question to which we have given first rank, "Why are there essents rather than nothing?" is the fundamental question of metaphysics. Metaphysics is a name for the pivotal point and core of all philosophy.

[In this introduction our treatment of the entire subject has been intentionally superficial and hence essentially vague. According to our explanation of the word ⟨*physis*⟩, it signifies the being of the essent. If the questioning is ⟨*peri physeōs*⟩, if it concerns the being of the essent, then the discussion has gone beyond ⟨*physis*⟩, beyond "physics" in the ancient sense, and essentially beyond ⟨*ta physika*⟩, beyond essents, and deals with being. From the very first "physics" has determined the essence and history of metaphysics. Even in the doctrines of being as pure act (Thomas Aquinas), as absolute concept (Hegel), as eternal recurrence of the identical will to power (Nietzsche), metaphysics has remained unalterably "physics."

But the inquiry into being as such is of a different nature and origin.

Within the purview of metaphysics and thinking on its level, we can, to be sure, consider the question about being as such as merely a mechanical repetition of the question about the essent as such. In this case the question about being as such is just another transcendental question, though one of a higher order. But this reinterpretation of the question about being as such bars the road to its appropriate unfolding.

However, this new interpretation comes readily to mind; it is bound to suggest itself, particularly as we have spoken in *Sein und Zeit* of a "transcendental horizon." But the "transcendental" there intended is not that of the subjective consciousness; rather, it defines itself in terms of the existential-ecstatic temporality of human being-there. Yet the reinterpretation of the question of being as such tends to take the same form as the question of the essent as such, chiefly because the essential origin of the question of the existent as such and with it the essence of metaphysics remain obscure. And this draws all questions that are in any way concerned with being into the indeterminate.

In the present attempt at an "introduction to metaphysics" I shall keep this confused state of affairs in mind.

In the current interpretation the "question of being" signifies the inquiry into the essent as such (metaphysics). But from the standpoint of *Sein und Zeit,* the "question of being" means the inquiry into being as such. This signification of the title is also the appropriate one from the standpoint of the subject matter and of linguistics; for the "question of being" in the sense of the metaphysical question regarding the essent as such does *not inquire* thematically into being. In this way of asking, being remains forgotten.

But just as ambiguous as the "question of being" referred to in the title is what is said about "forgetfulness of being." It is pointed out—quite correctly—that metaphysics inquires into the being of the essent and that it is therefore an obvious absurdity to impute a forgetfulness of being to metaphysics.

But if we consider the question of being in the sense of an inquiry into being as such, it becomes clear to anyone who follows our thinking that being as such is precisely hidden from metaphysics, and remains forgotten—and so radically that the forgetfulness of being, which itself falls into forgetfulness, is the unknown but enduring impetus to metaphysical questioning.

If for the treatment of the "question of being" in the indeterminate sense we choose the name "metaphysics," then the title of the present work is ambiguous. For at first sight the questioning seems to remain within the sphere of the essent as such, yet at the very first sentence it strives to depart from this sphere in order to consider and inquire into another realm. Actually the title of the work is deliberately ambiguous.

The fundamental question of this work is of a different kind from the leading question of metaphysics. Taking what was said in *Sein und Zeit* (pp. 21f. and 37f.) as a starting point, we inquired into the "*disclosure of being*." "Disclosure of being" means the unlocking of what forgetfulness of being closes and hides. And it is through this questioning that a light first falls on the essence of metaphysics that had hitherto also been hidden.]

"Introduction to metaphysics" means accordingly: an introduction to the asking of the fundamental question. But questions and particularly fundamental questions do not just occur like stones and water. Questions are not found ready-made like shoes and clothes and books. Questions are, and are only as they are actually asked. A leading into the asking of the fundamental questions is consequently not a going to something that lies and stands somewhere; no, this leading-to must first awaken and create the questioning. The leading is itself a questioning advance, a preliminary questioning. It is a leading for which in the very nature of things there can be no following. When we hear of disciples, "followers," as in a school of philosophy for example, it means that the nature of questioning is misunderstood. Such schools can exist only in the domain of scientific and technical work. Here everything has its definite hierarchical order. This work is also an indispensable part of philosophy and has today been lost. But the best technical ability can never replace the actual power of seeing and inquiring and speaking.

"Why are there essents rather than nothing?" That is the question. To state the interrogative sentence, even in a tone of questioning, is not yet to question. To repeat the interrogative sentence several times in succession does not necessarily breathe life into the questioning; on the contrary, saying the sentence over and over may well dull the questioning.

But even though the interrogative sentence is not the question and not the questioning, it must not be taken as a mere linguistic form of communication, as though, for example, the interrogative sentence were only a statement "about" a question. When I say to you "Why are there essents rather than nothing?" the purpose of my speaking and questioning is not to communicate to you the fact that a process of questioning is now at work within me. The spoken interrogative sentence can of course be interpreted in this way, but this means precisely that the questioning has not been heard. In this case you do not join me in questioning, nor do you question yourself. No sign of a questioning attitude or state of mind is awakened. Such a state of mind consists in a *willing* to know. Willing—that is no mere wishing or striving. Those who wish to know also seem to question; but they do not go beyond the stating of the question; they stop precisely where the question begins. To question is to will to know. He who wills, he who puts his whole existence into a will, is resolved. Resolve does not shift about; it does not shirk, but acts from out of the moment and never stops. Resolve is no mere decision to act, but the crucial beginning of action that anticipates and reaches through all action. To will is to be resolved. (The essence of willing is here carried back to determination *[Ent-schlossenheit, "unclosedness"]*. But the essence of resolve lies in the opening, the coming-out-of-cover *[Ent-borgenheit]* of human being-there into the clearing of being, and not in a storing up of energy for "action." See *Sein und Zeit,* §44 and §60. But its relation to being is one of letting-be. The idea that all willing should be grounded in letting-be offends the understanding. See my lecture *Vom Wesen der Wahrheit,* 1930.)

But to know means: to be able to stand in the truth. Truth is the manifestness of the essent. To know is accordingly the ability to stand *[stehen]* in the manifestness of the essent, to endure *[bestehen]* it. Merely to have information, however abundant, is not to know. Even if curricula and examination requirements concentrate this information into what is of the greatest practical importance, it still does not amount to knowledge. Even if this information, pruned down to the most indispensable needs, is "close to life," its possession is not knowledge. The man who possesses such information and has learned a few practical tricks, will still be perplexed in the presence of real reality, which is always different from what the philistine means by down-to-earth; he will always be a bungler. Why? Because he has no knowledge, for to know means *to be able to learn.*

In the common-sense view, to be sure, knowledge belongs to the man who has no further need to learn because he has finished learning. No, only that man is knowing who understands that he must keep learning over and over again and who above all, on the basis of this understanding, has attained to the point where he is always *able to learn.* This is much more difficult than to possess information.

Ability to learn presupposes ability to inquire. Inquiry is the willing to-know analyzed above: the resolve to be able to stand in the openness of the essent. Since we are concerned with the asking of the question that is first in rank, clearly the willing as well as the knowing is of a very special kind. So much the less will the interrogative sentence, even if it is uttered in an authentically questioning tone and even if the listener joins in the questioning, exhaustively reproduce the question. The questioning, which indeed is sounded in the interrogative sentence but which is still enclosed, wrapped up in the words, remains to be unwrapped. The questioning attitude must clarify and secure itself in this process, it must be consolidated by training.

Our next task lies in the development of the question "Why are there essents rather than nothing?" In what direction can it be asked? First of all the question is accessible in the interrogative sentence, which gives a kind of approximation of it. Hence its linguistic formulation must be correspondingly broad and loose. Let us consider our sentence in this respect. "Why are there essents rather than nothing?" The sentence has a caesura. "Why are there essents?" With these words the question is actually asked. The formulation of the question includes: 1) a definite indication of what is put into question, of what is *questioned;* 2) an indication of what the question is about, of what is asked. For it is clearly indicated what the question is about, namely the essent. What is asked after, that which is asked, is the why, i.e. the ground. What follows in the interrogative sentence, "rather than nothing," is only an appendage, which may be said to turn up of its own accord if for purposes of introduction we permit ourselves to speak loosely, a turn of phrase that says nothing further about the question or the object of questioning, an ornamental flourish. Actually the question is far more unambiguous and definite without such an appendage, which springs only from the prolixity of loose discourse. "Why are there essents?" The addition "rather than nothing" is dropped not only because we are striving for a strict formulation of the question but even more because it says nothing. For why should we go on to ask about nothing? Nothing is simply nothing. Here there is nothing more to inquire about. And above all, in talking about nothing or nothingness, we are not making the slightest advance toward the knowledge of the essent.

He who speaks of nothing does not know what he is doing. In speaking of nothing he makes it into a something. In speaking he speaks against what he intended. He contradicts himself. But discourse that contradicts itself offends against the fundamental rule of discourse (⟨*logos*⟩), against "logic." To speak of nothing is illogical. He who speaks and thinks illogically is unscientific. But he who goes so far as to speak of nothing in the realm of philosophy, where logic has its very home, exposes himself most particularly to the accusation of offending against the fundamental rule of all thinking. Such a speaking about nothing consists entirely of meaningless propositions. Moreover: he who takes the nothing seriously is allying himself with nothingness. He is patently promoting the spirit of negation and serving the cause of disintegration. Not only is speaking of nothing utterly repellent to thought; it also undermines all culture and all faith. What disregards the fundamental law of thought and also destroys faith and the will to build is pure nihilism.

On the basis of such considerations we shall do well, in our interrogative sentence, to cross out the superfluous words "rather than nothing" and limit the sentence to the simple and strict form: "Why are there essents?"

To this there would be no objection if . . . if in formulating our question, if altogether, in the asking of this question, we were as free as it may have seemed to us up to this point. But in asking this question we stand in a tradition. For philosophy has always, from time immemorial, asked about the ground of what is. With this question it began and with this question it will end, provided that it ends in greatness and not in an impotent decline. Ever since the question about the essent began, the question about the nonessent, about nothing, has gone side by side with it. And not only outwardly, in the manner of a by-product. Rather, the question about nothing has been asked with the same breadth, depth, and originality as the question about the essent. The manner of asking about nothing may be regarded as a gauge and hallmark for the manner of asking about the essent.

If we bear this in mind, the interrogative sentence uttered in the beginning, "Why are there essents rather than nothing?" seems to express the question about the essent far more adequately than the abbreviated version. It is not looseness of speech or prolixity that leads us to mention nothing. Nor is it an invention of ours; no, it is only strict observance of the original tradition regarding the meaning of the fundamental question.

Still, this speaking of nothing remains in general repellent to thought and in particular demoralizing. But what if both our concern for the fundamental rules of thought and our fear of nihilism, which both seem to counsel against speaking of nothing, should be based on a misunderstanding? And this indeed is the case. True, this misunderstanding is not accidental. It is rooted in long years of failure to understand the question about the essent. And this failure to understand arises from an increasingly hardened forgetfulness of being.

For it cannot be decided out of hand whether logic and its fundamental rules can, altogether, provide a standard for dealing with the question about the essent as such. It might be the other way around. Perhaps the whole body of logic as it is known to us, perhaps all the logic that we treat as a gift from heaven, is grounded in a very definite answer to the question about the essent; perhaps, in consequence, all thinking which solely follows the laws of thought prescribed by traditional logic is incapable from the very start of even understanding the question about the essent by its own resources, let alone actually unfolding the question and guiding it toward an answer. Actually it is only an appearance of strict, scientific method when we invoke the principle of contradiction and logic in general, in order to prove that all thinking and speaking about nothing are contradictory and therefore meaningless. In such a contention "logic" is regarded as a court of justice, established for all eternity, whose rights as first and last authority no rational man will impugn. Anyone who speaks against logic is therefore tacitly or explicitly accused of irresponsibility. And the mere accusation is taken as a proof and an argument relieving one of the need for any further, genuine reflection.

It is perfectly true that we cannot talk about nothing, as though it were a thing like the rain outside or a mountain or any object whatsoever. In principle, nothingness remains inaccessible to science. The man who wishes truly to speak about nothing must of necessity become unscientific. But this is a misfortune only so long as one supposes that scientific thinking is the only authentic rigorous thought, and that it alone can and must be made into the standard of philosophical thinking. But the reverse is true. All scientific thought is merely a derived form of philosophical thinking, which proceeded to freeze into its scientific cast. Philosophy never arises out of science or through science and it can never be accorded equal rank with the sciences. No, it is prior in rank, and not only "logically" or in a table representing the system of the sciences. Philosophy stands in a totally different realm and order. Only poetry stands in the same order as philosophy and its thinking, though poetry and thought are not the same thing. To speak of nothing will always remain a horror and an absurdity for science. But aside from the philosopher, the poet can do so—and not because, as common sense supposes, poetry is without strict rules, but because the spirit of poetry (only authentic and great poetry is meant) is essentially superior to the spirit that prevails in all mere science. By virtue of this superiority the poet always speaks as though the essent were being expressed and invoked for the first time. Poetry, like the thinking of the philosopher, has always so much world space to spare that in it each thing—a tree, a mountain, a house, the cry of a bird—loses all indifference and commonplaceness.

Authentic speaking about nothing always remains extraordinary. It cannot be vulgarized. It dissolves if it is placed in the cheap acid of a merely logical intelligence. Consequently true discourse about nothing can never be immediate like the description of a picture for example. Here I should like to cite a passage from one of Knut Hamsun's last works, *The Road Leads On*. The work forms a whole with *Vagabonds* and *August*. It describes the last years and end of this August, who embodies the uprooted modern man who can do everything equally well yet who cannot lose his ties with the extraordinary, because even in his weakness and despair he remains authentic and superior. In his last days August is alone in the high mountains. And the poet says: "Here he sits between his ears and all he hears is emptiness. An amusing conception, indeed. On the sea there were both motion and sound, something for the ear to feed upon, a chorus of waters. Here nothingness meets nothingness and the result is zero, not even a hole. Enough to make one shake one's head, utterly at a loss."*

We see that there is something very interesting about nothing. Let us then go back to our interrogative sentence; let us ask it through, and see whether this "rather than nothing" is merely a meaningless appendage or whether it does not have an essential meaning even in our provisional statement of the question.

Let us begin with the abbreviated, seemingly simpler, and ostensibly stricter form of the question: "Why are there essents?" When we inquire in this way, we start from the essent. The essent *is*. It is given, it confronts us; accordingly, it is to be found at any time, and it is, in certain realms, known to us. Now this essent, from which we start, is immediately questioned as to its ground. The questioning advances immediately toward a ground. Such a method is only an extension and enlargement, so to speak, of a method practiced in everyday life. Somewhere in the vineyard, for example, the vine-disease occurs; something incontestably present. We ask: where does it come from, where and what is the reason for it, the ground? Similarly the essent as a whole is present. We ask: where and what is the ground? This manner of questioning is represented in the simple formula: Why are there essents? Where and what is their ground? Tacitly we are asking after another and higher kind of essent. But here the question is not by any means concerned with the essent as such and as a whole.

But if we put the question in the form of our original interrogative sentence: "Why are there essents rather than nothing?" this addition prevents us in our questioning from beginning directly with an unquestionably given essent and, having scarcely

*Knut Hamsun, *The Road Leads On* (Coward-McCann, 1934), p. 508. Translated by Eugene Gay-Tifft.

begun, from continuing on to another expected essent as a ground. Instead this essent, through questioning, is held out into the possibility of nonbeing. Thereby the why takes on a very different power and penetration. Why is the essent torn away from the possibility of nonbeing? Why does it not simply keep falling back into nonbeing? Now the essent is no longer that which just happens to be present; it begins to waver and oscillate, regardless of whether or not we recognize the essent in all certainty, regardless of whether or not we apprehend it in its full scope. Henceforth the essent as such oscillates, insofar as we draw it into the question. The swing of the pendulum extends to the extreme and sharpest contrary possibility, to nonbeing and nothingness. And the search for the why undergoes a parallel change. It does not aim simply at providing an also present ground and explanation for what is present; now a ground is sought which will explain the emergence of the essent as an overcoming of nothingness. The ground that is now asked after is the ground of the decision for the essent over against nothingness, or more precisely, the ground for the oscillation of the essent, which sustains and unbinds us, half being, half not being, which is also why we can belong entirely to no thing, not even to ourselves; yet being-there *[Dasein]* is in every case mine.

[The qualification "in every case mine" means that being-there is allotted to me in order that my self should be being-there. But being there signifies: care of the ecstatically manifested being of the essent as such, not only of human being. Being-there is "in every case mine"; this means neither "posited through me" nor "apportioned to an individual ego." Being-there is *itself* by virtue of its essential relation to being in general. That is the meaning of the sentence that occurs frequently in *Sein und Zeit:* Being-there implies awareness of being.]

It is already becoming clearer that this "rather than nothing" is no superfluous appendage to the real question, but is an essential component of the whole interrogative sentence, which as a whole states an entirely different question from that intended in the question "Why are there essents?" With our question we place ourselves in the essent in such a way that it loses its self-evident character *as the essent.* The essent begins to waver between the broadest and most drastic extremes: "either essents—or nothing"—and thereby the questioning itself loses all solid foundation. Our questioning being-there is suspended, and in this suspense is nevertheless self-sustained.

But the essent is not changed by our questioning. It remains what it is and as it is. Our questioning is after all only a psycho-spiritual process in us which, whatever course it may take, cannot in any way affect the essent itself. True, the essent remains as it is manifested to us. But it cannot slough off the problematic fact that it might also not be what it is and as it is. We do not experience this possibility as something that we add to the essent by thinking; rather, the essent itself elicits this possibility, and in this possibility reveals itself. Our questioning only opens up the horizon, in order that the essent may dawn in such questionableness.

We still know far too little about the process of such questioning, and what we do know is far too crude. In this questioning we seem to belong entirely to ourselves. Yet it is this questioning that moves us into the open, provided that in questioning it transform itself (which all true questioning does), and cast a new space over everything and into everything.

The main thing is not to let ourselves be led astray by overhasty theories, but to experience things as they are on the basis of the first thing that comes to hand. This piece of chalk has extension; it is a relatively solid, grayish white thing with a definite shape, and apart from all that, it is a thing to write with. This particular thing has the attribute of lying here; but just as surely, it has the attribute of potentially not lying here and not being so large. The possibility of being guided along the blackboard and of being used up is not something that we add to the thing by thought. Itself, as this essent, is in this possibility; otherwise it would not be chalk as a writing material. Correspondingly, every essent has in it this potentiality in a different way. This potentiality belongs to the chalk. It has in itself a definite aptitude for a definite use. True, we are accustomed and inclined, in seeking this potentiality in the chalk, to say that we cannot see or touch it. But that is a prejudice, the elimination of which is part of the unfolding of our question. For the present our question is only to open up the essent in its wavering between nonbeing and being. Insofar as the essent resists the extreme possibility of nonbeing, it stands in being, but it has never caught up with or overcome the possibility of nonbeing.

We suddenly find ourselves speaking of the nonbeing and being of the essent, without saying how this being or nonbeing is related to the essent. Are the two terms the same? The essent and its being? What, for example, is "the essent" in this piece of chalk? The very question is ambiguous, because the word "the essent" can be understood in two respects, like the Greek ⟨to on⟩. The essent means first *that* which is at any time, in particular this grayish white, so-and-so-shaped, light, brittle mass. But "the essent" also means that which "brings it about," so to speak, that this thing is an essent rather than a nonessent, that which constitutes its being if it *is*. In accordance with this twofold meaning of the word "the essent," the Greek ⟨to on⟩ often has the second significance, not the essent itself, not that which is, but "is-ness," essentness, being. Over against this, "the essent" in the first sense signifies all or particular essent things themselves, in respect to themselves and not to their is-ness, their ⟨ousia⟩.

The first meaning of ⟨to on⟩ refers to ⟨ta onta⟩ (⟨entia⟩), the second to ⟨to einai⟩ (*esse*). We have listed what the essent is in the piece of chalk. This was relatively easy to do. It was also easy to see that the object named can also *not* be, that this chalk need ultimately not be here and not be. What then is being in distinction to what can stand in being or fall back into nonbeing—what is being in distinction to the essent? Is it the same as the essent? We ask the question once again. But in the foregoing we did not list being; we listed only material mass, grayish-white light, so-and-so-shaped, brittle. But where is the being situated? It must belong to the chalk, for this chalk *is*.

We encounter the essent everywhere; it sustains and drives us, enchants and fills us, elevates and disappoints us; but with all this, where is, and wherein consists, the being of the essent? One might reply: this distinction between the essent and its being may occasionally have an importance from the standpoint of language and even of meaning; this distinction can be effected in mere thought, i.e. in ideas and opinions, but is it certain that anything essent in the essent corresponds to the distinction? And even this merely cogitated distinction is questionable; for it remains unclear what is to be thought under the name of "being." Meanwhile it suffices to know the essent and secure our mastery over it. To go further and introduce being as distinct from it is artificial and leads to nothing.

We have already said a certain amount about this frequent question: What comes of such distinctions? Here we are going to concentrate on our undertaking. We ask: "Why are there essents rather than nothing?" And in this question we seemingly stick to the essent and avoid all empty brooding about being. But what really are we asking? Why the essent as such is. We are asking for the ground of the essent: that it is and is what it is, and that there is not rather nothing. Fundamentally we are asking about being. But how? We are asking about the being of the essent. We are questioning the essent in regard to its being.

But if we persevere in our questioning we shall actually be questioning forward, asking about being in respect to its ground, even if this question remains undeveloped and it remains undecided whether being itself is not in itself a ground and a sufficient ground. If we regard this question of being as the first question in order of rank, should we ask it without knowing how it stands with being and how being stands in its distinction to the essent? How shall we inquire into, not to say find, the ground for the being of the essent, if we have not adequately considered and understood being itself? This undertaking would be just as hopeless as if someone were to try to bring out the cause and ground of a fire, and yet claim that he need not worry about the actual course of the fire or examine the scene of it.

Thus it transpires that the question "Why are there essents rather than nothing?" compels us to ask the preliminary question: "How does it stand with being?"

Here we are asking about something which we barely grasp, which is scarcely more than the sound of a word for us, and which puts us in danger of serving a mere word idol when we proceed with our questioning. Hence it is all the more indispensable that we make it clear from the very outset how it stands at present with being and with our understanding of being. And in this connection the main thing is to impress it on our experience that we cannot immediately grasp the being of the essent itself, either through the essent or in the essent—or anywhere else.

A few examples may be helpful. Over there, across the street, stands the high school building. An essent. We can look over the building from all sides, we can go in and explore it from cellar to attic, and note everything we encounter in that building: corridors, staircases, schoolrooms, and their equipment. Everywhere we find essents and we even find them in a very definite arrangement. Now where is the being of this high school? For after all it is. The building is. If anything belongs to this essent, it is its being; yet we do not find the being inside it.

Nor does the being consist in the fact that we look at the essent. The building stands there even if we do not look at it. We can find it only because it already is. Moreover, this building's being does not by any means seem to be the same for everyone. For us, who look at it or ride by, it is different than for the pupils who sit in it; not because they see it only from within but because for them this building really is what it is and as it is. You can, as it were, smell the being of this building in your nostrils. The smell communicates the being of this essent far more immediately and truly than any description or inspection could ever do. But on the other hand the building's being is not based on this odor that is somewhere in the air.

How does it stand with being? Can you see being? We see essents; this chalk for example. But do we see being as we see color and light and shade? Or do we hear, smell, taste, feel being? We hear the motorcycle racing through the street. We hear the grouse gliding through the forest. But actually we hear only the whirring of the motor, the sound the grouse makes. As a matter of fact it is difficult to describe even the pure sound, and we do not ordinarily do so, because it is *not* what we commonly hear. [From the standpoint of sheer sound] we always hear *more.* We hear the flying bird, even though strictly speaking we should say: a grouse is nothing audible, it is no manner of tone that fits into a scale. And so it is with the other senses. We touch velvet, silk; we see them directly as this and that kind of essent, the one different from the other. Wherein lies and wherein consists being?

But we must take a wider look around us and consider the lesser and greater circle within which we spend our days and hours, wittingly and unwittingly, a circle whose limits shift continuously and which is suddenly broken through.

A heavy storm coming up in the mountains "is," or what here amounts to the same thing, "was" during the night. Wherein consists its being?

A distant mountain range under a broad sky . . . It "is." Wherein consists the being? When and to whom does it reveal itself? To the traveler who enjoys the landscape, or to the peasant who makes his living in it and from it, or to the meteorologist who is preparing a weather report? Who of these apprehends being? All and none. Or is what these men apprehend of the mountain range under the great sky only certain aspects of it, not the mountain range itself as it "is" as such, not that wherein its actual being consists? Who may be expected to apprehend this being? Or is it a non-sense, contrary to the sense of being, to inquire after what is in itself, behind those aspects? Does the being lie in the aspects?

The door of an early Romanesque church is an essent. How and to whom is its being revealed? To the connoisseur of art, who examines it and photographs it on an excursion, or to the abbot who on a holiday passes through this door with his monks, or to the children who play in its shadow on a summer's day? How does it stand with the being of this essent?

A state—*is*. By virtue of the fact that the state police arrest a suspect, or that so-and-so-many typewriters are clattering in a government building, taking down the words of ministers and state secretaries? Or "is" the state in a conversation between the chancellor and the British foreign minister? The state is. But where is being situated? Is it situated anywhere at all?

A painting by Van Gogh. A pair of rough peasant shoes, nothing else. Actually the painting represents nothing. But as to what *is* in that picture, you are immediately alone with it as though you yourself were making your way wearily homeward with your hoe on an evening in late fall after the last potato fires have died down. What is here? The canvas? The brush strokes? The spots of color?

What in all these things we have just mentioned is the being of the essent? We run (or stand) around in the world with our silly subtleties and conceit. But where in all this is being?

All the things we have named *are* and yet—when we wish to apprehend being, it is always as though we were reaching into the void. The being after which we inquire is almost like nothing, and yet we have always rejected the contention that the essent in its entirety *is not*.

But being remains unfindable, almost like nothing, or ultimately *quite* so. Then, in the end, the word "being" is no more than an empty word. It means nothing real, tangible, material. Its meaning is an unreal vapor. Thus in the last analysis Nietzsche was perfectly right in calling such "highest concepts" as being "the last cloudy streak of evaporating reality." Who would want to chase after such a vapor, when the very term is merely a name for a great fallacy! "Nothing indeed has exercised a more simple power of persuasion hitherto than the error of Being . . ."*

"Being"—a vapor and a fallacy? What Nietzsche says here of being is no random remark thrown out in the frenzy of preparation for his central, never finished work. No, this was his guiding view of being from the earliest days of his philosophical effort. It is the fundamental support and determinant of his philosophy. Yet even now this philosophy holds its ground against all the crude importunities of the scribblers who cluster round him more numerous with each passing day. And so far there seems to be no end in sight to this abuse of Nietzsche's work. In speaking here of Nietzsche, we mean to have nothing to do with all that—or with blind hero worship for that matter. The task in hand is too crucial and at the same time too sobering. It consists first of all, if we are to gain a true grasp of Nietzsche, in bringing his accomplishment to a full unfolding. Being a vapor, a fallacy? If this were so, the only possible consequence would be to abandon the question "Why are there essents as such and as a

*The Twilight of Idols, Nietzsche's Complete Works, Edinburgh and London, 16 (1911), 19, 22.

whole, rather than nothing?" For what good is the question if what it inquires into is only a vapor and a fallacy?

Does Nietzsche speak the truth? Or was he himself only the last victim of a long process of error and neglect, but as such the unrecognized witness to a new necessity?

Is it the fault of being that it is so involved? is it the fault of the word that it remains so empty? or are we to blame that with all our effort, with all our chasing after the essent, we have fallen out of being? And should we not say that the fault did not begin with us, or with our immediate or more remote ancestors, but lies in something that runs through Western history from the very beginning, a happening which the eyes of all the historians in the world will never perceive, but which nevertheless happens, which happened in the past and will happen in the future? What if it were possible that man, that nations in their greatest movements and traditions, are linked to being and yet had long fallen out of being, without knowing it, and that this was the most powerful and most central cause of their decline? (See *Sein und Zeit,* §38, in particular pp. 179f.)

We do not ask these questions incidentally, and still less do they spring from any particular outlook or state of mind; no, they are questions to which we are driven by that preliminary question which sprang necessarily from our main question "How does it stand with being?"—a sober question perhaps, but assuredly a very useless one. And yet a *question,* the question: is "being" a mere word and its meaning a vapor or is it the spiritual destiny of the Western world?

This Europe, in its ruinous blindness forever on the point of cutting its own throat, lies today in a great pincers, squeezed between Russia on one side and America on the other. From a metaphysical point of view, Russia and America are the same; the same dreary technological frenzy, the same unrestricted organization of the average man. At a time when the farthermost corner of the globe has been conquered by technology and opened to economic exploitation; when any incident whatever, regardless of where or when it occurs, can be communicated to the rest of the world at any desired speed; when the assassination of a king in France and a symphony concert in Tokyo can be "experienced" simultaneously; when time has ceased to be anything other than velocity, instantaneousness, and simultaneity, and time as history has vanished from the lives of all peoples; when a boxer is regarded as a nation's great man; when mass meetings attended by millions are looked on as a triumph—then, yes then, through all this turmoil a question still haunts us like a specter: What for?—Whither?—And what then?

The spiritual decline of the earth is so far advanced that the nations are in danger of losing the last bit of spiritual energy that makes it possible to see the decline (taken in relation to the history of "being"), and to appraise it as such. This simple observation has nothing to do with *Kulturpessimismus,* and of course it has nothing to do with any sort of optimism either; for the darkening of the world, the flight of the gods, the destruction of the earth, the transformation of men into a mass, the hatred and suspicion of everything free and creative, have assumed such proportions throughout the earth that such childish categories as pessimism and optimism have long since become absurd.

We are caught in a pincers. Situated in the center, our nation incurs the severest pressure. It is the nation with the most neighbors and hence the most endangered. With all this, it is the most metaphysical of nations. We are certain of this vocation, but our people will only be able to wrest a destiny from it if *within itself* it creates a resonance, a possibility of resonance for this vocation, and takes a creative view of its tradition. All this implies that this nation, as a historical nation, must move itself and thereby the history of the West beyond the center of their future "happening" and into the primordial realm of the powers of being. If the great decision regarding Europe is not to bring annihilation, that decision must be made in terms of new spiritual energies unfolding historically from out of the center.

To ask "How does it stand with being?" means nothing less than to recapture, to repeat *[wieder-holen]*, the beginning of our historical spiritual existence, in order to transform it into a new beginning. This is possible. It is indeed the crucial form of history, because it begins in the fundamental event. But we do not repeat a beginning by reducing it to something past and now known, which need merely be imitated; no, the beginning must be begun again, more radically, with all the strangeness, darkness, insecurity that attend a true beginning. Repetition as we understand it is anything but an improved continuation with the old methods of what has been up to now.

The question "How is it with being?" is included as a preliminary question in our central question "Why are there essents rather than nothing?" If we now begin to look into that which is questioned in our preliminary question, namely being, the full truth of Nietzsche's dictum is at once apparent. For if we look closely, what more is "being" to us than a mere word, an indeterminate meaning, intangible as a vapor? Nietzsche's judgment, to be sure, was meant in a purely disparaging sense. For him "being" is a delusion that should never have come about. Is "being," then, indeterminate, vague as a vapor? It is indeed. But we do not mean to sidestep this fact. On the contrary, we must see how much of a fact it is if we are to perceive its full implication.

Our questioning brings us into the landscape we must inhabit as a basic prerequisite, if we are to win back our roots in history. We shall have to ask why this fact, that for us "being" is no more than a word and a vapor, should have arisen precisely today, or whether and why it has existed for a long time. We must learn to see that this fact is not as harmless as it seems at first sight. For ultimately what matters is not that the word "being" remains a mere sound and its meaning a vapor, but that we have fallen away from what this word says and for the moment cannot find our way back; that it is for this and no other reason that the word "being" no longer applies to anything, that everything, if we merely take hold of it, dissolves like a tatter of cloud in the sunlight. Because this is so—that is why we ask about being. And we ask because we know that truths have never fallen into any nation's lap. The fact that people still cannot and do not wish to understand this question, even if it is asked in a still more fundamental form, deprives the question of none of its cogency.

Of course we can, seemingly with great astuteness and perspicacity, revive the old familiar argument to the effect that "being" is the most universal of concepts, that it covers anything and everything, even the nothing which also, in the sense that it is thought or spoken, "is" something. Beyond the domain of this most universal concept "being," there is, in the strictest sense of the word, nothing more, on the basis of which being itself could be more closely determined. The concept of being is an ultimate. Moreover, there is a law of logic that says: the more comprehensive a concept is—and what could be more comprehensive than the concept of "being"?—the more indeterminate and empty is its content.

For every normally thinking man—and we all should like to be normal men—this reasoning is immediately and wholly convincing. But the question now arises: does the designation of being as the most universal concept strike the essence of being, or is it not from the very outset such a misinterpretation that all questioning becomes hopeless? This then is the question: can being be regarded only as the most universal concept which inevitably occurs in all special concepts, or is being of an entirely different essence, and hence anything but an object of "ontology," provided we take this word in its traditional sense?

The word "ontology" was first coined in the seventeenth century. It marks the development of the traditional doctrine of the essent into a discipline of philosophy and a branch of the philosophical system. But the traditional doctrine was an academic classification and ordering of what for Plato and Aristotle and again for Kant was a question, though no longer to be sure a primordial one. And it is in this sense that the word "ontology" is used today. Under this title each school of philosophy has set up and described a branch within its system. But we can also take the word "ontology" in the "broadest sense," "without reference to ontological directions and tendencies" (cf. *Sein und Zeit,* p. 11, top). In this case "ontology" signifies the endeavor to make being manifest itself, and to do so by way of the question "how does it stand with being?" (and not only with the essent as such). But since thus far this question has not even been heard, let alone echoed; since it has been expressly rejected by the various schools of academic philosophy, which strive for an "ontology" in the traditional sense, it may be preferable to dispense in the future with the terms "ontology" and "ontological." Two modes of questioning which, as we now see clearly, are worlds apart, should not bear the same name.

We ask the questions "How does it stand with being?" "What is the meaning of being?" *not* in order to set up an ontology on the traditional style, much less to criticize the past mistakes of ontology. We are concerned with something totally different: to restore man's historical being-there—and that always includes our own future being-there in the totality of the history allotted to us—to the domain of being, which it was originally incumbent on man to open up for himself. All this, to be sure, in the limits within which philosophy can accomplish anything.

Out of the fundamental question of metaphysics, "Why are there essents rather than nothing?" we have separated the preliminary question, "How does it stand with being?" The relation between the two questions requires clarification, for it is of a special kind. Ordinarily a preliminary question is dealt with before and outside the main question, though in reference to it. But, in principle, philosophical questions are never dealt with as though we might some day cast them aside. Here the preliminary question is not by any means outside of the main question; rather, it is the flame which burns as it were in the asking of the fundamental question; it is the flaming center of all questioning. That is to say: it is crucial for the first asking of the fundamental question that in asking its *preliminary* question we derive the decisive fundamental attitude that is here essential. That is why we have related the question of being to the destiny of Europe, where the destiny of the earth is being decided—while our own historic being-there proves to be the center for Europe itself.

The question is:

Is being a mere word and its meaning a vapor, or does what is designated by the word "being" hold within it the historical destiny of the West?

To many ears the question may sound violent and exaggerated: for one might in a pinch suppose that a discussion of the question of being might be related in some very remote and indirect way to the decisive historical question of the earth, but assuredly not that the basic position and attitude of our questioning might be directly determined by the history of the human spirit on earth. And yet this relationship exists. Since our purpose is to set in motion the asking of the preliminary question, we must now show that, and to what extent, the asking of this question is an immediate and fundamental factor in the crucial historical question. For this demonstration it is necessary to anticipate an essential insight in the form of an assertion.

We maintain that this preliminary question and with it the fundamental question of metaphysics are historical questions through and through. But do not metaphysics and philosophy thereby become a historical science? Historical science after all investigates the temporal, while philosophy investigates the timeless. Philosophy is historical only insofar as it—like every work of the spirit—realizes itself in time. But in this sense the designation of metaphysical questioning as historical cannot characterize metaphysics, but merely expresses something obvious. Accordingly, the assertion is either meaningless and superfluous or else impossible, because it creates an amalgam of two fundamentally different kinds of science: philosophy and historical science.

In answer to this it must be said:

1. Metaphysics and philosophy are not sciences at all, and the fact that their questioning is basically historical cannot make them so.

2. Historical science does not determine a fundamental relation to history, but always presupposes such a relation. It is only for this reason that historical science can distort men's relation to history, which itself is always historical; or misinterpret it and degrade it to a mere knowledge of antiquities; or else deal with crucial fields in the light of this once established relation to history, and so produce cogent history. A historical relation between our historical being-there and history may become an object of knowledge and mark an advanced state of knowledge; but it need not. Moreover, all relations to history cannot be scientifically objectified and given a place in science, and it is precisely the essential ones that cannot. Historical science can never produce the historical relation to history. It can only illuminate a relation once supplied, ground it in knowledge, which is indeed an absolute necessity for the historical being-there of a wise people, and not either an "advantage" or a "disadvantage." Because it is only in philosophy—as *distinguished from all science*—that essential relations to the realm of what is take shape, this relation can, indeed must, for us today be a fundamentally historical one.

But for an understanding of our assertion that the "metaphysical" asking of the preliminary question is historical through and through, it is above all necessary to consider this: for us history is not synonymous with the past; for the past is precisely what is no longer happening. And much less is history the merely contemporary, which never happens but merely "passes," comes and goes by. History as happening is an acting and being acted upon which pass through the *present,* which are determined from out of the future, and which take over the past. It is precisely the present that vanishes in happening.

Our asking of the fundamental question of metaphysics is historical because it opens up the process of human being-there in its essential relations—i.e. its relations to the essent as such and as a whole—opens it up to unasked possibilities, futures, and at the same time binds it back to its past beginning, so sharpening it and giving it weight in its present. In this questioning our being-there is summoned to its history in the full sense of the word, called to history and to a decision in history. And this not after the fact, in the sense that we draw ethical, ideological lessons from it. No, the basic attitude of the questioning is in itself historical; it stands and maintains itself in happening, in giving out of happening for the sake of happening.

But we have not yet come to the essential reason why this inherently historical asking of the question about being is actually an integral part of history on earth. We have said that the world is darkening. The essential episodes of this darkening are: the flight of the gods, the destruction of the earth, the standardization of man, the preeminence of the mediocre.

What do we mean by world when we speak of a darkening of the world? World is always world of the *spirit*. The animal has no world nor any environment *[Umwelt]*. Darkening of the world means emasculation of the spirit, the disintegration, wasting away, repression, and misinterpretation of the spirit. We shall attempt to explain the emasculation of the spirit in one respect, that of misinterpretation. We have said: Europe lies in a pincers between Russia and America, which are metaphysically the same, namely in regard to their world character and their relation to the spirit. What makes the situation of Europe all the more catastrophic is that this enfeeblement of the spirit originated in Europe itself and—though prepared by earlier factors—was definitively determined by its own spiritual situation in the first half of the nineteenth century. It was then that occurred what is popularly and succinctly called the "collapse of German idealism." This formula is a kind of shield behind which the already dawning spirit-lessness, the dissolution of the spiritual energies, the rejection of all original inquiry into grounds and men's bond with the grounds, are hidden and masked. It was not German idealism that collapsed; rather, the age was no longer strong enough to stand up to the greatness, breadth, and originality of that spiritual world, i.e. truly to realize it, for to realize a philosophy means something very different from applying theorems and insights. The lives of men began to slide into a world which lacked that depth from out of which the essential always comes to man and comes back to man, so compelling him to become superior and making him act in conformity to a rank. All things sank to the same level, a surface resembling a blind mirror that no longer reflects, that casts nothing back. The prevailing dimension became that of extension and number. Intelligence no longer meant a wealth of talent, lavishly spent, and the command of energies, but only what could be learned by everyone, the practice of a routine, always associated with a certain amount of sweat and a certain amount of show. In America and in Russia this development grew into a boundless etcetera of indifference and always-the-sameness—so much so that the quantity took on a quality of its own. Since then the domination in those countries of a cross section of the indifferent mass has become something more than a dreary accident. It has become an active onslaught that destroys all rank and every world-creating impulse of the spirit, and calls it a lie. This is the onslaught of what we call the demonic (in the sense of destructive evil). There are many indications of the emergence of this demonism, identical with the increasing helplessness and uncertainty of Europe against it and within itself. One of these signs is the emasculation of the spirit through misinterpretation; we are still in the midst of this process. This misinterpretation of the spirit may be described briefly in four aspects.

1. The crux of the matter is the reinterpretation of the spirit as *intelligence,* or mere cleverness in examining and calculating given things and the possibility of changing them and complementing them to make new things. This cleverness is a matter of mere talent and practice and mass division of labor. The cleverness itself is subject to the possibility of organization, which is never true of the spirit. The attitude of the litterateur and esthete is merely a late consequence and variation of the spirit falsified into intelligence. Mere intelligence is a semblance of spirit, masking its absence.

2. The spirit falsified into intelligence thus falls to the level of a tool in the service of others, a tool the manipulation of which can be taught and learned. Whether this use of intelligence relates to the regulation and domination of the material conditions of production (as in Marxism) or in general to the intelligent ordering and explanation of everything that is present and already posited at any time (as in positivism), or whether it is applied to the organization and regulation of a nation's vital resources and race—in any case the spirit as intelligence becomes the impotent superstructure of something else, which, because it is without spirit or even opposed to the spirit, is taken for the actual reality. If the spirit is taken as intelligence, as is done in the most extreme form of Marxism, then it is perfectly correct to say, in defense against it, that in the order of the effective forces of human being-there, the spirit, i.e.

intelligence, must always be ranked below healthy physical activity and character. But this order becomes false once we understand the true essence of the spirit. For all true power and beauty of the body, all sureness and boldness in combat, all authenticity and inventiveness of the understanding, are grounded in the spirit and rise or fall only through the power or impotence of the spirit. The spirit is the sustaining, dominating principle, the first and the last, not merely an indispensable third factor.

3. As soon as the misinterpretation sets in that degrades the spirit to a tool, the energies of the spiritual process, poetry and art, statesmanship and religion, become subject to *conscious* cultivation and planning. They are split into branches. The spiritual world becomes culture and the individual strives to perfect himself in the creation and preservation of this culture. These branches become fields of free endeavor, which sets its own standards and barely manages to live up to them. These standards of production and consumption are called values. The cultural values preserve their meaning only by restricting themselves to an autonomous field: poetry for the sake of poetry, art for the sake of art, science for the sake of science.

Let us consider the example of science, which is of particular concern to us here at the university. The state of science since the turn of the century—it has remained unchanged despite a certain amount of house cleaning—is easy to see. Though today two seemingly different conceptions of science seem to combat one another—science as technical, practical, professional knowledge and science as cultural value per se—both are moving along the same downgrade of misinterpretation and emasculation of the spirit. They differ only in this: in the present situation the technical, practical conception of science as specialization can at least lay claim to frank and clear consistency, while the reactionary interpretation of science as a cultural value, now making its reappearance, seeks to conceal the impotence of the spirit behind an unconscious lie. The confusion of spiritlessness can even go so far as to lead the upholders of the technical, practical view of science to profess their belief in science as a cultural value; then the two understand each other perfectly in the same spiritlessness. We may choose to call the institution where the specialized sciences are grouped together for purposes of teaching and research a university, but this is no more than a name; the "university" has ceased to be a fundamental force for unity and responsibility. What I said here in 1929, in my inaugural address, is still true of the German university: "The scientific fields are still far apart. Their subjects are treated in fundamentally different ways. Today this hodgepodge of disciplines is held together only by the technical organization of the universities and faculties and preserves what meaning it has only through the practical aims of the different branches. The sciences have lost their roots in their essential ground" (*Was ist Metaphysik?* 1929, p. 8). Science today in all its branches is a technical, practical business of gaining and transmitting information. An awakening of the spirit cannot take its departure from such science. It is itself in need of an awakening.

4. The last misinterpretation of the spirit is based on the above mentioned falsifications which represent the spirit as intelligence, and intelligence as a serviceable tool which, along with its product, is situated in the realm of culture. In the end the spirit as utilitarian intelligence and the spirit as culture become holiday ornaments cultivated along with many other things. They are brought out and exhibited as a proof that there is no intention to combat culture or favor barbarism. In the beginning Russian Communism took a purely negative attitude but soon went over to propagandist tactics of this kind.

In opposition to this multiple misinterpretation of the spirit, we define the essence of the spirit briefly as follows (I shall quote from the address I delivered on the occasion of my appointment as rector, because of its succinct formulation): "Spirit is neither empty cleverness nor the irresponsible play of the wit, nor the boundless work of dismemberment carried on by the practical intelligence; much less is it world reason; no, spirit is a fundamental, knowing resolve toward the essence of being" (*Rektoratsrede,* p. 13). Spirit is the mobilization of the powers of the essent as such and as a whole. Where spirit prevails, the essent as such becomes always and at all times more essent. Thus the inquiry into the essent as such and as a whole, the asking of the question of being, is one of the essential and fundamental conditions for an awakening of the spirit and hence for an original world of historical being-there. It is indispensable if the peril of world darkening is to be forestalled and if our nation in the center of the Western world is to take on its historical mission. Here we can explain only in these broad outlines why the asking of the question of being is in itself through and through historical, and why, accordingly, our question as to whether being will remain a mere vapor for us or become the destiny of the West is anything but an exaggeration and a rhetorical figure.

But if our question about being has this essential and decisive character, we must above all take an absolutely serious view of *the fact* that gives the question its immediate necessity, the fact that for us being has become little more than a mere word and its meaning an evanescent vapor. This is not the kind of fact which merely confronts us as something alien and other, which we need merely note as an occurrence. It is a fact in which we stand. It is a state of our being-there. And by state, of course, I do not mean a quality that can be demonstrated only psychologically. Here state means our entire constitution, the way in which we ourselves are constituted in regard to being. Here we are not concerned with psychology but with our history in an essential respect. When we call it a "fact" that being for us is a mere word and vapor, we are speaking very provisionally. We are merely holding fast, establishing something which has not yet been thought through, for which we still have no locus, even if it looks as though this something were an occurrence among us, here and now, or "in" us, as we like to say.

One would like to integrate the individual fact that for us being remains no more than an empty word and an evanescent vapor with the more general fact that many words, and precisely the essential ones, are in the same situation; that the language in general is worn out and used up—an indispensable but masterless means of communication that may be used as one pleases, as indifferent as a means of public transport, as a street car which everyone rides in. Everyone speaks and writes away in the language, without hindrance and above all *without danger.* That is certainly true. And only a very few are capable of thinking through the full implications of this misrelation and unrelation of present-day being-there to language.

But the emptiness of the word "being," the total disappearance of its appellative force, is not merely a particular instance of the general exhaustion of language; rather, the destroyed relation to being as such is the actual reason for the general misrelation to language.

The organizations for the purification of the language and defense against its progressive barbarization are deserving of respect. But such efforts merely demonstrate all the more clearly that we no longer know what is at stake in language. Because the destiny of language is grounded in a nation's *relation to being,* the question of being will involve us deeply in the question of language. It is more than an outward accident that now, as we prepare to set forth, in all its implication, the fact of the evaporation of being, we find ourselves compelled to take linguistic considerations as our starting point.

BUILDING DWELLING THINKING

In what follows we shall try to think about dwelling and building. This thinking about building does not presume to discover architectural ideas, let alone to give rules for building. This venture in thought does not view building as an art or as a technique of construction; rather it traces building back into that domain to which everything that *is* belongs. We ask:

1. What is it to dwell?
2. How does building belong to dwelling?

I

We attain to dwelling, so it seems, only by means of building. The latter, building, has the former, dwelling, as its goal. Still, not every building is a dwelling. Bridges and hangars, stadiums and power stations are buildings but not dwellings; railway stations and highways, dams and market halls are built, but they are not dwelling places. Even so, these buildings are in the domain of our dwelling. That domain extends over these buildings and yet is not limited to the dwelling place. The truck driver is at home on the highway, but he does not have his shelter there; the working woman is at home in the spinning mill, but does not have her dwelling place there; the chief engineer is at home in the power station, but he does not dwell there. These buildings house man. He inhabits them and yet does not dwell in them, when to dwell means merely that we take shelter in them. In today's housing shortage even this much is reassuring and to the good; residential buildings do indeed provide shelter; today's houses may even be well planned, easy to keep, attractively cheap, open to air, light, and sun, but—do the houses in themselves hold any guarantee that *dwelling* occurs in them? Yet those buildings that are not dwelling places remain in turn determined by dwelling insofar as they serve man's dwelling. Thus dwelling would in any case be the end that presides over all building. Dwelling and building are related as end and means. However, as long as this is all we have in mind, we take dwelling and building as two separate activities, an idea that has something correct in it. Yet at the same time by the means-end schema we block our view of the essential relations. For building is not merely a means and a way toward dwelling—to build is in itself already to dwell. Who tells us this? Who gives us a standard at all by which we can take the measure of the nature of dwelling and building?

It is language that tells us about the nature of a thing, provided that we respect language's own nature. In the meantime, to be sure there rages round the earth an unbridled yet clever talking, writing, and broadcasting of spoken words. Man acts as though *he* were the shaper and master of language, while in fact *language* remains the master of man. Perhaps it is before all else man's subversion of *this* relation of dominance that drives his nature into alienation. That we retain a concern for care in speaking is all to the good, but it is of no help to us as long as language still serves us even then only as a means of expression. Among all the appeals that we human beings, on our part, can help to be voiced, language is the highest and everywhere the first.

Martin Heidegger, *Poetry, Language, Thought,* translated by Albert Hofstadter (New York: Harper & Row, 1975), pp. 145–161.

What, then, does *Bauen,* building, *mean?* The Old English and High German word for building, *buan,* means to dwell. This signifies: to remain, to stay in a place. The real meaning of the verb *bauen,* namely, to dwell, has been lost to us. But a covert trace of it has been preserved in the German word *Nachbar,* neighbor. The neighbor is in Old English the *neahgebur; neah,* near, and *gebur,* dweller. The Nachbar is the *Nachgebur,* the *Nachgebauer,* the near-dweller, he who dwells nearby. The verbs *buri, büren, beuren, beuron,* all signify dwelling, the abode, the place of dwelling. Now to be sure the old word *buan* not only tells us that *bauen,* to build, is really to dwell; it also gives us a clue as to how we have to think about the dwelling it signifies. When we speak of dwelling we usually think of an activity that man performs alongside many other activities. We work here and dwell there. We do not merely dwell—that would be virtual inactivity—we practice a profession, we do business, we travel and lodge on the way, now here, now there. *Bauen* originally means to dwell. Where the word *bauen* still speaks in its original sense it also says *how far* the nature of dwelling reaches. That is, *banen, buan, bhu, beo* are our word *bin* in the versions: *ich bin,* I am, *du bist,* you are, the imperative form *bis,* be. What then does *ich bin* mean? The old word *bauen,* to which the *bin* belongs, answers: *ich bin, du bist* mean: I dwell, you dwell. The way in which you are and I am, the manner in which we humans *are* on the earth, is *Buan,* dwelling. To be a human being means to be on the earth as a mortal. It means to dwell. The old word *bauen,* which says that man *is* insofar as he *dwells,* this word *bauen* however *also* means at the same time to cherish and protect, to preserve and care for, specifically to till the soil, to cultivate the vine. Such building only takes care—it tends the growth that ripens into its fruit of its own accord. Building in the sense of preserving and nurturing is not making anything. Shipbuilding and temple-building, on the other hand, do in a certain way make their own works. Here building, in contrast with cultivating, is a constructing. Both modes of building—building as cultivating, Latin *colere, cultura,* and building as the raising up of edifices, *aedificare*—are comprised within genuine building, that is, dwelling. Building as dwelling, that is, as being on the earth, however, remains for man's everyday experience that which is from the outset "habitual"—we inhabit it, as our language says so beautifully: it is the *Gewohnte.* For this reason it recedes behind the manifold ways in which dwelling is accomplished, the activities of cultivation and construction. These activities later claim the name of *bauen,* building, and with it the fact of building, exclusively for themselves. The real sense of *bauen,* namely dwelling, falls into oblivion.

At first sight this event looks as though it were no more than a change of meaning of mere terms. In truth, however, something decisive is concealed in it, namely, dwelling is not experienced as man's being; dwelling is never thought of as the basic character of human being.

That language in a way retracts the real meaning of the word *bauen,* which is dwelling, is evidence of the primal nature of these meanings; for with the essential words of language, their true meaning easily falls into oblivion in favor of foreground meanings. Man has hardly yet pondered the mystery of this process. Language withdraws from man its simple and high speech. But its primal call does not thereby become incapable of speech; it merely falls silent. Man, though, fails to heed this silence.

But if we listen to what language says in the word *bauen* we hear three things:

1. Building is really dwelling.
2. Dwelling is the manner in which mortals are on the earth.
3. Building as dwelling unfolds into the building that cultivates growing things and the building that erects buildings.

If we give thought to this threefold fact, we obtain a clue and note the following: as long as we do not bear in mind that all building is in itself a dwelling, we cannot even adequately *ask,* let alone properly decide, what the building of buildings might be in its nature. We do not dwell because we have built, but we build and have built because we dwell, that is, because we are *dwellers.* But in what does the nature of dwelling consist? Let us listen once more to what language says to us. The Old Saxon *wuon,* the Gothic *wunian,* like the old word *bauen,* mean to remain, to stay in a place. But the Gothic *wunian* says more distinctly how this remaining is experienced. *Wunian* means: to be at peace, to be brought to peace, to remain in peace. The word for peace, *Friede,* means the free, *das Frye,* and *fry* means: preserved from harm and danger: preserved from something, safeguarded. To free really means to spare. The sparing itself consists not only in the fact that we do not harm the one whom we spare. Real sparing is something *positive* and takes place when we leave something beforehand in its own nature, when we return it specifically to its being, when we "free" it in the real sense of the word into a preserve of peace. To dwell, to be set at peace, means to remain at peace within the free, the preserve, the free sphere that safeguards each thing in its nature. *The fundamental character of dwelling is this sparing and preserving.* It pervades dwelling in its whole range. That range reveals itself to us as soon as we reflect that human being consists in dwelling and, indeed, dwelling in the sense of the stay of mortals on the earth.

But "on the earth" already means "under the sky." Both of these *also* mean "remaining before the divinities" and include a "belonging to men's being with one another." By a *primal* oneness the four—earth and sky, divinities and mortals-belong together in one.

Earth is the serving bearer, blossoming and fruiting, spreading out in rock and water, rising up into plant and animal. When we say earth, we are already thinking of the other three along with it, but we give no thought to the simple oneness of the four.

The sky is the vaulting path of the sun, the course of the changing moon, the wandering glitter of the stars, the year's seasons and their changes, the light and dusk of day, the gloom and glow of night, the clemency and inclemency of the weather, the drifting clouds and blue depth of the ether. When we say sky, we are already thinking of the other three along with it, but we give no thought to the simple oneness of the four.

The divinities are the beckoning messengers of the godhead. Out of the holy sway of the godhead, the god appears in his presence or withdraws into his concealment. When we speak of the divinities, we are already thinking of the other three along with them, but we give no thought to the simple oneness of the four.

The mortals are the human beings. They are called mortals because they can die. To die means to be capable of death as death. Only man dies, and indeed continually, as long as he remains on earth, under the sky, before the divinities. When we speak of mortals, we are already thinking of the other three along with them, but we give no thought to the simple oneness of the four.

This simple oneness of the four we call *the fourfold.* Mortals *are* in the fourfold by *dwelling.* But the basic character of dwelling is to spare, to preserve. Mortal; dwell in the way they preserve the fourfold in its essential being, its presencing. Accordingly, the preserving that dwells is fourfold.

Mortals dwell in that they save the earth—taking the word in the old sense still known to Lessing. Saving does not only snatch something from a danger. To save really means to set something free into its own presencing. To save the earth is more than to exploit it or even wear it out. Saving the earth does not master the earth and does not subjugate it, which is merely one step from spoliation.

Mortals dwell in that they receive the sky as sky. They leave to the sun and the moon their journey, to the stars their courses, to the seasons their blessing and their inclemency; they do not turn night into day nor day into a harassed unrest.

Mortals dwell in that they await the divinities as divinities. In hope they hold up to the divinities what is unhoped for. They wait for intimations of their coming and do not mistake the signs of their absence. They do not make their gods for themselves and do not worship idols. In the very depth of misfortune they wait for the weal that has been withdrawn.

Mortals dwell in that they initiate their own nature—their being capable of death as death—into the use and practice of this capacity, so that there may be a good death. To initiate mortals into the nature of death in no way means to make death, as empty Nothing, the goal. Nor does it mean to darken dwelling by blindly staring toward the end.

In saving the earth, in receiving the sky, in awaiting the divinities, in initiating mortals, dwelling occurs as the fourfold preservation of the fourfold. To spare and preserve means: to take under our care, to look after the fourfold in its presencing. What we take under our care must be kept safe. But if dwelling preserves the fourfold, where does it keep the fourfold's nature? How do mortals make their dwelling such a preserving? Mortals would never be capable of it if dwelling were merely a staying on earth under the sky, before the divinities, among mortals. Rather, dwelling itself is always a staying with things. Dwelling, as preserving, keeps the fourfold in that with which mortals stay: in things.

Staying with things, however, is not merely something attached to this fourfold preserving as a fifth something. On the contrary: staying with things is the only way in which the fourfold stay within the fourfold is accomplished at any time in simple unity. Dwelling preserves the fourfold by bringing the presencing of the fourfold into things. But things themselves secure the fourfold *only when* they themselves as things are let be in their presencing. How is this done? In this way, that mortals nurse and nurture the things that grow, and specially construct things that do not grow. Cultivating and construction are building in the narrower sense. *Dwelling,* insofar as it keeps or secures the fourfold in things, is, as this keeping, *a building.* With this, we are on our way to the second question.

II

In what way does building belong to dwelling?

The answer to this question will clarify for us what building, understood by way of the nature of dwelling, really is. We limit ourselves to building in the sense of constructing things and inquire: what is a built thing? A bridge may serve as an example for our reflections.

The bridge swings over the stream "with ease and power." It does not just connect banks that are already there. The banks emerge as banks only as the bridge crosses the stream. The bridge designedly causes them to lie across from each other. One side is set off against the other by the bridge. Nor do the banks stretch along the stream as indifferent border strips of the dry land. With the banks, the bridge brings to the stream the one and the other expanse of the landscape lying behind them. It brings stream and bank and land into each other's neighborhood. The bridge *gathers* the earth as landscape around the stream. Thus it guides and attends the stream through the meadows. Resting upright in the stream's bed, the bridge-piers bear the swing of the arches that leave the stream's waters to run their course. The waters may wander on quiet and gay, the sky's floods from storm or thaw may shoot past the piers in torrential waves—the bridge is ready for the sky's weather and its fickle nature. Even where the bridge covers the stream, it holds its flow up to the sky by taking it for a moment under the vaulted gateway and then setting it free once more.

The bridge lets the stream run its course and at the same time grants their way to mortals so that they may come and go from shore to shore. Bridges lead in many ways. The city bridge leads from the precincts of the castle to the cathedral square; the river bridge near the country town brings wagons and horse teams to the surrounding villages. The old stone bridge's humble brook crossing gives to the harvest wagon its passage from the fields into the village and carries the lumber cart from the field path to the road. The highway bridge is tied into the network of long-distance traffic, paced as calculated for maximum yield. Always and ever differently the bridge escorts the lingering and hastening ways of men to and fro, so that they may get to other banks and in the end, as mortals, to the other side. Now in a high arch, now in a low, the bridge vaults over glen and stream—whether mortals keep in mind this vaulting of the bridge's course or forget that they, always themselves on their way to the last bridge, are actually striving to surmount all that is common and unsound in them in order to bring themselves before the haleness of the divinities. The bridge *gathers,* as a passage that crosses, before the divinities—whether we explicitly think of, and visibly *give thanks for,* their presence, as in the figure of the saint of the bridge, or whether that divine presence is obstructed or even pushed wholly aside.

The bridge *gathers* to itself in *its own* way earth and sky, divinities and mortals.

Gathering or assembly, by an ancient word of our language, is called "thing." The bridge is a thing—and, indeed, it is such as the gathering of the fourfold which we have described. To be sure, people think of the bridge as primarily and really *merely* a bridge; after that, and occasionally, it might possibly express much else besides; and as such an expression it would then become a symbol, for instance a symbol of those things we mentioned before. But the bridge, if it is a true bridge, is never first of all a mere bridge and then afterward a symbol. And just as little is the bridge in the first place exclusively a symbol, in the sense that it expresses something that strictly speaking does not belong to it. If we take the bridge strictly as such, it never appears as an expression. The bridge is a thing and *only that.* Only? As this thing it gathers the fourfold.

Our thinking has of course long been accustomed to *understate* the nature of the thing. The consequence, in the course of Western thought, has been that the thing is represented as an unknown X to which perceptible properties are attached. From this point of view, everything *that already belongs to the gathering nature of this thing* does, of course, appear as something that is afterward read into it. Yet the bridge would never be a mere bridge if it were not a thing.

To be sure, the bridge is a thing of its *own* kind; for it gathers the fourfold in *such* a way that it allows a *site* for it. But only something *that is itself* a location can make space for a site. The location is not already there before the bridge is. Before the bridge stands, there are of course many spots along the stream that can be occupied by something. One of them proves to be a location, and does so *because of the bridge.* Thus the bridge does not first come to a location to stand in it; rather, a location comes into existence only by virtue of the bridge. The bridge is a thing; it gathers the fourfold, but in such a way that it allows a site for the fourfold. By this site are determined the localities and ways by which a space is provided for.

Only things that are locations in this manner allow for spaces. What the word for space, *Raum, Rum,* designates is said by its ancient meaning. *Raum* means a place cleared or freed for settlement and lodging. A space is something that has been made room for, something that is cleared and free, namely within a boundary, Greek *peras.*

A boundary is not that at which something stops but, as the Greeks recognized, the boundary is that from which something *begins its presencing.* That is why the concept is that of *horismos,* that is, the horizon, the boundary. Space is in essence that for which room has been made, that which is let into its bounds. That for which room is made is always granted and hence is joined, that is, gathered, by virtue of a location, that is, by such a thing as the bridge. *Accordingly, spaces receive their being from locations and not from "space."*

Things which, as locations, allow a site we now in anticipation call buildings. They are so called because they are made by a process of building construction. Of what sort this making—building—must be, however, we find out only after we have first given thought to the nature of those things which of themselves require building as the process by which they are made. These things are locations that allow a site for the fourfold, a site that in each case provides for a space. The relation between location and space lies in the nature of these things *qua* locations, but so does the relation of the location to the man who lives at that location. Therefore we shall now try to clarify the nature of these things that we call buildings by the following brief consideration.

For one thing, what is the relation between location and space? For another, what is the relation between man and space?

The bridge is a location. As such a thing, it allows a space into which earth and heaven, divinities and mortals are admitted. The space allowed by the bridge contains many places variously near or far from the bridge. These places, however, may be treated as mere positions between which there lies a measurable distance; a distance, in Greek *stadion,* always has room made for it, and indeed by bare positions. The space that is thus made by positions is space of a peculiar sort. As distance or "stadion" it is what the same word, *stadion,* means in Latin, a *spatium,* an intervening space or interval. Thus nearness and remoteness between men and things can become mere distance, mere intervals of intervening space. In a space that is represented purely as spatium, the bridge now appears as a mere something at some position, which can be occupied at any time by something else or replaced by a mere marker. What is more, the mere dimensions of height, breadth, and depth can be abstracted from space as intervals. What is so abstracted we represent as the pure manifold of the three dimensions. Yet the room made by this manifold is also no longer determined by distances; it is no longer a *spatium,* but now no more than *extensio*—extension. But from space as *extensio* a further abstraction can be made, to analytic-algebraic relations. What these relations make room for is the possibility of the purely mathematical construction of manifolds with an arbitrary number of dimensions. The space provided for in this mathematical manner may be called "space," the "one" space as such. But in this sense "the" space, "space," contains no spaces and no places. We never find in it any locations, that is, things of the kind the bridge is. As against that, however, in the spaces provided for by locations there is always space as interval, and in this interval in turn there is space as pure extension. *Spatium* and *extensio* afford at any time the possibility of measuring things and what they make room for, according to distances, spans, and directions, and of computing these magnitudes. But the fact that they are *universally* applicable to everything that has extension can in no case make numerical magnitudes the ground of the nature of spaces and locations that are measurable with the aid of mathematics. How even modern physics was compelled by the facts themselves to represent the spatial medium of cosmic space as a field-unity determined by body as dynamic center, cannot be discussed here.

The spaces through which we go daily are provided for by locations; their nature is grounded in things of the type of buildings. If we pay heed to these relations between locations and spaces, between spaces and space, we get a clue to help us in thinking of the relation of man and space.

When we speak of man and space, it sounds as though man stood on one side, space on the other. Yet space is not something that faces man. It is neither an external object nor an inner experience. It is not that there are men, and over and above them *space;* for when I say "a man," and in saying this word think of a being who exists in a human manner—that is, who dwells—then by the name "man" I already name the stay within the fourfold among things. Even when we relate ourselves to those things that are not in our immediate reach, we are staying with the things themselves. We do not represent distant things merely in our mind—as the textbooks have it—so that only mental representations of distant things run through our minds and heads as substitutes for the things. If all of us now think, from where we are right here, of the old bridge in Heidelberg, this thinking toward that location is not a mere experience inside the persons present here; rather, it belongs to the nature of our thinking *of* that bridge that *in itself* thinking gets through, persists through, the distance to that location. From this spot right here, we are there at the bridge—we are by no means at some representational content in our consciousness. From right here we may even be much nearer to that bridge and to what it makes room for than someone who uses it daily as an indifferent river crossing. Spaces, and with them space as such—"space"—are always provided for already within the stay of mortals. Spaces open up by the fact that they are let into the dwelling of man. To say that mortals *are* is to say that *in dwelling* they persist through spaces by virtue of their stay among things and locations. And only because mortals pervade, persist through, spaces by their very nature are they able to go through spaces. But in going through spaces we do not give up our standing in them. Rather, we always go through spaces in such a way that we already experience them by staying constantly with near and remote locations and things. When I go toward the door of the lecture hall, I am already there, and I could not go to it at all if I were not such that I am there. I am never here only, as this encapsulated body; rather, I am there, that is, I already pervade the room, and only thus can I go through it.

Even when mortals turn "inward," taking stock of themselves, they do not leave behind their belonging to the fourfold. When, as we say, we come to our senses and reflect on ourselves, we come back to ourselves from things *without ever abandoning* our stay among things. Indeed, the loss of rapport with things that occurs in states of depression would be wholly impossible if even such a state were not still what it is as a human state: that is, a staying *with* things. Only if this stay already characterizes human being can the things among which we are also *fail* to speak to us, *fail* to concern us any longer.

Man's relation to locations, and through locations to spaces, inheres in his dwelling. The relationship between man and space is none other than dwelling, strictly thought and spoken.

When we think, in the manner just attempted, about the relation between location and space, but also about the relation of man and space, a light falls on the nature of the things that are locations and that we call buildings.

The bridge is a thing of this sort. The location allows the simple onefold of earth and sky, of divinities and mortals, to enter into a site by arranging the site into spaces. The location makes room for the fourfold in a double sense. The location *admits* the fourfold and it *installs* the fourfold. The two—making room in the sense of admitting and in the sense of installing—belong together. As a double space-making, the location is a shelter for the fourfold or, by the same token, a house. Things like such locations shelter or house men's lives. Things of this sort are housings, though not necessarily dwellings—houses in the narrower sense.

The making of such things is building. Its nature consists in this, that it corresponds to the character of these things. They are locations that allow spaces. This is why building, by virtue of constructing locations, is a founding and joining of spaces. Because building produces locations, the joining of the spaces of these locations necessarily brings with it space, as *spatium* and as *extensio,* into the thingly structure of buildings. But building never shapes pure "space" as a single entity. Neither directly nor indirectly. Nevertheless, because it produces things as locations, building is closer to the nature of spaces and to the origin of the nature of "space" than any geometry and mathematics. Building puts up locations that make space and a site for the fourfold. From the simple oneness in which earth and sky, divinities and mortals belong together, building *receives the directive* for its erecting of locations. Building takes over from the fourfold the standard for all the traversing and measuring of the spaces that in each case are provided for by the locations that have been founded. The edifices guard the fourfold. They are things that in their own way preserve the fourfold. To preserve the fourfold, to save the earth, to receive the sky, to await the divinities, to escort mortals—this fourfold preserving is the simple nature, the presencing, of dwelling. In this way, then, do genuine buildings give form to dwelling in its presencing and house this presence.

Building thus characterized is a distinctive letting-dwell. Whenever it *is* such in fact, building already *has* responded to the summons of the fourfold. All planning remains grounded on this responding, and planning in turn opens up to the designer the precincts suitable for his designs.

As soon as we try to think of the nature of constructive building in terms of a letting-dwell, we come to know more clearly what that process of making consists in by which building is accomplished. Usually we take production to be an activity whose performance has a result, the finished structure, as its consequence. It is possible to conceive of making in that way; we thereby grasp something that is correct, and yet never touch its nature, which is a producing that brings something forth. For building brings the fourfold *hither* into a thing, the bridge, and brings *forth* the thing as a location, out into what is already there, room for which is only now made *by* this location.

The Greek for "to bring forth or to produce" is *tikto.* The word *techne,* technique, belongs to the verb's root *tec.* To the Greeks *techne* means neither art nor handicraft but rather: to make something appear, within what is present, as this or that, in this way or that way. The Greeks conceive of *techne,* producing, in terms of letting appear. *Techne* thus conceived has been concealed in the tectonics of architecture since ancient times. Of late it still remains concealed, and more resolutely, in the technology of power machinery. But the nature of the erecting of buildings cannot be understood adequately in terms either of architecture or of engineering construction, nor in terms of a mere combination of the two. The erecting of buildings would not be suitably defined *even if* we were to think of it in the sense of the original Greek *techne* as *solely* a letting-appear, which brings something made, as something present, among the things that are already present.

The nature of building is letting dwell. Building accomplishes its nature in the raising of locations by the joining of their spaces. *Only if we are capable of dwelling, only then can we build.* Let us think for a while of a farmhouse in the Black Forest, which was built some two hundred years ago by the dwelling of peasants. Here the self-sufficiency of the power to let earth and heaven, divinities and mortals enter *in simple oneness* into things, ordered the house. It placed the farm on the wind-sheltered mountain slope looking south, among the meadows close to the spring. It gave it the wide overhanging shingle roof whose proper slope bears up under the burden of snow, and which, reaching deep down, shields the chambers against the storms of the long winter nights. It did not forget the altar corner behind the community table; it made room in its chamber for the hallowed places of childbed and the "tree of the dead"— for that is what they call a coffin there: the *Totenbaum*—and in this way it designed for the different generations under one roof the character of their journey through time. A craft which, itself sprung from dwelling, still uses its tools and frames as things, built the farmhouse.

Only if we are capable of dwelling, only then can we build. Our reference to the Black Forest farm in no way means that we should or could go back to building such houses; rather, it illustrates by a dwelling that *has been* how *it* was able to build.

Dwelling, however, is *the basic character* of Being in keeping with which mortals exist. Perhaps this attempt to think about dwelling and building will bring out somewhat more clearly that building belongs to dwelling and how it receives its nature from dwelling. Enough will have been gained if dwelling and building have become *worthy of questioning* and thus have remained *worthy of thought*.

But that thinking itself belongs to dwelling in the same sense as building, although in a different way, may perhaps be attested to by the course of thought here attempted.

Building and thinking are, each in its own way, inescapable for dwelling. The two, however, are also insufficient for dwelling so long as each busies itself with its own affairs in separation instead of listening to one another. They are able to listen if both—building and thinking—belong to dwelling, if they remain within their limits and realize that the one as much as the other comes from the workshop of long experience and incessant practice.

We are attempting to trace in thought the nature of dwelling. The next step on this path would be the question: what is the state of dwelling in our precarious age? On all sides we hear talk about the housing shortage, and with good reason. Nor is there just talk; there is action too. We try to fill the need by providing houses, by promoting the building of houses, planning the whole architectural enterprise. However hard and bitter, however hampering and threatening the lack of houses remains, the real plight of dwelling does not lie merely in a lack of houses. The *real plight of dwelling* is indeed older than the world wars with their destruction, older also than the increase of the earth's population and the condition of the industrial workers. The real dwelling plight lies in this, that mortals ever search anew for the nature of dwelling, that they *must ever learn to dwell*. What if man's homelessness consisted in this, that man still does not even think of the *real* plight of dwelling as *the* plight? Yet as soon as man *gives thought* to his homelessness, it is a misery no longer. Rightly considered and kept well in mind, it is the sole summons that calls mortals into their dwelling.

But how else can mortals answer this summons than by trying on *their* part, on their own, to bring dwelling to the fullness of its nature? This they accomplish when they build out of dwelling, and think for the sake of dwelling.

LUDWIG WITTGENSTEIN
1889–1951

Ludwig Wittgenstein was born into one of Vienna's leading families. His father, Karl, was a wealthy steel industrialist and his mother, Leopoldine, a concert pianist. Johannes Brahams, Gustaf Mahler, and Pablo Casals were frequent houseguests of the Wittgensteins. Educated at home by tutors, Wittgenstein showed great promise in mathematics and engineering. According to one report, he built a working sewing machine from matchsticks at age ten.

Wittgenstein remained home until age fifteen, when he enrolled at the *Linz Realschule,* where he studied engineering for two years before transferring to Berlin. In 1908, Wittgenstein enrolled at the University of Manchester, England, for studies in aerodynamics. While designing a propeller, Wittgenstein developed an interest in mathematics, which led him to Cambridge. There, from 1912 to 1913, he studied with Bertrand Russell. Russell later recalled one of his first encounters with Wittgenstein:

> At the end of his first term at Cambridge he came to me and said, "Will you please tell me whether I am a complete idiot or not?" I replied, "My dear fellow, I don't know. Why are you asking me?" He said, "Because if I am a complete idiot, I shall become an aeronaut; but, if not, I shall become a philosopher." I told him to write me something during the vacation on some philosophical subject and I would then tell him whether he was a complete idiot or not. At the beginning of the following term he brought me the fulfillment of this suggestion. After reading only one sentence, I said to him, "No, you must not become an aeronaut."*

*Bertrand Russell, *Portraits from Memory* (London: George Allen & Unwin, 1957), pp. 26–27.

Wittgenstein immersed himself in philosophical studies, filling notebooks with ideas. When World War I began in 1914, he enlisted as a machine-gunner in the Austrian army. While in the army, he continued his philosophical work, writing a short treatise in 1918 based on his notebooks. That same year, he was captured by the Italian army. In captivity, he managed to send a copy of this treatise to Russell, who considered it a work of genius and arranged for its publication as the *Tractatus Logico-Philosophicus* (1921). This was the only philosophical book Wittgenstein published during his lifetime.

Wittgenstein believed his *Tractatus* gave the definitive answer to all philosophical problems. Following the war, therefore, he left philosophy completely. After a course at a teacher's training college, he spent the next six years as a schoolteacher in remote Austrian villages. But teaching did not suit his temperament, and he was desperately unhappy. He resigned in 1926 and worked as a monastery gardener before moving back to Vienna to design a house for his sister. While in Vienna, Wittgenstein began talking philosophy again with Moritz Schlick, professor of philosophy at the University of Vienna, and with other professors who admired his *Tractatus*.

Philosophically revived, Wittgenstein returned to Cambridge in 1929, and, after submitting his now famous *Tractatus* as a doctoral dissertation, he became a research fellow of Trinity College. Again, Wittgenstein filled notebooks with philosophical reflections and prepared them for publication. But, with the exception of one paper, Wittgenstein never saw any of his new ideas in print; he always considered his newest thoughts incomplete or not yet adequately formulated.

For the rest of his life, Wittgenstein continued his association with Cambridge—though he never felt completely comfortable with academic life. On several occasions, he left the university, sometimes living in isolation in his hut in Norway. In 1939, he was appointed professor of philosophy at Cambridge, succeeding G.E. Moore. But before he could take the chair, World War II began, and he volunteered as a hospital orderly in London. He returned to Cambridge following the war, but he found his job so dreadful he resigned after two years. Living alone in Ireland, he completed his second major work, *Philosophical Investigations,* though again he could not bring himself to publish it. (It appeared posthumously in 1953.)

During a visit to the United States in 1949, his health began to deteriorate. On his return to Cambridge, doctors discovered prostate cancer, and he died eighteen months later, in 1951. Since his death, his literary executors have published over a dozen books of uncompleted manuscripts, notes, lectures, and letters.

*   *   *

Throughout his adult life, Wittgenstein was interested in philosophy as an activity rather than as a set of theories. He believed that the goal of philosophy is to remove or "dissolve" problems, and the primary means for doing this is analysis of language. According to Wittgenstein, most philosophical problems can be traced to a misuse of language. In one of his early notebooks he wrote:

> Philosophy gives no pictures of reality and can neither confirm nor confute scientific investigations. Philosophy teaches us the logical form of propositions: that is its fundamental task.*

*Ludwig Wittgenstein, *Notebooks 1914–1916* (London: Basil Blackwell, 1961), p. 93.

Thirty-five years later, he still maintained this philosophical position: "Philosophy is a battle against the bewitchment of our intelligence by means of language."*

But despite this theme, Wittgenstein developed two different ways to understand language. The early Wittgenstein created a "picture theory of meaning" that held that language consists of statements or propositions that picture the world. Just as a picture has something in common with that which it pictures, so language has a logical form in common with the world it pictures. This logical form is usually obscured by ordinary language, so the philosopher's job is to clear up ordinary language by crafting a language that more perfectly pictures the world. This perfected language will have to exclude many propositions (such as those in ethics, metaphysics, or religion), consigning them to silence. Our selection from the *Tractatus,* translated by D.F. Pears and B.F. McGuiness, presents this early theory.

Wittgenstein's early theory was adopted and modified by Moritz Schlick and his "Vienna Circle." This group developed a philosophy that came to be called "logical positivism." Like Wittgenstein, they worked on an ideal language, free from the ambiguities of ordinary discourse, that would clearly exhibit its logical form. They also held that such a language would exclude the propositions of ethics, metaphysics, and religion. (For more on logical positivism, see the introduction to Rudolf Carnap, pages 186–189.)

The early Wittgenstein, and the logical positivism that adapted many of his ideas, profoundly impacted the philosophy of the mid-twentieth century. But Wittgenstein himself moved to a different understanding of language: a "language game" theory. This theory found the earlier picture theory too narrow; a perfected language is neither possible nor desirable. As he explains in our selection from the *Investigations,* given here in the G.E.M. Anscombe translation, there are many kinds of meaningful sentences that share certain characteristics, but not others. Just as there is no one characteristic common to all games, so there is no one theory to explain all language uses. The proper way to understand a sentence is not to break it down into its constituent parts and analyze its logical form. Instead, we should examine the "forms of life" out of which the sentence arises, to see what "game" it is playing. "The meaning of a word," Wittgenstein wrote, "is its use in the language."

The later Wittgenstein was not interested in creating a perfect language. He sought rather to expose the underlying assumptions of language and the forms of life out of which our sentences arise. By understanding language in terms of the social environment that gives it birth, the later Wittgenstein encouraged a sociological understanding of language. Accordingly, Wittgenstein argued against the idea of a private language—a language apart from communal interactions.

The influence of Wittgenstein's early work peaked in the 1950s. But his later understanding of philosophy and his lifelong conception of philosophy as activity are still influential, particularly in the English-speaking world. For example, feminist philosophers have used Wittgenstein's insights to show how patriarchal language both influences and is influenced by social structures, and theologians have tried to understand the language of sacred texts by exploring their historical contexts. Wittgenstein's belief that the aim of philosophy is to dissolve problems—"To shew the fly the way out of the fly-bottle"—has continued to impress, or, as critics would say, to depress, philosophy.

---

*Ludwig Wittgenstein, *Philosophical Investigations* (New York: Macmillan, 1958), no. 109, p. 47.

*   *   *

Among the many general introductions to Wittgenstein's life and thought, Anthony Kenney, *Wittgenstein* (Cambridge, MA: Harvard University Press, 1973) still provides one of the best. Also helpful are George Pitcher, *The Philosophy of Wittgenstein* (Englewood Cliffs, NJ: Prentice Hall, 1964); David Pears, *Ludwig Wittgenstein* (New York: Viking Press, 1970); A.J. Ayer, *Wittgenstein* (Chicago: University of Chicago Press, 1985); Joachim Schulte, *Wittgenstein: An Introduction,* translated by William H. Brenner and John F. Holley (Albany, NY: SUNY Press, 1992); P.M.S. Hacker, *Wittgenstein's Place in Twentieth-Century Analytic Philosophy* (Oxford: Basil Blackwell, 1996); and the more specialized David G. Stern, *Wittgenstein on Mind and Language* (Oxford: Oxford University Press, 1995). Norman Malcolm, *Ludwig Wittgenstein: A Memoir* (London: Oxford University Press, 1958); K.T. Fann, ed., *Wittgenstein: The Man and His Philosophy* (New York: Delta, 1967); and O.K. Bouwsma, *Wittgenstein: Conversations, 1949–1951* (Indianapolis, IN: Hackett, 1986) all provide personal memoirs, whereas Allan Janik and Stephen Toulmin, *Wittgenstein's Vienna* (New York: Simon & Schuster, 1973) and Ray Monk, *Ludwig Wittgenstein: The Duty of Genius* (New York: Penguin Books, 1992) give biographies. For guides to Wittgenstein's two major works, see G.E.M. Anscombe, *An Introduction to Wittgenstein's "Tractatus"* (London: Hillary House, 1959); H.O. Mounce, *Wittgenstein's "Tractatus"* (Chicago: University of Chicago Press, 1981); Garth Hallett, *A Companion to Wittgenstein's "Philosophical Investigations"* (Ithaca, NY: Cornell University Press, 1977); G.P. Baker and P.M.S. Hacker, *Wittgenstein: Understanding and Meaning* (Chicago: University of Chicago Press, 1979); Marie McGinn, *Routledge Philosophy Guidebook to Wittgenstein and the Philosophical Investigations* (Oxford: Routledge, 1997); and William H. Brenner, *Wittgenstein's Philosophical Investigations* (Albany, NY: SUNY Press, 1999). Hans-Johann Glock, *A Wittgenstein Dictionary* (Oxford: Basil Blackwell, 1995) provides a useful reference work. Collections of essays include Irving Copi, ed., *Essays on Wittgenstein's "Tractatus"* (New York: Macmillan, 1966); George Pitcher, ed., *Wittgenstein's "Investigations"* (Garden City, NY: Anchor Doubleday, 1966); Peter A. French, Theodore E. Uehling, Jr., and Howard K. Wettstein, eds., *The Wittgenstein Legacy* (Notre Dame, IN: University of Notre Dame Press, 1992); Robert L. Arrington and Johann Glock, eds., *Wittgenstein and Quine* (Oxford: Routledge, 1996); and Hans Sluga and David G. Stern, eds., *The Cambridge Companion to Wittgenstein* (Cambridge: Cambridge University Press, 1996).

TRACTATUS LOGICO-PHILOSOPHICUS
(in part)

PREFACE

Perhaps this book will be understood only by someone who has himself already had the thoughts that are expressed in it—or at least similar thoughts.—So it is not a textbook.—Its purpose would be achieved if it gave pleasure to one person who read and understood it.

Ludwig Wittgenstein, *Tractatus Logico-Philosophicus,* Translated by D.F. Pears and B.F. McGuiness (London: Routledge & Kegan Paul PLC, 1972). Reprinted by permission of Routledge & Kegan Paul.

The book deals with the problems of philosophy, and shows, I believe, that the reason why these problems are posed is that the logic of our language is misunderstood. The whole sense of the book might be summed up in the following words: what can be said at all can be said clearly, and what we cannot talk about we must consign to silence.

Thus the aim of the book is to set a limit to thought, or rather—not to thought, but to the expression of thoughts: for in order to be able to set a limit to thought, we should have to find both sides of the limit thinkable (i.e. we should have to be able to think what cannot be thought).

It will therefore only be in language that the limit can be set, and what lies on the other side of the limit will simply be nonsense.

I do not wish to judge how far my efforts coincide with those of other philosophers. Indeed, what I have written here makes no claim to novelty in detail, and the reason why I give no sources is that it is a matter of indifference to me whether the thoughts that I have had have been anticipated by someone else.

I will only mention that I am indebted to Frege's great works and to the writings of my friend Mr. Bertrand Russell for much of the stimulation of my thoughts.

If this work has any value, it consists in two things: the first is that thoughts are expressed in it, and on this score the better the thoughts are expressed—the more the nail has been hit on the head—the greater will be its value.—Here I am conscious of having fallen a long way short of what is possible. Simply because my powers are too slight for the accomplishment of the task.—May others come and do it better.

On the other hand the *truth* of the thoughts that are here set forth seems to me unassailable and definitive. I therefore believe myself to have found, on all essential points, the final solution of the problems. And if I am not mistaken in this belief, then the second thing in which the value of this work consists is that it shows how little is achieved when these problems are solved.

TRACTATUS LOGICO-PHILOSOPHICUS

1*   The world is all that is the case.
1.1   The world is the totality of facts, not of things.
1.11   The world is determined by the facts, and by their being *all* the facts.
1.12   For the totality of facts determines what is the case, and also whatever is not the case.
1.13   The facts in logical space are the world.
1.2   The world divides into facts.
1.21   Each item can be the case or not the case while everything else remains the same.
2   What is the case—a fact—is the existence of states of affairs.
2.01   A state of affairs (a state of things) is a combination of objects (things).
2.011   It is essential to things that they should be possible constituents of states of affairs.
2.012   In logic nothing is accidental: if a thing *can* occur in a state of affairs, the possibility of the state of affairs must be written into the thing itself.

*[The decimal numbers assigned to the individual propositions indicate the logical importance of the propositions, the stress laid on them in my exposition. The propositions *n*.1, *n*.2, *n*.3, etc. are comments on proposition no. *n;* the propositions *n.m*1, *n.m*2, etc. are comments on proposition no. *n.m;* and so on.]

2.0121   It would seem to be a sort of accident, if it turned out that a situation would fit a thing that could already exist entirely on its own.

It things can occur in states of affairs, this possibility must be in them from the beginning.

(Nothing in the province of logic can be merely possible. Logic deals with every possibility and all possibilities are its facts.)

Just as we are quite unable to imagine spatial objects outside space or temporal objects outside time, so too there is *no* object that we can imagine excluded from the possibility of combining with others.

If I can imagine objects combined in states of affairs, I cannot imagine them excluded from the *possibility* of such combinations.

2.0122   Things are independent in so far as they can occur in all *possible* situations, but this form of independence is a form of connexion with states of affairs, a form of dependence. (It is impossible for words to appear in two different roles: by themselves, and in propositions.)

2.0123   If I know an object I also know all its possible occurrences in states of affairs. (Every one of these possibilities must be part of the nature of the object.)

A new possibility cannot be discovered later.

2.01231   If I am to know an object, though I need not know its external properties, I must know all its internal properties.

2.0124   If all objects are given, then at the same time all *possible* states of affairs are also given.

2.013   Each thing is, as it were, in a space of possible states of affairs. This space I can imagine empty, but I cannot imagine the thing without the space.

2.0131   A spatial object must be situated in infinite space. (A spatial point is an argument-place.)

A speck in the visual field, though it need not be red, must have some colour: it is, so to speak, surrounded by colour-space. Tones must have some pitch, objects of the sense of touch *some* degree of hardness, and so on.

2.014   Objects contain the possibility of all situations.

2.0141   The possibility of its occurring in states of affairs is the form of an object.

2.02   Objects are simple.

2.0201   Every statement about complexes can be resolved into a statement about their constituents and into the propositions that describe the complexes completely.

2.021   Objects make up the substance of the world. That is why they cannot be composite.

2.0211   If the world had no substance, then whether a proposition had sense would depend on whether another proposition was true.

2.0212   In that case we could not sketch out any picture of the world (true or false).

2.022   It is obvious that an imagined world, however different it may be from the real one, must have *something*—a form—in common with it.

2.023   Objects are just what constitute this unalterable form.

2.0231   The substance of the world *can* only determine a form, and not any material properties. For it is only by means of propositions that material properties are represented—only by the configuration of objects that they are produced.

2.0232   In a manner of speaking, objects are colourless.

2.0233   If two objects have the same logical form, the only distinction between them, apart from their external properties, is that they are different.

2.02331   Either a thing has properties that nothing else has, in which case we can immediately use a description to distinguish it from the others and refer to it; or, on the other hand, there are several things that have the whole set of their properties in common, in which case it is quite impossible to indicate one of them.

For if there is nothing to distinguish a thing, I cannot distinguish it, since if I do it will be distinguished after all.

2.024   Substance is what subsists independently of what is the case.

2.025   It is form and content.

2.0251   Space, time, and colour (being coloured) are forms of objects.

2.026   There must be objects, if the world is to have an unalterable form.

2.027   Objects, the unalterable, and the subsistent are one and the same.

2.0271   Objects are what is unalterable and subsistent; their configuration is what is changing and unstable.

2.0272   The configuration of objects produces states of affairs.

2.03   In a state of affairs objects fit into one another like the links of a chain.

2.031   In a state of affairs objects stand in a determinate relation to one another.

2.032   The determinate way in which objects are connected in a state of affairs is the structure of the state of affairs.

2.033   Its form is the possibility of its structure.

2.034   The structure of a fact consists of the structures of states of affairs.

2.04   The totality of existing states of affairs is the world.

2.05   The totality of existing states of affairs also determines which states of affairs do not exist.

2.06   The existence and non-existence of states of affairs is reality.
         (We also call the existence of states of affairs a positive fact, and their non-existence a negative fact.)

2.061   States of affairs are independent of one another.

2.062   From the existence or non-existence of one state of affairs it is impossible to infer the existence or non-existence of another.

2.063   The sum-total of reality is the world.

2.1   We picture facts to ourselves.

2.11   A picture presents a situation in logical space, the existence and non-existence of states of affairs.

2.12   A picture is a model of reality.

2.13   In a picture objects have the elements of the picture corresponding to them.

2.131   In a picture the elements of the picture are the representatives of objects.

2.14   What constitutes a picture is that its elements are related to one another in a determinate way.

2.141   A picture is a fact.

2.15   The fact that the elements of a picture are related to one another in a determinate way represents that things are related to one another in the same way.
         Let us call this connexion of its elements the structure of the picture, and let us call the possibility of this structure the pictorial form of the picture.

2.151   Pictorial form is the possibility that things are related to one another in the same way as the elements of the picture.

2.1511   *That* is how a picture is attached to reality; it reaches right out to it.

2.1512   It is laid against reality like a ruler.

2.15121 Only the end-points of the graduating lines actually *touch* the object that is to be measured.

2.1513   So a picture, conceived in this way, also includes the pictorial relationship, which makes it into a picture.

Composition in Yellow, Red, Blue and Black, 1921, by Piet Mondrian (1872–1944). The painter/draftsman Mondrian constructed nonobjective paintings with mathematical precision. The clarity of form and structure, together with the lack of any ornamentation, provides a visual metaphor for the precision and austerity of Wittgenstein's *Tractatus*. *(Giraudon/Art Resource, NY)*

2.1514   The pictorial relationship consists of the correlations of the picture's ele-
           ments with things.
2.1515   These correlations are, as it were, the feelers of the picture's elements,
           with which the picture touches reality.
2.16   If a fact is to be a picture, it must have something in common with what it
           depicts.
2.161   There must be something identical in a picture and what it depicts, to en-
           able the one to be a picture of the other at all.
2.17   What a picture must have in common with reality, in order to be able to
           depict it—correctly or incorrectly—in the way it does, is its pictorial form.
2.171   A picture can depict any reality whose form it has.
           A spatial picture can depict anything spatial, a coloured one anything
           coloured, etc.
2.172   A picture cannot, however, depict its pictorial form: it displays it.
2.173   A picture represents its subject from a position outside it. (Its standpoint is
           its representational form.) That is why a picture represents its subject cor-
           rectly or incorrectly.
2.174   A picture cannot, however, place itself outside its representational form.
2.18   What any picture, of whatever form, must have in common with reality, in
           order to be able to depict it—correctly or incorrectly—in any way at all, is
           logical form, i.e. the form of reality.
2.181   A picture whose pictorial form is logical form is called a logical picture.
2.182   Every picture is *at the same time* a logical one. (On the other hand, not
           every picture is, for example, a spatial one.)
2.19   Logical pictures can depict the world.
2.2   A picture has logico-pictorial form in common with what it depicts.
2.201   A picture depicts reality by representing a possibility of existence and
           non-existence of states of affairs.
2.202   A picture represents a possible situation in logical space.
2.203   A picture contains the possibility of the situation that it represents.
2.21   A picture agrees with reality or fails to agree; it is correct or incorrect, true
           or false.
2.22   What a picture represents it represents independently of its truth or falsity,
           by means of its pictorial form.
2.221   What a picture represents is its sense.
2.222   The agreement or disagreement of its sense with reality constitutes its
           truth or falsity.
2.223   In order to tell whether a picture is true or false we must compare it with
           reality.
2.224   It is impossible to tell from the picture alone whether it is true or false.
2.225   There are no pictures that are true *a priori*.
3   A logical picture of facts is a thought.
3.001   "A state of affairs is thinkable"—this means that we can picture it to our-
           selves.
3.01   The totality of true thoughts is a picture of the world.
3.02   A thought contains the possibility of the situation of which it is the
           thought. What is thinkable is possible too.
3.03   Thought can never be of anything illogical, since, if it were, we should
           have to think illogically.

3.031   It used to be said that God could create anything except what would be contrary to the laws of logic.—The reason being that we could not say what an "illogical" world would look like.

3.032   It is as impossible to represent in language anything that "contradicts logic" as it is in geometry to represent by its co-ordinates a figure that contradicts the laws of space, or to give the co-ordinates of a point that does not exist.

3.0321   Though a state of affairs that would contravene the laws of physics can be represented by us spatially, one that would contravene the laws of geometry cannot.

3.04   If a thought were correct , it would be a thought whose possibility ensured its truth.

3.05   *A priori* knowledge that a thought was true would be possible only if its truth were recognizable from the thought itself (without anything to compare it with).

3.1   In a proposition a thought finds an expression that can be perceived by the senses.

3.11   We use the perceptible sign of a proposition (spoken or written, etc.) as a projection of a possible situation.

The method of projection is to think out the sense of the proposition.

3.12   I call the sign with which we express a thought a propositional sign.—And a proposition is a propositional sign in its projective relation to the world.

3.13   A proposition includes all that the projection includes, but not what is projected.

Therefore, though what is projected is not itself included, its possibility is.

A proposition does not actually contain its sense, but does contain the possibility of expressing it.

("The content of a proposition" means the content of a proposition that has sense.)

A proposition contains the form, but not the content, of its sense.

3.14   What constitutes a propositional sign is that in it its elements (the words) stand in a determinate relation to one another.

A propositional sign is a fact.

3.141   A proposition is not a medley of words.—(Just as a theme in music is not a medley of notes.)

A proposition is articulated.

3.142   Only facts can express a sense, a set of names cannot.

3.143   Although a propositional sign is a fact, this is obscured by the usual form of expression in writing or print.

For in a printed proposition, for example, no essential difference is apparent between a propositional sign and a word.

(That is what made it possible for Frege to call a proposition a composite name.)

3.1431   The essence of a propositional sign is very clearly seen if we imagine one composed of spatial objects (such as tables, chairs, and books) instead of written signs.

Then the spatial arrangement of these things will express the sense of the proposition.

*   *   *

6.4   All propositions are of equal value.

6.41   The sense of the world must lie outside the world. In the world everything

is as it is, and everything happens as it does happen: in it no value exists—
and if it did, it would have no value.

If there is any value that does have value, it must lie outside the whole
sphere of what happens and is the case. For all that happens and is the case is
accidental.

What makes it non-accidental cannot lie *within* the world, since if it did it
would itself be accidental.

It must lie outside the world.

6.42   And so it is impossible for there to be propositions of ethics.

Propositions can express nothing of what is higher.

6.421   It is clear that ethics cannot be put into words. Ethics is transcendental.
(Ethics and aesthetics are one and the same.)

6.422   When an ethical law of the form, "Thou shalt . . .," is laid down, one's first
thought is, "And what if I do not do it?" It is clear, however, that ethics has
nothing to do with punishment and reward in the usual sense of the terms. So
our question about the consequences of an action must be unimportant.—At
least those consequences should not be events. For there must be something
right about the question we posed. There must indeed be some kind of ethical
reward and ethical punishment, but they must reside in the action itself.

(And it is also clear that the reward must be something pleasant and the
punishment something unpleasant.)

6.423   It is impossible to speak about the will in so far as it is the subject of ethical attributes.

And the will as a phenomenon is of interest only to psychology.

6.43   If good or bad acts of will do alter the world, it can only be the limits of
the world that they alter, not the facts, not what can be expressed by means of
language.

In short their effect must be that it becomes an altogether different world.
It must, so to speak, wax and wane as a whole.

The world of the happy man is a different one from that of the unhappy
man.

6.431   So too at death the world does not alter, but comes to an end.

6.4311   Death is not an event in life: we do not live to experience death.

If we take eternity to mean not infinite temporal duration but timelessness,
then eternal life belongs to those who live in the present.

Our life has no end in just the way in which our visual field has no limits.

6.4312   Not only is there no guarantee of the temporal immortality of the human
soul, that is to say of its eternal survival after death; but, in any case, this assumption completely fails to accomplish the purpose for which it has always
been intended. Or is some riddle solved by my surviving for ever? Is not this
eternal life itself as much of a riddle as our present life? The solution of the
riddle of life in space and time lies *outside* space and time.

(It is certainly not the solution of any problems of natural science that is
required.)

6.432   *How* things are in the world is a matter of complete indifference for what
is higher. God does not reveal himself *in* the world.

6.4321   The facts all contribute only to setting the problem, not to its solution.

6.44   It is not *how* things are in the world that is mystical, but *that* it exists.

6.45   To view the world *sub specie aeterni* is to view it as a whole—a limited
whole.

Feeling the world as a limited whole—it is this that is mystical.

6.5   When the answer cannot be put into words, neither can the question be put into words.

The riddle does not exist.

If a question can be framed at all, it is also *possible* to answer it.

6.51   Scepticism is *not* irrefutable, but obviously nonsensical, when it tries to raise doubts where no questions can be asked.

For doubt can exist only where a question exists, a question only where an answer exists, and an answer only where something *can be said.*

6.52   We feel that even when *all possible* scientific questions have been answered, the problems of life remain completely untouched. Of course there are then no questions left, and this itself is the answer.

6.521   The solution of the problem of life is seen in the vanishing of the problem.

(Is not this the reason why those who have found after a long period of doubt that the sense of life became clear to them have then been unable to say what constituted that sense?)

6.522   There are, indeed, things that cannot be put into words. They *make themselves manifest.* They are what is mystical.

6.53   The correct method in philosophy would really be the following: to say nothing except what can be said, i.e. propositions of natural science—i.e. something that has nothing to do with philosophy—and then, whenever someone else wanted to say something metaphysical, to demonstrate to him that he had failed to give a meaning to certain signs in his propositions. Although it would not be satisfying to the other person—he would not have the feeling that we were teaching him philosophy—*this* method would be the only strictly correct one.

6.54   My propositions serve as elucidations in the following way: anyone who understands me eventually recognizes them as nonsensical, when he has used them—as steps—to climb up beyond them. (He must, so to speak, throw away the ladder after he has climbed up it.)

He must transcend these propositions, and then he will see the world aright.

7   What we cannot speak about we must consign to silence.

PHILOSOPHICAL INVESTIGATIONS
(in part)

1. "When they (my elders) named some object, and accordingly moved towards something, I saw this and I grasped that the thing was called by the sound they uttered when they meant to point it out. Their intention was shewn by their bodily movements, as it were the natural language of all peoples: the expression of the face, the play of the

Reprinted with permission of Blackwell Publisher from Ludwig Wittgenstein: *Philosophical Investigations*, 3rd edition, 1–47, 65–71, 241, 257–258, 305, 309, translated by G.E.M. Anscombe.

eyes, the movement of other parts of the body, and the tone of voice which expresses our state of mind in seeking, having, rejecting, or avoiding something. Thus, as I heard words repeatedly used in their proper places in various sentences, I gradually learnt to understand what objects they signifed; and after I had trained my mouth to form these signs, I used them to express my own desires" (Augustine, *Confessions,* I. 8).

These words, it seems to me, give us a particular picture of the essence of human language. It is this: the individual words in language name objects—sentences are combinations of such names. In this picture of language we find the roots of the following idea: Every word has a meaning. This meaning is correlated with the word. It is the object for which the word stands.

Augustine does not speak of there being any difference between kinds of word. If you describe the learning of language in this way you are, I believe, thinking primarily of nouns like "table," "chair," "bread," and of people's names, and only secondarily of the names of certain actions and properties; and of the remaining kinds of word as something that will take care of itself.

Now think of the following use of language: I send someone shopping. I give him a slip marked "five red apples." He takes the slip to the shopkeeper, who opens the drawer marked "apples"; then he looks up the word "red" in a table and finds a colour sample opposite it; then he says the series of cardinal numbers—I assume that he knows them by heart—up to the word "five" and for each number he takes an apple of the same colour as the sample out of the drawer. It is in this and similar ways that one operates with words. "But how does he know where and how he is to look up the word 'red' and what he is to do with the word 'five'?" Well, I assume that he acts as I have described. Explanations come to an end somewhere.—But what is the meaning of the word "five"?—No such thing was in question here, only how the word "five" is used.

2. That philosophical concept of meaning has its place in a primitive idea of the way language functions. But one can also say that it is the idea of a language more primitive than ours.

Let us imagine a language for which the description given by Augustine is right. The language is meant to serve for communication between a builder A and an assistant B. A is building with building-stones: there are blocks, pillars, slabs and beams. B has to pass the stones, and that in the order in which A needs them. For this purpose they use a language consisting of the words "block," "pillar," "slab," "beam." A calls them out;—B brings the stone which he has learnt to bring at such-and-such a call.— Conceive this as a complete primitive language.

3. Augustine, we might say, does describe a system of communication; only not everything that we call language is this system. And one has to say this in many cases where the question arises "Is this an appropriate description or not?" The answer is: "Yes, it is appropriate, but only for this narrowly circumscribed region, not for the whole of what you were claiming to describe."

It is as if someone were to say: "A game consists in moving objects about on a surface according to certain rules . . ."—and we replied: You seem to be thinking of board games, but there are others. You can make your definition correct by expressly restricting it to those games.

4. Imagine a script in which the letters were used to stand for sounds, and also as signs of emphasis and punctuation. (A script can be conceived as a language for describing sound-patterns.) Now imagine someone interpreting that script as if there were simply a correspondence of letters to sounds and as if the letters had not also completely different functions. Augustine's conception of language is like such an over-simple conception of the script.

5. If we look at the example in ¶1, we may perhaps get an inkling how much this general notion of the meaning of a word surrounds the working of language with a haze which makes clear vision impossible. It disperses the fog to study the phenomena of language in primitive kinds of application in which one can command a clear view of the aim and functioning of the words.

A child uses such primitive forms of language when it learns to talk. Here the teaching of language is not explanation, but training.

6. We could imagine that the language of ¶2 was the *whole* language of A and B; even the whole language of a tribe. The children are brought up to perform *these* actions, to use these words as they do so, and to react in *this* way to the words of others.

An important part of the training will consist in the teacher's pointing to the objects, directing the child's attention to them, and at the same time uttering a word; for instance, the word "slab" as he points to that shape. (I do not want to call this "ostensive definition," because the child cannot as yet ask what the name is. I will call it "ostensive teaching of words." I say that it will form an important part of the training, because it is so with human beings; not because it could not be imagined otherwise.) This ostensive teaching of words can be said to establish an association between the word and the thing. But what does this mean? Well, it may mean various things; but one very likely thinks first of all that a picture of the object comes before the child's mind when it hears the word. But now, if this does happen—is it the purpose of the word?— Yes, it *may* be the purpose.—I can imagine such a use of words (of series of sounds). (Uttering a word is like striking a note on the keyboard of the imagination.) But in the language of ¶2 it is *not* the purpose of the words to evoke images. (It may, of course, be discovered that that helps to attain the actual purpose.)

But if the ostensive teaching has this effect,—am I to say that it effects an understanding of the word? Don't you understand the call "Slab!" if you act upon it in such-and-such a way?—Doubtless the ostensive teaching helped to bring this about; but only together with a particular training. With different training the same ostensive teaching of these words would have effected a quite different understanding.

"I set the brake up by connecting up rod and lever."—Yes, given the whole of the rest of the mechanism. Only in conjunction with that is it a brake-lever, and separated from its support it is not even a lever; it may be anything, or nothing.

7. In the practice of the use of language (2) one party calls out the words, the other acts on them. In instruction in the language the following process will occur: the learner *names* the objects; that is, he utters the word when the teacher points to the stone.—And there will be this still simpler exercise: the pupil repeats the words after the teacher— both of these being processes resembling language.

We can also think of the whole process of using words in (2) as one of those games by means of which children learn their native language. I will call these games "language-games" and will sometimes speak of a primitive language as a language-game.

And the processes of naming the stones and of repeating words after someone might also be called language-games. Think of much of the use of words in games like ring-a-ring-a-roses.

I shall also call the whole, consisting of language and the actions into which it is woven, the "language-game."

8. Let us now look at an expansion of language (2). Besides the four words "block," "pillar," etc., let it contain a series of words used as the shopkeeper in (I) used the numerals (it can be the series of letters of the alphabet); further, let there be two words, which may as well be "there" and "this" (because this roughly indicates their purpose), that are used in connexion with a pointing gesture; and finally a number of colour sam-

ples. A gives an order like: "d—slab—there." At the same time he shews the assistant a colour sample, and when he says "there" he points to a place on the building site. From the stock of slabs B takes one for each letter of the alphabet up to "d," of the same colour as the sample, and brings them to the place indicated by A.—On other occasions A gives the order "this—there." At "this" he points to a building stone. And so on.

9. When a child learns this language, it has to learn the series of 'numerals' a, b, c, ... by heart. And it has to learn their use.—Will this training include ostensive teaching of the words?—Well, people will, for example, point to slabs and count: "a, b, c slabs."—Something more like the ostensive teaching of the words "block," "pillar," etc. would be the ostensive teaching of numerals that serve not to count but to refer to groups of objects that can be taken in at a glance. Children do learn the use of the first five or six cardinal numerals in this way.

Are "there" and "this" also taught ostensively?—Imagine how one might perhaps teach their use. One will point to places and things—but in this case the pointing occurs in the *use* of the words too and not merely in learning the use.—

10. Now what do the words of this language *signify?*—What is supposed to shew what they signify, if not the kind of use they have? And we have already described that. So we are asking for the expression "This word signifies this" to be made a part of the description. In other words the description ought to take the form: "The word . . . signifies . . ."

Of course, one can reduce the description of the use of the word "slab" to the statement that this word signifies this object. This will be done when, for example, it is merely a matter of removing the mistaken idea that the word "slab" refers to the shape of building-stone that we in fact call a "block"— but the kind of '*referring*' this is, that is to say the use of these words for the rest, is already known.

Equally one can say that the signs "a," "b," etc. signify numbers; when for example this removes the mistaken idea that "a," "b," "c," play the part actually played in language by "block," "slab," "pillar." And one can also say that "c" means this number and not that one; when for example this serves to explain that the letters are to be used in the order a, b, c, d, etc. and not in the order a, b, d, c.

But assimilating the descriptions of the uses of words in this way cannot make the uses themselves any more like one another. For, as we see, they are absolutely unlike.

11. Think of the tools in a toolbox: there is a hammer, pliers, a saw, a screwdriver, a rule, a glue-pot, glue, nails and screws.—The functions of words are as diverse as the functions of these objects. (And in both cases there are similarities.)

Of course, what confuses us is the uniform appearance of words when we hear them spoken or meet them in script and print. For their *application* is not presented to us so clearly. Especially when we are doing philosophy!

12. It is like looking into the cabin of a locomotive. We see handles all looking more or less alike. (Naturally, since they are all supposed to be handled.) But one is the handle of a crank which can be moved continuously (it regulates the opening of a valve); another is the handle of a switch, which has only two effective positions, it is either off or on; a third is the handle of a brake-lever, the harder one pulls on it, the harder it brakes; a fourth, the handle of a pump: it has an effect only so long as it is moved to and fro.

13. When we say: "Every word in language signifies something" we have so far said *nothing whatever;* unless we have explained exactly what distinction we wish to make. (It might be, of course, that we wanted to distinguish the words of language [8] from words 'without meaning' such as occur in Lewis Carroll's poems, or words like "Lilliburlero" in songs.)

14. Imagine someone's saying: "*All* tools serve to modify something. Thus the hammer modifies the position of the nail, the saw the shape of the board, and so on."—And what is modified by the rule, the glue-pot, the nails?—"Our knowledge of a thing's length, the temperature of the glue, and the solidity of the box." Would anything be gained by this assimilation of expressions?—

15. The word "to signify" is perhaps used in the most straightforward way when the object signified is marked with the sign. Suppose that the tools A uses in building bear certain marks. When A shews his assistant such a mark, he brings the tool that has that mark on it.

It is in this and more or less similar ways that a name means and is given to a thing.—It will often prove useful in philosophy to say to ourselves: naming something is like attaching a label to a thing.

16. What about the colour samples that A shews to B: are they part of the *language*? Well, it is as you please. They do not belong among the words; yet when I say to someone: "Pronounce the word 'the'," you will count the second "the" as part of the sentence. Yet it has a role just like that of a colour-sample in language-game (8); that is, it is a sample of what the other is meant to say.

It is most natural, and causes least confusion, to reckon the samples among the instruments of the language.

((Remark on the reflexive pronoun "*this* sentence."))

17. It will be possible to say: In language (8) we have different kinds *of word*. For the functions of the word "slab" and the word "block" are more alike than those of "slab" and "d." But how we group words into kinds will depend on the aim of the classification,—and on our own inclination.

Think of the different points of view from which one can classify tools or chessmen.

18. Do not be troubled by the fact that languages (2) and (8) consist only of orders. If you want to say that this shews them to be incomplete, ask yourself whether our language is complete;—whether it was so before the symbolism of chemistry and the notation of the infinitesimal calculus were incorporated in it; for these are, so to speak, suburbs of our language. (And how many houses or streets does it take before a town begins to be a town?) Our language can be seen as an ancient city: a maze of little streets and squares, of old and new houses, and of houses with additions from various periods; and this surrounded by a multitude of new boroughs with straight regular streets and uniform houses.

19. It is easy to imagine a language consisting only of orders and reports in battle.—Or a language consisting only of questions and expressions for answering yes and no. And innumerable others.—And to imagine a language means to imagine a form of life.

But what about this: is the call "Slab!" in example (2) a sentence or a word?—If a word, surely it has not the same meaning as the like-sounding word of our ordinary language, for in ¶2 it is a call. But if a sentence, it is surely not the elliptical sentence: "Slab!" of our language. As far as the first question goes you can call "Slab!" a word and also a sentence; perhaps it could be appropriately called a 'degenerate sentence' (as one speaks of a degenerate hyperbola); in fact it is our 'elliptical' sentence.—But that is surely only a shortened form of the sentence "Bring me a slab," and there is no such sentence in example (2).—But why should I not on the contrary have called the sentence "Bring me a slab" a *lengthening* of the sentence "Slab!"?—Because if you shout "Slab!" you really mean: "Bring me a slab."—But how do you do this: how do you mean that while you say "Slab!"? Do you say the unshortened sentence to yourself? And why should I translate the call "Slab!" into a different expression in order to say what someone means by it? And if they mean the same thing—why should I not say: "When he says 'Slab!' he means 'Slab!' "? Again, if you can mean "Bring me the slab," why should you not be able to mean "Slab!"? But when I call "Slab!" then what I want is, *that he should bring me a slab!*—Certainly, but does 'wanting this' consist in thinking in some form or other a different sentence from the one you utter?—

20. But now it looks as if when someone says "Bring me a slab" he could mean this expression as *one* long word corresponding to the single word "Slab!" Then can one mean it sometimes as one word and sometimes as four? And how does one usually mean it? I think we shall be inclined to say: we mean the sentence as four words when we use it in contrast with other sentences such as "*Hand* me a slab," "Bring *him* a slab," "Bring *two* slabs," etc.; that is, in contrast with sentences containing the separate words of our command in other combinations.—But what does using one sentence in contrast with others consist in? Do the others, perhaps, hover before one's mind? *All* of them? And *while* one is saying the one sentence, or before, or afterwards?—No. Even if such an explanation rather tempts us, we need only think for a moment of what actually happens in order to see that we are going astray here. We say that we use the command in contrast with other sentences because *our language* contains the possibility of those other sentences. Someone who did not understand our language, a foreigner, who had fairly often heard someone giving the order: "Bring me a slab!" might believe that this whole series of sounds was one word corresponding perhaps to the word for "building-stone" in his language. If he himself had then given this order perhaps he would have pronounced it differently, and we should say: he pronounces it so oddly because he takes it for a *single* word.—But then, is there not also something different going on in him when he pronounces it,—something corresponding to the fact that he conceives the sentence as a single word?—Either the same thing may go on in him, or something different. For what goes on in you when you give such an order? Are you conscious of its consisting of four words *while* you are uttering it? Of course you have a mastery of this language—which contains those other sentences as well—but is this having a mastery something that *happens* while you are uttering the sentence?—And I have admitted that the foreigner will probably pronounce a sentence differently if he conceives it differently; but what we call his wrong conception *need* not lie in anything that accompanies the utterance of the command.

The sentence is 'elliptical,' not because it leaves out something that we think when we utter it, but because it is shortened—in comparison with a particular paradigm of our grammar.—Of course one might object here: "You grant that the shortened and the unshortened sentence have the same sense.—What is this sense, then? Isn't there a verbal expression for this sense?" But doesn't the fact that sentences have the same sense consist in their having the same *use?*—(In Russian one says "stone red" instead of "the stone is red"; do they feel the copula to be missing in the sense, or attach it in *thought?*)

21. Imagine a language-game in which A asks and B reports the number of slabs or blocks in a pile, or the colours and shapes of the building-stones that are stacked in such-and-such a place.—Such a report might run: "Five slabs." Now what is the difference between the report or statement "Five slabs" and the order "Five slabs!"?—Well, it is the part which uttering these words plays in the language-game. No doubt the tone of voice and the look with which they are uttered, and much else besides, will also be different. But we could also imagine the tone's being the same—for an order and a report can be spoken in a *variety* of tones of voice and with various expressions of face—the difference being only in the application. (Of course, we might use the words "statement" and "command" to stand for grammatical forms of sentence and intonations; we do in fact call "Isn't the weather glorious to-day?" a question, although it is used as a statement.) We could imagine a language in which *all* statements had the

form and tone of rhetorical questions; or every command the form of the question "Would you like to . . .?" Perhaps it will then be said: "What he says has the form of a question but is really a command,"—that is, has the function of a command in the technique of using the language. (Similarly one says "You will do this" not as a prophecy but as a command. What makes it the one or the other?)

22. Frege's idea that every assertion contains an assumption, which is the thing that is asserted, really rests on the possibility found in our language of writing every statement in the form: "It is asserted that such-and-such is the case."—But "that such-and-such is the case" is not a sentence in our language—so far it is not a *move* in the language-game. And if I write, not "It is asserted that . . . .," but "It is asserted: such-and-such is the case," the words "It is asserted" simply become superfluous.

We might very well also write every statement in the form of a question followed by a "Yes"; for instance: "Is it raining? Yes!" Would this shew that every statement contained a question?

Of course we have the right to use an assertion sign in contrast with a question-mark, for example, or if we want to distinguish an assertion from a fiction or a supposition. It is only a mistake if one thinks that the assertion consists of two actions, entertaining and asserting (assigning the truth-value, or something of the kind), and that in performing these actions we follow the propositional sign roughly as we sing from the musical score. Reading the written sentence loud or soft is indeed comparable with singing from a musical score, but '*meaning*' (thinking) the sentence that is read is not.

Frege's assertion sign marks the *beginning of the sentence*. Thus its function is like that of the full-stop. It distinguishes the whole period from a clause *within* the period. If I hear someone say "it's raining" but do not know whether I have heard the beginning and end of the period, so far this sentence does not serve to tell me anything.

23. But how many kinds of sentences are there? Say assertion, question, and command?—There are *countless* kinds: countless different kinds of use of what we call "symbols," "words," "sentences." And this multiplicity is not something fixed, given once for all; but new types of language, new language-games, as we may say, come into existence, and others become obsolete and get forgotten. (We can get a *rough picture* of this from the changes in mathematics.)

Here the term "language-*game*" is meant to bring into prominence the fact that the *speaking* of language is part of an activity, or of a form of life.

Review the multiplicity of language-games in the following examples, and in others:

> Giving orders, and obeying them—
> Describing the appearance of an object, or giving its measurements—
> Constructing an object from a description (a drawing)—
> Reporting an event—
> Speculating about an event—
> Forming and testing a hypothesis—
> Presenting the results of an experiment in tables and diagrams—
> Making up a story; and reading it—
> Play-acting—
> Singing catches—
> Guessing riddles—
> Making a joke; telling it—
> Solving a problem in practical arithmetic—

Translating from one language into another—
Asking, thanking, cursing, greeting, praying.

Imagine a picture representing a boxer in a particular stance. Now, this picture can be used to tell someone how he should stand, should hold himself; or how he should not hold himself; or how a particular man did stand in such-and-such a place; and so on. One might (using the language of chemistry) call this picture a proposition-radical. This will be how Frege thought of the "assumption." [Note added by Wittgenstein.]

—It is interesting to compare the multiplicity of the tools in language and of the ways they are used, the multiplicity of kinds of word and sentence, with what logicians have said about the structure of language. (Including the author of the *Tractatus Logico-Philosophicus.*)

24. If you do not keep the multiplicity of language-games in view you will perhaps be inclined to ask questions like: "What is a question?"—Is it the statement that I do not know such-and-such, or the statement that I wish the other person would tell me . . . ? Or is it the description of my mental state of uncertainty?—And is the cry "Help!" such a description?

Think how many different kinds of thing are called "description": description of a body's position by means of its co-ordinates; description of a facial expression; description of a sensation of touch; of a mood.

Of course it is possible to substitute the form of statement or description for the usual form of question: "I want to know whether . . ." or "I am in doubt whether . . ."— but this does not bring the different language-games any closer together.

The significance of such possibilities of transformation, for example of turning all statements into sentences beginning "I think" or "I believe" (and thus, as it were, into descriptions of my inner life) will become clearer in another place. (Solipsism.)

25. It is sometimes said that animals do not talk because they lack the mental capacity. And this means: "they do not think, and that is why they do not talk." But— they simply do not talk. Or to put it better: they do not use language—if we except the most primitive forms of language.—Commanding, questioning, recounting, chatting, are as much a part of our natural history as walking, eating, drinking, playing.

26. One thinks that learning language consists in giving names to objects. Viz., to human beings, to shapes, to colours, to pains, to moods, to numbers, etc. To repeat—naming is something like attaching a label to a thing. One can say that this is preparatory to the use of a word. But *what* is it a preparation *for?*

27. "We name things and then we can talk about them: can refer to them in talk."—As if what we did next were given with the mere act of naming. As if there were only one thing called "talking about a thing." Whereas in fact we do the most various things with our sentences. Think of exclamations alone, with their completely different functions.

Water!
Away!
Ow!
Help!
Fine!
No!

Are you inclined still to call these words "names of objects"?

In languages (2) and (8) there was no such thing as asking something's name. This, with its correlate, ostensive definition, is, we might say, a language-game on its own. That is really to say: we are brought up, trained, to ask: "What is that called?"— upon which the name is given. And there is also a language-game of inventing a name for something, and hence of saying, "This is . . . ." and then using the new name. (Thus, for example, children give names to their dolls and then talk about them and to them. Think in this connexion how singular is the use of a person's name to *call* him!)

28. Now one can ostensively define a proper name, the name of a colour, the name of a material, a numeral, the name of a point of the compass and so on. The definition of the number two, "That is called 'two'"—pointing to two nuts—is perfectly exact.—But how can two be defined like that? The person one gives the definition to doesn't know what one wants to call "two"; he will suppose that "two" is the name given to *this* group of nuts!—He *may* suppose this; but perhaps he does not. He might make the opposite mistake; when I want to assign a name to this group of nuts, he might understand it as a numeral. And he might equally well take the name of a person, of which I give an ostensive definition, as that of a colour, of a race, or even of a point of the compass. That is to say: an ostensive definition can be variously interpreted in *every* case.

29. Perhaps you say: two can only be ostensively defined in *this* way: "This *number* is called 'two.'" For the word "number" here shews what place in language, in grammar, we assign to the word. But this means that the word "number" must be explained before the ostensive definition can be understood.—The word "number" in the definition does indeed shew this place; does shew the post at which we station the word. And we can prevent misunderstandings by saying: "This *colour* is called so-and-so," "This *length* is called so-and-so," and so on. That is to say: misunderstandings are sometimes averted in this way. But is there only *one* way of taking the word "colour" or "length"?—Well, they just need defining.—Defining, then, by means of other words! And what about the last definition in this chain? (Do not say: "There isn't a 'last' definition." That is just as if you chose to say: "There isn't a last house in this road; one can always build an additional one.")

Whether the word "number" is necessary in the ostensive definition depends on whether without it the other person takes the definition otherwise than I wish. And that will depend on the circumstances under which it is given, and on the person I give it to.

And how he 'takes' the definition is seen in the use that he makes of the word defined.

30. So one might say: the ostensive definition explains the use—the meaning— of the word when the overall role of the word in language is clear. Thus if I know that someone means to explain a colour-word to me the ostensive definition "That is called 'sepia'" will help me to understand the word.—And you can say this, so long as you do not forget that all sorts of problems attach to the words "to know" or "to be clear."

One has already to know (or be able to do) something in order to be capable of asking a thing's name. But what does one have to know?

Could one define the word "red" by pointing to something that was *not red*? That would be as if one were supposed to explain the word "*modest*" to someone whose English was weak, and one pointed to an arrogant man and said "That man is *not* modest." That it is ambiguous is no argument against such a method of definition. Any definition can be misunderstood.

But it might well be asked: are we still to call this "definition"?—For, of course, even if it has the same practical consequences, the same *effect* on the learner, it plays a different part in the calculus from what we ordinarily call "ostensive definition" of the word "red." [Note added by Wittgenstein.]

---

31. When one shews someone the king in chess and says: "This is the king," this does not tell him the use of this piece—unless he already knows the rules of the game up to this last point: the shape of the king. You could imagine his having learnt the rules of the game without ever having been shewn an actual piece. The shape of the chessman corresponds here to the sound or shape of a word.

One can also imagine someone's having learnt the game without ever learning or formulating rules. He might have learnt quite simple board-games first, by watching, and have progressed to more and more complicated ones. He too might be given the explanation "This is the king,"—if, for instance, he were being shewn chessmen of a shape he was not used to. This explanation again only tells him the use of the piece because, as we might say, the place for it was already prepared. Or even: we shall only say that it tells him the use, if the place is already prepared. And in this case it is so, not because the person to whom we give the explanation already knows rules, but because in another sense he is already master of a game.

Consider this further case: I am explaining chess to someone; and I begin by pointing to a chessman and saying: "This is the king; it can move like this, ... and so on."—In this case we shall say: the words "This is the king" (or "This is called the 'king'") are a definition only if the learner already 'knows what a piece in a game is.' That is, if he has already played other games, or has watched other people playing 'and understood'—*and similar things.* Further, only under these conditions will he be able to ask relevantly in the course of learning the game: "What do you call this?"—that is, this piece in a game.

We may say: only someone who already knows how to do something with it can significantly ask a name.

And we can imagine the person who is asked replying: "Settle the name yourself"—and now the one who asked would have to manage everything for himself.

32. Someone coming into a strange country will sometimes learn the language of the inhabitants from ostensive definitions that they give him; and he will often have to guess the meaning of these definitions; and will guess sometimes right, sometimes wrong.

And now, I think, we can say: Augustine describes the learning of human language as if the child came into a strange country and did not understand the language of the country; that is, as if it already had a language, only not this one. Or again: as if the child could already *think,* only not yet speak. And "think" would here mean something like "talk to itself."

33. Suppose, however, someone were to object: "It is not true that you must already be master of a language in order to understand an ostensive definition: all you need—of course I—is to know or guess what the person giving the explanation is pointing to. That is, whether for example to the shape of the object, or to its colour, or to its number, and so on." And what does 'pointing to the shape,' 'pointing to the colour' consist in? Point to a piece of paper.—And now point to its shape—now to its colour—now to its number (that sounds queer).—How did you do it?—You will say that you 'meant' a different thing each time you pointed. And if I ask how that is done, you will say you concentrated your attention on the colour, the shape, etc. But I ask again: how is *that* done?

Suppose someone points to a vase and says "Look at that marvelous blue—the shape isn't the point."—Or: "Look at the marvelous shape—the colour doesn't matter." Without doubt you will do something *different* when you act upon these two invitations. But do you always do the *same* thing when you direct your attention to the colour? Imagine various different cases. To indicate a few:

"Is this blue the same as the blue over there? Do you see any difference?"—

You are mixing paint and you say "It's hard to get the blue of this sky."

"It's turning fine, you can already see blue sky again."

"Look what different effects these two blues have."

"Do you see the blue book over there? Bring it here."

"This blue signal-light means. . . ."

"What's this blue called?—Is it 'indigo'?"

You sometimes attend to the colour by putting your hand up to keep the outline from view; or by not looking at the outline of the thing; sometimes by staring at the object and trying to remember where you saw that colour before.

You attend to the shape, sometimes by tracing it, sometimes by screwing up your eyes so as not to see the colour clearly, and in many other ways. I want to say: This is the sort of thing that happens while one 'directs one's attention to this or that.' But it isn't these things by themselves that make us say someone is attending to the shape, the colour, and so on. Just as a move in chess doesn't consist simply in moving a piece in such-and-such a way on the board—nor yet in one's thoughts and feelings as one makes the move: but in the circumstances that we call "playing a game of chess," "solving a chess problem," and so on.

34. But suppose someone said: "I always do the same thing when I attend to the shape: my eye follows the outline and I feel. . . ." And suppose this person to give someone else the ostensive definition "That is called a 'circle,'" pointing to a circular object and having all these experiences cannot his hearer still interpret the definition differently, even though he sees the other's eyes following the outline, and even though he feels what the other feels? That is to say: this 'interpretation' may also consist in how he now makes use of the word; in what he points to, for example, when told: "Point to a circle."—For neither the expression "to intend the definition in such-and-such a way" nor the expression "to interpret the definition in such-and-such a way" stands for a process which accompanies the giving and hearing of the definition.

35. There are, of course, what can be called "characteristic experiences" of pointing to (e.g.) the shape. For example, following the outline with one's finger or with one's eyes as one points.—But *this* does not happen in all cases in which I 'mean the shape,' and no more does any other one characteristic process occur in all these cases.—Besides, even if something of the sort did recur in all cases, it would still depend on the circumstances—that is, on what happened before and after the pointing—whether we should say "He pointed to the shape and not to the colour."

For the words "to point to the shape," "to mean the shape," and so on, are not used in the same way as *these:* "to point to this book (not to that one)," "to point to the chair, not the table," and so on.—Only think how differently we *learn* the use of the words "to point to this thing," "to point to that thing," and on the other hand "to point to the colour, not the shape," "to mean the colour," and so on.

To repeat: in certain cases, especially when one points 'to the shape' or 'to the number' there are characteristic experiences and ways of pointing—'characteristic' because they recur often (not always) when shape or number are 'meant.' But do you also know of an experience characteristic of pointing to a piece in a game *as a piece in a game?* All the same one can say: "I mean that this *piece* is called the 'king,' not this particular bit of wood I am pointing to." (Recognizing, wishing, remembering, etc.)

36. And we do here what we do in a host of similar cases: because we cannot specify any *one* bodily action which we call pointing to the shape (as opposed, for example, to the colour), we say that a *spiritual* [mental, intellectual] activity corresponds to these words.

Where our language suggests a body and there is none: there, we should like to say, is a *spirit.*

37. What is the relation between name and thing named?—Well, what is it? Look at language-game (2) or at another one: there you can see the sort of thing this relation consists in. This relation may also consist, among many other things, in the fact that hearing the name calls before our mind the picture of what is named; and it also consists, among other things, in the name's being written on the thing named or being pronounced when that thing is pointed at.

38. But what, for example, is the word "this" the name of in language-game (8) or the word "that" in the ostensive definition "that is called. . . ."?—If you do not want to produce confusion you will do best not to call these words names at all.—Yet, strange to say, the word "this" has been called the only *genuine* name; so that anything else we call a name was one only in an inexact, approximate sense.

This queer conception springs from a tendency to sublime the logic of our language—as one might put it. The proper answer to it is: we call very different things "names"; the word "name" is used to characterize many different kinds of use of a word, related to one another in many different ways;—but the kind of use that "this" has is not among them.

What is it to mean the words *"That* is blue" at one time as a statement about the object one is pointing to—at another as an explanation of the word "blue"? Well, in the second case one really means "That is called 'blue.'"—Then can one at one time mean the word "is" as "is called" and the word "blue" as "'blue,'" and another time mean "is" really as "is"?

It is also possible for someone to get an explanation of the words out of what was intended as a piece of information. [Marginal note: Here lurks a crucial superstition.]

Can I say "bububu" and mean "If it doesn't rain I shall go for a walk"?—It is only in a language that I can mean something by something. This shews clearly that the grammar of "to mean" is not like that of the expression "to imagine" and the like. [Note added by Wittgenstein.]

It is quite true that, in giving an ostensive definition for instance, we often point to the object named and say the name. And similarly, in giving an ostensive definition for instance, we say the word "this" while pointing to a thing. And also the word "this" and a name often occupy the same position in a sentence. But it is precisely characteristic of a name that it is defined by means of the demonstrative expression "That is N" (or "That is called 'N'"). But do we also give the definitions: "That is called 'this,'" or "This is called 'this'"?

This is connected with the conception of naming as, so to speak, an occult process. Naming appears as a *queer* connexion of a word with an object.—And you really get such a queer connexion when the philosopher tries to bring out *the* relation between name and thing by staring at an object in front of him and repeating a name or even the word "this" innumerable times. For philosophical problems arise when language *goes on holiday.* And *here* we may indeed fancy naming to be some remarkable act of mind, as it were a baptism of an object. And we can also say the word "this" *to* the object, as it were *address* the object as "this"—a queer use of this word, which doubtless only occurs in doing philosophy.

39. But why does it occur to one to want to make precisely this word into a name, when it evidently is *not* a name?—That is just the reason. For one is tempted to make an objection against what is ordinarily called a name. It can be put like this: *a name ought really to signify a simple.* And for this one might perhaps give the following reasons: The word "Excalibur," say, is a proper name in the ordinary sense. The sword Excalibur consists of parts combined in a particular way. If they are combined differently Excalibur does not exist. But it is clear that the sentence "Excalibur has a sharp blade" makes sense whether Excalibur is still whole or is broken up. But if "Excalibur" is the name of an object, this object no longer exists when Excalibur is broken in pieces; and as no object would then correspond to the name it would have no meaning. But then the sentence "Excalibur has a sharp blade" would contain a word that had no meaning, and hence the sentence would be nonsense. But it does make sense; so there must always be something corresponding to the words of which it consists. So the word "Excalibur" must disappear when the sense is analysed and its place be taken by words which name simples. It will be reasonable to call these words the real names.

40. Let us first discuss *this* point of the argument: that a word has no meaning if nothing corresponds to it.—It is important to note that the word "meaning" is being used illicitly if it is used to signify the thing that 'corresponds' to the word. That is to confound the meaning of a name with the *bearer* of the name. When Mr. N. N. dies one says that the bearer of the name dies, not that the meaning dies. And it would be nonsensical to say that, for if the name ceased to have meaning it would make no sense to say "Mr. N. N. is dead."

41. In §15 we introduced proper names into language (8). Now suppose that the tool with the name "N" is broken. Not knowing this, A gives B the sign "N." Has this sign meaning now or not?—What is B to do when he is given it?—We have not settled anything about this. One might ask: what *will* he do? Well, perhaps he will stand there at a loss, or shew A the pieces. Here one *might* say: "N" has become meaningless; and this expression would mean that the sign "N" no longer had a use in our language-game (unless we gave it a new one). "N" might also become meaningless because, for whatever reason, the tool was given another name and the sign "N" no longer used in the language-game.—But we could also imagine a convention whereby B has to shake his head in reply if A gives him the sign belonging to a tool that is broken.—In this way the command "N" might be said to be given a place in the language-game even when the tool no longer exists, and the sign "N" to have meaning even when its bearer ceases to exist.

42. But has for instance a name which has *never* been used for a tool also got a meaning in that game? Let us assume that "X" is such a sign and that A gives this sign to B—well, even such signs could be given a place in the language-game, and B might have, say, to answer them too with a shake of the head. (One could imagine this as a sort of joke between them.)

43. For a *large* class of cases—though not for all—in which we employ the word "meaning" it can be defined thus: the meaning of a word is its use in the language.

And the *meaning* of a name is sometimes explained by pointing to its *bearer.*

44. We said that the sentence "Excalibur has a sharp blade" made sense even when Excalibur was broken in pieces. Now this is so because in this language-game a name is also used in the absence of its bearer. But we can imagine a language-game with names (that is, with signs which we should certainly include among names) in

which they are used only in the presence of the bearer; and so could always be replaced by a demonstrative pronoun and the gesture of pointing.

45. The demonstrative "this" can never be without a bearer. It might be said: "so long as there is a *this,* the word 'this' has a meaning too, whether *this* is simple or complex." But that does not make the word into a name. On the contrary: for a name is not used with, but only explained by means of, the gesture of pointing.

46. What lies behind the idea that names really signify simples?—

Socrates says in the *Theaetetus:* "If I make no mistake, I have heard some people say this: there is no definition of the primary elements—so to speak—out of which we and everything else are composed; for everything that exists in its own right can only be *named,* no other determination is possible, neither that it *is* nor that it *is not.* . . . But what exists in its own right has to be . . . named without any other determination. In consequence it is impossible to give an account of any primary element; for it, nothing is possible but the bare name; its name is all it has. But just as what consists of these primary elements is itself complex, so the names of the elements become descriptive language by being compounded together. For the essence of speech is the composition of names."

Both Russell's 'individuals' and my 'objects' (*Tractatus Logico-Philosophicus*) were such primary elements.

47. But what are the simple constituent parts of which reality is composed?— What are the simple constituent parts of a chair?—The bits of wood of which it is made? Or the molecules, or the atoms?—"Simple" means: not composite. And here the point is: in what sense 'composite'? It makes no sense at all to speak absolutely of the 'simple parts of a chair.'

Again: Does my visual image of this tree, of this chair, consist of parts? And what are its simple component parts? Multi-colouredness is one kind of complexity; another is, for example, that of a broken outline composed of straight bits. And a curve can be said to be composed of an ascending and a descending segment.

If I tell someone without any further explanation: "What I see before me now is composite," he will have the right to ask: "What do you mean by 'composite'? For there are all sorts of things that that can mean!"—The question "Is what you see composite?" makes good sense if it is already established what kind of complexity—that is, which particular use of the word—is in question. If it had been laid down that the visual image of a tree was to be called "composite" if one saw not just a single trunk, but also branches, then the question "Is the visual image of this tree simple or composite?" and the question "What are its simple component parts?" would have a clear sense—a clear use. And of course the answer to the second question is not "The branches" (that would be an answer to the *grammatical* question: "What are here called 'simple component parts'?") but rather a description of the individual branches.

But isn't a chessboard, for instance, obviously, and absolutely, composite?— You are probably thinking of the composition out of thirty-two white and thirty-two black squares. But could we not also say, for instance, that it was composed of the colours black and white and the schema of squares? And if there are quite different ways of looking at it, do you still want to say that the chessboard is absolutely 'composite'?—Asking "Is this object composite?" *outside* a particular language-game is like what a boy once did, who had to say whether the verbs in certain sentences were in the active or passive voice, and who racked his brains over the question whether the verb "to sleep" meant something active or passive.

We use the word "composite" (and therefore the word "simple") in an enormous number of different and differently related ways. (Is the colour of a square on a chessboard simple, or does it consist of pure white and pure yellow? And is white simple, or does it consist of the colours of the rainbow?—Is this length of 2 cm. simple, or does it consist of two parts, each 1 cm. long? But why not of one bit 3 cm. long, and one bit 1 cm. long measured in the opposite direction?)

To the *philosophical* question: "Is the visual image of this tree composite, and what are its component parts?" the correct answer is: "That depends on what you understand by 'composite'." (And that is of course not an answer but a rejection of the question.)

*   *   *

65. Here we come up against the great question that lies behind all these considerations.—For someone might object against me: "You take the easy way out! You talk about all sorts of language-games, but have nowhere said what the essence of a language-game, and hence of language, is: what is common to all these activities, and what makes them into language or parts of language. So you let yourself off the very part of the investigation that once gave you yourself most headache, the part about the *general form of propositions* and of language."

And this is true.—Instead of producing something common to all that we call language, I am saying that these phenomena have no one thing in common which makes us use the same word for all,—but that they are *related* to one another in many different ways. And it is because of this relationship, or these relationships, that we call them all "language." I will try to explain this.

66. Consider for example the proceedings that we call "games." I mean board-games, card-games, ball-games, Olympic games, and so on. What is common to them all?—Don't say: "There *must* be something common, or they would not be called 'games'"—but *look* and *see* whether there is anything common to all.—For if you look at them you will not see something that is common to *all,* but similarities, relationships, and a whole series of them at that. To repeat: don't think, but look!—Look for example at board-games, with their multifarious relationships. Now pass to card-games; here you find many correspondences with the first group, but many common features drop out, and others appear. When we pass next to ball-games, much that is common is retained, but much is lost.—Are they all 'amusing'? Compare chess with noughts and crosses. Or is there always winning and losing, or competition between players? Think of patience. In ball-games there is winning and losing; but when a child throws his ball at the wall and catches it again, this feature has disappeared. Look at the parts played by skill and luck; and at the difference between skill in chess and skill in tennis. Think now of games like ring-a-ring-a-roses; here is the element of amusement, but how many other characteristic features have disappeared! And we can go through the many, many other groups of games in the same way; can see how similarities crop up and disappear.

And the result of this examination is: we see a complicated network of similarities overlapping and criss-crossing: sometimes overall similarities, sometimes similarities of detail.

67. I can think of no better expression to characterize these similarities than "family resemblances"; for the various resemblances between members of a family: build, features, colour of eyes, gait, temperament, etc., etc. overlap and criss-cross in the same way.—And I shall say: "games" form a family.

And for instance the kinds of number form a family in the same way. Why do we call something a "number"? Well, perhaps because it has a—direct—relationship with several things that have hitherto been called number; and this can be said to give it an indirect relationship to other things we call the same name. And we extend our concept of number as in spinning a thread we twist fibre on fibre. And the strength of the thread does not reside in the fact that some one fibre runs through its whole length, but in the overlapping of many fibres.

But if someone wished to say: "There is something common to all these constructions—namely the disjunction of all their common properties"—I should reply: Now you are only playing with words. One might as well say: "Something runs through the whole thread—namely the continuous overlapping of those fibres."

68. "All right: the concept of number is defined for you as the logical sum of these individual interrelated concepts: cardinal numbers, rational numbers, real numbers, etc.; and in the same way the concept of a game as the logical sum of a corresponding set of sub-concepts."—It need not be so. For I *can* give the concept 'number' rigid limits in this way, that is, use the word "number" for a rigidly limited concept, but I can also use it so that the extension of the concept is *not* closed by a frontier. And this is how we do use the word "game." For how is the concept of a game bounded? What still counts as a game and what no longer does? Can you give the boundary? No. You can *draw* one; for none has so far been drawn. (But that never troubled you before when you used the word "game.")

"But then the use of the word is unregulated, the 'game' we play with it is unregulated."—It is not everywhere circumscribed by rules; but no more are there any rules for how high one throws the ball in tennis, or how hard; yet tennis is a game for all that and has rules too.

69. How should we explain to someone what a game is? I imagine that we should describe *games* to him, and we might add: "This *and similar things* are called 'games'." And do we know any more about it ourselves? Is it only other people whom we cannot tell exactly what a game is?—But this is not ignorance. We do not know the boundaries because none have been drawn. To repeat, we can draw a boundary—for a special purpose. Does it take that to make the concept usable? Not at all! (Except for that special purpose.) No more than it took the definition: 1 pace = 75 cm to make the measure of length 'one pace' usable. And if you want to say "But still, before that it wasn't an exact measure," then I reply: very well, it was an inexact one.—Though you still owe me a definition of exactness.

70. "But if the concept 'game' is uncircumscribed like that, you don't really know what you mean by a 'game'."—When I give the description: "The ground was quite covered with plants"—do you want to say I don't know what I am talking about until I can give a definition of a plant?

My meaning would be explained by, say, a drawing and the words "The ground looked roughly like this." Perhaps I even say "it looked *exactly* like this."—Then were just *this* grass and *these* leaves there, arranged just like this? No, that is not what it means. And I should not accept any picture as exact in *this* sense.

Someone says to me: "Shew the children a game." I teach them gaming with dice, and the other says "I didn't mean that sort of game." Must the exclusion of the game with dice have come before his mind when he gave me the order? [Note added by Wittgenstein.]

71. One might say that the concept 'game' is a concept with blurred edges.—"But is a blurred concept a concept at all?"—Is an indistinct photograph a picture of a person at all? Is it even always an advantage to replace an indistinct picture by a sharp one? Isn't the indistinct one often exactly what we need?

Frege compares a concept to an area and says that an area with vague boundaries cannot be called an area at all. This presumably means that we cannot do anything with it.—But is it senseless to say: "Stand roughly there"? Suppose that I were standing with someone in a city square and said that. As I say it I do not draw any kind of boundary, but perhaps point with my hand—as if I were indicating a particular *spot*. And this is just how one might explain to someone what a game is. One gives examples and intends them to be taken in a particular way.—I do not, however, mean by this that he is supposed to see in those examples that common thing which I—for some reason—was unable to express; but that he is now to *employ* those examples in a particular way. Here giving examples is not an *indirect* means of explaining—in default of a better. For any general definition can be misunderstood too. The point is that *this* is how we play the game. (I mean the language-game with the word "game.")

* * *

241. "So you are saying that human agreement decides what is true and what is false?"—It is what human beings say that is true and false; and they agree in the *language* they use. That is not agreement in opinions but in form of life.

* * *

257. "What would it be like if human beings shewed no outward signs of pain (did not groan, grimace, etc.)? Then it would be impossible to teach a child the use of the word 'tooth-ache'."—Well, let's assume the child is a genius and itself invents a name for the sensation!—But then, of course, he couldn't make himself understood when he used the word.—So does he understand the name, without being able to explain its meaning to anyone?—But what does it mean to say that he has 'named his pain'?—How has he done this naming of pain?! And whatever he did, what was its purpose?—When one says "He gave a name to his sensation" one forgets that a great deal of stage-setting in the language is presupposed if the mere act of naming is to make sense. And when we speak of someone's having given a name to pain, what is presupposed is the existence of the grammar of the word "pain"; it shews the post where the new word is stationed.

258. Let us imagine the following case. I want to keep a diary about the recurrence of a certain sensation. To this end I associate it with the sign "S" and write this sign in a calendar for every day on which I have the sensation. I will remark first of all that a definition of the sign cannot be formulated.—But still I can give myself a kind of ostensive definition.—How? Can I point to the sensation? Not in the ordinary sense. But I speak, or write the sign down, and at the same time I concentrate my attention on the sensation—and so, as it were, point to it inwardly.—But what is this ceremony for? for that is all it seems to be! A definition surely serves to establish the meaning of a sign.—Well, that is done precisely by the concentrating of my attention; for in this way I impress on myself the connexion between the sign and the sensation.—But "I impress it on myself" can only mean: this process brings it about that I remember the connexion *right* in the future. But in the present case I have no criterion of correctness.

One would like to say: whatever is going to seem right to me is right. And that only means that here we can't talk about 'right.'

*   *   *

305. "But you surely cannot deny that, for example, in remembering, an inner process takes place."—What gives the impression that we want to deny anything? When one says "Still, an inner process does take place here"—one wants to go on: "After all, you *see* it." And it is this inner process that one means by the word "remembering."—The impression that we wanted to deny something arises from our setting our faces against the picture of the 'inner process.' What we deny is that the picture of the inner process gives us the correct idea of the use of the word "to remember." We say that this picture with its ramifications stands in the way of our seeing the use of the word as it is.

*   *   *

309. What is your aim in philosophy?—To shew the fly the way out of the fly-bottle.

A.J. AYER
1910–1989

Alfred Jules Ayer was born in London, the only child of immigrant parents. His father, Jules Ayer, was a Swiss-born businessman, and his mother, Reine Citroen Ayer, was a Dutch Jew whose distant cousin had founded the well-known Citroen automobile company. At age seven, Ayer was sent to boarding school at Eastbourne, and at age twelve he won an academic scholarship to prestigious Eton College. For the next six years, he studied the classics, enjoyed the theater, and participated actively in sports (he was quite good at tennis and fantasized about becoming a professional cricket player). During this time, he also gave up all religious belief.

In 1928, Ayer won a scholarship in classics to Christ Church College, Oxford. There he studied philosophy as well as Greek and Roman history. He was fascinated by the philosophy of the early Wittgenstein and spent time in Cambridge with the philosopher. After graduation, he became a lecturer at Christ Church; but the college had overhired, and he was given a two-term leave. He used this time to visit Austria, where he met Moritz Schlick and became an enthusiastic member of the "Vienna Circle" of logical positivists. Returning to Oxford full of zeal for the new philosophy, he wrote his most famous book, *Language, Truth, and Logic* (1936). The twenty-six-year-old Ayer immediately became the leading apologist for logical positivism in the English-speaking world.

After five years as a research student at Christ Church and after service in the Welsh Guards during World War II, Ayer became Fellow and Dean of Wadham, Oxford. In 1946, he was elected Grote Professor of Philosophy of Mind and Logic at University College, London. During this time he wrote extensively, modifying some of the brasher statements of his earlier writings. His major work from this period was his theory of knowledge, *The Problem of Knowledge* (1956). In addition to writing, Ayer served as editor of the Pelican Philosophy Series and president of the Aristotelian Society, was an activist in liberal political causes, and appeared as a regular guest on the BBC television program "The Brains Trust." In 1960, he returned to Oxford as Wykeham Professor of Logic. While at Oxford, he also lectured throughout the world. Though obliged to retire from his chair at Oxford at age sixty-seven, Ayer continued to write and teach until his death in 1989.

A year before his death, Ayer had a "somewhat agonising but very astonishing experience" when his heart stopped beating for four minutes. In an article entitled "What I Saw When I Was Dead . . .," Ayer described the incident:

> I was confronted by a red light, exceedingly bright, and also very painful, even when I turned away from it. I was aware that this light was responsible for the government of the universe.*

In the same article, Ayer made it clear that this event in no way shook his atheistic convictions.

*   *   *

Logical positivism has its roots in the empiricism of David Hume and the language theory of the early Wittgenstein. Hume had divided all meaningful ideas into two classes—those concerned with "relations of ideas" and those concerned with "matters of fact." The *a priori* propositions of logic and pure mathematics (known as "analytic" propositions) comprise the former class and propositions that depend on observation and experimentation (known as "synthetic") comprise the latter. But metaphysical ideas did not fit either class and hence were considered vacuous or meaningless. Wittgenstein's early *Tractatus* called for a philosophical language stripped of such meaningless statements:

> The correct method in philosophy would really be the following: to say nothing except what can be said, i.e. propositions of natural science—i.e. something that has nothing to do with philosophy—and then, whenever someone else wanted to say something metaphysical, to demonstrate to him that he had failed to give a meaning to certain signs in his propositions. . . . [T]his method would be the only strictly correct one.

Ayer, together with Moritz Schlick and the rest of the Vienna Circle, sought to develop this "correct" philosophy. The members of the circle called themselves "positivists" because they wanted to eliminate all metaphysical pseudo-propositions and to show that only logic, mathematics, and the natural sciences provide genuine knowledge. They were "logical" positivists because they claimed that the logical analysis of supposed metaphysical assertions will not show them to be *false* but rather *meaningless.*

To determine which propositions were meaningful and which were not, logical positivists such as Ayer developed a verification criterion of meaning. In our

---

*Spectator, 16 July 1988, as quoted in A.J. Ayer, *The Philosophy of A.J. Ayer,* edited by Lewis E. Hahn (LaSalle, IL: Open Court, 1992), p. 48.

selection from *Language, Truth, and Logic,* Ayer gives this version of the criterion for synthetic propositions:

> We say that a sentence is factually significant to any given person, if, and only if, he knows how to verify the proposition which it purports to express—that is, if he knows what observations would lead him, under certain conditions, to accept the proposition as being true, or reject it as being false.

Ayer immediately makes three qualifications to this principle. In the first place, he points out that he is only talking about "verifiability in principle." It might not be practically possible for me at this time, for example, to verify or falsify the existence of Tasmanian Devils on the island of Tasmania, but there is nothing in *principle* to keep me from doing so. Second, he distinguishes between "strong" and "weak" verification. A proposition is verifiable in the strong sense "if, and only if, its truth could be conclusively established in experience." But this "strong" verification would eliminate all general propositions such as "a body tends to expand when it is heated" since such truths cannot be "conclusively" established by a finite number of observations. Instead, Ayer opted for a weaker sense of verification: "Would any observations be relevant to the determination of its truth or falsehood?" Finally, Ayer made it clear that his criterion applies only to *synthetic* propositions. The propositions of philosophy, including the verification criterion itself, are "held to be linguistically necessary, and so analytic."

This last qualification points to a problem that was to vex the logical positivists: How does one verify the verification criterion? What observations would lead one to accept the proposition previously given ("We say that a sentence is factually significant . . .") as true, or reject it as false? In the *Tractatus,* Wittgenstein had noticed this problem with self-reference and concluded that the propositions that made up the *Tractatus* itself were "nonsense"—but that one could still use them to "see the world aright." Ayer sought to avoid the problem by claiming that the verification criterion was analytic, a mere tautology, and so not subject to the criterion. But if the criterion is only a tautology, it would tell us nothing about the world. How could it then function as a test of meaning and what prevents it from being completely arbitrary?

In his later writings Ayer tried different ways of grounding the verification criterion, as did other positivists, but none of these attempts has satisfied contemporary philosophers. Partially as a result of the problems involved in developing a credible verification criterion, logical positivism no longer exists as a movement. But the spirit of hard-nosed positivistic empiricism is still with us.

*   *   *

For works on logical positivism, see R.W. Ashby, "Logical Positivism," in D.J. O'Connor, ed., *A Critical History of Western Philosophy* (New York: The Free Press, 1964); Peter Achinstein and Stephen F. Barker, *The Legacy of Logical Positivism* (Baltimore: The Johns Hopkins University Press, 1969); Barry R. Gross, *Analytic Philosophy: An Historical Introduction* (New York: Pegasus, 1970); Frederick C. Copleston, *Contemporary Philosophy: Studies of Logical Positivism and Existentialism* (New York: Barnes & Noble, 1979); and Oswald Hanfling, *Logical Positivism* (New York: Columbia University Press, 1981). For a collection of primary source readings, see Oswald Hanfling, ed., *Essential Readings in Logical Positivism* (Oxford: Blackwell, 1981).

A good text for specific aspects of Ayer's thought is A.J. Ayer, *The Philosophy of A.J. Ayer,* edited by Lewis E. Hahn (La Salle, IL: Open Court, 1992), another volume in the outstanding Library of Living Philosophers Series. John Foster, *Ayer* (London: Routledge, 1985), gives a detailed discussion of Ayer's ideas, while Graham Macdonald and Crispin Wright, eds., *Fact, Science, and Morality: Essays on A.J. Ayer's "Language, Truth, and Logic"* (New York: Blackwell, 1987), and Barry Gower, ed., *Logical Positivism in Perspective: Essays on "Language, Truth and Logic"* (London: Croom Helm, 1987), gather essays on Ayer's most important work. A general collection of essays is A. Phillips Griffiths, ed., *A.J. Ayer Memorial Essays* (Cambridge: Cambridge University Press, 1991).

LANGUAGE, TRUTH AND LOGIC
(in part)

PREFACE TO FIRST EDITION

The views which are put forward in this treatise derive from the doctrines of Bertrand Russell and Wittgenstein, which are themselves the logical outcome of the empiricism of Berkeley and David Hume. Like Hume, I divide all genuine propositions into two classes: those which, in his terminology, concern "relations of ideas," and those which concern "matters of fact." The former class comprises the *a priori* propositions of logic and pure mathematics, and these I allow to be necessary and certain only because they are analytic. That is, I maintain that the reason why these propositions cannot be confuted in experience is that they do not make any assertion about the empirical world, but simply record our determination to use symbols in a certain fashion. Propositions concerning empirical matters of fact, on the other hand, I hold to be hypotheses, which can be probable but never certain. And in giving an account of the method of their validation I claim also to have explained the nature of truth.

To test whether a sentence expresses a genuine empirical hypothesis, I adopt what may be called a modified verification principle. For I require of an empirical hypothesis, not indeed that it should be conclusively verifiable, but that some possible sense-experience should be relevant to the determination of its truth or falsehood. If a putative proposition fails to satisfy this principle, and is not a tautology, then I hold that it is metaphysical, and that, being metaphysical, it is neither true nor false but literally senseless. It will be found that much of what ordinarily passes for philosophy is metaphysical according to this criterion, and, in particular, that it can not be significantly asserted that there is a non-empirical world of values, or that men have immortal souls, or that there is a transcendent God.

A.J. Ayer, *Language, Truth and Logic.* New York: Dover Publications, 1936. Reprinted by permission.

As for the propositions of philosophy themselves, they are held to be linguistically necessary, and so analytic. And with regard to the relationship of philosophy and empirical science, it is shown that the philosopher is not in a position to furnish speculative truths, which would, as it were, compete with the hypotheses of science, nor yet to pass *a priori* judgements upon the validity of scientific theories, but that his function is to clarify the propositions of science by exhibiting their logical relationships, and by defining the symbols which occur in them. Consequently I maintain that there is nothing in the nature of philosophy to warrant the existence of conflicting philosophical "schools." And I attempt to substantiate this by providing a definitive solution of the problems which have been the chief sources of controversy between philosophers in the past.

The view that philosophizing is an activity of analysis is associated in England with the work of G.E. Moore and his disciples. But while I have learned a great deal from Professor Moore, I have reason to believe that he and his followers are not prepared to adopt such a thoroughgoing phenomenalism as I do, and that they take a rather different view of the nature of philosophical analysis. The philosophers with whom I am in the closest agreement are those who compose the "Viennese circle," under the leadership of Moritz Schlick, and are commonly known as logical positivists. And of these I owe most to Rudolf Carnap. Further, I wish to acknowledge my indebtedness to Gilbert Ryle, my original tutor in philosophy, and to Isaiah Berlin, who have discussed with me every point in the argument of this treatise, and made many valuable suggestions, although they both disagree with much of what I assert. . . .

CHAPTER 1: THE ELIMINATION OF METAPHYSICS

The traditional disputes of philosophers are, for the most part, as unwarranted as they are unfruitful. The surest way to end them is to establish beyond question what should be the purpose and method of a philosophical enquiry. And this is by no means so difficult a task as the history of philosophy would lead one to suppose. For if there are any questions which science leaves it to philosophy to answer, a straightforward process of elimination must lead to their discovery.

We may begin by criticising the metaphysical thesis that philosophy affords us knowledge of a reality transcending the world of science and common sense. Later on, when we come to define metaphysics and account for its existence, we shall find that it is possible to be a metaphysician without believing in a transcendent reality; for we shall see that many metaphysical utterances are due to the commission of logical errors, rather than to a conscious desire on the part of their authors to go beyond the limits of experience. But it is convenient for us to take the case of those who believe that it is possible to have knowledge of a transcendent reality as a starting-point for our discussion. The arguments which we use to refute them will subsequently be found to apply to the whole of metaphysics.

One way of attacking a metaphysician who claimed to have knowledge of a reality which transcended the phenomenal world would be to enquire from what premises his propositions were deduced. Must he not begin, as other men do, with the evidence of his senses? And if so, what valid process of reasoning can possibly lead him to the conception of a transcendent reality? Surely from empirical premises nothing whatsoever concerning the properties, or even the existence, of anything super-empirical can legitimately be inferred. But this objection would be met by a denial on the part of the metaphysician that his assertions were ultimately based on the evidence of his senses. He would say that he was endowed with a faculty of intellectual intuition which enabled him to know facts that could not be known through sense-experience. And even if it could be shown that he was relying on empirical premises, and that his venture into a non-empirical world was therefore logically unjustified, it would not follow that the assertions which he made concerning this non-empirical world could not be true. For the fact that a conclusion does not follow from its putative premise is not sufficient to show that it is false. Consequently one cannot overthrow a system of transcendent metaphysics merely by criticising the way in which it comes into being. What is required is rather a criticism of the nature of the actual statements which comprise it. And this is the line of argument which we shall, in fact, pursue. For we shall maintain that no statement which refers to a "reality" transcending the limits of all possible sense-experience can possibly have any literal significance; from which it must follow that the labours of those who have striven to describe such a reality have all been devoted to the production of nonsense.

It may be suggested that this is a proposition which has already been proved by Kant. But although Kant also condemned transcendent metaphysics, he did so on different grounds. For he said that the human understanding was so constituted that it lost itself in contradictions when it ventured out beyond the limits of possible experience and attempted to deal with things in themselves. And thus he made the impossibility of a transcendent metaphysic not, as we do, a matter of logic, but a matter of fact. He asserted, not that our minds could not conceivably have had the power of penetrating beyond the phenomenal world, but merely that they were in fact devoid of it. And this leads the critic to ask how, if it is possible to know only what lies within the bounds of sense-experience, the author can be justified in asserting that real things do exist beyond, and how he can tell what are the boundaries beyond which the human understanding may not venture, unless he succeeds in passing them himself. As Wittgenstein says, "in order to draw a limit to thinking, we should have to think both sides of this limit,"* a truth to which Bradley gives a special twist in maintaining that the man who is ready to prove that metaphysics is impossible is a brother metaphysician with a rival theory of his own.**

Whatever force these objections may have against the Kantian doctrine, they have none whatsoever against the thesis that I am about to set forth. It cannot here be said that the author is himself overstepping the barrier he maintains to be impassable. For the fruitlessness of attempting to transcend the limits of possible sense-experience will be deduced, not from a psychological hypothesis concerning the actual constitution of the human mind, but from the rule which determines the literal significance of language. Our charge against the metaphysician is not that he attempts to employ the understanding in a field where it cannot profitably venture, but that he produces sentences which fail to conform to the conditions under which alone a sentence can be literally significant. Nor are we ourselves obliged to talk nonsense in order to show that all sentences of a certain type are necessarily devoid of literal significance. We need only formulate the criterion which enables us to test whether a sentence expresses a genuine proposition about a matter of fact, and then point out that the sentences under consideration fail to satisfy it. And this we shall now proceed to do. We shall first of all

---

*Tractatus Logico-Philosophicus, Preface.
**Bradley, Appearance and Reality, 2nd ed., p. 1.

formulate the criterion in somewhat vague terms, and then give the explanations which are necessary to render it precise.

The criterion which we use to test the genuineness of apparent statements of fact is the criterion of verifiability. We say that a sentence is factually significant to any given person, if, and only if, he knows how to verify the proposition which it purports to express—that is, if he knows what observations would lead him, under certain conditions, to accept the proposition as being true, or reject it as being false. If, on the other hand, the putative proposition is of such a character that the assumption of its truth, or falsehood, is consistent with any assumption whatsoever concerning the nature of his future experience, then, as far as he is concerned, it is, if not a tautology, a mere pseudo-proposition. The sentence expressing it may be emotionally significant to him; but it is not literally significant. And with regard to questions the procedure is the same. We enquire in every case what observations would lead us to answer the question, one way or the other; and, if none can be discovered, we must conclude that the sentence under consideration does not, as far as we are concerned, express a genuine question, however strongly its grammatical appearance may suggest that it does.

As the adoption of this procedure is an essential factor in the argument of this book, it needs to be examined in detail.

In the first place, it is necessary to draw a distinction between practical verifiability, and verifiability in principle. Plainly we all understand, in many cases believe, propositions which we have not in fact taken steps to verify. Many of these are propositions which we could verify if we took enough trouble. But there remain a number of significant propositions, concerning matters of fact, which we could not verify even if we chose; simply because we lack the practical means of placing ourselves in the situation where the relevant observations could be made. A simple and familiar example of such a proposition is the proposition that there are mountains on the farther side of the moon. No rocket has yet been invented which would enable me to go and look at the farther side of the moon, so that I am unable to decide the matter by actual observation. But I do know what observations would decide it for me, if, as is theoretically conceivable, I were once in a position to make them. And therefore I say that the proposition is verifiable in principle, if not in practice, and is accordingly significant. On the other hand, such a metaphysical pseudo-proposition as "the Absolute enters into, but is itself incapable of, evolution and progress," is not even in principle verifiable. For one cannot conceive of an observation which would enable one to determine whether the Absolute did, or did not, enter into evolution and progress. Of course it is possible that the author of such a remark is using English words in a way in which they are not commonly used by English-speaking people, and that he does, in fact, intend to assert something which could be empirically verified. But until he makes us understand how the proposition that he wishes to express would be verified, he fails to communicate anything to us. And if he admits, as I think the author of the remark in question would have admitted, that his words were not intended to express either a tautology or a proposition which was capable, at least in principle, of being verified, then it follows that he has made an utterance which has no literal significance even for himself.

A further distinction which we must make is the distinction between the "strong" and the "weak" sense of the term "verifiable." A proposition is said to be verifiable, in the strong sense of the term, if, and only if, its truth could be conclusively established in experience. But it is verifiable, in the weak sense, if it is possible for experience to render it probable. In which sense are we using the term when we say that a putative proposition is genuine only if it is verifiable?

It seems to me that if we adopt conclusive verifiability as our criterion of significance, as some positivists have proposed, our argument will prove too much. Consider, for example, the case of general propositions of law—such propositions, namely, as "arsenic is poisonous"; "all men are mortal"; "a body tends to expand when it is heated." It is of the very nature of these propositions that their truth cannot be established with certainty by any finite series of observations. But if it is recognised that such general propositions of law are designed to cover an infinite number of cases, then it must be admitted that they cannot, even in principle, be verified conclusively. And then, if we adopt conclusive verifiability as our criterion of significance, we are logically obliged to treat these general propositions of law in the same fashion as we treat the statements of the metaphysician.

In face of this difficulty, some positivists have adopted the heroic course of saying that these general propositions are indeed pieces of nonsense, albeit an essentially important type of nonsense. But here the introduction of the term "important" is simply an attempt to hedge. It serves only to mark the authors' recognition that their view is somewhat too paradoxical, without in any way removing the paradox. Besides, the difficulty is not confined to the case of general propositions of law, though it is there revealed most plainly. It is hardly less obvious in the case of propositions about the remote past. For it must surely be admitted that, however strong the evidence in favour of historical statements may be, their truth can never become more than highly probable. And to maintain that they also constituted an important, or unimportant, type of nonsense would be unplausible, to say the very least. Indeed, it will be our contention that no proposition, other than a tautology, can possibly be anything more than a probable hypothesis. And if this is correct, the principle that a sentence can be factually significant only if it expresses what is conclusively verifiable is self-stultifying as a criterion of significance. For it leads to the conclusion that it is impossible to make a significant statement of fact at all.

Nor can we accept the suggestion that a sentence should be allowed to be factually significant if, and only if, it expresses something which is definitely confutable by experience. Those who adopt this course assume that, although no finite series of observations is ever sufficient to establish the truth of a hypothesis beyond all possibility of doubt, there are crucial cases in which a single observation, or series of observations, can definitely confute it. But, as we shall show later on, this assumption is false. A hypothesis cannot be conclusively confuted any more than it can be conclusively verified. For when we take the occurrence of certain observations as proof that a given hypothesis is false, we presuppose the existence of certain conditions. And though, in any given case, it may be extremely improbable that this assumption is false, it is not logically impossible. We shall see that there need be no self-contradiction in holding that some of the relevant circumstances are other than we have taken them to be, and consequently that the hypothesis has not really broken down. And if it is not the case that any hypothesis can be definitely confuted, we cannot hold that the genuineness of a proposition depends on the possibility of its definite confutation.

Accordingly, we fall back on the weaker sense of verification. We say that the question that must be asked about any putative statement of fact is not, Would any observations make its truth or falsehood logically certain? but simply, Would any observations be relevant to the determination of its truth or falsehood? And it is only if a negative answer is given to this second question that we conclude that the statement under consideration is nonsensical.

To make our position clearer, we may formulate it in another way. Let us call a proposition which records an actual or possible observation an experiential proposition. Then we may say that it is the mark of a genuine factual proposition, not that it should be equivalent to an experiential proposition, or any finite number of experiential propositions, but simply that some experiential propositions can be deduced from it in conjunction with certain other premises without being deducible from those other premises alone.

This criterion seems liberal enough. In contrast to the principle of conclusive verifiability, it clearly does not deny significance to general propositions or to propositions about the past. Let us see what kinds of assertion it rules out.

A good example of the kind of utterance that is condemned by our criterion as being not even false but nonsensical would be the assertion that the world of sense-experience was altogether unreal. It must, of course, be admitted that our senses do sometimes deceive us. We may, as the result of having certain sensations, expect certain other sensations to be obtainable which are, in fact, not obtainable. But, in all such cases, it is further sense-experience that informs us of the mistakes that arise out of sense-experience. We say that the senses sometimes deceive us, just because the expectations to which our sense-experiences give rise do not always accord with what we subsequently experience. That is, we rely on our senses to substantiate or confute the judgements which are based on our sensations. And therefore the fact that our perceptual judgements are sometimes found to be erroneous has not the slightest tendency to show that the world of sense-experience is unreal. And, indeed, it is plain that no conceivable observation, or series of observations, could have any tendency to show that the world revealed to us by sense-experience was unreal. Consequently, anyone who condemns the sensible world as a world of mere appearance, as opposed to reality, is saying something which, according to our criterion of significance, is literally nonsensical.

An example of a controversy which the application of our criterion obliges us to condemn as fictitious is provided by those who dispute concerning the number of substances that there are in the world. For it is admitted both by monists, who maintain that reality is one substance, and by pluralists, who maintain that reality is many, that it is impossible to imagine any empirical situation which would be relevant to the solution of their dispute. But if we are told that no possible observation could give any probability either to the assertion that reality was one substance or to the assertion that it was many, then we must conclude that neither assertion is significant. We shall see later on that there are genuine logical and empirical questions involved in the dispute between monists and pluralists. But the metaphysical question concerning "substance" is ruled out by our criterion as spurious.

A similar treatment must be accorded to the controversy between realists and idealists, in its metaphysical aspect. A simple illustration, which I have made use of in a similar argument elsewhere, will help to demonstrate this. Let us suppose that a picture is discovered and the suggestion made that it was painted by Goya. There is a definite procedure for dealing with such a question. The experts examine the picture to see in what way it resembles the accredited works of Goya, and to see if it bears any marks which are characteristic of a forgery; they look up contemporary records for evidence of the existence of such a picture, and so on. In the end, they may still disagree, but each one knows what empirical evidence would go to confirm or discredit his opinion. Suppose, now, that these men have studied philosophy, and some of them proceed to maintain that this picture is a set of ideas in the perceiver's mind, or in God's mind, others that it is objectively real. What possible experience could any of them have which would be relevant to the solution of this dispute one way or the other? In the ordinary sense of the term "real," in which it is opposed to "illusory," the reality of the picture is not in doubt. The disputants have satisfied themselves that the picture is real, in this sense, by obtaining a correlated series of sensations of sight and sensations of touch. Is there any similar process by which they could discover whether the picture was real, in the sense in which the term "real" is opposed to "ideal"? Clearly there is none. But, if that is so, the problem is fictitious according to our criterion. This does not mean that the realist-idealist controversy may be dismissed without further ado. For it can legitimately be regarded as a dispute concerning the analysis of existential propositions, and so as involving a logical problem which, as we shall see, can be definitively solved. What we have just shown is that the question at issue between idealists and realists becomes fictitious when, as is often the case, it is given a metaphysical interpretation.

There is no need for us to give further examples of the operation of our criterion of significance. For our object is merely to show that philosophy, as a genuine branch of knowledge, must be distinguished from metaphysics. We are not now concerned with the historical question how much of what has traditionally passed for philosophy is actually metaphysical. We shall, however, point out later on that the majority of the "great philosophers" of the past were not essentially metaphysicians, and thus reassure those who would otherwise be prevented from adopting our criterion by considerations of piety.

As to the validity of the verification principle . . . it will be shown that all propositions which have factual content are empirical hypotheses; and that the function of an empirical hypothesis is to provide a rule for the anticipation of experience. And this means that every empirical hypothesis must be relevant to some actual, or possible, experience, so that a statement which is not relevant to any experience is not an empirical hypothesis, and accordingly has no factual content. But this is precisely what the principle of verifiability asserts.

It should be mentioned here that the fact that the utterances of the metaphysician are nonsensical does not follow simply from the fact that they are devoid of factual content. It follows from that fact, together with the fact that they are not *a priori* propositions. . . . *a priori* propositions, which have always been attractive to philosophers on account of their certainty, owe this certainty to the fact that they are tautologies. We may accordingly define a metaphysical sentence as a sentence which purports to express a genuine proposition, but does, in fact, express neither a tautology nor an empirical hypothesis. And as tautologies and empirical hypotheses form the entire class of significant propositions, we are justified in concluding that all metaphysical assertions are nonsensical. Our next task is to show how they come to be made.

The use of the term "substance," to which we have already referred, provides us with a good example of the way in which metaphysics mostly comes to be written. It happens to be the case that we cannot, in our language, refer to the sensible properties of a thing without introducing a word or phrase which appears to stand for the thing itself as opposed to anything which may be said about it. And, as a result of this, those who are infected by the primitive superstition that to every name a single real entity must correspond assume that it is necessary to distinguish logically between the thing itself and any, or all, of its sensible properties. And so they employ the term "substance" to refer to the thing itself. But from the fact that we happen to employ a single word to refer to a thing, and make that word the grammatical subject of the sentences in which we refer to the sensible appearances of the thing, it does not by any means follow that the thing itself is a "simple entity," or that it cannot be defined in terms of the totality of its appearances. It is true that in talking of "its" appearances we appear to distinguish the thing from the appearances, but that is simply an accident of linguistic usage. Logical analysis shows that what makes these "appearances" the "appearances of" the same thing is not their relationship to an entity other than themselves, but their relationship to one another. The metaphysician fails to see this because he is misled by a superficial grammatical feature of his language.

A simpler and clearer instance of the way in which a consideration of grammar leads to metaphysics is the case of the metaphysical concept of Being. The origin of our temptation to raise questions about Being, which no conceivable experience would enable us to answer, lies in the fact that, in our language, sentences which express existential propositions and sentences which express attributive propositions may be of the same grammatical form. For instance, the sentences "Martyrs exist" and "Martyrs suffer" both consist of a noun followed by an intransitive verb, and the fact that they have grammatically the same appearance leads one to assume that they are of the same logical type. It is seen that in the proposition "Martyrs suffer," the members of a certain species are credited with a certain attribute, and it is sometimes assumed that the same thing is true of such a proposition as "Martyrs exist." If this were actually the case, it would, indeed, be as legitimate to speculate about the Being of martyrs as it is to speculate about their suffering. But, as Kant pointed out, existence is not an attribute. For, when we ascribe an attribute to a thing, we covertly assert that it exists: so that if existence were itself an attribute, it would follow that all positive existential propositions were tautologies, and all negative existential propositions self-contradictory; and this is not the case. So that those who raise questions about Being which are based on the assumption that existence is an attribute are guilty of following grammar beyond the boundaries of sense.

A similar mistake has been made in connection with such propositions as "Unicorns are fictitious." Here again the fact that there is a superficial grammatical resemblance between the English sentences "Dogs are faithful" and "Unicorns are fictitious," and between the corresponding sentences in other languages, creates the assumption that they are of the same logical type. Dogs must exist in order to have the property of being faithful, and so it is held that unless unicorns in some way existed they could not have the property of being fictitious. But, as it is plainly self-contradictory to say that fictitious objects exist, the device is adopted of saying that they are real in some non-empirical sense—that they have a mode of real being which is different from the mode of being of existent things. But since there is no way of testing whether an object is real in this sense, as there is for testing whether it is real in the ordinary sense, the assertion that fictitious objects have a special non-empirical mode of real being is devoid of all literal significance. It comes to be made as a result of the assumption that being fictitious is an attribute. And this is a fallacy of the same order as the fallacy of supposing that existence is an attribute, and it can be exposed in the same way.

In general, the postulation of real non-existent entities results from the superstition, just now referred to, that, to every word or phrase that can be the grammatical subject of a sentence, there must somewhere be a real entity corresponding. For as there is no place in the empirical world for many of these "entities," a special non-empirical world is invoked to house them. To this error must be attributed, not only the utterances of a Heidegger, who bases his metaphysics on the assumption that "Nothing" is a name which is used to denote something peculiarly mysterious, but also the prevalence of such problems as those concerning the reality of propositions and universals whose senselessness, though less obvious, is no less complete.

These few examples afford a sufficient indication of the way in which most metaphysical assertions come to be formulated. They show how easy it is to write sentences which are literally nonsensical without seeing that they are nonsensical. And thus we see that the view that a number of the traditional "problems of philosophy" are metaphysical, and consequently fictitious, does not involve any incredible assumptions about the psychology of philosophers.

Among those who recognise that if philosophy is to be accounted a genuine branch of knowledge it must be defined in such a way as to distinguish it from metaphysics, it is fashionable to speak of the metaphysician as a kind of misplaced poet. As his statements have no literal meaning, they are not subject to any criteria of truth or falsehood: but they may still serve to express, or arouse, emotion, and thus be subject to ethical or aesthetic standards. And it is suggested that they may have considerable value, as means of moral inspiration, or even as works of art. In this way, an attempt is made to compensate the metaphysician for his extrusion from philosophy.

I am afraid that this compensation is hardly in accordance with his deserts. The view that the metaphysician is to be reckoned among the poets appears to rest on the assumption that both talk nonsense. But this assumption is false. In the vast majority of cases the sentences which are produced by poets do have literal meaning. The difference between the man who uses language scientifically and the man who uses it emotively is not that the one produces sentences which are incapable of arousing emotion, and the other sentences which have no sense, but that the one is primarily concerned with the expression of true propositions, the other with the creation of a work of art. Thus, if a work of science contains true and important propositions, its value as a work of science will hardly be diminished by the fact that they are inelegantly expressed. And similarly, a work of art is not necessarily the worse for the fact that all the propositions comprising it are literally false. But to say that many literary works are largely composed of falsehoods is not to say that they are composed of pseudo-propositions. It is, in fact, very rare for a literary artist to produce sentences which have no literal meaning. And where this does occur, the sentences are carefully chosen for their rhythm and balance. If the author writes nonsense, it is because he considers it most suitable for bringing about the effects for which his writing is designed.

The metaphysician, on the other hand, does not intend to write nonsense. He lapses into it through being deceived by grammar, or through committing errors of reasoning, such as that which leads to the view that the sensible world is unreal. But it is not the mark of a poet simply to make mistakes of this sort. There are some, indeed, who would see in the fact that the metaphysician's utterances are senseless a reason against the view that they have aesthetic value. And, without going so far as this, we may safely say that it does not constitute a reason for it.

It is true, however, that although the greater part of metaphysics is merely the embodiment of humdrum errors, there remain a number of metaphysical passages which are the work of genuine mystical feeling; and they may more plausibly be held to have moral or aesthetic value. But, as far as we are concerned, the distinction between the kind of metaphysics that is produced by a philosopher who has been duped by grammar, and the kind that is produced by a mystic who is trying to express the inexpressible, is of no great importance: what is important to us is to realise that even the utterances of the metaphysician who is attempting to expound a vision are literally senseless; so that henceforth we may pursue our philosophical researches with as little regard for them as for the more inglorious kind of metaphysics which comes from a failure to understand the workings of our language.

HANS-GEORG GADAMER
1900–

Hans-Georg Gadamer grew up in the Silesian town of Breslau—what is now Wroclaw, Poland. His father, a pharmaceutical chemist, firmly believed in the natural sciences and found it difficult to comprehend his son's interests in literature, theater, and philosophy. As a boy, Gadamer was taken with Prussian patriotic fervor and spent part of each summer vacation in mock military maneuvers. When real fighting broke out in 1914, however, Gadamer found war less glamorous. The higher classes at his *gymnasium* were depleted by the draft, and many of his older classmates died on the battlefields in the First World War.

Gadamer studied philosophy at the University of Marburg, a school with a strong philosophical tradition. In 1922, as he was completing his studies, he was stricken with polio and forced to live in an almost hermetic environment. But using his quarantine wisely, he worked on his doctoral dissertation. By 1923, he had received his doctorate, found time for marriage, and moved with his new wife to Freiburg for study with Husserl and Heidegger.

Although he respected Husserl, Heidegger had the greatest influence on Gadamer. Early each morning in Freiburg, Gadamer would join a group of students to study Aristotle with Heidegger. The students considered Heidegger a genius and were in awe of both his content and style. The effects of this infatuation may not have been entirely positive, as Gadamer later noted: "We were an arrogant little in-group and easily let our pride in our teacher and his manner of working go to our heads."* When Heidegger left Freiburg for Marburg,

*Hans-Georg Gadamer, *Philosophical Apprenticeships,* translated by Robert R. Sullivan (Cambridge, MA: MIT Press, 1985), p. 49.

198

Gadamer followed his mentor back to his alma mater. For the next five years, Gadamer studied with Heidegger, who was completing his famed *Being and Time*. During this period, Gadamer worked on his "habilitation," the traditional second dissertation required for teachers in the German university system, completing it just after Heidegger returned once again to Freiburg in 1928.

For the next nine years, Gadamer taught at Marburg as an unsalaried lecturer seeking a chair of philosophy. Though generally successful as a lecturer, students and colleagues complained about the complexity of his presentations. As Gadamer himself later noted, "My friends . . . invented a new scientific unit: it was called a 'Gad' and designated a certain measure of unnecessary complexity."* Following the Nazi Party takeover in 1933, Gadamer's job prospects diminished. Although he had not spoken out clearly against the Nazis, he would not collaborate as his mentor Heidegger had done. Nevertheless, following a period at a "rehabilitation camp," Gadamer was given a professorial title in 1937.

In 1938, Gadamer moved to the University of Leipzig, where he taught philosophy during the Second World War. Despite its following official Nazi policies, Gadamer found the university surprisingly free of governmental interference. Although the war years were difficult, especially the Allied carpet bombing, Gadamer's teaching flourished. When the war ended, Gadamer was named rector by the occupying Russian forces, and he set about rebuilding the university.

Two years later, Gadamer left what had become East Germany, accepting the chair of philosophy at the University of Frankfurt. In 1949, Gadamer was named successor to Karl Jaspers at the University of Heidelberg. It was here, at age sixty, that he wrote his most famous work, *Truth and Method* (1960).

Since his retirement in 1968, Gadamer has remained active in philosophy. He has held numerous debates with fellow German philosopher Jürgen Habermas, and in 1981 he had a famous encounter with the French philosopher Derrida (see the suggested readings for studies of these exchanges). Despite his age, Gadamer has published over twenty books in retirement, one as recently as 1993.

* * *

Gadamer's thought can best be called philosophical hermeneutics. Hermeneutics, or the art of understanding, has traditionally been concerned with the correct interpretation of texts. Accordingly, the goal of hermeneutics is to find those scientific or objective methods of interpretation that, when applied to texts, yield truth. But for Gadamer, the task of hermeneutics is more fundamental: to explain how understanding is possible at all.

As Gadamer explains in our selection from *Truth and Method,* translated by W. Glen-Doepel, any theory must begin by acknowledging the *hermeneutical circle.* The theologian Friedrich Schleiermacher (1768–1834) had demonstrated the interdependence between a whole sentence and its parts. To understand a sentence, one must understand the meaning of its words. On the other hand, one cannot understand the precise meaning of a word without understanding the (sentence) context of which it is a part. Heidegger held that this hermeneutical circle was not merely a question of

*Quoted in Joel C. Weinsheimer, *Gadamer's Hermeneutics: A Reading of Truth and Method* (New Haven, CT: Yale University Press, 1985), p. x. Weinsheimer goes on to add, "Even *Truth and Method,* it is not disrespectful to say, is perhaps too complex by a 'Gad' or two."

the procedure for understanding parts and wholes. Instead, Heidegger claimed, "In the circle is hidden a positive possibility of the most primordial kind of knowing." This primordial knowing begins by acknowledging the *fore-structures* that condition interpretation, while continuing to gaze "on the things themselves."

Gadamer calls these fore-structures *prejudices,* and argues that they play a constitutive role in hermeneutics. "Prejudice," Gadamer points out, "means a judgment that is rendered before all the elements that determine a situation have been finally examined," and this need not have a negative connotation. Hasty prejudice is problematic, but prejudice born of the "respect we have for others and their authority" is both inevitable and essential for understanding. What we must guard against is not known prejudice, but the "tyranny of hidden prejudices that [make] us deaf to what speaks to us in tradition." The Enlightenment, for example, betrayed a fundamental "prejudice against prejudice itself," and accepted "no authority and [decided] everything before the judgment seat of reason." But by this hidden prejudice, Enlightenment thinkers cut themselves off from history and tradition, which are the ground of meaning.

Contrary to Enlightenment "objective" reason, Gadamer claims "all understanding is interpretation." But all interpretation is not subjective—at least not in the sense of being the interpretation of the solitary, isolated subject. Instead, all human understanding is heavy with tradition and history. "It is not really ourselves who understand," says Gadamer, "it is always a past that allows us to say, 'I have understood.'"* Understanding is not something we do as subjects so much as something that happens to us because of our place in history. As Gadamer concludes, *"Understanding is, essentially, a historically effected event."*

Given these ideas of prejudice, understanding, and interpretation, how does Gadamerian hermeneutics work? In the first place, we begin by acknowledging the centrality of language: "Language is the universal medium in which understanding itself is realized."** Second, we must look to application. In the case of a text, "there is a tension . . . in the play between the traditionary text's strangeness and familiarity to us, between being a historically intended, distanciated object and belonging to a tradition." By applying the text to the interpreter's present, one can overcome the gap of "temporal distance" and begin to understand. Such application will involve not only asking questions of the text in order to open it up to new possibilities, but also listening to the text as it asks questions of the interpreter and discloses the original situation that called it into being.

The event of understanding, therefore, can best be understood as a conversation between the text and the interpreter. Just as dialogue has no external grounding that validates it, so also no objective or scientific basis substantiates understanding: "In genuine conversation there is no last word just as there is no first word." There can be no claim to definitive knowledge beyond "the acknowledgment of the finitude of human being in itself." But *truth,* understood as openness to a possible mode of being-in-the world, is possible: "The dialectic of experience has its own fulfillment not in definitive knowledge, but in that openness to experience that is encouraged by experience itself."***

*Truth and Method, p. 58.
**Ibid., p. 350.
***Ibid., p. 319.

*   *   *

The classic introductions to philosophical hermeneutics are Richard E. Palmer, *Hermeneutics: Interpretation Theory in Schleiermacher, Dilthey, Heidegger, and Gadamer* (Evanston, IL: Northwestern University Press, 1969) and David Couzens Hoy, *The Critical Circle: Literature, History, and Philosophical Hermeneutics* (Berkeley: University of California Press, 1978). More recent introductory surveys include G.B. Madison, *The Hermeneutics of Postmodernity* (Bloomington: Indiana University Press, 1988); Joel Weinsheimer, *Philosophical Hermeneutics and Literary Theory* (New Haven, CT: Yale University Press, 1991); and Jean Grondin, *Sources of Hermeneutics* (Albany, NY: SUNY Press, 1995).

For an introduction to Gadamer's thought, see Georgia Warnke, *Gadamer: Hermeneutics, Tradition and Reason* (Stanford, CA: Stanford University Press, 1987). Joel C. Weinsheimer, *Gadamer's Hermeneutics: A Reading of Truth and Method* (New Haven, CT: Yale University Press, 1985) and Lawrence K. Schmidt, ed., *The Specter of Relativism* (Evanston, IL: Northwestern University Press, 1995) are guides to Gadamer's *magnum opus*. Comparative studies include Diane P. Michelfelder and Richard E. Palmer, eds., *Dialogue and Deconstruction: The Gadamer-Derrida Encounter* (Albany, NY: SUNY Press, 1989); Jerald Wallulis, *The Hermeneutics of Life History: Personal Achievement and History in Gadamer, Habermas, and Erickson* (Evanston, IL: Northwestern University Press, 1990); R. Christopher Smith, *Hermeneutics and Human Finitude: Towards a Theory of Ethical Understanding* (New York: Fordham University Press, 1991); and Demetrius Teigas, *Knowledge and Hermeneutic Understanding: A Study of the Habermas-Gadamer Debate* (Lewisburg, PA: Bucknell University Press, 1995). For collections of critical essays, see Brice R. Wachterhauser, ed., *Hermeneutics and Modern Philosophy* (Albany, NY: SUNY Press, 1986); Kathleen Wright, ed., *Festivals of Interpretation: Essays on Hans-Georg Gadamer's Work* (Albany, NY: SUNY Press, 1990); Hugh J. Silverman, ed., *Gadamer and Hermeneutics* (New York: Routledge, 1991); and Hans Herbert Kögler, *The Power of Dialogue: Critical Hermeneutics after Gadamer and Foucault,* translated by Paul Hendrickson (Cambridge, MA: MIT Press, 1996).

TRUTH AND METHOD (in part)

Part II: The Extension of the Question of Truth
to Understanding in the Human Sciences

Section II: Elements of a Theory of Hermeneutic Experience

CHAPTER 1: THE ELEVATION OF THE HISTORICITY OF UNDERSTANDING TO THE STATUS OF A HERMENEUTIC PRINCIPLE

(A) THE HERMENEUTIC CIRCLE AND THE PROBLEM OF PREJUDICES

(I) Heidegger's Disclosure of the Fore-Structure of Understanding

Heidegger entered into the problems of historical hermeneutics and critique only in order to explicate the fore-structure of understanding for the purposes of ontology.* Our question, by contrast, is how hermeneutics, once freed from the ontological obstructions of the scientific concept of objectivity, can do justice to the historicity of understanding. Hermeneutics has traditionally understood itself as an art or technique.** This is true even of Dilthey's expansion of hermeneutics into an organon of the human sciences. One might wonder whether there is such an art or technique of understanding—we shall come back to the point. But at any rate we can inquire into the consequences for the hermeneutics of the human sciences of the fact that Heidegger derives the circular structure of understanding from the temporality of Dasein. These consequences do not need to be such that a theory is applied to practice so that the latter is performed differently—i.e., in a way that is technically correct. They could also consist in correcting (and refining) the way in which constantly exercised understanding understands itself—a process that would benefit the art of understanding at most only indirectly.

Hence we will once more examine Heidegger's description of the hermeneutical circle in order to make its new fundamental significance fruitful for our purposes. Heidegger writes, "It is not to be reduced to the level of a vicious circle, or even of a circle which is merely tolerated. In the circle is hidden a positive possibility of the most primordial kind of knowing, and we genuinely grasp this possibility only when we have understood that our first, last, and constant task in interpreting is never to allow our fore-having, fore-sight, and fore-conception to be presented to us by fancies and popular conceptions, but rather to make the scientific theme secure by working out these fore-structures in terms of the things themselves" (*Being and Time,* p. 153).

---

*Heidegger, *Sein und Zeit,* pp. 312ff.
**Cf. Schleiermacher's *Hermeneutik,* ed. Heinz Kimmerle in *Abhandlungen der Heidelberger Akademie* (1959), 2nd *Abhandlung,* which is explicitly committed to the old ideal of an art formulated in rules (p. 127, n.: "I . . . hate it when theory does not go beyond nature and the bases of art, whose object it is").

Hans-Georg Gadamer, *Truth and Method,* 2nd revised edition, translation revised by Joel Weinsheimer and Donald G. Marshall (London: Sheed and Ward, 1989), pp. 265–300.

What Heidegger is working out here is not primarily a prescription for the practice of understanding, but a description of the way interpretive understanding is achieved. The point of Heidegger's hermeneutical reflection is not so much to prove that there is a circle as to show that this circle possesses an ontologically positive significance. The description as such will be obvious to every interpreter who knows what he is about.* All correct interpretation must be on guard against arbitrary fancies and the limitations imposed by imperceptible habits of thought, and it must direct its gaze "on the things themselves" (which, in the case of the literary critic, are meaningful texts, which themselves are again concerned with objects). For the interpreter to let himself be guided by the things themselves is obviously not a matter of a single, "conscientious" decision, but is "the first, last, and constant task." For it is necessary to keep one's gaze fixed on the thing throughout all the constant distractions that originate in the interpreter himself. A person who is trying to understand a text is always projecting. He projects a meaning for the text as a whole as soon as some initial meaning emerges in the text. Again, the initial meaning emerges only because he is reading the text with particular expectations in regard to a certain meaning. Working out this fore-projection, which is constantly revised in terms of what emerges as he penetrates into the meaning, is understanding what is there.

This description is, of course, a rough abbreviation of the whole. The process that Heidegger describes is that every revision of the fore-projection is capable of projecting before itself a new projection of meaning; rival projects can emerge side by side until it becomes clearer what the unity of meaning is; interpretation begins with fore-conceptions that are replaced by more suitable ones. This constant process of new projection constitutes the movement of understanding and interpretation. A person who is trying to understand is exposed to distraction from fore-meanings that are not borne out by the things themselves. Working out appropriate projections, anticipatory in nature, to be confirmed "by the things" themselves, is the constant task of understanding. The only "objectivity" here is the confirmation of a fore-meaning in its being worked out. Indeed, what characterizes the arbitrariness of inappropriate fore-meanings if not that they come to nothing in being worked out? But understanding realizes its full potential only when the fore-meanings that it begins with are not arbitrary. Thus it is quite right for the interpreter not to approach the text directly, relying solely on the fore-meaning already available to him, but rather explicitly to examine the legitimacy—i.e., the origin and validity—of the fore-meanings dwelling within him.

This basic requirement must be seen as the radicalization of a procedure that we in fact exercise whenever we understand anything. Every text presents the task of not simply leaving our own linguistic usage unexamined—or in the case of a foreign language the usage that we are familiar with from writers or from daily intercourse. Rather, we regard our task as deriving our understanding of the text from the linguistic usage of the time or of the author. The question is, of course, how this general require-

---

*Cf. Emil Staiger's description, which accords with that of Heidegger, in *Die Kunst der Interpretation*, pp. 11ff. I do not, however, agree that the work of a literary critic begins only "when we are in the situation of a contemporary reader." This is something we never are, and yet we are capable of understanding, although we can never achieve a definite "personal or temporal identity" with the author . . . [See also my "Vom Zirkel des Verstehens," *Kleine Schriften,* IV, 54–61 (GW, 11, 57–65) and the criticism of W. Stegmuller, *Der sogenannte Zirkel des Verstehens* (Darmstadt, 1974). The objection raised from a logical point of view against talk of the "hermeneutic circle" fails to recognize that this concept makes no claim to scientific proof, but presents a logical metaphor, known to rhetoric ever since Schleiermacher. Rightly opposed to this misunderstanding is Karl-Otto Apel, *Transformationen der Philosophie* (2 vols.; Frankfurt, 1973), 11, 83, 89, 216, and passim.]

ment can be fulfilled. Especially in the field of semantics we are confronted with the problem that our own use of language is unconscious. How do we discover that there is a difference between our own customary usage and that of the text?

I think we must say that generally we do so in the experience of being pulled up short by the text. Either it does not yield any meaning at all or its meaning is not compatible with what we had expected. This is what brings us up short and alerts us to a possible difference in usage. Someone who speaks the same language as I do uses the words in the sense familiar to me—this is a general presupposition that can be questioned only in particular cases. The same thing is true in the case of a foreign language: we all think we have a standard knowledge of it and assume this standard usage when we are reading a text.

What is true of fore-meanings that stem from usage, however, is equally true of the fore-meanings concerning content with which we read texts, and which make up our fore-understanding. Here too we may ask how we can break the spell of our own fore-meanings. There can, of course, be a general expectation that what the text says will fit perfectly with my own meanings and expectations. But what another person tells me, whether in conversation, letter, book, or whatever, is generally supposed to be his own and not my opinion; and this is what I am to take note of without necessarily having to share it. Yet this presupposition is not something that makes understanding easier, but harder, since the fore-meanings that determine my own understanding can go entirely unnoticed. If they give rise to misunderstandings, how can our misunderstandings of a text be perceived at all if there is nothing to contradict them? How can a text be protected against misunderstanding from the start?

If we examine the situation more closely, however, we find that meanings cannot be understood in an arbitrary way. Just as we cannot continually misunderstand the use of a word without its affecting the meaning of the whole, so we cannot stick blindly to our own fore-meaning about the thing if we want to understand the meaning of another. Of course this does not mean that when we listen to someone or read a book we must forget all our fore-meanings concerning the content and all our own ideas. All that is asked is that we remain open to the meaning of the other person or text. But this openness always includes our situating the other meaning in relation to the whole of our own meanings or ourselves in relation to it. Now, the fact is that meanings represent a fluid multiplicity of possibilities (in comparison to the agreement presented by a language and a vocabulary), but within this multiplicity of what can be thought—i.e., of what a reader can find meaningful and hence expect to find—not everything is possible; and if a person fails to hear what the other person is really saying, he will not be able to fit what he has misunderstood into the range of his own various expectations of meaning. Thus there is a criterion here also. *The hermeneutical task becomes of itself a questioning of things* and is always in part so defined. This places hermeneutical work on a firm basis. A person trying to understand something will not resign himself from the start to relying on his own accidental fore-meanings, ignoring as consistently and stubbornly as possible the actual meaning of the text until the latter becomes so persistently audible that it breaks through what the interpreter imagines it to be. Rather, a person trying to understand a text is prepared for it to tell him something. That is why a hermeneutically trained consciousness must be, from the start, sensitive to the text's alterity [otherness]. But this kind of sensitivity involves neither "neutrality" with respect to content nor the extinction of one's self, but the fore-grounding and appropriation of one's own fore-meanings and prejudices. The important thing is to be aware of one's own bias, so that the text can present itself in all its otherness and thus assert its own truth against one's own fore-meanings.

When Heidegger disclosed the forestructure of understanding in what is considered merely "reading what is there," this was a completely correct phenomenological description. He also exemplified the task that follows from this. In *Being and Time* he gave the general hermeneutical problem a concrete form in the question of being.* In order to explain the hermeneutical situation of the question of being in terms of forehaving, fore-sight, and fore-conception, he critically tested his question, directed at metaphysics, on important turning points in the history of metaphysics. Here he was only doing what historical-hermeneutical consciousness requires in every case. Methodologically conscious understanding will be concerned not merely to form anticipatory ideas, but to make them conscious, so as to check them and thus acquire right understanding from the things themselves. This is what Heidegger means when he talks about making our scientific theme "secure" by deriving our fore-having, fore-sight and fore-conception from the things themselves.

It is not at all a matter of securing ourselves against the tradition that speaks out of the text then, but, on the contrary, of excluding everything that could hinder us from understanding it in terms of the subject matter. It is the tyranny of hidden prejudices that makes us deaf to what speaks to us in tradition. Heidegger's demonstration that the concept of consciousness in Descartes and of spirit in Hegel is still influenced by Greek substance ontology, which sees being in terms of what is present, undoubtedly surpasses the self-understanding of modern metaphysics, yet not in an arbitrary, willful way, but on the basis of a "fore-having" that in fact makes this tradition intelligible by revealing the ontological premises of the concept of subjectivity. On the other hand, Heidegger discovers in Kant's critique of "dogmatic" metaphysics the idea of a metaphysics of finitude which is a challenge to his own ontological scheme. Thus he "secures" the scientific theme by framing it within the understanding of tradition and so putting it, in a sense, at risk. All of this is a concretization of the historical consciousness involved in understanding.

The recognition that all understanding inevitably involves some prejudice gives the hermeneutical problem its real thrust. In light of this insight it appears that *historicism, despite its critique of rationalism and of natural law philosophy, is based on the modern Enlightenment and unwittingly shares its prejudices.* And there is one prejudice of the Enlightenment that defines its essence: the fundamental prejudice of the Enlightenment is the prejudice against prejudice itself, which denies tradition its power.

The history of ideas shows that not until the Enlightenment does *the concept of prejudice* acquire the negative connotation familiar today. Actually "prejudice" means a judgment that is rendered before all the elements that determine a situation have been finally examined. In German legal terminology a "prejudice" is a provisional legal verdict before the final verdict is reached. For someone involved in a legal dispute, this kind of judgment against him affects his chances adversely. Accordingly, the French *préjudice,* as well as the Latin *praejudicium,* means simply "adverse effect," "disadvantage," "harm." But this negative sense is only derivative. The negative consequence depends precisely on the positive validity, the value of the provisional decision as a prejudgment, like that of any precedent.

Thus "prejudice" certainly does not necessarily mean a false judgment, but part of the idea is that it can have either a positive or a negative value. This is clearly due to the influence of the Latin *praejudicium.* There are such things as *préjugés légitimes.* This seems a long way from our current use of the word. The German *Vorurteil,* like

---

Sein und Zeit, pp. 312ff.

the English "prejudice" and even more than the French *préjugé,* seems to have been limited in its meaning by the Enlightenment critique of religion simply to the sense of an "unfounded judgment."* The only thing that gives a judgment dignity is its having a basis, a methodological justification (and not the fact that it may actually be correct). For the Enlightenment the absence of such a basis does not mean that there might be other kinds of certainty, but rather that the judgment has no foundation in the things themselves—i.e., that it is "unfounded." This conclusion follows only in the spirit of rationalism. It is the reason for discrediting prejudices and the reason scientific knowledge claims to exclude them completely.

In adopting this principle, modern science is following the rule of Cartesian doubt, accepting nothing as certain that can in any way be doubted, and adopting the idea of method that follows from this rule. In our introductory observations we have already pointed out how difficult it is to harmonize the historical knowledge that helps to shape our historical consciousness with this ideal and how difficult it is, for that reason, to comprehend its true nature on the basis of the modern conception of method. This is the place to turn those negative statements into positive ones. The concept of "prejudice" is where we can start.

(II) The Discrediting of Prejudice by the Enlightenment

If we consider the Enlightenment doctrine of prejudice, we find that it makes the following division: we must make a basic distinction between the prejudice due to human authority and that due to overhastiness.** This distinction is based on the origin of prejudices in the persons who have them. Either the respect we have for others and their authority leads us into error, or else an overhastiness in ourselves. That authority is a source of prejudices accords with the well-known principle of the Enlightenment that Kant formulated: Have the courage to make use of your own understanding.*** Although this distinction is certainly not limited to the role that prejudices play in understanding texts, its chief application is still in the sphere of hermeneutics, for Enlightenment critique is primarily directed against the religious tradition of Christianity—i.e., the Bible. By treating the Bible as a historical document, biblical criticism endangers its own dogmatic claims. This is the real radicality of the modern Enlightenment compared to all other movements of enlightenment: it must assert itself against the Bible and dogmatic interpretation of it.† It is therefore particularly concerned with the hermeneutical problem. It wants to understand tradition correctly—i.e., rationally and without prejudice. But there is a special difficulty about this, since the sheer fact that something is written down gives it special authority. It is not altogether easy to realize that what is written down can be untrue. The written word has the tangible quality

---

*Cf. Leo Strauss, *Die Religionskritik Spinozas,* p. 163: "The word 'prejudice' is the most suitable expression for the great aim of the Enlightenment, the desire for free, untrammeled verification; the Vorurteil is the unambiguous polemical correlate of the very ambiguous word 'freedom'."

**Praeiudicium auctoritatis et precipitantiae,* which we find as early as Christian Thomasius' *Lectiones de praeiudiciis* (1689/90) and his *Einleitung der Vernunftlehre,* ch. 13, §§ 39–40. Cf. the article in Walch, *Philosophisches Lexikon* (1726), pp. 2794ff.

***At the beginning of his essay, "What Is Enlightenment?" (1784).

†The enlightenment of the classical world, the fruit of which was Greek philosophy and its culmination in sophism, was quite different in nature and hence permitted a thinker like Plato to use philosophical myths to convey the religious tradition and the dialectical method of philosophizing. Cf. Erich Frank, *Philosophische Erkenntnis und religiöse Wahrheit,* pp. 31ff., and my review of it in the *Theologische Rundschau* (1950), pp. 260–266. And see especially Gerhard Krüger, *Einsicht und Leidenschaft* (2nd ed., 1951).

of something that can be demonstrated and is like a proof. It requires a special critical effort to free oneself from the prejudice in favor of what is written down and to distinguish here also, no less than in the case of oral assertions, between opinion and truth.* In general, the Enlightenment tends to accept no authority and to decide everything before the judgment seat of reason. Thus the written tradition of Scripture, like any other historical document, can claim no absolute validity; the possible truth of the tradition depends on the credibility that reason accords it. It is not tradition but reason that constitutes the ultimate source of all authority. What is written down is not necessarily true. We can know better: this is the maxim with which the modern Enlightenment approaches tradition and which ultimately leads it to undertake historical research.** It takes tradition as an object of critique, just as the natural sciences do with the evidence of the senses. This does not necessarily mean that the "prejudice against prejudices" was everywhere taken to the extremes of free thinking and atheism, as in England and France. On the contrary, the German Enlightenment recognized the "true prejudices" of the Christian religion. Since the human intellect is too weak to manage without prejudices, it is at least fortunate to have been educated with true prejudices.

It would be valuable to investigate to what extent this kind of modification and moderation of the Enlightenment*** prepared the way for the rise of the romantic movement in Germany, as undoubtedly did the critique of the Enlightenment and the revolution by Edmund Burke. But none of this alters the fundamental fact. True prejudices must still finally be justified by rational knowledge, even though the task can never be fully completed.

Thus the criteria of the modern Enlightenment still determine the self-understanding of historicism. They do so not directly, but through a curious refraction caused by romanticism. This can be seen with particular clarity in the fundamental schema of the philosophy of history that romanticism shares with the Enlightenment and that precisely through the romantic reaction to the Enlightenment became an unshakable premise: the schema of the conquest of ⟨*mythos*⟩ by ⟨*logos*⟩. What gives this schema its validity is the presupposition of the progressive retreat of magic in the world. It is supposed to represent progress in the history of the mind, and precisely because romanticism disparages this development, it takes over the schema itself as a self-evident truth. It shares the presupposition of the Enlightenment and only reverses its values, seeking to establish the validity of what is old simply on the fact that it is old: the "gothic" Middle Ages, the Christian European community of states, the permanent structure of society, but also the simplicity of peasant life and closeness to nature.

In contrast to the Enlightenment's faith in perfection, which thinks in terms of complete freedom from "superstition" and the prejudices of the past, we now find that olden times—the world of myth, unreflective life, not yet analyzed away by consciousness, in a "society close to nature," the world of Christian chivalry—all these acquire a

---

*A good example of this is the length of time it has taken for the authority of the historical writing of antiquity to be destroyed in historical studies and how slowly the study of archives and the research into sources have established themselves (cf. R.G. Collingwood, *Autobiography* [Oxford, 1939], ch. 11, where he more or less draws a parallel between turning to the study of sources and the Baconian revolution in the study of nature).

**Cf. what we said about Spinoza's *Theological-Political Treatise,* pp. 181f. above. [not in this selection.—FB]

***As we find, for example, in G.F. Meier's *Beiträge zu der Lehre von den Vorurteilen des menschlichen Geschlechts* (1766).

romantic magic, even a priority over truth.* Reversing the Enlightenment's presupposition results in the paradoxical tendency toward restoration—i.e., the tendency to reconstruct the old because it is old, the conscious return to the unconscious, culminating in the recognition of the superior wisdom of the primeval age of myth. But the romantic reversal of the Enlightenment's criteria of value actually perpetuates the abstract contrast between myth and reason. All criticism of the Enlightenment now proceeds via this romantic mirror image of the Enlightenment. Belief in the perfectibility of reason suddenly changes into the perfection of the "mythical" consciousness and finds itself reflected in a paradisiacal primal state before the "fall" of thought.**

In fact the presupposition of a mysterious darkness in which there was a mythical collective consciousness that preceded all thought is just as dogmatic and abstract as that of a state of perfect enlightenment or of absolute knowledge. Primeval wisdom is only the counterimage of "primeval stupidity." All mythical consciousness is still knowledge, and if it knows about divine powers, then it has progressed beyond mere trembling before power (if this is to be regarded as the primeval state), but also beyond a collective life contained in magic rituals (as we find in the early Orient). It knows about itself, and in this knowledge it is no longer simply outside itself.***

There is the related point that even the contrast between genuine mythical thinking and pseudomythical poetic thinking is a romantic illusion based on a prejudice of the Enlightenment: namely that the poetic act no longer shares the binding quality of myth because it is a creation of the free imagination. It is the old quarrel between the poets and the philosophers in the modern garb appropriate to the age of belief in science. It is now said, not that poets tell lies, but that they are incapable of saying anything true; they have only an aesthetic effect and, through their imaginative creations, they merely seek to stimulate the imagination and vitality of their hearers or readers.

Another case of romantic refraction is probably to be found in the concept of an "organic society," which Ladendorf (217) says was introduced by H. Leo.[†] In Karl Marx it appears as a kind of relic of natural law that limits the validity of his socioeconomic theory of the class struggle.[††] Does the idea go back to Rousseau's description of society before the division of labor and the introduction of property?[§] At any rate, Plato had already demonstrated the illusory nature of this political theory in his ironical account of a state of nature in the third book of the Republic.[§§]

These romantic revaluations give rise to historical science in the nineteenth century. It no longer measures the past by the standards of the present, as if they were an absolute, but it ascribes to past ages a value of their own and can even acknowledge their superiority in one respect or another. The great achievements of romanticism—the revival of the past, the discovery of the voices of the peoples in their songs, the col-

---

*I have analyzed an example of this process in a little study on Immermann's "Chiliastische Sonette," *Kleine Schriften,* 11, 136–147 (GW, IX).

**See my "Mythos und Vernunft," *Kleine Schriften,* IV, 48–53 (GW, VIII) and "Mythos und Wissenschaft," GW, VIII.

***Horkheimer and Adorno seem to me right in their analysis of the "dialectic of the Enlightenment" (although I must regard the application of sociological concepts such as "bourgeois" to Odysseus as a failure of historical reflection, if not, indeed, a confusion of Homer with Johann Heinrich Voss [author of the standard German translation of Homer], who had already been criticized by Goethe).

[†]H. Leo, *Studien und Skizzen zu einer Naturlehre des Staates* (1833).

[††]Cf. the reflections on this important question by G. von Lukács in his *History and Class Consciousness,* tr. Rodney Livingstone (1923; Cambridge, MA: MIT Press, 1971).

[§]Rousseau, *Discourse on the Origin of Inequality.*

[§§]Cf. my "Plato and the Poets," in *Dialogue and Dialectic: Eight Hermeneutical Studies on Plato,* tr. P. Christopher Smith (New Haven, CT: Yale University Press, 1980), pp. 54f.

lecting of fairy tales and legends, the cultivation of ancient customs, the discovery of the worldviews implicit in languages, the study of the "religion and wisdom of India"—all contributed to the rise of historical research, which was slowly, step by step, transformed from intuitive revival into detached historical knowledge. The fact that it was romanticism that gave birth to the historical school confirms that the romantic retrieval of origins is itself based on the Enlightenment. Nineteenth-century historiography is its finest fruit and sees itself precisely as the fulfillment of the Enlightenment, as the last step in the liberation of the mind from the trammels of dogma, the step to objective knowledge of the historical world, which stands on a par with the knowledge of nature achieved by modern science.

The fact that the restorative tendency of romanticism could combine with the fundamental concerns of the Enlightenment to create the historical sciences simply indicates that the same break with the continuity of meaning in tradition lies behind both. If the Enlightenment considers it an established fact that all tradition that reason shows to be impossible (i.e., nonsense) can only be understood historically—i.e., by going back to the past's way of looking at things—then the historical consciousness that emerges in romanticism involves a radicalization of the Enlightenment. For nonsensical tradition, which had been the exception, has become the general rule for historical consciousness. Meaning that is generally accessible through reason is so little believed that the whole of the past—even, ultimately, all the thinking of one's contemporaries—is understood only "historically." Thus the romantic critique of the Enlightenment itself ends in enlightenment, for it evolves as historical science and draws everything into the orbit of historicism. The basic discreditation of all prejudices, which unites the experimental fervor of the new natural sciences during the Enlightenment, is universalized and radicalized in the historical Enlightenment.

This is the point at which the attempt to critique historical hermeneutics has to start. The overcoming of all prejudices, this global demand of the Enlightenment, will itself prove to be a prejudice, and removing it opens the way to an appropriate understanding of the finitude which dominates not only our humanity but also our historical consciousness.

Does being situated within traditions really mean being subject to prejudices and limited in one's freedom? Is not, rather, all human existence, even the freest, limited and qualified in various ways? If this is true, the idea of an absolute reason is not a possibility for historical humanity. Reason exists for us only in concrete, historical terms—i.e., it is not its own master but remains constantly dependent on the given circumstances in which it operates. This is true not only in the sense in which Kant, under the influence of the skeptical critique of Hume, limited the claims of rationalism to the a priori element in the knowledge of nature; it is still truer of historical consciousness and the possibility of historical knowledge. For that man is concerned here with himself and his own creations (Vico) is only an apparent solution of the problem posed by historical knowledge. Man is alien to himself and his historical fate in a way quite different from the way nature, which knows nothing of him, is alien to him.

The epistemological question must be asked here in a fundamentally different way. We have shown above that Dilthey probably saw this, but he was not able to escape his entanglement in traditional epistemology. Since he started from the awareness of "experiences" *[Erlebnisse]*, he was unable to build a bridge to the historical realities, because the great historical realities of society and state always have a predeterminate influence on any "experience." Self-reflection and autobiography—Dilthey's starting points—are not primary and are therefore not an adequate basis for the hermeneutical problem, because through them history is made private once more. In

fact history does not belong to us; we belong to it. Long before we understand ourselves through the process of self-examination, we understand ourselves in a self-
evident way in the family, society, and state in which we live. The focus of subjectivity
is a distorting mirror. The self-awareness of the individual is only a flickering in the
closed circuits of historical life. *That is why the prejudices of the individual, far more
than his judgments, constitute the historical reality of his being.*

(B) PREJUDICES AS CONDITIONS OF UNDERSTANDING

(I) THE REHABILITATION OF AUTHORITY AND TRADITION

Here is the point of departure for the hermeneutical problem. This is why we examined the Enlightenment's discreditation of the concept of "prejudice." What appears
to be a limiting prejudice from the viewpoint of the absolute self-construction of reason in fact belongs to historical reality itself. If we want to do justice to man's finite,
historical mode of being, it is necessary to fundamentally rehabilitate the concept of
prejudice and acknowledge the fact that there are legitimate prejudices. Thus we can
formulate the fundamental epistemological question for a truly historical hermeneutics
as follows: what is the ground of the legitimacy of prejudices? What distinguishes legitimate prejudices from the countless others which it is the undeniable task of critical
reason to overcome?

We can approach this question by taking the Enlightenment's critical theory of
prejudices, as set out above, and giving it a positive value. The division of prejudices
into those of "authority" and those of "overhastiness" is obviously based on the fundamental presupposition of the Enlightenment, namely that methodologically disciplined
use of reason can safeguard us from all error. This was Descartes' idea of method.
Overhastiness is the source of errors that arise in the use of one's own reason. Authority, however, is responsible for one's not using one's own reason at all. Thus the division is based on a mutually exclusive antithesis between authority and reason. The
false prepossession in favor of what is old, in favor of authorities, is what has to be
fought. Thus the Enlightenment attributes to Luther's reforms the fact that "the prejudice of human prestige, especially that of the philosophical [he means Aristotle] and
the Roman pope, was greatly weakened."* The Reformation, then, gives rise to a flour-
ishing hermeneutics which teaches the right use of reason in understanding traditionary
texts. Neither the doctrinal authority of the pope nor the appeal to tradition can obviate
the work of hermeneutics, which can safeguard the reasonable meaning of a text
against all imposition.

This kind of hermeneutics need not lead to the radical critique of religion that we
found, for example, in Spinoza. Rather, the possibility of supernatural truth can remain
entirely open. Thus especially in the field of German popular philosophy, the Enlightenment limited the claims of reason and acknowledged the authority of Bible and
church. We read in Walch, for example, that he distinguishes between the two classes
of prejudice—authority and overhastiness—but considers them two extremes, between
which it is necessary to find the right middle path, namely a mediation between reason
and biblical authority. Accordingly, he regards prejudices deriving from overhastiness
as prejudices in favor of the new, a predisposition to the overhasty rejection of truths

---

*Walch, *Philosophisches Lexicon* (1726), p. 1013.

simply because they are old and attested by authorities.* Thus he disputes the British free thinkers (such as Collins and others) and defends the historical faith against the norm of reason. Here the meaning of prejudice deriving from overhastiness is given a conservative reinterpretation.

There can be no doubt, however, that the real consequence of the Enlightenment is different: namely the subjection of all authority to reason. Accordingly, prejudice from overhastiness is to be understood as Descartes understood it—i.e., as the source of all error in the use of reason. This fits in with the fact that after the victory of the En-lightenment, when hermeneutics was freed from all dogmatic ties, the old division re-turns in a new guise. Thus Schleiermacher distinguishes between partiality and over-hastiness as the causes of misunderstanding.** To the lasting prejudices due to partiality he contrasts the momentary ones due to overhastiness, but only the former are of interest to those concerned with scientific method. It no longer even occurs to Schleiermacher that among the prejudices in favor of authorities there might be some that are true—yet this was implied in the concept of authority in the first place. His al-teration of the traditional division of prejudices documents the victory of the Enlight-enment. Partiality now means only an individual limitation of understanding: "The one-sided preference for what is close to one's own sphere of ideas."

In fact, however, the decisive question is concealed behind the concept of par-tiality. That the prejudices determining what I think are due to my own partiality is a judgment based on the standpoint of their having been dissolved and enlightened, and it holds only for unjustified prejudices. If, on the other hand, there are justified preju-dices productive of knowledge, then we are back to the problem of authority. Hence the radical consequences of the Enlightenment, which are still to be found in Schleier-macher's faith in method, are not tenable.

The Enlightenment's distinction between faith in authority and using one's own reason is, in itself, legitimate. If the prestige of authority displaces one's own judg-ment, then authority is in fact a source of prejudices. But this does not preclude its being a source of truth, and that is what the Enlightenment failed to see when it deni-grated all authority. To be convinced of this, we need only consider one of the greatest forerunners of the European Enlightenment, namely Descartes. Despite the radicalness of his methodological thinking, we know that Descartes excluded morality from the total reconstruction of all truths by reason. This was what he meant by his provisional morality. It seems to me symptomatic that he did not in fact elaborate his definitive morality and that its principles, as far as we can judge from his letters to Elizabeth, contain hardly anything new. It is obviously unthinkable to defer morality until mod-ern science has progressed enough to provide a new basis for it. In fact the denigration of authority is not the only prejudice established by the Enlightenment. It also distorted the very concept of authority. Based on the Enlightenment conception of reason and freedom, the concept of authority could be viewed as diametrically opposed to reason and freedom: to be, in fact, blind obedience. This is the meaning that we find in the language critical of modern dictatorships.

But this is not the essence of authority. Admittedly, it is primarily persons that have authority; but the authority of persons is ultimately based not on the subjection and abdication of reason but on an act of acknowledgment and knowledge—the knowledge, namely, that the other is superior to oneself in judgment and insight and that for this reason his judgment takes precedence—i.e., it has priority over one's own.

---

*Walch, *op. cit.*, pp. 1006ff. under the entry "Freiheit zu gedenken."
**Schleiermacher, *Werke,* 1, part 7, 31.

This is connected with the fact that authority cannot actually be bestowed but is earned, and must be earned if someone is to lay claim to it. It rests on acknowledgment and hence on an act of reason itself which, aware of its own limitations, trusts to the better insight of others. Authority in this sense, properly understood, has nothing to do with blind obedience to commands. Indeed, authority has to do not with obedience but rather with knowledge. It is true that authority implies the capacity to command and be obeyed. But this proceeds only from the authority that a person has. Even the anonymous and impersonal authority of a superior which derives from his office is not ultimately based on this hierarchy, but is what makes it possible. Here also its true basis is an act of freedom and reason that grants the authority of a superior fundamentally because he has a wider view of things or is better informed—i.e., once again, because he knows more.* Thus, acknowledging authority is always connected with the idea that what the authority says is not irrational and arbitrary but can, in principle, be discovered to be true. This is the essence of the authority claimed by the teacher, the superior, the expert. The prejudices that they implant are legitimized by the person who presents them. But in this way they become prejudices not just in favor of a person but a content, since they effect the same disposition to believe something that can be brought about in other ways—e.g., by good reasons. Thus the essence of authority belongs in the context of a theory of prejudices free from the extremism of the Enlightenment.

Here we can find support in the romantic criticism of the Enlightenment; for there is one form of authority particularly defended by romanticism, namely tradition. That which has been sanctioned by tradition and custom has an authority that is nameless, and our finite historical being is marked by the fact that the authority of what has been handed down to us—and not just what is clearly grounded—always has power over our attitudes and behavior. All education depends on this, and even though, in the case of education, the educator loses his function when his charge comes of age and sets his own insight and decisions in the place of the authority of the educator, becoming mature does not mean that a person becomes his own master in the sense that he is freed from all tradition. The real force of morals, for example, is based on tradition. They are freely taken over but by no means created by a free insight or grounded on reasons. This is precisely what we call tradition: the ground of their validity. And in fact it is to romanticism that we owe this correction of the Enlightenment: that tradition has a justification that lies beyond rational grounding and in large measure determines our institutions and attitudes. What makes classical ethics superior to modern moral philosophy is that it grounds the transition from ethics to "politics," the art of right legislation, on the indispensability of tradition.** By comparison, the modern Enlightenment is abstract and revolutionary.

The concept of tradition, however, has become no less ambiguous than that of authority, and for the same reason—namely that what determines the romantic under-

---

*(It seems to me that the tendency to acknowledge authority, as for instance in Karl Jaspers, *Von der Wahrheit,* pp. 766ff., and Gerhard Krüger, *Freiheit und Weltverwaltung,* pp. 231ff., lacks an intelligible basis so long as this proposition is not acknowledged.) The notorious statement, "The party (or the Leader) is always right" is not wrong because it claims that a certain leadership is superior, but because it serves to shield the leadership, by a dictatorial decree, from any criticism that might be true. True authority does not have to be authoritarian. (This issue has meanwhile been much debated, particularly in my exchange with Jürgen Habermas. See *Hermeneutik und Ideologiekritik,* ed. Jürgen Habermas (Frankfurt, 1977) and my lecture at Solothurn, "Über den Zusammenhang von Autorität und kritischer Freiheit," *Schweizer Archiv für Neurologie, Neurochirurgie und Psychiatrie* 133 (1983), 11–16. Arnold Gehlen especially has worked out the role of institutions.)

**Cf. Aristotle, *Nichomachean Ethics,* X, 10.

standing of tradition is its abstract opposition to the principle of enlightenment. Romanticism conceives of tradition as an antithesis to the freedom of reason and regards it as something historically given, like nature. And whether one wants to be revolutionary and oppose it or preserve it, tradition is still viewed as the abstract opposite of free self-determination, since its validity does not require any reasons but conditions us without our questioning it. Of course, the romantic critique of the Enlightenment is not an instance of tradition's automatic dominance of tradition, of its persisting unaffected by doubt and criticism. Rather, a particular critical attitude again addresses itself to the truth of tradition and seeks to renew it. We can call it "traditionalism."

It seems to me, however, that there is no such unconditional antithesis between tradition and reason. However problematical the conscious restoration of old or the creation of new traditions may be, the romantic faith in the "growth of tradition," before which all reason must remain silent, is fundamentally like the Enlightenment, and just as prejudiced. The fact is that in tradition there is always an element of freedom and of history itself. Even the most genuine and pure tradition does not persist because of the inertia of what once existed. It needs to be affirmed, embraced, cultivated. It is, essentially, preservation, and it is active in all historical change. But preservation is an act of reason, though an inconspicuous one. For this reason, only innovation and planning appear to be the result of reason. But this is an illusion. Even where life changes violently, as in ages of revolution, far more of the old is preserved in the supposed transformation of everything than anyone knows, and it combines with the new to create a new value. At any rate, preservation is as much a freely chosen action as are revolution and renewal. That is why both the Enlightenment's critique of tradition and the romantic rehabilitation of it lag behind their true historical being.

These thoughts raise the question of whether in the hermeneutics of the human sciences the element of tradition should not be given its full value. Research in the human sciences cannot regard itself as in an absolute antithesis to the way in which we, as historical beings, relate to the past. At any rate, our usual relationship to the past is not characterized by distancing and freeing ourselves from tradition. Rather, we are always situated within traditions, and this is no objectifying process—i.e., we do not conceive of what tradition says as something other, something alien. It is always part of us, a model or exemplar, a kind of cognizance that our later historical judgment would hardly regard as a kind of knowledge but as the most ingenuous affinity with tradition.

Hence in regard to the dominant epistemological methodologism we must ask: has the rise of historical consciousness really divorced our scholarship from this natural relation to the past? Does understanding in the human sciences understand itself correctly when it relegates the whole of its own historicality to the position of prejudices from which we must free ourselves? Or does "unprejudiced scholarship" share more than it realizes with that naive openness and reflection in which traditions live and the past is present?

In any case, understanding in the human sciences shares one fundamental condition with the life of tradition: it lets itself be *addressed* by tradition. Is it not true of the objects that the human sciences investigate, just as for the contents of tradition, that what they are really about can be experienced only when one is addressed by them? However mediated this significance may be, and though it may proceed from a historical interest that appears to bear no relation to the present—even in the extreme case of "objective" historical research—the real fulfillment of the historical task is to determine anew the significance of what is examined. But the significance exists at the beginning of any such research as well as at the end: in choosing the theme to be investigated, awakening the desire to investigate, gaining a new problematic.

At the beginning of all historical hermeneutics, then, the *abstract antithesis between tradition and historical research, between history and the knowledge of it, must be discarded.* The effect *[Wirkung]* of a living tradition and the effect of historical study must constitute a unity of effect, the analysis of which would reveal only a texture of reciprocal effects.* Hence we would do well not to regard historical consciousness as something radically new—as it seems at first—but as a new element in what has always constituted the human relation to the past. In other words, we have to recognize the element of tradition in historical research and inquire into its hermeneutic productivity.

That an element of tradition affects the human sciences despite the methodological purity of their procedures, an element that constitutes their real nature and distinguishing mark, is immediately clear if we examine the history of research and note the difference between the human and natural sciences with regard to their history. Of course none of man's finite historical endeavors can completely erase the traces of this finitude. The history of mathematics or of the natural sciences is also a part of the history of the human spirit and reflects its destinies. Nevertheless, it is not just historical naivete when the natural scientist writes the history of his subject in terms of the present state of knowledge. For him errors and wrong turnings are of historical interest only, because the progress of research is the self-evident standard of examination. Thus it is only of secondary interest to see how advances in the natural sciences or in mathematics belong to the moment in history at which they took place. This interest does not affect the epistemic value of discoveries in those fields.

There is, then, no need to deny that elements of tradition can also affect the natural sciences—e.g., particular lines of research are preferred at particular places. But scientific research as such derives the law of its development not from these circumstances but from the law of the object it is investigating, which conceals its methodical efforts.**

It is clear that the human sciences cannot be adequately described in terms of this conception of research and progress. Of course it is possible to write a history of the solution of a problem—e.g., the deciphering of barely legible inscriptions—in which the only interest is in ultimately reaching the final result. Were this not so, it would have been impossible for the human sciences to have borrowed the methodology of the natural ones, as happened in the last century. But what the human sciences share with the natural is only a subordinate element of the work done in the human sciences.

This is shown by the fact that the great achievements in the human sciences almost never become outdated. A modern reader can easily make allowances for the fact that, a hundred years ago, less knowledge was available to a historian, and he therefore made judgments that were incorrect in some details. On the whole, he would still rather read Droysen or Mommsen than the latest account of the subject from the pen of a historian living today. What is the criterion here? Obviously the value and importance of research cannot be measured by a criterion based in the subject matter. Rather, the subject matter appears truly significant only when it is properly portrayed for us.

---

*I don't agree with Scheler that the preconscious pressure of tradition decreases as historical study proceeds (*Stellung des Menschen im Kosmos,* p. 37). The independence of historical study implied in this view seems to me a liberal fiction of a sort that Scheler is generally able to see through. (Cf. similarly in his *Nachlass,* 1, 228ff., where he affirms his faith in enlightenment through historical study or sociology of knowledge.)

**(The question appears much more complicated since Thomas Kuhn's *The Structure of Scientific Revolutions* [Chicago, 1963] and *The Essential Tension: Selected Studies in Scientific Tradition and Change* [Chicago, 1977].)

Thus we are certainly interested in the subject matter, but it acquires its life only from the light in which it is presented to us. We accept the fact that the subject presents different aspects of itself at different times or from different standpoints. We accept the fact that these aspects do not simply cancel one another out as research proceeds, but are like mutually exclusive conditions that exist by themselves and combine only in us. Our historical consciousness is always filled with a variety of voices in which the echo of the past is heard. Only in the multifariousness of such voices does it exist: this constitutes the nature of the tradition in which we want to share and have a part. Modern historical research itself is not only research, but the handing down of tradition. We do not see it only in terms of progress and verified results; in it we have, as it were, a new experience of history whenever the past resounds with a new voice.

Why is this so? Obviously, in the human sciences we cannot speak of an object of research in the same sense as in the natural sciences, where research penetrates more and more deeply into nature. Rather, in the human sciences the particular research questions concerning tradition that we are interested in pursuing are motivated in a special way by the present and its interests. The theme and object of research are actually constituted by the motivation of the inquiry.* Hence historical research is carried along by the historical movement of life itself and cannot be understood teleologically in terms of the object into which it is inquiring. Such an "object in itself" clearly does not exist at all. This is precisely what distinguishes the human sciences from the natural sciences. Whereas the object of the natural sciences can be described idealiter as what would be known in the perfect knowledge of nature, it is senseless to speak of a perfect knowledge of history, and for this reason it is not possible to speak of an "object in itself" toward which its research is directed.**

(II) The Example of the Classical***

Of course it is a lot to ask that the self-understanding of the human sciences detach itself, in the whole of its activity, from the model of the natural sciences and regard the historical movement of the things they are concerned with not simply as an impairment of their objectivity, but as something of positive value. In the recent development of the human sciences, however, there are starting points for a reflection that would really do justice to the problem. The naive schema of history-as-research no longer dominates the way the human sciences conceive of themselves. The advancement of inquiry is no longer universally conceived of as an expansion or penetration into new fields or material, but instead as raising the inquiry to a higher stage of reflection. But even where this happens, one is still thinking teleologically, from the viewpoint of progressive research, in a way appropriate to a research scientist. But a hermeneutical consciousness is gradually growing that is infusing research with a spirit of self-reflection; this is true, above all, in those human sciences that have the oldest tradition. Thus the study of classical antiquity, after it had worked over the whole extent of the available transmitted texts, continually applied itself again, with more subtle questions, to its favorite objects of study. This introduced something of an element of

*(That K.–G. Faber in his thorough discussion in *Theorie der Geschichtswissenschaft* [2nd ed., Munich, 1972], p. 25, cannot quote this statement without placing an ironic exclamation mark after "constituted" obliges me to ask how else one defines a "historical fact"?)

**(Now, in the light of the past three decades of work in the philosophy of science, I willingly acknowledge that even this formulation is too undifferentiated.)

***(See my "Zwischen Phänomenologie und Dialektik: Versuch einer Selbstkritik," *GW*, 11.)

self-criticism by inviting reflection on what constituted the real merit of its favorite objects. The concept of the classical, which since Droysen's discovery of Hellenism had been reduced by historical thinking to a mere stylistic concept, now acquired a new scholarly legitimacy.

It requires hermeneutical reflection of some sophistication to discover how it is possible for a normative concept such as the classical to acquire or regain its scholarly legitimacy. For it follows from the self-understanding of historical consciousness that all of the past's normative significance has been finally dissolved by sovereign historical reason. Only at the beginnings of historicism, as for example in Winckelmann's epoch-making work, had the normative element been a real motive of historical research.

The concept of classical antiquity and of the classical—which dominated pedagogical thought in particular since the days of German classicism—combined both a normative and a historical side. A particular stage in the historical development of humanity was thought to have produced a mature and perfect form of the human. This mediation between the normative and historical senses of the concept goes back to Herder. But Hegel still preserved this mediation, even though he gave it a different emphasis, namely in terms of the history of philosophy. For him classical art retained its special distinction by being regarded as the "religion of art." Since this form of spirit is past, it is exemplary only in a qualified sense. The fact that it is a past art testifies to the "past" character of art in general. In this way Hegel systematically justified the historicization of the concept of the classical, and he began the process of development that finally changed the classical into a descriptive stylistic concept—one that describes the short-lived harmony of measure and fullness that comes between archaic rigidity and baroque dissolution. Since it became part of the aesthetic vocabulary of historical studies, the concept of the classical retains the sense of a normative content only in an unacknowledged way.

Symptomatic of renewed historical self-criticism was that after the First World War classical philology started to examine itself under the banner of a new humanism, and hesitantly again acknowledged the combination of normative and historical elements in "the classical."* In so doing, it proved impossible (however one tried) to interpret the concept of the classical—which arose in antiquity and canonized certain writers—as if it expressed the unity of a stylistic ideal.** On the contrary, as a stylistic term the ancient concept was wholly ambiguous. Today when we use classical as a historical stylistic concept whose clear meaning is defined by its being set against what came before and after, this concept has become quite detached from the ancient one. The concept of the classical now signifies a period of time, a phase of historical development but not a suprahistorical value.

In fact, however, the normative element in the concept of the classical has never completely disappeared. Even today it is still the basis of the idea of liberal education. The philologist is rightly dissatisfied with simply applying to his texts the historical stylistic concept that developed through the history of the plastic arts. The question whether Homer too is "classical" shatters the notion that the classical is merely a historical category of style analogous to categories of style used in the history of art—an

*The congress at Naumburg on the classical (1930), which was completely dominated by Werner Jaeger, is as much an example of this as the founding of the periodical *Die Antike*. Cf. *Das Problem des Klassischen und die Antike* (1931).
**Cf. the legitimate criticism that A. Körte made of the Naumburg lecture by J. Stroux, in the *Berichte der Sächsischen Akademie der Wissenchaften*, 86 (1934), and my note in *Gnomon*, 11 (1935), 612f. [repr. in GW, V, 350–353].

instance of the fact that historical consciousness always includes more than it admits of itself.

If we try to see what this implies, we might say that the classical is a truly historical category, precisely because it is more than a concept of a period or of a historical style, and yet it nevertheless does not try to be the concept of a suprahistorical value. It does not refer to a quality that we ascribe to particular historical phenomena but to a notable mode of being historical: the historical process of preservation *[Bewahrung]* that, through constantly proving itself *[Bewahrung],* allows something true *[ein Wahres]* to come into being. It is not at all the case, as the historical mode of thought would have us believe, that the value judgment which accords something the status of a classic was in fact destroyed by historical reflection and its criticism of all teleological construals of the process of history. Rather, through this criticism the value judgment implicit in the concept of the classical acquires a new, special legitimacy. The classical is something that resists historical criticism because its historical dominion, the binding power of the validity that is preserved and handed down, precedes all historical reflection and continues in it.

To take the key example of the blanket concept of "classical antiquity," it is, of course, unhistorical to devalue Hellenism as an age of the decline and fall of classicism, and Droysen has rightly emphasized its place in the continuity of world history and stressed the importance of Hellenism for the birth and spread of Christianity. But he would not have needed to undertake this historical theodicy if there had not always been a prejudice in favor of the classical and if the culture of "humanism" had not held on to "classical antiquity" and preserved it within Western culture as the heritage of the past. The classical is fundamentally something quite different from a descriptive concept used by an objectivizing historical consciousness. It is a historical reality to which historical consciousness belongs and is subordinate. The "classical" is something raised above the vicissitudes of changing times and changing tastes. It is immediately accessible, not through that shock of recognition, as it were, that sometimes characterizes a work of art for its contemporaries and in which the beholder experiences a fulfilled apprehension of meaning that surpasses all conscious expectations. Rather, when we call something classical, there is a consciousness of something enduring, of significance that cannot be lost and that is independent of all the circumstances of time—a kind of timeless present that is contemporaneous with every other present.

So the most important thing about the concept of the classical (and this is wholly true of both the ancient and the modern use of the word) is the normative sense. But insofar as this norm is related retrospectively to a past greatness that fulfilled and embodied it, it always contains a temporal quality that articulates it historically. So it is not surprising that, with the rise of historical reflection in Germany which took Winckelmann's classicism as its standard, a historical concept of a time or period detached itself from what was regarded as classical in Winckelmann's sense. It denoted a quite specific stylistic ideal and, in a historically descriptive way, also a time or period that fulfilled this ideal. From the distance of the epigones who set up the criterion, this stylistic ideal seemed to designate a historic moment that belonged to the past. Accordingly, the concept of the classical came to be used in modern thought to describe the whole of "classical antiquity" when humanism again proclaimed the exemplarity of this antiquity. It was reviving an ancient usage, and with some justification, for those ancient authors who were "discovered" by humanism were the same ones who in late antiquity comprised the canon of classics.

They were preserved in the history of Western culture precisely because they became canonical as the writers of the "school." But it is easy to see how the historical

stylistic concept was able to adopt this usage. For although there is a normative consciousness behind this concept, there is still a retrospective element. What gives birth
to the classical norm is an awareness of decline and distance. It is not by accident that
the concept of the classical and of classical style emerges in late periods. Callimachus
and Tacitus' *Dialogue on Oratory* played a decisive role in this connection.* But there
is something else. The authors regarded as classical are, as we know, always the representatives of particular literary genres. They were considered the culmination of the
norm of that literary genre, an ideal that literary criticism makes plain in retrospect. If
we now examine these generic norms historically—i.e., if we consider their history—
then the classical is seen as a stylistic phase, a climax that articulates the history of the
genre in terms of before and after. Insofar as the climactic points in the history of genres belong largely within the same brief period of time, within the totality of the historical development of classical antiquity, the classical refers to such a period and thus
also becomes a concept denoting a period and fuses with a concept of style.

As such a historical stylistic concept, the concept of the classical is capable of
being extended to any "development" to which an immanent ⟨*telos*⟩ gives unity. And
in fact all cultures have high periods, when a particular civilization is marked by special achievements in all fields. Thus, via its particular historical fulfillment, the classical as a general concept of value again becomes a general historical stylistic concept.

Although this is an understandable development, the historicization of the concept also involves its uprooting, and that is why when historical consciousness started
to engage in self-criticism, it reinstated the normative element in the concept of the
classical as well as the historical uniqueness of its fulfillment. Every "new humanism"
shares with the first and oldest the consciousness of belonging in an immediate way
and being bound to its model—which, as something past, is unattainable and yet present. Thus the classical epitomizes a general characteristic of historical being: preservation amid the ruins of time. The general nature of tradition is such that only the part of
the past that is not past offers the possibility of historical knowledge. The classical,
however, as Hegel says, is "that which is self-significant *[selbst bedeutende]* and hence
also self-interpretive *[selber Deutende]*."** But that ultimately means that the classical
preserves itself precisely because it is significant in itself and interprets itself; i.e., it
speaks in such a way that it is not a statement about what is past—documentary evidence that still needs to be interpreted—rather, it says something to the present as if it
were said specifically to it. What we call "classical" does not first require the overcoming of historical distance, for in its own constant mediation it overcomes this distance
by itself. The classical, then, is certainly "timeless," but this timelessness is a mode of
historical being.

Of course this is not to deny that works regarded as classical present tasks of historical understanding to a developed historical consciousness, one that is aware of historical distance. The aim of historical consciousness is not to use the classical model in
the direct way, like Palladio or Corneille, but to know it as a historical phenomenon
that can be understood solely in terms of its own time. But understanding it will always

---

*Thus Tacitus' *Dialogue on Oratory* rightly received special attention in the Naumburg discussions
on the classical. The reasons for the decline of rhetoric include the recognition of its former greatness, i.e., a
normative awareness. Bruno Snell is correct when he points out that the historical stylistic concepts of
"baroque," "archaic," etc. all presuppose a relation to the normative concept of the classical and have only
gradually lost their pejorative sense ("Wesen und Wirklichkeit des Menschen," *Festschrift für H. Plessner*,
pp. 333ff.).

**Hegel, *Ästhetik*, 11, 3.

involve more than merely historically reconstructing the past "world" to which the work belongs. Our understanding will always retain the consciousness that we too belong to that world, and correlatively, that the work too belongs to our world.

This is just what the word "classical" means: that the duration of a work's power to speak directly is fundamentally unlimited.* However much the concept of the classical expresses distance and unattainability and is part of cultural consciousness, the phrase "classical culture" still implies something of the continuing validity of the classical. Cultural consciousness manifests an ultimate community and sharing with the world from which a classical work speaks.

This discussion of the concept of the classical claims no independent significance, but serves only to evoke a general question, namely: Does the kind of historical mediation between the past and the present that characterizes the classical ultimately underlie all historical activity as its effective substratum? Whereas romantic hermeneutics had taken homogeneous human nature as the unhistorical substratum of its theory of understanding and hence had freed the congenial interpreter from all historical conditions, the self-criticism of historical consciousness leads finally to recognizing historical movement not only in events but also in understanding itself. *Understanding is to be thought of less as a subjective act than as participating in an event of tradition*, a process of transmission in which past and present are constantly mediated. This is what must be validated by hermeneutic theory, which is far too dominated by the idea of a procedure, a method.

(III) The Hermeneutic Significance of Temporal Distance**

Let us next consider how hermeneutics goes about its work. What consequences for understanding follow from the fact that belonging to a tradition is a condition of hermeneutics? We recall the hermeneutical rule that we must understand the whole in terms of the detail and the detail in terms of the whole. This principle stems from ancient rhetoric, and modern hermeneutics has transferred it to the art of understanding. It is a circular relationship in both cases. The anticipation of meaning in which the whole is envisaged becomes actual understanding when the parts that are determined by the whole themselves also determine this whole.

We know this from learning ancient languages. We learn that we must "construe" a sentence before we attempt to understand the linguistic meaning of the individual parts of the sentence. But the process of construal is itself already governed by an expectation of meaning that follows from the context of what has gone before. It is of course necessary for this expectation to be adjusted if the text calls for it. This means, then, that the expectation changes and that the text unifies its meaning around another expectation. Thus the movement of understanding is constantly from the whole to the part and back to the whole. Our task is to expand the unity of the understood meaning centrifugally. The harmony of all the details with the whole is the criterion of correct understanding. The failure to achieve this harmony means that understanding has failed.

---

*Friedrich Schlegel, *Fragmente*, ed. Minor, no. 20, draws the hermeneutical consequence: "A classical work of literature is one that can never be completely understood. But it must also be one from which those who are educated and educating themselves must always desire to learn more."

**(Here especially, see my "Zwischen Phänomenologie und Dialektik: Versuch einer Selbstkritik," *GW*, 11, 3ff.)

Schleiermacher elaborated this hermeneutic circle of part and whole in both its objective and its subjective aspects. As the single word belongs in the total context of the sentence, so the single text belongs in the total context of a writer's work, and the latter in the whole of the literary genre or of literature. At the same time, however, the same text, as a manifestation of a creative moment, belongs to the whole of its author's inner life. Full understanding can take place only within this objective and subjective whole. Following this theory, Dilthey speaks of "structure" and of the "centering in a mid-point," which permits one to understand the whole. In this (as we have already said above) he is applying to the historical world what has always been a principle of all textual interpretation: namely that a text must be understood in its own terms.

The question is, however, whether this is an adequate account of the circular movement of understanding. Here we must return to what we concluded from our analysis of Schleiermacher's hermeneutics. We can set aside Schleiermacher's ideas on subjective interpretation. When we try to understand a text, we do not try to transpose ourselves into the author's mind but, if one wants to use this terminology, we try to transpose ourselves into the perspective within which he has formed his views. But this simply means that we try to understand how what he is saying could be right. If we want to understand, we will try to make his arguments even stronger. This happens even in conversation, and it is *a fortiori* true of understanding what is written down that we are moving in a dimension of meaning that is intelligible in itself and as such offers no reason for going back to the subjectivity of the author. The task of hermeneutics is to clarify this miracle of understanding, which is not a mysterious communion of souls, but sharing in a common meaning.

But even Schleiermacher's description of the objective side of this circle does not get to the heart of the matter. We have seen that the goal of all attempts to reach an understanding is agreement concerning the subject matter. Hence the task of hermeneutics has always been to establish agreement where there was none or where it had been disturbed in some way. The history of hermeneutics confirms this if, for example, we think of Augustine, who sought to mediate the Gospel with the Old Testament;* or early Protestantism, which faced the same problem;** or, finally, the Enlightenment, when (almost as if renouncing the possibility of agreement) it was supposed that a text could be "fully understood" only by means of historical interpretation. It is something qualitatively new when romanticism and Schleiermacher universalize historical consciousness by denying that the binding form of the tradition from which they come and in which they are situated provides a solid basis for all hermeneutic endeavor.

One of the immediate predecessors of Schleiermacher, the philologist Friedrich Ast, still had a view of hermeneutical work that was markedly concerned with content, since for him its purpose was to establish harmony between the worlds of classical antiquity and Christianity, between a newly discovered genuine antiquity and the Christian tradition. This is something new. In contrast to the Enlightenment, this hermeneutics no longer evaluates and rejects tradition according to the criterion of natural reason. But in its attempt to bring about a meaningful agreement between the two traditions to which it sees itself as belonging, this kind of hermeneutics is still pursuing the task of all preceding hermeneutics, namely to bring about agreement *in content.*

In going beyond the "particularity" of this reconciliation of the ancient classical world and Christianity, Schleiermacher and, following him, nineteenth-century science conceive the task of hermeneutics in a way that is *formally* universal. They were able

---

*(See G. Ripanti, *Agostino teoretico del'interpretazione* [Brescia, 1980].)
**(See M. Flacius, *Clavis Scripturae sacrae seu de Sermone sacrarum literarum,* book II [1676].)

to harmonize it with the natural sciences' ideal of objectivity, but only by ignoring the concretion of historical consciousness in hermeneutical theory.

Heidegger's description and existential grounding of the hermeneutic circle, by contrast, constitute a decisive turning point. Nineteenth-century hermeneutic theory often discussed the circular structure of understanding, but always within the framework of a formal relation between part and whole—or its subjective reflex, the intuitive anticipation of the whole and its subsequent articulation in the parts. According to this theory, the circular movement of understanding runs backward and forward along the text, and ceases when the text is perfectly understood. This view of understanding came to its logical culmination in Schleiermacher's theory of the divinatory act, by means of which one places oneself entirely within the writer's mind and from there resolves all that is strange and alien about the text. In contrast to this approach, Heidegger describes the circle in such a way that the understanding of the text remains permanently determined by the anticipatory movement of fore-understanding. The circle of whole and part is not dissolved in perfect understanding but, on the contrary, is most fully realized.

The circle, then, is not formal in nature. It is neither subjective nor objective, but describes understanding as the interplay of the movement of tradition and the movement of the interpreter. The anticipation of meaning that governs our understanding of a text is not an act of subjectivity, but proceeds from the commonality that binds us to the tradition. But this commonality is constantly being formed in our relation to tradition. Tradition is not simply a permanent precondition; rather, we produce it ourselves inasmuch as we understand, participate in the evolution of tradition, and hence further determine it ourselves. Thus the circle of understanding is not a "methodological" circle, but describes an element of the ontological structure of understanding.

The circle, which is fundamental to all understanding, has a further hermeneutic implication which I call the "fore-conception of completeness." But this, too, is obviously a formal condition of all understanding. It states that only what really constitutes a unity of meaning is intelligible. So when we read a text we always assume its completeness, and only when this assumption proves mistaken—i.e., the text is not intelligible—do we begin to suspect the text and try to discover how it can be remedied. The rules of such textual criticism can be left aside, for the important thing to note is that applying them properly depends on understanding the content.

The fore-conception of completeness that guides all our understanding is, then, always determined by the specific content. Not only does the reader assume an immanent unity of meaning, but his understanding is likewise guided by the constant transcendent expectations of meaning that proceed from the relation to the truth of what is being said. Just as the recipient of a letter understands the news that it contains and first sees things with the eyes of the person who wrote the letter—i.e., considers what he writes as true, and is not trying to understand the writer's peculiar opinions as such—so also do we understand traditionary texts on the basis of expectations of meaning drawn from our own prior relation to the subject matter. And just as we believe the news reported by a correspondent because he was present or is better informed, so too are we fundamentally open to the possibility that the writer of a transmitted text is better informed than we are, with our prior opinion. It is only when the attempt to accept what is said as true fails that we try to "understand" the text psychologically or historically, as another's opinion.* The prejudice of completeness, then, implies not only this

---

*In a lecture on aesthetic judgment at a conference in Venice in 1958 I tried to show that it too, like historical judgment, is secondary in character and confirms the "anticipation of completeness." ["On the Problematic Character of Aesthetic Consciousness," tr. E. Kelly, *Graduate Faculty Philosophy Journal* (New School for Social Research) 9 (1982), 31–40.]

formal element—that a text should completely express its meaning—but also that what it says should be the complete truth.

Here again we see that understanding means, primarily, to understand the content of what is said, and only secondarily to isolate and understand another's meaning as such. Hence the most basic of all hermeneutic preconditions remains one's own fore-understanding, which comes from being concerned with the same subject. This is what determines what can be realized as unified meaning and thus determines how the fore-conception of completeness is applied.*

Thus the meaning of "belonging"—i.e., the element of tradition in our historical-hermeneutical activity—is fulfilled in the commonality of fundamental, enabling prejudices. Hermeneutics must start from the position that a person seeking to understand something has a bond to the subject matter that comes into language through the traditionary text and has, or acquires, a connection with the tradition from which the text speaks. On the other hand, hermeneutical consciousness is aware that its bond to this subject matter does not consist in some self-evident, unquestioned unanimity, as is the case with the unbroken stream of tradition. Hermeneutic work is based on a polarity of familiarity and strangeness; but this polarity is not to be regarded psychologically, with Schleiermacher, as the range that covers the mystery of individuality, but truly hermeneutically—i.e., in regard to what has been said: the language in which the text addresses us, the story that it tells us. Here too there is a tension. It is in the play between the traditionary text's strangeness and familiarity to us, between being a historically intended, distanciated object and belonging to a tradition. *The true locus of hermeneutics is this in-between.*

Given the intermediate position in which hermeneutics operates, it follows that its work is not to develop a procedure of understanding, but to clarify the conditions in which understanding takes place. But these conditions do not amount to a "procedure" or method which the interpreter must of himself bring to bear on the text; rather, they must be given. The prejudices and fore-meanings that occupy the interpreter's consciousness are not at his free disposal. He cannot separate in advance the productive prejudices that enable understanding from the prejudices that hinder it and lead to misunderstandings.

Rather, this separation must take place in the process of understanding itself, and hence hermeneutics must ask how that happens. But that means it must foreground what has remained entirely peripheral in previous hermeneutics: temporal distance and its significance for understanding.

This point can be clarified by comparing it with the hermeneutic theory of romanticism. We recall that the latter conceived of understanding as the reproduction of

---

*There is one exception to this anticipation of completeness, namely the case of writing that is presenting something in disguise, e.g., a roman à clef. This presents one of the most difficult hermeneutical problems (cf. the interesting remarks by Leo Strauss in *Persecution and the Art of Writing*). This exceptional hermeneutical case is of special significance, in that it goes beyond interpretation of meaning in the same way as when historical source criticism goes back behind the tradition. Although the task here is not a historical, but a hermeneutical one, it can be performed only by using understanding of the subject matter as a key to discover what is behind the disguise—just as in conversation we understand irony to the extent to which we are in agreement with the other person on the subject matter. Thus the apparent exception confirms that understanding involves agreement. [I doubt that Strauss is right in the way he carries out his theory, for instance in his discussion of Spinoza. Dissembling meaning implies a high degree of consciousness. Accommodation, conforming, and so on do not have to occur consciously. In my view, Strauss did not sufficiently see this. See op. cit., pp. 223ff. and my "Hermeneutics and Historicism," Supplement I below. These problems have meanwhile been much disputed, in my view, on too narrowly semantic a basis. See Donald Davidson, *Inquiries into Truth and Interpretation* (Oxford, 1984).]

an original production. Hence it was possible to say that one should be able to understand an author better than he understood himself. We examined the origin of this statement and its connection with the aesthetics of genius, but must now come back to it, since our present inquiry lends it a new importance.

That subsequent understanding is superior to the original production and hence can be described as superior understanding does not depend so much on the conscious realization that places the interpreter on the same level as the author (as Schleiermacher said) but instead denotes an insuperable difference between the interpreter and the author that is created by historical distance. Every age has to understand a transmitted text in its own way, for the text belongs to the whole tradition whose content interests the age and in which it seeks to understand itself. The real meaning of a text, as it speaks to the interpreter, does not depend on the contingencies of the author and his original audience. It certainly is not identical with them, for it is always co-determined also by the historical situation of the interpreter and hence by the totality of the objective course of history. A writer like Chladenius, who does not yet view understanding in terms of history, is saying the same thing in a naive, ingenuous way when he says that an author does not need to know the real meaning of what he has written; and hence the interpreter can, and must, often understand more than he. But this is of fundamental importance. Not just occasionally but always, the meaning of a text goes beyond its author. That is why understanding is not merely a reproductive but always a productive activity as well. Perhaps it is not correct to refer to this productive element in understanding as "better understanding." For this phrase is, as we have shown, a principle of criticism taken from the Enlightenment and revised on the basis of the aesthetics of genius. Understanding is not, in fact, understanding better, either in the sense of superior knowledge of the subject because of clearer ideas or in the sense of fundamental superiority of conscious over unconscious production. It is enough to say that we understand in a different way, if we understand at all.

Such a conception of understanding breaks right through the circle drawn by romantic hermeneutics. Since we are now concerned not with individuality and what it thinks but with the truth of what is said, a text is not understood as a mere expression of life but is taken seriously in its claim to truth. That this is what is meant by "understanding" was once self-evident (we need only recall Chladenius). But this dimension of the hermeneutical problem was discredited by historical consciousness and the psychological turn that Schleiermacher gave to hermeneutics, and could only be regained when the aporias of historicism came to light and led finally to the fundamentally new development to which Heidegger, in my view, gave the decisive impetus. For the hermeneutic productivity of temporal distance could be understood only when Heidegger gave understanding an ontological orientation by interpreting it as an "existential" and when he interpreted Dasein's mode of being in terms of time.

Time is no longer primarily a gulf to be bridged because it separates; it is actually the supportive ground of the course of events in which the present is rooted. Hence temporal distance is not something that must be overcome. This was, rather, the naive assumption of historicism, namely that we must transpose ourselves into the spirit of the age, think with its ideas and its thoughts, not with our own, and thus advance toward historical objectivity. In fact the important thing is to recognize temporal distance as a positive and productive condition enabling understanding. It is not a yawning abyss but is filled with the continuity of custom and tradition, in the light of which everything handed down presents itself to us. Here it is not too much to speak of the genuine productivity of the course of events. Everyone is familiar with the curious impotence of our judgment where temporal distance has not given us sure criteria. Thus the judgment of contemporary works of art is desperately uncertain for the scholarly consciousness. Obviously we approach such creations with unverifiable prejudices, presuppositions that have too great an influence over us for us to know about them; these can give contemporary creations an extra resonance that does not correspond to their true content and significance. Only when all their relations to the present time have faded away can their real nature appear, so that the understanding of what is said in them can claim to be authoritative and universal.

In historical studies this experience has led to the idea that objective knowledge can be achieved only if there has been a certain historical distance. It is true that what a thing has to say, its intrinsic content, first appears only after it is divorced from the fleeting circumstances that gave rise to it. The positive conditions of historical under-standing include the relative closure of a historical event, which allows us to view it as a whole, and its distance from contemporary opinions concerning its import. The im-plicit presupposition of historical method, then, is that the permanent significance of something can first be known objectively only when it belongs to a closed context—in other words, when it is dead enough to have only historical interest. Only then does it seem possible to exclude the subjective involvement of the observer. This is, in fact, a paradox, the epistemological counterpart to the old moral problem of whether anyone can be called happy before his death. Just as Aristotle showed how this kind of prob-lem can serve to sharpen the powers of human judgment,* so hermeneutical reflection cannot fail to find here a sharpening of the methodological self-consciousness of sci-ence. It is true that certain hermeneutic requirements are automatically fulfilled when a historical context has come to be of only historical interest. Certain sources of error are automatically excluded. But it is questionable whether this is the end of the hermeneu-tical problem. Temporal distance obviously means something other than the extinction of our interest in the object. It lets the true meaning of the object emerge fully. But the discovery of the true meaning of a text or a work of art is never finished; it is in fact an infinite process. Not only are fresh sources of error constantly excluded, so that all kinds of things are filtered out that obscure the true meaning; but new sources of un-derstanding are continually emerging that reveal unsuspected elements of meaning. The temporal distance that performs the filtering process is not fixed, but is itself un-dergoing constant movement and extension. And along with the negative side of the filtering process brought about by temporal distance there is also the positive side, namely the value it has for understanding. It not only lets local and limited prejudices die away, but allows those that bring about genuine understanding to emerge clearly as such.

Often temporal distance** can solve question of critique in hermeneutics, namely how to distinguish the true prejudices, by which we understand, from the false ones, by which we misunderstand. Hence the hermeneutically trained mind will also include historical consciousness. It will make conscious the prejudices governing our own understanding, so that the text, as another's meaning, can be isolated and valued on its own. Foregrounding *[abheben]* a prejudice clearly requires suspending its valid-ity for us. For as long as our mind is influenced by a prejudice, we do not consider it a judgment. How then can we foreground it? It is impossible to make ourselves aware of a prejudice while it is constantly operating unnoticed, but only when it is, so to speak,

---

Nicomachean Ethics, I, 7.
**[I have here softened the original text ("It is only temporal distance that can solve . . ."): it is dis-tance, not only temporal distance, that makes this hermeneutic problem solvable. See also *GW*, II, 64. Trans-lator's note.]

provoked. The encounter with a traditionary text can provide this provocation. For what leads to understanding must be something that has already asserted itself in its own separate validity. Understanding begins, as we have already said above, when something addresses us. This is the first condition of hermeneutics. We now know what this requires, namely the fundamental suspension of our own prejudices. But all suspension of judgments and hence, a fortiori, of prejudices, has the logical structure of a *question.*

The essence of the *question* is to open up possibilities and keep them open. If a prejudice becomes questionable in view of what another person or a text says to us, this does not mean that it is simply set aside and the text or the other person accepted as valid in its place. Rather, historical objectivism shows its naivete in accepting this disregarding of ourselves as what actually happens. In fact our own prejudice is properly brought into play by being put at risk. Only by being given full play is it able to experience the other's claim to truth and make it possible for him to have full play himself.

The naivete of so-called historicism consists in the fact that it does not undertake this reflection, and in trusting to the fact that its procedure is methodical, it forgets its own historicity. We must here appeal from a badly understood historical thinking to one that can better perform the task of understanding. Real historical thinking must take account of its own historicity. Only then will it cease to chase the phantom of a historical object that is the object of progressive research, and learn to view the object as the counterpart of itself and hence understand both. The true historical object is not an object at all, but the unity of the one and the other, a relationship that constitutes both the reality of history and the reality of historical understanding.* A hermeneutics adequate to the subject matter would have to demonstrate the reality and efficacy of history within understanding itself. I shall refer to this as "history of effect." *Understanding is, essentially, a historically effected event.*

*(Here constantly arises the danger of "appropriating" the other person in one's own understanding and thereby failing to recognize his or her otherness.)

JEAN-PAUL SARTRE
1905–1980

In addition to being one of the leading philosophers of the twentieth century, Jean-Paul Sartre was also an essayist, novelist, playwright, and editor. His name has become synonymous with existentialism, a movement that exploded beyond the boundaries of the academy to enter virtually every area of Western culture. Sartre himself became as famous as the philosophy he taught, and at his death in 1980 almost fifty thousand people accompanied his casket to Paris's Montparnasse Cemetery.

Jean-Paul-Charles-Aymard Sartre was born in Paris in 1905, the only child of naval officer Jean-Baptiste Sartre and his wife Anne-Marie Schweitzer Sartre. Barely a year after his birth, his father died. Jean-Paul and his mother moved in with her parents. Sartre's maternal grandfather, a German-language teacher, had a study filled with books; this room fascinated the young Sartre. He taught himself to read, and by the age of eight he had read such French classics as *Madame Bovary*. While still a boy, his devotion to books overwhelmed all other devotions—including that to religion. From about the age of twelve, Sartre said that he was a confirmed atheist. He did exceptionally well in his studies, exhibiting a clear independence of mind. One of his teachers noted on his report card: "Excellent student: mind already lively, good at discussing questions, but needs to depend a little less on himself."

In 1924, Sartre enrolled at the prestigious École Normale Supérieure. Over the next four years, he studied for the *agrégation* in philosophy (the highest degree except for the doctorate in the French system), but surprisingly he failed the written examination on his first attempt. He retook the examination a year later and placed first.

Guernica, 1937, by Pablo Picasso (1881–1973). In 1937 the city of Guernica was destroyed by German bombers simply for the purpose of testing their new weapons. Sartre's friend Picasso created this painting to memorialize the innocent sacrifice of the Spanish people. This representation of broken, fragmented pieces of humanity wrung by pain and anxiety capture well the reality of death and violence. Sartre insisted that to live fully one must squarely face such suffering. *(Museo del Prador, Madrid)*

The person who took second in that 1929 examination was his study partner, Simone de Beauvoir. That same year, Sartre suggested to her that they take "a two-year lease" on each other. Though neither believed in the bourgeois institution of marriage, and each had a variety of lovers, the two remained "companions" for life.

Over the next ten years, Sartre served briefly in the army, studied in Berlin, taught at a number of lycées, and began writing. Among his early publications were the philosophical novel *Nausea* (1938) and the collection of short stories *The Wall* (1939).

In 1939, Sartre was called up for active duty by the French army. Within the year, he was captured by the Germans. Released a few months later, he seemed to return to a quiet life of teaching and writing. But Sartre was secretly a member of the French resistance. He was never involved in the armed resistance but worked with the intellectual resistance group Socialism and Liberty. Even during the war, Sartre continued his writing, and in 1943 he published his most important philosophical text, *Being and Nothingness*. Three years later, *Existentialism Is a Humanism,* his most widely read philosophical work, was published.

After the war, Sartre retired from teaching and, with Maurice Merleau Ponty and de Beauvoir, founded the influential journal *Les Temps modernes.* He was awarded the Nobel Prize for literature in 1964 but refused to accept it. Together with de Beauvoir, he spent the rest of his life writing and promoting revolutionary political causes. Frequently joining students or union workers in demonstrations, Sartre even served as president of the International War Crimes Tribunal, which condemned U.S. intervention in Vietnam. He was attracted to Marxist thought—though he frequently criticized the French Communist Party for its inadequacies. The discrepancies between the determinism of Marxist theory and

Sartre's existentialist emphasis on radical freedom have been the subject of many books. (See the suggested readings.)

Throughout his life, Sartre preferred the pleasures of the café over the joys of the hearth. For years he and de Beauvoir were fixtures at La Coupole, a restaurant on the Left Bank of Paris frequented by artists. But eventually his health deteriorated, exacerbated by his frequent use of amphetamines, and he was forced to retire to his apartment. After an agonizingly slow decline, Sartre died in 1980.

*   *   *

Like Heidegger before him, Sartre was fascinated with "being." According to Sartre, there are two categories of being: "being-in-itself" (*étre en-soi*) and "being-for-itself" (*étre pour-soi*). *Being-in-itself* is complete in itself, "solid," fixed, and totally given: "Uncreated, without reason for being, without connection with any other being, being-in-itself is superfluous for all eternity." Like Parmenides' One, being-in-itself simply is. This is the being of rocks and trees. This being-in-itself has no sufficient reason for being, no purpose or meaning— it is "absurd."

Being-for-itself, on the other hand, is incomplete and fluid and without a determined structure. Being-for-itself is the being of human consciousness that at every moment is freely choosing its future. This consciousness arises by virtue of its power of negation, based on freedom: "[Consciousness] constitutes itself in its own flesh as the nihilation of a possibility which another human reality projects as its possibility. For that reason it must arise in the world as a Not." Individual consciousness constitutes itself by freely rejecting all roles that others try to force upon it. It is precisely in the act of saying "No" to all attempts to make me into a being-in-itself that I create myself as a being-for-itself.

In creating myself, I do not choose what I will become on the basis of preexisting values. There are no eternal values, no givens for me to use. Dostoevsky's character Ivan Karamazov had claimed, "If there is no God, all things are lawful." Sartre agreed and added that since there was no God, all things are, indeed, lawful. In fact, there is no possible justification for any choice I might make, since justification implies an appeal to given values. I am free to choose my values without any external justification.

Although this freedom is complete, it is not absolute. In the first place, as a free being, I encounter other free beings. My world is interrupted when the "other" gives me "the look." By looking at me, the other objectifies me, makes me a part of his or her world, part of his or her freedom: "Thus being-seen constitutes me as a being without defenses for a freedom which is not my freedom." But I can regain my freedom by looking back and by an act of will transforming the other into an object for me. (This world of people-objects led Sartre to exclaim, "Hell is other people.")

Second, I must acknowledge the "facticity" found in existence. I cannot change the fact that this tree is in front of me or that I cannot walk through it. But even here my freedom still prevails. I freely create the *meaning* of this tree as an object to climb or as a source of lumber or as a thing to be preserved or as a biological specimen. In creating these meanings, I create the world in which I live.

Some people are unwilling to face up to this radical freedom and turn their power of negation inward upon consciousness itself. In our selection from *Being and Nothingness,* translated by Hazel E. Barnes, Sartre calls this negative turn "bad faith." To live in bad faith is to deny oneself as a being-for-itself in order to become a being-in-itself; it is to blame others or circumstances for what one has become. This mode of being is bad faith because it refuses to acknowledge that only the individual determines the meanings of externals. Furthermore, one always has alternatives (for example, no matter the circumstances, one could always commit suicide), and so one's choice is always free.

In *Existentialism Is a Humanism,* translated here by Bernard Frechtman, Sartre expands on this freedom while defending the basic ideas of existentialism. He begins by discussing human artifacts, such as a book or a paper-cutter. An object like a paper-cutter begins as an essence, that is, as an "ensemble of both the production routines and the properties which enable it to be both produced and defined." One conceives of a paper-cutter (essentially) and how to make it and only then does one construct it. The essence of a paper-cutter precedes its existence. According to Sartre, theists believe that God does the same with human beings. First God conceives of humans and then creates them. But Sartre says that there is no God, and hence no preexisting human essence: "There is no human nature, since there is no God to conceive it." Instead, "Man is nothing else but what he makes of himself." For humans, existence precedes essence.

When one realizes the implications of this atheism and the primacy of freedom, one is brought to anguish and forlornness. But Sartre strongly denied that this state necessarily led to despair. Even though all my actions are indeed ultimately futile because of my eventual death, and existence is in fact absurd, I can still choose my actions and so give my life meaning. As Sartre concluded, "In this sense existentialism is optimistic, a doctrine of action."

*   *   *

There are many studies of existentialism; see especially Gabriel Marcel, *The Philosophy of Existentialism,* translated by Manya Harari (New York: Citadel Press, 1956); Hazel E. Barnes, *An Existentialist Ethic* (Chicago: University of Chicago Press, 1967); and William Barrett's two books, *Irrational Man* (Garden City, NY: Doubleday, 1962) and *What Is Existentialism?* (New York: Grove Press, 1964). For primary source materials, see Walter Kaufmann, ed., *Existentialism from Dostoevsky to Sartre* (New York: Viking Press, 1956) and Charles Guignon and Derk Pereboom, *Existentialism: Basic Texts* (Indianapolis, IN: Hackett, 1994).

For biographies of Sartre, see Annie Cohen-Solal, *Sartre: A Life,* translated by Anna Cancogni (New York: Pantheon Books, 1987); John Gerassi, *Jean-Paul Sartre: Hated Conscience of His Century* (Chicago: University of Chicago Press, 1989); and Simone de Beauvoir's recounting of Sartre's final days, *Adieux: A Farewell to Sartre* (New York: Pantheon, 1984). For general introductions to Sartre's thought, see Mary Warnock, *The Philosophy of Sartre* (London: Hutchinson, 1965); Anthony Manser, *Sartre: A Philosophic Study* (London: Athlone Press, 1966); Arthur C. Danto, *Jean-Paul Sartre* (New York: Viking Press, 1975); and Peter Caws, *Sartre* (London: Routledge & Kegan Paul, 1979). Iris Murdoch, *Sartre: Romantic Rationalist* (New Haven, CT: Yale University Press, 1959) explores the philosophical ideas in Sartre's novels. There are several discussions of Sartre's Marxism, including W. Desan, *The Marxism of Jean-Paul Sartre* (Garden City, NY: Doubleday, 1965); Mark Poster, *Sartre's Marxism* (Cambridge: Cambridge University Press, 1982); and Thomas R. Flynn,

Sartre and Marxist Existentialism: The Test Case of Collective Responsibility (Chicago: University of Chicago Press, 1984). For collections of essays, see Edith Kern, ed., *Sartre: A Collection of Critical Essays* (Englewood Cliffs, NJ: Prentice Hall, 1962); Mary Warnock, ed., *Sartre* (Garden City, NY: Anchor Doubleday, 1971); Hugh J. Silverman and Frederick A. Elliston, eds., *Jean-Paul Sartre: Contemporary Approaches to His Philosophy* (Pittsburgh, PA: Duquesne University Press, 1980); Paul A. Schilpp, ed., *The Philosophy of Jean-Paul Sartre* (La Salle, IL: Open Court, 1981); Christina Howells, ed., *The Cambridge Companion to Sartre* (Cambridge: Cambridge University Press, 1992); and the multi-volume William L. McBride, *Sartre and Existentialism* (Hamden, CT: Garland, 1997).

BEING AND NOTHINGNESS (in part)

CHAPTER 2: BAD FAITH

I. BAD FAITH AND FALSEHOOD

The human being is not only the being by whom *négatités* are disclosed in the world; he is also the one who can take negative attitudes with respect to himself. In our Introduction we defined consciousness as "a being such that in its being, its being is in question in so far as this being implies a being other than itself." But now that we have examined the meaning of "the question," we can at present also write the formula thus: "Consciousness is a being, the nature of which is to be conscious of the nothingness of its being." In a prohibition or a veto, for example, the human being denies a future transcendence. But this negation is not explicative. My consciousness is not restricted to *envisioning a négatité*. It constitutes itself in its own flesh as the nihilation of a possibility which another human reality projects as its possibility. For that reason it must arise in the world as a Not; it is as a Not that the slave first apprehends the master, or that the prisoner who is trying to escape sees the guard who is watching him. There are even men (e.g., caretakers, overseers, gaolers) whose social reality is uniquely that of the Not, who will live and die, having forever been only a Not upon the earth. Others so as to make the Not a part of their very subjectivity establish their human personality as a perpetual negation. This is the meaning and function of what Scheler calls "the man of resentment"—in reality, the Not. But there exist more subtle behaviors, the description of which will lead us further into the inwardness of consciousness. Irony is one of these. In irony a man annihilates what he posits within one and the same act; he leads us to believe in order not to be believed; he affirms to deny and denies to affirm; he creates a positive object but it has no being other than its nothingness. Thus attitudes of negation toward the self permit us to raise a new question: What are we to say

Jean-Paul Sartre, *Being and Nothingness,* translated by Hazel E. Barnes (New York: Philosophical Library, 1956). Reprinted by permission.

is the being of man who has the possibility of denying himself? But it is out of the question to discuss the attitude of "self-negation" in its universality. The kinds of behavior which can be ranked under this heading are too diverse; we risk retaining only the abstract form of them. It is best to choose and to examine one determined attitude which is essential to human reality and which is such that consciousness instead of directing its negation outward turns it toward itself. This attitude, it seems to me, is *bad faith (mauvaise foi)*.

Frequently this is identified with falsehood. We say indifferently of a person that he shows signs of bad faith or that he lies to himself. We shall willingly grant that bad faith is a lie to oneself, on condition that we distinguish the lie to oneself from lying in general. Lying is a negative attitude we will agree to that. But this negation does not bear on consciousness itself, it aims only at the transcendent. The essence of the lie implies in fact that the liar actually is in complete possession of the truth which he is hiding. A man does not lie about what he is ignorant of; he does not lie when he spreads an error of which he himself is the dupe; he does not lie when he is mistaken. The ideal description of the liar would be a cynical consciousness, affirming truth within himself, denying it in his words, and denying that negation as such. Now this doubly negative attitude rests on the transcendent; the fact expressed is transcendent since it does not exist, and the original negation rests on a *truth;* that is, on a particular type of transcendence. As for the inner negation which I effect correlatively with the affirmation for myself of the truth, this rests on words, that is, on an event in the world. Furthermore the inner disposition of the liar is positive; it could be the object of an affirmative judgment. The liar intends to deceive and he does not seek to hide this intention from himself nor to disguise the translucency of consciousness; on the contrary, he has recourse to it when there is a question of deciding secondary behavior. It explicitly exercises a regulatory control over all attitudes. As for his flaunted intention of telling the truth ("I'd never want to deceive you! This is true! I swear it!")— all this, of course, is the object of an inner negation, but also it is not recognized by the liar as his intention. It is played, imitated, it is the intention of the character which he plays in the eyes of his questioner, but this character, precisely because he does not exist, is a transcendent. Thus the lie does not put into the play the inner structure of present consciousness; all the negations which constitute it bear on objects which by this fact are removed from consciousness. The lie then does not require special ontological foundation, and the explanations which the existence of negation in general requires are valid without change in the case of deceit. Of course we have described the ideal lie; doubtless it happens often enough that the liar is more or less the victim of his lie, that he half persuades himself of it. But these common, popular forms of the lie are also degenerate aspects of it; they represent intermediaries between falsehood and bad faith. The lie is a behavior of transcendence.

The lie is also a normal phenomenon of what Heidegger calls the "*Mit-sein*" ["being with" others]. It presupposes my existence, the existence of the *Other,* my existence *for* the Other, and the existence of the Other *for* me. Thus there is no difficulty in holding that the liar must make the project of the lie in entire clarity and that he must possess a complete comprehension of the lie and of the truth which he is altering. It is sufficient that an over-all opacity hide his intentions from the *Other;* it is sufficient that the Other can take the lie for truth. By the lie consciousness affirms that it exists by nature as *hidden from the Other;* it utilizes for its own profit the ontological duality of myself and myself in the eyes of the Other.

The situation can not be the same for bad faith if this, as we have said, is indeed a lie to oneself. To be sure, the one who practices bad faith is hiding a displeasing truth or presenting as truth a pleasing untruth. Bad faith then has in appearance the structure of falsehood. Only what changes everything is the fact that in bad faith it is from my-self that I am hiding the truth. Thus the duality of the deceiver and the deceived does not exist here. Bad faith on the contrary implies in essence the unity of a *single* consciousness. This does not mean that it can not be conditioned by the *Mit-sein* like all other phenomena of human reality, but the *Mit-sein* can call forth bad faith only by presenting itself as a *situation* which bad faith permits surpassing; bad faith does not come from outside to human reality. One does not undergo his bad faith; one is not infected with it; it is not a state. But consciousness affects itself with bad faith. There must be an original intention and a project of bad faith; this project implies a comprehension of bad faith as such and a pre-reflective apprehension (of) consciousness as affecting itself with bad faith. It follows first that the one to whom the lie is told and the one who lies are one and the same person, which means that I must know in my capacity as deceiver the truth which is hidden from me in my capacity as the one deceived. Better yet I must know the truth very exactly *in order* to conceal it more carefully— and this not at two different moments, which at a pinch would allow us to reestablish a semblance of duality—but in the unitary structure of a single project. How then can the lie subsist if the duality which conditions it is suppressed?

To this difficulty is added another which is derived from the total translucency of consciousness. That which affects itself with bad faith must be conscious (of) its bad faith since the being of consciousness is consciousness of being. It appears then that I must be in good faith, at least to the extent that I am conscious of my bad faith. But then this whole psychic system is annihilated. We must agree in fact that if I deliberately and cynically attempt to lie to myself, I fail completely in this undertaking; the lie falls back and collapses beneath my look; it is ruined *from behind* by the very consciousness of lying to myself which pitilessly constitutes itself well within my project as its very condition. We have here an evanescent phenomenon which exists only in and through its own differentiation. To be sure, these phenomena are frequent and we shall see that there is in fact an "evanescence" of bad faith, which, it is evident, vacillates continually between good faith and cynicism: Even though the existence of bad faith is very precarious, and though it belongs to the kind of psychic structures which we might call "metastable," [Sartre's word for "subject to sudden changes"] it presents nonetheless an autonomous and durable form. It can even be the normal aspect of life for a very great number of people. A person can *live* in bad faith, which does not mean that he does not have abrupt awakenings to cynicism or to good faith, but which implies a constant and particular style of life. Our embarrassment then appears extreme since we can neither reject nor comprehend bad faith.

*   *   *

II. PATTERNS OF BAD FAITH

If we wish to get out of this difficulty, we should examine more closely the patterns of bad faith and attempt a description of them. This description will permit us perhaps to fix more exactly the conditions for the possibility of bad faith; that is, to reply to the question we raised at the outset: "What must be the being of man if he is to be capable of bad faith?"

Take the example of a woman who has consented to go out with a particular man for the first time. She knows very well the intentions which the man who is speaking to her cherishes regarding her. She knows also that it will be necessary sooner or later for her to make a decision. But she does not want to realize the urgency; she concerns herself only with what is respectful and discreet in the attitude of her companion. She does not apprehend this conduct as an attempt to achieve what we call "the first approach"; that is, she does not want to see possibilities of temporal development which his conduct presents. She restricts this behavior to what is in the present; she does not wish to read in the phrases which he addresses to her anything other than their explicit meaning. If he says to her, "I find you so attractive!" she disarms this phrase of its sexual background; she attaches to the conversation and to the behavior of the speaker, the immediate meanings, which she imagines as objective qualities. The man who is speaking to her appears to her sincere and respectful as the table is round or square, as the wall coloring is blue or gray. The qualities thus attached to the person she is listening to are in this way fixed in a permanence like that of things, which is no other than the projection of the strict present of the qualities into the temporal flux. This is because she does not quite know what she wants. She is profoundly aware of the desire which she inspires, but the desire cruel and naked would humiliate and horrify her. Yet she would find no charm in a respect which would be only respect. In order to satisfy her, there must be a feeling which is addressed wholly to her *personality*—i.e., to her full freedom—and which would be a recognition of her freedom. But at the same time this feeling must be wholly desire; that is, it must address itself to her body as object. This time then she refuses to apprehend the desire for what it is; she does not even give it a name; she recognizes it only to the extent that it transcends itself toward admiration, esteem, respect and that it is wholly absorbed in the more refined forms which it produces, to the extent of no longer figuring anymore as a sort of warmth and density. But then suppose he takes her hand. This act of her companion risks changing the situation by calling for an immediate decision. To leave the hand there is to consent in herself to flirt, to engage herself. To withdraw it is to break the troubled and unstable harmony which gives the hour its charm. The aim is to postpone the moment of decision as long as possible. We know what happens next; the young woman leaves her hand there, but she *does not notice* that she is leaving it. She does not notice because it happens by chance that she is at this moment all intellect. She draws her companion up to the most lofty regions of sentimental speculation; she speaks of Life, of her life, she shows herself in her essential aspect—a personality, a consciousness. And during this time the divorce of the body from the soul is accomplished; the hand rests inert between the warm hands of her companion—neither consenting nor resisting—a thing.

We shall say that this woman is in bad faith. But we see immediately that she uses various procedures in order to maintain herself in this bad faith. She has disarmed the actions of her companion by reducing them to being only what they are; that is, to existing in the mode of the in-itself. But she permits herself to enjoy his desire, to the extent that she will apprehend it as not being what it is, will recognize its transcendence. Finally, while sensing profoundly the presence of her own body—to the degree of being disturbed perhaps—she realizes herself as *not being* her own body, and she contemplates it as though from above as a passive object to which events can *happen* but which can neither provoke them nor avoid them because all its possibilities are outside of it. What unity do we find in these various aspects of bad faith? It is a certain art of forming contradictory concepts which unite in themselves both an idea and the negation of that idea. The basic concept which is thus engendered utilizes the double property of the human being, who is at once a *facticity* and a *transcendence*. These two aspects of human reality are and ought to be capable of a valid coordination. But bad faith does not wish either to coordinate them nor to surmount them in a synthesis. Bad faith seeks to affirm their identity while preserving their differences. It must affirm facticity as *being* transcendence and transcendence as *being* facticity, in such a way that at the instant when a person apprehends the one, he can find himself abruptly faced with the other.

We can find the prototype of formulae of bad faith in certain famous expressions which have been rightly conceived to produce their whole effect in a spirit of bad faith. Take for example the title of a work by Jacques Chardonne, *Love Is Much More than Love.** We see here how unity is established between present love in its facticity—"the contact of two skins," sensuality, egoism, Proust's mechanism of jealousy, Adler's battle of the sexes, *etc.*—and love as transcendence—Mauriac's "river of fire," the longing for the infinite, Plato's *eros,* Lawrence's deep cosmic intuition, etc. Here we leave facticity to find ourselves suddenly beyond the present and the factual condition of man, beyond the psychological, in the heart of metaphysics. On the other hand, the title of a play by Sarment, *I Am Too Great for Myself,*** which also presents characters in bad faith, throws us first into full transcendence in order suddenly to imprison us within the narrow limits of our factual essence. We will discover this structure again in the famous sentence: "He has become what he was" or in its no less famous opposite: "Eternity at last changes each man into himself." It is well understood that these various formulae have only the appearance of bad faith; they have been conceived in this paradoxical form explicitly to shock the mind and discountenance it by an enigma. But it is precisely this appearance which is of concern to us. What counts here is that the formulae do not constitute new, solidly structured ideas; on the contrary, they are formed so as to remain in perpetual disintegration and so that we may slide at any time from naturalistic present to transcendence and vice versa.

We can see the use which bad faith can make of these judgments which all aim at establishing that I am not what I am. If I were only what I am, I could, for example, seriously consider an adverse criticism which someone makes of me, question myself scrupulously, and perhaps be compelled to recognize the truth in it. But thanks to transcendence, I am not subject to all that I am. I do not even have to discuss the justice of the reproach. As Suzanne says to Figaro, "To prove that I am right would be to recognize that I can be wrong." I am on a plane where no reproach can touch me since what I really am is my transcendence. I flee from myself, I escape myself, I leave my tattered garment in the hands of the fault-finder. But the ambiguity necessary for bad faith comes from the fact that I affirm here that I am my transcendence in the mode of being of a thing. It is only thus, in fact, that I can feel that I escape all reproaches. It is in the sense that our young woman purifies the desire of anything humiliating by being willing to consider it only as pure transcendence, which she avoids even naming. But inversely "I Am Too Great for Myself," while showing our transcendence changed into facticity, is the source of an infinity of excuses for our failures or our weaknesses. Similarly the young coquette maintains transcendence to the extent that the respect, the esteem manifested by the actions of her admirer are already on the plane of the transcendent. But she arrests this transcendence, she glues it down with all the facticity of the present; respect is nothing other than respect, it is an arrested surpassing which no longer surpasses itself toward anything.

But although this *metastable* concept of "transcendence-facticity" is one of the most basic instruments of bad faith, it is not the only one of its kind. We can equally

---

L'amour, c'est beaucoup plus que l'amour.
**Je suis trop grand pour moi.*

well use another kind of duplicity derived from human reality which we will express roughly by saying that its being-for-itself implies complementarily a being-for-others. Upon any one of my conducts it is always possible to converge two looks, mine and that of the Other. The conduct will not present exactly the same structure in each case. But as we shall see later, as each look perceives it, there is between these two aspects of my being, no difference between appearance and being—as if I were to myself the truth of myself and as if the Other possessed only a deformed image of me. The equal dignity of being, possessed by my being-for-others and by my being-for-myself permits a perpetually disintegrating synthesis and a perpetual game of escape from the for-itself to the for-others and from the for-others to the for-itself. We have seen also the use which our young lady made of our being-in-the-midst-of-the-world—*i.e.*, of our inert presence as a passive object among other objects—in order to relieve herself suddenly from the functions of her being-in-the-world—that is, from the being which causes there to be a world by projecting itself beyond the world toward its own possibilities. Let us note finally the confusing syntheses which play on the nihilating ambiguity of these temporal ⟨*ekstases*⟩, affirming at once that I am what I have been (the man who deliberately arrests *himself* at one period in his life and refuses to take into consideration the later changes) and that I am not what I have been (the man who in the face of reproaches or rancor dissociates himself from his past by insisting on his freedom and on his perpetual re-creation). In all these concepts, which have only a transitive role in the reasoning and which are eliminated from the conclusion (like hypochondriacs in the calculations of physicians), we find again the same structure. We have to deal with human reality as a being which is what it is not and which is not what it is.

But what exactly is necessary in order for these concepts of disintegration to be able to receive even a pretence of existence, in order for them to be able to appear for an instant to consciousness, even in a process of evanescence? A quick examination of the idea of sincerity, the antithesis of bad faith, will be very instructive in this connection. Actually sincerity presents itself as a demand and consequently is not a state. Now what is the ideal to be attained in this case? It is necessary that a man be *for himself* only what he is. But is this not precisely the definition of the in-itself—or if you prefer—the principle of identity? To posit as an ideal the being of things, is this not to assert by the same stroke that this being does not belong to human reality and that the principle of identity, far from being a universal axiom universally applied, is only a synthetic principle enjoying a merely regional universality? Thus in order that the concepts of bad faith can put us under illusion at least for an instant, in order that the candor of "pure hearts" (cf. Gide, Kessel) can have validity for human reality as an ideal, the principle of identity must not represent a constitutive principle of human reality and human reality must not be necessarily what it is but must be able to be what it is not. What does this mean?

If man is what he is, bad faith is for ever impossible and candor ceases to be his ideal and becomes instead his being. But is man what he is? And more generally, how can he be what he is when he exists as consciousness of being? If candor or sincerity is a universal value, it is evident that the maxim "one must be what one is" does not serve solely as a regulating principle for judgments and concepts by which I express what I am. It posits not merely an ideal of knowing but an ideal of being; it proposes for us an absolute equivalence of being with itself as a prototype of being. In this sense it is necessary that we *make ourselves* what we are. But what are we then if we have the constant obligation to make ourselves what we are, if our mode of being is having the obligation to be what we are?

Let us consider this waiter in the café. His movement is quick and forward, a little too precise, a little too rapid. He comes toward the patrons with a step a little too quick. He bends forward a little too eagerly; his voice, his eyes express an interest a little too solicitous for the order of the customer. Finally there he returns, trying to imitate in his walk the inflexible stiffness of some kind of automaton while carrying his tray with the recklessness of a tight-rope-walker by putting it in a perpetually unstable, perpetually broken equilibrium which he perpetually reestablishes by a light movement of the arm and hand. All his behavior seems to us a game. He applies himself to chaining his movements as if they were mechanisms, the one regulating the other; his gestures and even his voice seem to be mechanisms; he gives himself the quickness and pitiless rapidity of things. He is playing, he is amusing himself. But what is he playing? We need not watch long before we can explain it: he is playing *at being* a waiter in a café. There is nothing there to surprise us. The game is a kind of marking out and investigation. The child plays with his body in order to explore it, to take inventory of it; the waiter in the café plays with his condition in order to *realize* it. This obligation is not different from that which is imposed on all tradesmen. Their condition is wholly one of ceremony. The public demands of them that they realize it as a ceremony; there is the dance of the grocer, of the tailor, of the auctioneer, by which they endeavour to persuade their clientele that they are nothing but a grocer, an auctioneer, a tailor. A grocer who dreams is offensive to the buyer, because such a grocer is not wholly a grocer. Society demands that he limit himself to his function as a grocer, just as the soldier at attention makes himself into a soldier-thing with a direct regard which does not see at all, which is no longer meant to see, since it is the rule and not the interest of the moment which determines the point he must fix his eyes on (the sight "fixed at ten paces"). There are indeed many precautions to imprison a man in what he is, as if we lived in perpetual fear that he might escape from it, that he might break away and suddenly elude his condition.

In a parallel situation, from within, the waiter in the café can not be immediately a café waiter in the sense that this inkwell *is* an inkwell, or the glass is a glass. It is by no means that he can not form reflective judgments or concepts concerning his condition. He knows well what it "means": the obligation of getting up at five o'clock, of sweeping the floor of the shop before the restaurant opens, of starting the coffee pot going, etc. He knows the rights which it allows: the right to the tips, the right to belong to a union, etc. But all these concepts, all these judgments refer to the transcendent. It is a matter of abstract possibilities, of rights and duties conferred on a "person possessing rights." And it is precisely this person *who I have to be* (if I am the waiter in question) and who I am not. It is not that I do not wish to be this person or that I want this person to be different. But rather there is no common measure between his being and mine. It is a "representation" for others and for myself, which means that I can be he only in *representation*. But if I represent myself as him, I am not he; I am separated from him as the object from the subject, separated by *nothing,* but this nothing isolates me from him. I can not be he, I can only play *at being* him; that is, imagine to myself that I am he. And thereby I affect him with nothingness. In vain do I fulfill the functions of a café waiter. I can be he only in the neutralized mode, as the actor is Hamlet, by mechanically making the *typical gestures* of my state and by aiming at myself as an imaginary café waiter through those gestures taken as an "analogue." What I attempt to realize is a being-in-itself of the café waiter, as if it were not just in my power to confer their value and their urgency upon my duties and the rights of my position, as if it were not my free choice to get up each morning at five o'clock or to remain in bed, even though it meant getting fired. As if from the very fact that I sustain this role in existence I did not transcend it on every side, as if I did not constitute myself as one *beyond* my condition. Yet there is no doubt that I am in a sense a café waiter—otherwise could I not just as well call myself a diplomat or a reporter? But if I am one, this can not be in the mode of being-in-itself. I am a waiter in the mode of *being what I am not.*

Furthermore we are dealing with more than mere social positions; I am never any one of my attitudes, any one of my actions. The good speaker is the one who plays at speaking, because he can not *be speaking.* The attentive pupil who wishes to be attentive, his eyes riveted on the teacher, his ears open wide, so exhausts himself in playing the attentive role that he ends up by no longer hearing anything. Perpetually absent to my body, to my acts, I am despite myself that "divine absence" of which Valéry speaks. I can not say either that I *am* here or that I *am* not here, in the sense that we say "that box of matches *is* on the table"; this would be to confuse my "being-in-the-world" with a "being-in-the-midst-of-the-world." Nor that I *am* standing, nor that I *am* seated; this would be to confuse my body with the idiosyncratic totality of which it is only one of the structures. On all sides I escape being and yet—I am.

But take a mode of being which concerns only myself: I am sad. One might think that surely I am the sadness in the mode of being what I am. What is the sadness, however, if not the intentional unity which comes to reassemble and animate the totality of my *conduct*? It is the meaning of this dull look with which I view the world, of my bowed shoulders, of my lowered head, of the listlessness in my whole body. But at the very moment when I adopt each of these attitudes, do I not know that I shall not be able to hold on to it? Let a stranger suddenly appear and I will lift up my head, I will assume a lively cheerfulness. What will remain of my sadness except that I obligingly promise it an appointment for later after the departure of the visitor? Moreover is not this sadness itself a conduct? Is it not consciousness which affects itself with sadness as a magical recourse against a situation too urgent? And in this case even, should we not say that being sad means first to make oneself sad? That may be, someone will say, but after all doesn't giving oneself the being of sadness mean to receive this being? It makes no difference from where I receive it. The fact is that a consciousness which affects itself with sadness is sad precisely for this reason. But it is difficult to comprehend the nature of consciousness; the being-sad is not a ready-made being which I give to myself as I can give this book to my friend. I do not possess the property of *affecting myself with being.* If I make myself sad, I must continue to make myself sad from beginning to end. I can not treat my sadness as an impulse finally achieved and put it on file without recreating it, nor can I carry it in the manner of an inert body which continues its movement after the initial shock. There is no inertia in consciousness. If I make myself sad, it is because I *am* not sad—the being of the sadness escapes me by and in the very act by which I affect myself with it. The being-in-itself of sadness perpetually haunts my consciousness (of) being sad, but it is as a value which I can not realize; it stands as a regulative meaning of my sadness, not as its constitutive modality.

Someone may say that my consciousness at least is, whatever may be the object or the state of which it makes itself consciousness. But how do we distinguish my consciousness (of) being sad from sadness? Is it not all one? It is true in a way that my consciousness is, if one means by this that for another it is a part of the totality of being on which judgments can be brought to bear. But it should be noted, as Husserl clearly understood, that my consciousness appears originally to the Other as an absence. It is the object always present as the *meaning* of all my attitudes and all my conduct—and always absent, for it gives itself to the intuition of another as a perpetual question— still better, as a perpetual freedom. When Pierre looks at me, I know of course that he is looking at me. His eyes, things in the world, are fixed on my body, a thing in the world—that is the objective fact of which I can say: it *is*. But it is also a fact *in the world*. The meaning of this look is not a fact in the world, and this is what makes me uncomfortable. Although I make smiles, promises, threats, nothing can get hold of the approbation, the free judgment which I seek; I know that it is always beyond. I sense it in my very attitude, which is no longer like that of the worker toward the things he uses as instruments. My reactions, to the extent that I project myself toward the Other, are no longer for myself but are rather mere *presentations;* they await being constituted as graceful or uncouth, sincere or insincere, etc., by an apprehension which is always beyond my efforts to provoke, an apprehension which will be provoked by my efforts only if of itself it lends them force (that is, only in so far as it causes itself to be provoked from the outside), *which is its own mediator with the transcendent.* Thus the objective fact of the being-in-itself of the consciousness of the Other is posited in order to disappear in negativity and in freedom: consciousness of the Other is as not-being; its being-in-itself "here and now" is not-to-be.

CONSCIOUSNESS OF THE *OTHER IS WHAT IT IS NOT.*

Furthermore the being of my own consciousness does not appear to me as the consciousness of the Other. It is because it makes itself, since its being is consciousness of being. But this means that making sustains being; consciousness has to be its own being, it is never sustained by being; it sustains being in the heart of subjectivity, which means once again that it is inhabited by being but that it is not being: *consciousness is not what it is.*

Under these conditions what can be the significance of the ideal of sincerity except as a task impossible to achieve, of which the very meaning is in contradiction with the structure of my consciousness. To be sincere, we said, is to be what one is. That supposes that I am not originally what I am. But here naturally Kant's "You ought, therefore you can" is implicitly understood. I can *become* sincere; this is what my duty and my effort to achieve sincerity imply. But we definitely establish that the original structure of "not being what one is" renders impossible in advance all movement toward being in itself or "being what one is." And this impossibility is not hidden from consciousness; on the contrary, it is the very stuff of consciousness; it is the embarrassing constraint which we constantly experience; it is our very incapacity to recognize ourselves, to constitute ourselves as being what we are. It is this necessity which means that, as soon as we posit ourselves as a certain being, by a legitimate judgment, based on inner experience or correctly deduced from *a priori* or empirical premises, then by that very positing we surpass this being—and that not toward another being but toward emptiness, toward nothing.

How then can we blame another for not being sincere or rejoice in our own sincerity since this sincerity appears to us at the same time to be impossible? How can we in conversation, in confession, in introspection, even attempt sincerity since the effort will by its very nature be doomed to failure and since at the very time when we announce it we have a prejudicative comprehension of its futility? In introspection I try to determine exactly what I am, to make up my mind to be my true self without delay—even though it means consequently to set about searching for ways to change myself. But what does this mean if not that I am constituting myself as a thing? Shall I determine the ensemble of purposes and motivations which have pushed me to do this or that action? But this is already to postulate a causal determinism which constitutes the flow of my states of consciousness as a succession of physical states. Shall I uncover in myself "drives," even though it be to affirm them in shame? But is this not deliberately to forget that these drives are realized with my consent, that they are not forces of nature but that I lend them their efficacy by a perpetually renewed decision concerning their value. Shall I pass judgment on my character, on my nature? Is this not to veil from myself at that moment what I know only too well, that I thus judge a past to which by definition my present is not subject? The proof of this is that the same man who in sincerity posits that he is what in actuality he was, is indignant at the reproach of another and tries to disarm it by asserting that he can no longer be what he was. We are readily astonished and upset when the penalties of the court affect a man who in his new freedom is no longer the guilty person he was. But at the same time we require of this man that he recognize himself as being this guilty one. What then is sincerity except precisely a phenomenon of bad faith? Have we not shown indeed that in bad faith human reality is constituted as a being which is what it is not and which is not what it is?

Let us take an example: A homosexual frequently has an intolerable feeling of guilt, and his whole existence is determined in relation to this feeling. One will readily foresee that he is in bad faith. In fact it frequently happens that this man, while recognizing his homosexual inclination, while avowing each and every particular misdeed which he has committed, refuses with all his strength to consider himself "*a paederast.*" His case is always "different," peculiar; there enters into it something of a game, of chance, of bad luck; the mistakes are all in the past; they are explained by a certain conception of the beautiful which women can not satisfy; we should see in them the results of a restless search, rather than the manifestations of a deeply rooted tendency, etc., etc. Here is assuredly a man in bad faith who borders on the comic since, acknowledging all the facts which are imputed to him, he refuses to draw from them the conclusion which they impose. His friend, who is his most severe critic, becomes irritated with this duplicity. The critic asks only one thing—and perhaps then he will show himself indulgent: that the guilty one recognize himself as guilty, that the homosexual declare frankly—whether humbly or boastfully matters little—"I am a paederast." We ask here: Who is in bad faith? The homosexual or the champion of sincerity?

The homosexual recognizes his faults, but he struggles with all his strength against the crushing view that his mistakes constitute for him a destiny. He does not wish to let himself be considered as a thing. He has an obscure but strong feeling that an homosexual is not an homosexual as this table is a table or as this red-haired man is red-haired. It seems to him that he has escaped from each mistake as soon as he has posited it and recognized it; he even feels that the psychic duration by itself cleanses him from each misdeed, constitutes for him an undetermined future, causes him to be born anew. Is he wrong? Does he not recognize in himself the peculiar, irreducible character of human reality? His attitude includes then an undeniable comprehension of truth. But at the same time he needs this perpetual rebirth, this constant escape in order to live; he must constantly put himself beyond reach in order to avoid the terrible judgment of collectivity. Thus he plays on the word *being*. He would be right actually if he understood the phrase, "I am not a paederast" in the sense of "I am not what I am." That is, if he declared to himself, "To the extent that a pattern of conduct is defined as the conduct of a paederast and to the extent that I have adopted this conduct, I am a paederast. But to the extent that human reality can not be finally defined by patterns of conduct, I am not one." But instead he slides surreptitiously towards a different connotation of the word "being." He understands "not being" in the sense of "not-being-in-itself." He lays claim to "not being a paederast" in the sense in which this table is not an inkwell. He is in bad faith.

But the champion of sincerity is not ignorant of the transcendence of human reality, and he knows how at need to appeal to it for his own advantage. He makes use of it even and brings it up in the present argument. Does he not wish, first in the name of sincerity, then of freedom, that the homosexual reflect on himself and acknowledge himself as an homosexual? Does he not let the other understand that such a confession will win indulgence for him? What does this mean if not that the man who will acknowledge himself as an homosexual will no longer be the same as the homosexual whom he acknowledges being and that he will escape into the region of freedom and of good will? The critic asks the man then to be what he is in order no longer to be what he is. It is the profound meaning of the saying, "A sin confessed is half pardoned." The critic demands of the guilty one that he constitute himself as a thing, precisely in order no longer to treat him as a thing. And this contradiction is constitutive of the demand of sincerity. Who can not see how offensive to the Other and how reassuring for me is a statement such as, "He's just a paederast," which removes a disturbing freedom from a trait and which aims at henceforth constituting all the acts of the Other as consequences following strictly from his essence. That is actually what the critic is demanding of his victim—that he constitute himself as a thing, that he should entrust his freedom to his friend as a fief, in order that the friend should return it to him subsequently—like a suzerain to his vassal. The champion of sincerity is in bad faith to the degree that in order to reassure himself, he pretends to judge, to the extent that he demands that freedom as freedom constitute itself as a thing. We have here only one episode in that battle to the death of consciousnesses which Hegel calls "the relation of the master and the slave." A person appeals to another and demands that in the name of his nature as consciousness he should radically destroy himself as consciousness, but while making this appeal he leads the other to hope for a rebirth beyond this destruction.

Very well, someone will say, but our man is abusing sincerity, playing one side against the other. We should not look for sincerity in the relation of the *Mit-sein* but rather where it is pure—in the relations of a person with himself. But who can not see that objective sincerity is constituted in the same way? Who can not see that the sincere man constitutes himself as a thing in order to escape the condition of a thing by the same act of sincerity? The man who confesses that he is evil has exchanged his disturbing "freedom-for-evil" for an inanimate character of evil; he *is* evil, he clings to himself, he is what he is. But by the same stroke, he escapes from that *thing,* since it is he who contemplates it, since it depends on him to maintain it under his glance or to let it collapse in an infinity of particular acts. He derives a *merit* from his sincerity, and the deserving man is not the evil man as he is evil but as he is beyond his evilness. At the same time the evil is disarmed since it is nothing, save on the plane of determinism, and since in confessing it, I posit my freedom in respect to it; my future is virgin; everything is allowed to me.

Thus the essential structure of sincerity does not differ from that of bad faith since the sincere man constitutes himself as what he is *in order not to be it.* This explains the truth recognized by all that one can fall into bad faith through being sincere. As Valéry pointed out, this is the case with Stendhal. Total, constant sincerity as a constant effort to adhere to oneself is by nature a constant effort to dissociate oneself from oneself. A person frees himself from himself by the very act by which he makes himself an object for himself. To draw up a perpetual inventory of what one is means constantly to re-deny oneself and to take refuge in a sphere where one is no longer anything but a pure, free regard. The goal of bad faith, as we said, is to put oneself out of reach; it is an escape. Now we see that we must use the same terms to define sincerity. What does this mean?

In the final analysis the goal of sincerity and the goal of bad faith are not so different. To be sure, there is a sincerity which bears on the past and which does not concern us here; I am sincere if I confess *having had* this pleasure or that intention. We shall see that if this sincerity is possible, it is because in his fall into the past, the being of man is constituted as a being-in-itself. But here our concern is only with the sincerity which aims at itself in present immanence. What is its goal? To bring me to confess to myself what I am in order that I may finally coincide with my being; in a word, to cause myself to be, in the mode of the in-itself, what I am in the mode of "not being what I am." Its assumption is that fundamentally I am already, in the mode of the in-itself, what I have to be. Thus we find at the base of sincerity a continual game of mirror and reflection, a perpetual passage from the being which is what it is, to the being which is not what it is and inversely from the being which is not what it is to the being which is what it is. And what is the goal of bad faith? To cause me to be what I am, in the mode of "not-being-what-one-is," or not to be what I am in the mode of "being-what-one-is." We find here the same game of mirrors. In fact in order for me to have an intention of sincerity, I must at the outset simultaneously be and not be what I am. Sincerity does not assign to me a mode of being or a particular quality, but in relation to that quality it aims at making me pass from one mode of being to another mode of being. This second mode of being, the ideal of sincerity, I am prevented by nature from attaining; and at the very moment when I struggle to attain it, I have a vague prejudicative comprehension that I shall not attain it. But all the same, in order for me to be able to conceive an intention in bad faith, I must have such a nature that within my being I escape from my being. If I were sad or cowardly in the way in which this inkwell is an inkwell, the possibility of bad faith could not even be conceived. Not only should I be unable to escape from my being; I could not even imagine that I could escape from it. But if bad faith is possible by virtue of a simple project, it is because so far as my being is concerned, there is no difference between being and non-being if I am cut off from my project.

Bad faith is possible only because sincerity is conscious of missing its goal inevitably, due to its very nature. I can try to apprehend myself as "*not being cowardly*," when I *am* so, only on condition that the "being cowardly" is itself "in question" at the very moment when it exists, on condition that it is itself *one* question, that at the very moment when I wish to apprehend it, it escapes me on all sides and annihilates itself. The condition under which I can attempt an effort in bad faith is that in one sense, I *am not* this coward which I do not wish to be. But if I were not cowardly in the simple mode of not-being-what-one-is-not, I would be "in good faith" by declaring that I am not cowardly. Thus this inapprehensible coward is evanescent; in order for me not to be cowardly, I must in some way also be cowardly. That does not mean that I must be "a little" cowardly, in the sense that "a little" signifies "to a certain degree cowardly—and not cowardly to a certain degree." No. I must at once both be and not be totally and in all respects a coward. Thus in this case bad faith requires that I should not be what I am; that is, that there be an imponderable difference separating being from non-being in the mode of being of human reality.

But bad faith is not restricted to denying the qualities which I possess, to not seeing the being which I am. It attempts also to constitute myself as being what I am not. It apprehends me positively as courageous when I am not so. And that is possible, once again, only if I am what I am not; that is, if non-being in me does not have being even as non-being. Of course necessarily I am not courageous; otherwise bad faith would not be bad faith. But in addition my effort in bad faith must include the ontological comprehension that even in my usual being what I am, I am not it really and that there is no such difference between the being of "being-sad," for example—which I am in the mode of not being what I am—and the "non-being" of not-being-courageous which I wish to hide from myself. Moreover it is particularly requisite that the very negation of being should be itself the object of a perpetual nihilation, that the very meaning of "non-being" be perpetually in question in human reality. If I were not courageous in the way in which this inkwell is not a table; that is, if I were isolated in my cowardice, propped firmly against it, incapable of putting it in relation to its opposite, if I were not capable of *determining* myself as cowardly—that is, to deny courage to myself and thereby to escape my cowardice in the very moment that I posit it—if it were not on principle *impossible* for me to coincide with my *not-being-courageous* as well as with my being—courageous—then any project of bad faith would be prohibited me. Thus in order for bad faith to be possible, sincerity itself must be in bad faith. The condition of the possibility for bad faith is that human reality, in its most immediate being, in the intrastructure of the pre-reflective *cogito,* must be what it is not and not be what it is.

III. THE "FAITH" OF BAD FAITH

We have indicated for the moment only those conditions which render bad faith conceivable, the structures of being which permit us to form concepts of bad faith. We can not limit ourselves to these considerations; we have not yet distinguished bad faith from falsehood. The two-faced concepts which we have described would without a doubt be utilized by a liar to discountenance his questioner, although their two-faced quality being established on the being of man and not on some empirical circumstance can and ought to be evident to all. The true problem of bad faith stems evidently from the fact that bad faith is *faith.* It can not be either a cynical lie or certainty—if certainty is the intuitive possession of the object. But if we take belief as meaning the adherence of being to its object when the object is not given or is given indistinctly, then bad faith is belief; and the essential problem of bad faith is a problem of belief.

How can we believe by bad faith in the concepts which we forge expressly to persuade ourselves? We must note in fact that the project of bad faith must be itself in bad faith. I am not only in bad faith at the end of my effort when I have constructed my two-faced concepts and when I have persuaded myself. In truth, I have not persuaded myself; to the extent that I could be so persuaded, I have always been so. And at the very moment when I was disposed to put myself in bad faith, I of necessity was in bad faith with respect to this same disposition. For me to have represented it to myself as bad faith would have been cynicism; to believe it sincerely innocent would have been in good faith. The decision to be in bad faith does not dare to speak its name; it believes itself and does not believe itself in bad faith; it believes itself and does not believe itself in good faith. It is this which from the upsurge of bad faith, determines the later attitude and, as it were, the *Weltanschauung* of bad faith.

Bad faith does not hold the norms and criteria of truth as they are accepted by the critical thought of good faith. What it decides first, in fact, is the nature of truth. With bad faith a truth appears, a method of thinking, a type of being which is like that of objects; the ontological characteristic of the world of bad faith with which the subject suddenly surrounds himself is this: that here being is what it is not, and is not what it is. Consequently a peculiar type of evidence appears: *non-persuasive* evidence. Bad faith apprehends evidence but it is resigned in advance to not being fulfilled by this evidence, to not being persuaded and transformed into good faith. It makes itself humble and modest; it is not ignorant, it says, that faith is decision and that after each intuition, it must decide and will what it is. Thus bad faith in its primitive project and in its coming into the world decides on the exact nature of its requirements. It stands forth in the firm resolution *not to demand too much,* to count itself satisfied when it is barely persuaded, to force itself in decisions to adhere to uncertain truths. This original project of bad faith is a decision in bad faith on the nature of faith. Let us understand clearly that there is no question of a reflective, voluntary decision, but of a spontaneous determination of our being. One *puts oneself* in bad faith as one goes to sleep and one is in bad faith as one dreams. Once this mode of being has been realized, it is as difficult to get out of it as to wake oneself up; bad faith is a type of being in the world, like waking or dreaming, which by itself tends to perpetuate itself, although its structure is of the *metastable* type. But bad faith is conscious of its structure, and it has taken precautions by deciding that the *metastable* structure is the structure of being and that non-persuasion is the structure of all convictions. It follows that if bad faith is faith and if it includes in its original project its own negation (it determines itself to be not quite convinced in order to convince itself that I am what I am not), then to start with, a faith which wishes itself to be not quite convinced must be possible. What are the conditions for the possibility of such a faith?

I believe that my friend Pierre feels friendship for me. I believe it in good *faith.* I believe it but I do not have for it any self-evident intuition, for the nature of the object does not lend itself to intuition. I *believe* it; that is, I allow myself to give in to all impulses to trust it; I decide to believe in it, and to maintain myself in this decision; I conduct myself, finally, as if I were certain of it—and all this in the synthetic unity of one and the same attitude. This which I define as good faith is what Hegel would call the *immediate.* It is simple faith. Hegel would demonstrate at once that the immediate calls for mediation and that belief by becoming *belief for itself,* passes to the state of non-belief. If *I believe* that my friend Pierre likes me, this means that his friendship appears to me as the meaning of all his acts. Belief is a particular consciousness of *the meaning* of Pierre's acts. But if I know that I believe, the belief appears to me as pure subjective determination without external correlative. This is what makes the very word "to believe" a term utilized indifferently to indicate the unwavering firmness of belief ("My God, I believe in you") and its character as disarmed and strictly subjective. ("Is Pierre my friend? I do not know; I believe so.") But the nature of consciousness is such that in it the mediate and the immediate are one and the same being. To believe is to know that one believes, and to know that one believes is no longer to believe. Thus to believe is not to believe any longer because that is only to believe—this in the unity of one and the same non-thetic self-consciousness. To be sure, we have here forced the description of the phenomenon by designating it with the word *to know;* non-thetic consciousness is not to *know.* But it is in its very translucency at the origin of all knowing. Thus the non-thetic consciousness (of) believing is destructive of belief. But at the same time the very law of the pre-reflective *cogito* implies that the being of believing ought to be the consciousness of believing.

Thus belief is a being which questions its own being, which can realize itself only in its destruction, which can manifest itself to itself only by denying itself. It is a being for which to be is to appear and to appear is to deny itself. To believe is not-to-believe. We see the reason for it; the being of consciousness is to exist by itself, then to make itself be and thereby to pass beyond itself. In this sense consciousness is perpetually escaping itself, belief becomes non-belief, the immediate becomes mediation, the absolute becomes relative, and the relative becomes absolute. The ideal of good faith (to believe what one believes) is, like that of sincerity (to be what one is), an ideal of being-in-itself. Every belief is a belief that falls short; one never wholly believes what one believes. Consequently the primitive project of bad faith is only the utilization of this self-destruction of the fact of consciousness. If every belief in good faith is an impossible belief, then there is a place for every impossible belief. My inability to *believe* that I am courageous will not discourage me since every belief involves not quite believing. I shall define this impossible belief as *my* belief. To be sure, I shall not be able to hide from myself that I believe in order not to believe and that I do not believe *in order* to believe. But the subtle, total annihilation of bad faith by itself can not surprise me; it exists at the basis of all faith. What is it then? At the moment when I wish to believe myself courageous I know that I am a coward. And this certainly would come to destroy my belief. But *first,* I am not any more courageous than cowardly, if we are to understand this in the mode of being of the-in-itself. In the second place, I do not *know* that I am courageous; such a view of myself can be accompanied only by *belief,* for it surpasses pure reflective certitude. In the third place, it is very true that bad faith does not succeed in believing what it wishes to believe. But it is precisely as the acceptance of not believing what it believes that it is bad faith. Good faith wishes to flee the "not-believing-what-one-believes" by finding refuge in being. Bad faith flees being by taking refuge in "not-believing-what-one-believes." It has disarmed all beliefs in advance—those which it would like to take hold of and, by the same stroke, the others, those which it wishes to flee. In *willing* this self-destruction of belief, from which science escapes by searching for evidence, it ruins the beliefs which are opposed to it, which reveal themselves as *being only* belief. Thus we can better understand the original phenomenon of bad faith.

In bad faith there is no cynical lie nor knowing preparation for deceitful concepts. But the first act of bad faith is to flee what it can not flee, to flee what it is. The very project of flight reveals to bad faith an inner disintegration in the heart of being, and it is this disintegration which bad faith wishes to be. In truth, the two immediate attitudes which we can take in the face of our being are conditioned by the very nature of this being and its immediate relation with the in-itself. Good faith seeks to flee the inner disintegration of my being in the direction of the in-itself which it should be and is not. Bad faith seeks to flee the in-itself by means of the inner disintegration of my being. But it denies this very disintegration as it denies that it is itself bad faith. Bad faith seeks by means of "not-being-what-one-is" to escape from the in-itself which I am not in the mode of being what one is not. It denies itself as bad faith and aims at the in-itself which I am not in the mode of "not-being-what-one-is-not."* If bad faith is possible, it is because it is an immediate, permanent threat to every project of the human being; it is because consciousness conceals in its being a permanent risk of bad faith. The origin of this risk is the fact that the nature of consciousness simultaneously is to be what it is not and not to be what it is. In the light of these remarks we can now approach the ontological study of consciousness, not as the totality of the human being, but as the instantaneous nucleus of this being.

---

*If it is indifferent whether one is in good or in bad faith, because bad faith reapprehends good faith and slides to the very origin of the project of good faith, that does not mean that we can not radically escape bad faith. But this supposes a self-recovery of being which was previously corrupted. This self-recovery we shall call authenticity, the description of which has no place here.

EXISTENTIALISM IS A HUMANISM

I should like on this occasion to defend existentialism against some charges which have been brought against it.

First, it has been charged with inviting people to remain in a kind of desperate quietism because, since no solutions are possible, we should have to consider action in this world as quite impossible. We should then end up in a philosophy of contemplation; and since contemplation is a luxury, we come in the end to a bourgeois philosophy. The communists in particular have made these charges.

On the other hand, we have been charged with dwelling on human degradation, with pointing up everywhere the sordid, shady, and slimy, and neglecting the gracious and beautiful, the bright side of human nature; for example, according to Mlle. Mercier, a Catholic critic, with forgetting the smile of the child. Both sides charge us with having ignored human solidarity, with considering man as an isolated being. The communists say that the main reason for this is that we take pure subjectivity, *the Cartesian I think,* as our starting point; in other words, the moment in which man becomes fully aware of what it means to him to be an isolated being; as a result, we are unable to return to a state of solidarity with the men who are not ourselves, a state which we can never reach in the *cogito.*

From the Christian standpoint, we are charged with denying the reality and seriousness of human undertakings, since, if we reject God's commandments and the eternal verities, there no longer remains anything but pure caprice, with everyone permitted to do as he pleases and incapable, from his own point of view, of condemning the points of view and acts of others.

I shall try today to answer these different charges. Many people are going to be surprised at what is said here about humanism. We shall try to see in what sense it is to be understood. In any case, what can be said from the very beginning is that by existentialism we mean a doctrine which makes human life possible and, in addition, declares that every truth and every action implies a human setting and a human subjectivity.

As is generally known, the basic charge against us is that we put the emphasis on the dark side of human life. Someone recently told me of a lady who, when she let slip a vulgar word in a moment of irritation, excused herself by saying, "I guess I'm becoming an existentialist." Consequently, existentialism is regarded as something ugly; that is why we are said to be naturalists; and if we are, it is rather surprising that in this day and age we cause so much more alarm and scandal than does naturalism, properly so called. The kind of person who can take in his stride such a novel as Zola's *The Earth* is disgusted as soon as he starts reading an existentialist novel; the kind of person who is resigned to the wisdom of the ages—which is pretty sad—finds us even sadder. Yet, what can be more disillusioning than saying "true charity begins at home" or "a scoundrel will always return evil for good"?

We know the commonplace remarks made when this subject comes up, remarks which always add up to the same thing: we shouldn't struggle against the powers-that-be; we shouldn't resist authority; we shouldn't try to rise above our station; any action

Jean-Paul Sartre, *Existentialism Is a Humanism,* translated by Bernard Frechtman (New York: Philosophical Library, 1947). Reprinted by permission.

which doesn't conform to authority is romantic; any effort not based on past experience is doomed to failure; experience shows that man's bent is always toward trouble, that there must be a strong hand to hold him in check, if not, there will be anarchy. There are still people who go on mumbling these melancholy old saws, the people who say, "It's only human!" whenever a more or less repugnant act is pointed out to them, the people who glut themselves on *chansons réalistes;* these are the people who accuse existentialism of being too gloomy, and to such an extent that I wonder whether they are complaining about it, not for its pessimism, but much rather its optimism. Can it be that what really scares them in the doctrine I shall try to present here is that it leaves to man a possibility of choice? To answer this question, we must re-examine it on a strictly philosophical plane. What is meant by the term *existentialism*?

Most people who use the word would be rather embarrassed if they had to explain it, since, now that the word is all the rage, even the work of a musician or painter is being called existentialist. A gossip columnist in *Clartés* signs himself *The Existentialist,* so that by this time the word has been so stretched and has taken on so broad a meaning, that it no longer means anything at all. It seems that for want of an avant-garde doctrine analogous to surrealism, the kind of people who are eager for scandal and flurry turn to this philosophy which in other respects does not at all serve their purposes in this sphere.

Actually, it is the least scandalous, the most austere of doctrines. It is intended strictly for specialists and philosophers. Yet it can be defined easily. What complicates matters is that there are two kinds of existentialist; first, those who are Christian, among whom I would include Jaspers and Gabriel Marcel, both Catholic; and on the other hand the atheistic existentialists, among whom I class Heidegger, and then the French existentialists and myself. What they have in common is that they think that existence precedes essence, or, if you prefer, that subjectivity must be the starting point.

Just what does that mean? Let us consider some object that is manufactured, for example, a book or a paper-cutter: here is an object which has been made by an artisan whose inspiration came from a concept. He referred to the concept of what a paper-cutter is and likewise to a known method of production, which is part of the concept, something which is, by and large, a routine. Thus, the paper-cutter is at once an object produced in a certain way and, on the other hand, one having a specific use; and one cannot postulate a man who produces a paper-cutter but does not know what it is used for. Therefore, let us say that, for the paper-cutter, essence—that is, the ensemble of both the production routines and the properties which enable it to be both produced and defined—precedes existence. Thus, the presence of the paper-cutter or book in front of me is determined. Therefore, we have here a technical view of the world whereby it can be said that production precedes existence.

When we conceive God as the Creator, He is generally thought of as a superior sort of artisan. Whatever doctrine we may be considering, whether one like that of Descartes or that of Leibnitz, we always grant that will more or less follows understanding or, at the very least, accompanies it, and that when God creates He knows exactly what He is creating. Thus, the concept of man in the mind of God is comparable to the concept of paper-cutter in the mind of the manufacturer, and, following certain techniques and a conception, God produces man, just as the artisan, following a definition and a technique, makes a paper-cutter. Thus, the individual man is the realization of a certain concept in the divine intelligence.

In the eighteenth century, the atheism of the *philosophes* discarded the idea of God, but not so much for the notion that essence precedes existence. To a certain extent, this idea is found everywhere; we find it in Diderot, in Voltaire, and even in Kant. Man has a human nature; this human nature, which is the concept of the human, is found in all men, which means that each man is a particular example of a universal concept, man. In Kant, the result of this universality is that the wild-man, the natural man, as well as the bourgeois, are circumscribed by the same definition and have the same basic qualities. Thus, here too the essence of man precedes the historical existence that we find in nature.

Atheistic existentialism, which I represent, is more coherent. It states that if God does not exist, there is at least one being in whom existence precedes essence, a being who exists before he can be defined by any concept, and that this being is man, or, as Heidegger says, human reality. What is meant here by saying that existence precedes essence? It means that, first of all, man exists, turns up, appears on the scene, and, only afterwards, defines himself. If man, as the existentialist conceives him, is indefinable, it is because at first he is nothing. Only afterward will he be something, and he himself will have made what he will be. Thus, there is no human nature, since there is no God to conceive it. Not only is man what he conceives himself to be, but he is also only what he wills himself to be after this thrust toward existence.

Man is nothing else but what he makes of himself. Such is the first principle of existentialism. It is also what is called subjectivity, the name we are labeled with when charges are brought against us. But what do we mean by this, if not that man has a greater dignity than a stone or table? For we mean that man first exists, that is, that man first of all is the being who hurls himself toward a future and who is conscious of imagining himself as being in the future. Man is at the start a plan which is aware of itself, rather than a patch of moss, a piece of garbage, or a cauliflower; nothing exists prior to this plan; there is nothing in heaven; man will be what he will have planned to be. Not what he will want to be. Because by the word "will" we generally mean a conscious decision, which is subsequent to what we have already made of ourselves. I may want to belong to a political party, write a book, get married; but all that is only a manifestation of an earlier, more spontaneous choice that is called "will." But if existence really does precede essence, man is responsible for what he is. Thus, existentialism's first move is to make every man aware of what he is and to make the full responsibility of his existence rest on him. And when we say that a man is responsible for himself, we do not only mean that he is responsible for his own individuality, but that he is responsible for all men.

The word subjectivism has two meanings, and our opponents play on the two. Subjectivism means, on the one hand, that an individual chooses and makes himself; and, on the other, that it is impossible for man to transcend human subjectivity. The second of these is the essential meaning of existentialism. When we say that man chooses his own self, we mean that every one of us does likewise; but we also mean by that that in making this choice he also chooses all men. In fact, in creating the man that we want to be, there is not a single one of our acts which does not at the same time create an image of man as we think he ought to be. To choose to be this or that is to affirm at the same time the value of what we choose, because we can never choose evil. We always choose the good, and nothing can be good for us without being good for all.

If, on the other hand, existence precedes essence, and if we grant that we exist and fashion our image at one and the same time, the image is valid for everybody and for our whole age. Thus, our responsibility is much greater than we might have supposed, because it involves all mankind. If I am a workingman and choose to join a Christian trade-union rather than be a communist, and if by being a member I want to show that the best thing for man is resignation, that the kingdom of man is not of this world, I am not only involving my own case—I want to be resigned for everyone. As a result, my action has involved all humanity. To take a more individual matter, if I want to marry, to have children; even if this marriage depends solely on my own circumstances or passion or wish, I am involving all humanity in monogamy and not merely myself. Therefore, I am responsible for myself and for everyone else. I am creating a certain image of man of my own choosing. In choosing myself, I choose man.

This helps us understand what the actual content is of such rather grandiloquent words as anguish, forlornness, despair. As you will see, it's all quite simple.

First, what is meant by anguish? The existentialists say at once that man is in anguish. What that means is this: the man who involves himself and who realizes that he is not only the person he chooses to be, but also a law-maker who is, at the same time, choosing all mankind as well as himself, can not help escape the feeling of his total and deep responsibility. Of course, there are many people who are not anxious; but we claim that they are hiding their anxiety, that they are fleeing from it. Certainly, many people believe that when they do something, they themselves are the only ones involved, and when someone says to them, "What if everyone acted that way?" they shrug their shoulders and answer, "Everyone doesn't act that way." But really, one should always ask himself, "What would happen if everybody looked at things that way?" There is no escaping this disturbing thought except by a kind of double-dealing. A man who lies and makes excuses for himself by saying "not everybody does that," is someone with an uneasy conscience, because the act of lying implies that a universal value is conferred upon the lie.

Anguish is evident even when it conceals itself. This is the anguish that Kierkegaard called the anguish of Abraham. You know the story: an angel has ordered Abraham to sacrifice his son; if it really were an angel who has come and said, "You are Abraham, you shall sacrifice your son," everything would be all right. But everyone might first wonder, "Is it really an angel, and am I really Abraham? What proof do I have?"

There was a mad woman who had hallucinations; someone used to speak to her on the telephone and give her orders. Her doctor asked her, "Who is it who talks to you?" She answered, "He says it's God." What proof did she really have that it was God? If an angel comes to me, what proof is there that it's an angel? And if I hear voices, what proof is there that they come from heaven and not from hell, or from the subconscious, or a pathological condition? What proves that they are addressed to me? What proof is there that I have been appointed to impose my choice and my conception of man on humanity? I'll never find any proof or sign to convince me of that. If a voice addresses me, it is always for me to decide that this is the angel's voice; if I consider that such an act is a good one, it is I who will choose to say that it is good rather than bad.

Now, I'm not being singled out as an Abraham, and yet at every moment I'm obliged to perform exemplary acts. For every man, everything happens as if all mankind had its eyes fixed on him and were guiding itself by what he does. And every man ought to say to himself, "Am I really the kind of man who has the right to act in such a way that humanity might guide itself by my actions?" And if he does not say that to himself, he is masking his anguish.

There is no question here of the kind of anguish which would lead to quietism, to inaction. It is a matter of a simple sort of anguish that anybody who has had responsibilities is familiar with. For example, when a military officer takes the responsibility for an attack and sends a number of men to death, he chooses to do so, and in the main he alone makes the choice. Doubtless, orders come from above, but they are too broad; he interprets them, and on this interpretation depend the lives of ten or fourteen or twenty men. In making a decision he can not help having a certain anguish. All leaders know this anguish. That doesn't keep them from acting; on the contrary, it is the very condition of their action. For it implies that they envisage a number of possibilities, and when they choose one, they realize that it has value only because it is chosen. We shall see that this kind of anguish, which is the kind that existentialism describes, is explained, in addition, by a direct responsibility to the other men whom it involves. It is not a curtain separating us from action, but is part of action itself.

When we speak of forlornness, a term Heidegger was fond of, we mean only that God does not exist and that we have to face all the consequences of this. The existentialist is strongly opposed to a certain kind of secular ethics which would like to abolish God with the least possible expense. About 1880, some French teachers tried to set up a secular ethic which went something like this: God is a useless and costly hypothesis; we are discarding it; but, meanwhile, in order for there to be an ethics, a society, a civilization, it is essential that certain values be taken seriously and that they be considered as having an *a priori* existence. It must be obligatory, *a priori,* to be honest, not to lie, not to beat your wife, to have children, etc., etc. So we're going to try a little device which will make it possible to show that values exist all the same, inscribed in a heaven of ideas, though otherwise God does not exist. In other words—and this, I believe, is the tendency of everything called reformism in France—nothing will be changed if God does not exist. We shall find ourselves with the same norms of honesty, progress, and humanism, and we shall have made of God an outdated hypothesis which will peacefully die off by itself.

The existentialist, on the contrary, thinks it very distressing that God does not exist, because all possibility of finding values in a heaven of ideas disappears along with Him; there can no longer be an *a priori* Good, since there is no infinite and perfect consciousness to think it. Nowhere is it written that the Good exists, that we must be honest, that we must not lie; because the fact is we are on a plane where there are only men. Dostoevski said, "If God didn't exist, everything would be possible." That is the very starting point of existentialism. Indeed, everything is permissible if God does not exist, and as a result man is forlorn, because neither within him nor without does he find anything to cling to. He can't start making excuses for himself.

If existence really does precede essence, there is no explaining things away by reference to a fixed and given human nature. In other words, there is not determinism, man is free, man is freedom. On the other hand, if God does not exist, we find no values or commands to turn to which legitimize our conduct. So, in the bright realm of values, we have no excuse behind us, nor justification before us. We are alone, with no excuses.

That is the idea I shall try to convey when I say that man is condemned to be free. Condemned, because he did not create himself, yet, in other respects is free; because, once thrown into the world, he is responsible for everything he does. The existentialist does not believe in the power of passion. He will never agree that a sweeping passion is a ravaging torrent which fatally leads a man to certain acts and is therefore an excuse. He thinks that man is responsible for his passion.

The existentialist does not think man is going to help himself by finding in the world some omen by which to orient himself. Because he thinks that man will interpret the omen to suit himself. Therefore, he thinks that man, with no support and no aid, is condemned every moment to invent man. Ponge, in a very fine article, has said, "Man is the future of man." That's exactly it. But if it is taken to mean that this future is recorded in heaven, that God sees it, then it is false, because it would really no longer be a future. If it is taken to mean that, whatever a man may be, there is a future to be forged, a virgin future before him, then this remark is sound. But then we are forlorn.

To give you an example which will enable you to understand forlornness better, I shall cite the case of one of my students who came to see me under the following circumstances: his father was on bad terms with his mother, and, moreover, was inclined to be a collaborationist; his older brother had been killed in the German offensive of 1940, and the young man, with somewhat immature but generous feelings, wanted to avenge him. His mother lived alone with him, very much upset by the half-treason of her husband and the death of her older son; the boy was her only consolation.

The boy was faced with the choice of leaving for England and joining the Free French Forces—that is, leaving his mother behind—or remaining with his mother and helping her to carry on. He was fully aware that the woman lived only for him and that his going-off—and perhaps his death—would plunge her into despair. He was also aware that every act that he did for his mother's sake was a sure thing, in the sense that it was helping her to carry on, whereas every effort he made toward going off and fighting was an uncertain move which might run aground and prove completely useless; for example, on his way to England he might, while passing through Spain, be detained indefinitely in a Spanish camp; he might reach England or Elgiers and be stuck in an office at a desk job. As a result, he was faced with two very different kinds of action: one, concrete, immediate, but concerning only one individual; the other concerned an incomparably vaster group, a national collectivity, but for that very reason was dubious, and might be interrupted en route. And, at the same time, he was wavering between two kinds of ethics. On the one hand, an ethics of sympathy, of personal devotion; on the other, a broader ethics, but one whose efficacy was more dubious. He had to choose between the two.

Who could help him choose? Christian doctrine? No. Christian doctrine says, "Be charitable, love your neighbor, take the more rugged path, etc., etc." But which is the more rugged path? Whom should he love as a brother? The fighting man or his mother? Which does the greater good, the vague act of fighting in a group, or the concrete one of helping a particular human being to go on living? Who can decide *a priori*? Nobody. No book of ethics can tell him. The Kantian ethics says, "Never treat any person as a means, but as an end." Very well, if I stay with my mother, I'll treat her as an end and not as a means; but by virtue of this very fact, I'm running the risk of treating the people around me who are fighting, as means; and, conversely, if I go to join those who are fighting, I'll be treating them as an end, and, by doing that, I run the risk of treating my mother as a means.

If values are vague, and if they are always too broad for the concrete and specific case that we are considering, the only thing left for us is to trust our instincts. That's what this young man tried to do; and when I saw him, he said, "In the end, feeling is what counts. I ought to choose whichever pushes me in one direction. If I feel that I love my mother enough to sacrifice everything else for her—my desire for vengeance, for action, for adventure—then I'll stay with her. If, on the contrary, I feel that my love for my mother isn't enough, I'll leave."

But how is the value of a feeling determined? What gives his feeling for his mother value? Precisely the fact that he remained with her. I may say that I like so-and-so well enough to sacrifice a certain amount of money for him, but I may say so only if I've done it. I may say "I love my mother well enough to remain with her" if I have remained with her. The only way to determine the value of this affection is, precisely, to perform an act which confirms and defines it. But, since I require this affection to justify my act, I find myself caught in a vicious circle.

On the other hand, Gide has well said that a mock feeling and a true feeling are almost indistinguishable; to decide that I love my mother and will remain with her, or to remain with her by putting on an act, amount somewhat to the same thing. In other words, the feeling is formed by the acts one performs; so, I can not refer to it in order to act upon it. Which means that I can neither seek within myself the true condition which will impel me to act, nor apply to a system of ethics for concepts which will permit me to act. You will say, "At least, he did go to a teacher for advice." But if you seek advice from a priest, for example, you have chosen this priest; you already knew, more or less, just about what advice he was going to give you. In other words, choosing your adviser is involving yourself. The proof of this is that if you are a Christian, you will say, "Consult a priest." But some priests are collaborating, some are just marking time, some are resisting. Which to choose? If the young man chooses a priest who is resisting or collaborating, he has already decided on the kind of advice he's going to get. Therefore, in coming to see me he knew the answer I was going to give him, and I had only one answer to give: "You're free, choose, that is, invent." No general ethics can show you what is to be done; there are no omens in the world. The Catholics will reply, "But there are." Granted—but, in any case, I myself choose the meaning they have.

When I was a prisoner, I knew a rather remarkable young man who was a Jesuit. He had entered the Jesuit order in the following way: he had a number of very bad breaks; in childhood, his father died, leaving him in poverty, and he was a scholarship student at a religious institution where he was constantly made to feel that he was being kept out of charity; then, he failed to get any of the honors and distinctions that children like; later on, at about eighteen, he bungled a love affair; finally, at twenty-two, he failed in military training, a childish enough matter, but it was the last straw.

This young fellow might well have felt that he had botched everything. It was a sign of something, but of what? He might have taken refuge in bitterness or despair. But he very wisely looked upon all this as a sign that he was not made for secular triumphs, and that only the triumphs of religion, holiness, and faith were open to him. He saw the hand of God in all this, and so he entered the order. Who can help seeing that he alone decided what the sign meant?

Some other interpretation might have been drawn from this series of setbacks; for example, that he might have done better to turn carpenter or revolutionist. Therefore, he is fully responsible for the interpretation. Forlornness implies that we ourselves choose our being. Forlornness and anguish go together.

As for despair, the term has a very simple meaning. It means that we shall confine ourselves to reckoning only with what depends upon our will, or on the ensemble of probabilities which make our action possible. When we want something, we always have to reckon with probabilities. I may be counting on the arrival of a friend. The friend is coming by rail or street-car; this supposes that the train will arrive on schedule, or that the street-car will not jump the track. I am left in the realm of possibility; but possibilities are to be reckoned with only to the point where my action comports with the ensemble of these possibilities, and no further. The moment the possibilities I am considering are not rigorously involved by my action, I ought to disengage myself from them, because no God, no scheme, can adapt the world and its possibilities to my will. When Descartes said, "Conquer yourself rather than the world," he meant essentially the same thing.

The Marxists to whom I have spoken reply, "You can rely on the support of others in your action, which obviously has certain limits because you're not going to live forever. That means: rely on both what others are doing elsewhere to help you, in China, in Russia, and what they will do later on, after your death, to carry on the action and lead it to its fulfillment, which will be the revolution. You even *have* to rely upon that, otherwise you're immoral." I reply at once that I will always rely on fellow-fighters insofar as these comrades are involved with me in a common struggle, in the unity of a party or a group in which I can more or less make my weight felt; that is, one whose ranks I am in as a fighter and whose movements I am aware of at every moment. In such a situation, relying on the unity and will of the party is exactly like counting on the fact that the train will arrive on time, or that the car won't jump the track. But, given that man is free and that there is no human nature for me to depend on, I can not count on men whom I do not know by relying on human goodness or man's concern for the good of society. I don't know what will become of the Russian revolution; I may make an example of it to the extent that at the present time it is apparent that the proletariat plays a part in Russia that it plays in no other nation. But I can't swear that this will inevitably lead to a triumph of the proletariat. I've got to limit myself to what I see.

Given that men are free and that tomorrow they will freely decide what man will be, I can not be sure that, after my death, fellow-fighters will carry on my work to bring it to its maximum perfection. Tomorrow, after my death, some men may decide to set up Fascism, and the others may be cowardly and muddled enough to let them do it. Fascism will then be the human reality, so much the worse for us.

Actually, things will be as man will have decided they are to be. Does that mean that I should abandon myself to quietism? No. First, I should involve myself; then, act on the old saw, "Nothing ventured, nothing gained." Nor does it mean that I shouldn't belong to a party, but rather that I shall have no illusions and shall do what I can. For example, suppose I ask myself, "Will socialization, as such, ever come about?" I know nothing about it. All I know is that I'm going to do everything in my power to bring it about. Beyond that, I can't count on anything. Quietism is the attitude of people who say, "Let others do what I can't do." The doctrine I am presenting is the very opposite of quietism, since it declares, "There is no reality except in action." Moreover, it goes further, since it adds, "Man is nothing else than his plan; he exists only to the extent that he fulfills himself; he is therefore nothing else than the ensemble of his acts, nothing else than his life."

According to this, we can understand why our doctrine horrifies certain people. Because often the only way they can bear their wretchedness is to think, "Circumstances have been against me. What I've been and done doesn't show my true worth. To be sure, I've had no great love, no great friendship, but that's because I haven't met a man or woman who was worthy. The books I've written haven't been very good because I haven't had the proper leisure. I haven't had children to devote myself to because I didn't find a man with whom I could have spent my life. So there remains within me, unused and quite viable, a host of propensities, inclinations, possibilities, that one wouldn't guess from the mere series of things I've done."

Now, for the existentialist there is really no love other than one which manifests itself in a person's being in love. There is no genius other than one which is expressed in works of art; the genius of Proust is the sum of Proust's works; the genius of Racine is his series of tragedies. Outside of that, there is nothing. Why say that Racine could have written another tragedy, when he didn't write it? A man is involved in life, leaves his impress on it, and outside of that there is nothing. To be sure, this may seem a harsh thought to someone whose life hasn't been a success. But, on the other hand, it prompts people to understand that reality alone is what counts, that dreams, expectations, and hopes warrant no more than to define a man as a disappointed dream, as miscarried hopes, as vain expectations. In other words, to define him negatively and not positively. However, when we say, "You are nothing else than your life," that does not imply that the artist will be judged solely on the basis of his works of art; a thousand other things will contribute toward summing him up. What we mean is that a man is nothing else than a series of undertakings, that he is the sum, the organization, the ensemble of the relationships which make up these undertakings.

When all is said and done, what we are accused of, at bottom, is not our pessimism, but an optimistic toughness. If people throw up to us our works of fiction in which we write about people who are soft, weak, cowardly, and sometimes even downright bad, it's not because these people are soft, weak, cowardly, or bad; because if we were to say, as Zola did, that they are that way because of heredity, the workings of environment, society, because of biological or psychological determinism, people would be reassured. They would say, "Well, that's what we're like, no one can do anything about it." But when the existentialist writes about a coward, he says that this coward is responsible for his cowardice. He's not like that because he has a cowardly heart or lung or brain; he's not like that on account of his physiological makeup; but he's like that because he has made himself a coward by his acts. There's no such thing as a cowardly constitution; there are nervous constitutions; there is poor blood, as the common people say, or strong constitutions. But the man whose blood is poor is not a coward on that account, for what makes cowardice is the act of renouncing or yielding. A constitution is not an act; the coward is defined on the basis of the acts he performs. People feel, in a vague sort of way, that this coward we're talking about is guilty of being a coward, and the thought frightens them. What people would like is that a coward or a hero be born that way.

One of the complaints most frequently made about *The Ways of Freedom** can be summed up as follows: "After all, these people are so spineless, how are you going to make heroes out of them?" This objection almost makes me laugh, for it assumes that people are born heroes. That's what people really want to think. If you're born cowardly, you may set your mind perfectly at rest; there's nothing you can do about it; you'll be cowardly all your life, whatever you may do. If you're born a hero, you may set your mind just as much at rest; you'll be a hero all your life; you'll drink like a hero and eat like a hero. What the existentialist says is that the coward makes himself cowardly, that the hero makes himself heroic. There's always a possibility for the coward not to be cowardly any more and for the hero to stop being heroic. What counts is total involvement; some one particular action or set of circumstances is not total involvement.

Thus, I think we have answered a number of the charges concerning existentialism. You see that it can not be taken for a philosophy of quietism, since it defines man in terms of action; nor for a pessimistic description of man—there is no doctrine more optimistic, since man's destiny is within himself; nor for an attempt to discourage man from acting, since it tells him that the only hope is in his acting and that action is the only thing that enables a man to live. Consequently, we are dealing here with an ethic of action and involvement.

Nevertheless, on the basis of a few notions like these, we are still charged with immuring man in his private subjectivity. There again we're very much misunderstood. Subjectivity of the individual is indeed our point of departure, and this for strictly philosophic reasons. Not because we are bourgeois, but because we want a doctrine based on truth and not a lot of fine theories, full of hope but with no real basis. There can be no other truth to take off from than this: *I think; therefore I exist.* There we have the absolute truth of consciousness becoming aware of itself. Every theory which takes man out of the moment in which he becomes aware of himself is, at its

---

*[*Les Chemins de la Liberté*, A trilogy of novels of which two —*L'Age de Raison (The Age of Reason)* and *Le Sursis (The Reprieve)*—had been published at the time of this article.]

very beginning, a theory which confounds truth, for outside the Cartesian *cogito,* all views are only probable, and a doctrine of probability which is not bound to a truth dissolves into thin air. In order to describe the probable, you must have a firm hold on the true. Therefore, before there can be any truth whatsoever, there must be an absolute truth; and this one is simple and easily arrived at; it's on everyone's doorstep; it's a matter of grasping it directly.

Secondly, this theory is the only one which gives man dignity, the only one which does not reduce him to an object. The effect of all materialism is to treat all men, including the one philosophizing, as objects, that is, as an ensemble of determined reactions in no way distinguished from the ensemble of qualities and phenomena which constitute a table or a chair or a stone. We definitely wish to establish the human realm as an ensemble of values distinct from the material realm. But the subjectivity that we have thus arrived at, and which we have claimed to be truth, is not a strictly individual subjectivity, for we have demonstrated that one discovers in the *cogito* not only himself, but others as well.

The philosophies of Descartes and Kant to the contrary, through the *I think* we reach our own self in the presence of others, and the others are just as real to us as our own self. Thus, the man who becomes aware of himself through the *cogito* also perceives all others, and he perceives them as the condition of his own existence. He realizes that he can not be anything (in the sense that we say that someone is witty or nasty or jealous) unless others recognize it as such. In order to get any truth about myself, I must have contact with another person. The other is indispensable to my own existence, as well as to my knowledge about myself. This being so, in discovering my inner being I discover the other person at the same time, like a freedom placed in front of me which thinks and wills only for or against me. Hence, let us at once announce the discovery of a world which we shall call intersubjectivity; this is the world in which man decides what he is and what others are.

Besides, if it is impossible to find in every man some universal essence which would be human nature, yet there does exist a universal human condition. It's not by chance that today's thinkers speak more readily of man's condition than of his nature. By condition they mean, more or less definitely, the *a priori* limits which outline man's fundamental situation in the universe. Historical situations vary; a man may be born a slave in a pagan society or a feudal lord or a proletarian. What does not vary is the necessity for him to exist in the world, to be at work there, to be there in the midst of other people, and to be mortal there. The limits are neither subjective nor objective, or, rather, they have an objective and a subjective side. Objective because they are to be found everywhere and are recognizable everywhere; subjective because they are lived and are nothing if man does not live them, that is, freely determine his existence with reference to them. And though the configurations may differ, at least none of them are completely strange to me, because they all appear as attempts either to pass beyond these limits or recede from them or deny them or adapt to them. Consequently, every configuration, however individual it may be, has a universal value.

Every configuration, even the Chinese, the Indian, or the Negro, can be understood by a Westerner. "Can be understood" means that by virtue of a situation that he can imagine, a European of 1945 can, in like manner, push himself to his limits and reconstitute within himself the configuration of the Chinese, the Indian, or the African. Every configuration has universality in the sense that every configuration can be understood by every man. This does not at all mean that this configuration defines man forever, but that it can be met with again. There is always a way to understand the idiot, the child, the savage, the foreigner, provided one has the necessary information.

In this sense we may say that there is a universality of man; but it is not given, it is perpetually being made. I build the universal in choosing myself; I build it in understanding the configuration of every other man, whatever age he might have lived in. This absoluteness of choice does not do away with the relativeness of each epoch. At heart, what existentialism shows is the connection between the absolute character of free involvement, by virtue of which every man realizes himself in realizing a type of mankind, an involvement always comprehensible in any age whatsoever and by any person whosoever, and the relativeness of the cultural ensemble which may result from such a choice; it must be stressed that the relativity of Cartesianism and the absolute character of Cartesian involvement go together. In this sense, you may, if you like, say that each of us performs an absolute act in breathing, eating, sleeping, or behaving in any way whatever. There is no difference between being free, like a configuration, like an existence which chooses its essence, and being absolute. There is no difference between being an absolute temporarily localized, that is, localized in history, and being universally comprehensible.

This does not entirely settle the objection to subjectivism. In fact, the objection still takes several forms. First, there is the following: we are told, "So you're able to do anything, no matter what!" This is expressed in various ways. First we are accused of anarchy; then they say, "You're unable to pass judgment on others, because there's no reason to prefer one configuration to another"; finally they tell us, "Everything is arbitrary in this choosing of yours. You take something from one pocket and pretend you're putting it into the other."

These three objections aren't very serious. Take the first objection. "You're able to do anything, no matter what" is not to the point. In one sense choice is possible, but what is not possible is not to choose. I can always choose, but I ought to know that if I do not choose, I am still choosing. Though this may seem purely formal, it is highly important for keeping fantasy and caprice within bounds. If it is true that in facing a situation, for example, one in which, as a person capable of having sexual relations, of having children, I am obliged to choose an attitude, and if I in any way assume responsibility for a choice which, in involving myself, also involves all mankind, this has nothing to do with caprice, even if no *a priori* value determines my choice.

If anybody thinks that he recognizes here Gide's theory of the arbitrary act, he fails to see the enormous difference between this doctrine and Gide's. Gide does not know what a situation is. He acts out of pure caprice. For us, on the contrary, man is in an organized situation in which he himself is involved. Through his choice, he involves all mankind, and he can not avoid making a choice: either he will remain chaste, or he will marry without having children, or he will marry and have children; anyhow, whatever he may do, it is impossible for him not to take full responsibility for the way he handles this problem. Doubtless, he chooses without referring to preestablished values, but it is unfair to accuse him of caprice. Instead, let us say that moral choice is to be compared to the making of a work of art. And before going any further, let it be said at once that we are not dealing here with an aesthetic ethics, because our opponents are so dishonest that they even accuse us of that. The example I've chosen is a comparison only.

Having said that, may I ask whether anyone has ever accused an artist who has painted a picture of not having drawn his inspiration from rules set up *a priori*? Has anyone ever asked, "What painting ought he to make?" It is clearly understood that there is no definite painting to be made, that the artist is engaged in the making of his painting, and that the painting to be made is precisely the painting he will have made. It is clearly understood that there are no *a priori* aesthetic values, but that there are values which appear subsequently in the coherence of the painting, in the correspondence between what the artist intended and the result. Nobody can tell what the painting of tomorrow will be like. Painting can be judged only after it has once been made. What connection does that have with ethics? We are in the same creative situation. We never say that a work of art is arbitrary. When we speak of a canvas of Picasso, we never say that it is arbitrary; we understand quite well that he was making himself what he is at the very time he was painting, that the ensemble of his work is embodied in his life.

The same holds on the ethical plane. What art and ethics have in common is that we have creation and invention in both cases. We can not decide *a priori* what there is to be done. I think that I pointed that out quite sufficiently when I mentioned the case of the student who came to see me, and who might have applied to all the ethical systems, Kantian or otherwise, without getting any sort of guidance. He was obliged to devise his law himself. Never let it be said by us that this man—who, taking affection, individual action, and kindheartedness toward a specific person as his ethical first principle, chooses to remain with his mother, or who, preferring to make a sacrifice, chooses to go to England—has made an arbitrary choice. Man makes himself. He isn't ready made at the start. In choosing his ethics, he makes himself, and force of circumstances is such that he can not abstain from choosing one. We define man only in relationship to involvement. It is therefore absurd to charge us with arbitrariness of choice.

In the second place, it is said that we are unable to pass judgment on others. In a way this is true, and in another way, false. It is true in this sense, that, whenever a man sanely and sincerely involves himself and chooses his configuration, it is impossible for him to prefer another configuration, regardless of what his own may be in other respects. It is true in this sense, that we do not believe in progress. Progress is betterment. Man is always the same. The situation confronting him varies. Choice always remains a choice in a situation. The problem has not changed since the time one could choose between those for and those against slavery, for example, at the time of the Civil War, and the present time, when one can side with the Maquis Resistance Party, or with the Communists.

But, nevertheless, one can still pass judgment, for, as I have said, one makes a choice in relationship to others. First, one can judge (and this is perhaps not a judgment of value, but a logical judgment) that certain choices are based on error and others on truth. If we have defined man's situation as a free choice, with no excuses and no recourse, every man who takes refuge behind the excuse of his passions, every man who sets up a determinism, is a dishonest man.

The objection may be raised, "But why mayn't he choose himself dishonestly?" I reply that I am not obliged to pass moral judgment on him, but that I do define his dishonesty as an error. One can not help considering the truth of the matter. Dishonesty is obviously a falsehood because it belies the complete freedom of involvement. On the same grounds, I maintain that there is also dishonesty if I choose to state that certain values exist prior to me; it is self-contradictory for me to want them and at the same state that they are imposed on me. Suppose someone says to me, "What if I want to be dishonest?" I'll answer, "There's no reason for you not to be, but I'm saying that that's what you are, and that the strictly coherent attitude is that of honesty."

Besides, I can bring moral judgment to bear. When I declare that freedom in every concrete circumstance can have no other aim than to want itself, if man has once become aware that in his forlornness he imposes values, he can no longer want but one thing, and that is freedom, as the basis of all values. That doesn't mean that he wants it in the abstract. It means simply that the ultimate meaning of the acts of honest men is the quest for freedom as such. A man who belongs to a communist or revolutionary union wants concrete goals; these goals imply an abstract desire for freedom; but this freedom is wanted in something concrete. We want freedom for freedom's sake and in every particular circumstance. And in wanting freedom we discover that it depends entirely on the freedom of others, and that the freedom of others depends on ours. Of course, freedom as the definition of man does not depend on others, but as soon as there is involvement, I am obliged to want others to have freedom at the same time that I want my own freedom. I can take freedom as my goal only if I take that of others as a goal as well. Consequently, when, in all honesty, I've recognized that man is a being in whom existence precedes essence, that he is a free being who, in various circumstances, can want only his freedom, I have at the same time recognized that I can want only the freedom of others.

Therefore, in the name of this will for freedom, which freedom itself implies, I may pass judgment on those who seek to hide from themselves the complete arbitrariness and the complete freedom of their existence. Those who hide their complete freedom from themselves out of a spirit of seriousness or by means of deterministic excuses, I shall call cowards; those who try to show that their existence was necessary, when it is the very contingency of man's appearance on earth, I shall call stinkers. But cowards or stinkers can be judged only from a strictly unbiased point of view.

Therefore though the content of ethics is variable, a certain form of it is universal. Kant says that freedom desires both itself and the freedom of others. Granted. But he believes that the formal and the universal are enough to constitute an ethics. We, on the other hand, think that principles which are too abstract run aground in trying to decide action. Once again, take the case of the student. In the name of what, in the name of what great moral maxim do you think he could have decided, in perfect peace of mind, to abandon his mother or to stay with her? There is no way of judging. The content is always concrete and thereby unforeseeable; there is always the element of invention. The one thing that counts is knowing whether the inventing that has been done has been done in the name of freedom.

For example, let us look at the following two cases. You will see to what extent they correspond, yet differ. Take *The Mill on the Floss*. We find a certain young girl, Maggie Tulliver, who is an embodiment of the value of passion and who is aware of it. She is in love with a young man, Stephen, who is engaged to an insignificant young girl. This Maggie Tulliver, instead of heedlessly preferring her own happiness, chooses, in the name of human solidarity, to sacrifice herself and give up the man she loves. On the other hand, Sanseverina, in *The Charterhouse of Parma*, believing that passion is man's true value, would say that a great love deserves sacrifices; that it is to be preferred to the banality of the conjugal love that would tie Stephen to the young ninny he had to marry. She would choose to sacrifice the girl and fulfill her happiness; and, as Stendhal shows, she is even ready to sacrifice herself for the sake of passion, if this life demands it. Here we are in the presence of two strictly opposed moralities. I claim that they are much the same thing; in both cases what has been set up as the goal is freedom.

You can imagine two highly similar attitudes: one girl prefers to renounce her love out of resignation; another prefers to disregard the prior attachment of the man she loves out of sexual desire. On the surface these two actions resemble those we've just described. However, they are completely different. Sanseverina's attitude is much nearer that of Maggie Tulliver, one of heedless rapacity.

Thus, you see that the second charge is true and, at the same time, false. One may choose anything if it is on the grounds of free involvement.

The third objection is the following: "You take something from one pocket and put it into the other. That is, fundamentally, values aren't serious, since you choose them." My answer to this is that I'm quite vexed that that's the way it is; but if I've discarded God the Father, there has to be someone to invent values. You've got to take things as they are. Moreover, to say that we invent values means nothing else but this: life has no meaning *a priori*. Before you come alive, life is nothing; it's up to you to give it a meaning, and value is nothing else but the meaning that you choose. In that way, you see, there is a possibility of creating a human community.

I've been reproached for asking whether existentialism is humanistic. It's been said, "But you said in *Nausea* that the humanists were all wrong. You made fun of a certain kind of humanist. Why come back to it now?" Actually, the word humanism has two very different meanings. By humanism one can mean a theory which takes man as an end and as a higher value. Humanism in this sense can be found in Cocteau's tale *Around the World in Eighty Hours* when a character, because he is flying over some mountains in an airplane, declares, "Man is simply amazing." That means that I, who did not build the airplanes, shall personally benefit from these particular inventions, and that I, as man, shall personally consider myself responsible for, and honored by, acts of a few particular men. This would imply that we ascribe a value to man on the basis of the highest deeds of certain men. This humanism is absurd, because only the dog or the horse would be able to make such an overall judgment about man, which they are careful not to do, at least to my knowledge.

But it can not be granted that a man may make a judgment about man. Existentialism spares him from any such judgment. The existentialist will never consider man as an end because he is always in the making. Nor should we believe that there is a mankind to which we might set up a cult in the manner of Auguste Comte. The cult of mankind ends in the self-enclosed humanism of Comte, and, let it be said, of fascism. This kind of humanism we can do without.

But there is another meaning of humanism. Fundamentally it is this: man is constantly outside of himself; in projecting himself, in losing himself outside of himself, he makes for man's existing; and, on the other hand, it is by pursuing transcendent goals that he is able to exist; man, being this state of passing-beyond, and seizing upon things only as they bear upon this passing-beyond, is at the heart, at the center of this passing-beyond. There is no universe other than a human universe, the universe of human subjectivity. This connection between transcendency, as a constituent element of man—not in the sense that God is transcendent, but in the sense of passing beyond—and subjectivity, in the sense that man is not closed in on himself but is always present in a human universe, is what we call existentialism humanism. Humanism, because we remind man that there is no law-maker other than himself, and that in his forlornness he will decide by himself; because we point out that man will fulfill himself as man, not in turning toward himself, but in seeking outside of himself a goal which is just this liberation, just this particular fulfillment.

From these few reflections it is evident that nothing is more unjust than the objections that have been raised against us. Existentialism is nothing else than an attempt to draw all the consequences of a coherent atheistic position. It isn't trying to plunge man into despair at all. But if one calls every attitude of unbelief despair, like the Christians, then the word is not being used in its original sense. Existentialism isn't so atheistic that it wears itself out showing that God doesn't exist. Rather, it declares that even if God did exist, that would change nothing. There you've got our point of view. Not that we believe that God exists, but we think that the problem of His existence is not the issue. In this sense existentialism is optimistic, a doctrine of action, and it is plain dishonesty for Christians to make no distinction between their own despair and ours and then to call us despairing.

SIMONE DE BEAUVOIR
1908–1986

Simone Lucie Ernestine Marie Bertrand de Beauvoir was the elder of two daughters born to attorney Georges Bertrand de Beauvoir and Françoise Brasseur de Beauvoir. The noble-sounding "de" in their name indicated some family prestige, but they were only comfortable, not wealthy. Apart from a five-year period during adulthood, de Beauvoir spent her entire life in the Montparnasse district of Paris. Her mother was a devout Catholic, and as a young girl de Beauvoir regularly attended church and went to confession. She studied in a Catholic school and considered God her personal companion. However, by adolescence she had given up her faith. She later recounted that this loss of belief was both freeing and terrifying: "Alone: for the first time I understood the terrible significance of that word. Alone: without a witness, without anyone to speak to, without refuge."

After the First World War, de Beauvoir's father suffered financial setbacks. He was forced to tell his daughters he could not provide them a dowry and concluded, "My dears, you'll never marry; you'll have to work for your livings." De Beauvoir decided to pursue a career as a philosophy teacher. She was drawn to philosophy because

It went straight to essentials. . . . I had always wanted to know *everything;* philosophy would allow me to satisfy this desire, for it aimed at total reality.*

*Simone de Beauvoir, *Memoirs of a Dutiful Daughter* (NY: Harper & Row, 1959), p. 158.

259

She enrolled at the Institut Sainte-Marie in 1925 and studied there for the next four years, simultaneously hearing lectures at the Institut Catholique and the Sorbonne.

In 1929, de Beauvoir met Jean-Paul Sartre and studied with him for the *agrégation* in philosophy (which he had failed the previous year). After both passed the examination with high honors, she agreed to a "two-year lease" relationship with Sartre. During this period she was an assistant at a lycée in Paris. In 1931, de Beauvoir accepted a full-time position at a lycée in Marseille and a year later moved to nearby Rouen. Though Sartre took a similar position at a lycée in Le Havre, on the opposite side of the country, their relationship continued. In fact, their "two-year lease" became a lifelong companionship, though they never married and were free to have "contingent" relationships.

By 1936, de Beauvoir was back in her beloved Montparnasse, Paris. For the next eight years, she taught at various lycées in Paris until the involvement of a student in her unusual life-style led to charges of corrupting a minor, and she was suspended. Though reinstated, she resigned in 1944 and supported herself for the rest of her life by her writings. Her first novel, *She Came to Stay,* was published that year to critical acclaim and financial success. She was heralded (with Albert Camus and Sartre) as one of the leaders of the new existentialist movement. The following year with Maurice Merleau-Ponty and Sartre she founded the influential journal *Les Temps modernes* and served as an editor and contributor to the magazine.

In her later years, de Beauvoir became increasingly involved in political issues. With Sartre, she visited Cuba, attended the International War Crimes Tribunal on U.S. War Crimes in Vietnam, and joined the student demonstrations at the Sorbonne. On her own, she worked vigorously for such feminist issues as legalized abortion and care for unmarried mothers. While leading the involved life of a left-wing political activist, de Beauvoir published a total of five novels, two collections of stories, and a play. She also published five volumes of memoirs, giving a picture of France in the twentieth century and of her relationship to Sartre. But de Beauvoir is best known for her philosophical works, especially the groundbreaking feminist text *The Second Sex* (1949).

*   *   *

The Second Sex is actually two separate volumes united around the question, "What is woman?" The first section, entitled "Facts and Myths," explores biology, psychology, sociology, history, myth, and literature to explain the answers given to this basic question. The second section, "Woman's Life Today," focuses on women's various roles and explores ways to move beyond these roles.

In the introduction to the work, reprinted here in the H.M. Parshley translation, de Beauvoir presents the basic categories that will guide her exploration of what it means to be woman. According to de Beauvoir, woman is the "second sex" because she is defined by man. Borrowing terminology from Sartre, she claims, "He is the Subject, he is the Absolute—she is the Other." Man sets himself up as the standard, the "One"—the definition of what it is to be human—so that immediately woman becomes the "Other." As the "Other," woman is relegated to existence as *"en-soi"*: a being-in-itself, an object. Woman is not able to exist as *"pour-soi,"* a being-for-itself. She cannot choose her existence because her role is already defined for her as the "Other."

De Beauvoir goes on to ask why women allow this to happen: "Why is it that women do not dispute male sovereignty?" After all, throughout history other groups have been treated as the "Other" and have redefined themselves. Why not women? Later in the book, de Beauvoir speculates that a woman's identity as the "Other" derives in part from her body—especially her reproductive capacity. But in our selection, she points outs that women have always (with rare exceptions) been subordinated to men, "and hence their dependency is not the result of a historical event or a social change—it was not something that *occurred*." Women have accepted their role as the "Other" because otherness "lacks the contingent or incidental nature of historical facts." Women have no past, no history of their own. They are not grouped together as women, they have no solidarity of employment since as a rule they work dispersed among men. In short, they do not have the "concrete means for organizing themselves into a unit which can stand face to face with the correlative unit."

The goal of *The Second Sex* is to move beyond analysis to a "concrete means" for organizing women. According to de Beauvoir, there must be two changes in order to accomplish this goal: (1) Women need to act as authentic subjects choosing their own histories and (2) society must be changed to make this possible. The first of these needed changes reflects de Beauvoir's existentialism, the second her Marxism.

Whereas traditionalists condemned the entire work, feminist critics raised questions about some of de Beauvoir's specific analyses. Many contemporary feminists claim that she did not go to the roots of patriarchy and its pervasive infection of even our language. Other feminists question her existentialist or Marxist assumptions (and her apparent hostility to the female body). But most feminists salute de Beauvoir for calling attention to feminist issues. As one writer put it, *The Second Sex* is for feminists "the base line from which other works either explicitly . . . or implicitly . . . take off."

*   *   *

There are several biographies of de Beauvoir, including Axel Madsen, *Hearts and Minds: The Common Journey of Simone de Beauvoir and Jean-Paul Sartre* (New York: Morrow, 1977); Carol Ascher, *Simone de Beauvoir: A Life of Freedom* (Boston: Beacon Press, 1981); Claude Francis, *Simone de Beauvoir: A Life, A Love Story,* translated by Lisa Nesselson (New York: St. Martin's Press, 1987); and the thorough Deirdre Bair, *Simone de Beauvoir: A Biography* (New York: Summit Books, 1990). General studies of her writings include Terry Keefe, *Simone de Beauvoir: A Study of Her Writings* (Totowa, NJ: Barnes & Noble, 1983); Judith Okely, *Simone de Beauvoir: A Re-reading* (London: Virago Press, 1986); Renee Winegarten, *Simone de Beauvoir: A Critical View* (New York: St. Martin's Press, 1988); Catharine Savage Brosman, *Simone de Beauvoir Revisited* (Boston: Twayne, 1991); and Margaret Crosland, *Simone de Beauvoir: The Woman and Her Work* (London: Heinemann, 1992). For material on her feminist theories specifically, see Jean Leighton, *Simone de Beauvoir on Woman* (Rutherford, NJ: Fairleigh Dickinson University Press, 1975); Mary Evans, *Simone de Beauvoir: A Feminist Mandarin* (London: Tavistock, 1985); Rosemarie Tong, *Feminist Thought: A Comprehensive Introduction* (Boulder, CO: Westview Press, 1989); Toril Moi, *Feminist Theory & Simone de Beauvoir* (Oxford: Blackwell, 1990); Margaret A. Simons, ed., *Feminist Interpretations of Simone* de Beauvoir (College Park, PA: Pennsylvania State University Press, 1995); and Debra B. Bergoffen, *The Philosophy of Simone de Beauvoir: Gendered Phenomenologies, Erotic Generosities* (Albany, NY: SUNY Press, 1996). Alice Schwarzer, *After "The Second Sex": Conversations with Simone de Beauvoir* (New York: Pantheon Books, 1984), gives de Beauvoir's reflections on her classic, whereas Donald L. Hatcher, *Understanding "The Second Sex"* (New York: Peter Lang, 1984) provides a philosophical appraisal of that work.

THE SECOND SEX (in part)

Introduction

For a long time I have hesitated to write a book on woman. The subject is irritating, especially to women; and it is not new. Enough ink has been spilled in the quarreling over feminism, now practically over, and perhaps we should say no more about it. It is still talked about, however, for the voluminous nonsense uttered during the last century seems to have done little to illuminate the problem. After all, is there a problem? And if so, what is it? Are there women, really? Most assuredly the theory of the eternal feminine still has its adherents who will whisper in your ear: "Even in Russia women still are *women*"; and other erudite persons—sometimes the very same—say with a sigh: "Woman is losing her way, woman is lost." One wonders if women still exist, if they will always exist, whether or not it is desirable that they should, what place they occupy in this world, what their place should be. "What has become of women?" was asked recently in an ephemeral magazine.

But first we must ask: what is a woman? "*Tota mulier in utero*," says one, "woman is a womb." But in speaking of certain women, connoisseurs declare that they are not women, although they are equipped with a uterus like the rest. All agree in recognizing the fact that females exist in the human species; today as always they make up about one half of humanity. And yet we are told that femininity is in danger; we are exhorted to be women, remain women, become women. It would appear, then, that every female human being is not necessarily a woman; to be so considered she must share in that mysterious and threatened reality known as femininity. Is this attribute something secreted by the ovaries? Or is it a Platonic essence, a product of the philosophic imagination? Is a rustling petticoat enough to bring it down to earth? Although some women try zealously to incarnate this essence, it is hardly patentable. It is frequently described in vague and dazzling terms that seem to have been borrowed from the vocabulary of the seers, and indeed in the times of St. Thomas it was considered an essence as certainly defined as the somniferous virtue of the poppy.

But conceptualism has lost ground. The biological and social sciences no longer admit the existence of unchangeably fixed entities that determine given characteristics, such as those ascribed to woman, the Jew, or the Negro. Science regards any characteristic as a reaction dependent in part upon a *situation.* If today femininity no longer exists, then it never existed. But does the word *woman,* then, have no specific content? This is stoutly affirmed by those who hold to the philosophy of the enlightenment, of rationalism, of nominalism; women, to them, are merely the human beings arbitrarily designated by the word woman. Many American women particularly are prepared to think that there is no longer any place for woman as such; if a backward individual still takes herself for a woman, her friends advise her to be psychoanalyzed and thus get rid of this obsession. In regard to a work, *Modern Woman: The Lost Sex,* which in other respects has its irritating features, Dorothy Parker has written: "I cannot be just to books which treat of woman as woman. . . . My idea is that all of us, men as well as women, should be regarded as human beings." But nominalism is a rather inadequate doctrine, and the antifemininists have had no trouble in showing that women simply *are not* men. Surely woman is, like man, a human being; but such a declaration is abstract. The fact is that every concrete human being is always a singular, separate individual. To decline to accept such notions as the eternal feminine, the black soul, the Jewish character, is not to deny that Jews, Negroes, women exist today—this denial does not represent a liberation for those concerned, but rather a flight from reality. Some years ago a well-known woman writer refused to permit her portrait to appear in a series of photographs especially devoted to women writers; she wished to be counted among the men. But in order to gain this privilege she made use of her husband's influence! Women who assert that they are men lay claim none the less to masculine consideration and respect. I recall also a young Trotskyite standing on a platform at a boisterous meeting and getting ready to use her fists, in spite of her evident fragility. She was denying her feminine weakness; but it was for love of a militant male whose equal she wished to be. The attitude of defiance of many American women proves that they are haunted by a sense of their femininity. In truth, to go for a walk with one's eyes open is enough to demonstrate that humanity is divided into two classes of individuals whose clothes, faces, bodies, smiles, gaits, interests, and occupations are manifestly different. Perhaps these differences are superficial, perhaps they are destined to disappear. What is certain is that right now they do most obviously exist.

If her functioning as a female is not enough to define woman, if we decline also to explain her through "the eternal feminine," and if nevertheless we admit, provisionally, that women do exist, then we must face the question: what is a woman?

To state the question is, to me, to suggest, at once, a preliminary answer. The fact that I ask it is in itself significant. A man would never get the notion of writing a book on the peculiar situation of the human male. But if I wish to define myself, I must first of all say: "I am a woman"; on this truth must be based all further discussion. A man never begins by presenting himself as an individual of a certain sex; it goes without saying that he is a man. The terms *masculine* and *feminine* are used symmetrically only as a matter of form, as on legal papers. In actuality the relation of the two sexes is not quite like that of two electrical poles, for man represents both the positive and the neutral, as is indicated by the common use of man to designate human beings in general; whereas woman represents only the negative, defined by limiting criteria, without reciprocity. In the midst of an abstract discussion it is vexing to hear a man say: "You think thus and so because you are a woman"; but I know that my only defense is to reply: "I think thus and so because it is true," thereby removing my subjective self from the argument. It would be out of the question to reply: "And you think the contrary because you are a man," for it is understood that the fact of being a man is no peculiarity. A man is in the right in being a man; it is the woman who is in the wrong. It amounts to this: just as for the ancients there was an absolute vertical with reference to which the oblique was defined, so there is an absolute human type, the masculine. Woman has ovaries, a uterus; these peculiarities imprison her in her subjectivity, circumscribe her within the limits of her own nature. It is often said that she thinks with her glands. Man superbly ignores the fact that his anatomy also includes glands, such as the testicles, and that they secrete hormones. He thinks of his body as a direct and normal connection with the world, which he believes he apprehends objectively, whereas he regards the body of woman as a hindrance, a prison, weighed down by everything peculiar to it. "The female is a female by virtue of a certain *lack* of qualities," said Aristotle; "we should regard the female nature as afflicted with a natural defectiveness." And St. Thomas for his part pronounced woman to be an "imperfect man," an "incidental" being. This is symbolized in Genesis where Eve is depicted as made from what Bossuet called "a supernumerary bone" of Adam.

Thus humanity is male and man defines woman not in herself but as relative to him; she is not regarded as an autonomous being. Michelet writes: "Woman, the relative being. . . ." And Benda is most positive in his *Rapport d'Uriel: "The body of man makes sense in itself quite apart from that of woman, whereas the latter seems wanting in significance by itself. . . . Man can think of himself without woman. She cannot think of herself without man." And she is simply what man decrees;* thus she is called "the sex," by which is meant that she appears essentially to the male as a sexual being. For him she is sex—absolute sex, no less. She is defined and differentiated with reference to man and not he with reference to her; she is the incidental, the inessential as opposed to the essential. He is the Subject, he is the Absolute—she is the Other.*

The category of the Other is as primordial as consciousness itself. In the most primitive societies, in the most ancient mythologies, one finds the expression of a duality—that of the Self and the Other. This duality was not originally attached to the division of the sexes; it was not dependent upon any empirical facts. It is revealed in such works as that of Granet on Chinese thought and those of Dumezil on the East Indies and Rome. The feminine element was at first no more involved in such pairs as Varuna-Mitra, Uranus-Zeus, Sun-Moon, and Day-Night than it was in the contrasts between Good and Evil, lucky and unlucky auspices, right and left, God and Lucifer. Otherness is a fundamental category of human thought.

Thus it is that no group ever sets itself up as the One without at once setting up the Other over against itself. If three travelers chance to occupy the same compartment, that is enough to make vaguely hostile "others" out of all the rest of the passengers on

---

*L. Lévinas expresses this idea most explicitly in his essay *Temps et l'Autre.* "Is there not a case in which otherness, alterity *[altérité],* unquestionably marks the nature of a being, as its essence, an instance of otherness not consisting purely and simply in the opposition of two species of the same genus? I think that the feminine represents the contrary in its absolute sense, this contrariness being in no wise affected by any relation between it and its correlative and thus remaining absolutely other. Sex is not a certain specific difference . . . no more is the sexual difference a mere contradiction. . . . Nor does this difference lie in the duality of two complementary terms, for two complementary terms imply a pre-existing whole. . . . Otherness reaches its full flowering in the feminine, a term of the same rank as consciousness but of opposite meaning."

I suppose that Lévinas does not forget that woman, too, is aware of her own consciousness, or ego. But it is striking that he deliberately takes a man's point of view, disregarding the reciprocity of subject and object. When he writes that woman is mystery, he implies that she is mystery for man. Thus his description, which is intended to be objective, is in fact an assertion of masculine privilege.

the train. In small-town eyes all persons not belonging to the village are "strangers" and suspect; to the native of a country all who inhabit other countries are "foreigners"; Jews are "different" for the anti-Semite, Negroes are "inferior" for American racists, aborigines are "natives" for colonists, proletarians are the "lower class" for the privileged.

Lévi-Strauss, at the end of a profound work on the various forms of primitive societies, reaches the following conclusion: "Passage from the state of Nature to the state of Culture is marked by man's ability to view biological relations as a series of contrasts; duality, alternation, opposition, and symmetry, whether under definite or vague forms, constitute not so much phenomena to be explained as fundamental and immediately given data of social reality." These phenomena would be incomprehensible if in fact human society were simply a *Mitsein* or fellowship based on solidarity and friendliness. Things become clear, on the contrary, if, following Hegel, we find in consciousness itself a fundamental hostility toward every other consciousness; the subject can be posed only in being opposed—he sets himself up as the essential, as opposed to the other, the inessential, the object.

But the other consciousness, the other ego, sets up a reciprocal claim. The native traveling abroad is shocked to find himself in turn regarded as a "stranger" by the natives of neighboring countries. As a matter of fact, wars, festivals, trading, treaties, and contests among tribes, nations, and classes tend to deprive the concept *Other* of its absolute sense and to make manifest its relativity; willy-nilly, individuals and groups are forced to realize the reciprocity of their relations. How is it, then, that this reciprocity has not been recognized between the sexes, that one of the contrasting terms is set up as the sole essential, denying any relativity in regard to its correlative and defining the latter as pure otherness? Why is it that women do not dispute male sovereignty? No subject will readily volunteer to become the object, the inessential; it is not the Other who, in defining himself as the Other, establishes the One. The Other is posed as such by the One in defining himself as the One. But if the Other is not to regain the status of being the One, he must be submissive enough to accept this alien point of view. Whence comes this submission in the case of woman?

There are, to be sure, other cases in which a certain category has been able to dominate another completely for a time. Very often this privilege depends upon inequality of numbers—the majority imposes its rule upon the minority or persecutes it. But women are not a minority, like the American Negroes or the Jews; there are as many women as men on earth. Again, the two groups concerned have often been originally independent; they may have been formerly unaware of each other's existence, or perhaps they recognized each other's autonomy. But a historical event has resulted in the subjugation of the weaker by the stronger. The scattering of the Jews, the introduction of slavery into America, the conquests of imperialism are examples in point. In these cases the oppressed retained at least the memory of former days; they possessed in common a past, a tradition, sometimes a religion or a culture.

The parallel drawn by Bebel between women and the proletariat is valid in that neither ever formed a minority or a separate collective unit of mankind. And instead of a single historical event it is in both cases a historical development that explains their status as a class and accounts for the membership of *particular individuals* in that class. But proletarians have not always existed, whereas there have always been women. They are women in virtue of their anatomy and physiology. Throughout history they have always been subordinated to men, and hence their dependency is not the result of a historical event or a social change—it was not something that *occurred*. The reason why otherness in this case seems to be an absolute is in part that it lacks the contingent or incidental nature of historical facts. A condition brought about at a certain time can be abolished at some other time, as the Negroes of Haiti and others have proved; but it might seem that a natural condition is beyond the possibility of change. In truth, however, the nature of things is no more immutably given, once for all, than is historical reality. If woman seems to be the inessential which never becomes the essential, it is because she herself fails to bring about this change. Proletarians say "We"; Negroes also. Regarding themselves as subjects, they transform the bourgeois, the whites, into "others." But women do not say "We," except at some congress of feminists or similar formal demonstration; men say "women," and women use the same word in referring to themselves. They do not authentically assume a subjective attitude. The proletarians have accomplished the revolution in Russia, the Negroes in Haiti, the Indo-Chinese are battling for it in Indo-China; but the women's effort has never been anything more than a symbolic agitation. They have gained only what men have been willing to grant; they have taken nothing, they have only received.

The reason for this is that women lack concrete means for organizing themselves into a unit which can stand face to face with the correlative unit. They have no past, no history, no religion of their own; and they have no such solidarity of work and interest as that of the proletariat. They are not even promiscuously herded together in the way that creates community feeling among the American Negroes, the ghetto Jews, the workers of Saint-Denis, or the factory hands of Renault. They live dispersed among the males, attached through residence, housework, economic condition, and social standing to certain men—fathers or husbands—more firmly than they are to other women. If they belong to the bourgeoisie, they feel solidarity with men of that class, not with proletarian women; if they are white, their allegiance is to white men, not to Negro women. The proletariat can propose to massacre the ruling class, and a sufficiently fanatical Jew or Negro might dream of getting sole possession of the atomic bomb and making humanity wholly Jewish or black; but woman cannot even dream of exterminating the males. The bond that unites her to her oppressors is not comparable to any other. The division of the sexes is a biological fact, not an event in human history. Male and female stand opposed within a primordial *Mitsein,* and woman has not broken it. The couple is a fundamental unity with its two halves riveted together, and the cleavage of society along the line of sex is impossible. Here is to be found the basic trait of woman: she is the Other in a totality of which the two components are necessary to one another.

One could suppose that this reciprocity might have facilitated the liberation of woman. When Hercules sat at the feet of Omphale and helped with her spinning, his desire for her held him captive; but why did she fail to gain a lasting power? To revenge herself on Jason, Medea killed their children; and this grim legend would seem to suggest that she might have obtained a formidable influence over him through his love for his offspring. In *Lysistrata* Aristophanes gaily depicts a band of women who joined forces to gain social ends through the sexual needs of their men; but this is only a play. In the legend of the Sabine women, the latter soon abandoned their plan of remaining sterile to punish their ravishers. In truth woman has not been socially emancipated through man's need—sexual desire and the desire for offspring—which makes the male dependent for satisfaction upon the female.

Master and slave, also, are united by a reciprocal need, in this case economic, which does not liberate the slave. In the relation of master to slave the master does not make a point of the need that he has for the other; he has in his grasp the power of satisfying this need through his own action; whereas the slave, in his dependent condition, his hope and fear, is quite conscious of the need he has for his master. Even if the

Migrant Mother, 1936, by Dorothea Lange (1895–1965). This powerful photograph of a migrant mother in central California reveals both anxiety and strength. *(The Oakland Museum)*

need is at bottom equally urgent for both, it always works in favor of the oppressor and against the oppressed. That is why the liberation of the working class, for example, has been slow.

Now, woman has always been man's dependent, if not his slave; the two sexes have never shared the world in equality. And even today woman is heavily handicapped, though her situation is beginning to change. Almost nowhere is her legal status the same as man's, and frequently it is much to her disadvantage. Even when her rights are legally recognized in the abstract, long-standing custom prevents their full expression in the mores. In the economic sphere men and women can almost be said to make up two castes; other things being equal, the former hold the better jobs, get higher wages, and have more opportunity for success than their new competitors. In industry and politics men have a great many more positions and they monopolize the most important posts. In addition to all this, they enjoy a traditional prestige that the education of children tends in every way to support, for the present enshrines the past—and in the past all history has been made by men. At the present time, when women are beginning to take part in the affairs of the world, it is still a world that belongs to men—they have no doubt of it at all and women have scarcely any. To decline to be the Other, to refuse to be a party to the deal—this would be for women to renounce all the advantages conferred upon them by their alliance with the superior caste. Man-the-sovereign will provide woman-the-liege with material protection and will undertake the moral justification of her existence; thus she can evade at once both economic risk and the metaphysical risk of a liberty in which ends and aims must be contrived without assistance. Indeed, along with the ethical urge of each individual to affirm his subjective existence, there is also the temptation to forgo liberty and become a thing. This is an inauspicious road, for he who takes it—passive, lost, ruined—becomes henceforth the creature of another's will, frustrated in his transcendence and deprived of every value. But it is an easy road; on it one avoids the strain involved in undertaking an authentic existence. When man makes of woman the *Other,* he may, then, expect her to manifest deep-seated tendencies toward complicity. Thus, woman may fail to lay claim to the status of subject because she lacks definite resources, because she feels the necessary bond that ties her to man regardless of reciprocity, and because she is often very well pleased with her role as the *Other.*

But it will be asked at once: how did all this begin? It is easy to see that the duality of the sexes, like any duality, gives rise to conflict. And doubtless the winner will assume the status of absolute. But why should man have won from the start? It seems possible that women could have won the victory; or that the outcome of the conflict might never have been decided. How is it that this world has always belonged to the men and that things have begun to change only recently? Is this change a good thing? Will it bring about an equal sharing of the world between men and women?

These questions are not new, and they have often been answered. But the very fact that woman *is the Other* tends to cast suspicion upon all the justifications that men have ever been able to provide for it. These have all too evidently been dictated by men's interest. A little-known feminist of the seventeenth century, Poulain de la Barre, put it this way: "All that has been written about women by men should be suspect, for the men are at once judge and party to the lawsuit." Everywhere, at all times, the males have displayed their satisfaction in feeling that they are the lords of creation. "Blessed be God . . . that He did not make me a woman," say the Jews in their morning prayers, while their wives pray on a note of resignation: "Blessed be the Lord, who created me according to His will." The first among the blessings for which Plato thanked the gods was that he had been created free, not enslaved; the second, a man, not a woman. But the males could not enjoy this privilege fully unless they believed it to be founded on the absolute and the eternal; they sought to make the fact of their supremacy into a right. "Being men, those who have made and compiled the laws have favored their own sex, and jurists have elevated these laws into principles," to quote Poulain de la Barre once more.

Legislators, priests, philosophers, writers, and scientists have striven to show that the subordinate position of woman is willed in heaven and advantageous on earth. The religions invented by men reflect this wish for domination. In the legends of Eve and Pandora men have taken up arms against women. They have made use of philosophy and theology, as the quotations from Aristotle and St. Thomas have shown. Since ancient times satirists and moralists have delighted in showing up the weaknesses of women. We are familiar with the savage indictments hurled against women throughout French literature. Montherlant, for example, follows the tradition of Jean de Meung, though with less gusto. This hostility may at times be well founded, often it is gratuitous; but in truth it more or less successfully conceals a desire for self-justification. As Montaigne says, "It is easier to accuse one sex than to excuse the other." Sometimes what is going on is clear enough. For instance, the Roman law limiting the rights of woman cited "the imbecility, the instability of the sex" just when the weakening of family ties seemed to threaten the interests of male heirs. And in the effort to keep the married woman under guardianship, appeal was made in the sixteenth century to the authority of St. Augustine, who declared that "woman is a creature neither decisive nor constant," at a time when the single woman was thought capable of managing her property. Montaigne understood clearly how arbitrary and unjust was woman's appointed lot: "Women are not in the wrong when they decline to accept the rules laid down for them, since the men make these rules without consulting them. No wonder intrigue and strife abound." But he did not go so far as to champion their cause.

It was only later, in the eighteenth century, that genuinely democratic men began to view the matter objectively. Diderot, among others, strove to show that woman is, like man, a human being. Later John Stuart Mill came fervently to her defense. But these philosophers displayed unusual impartiality. In the nineteenth century the feminist quarrel became again a quarrel of partisans. One of the consequences of the industrial revolution was the entrance of women into productive labor, and it was just here that the claims of the feminists emerged from the realm of theory and acquired an economic basis, while their opponents became the more aggressive. Although landed property lost power to some extent, the bourgeoisie clung to the old morality that found the guarantee of private property in the solidity of the family. Woman was ordered back into the home the more harshly as her emancipation became a real menace. Even within the working class the men endeavored to restrain woman's liberation, because they began to see the women as dangerous competitors—the more so because they were accustomed to work for lower wages.

In proving woman's inferiority, the antifeminists then began to draw not only upon religion, philosophy, and theology, as before, but also upon science—biology, experimental psychology, etc. At most they were willing to grant "equality in difference" to the *other* sex. That profitable formula is most significant; it is precisely like the "equal but separate" formula of the Jim Crow laws aimed at the North American Negroes. As is well known, this socalled equalitarian segregation has resulted only in the most extreme discrimination. The similarity just noted is in no way due to chance, for whether it is a race, a caste, a class, or a sex that is reduced to a position of inferiority, the methods of justification are the same. "The eternal feminine" corresponds to "the black soul" and to "the Jewish character." True, the Jewish problem is on the whole very different from the other two—to the anti-Semite the Jew is not so much an inferior as he is an enemy for whom there is to be granted no place on earth, for whom annihilation is the fate desired. But there are deep similarities between the situation of woman and that of the Negro. Both are being emancipated today from a like paternalism, and the former master class wishes to "keep them in their place"—that is, the place chosen for them. In both cases the former masters lavish more or less sincere eulogies, either on the virtues of "the good Negro" with his dormant, childish, merry soul—the submissive Negro—or on the merits of the woman who is "truly feminine"—that is, frivolous, infantile, irresponsible—the submissive woman. In both cases the dominant class bases its argument on a state of affairs that it has itself created. As George Bernard Shaw puts it, in substance, "The American white relegates the black to the rank of shoeshine boy; and he concludes from this that the black is good for nothing but shining shoes." This vicious circle is met with in all analogous circumstances; when an individual (or a group of individuals) is kept in a situation of inferiority, the fact is that he is inferior. But the significance of the verb *to be* must be rightly understood here; it is in bad faith to give it a static value when it really has the dynamic Hegelian sense of "to have become." Yes, women on the whole *are* today inferior to men; that is, their situation affords them fewer possibilities. The question is: should that state of affairs continue?

Many men hope that it will continue; not all have given up the battle. The conservative bourgeoisie still see in the emancipation of women a menace to their morality and their interests. Some men dread feminine competition. Recently a male student wrote in the *Hebdo-Latin:* "Every woman student who goes into medicine or law robs us of a job." He never questioned his rights in this world. And economic interests are not the only ones concerned. One of the benefits that oppression confers upon the oppressors is that the most humble among them is made to *feel* superior; thus, a "poor white" in the South can console himself with the thought that he is not a "dirty nigger"—and the more prosperous whites cleverly exploit this pride.

Similarly, the most mediocre of males feels himself a demigod as compared with women. It was much easier for M. de Montherlant to think himself a hero when he faced women (and women chosen for his purpose) than when he was obliged to act the man among men—something many women have done better than he, for that matter. And in September 1948, in one of his articles in the *Figaro littéraire,* Claude Mauriac—whose great originality is admired by all—could write regarding woman: "We listen on a tone *[sic!]* of polite indifference . . . to the most brilliant among them, well knowing that her wit reflects more or less luminously ideas that come from *us.*" Evidently the speaker referred to is not reflecting the ideas of Mauriac himself, for no one knows of his having any. It may be that she reflects ideas originating with men, but then, even among men there are those who have been known to appropriate ideas not their own; and one can well ask whether Claude Mauriac might not find more interesting a conversation reflecting Descartes, Marx, or Gide rather than himself. What is really remarkable is that by using the questionable we he identifies himself with St. Paul, Hegel, Lenin, and Nietzsche, and from the lofty eminence of their grandeur looks down disdainfully upon the bevy of women who make bold to converse with him on a footing of equality. In truth, I know of more than one woman who would refuse to suffer with patience Mauriac's "tone of polite indifference."

I have lingered on this example because the masculine attitude is here displayed with disarming ingenuousness. But men profit in many more subtle ways from the otherness, the alterity of woman. Here is miraculous balm for those afflicted with an inferiority complex, and indeed no one is more arrogant toward women, more aggressive or scornful, than the man who is anxious about his virility. Those who are not fear-ridden in the presence of their fellow men are much more disposed to recognize a fellow creature in woman; but even to these the myth of Woman, the Other, is precious for many reasons.* They cannot be blamed for not cheerfully relinquishing all the benefits they derive from the myth, for they realize what they would lose in relinquishing woman as they fancy her to be, while they fail to realize what they have to gain from the woman of tomorrow. Refusal to pose oneself as the Subject, unique and absolute, requires great self-denial. Furthermore, the vast majority of men make no such claim explicitly. They do not *postulate* woman as inferior, for today they are too thoroughly imbued with the ideal of democracy not to recognize all human beings as equals.

In the bosom of the family, woman seems in the eyes of childhood and youth to be clothed in the same social dignity as the adult males. Later on, the young man, desiring and loving, experiences the resistance, the independence of the woman desired and loved; in marriage, he respects woman as wife and mother, and in the concrete events of conjugal life she stands there before him as a free being. He can therefore feel that social subordination as between the sexes no longer exists and that on the whole, in spite of differences, woman is an equal. As, however, he observes some points of inferiority—the most important being unfitness for the professions—he attributes these to natural causes. When he is in a co-operative and benevolent relation with woman, his theme is the principle of abstract equality, and he does not base his attitude upon such inequality as may exist. But when he is in conflict with her, the situation is reversed: his theme will be the existing inequality, and he will even take it as justification for denying abstract equality.**

So it is that many men will affirm as if in good faith that women *are* the equals of man and that they have nothing to clamor for, while *at the same* time they will say that women can never be the equals of man and that their demands are in vain. It is, in point of fact, a difficult matter for man to realize the extreme importance of social discriminations which seem outwardly insignificant but which produce in woman moral and intellectual effects so profound that they appear to spring from her original nature. The most sympathetic of men never fully comprehend woman's concrete situation. And there is no reason to put much trust in the men when they rush to the defense of privileges whose full extent they can hardly measure. We shall not, then, permit ourselves to be intimidated by the number and violence of the attacks launched against women, nor to be entrapped by the self-seeking eulogies bestowed on the "true woman," nor to profit by the enthusiasm for woman's destiny manifested by men who would not for the world have any part of it.

We should consider the arguments of the feminists with no less suspicion, however, for very often their controversial aim deprives them of all real value. If the "woman question" seems trivial, it is because masculine arrogance has made of it a "quarrel"; and when quarreling one no longer reasons well. People have tirelessly sought to prove that woman is superior, inferior, or equal to man. Some say that, having been created after Adam, she is evidently a secondary being; others say on the con-

---

*A significant article on this theme by Michel Carrouges appeared in No. 292 of the *Cahiers du Sud*. He writes indignantly: "Would that there were no woman-myth at all but only a cohort of cooks, matrons, prostitutes, and bluestockings serving functions of pleasure or usefulness!" That is to say, in his view woman has no existence in and for herself; he thinks only of her *function* in the male world. Her reason for existence lies in man. But then, in fact, her poetic "function" as a myth might be more valued than any other. The real problem is precisely to find out why woman should be defined with relation to man.

**For example, a man will say that he considers his wife in no wise degraded because she has no gainful occupation. The profession of housewife is just as lofty, and so on. But when the first quarrel comes, he will exclaim: "Why, you couldn't make your living without me!"

trary that Adam was only a rough draft and that God succeeded in producing the human being in perfection when He created Eve. Woman's brain is smaller; yes, but it is relatively larger. Christ was made a man; yes, but perhaps for his greater humility. Each argument at once suggests its opposite, and both are often fallacious. If we are to gain understanding, we must get out of these ruts; we must discard the vague notions of superiority, inferiority, equality which have hitherto corrupted every discussion of the subject and start afresh.

Very well, but just how shall we pose the question? And, to begin with, who are we to propound it at all? Man is at once judge and party to the case; but so is woman. What we need is an angel—neither man nor woman—but where shall we find one? Still, the angel would be poorly qualified to speak, for an angel is ignorant of all the basic facts involved in the problem. With a hermaphrodite we should be no better off, for here the situation is most peculiar; the hermaphrodite is not really the combination of a whole man and a whole woman, but consists of parts of each and thus is neither. It looks to me as if there are, after all, certain women who are best qualified to elucidate the situation of woman. Let us not be misled by the sophism that because Epimenides was a Cretan he was necessarily a liar; it is not a mysterious essence that compels men and women to act in good or in bad faith; it is their situation that inclines them more or less toward the search for truth. Many of today's women, fortunate in the restoration of all the privileges pertaining to the estate of the human being, can afford the luxury of impartiality—we even recognize its necessity. We are no longer like our partisan elders; by and large we have won the game. In recent debates on the status of women the United Nations has persistently maintained that the equality of the sexes is now becoming a reality, and already some of us have never had to sense in our femininity an inconvenience or an obstacle. Many problems appear to us to be more pressing than those which concern us in particular, and this detachment even allows us to hope that our attitude will be objective. Still, we know the feminine world more intimately than do the men because we have our roots in it, we grasp more immediately than do men what it means to a human being to be feminine; and we are more concerned with such knowledge. I have said that there are more pressing problems, but this does not prevent us from seeing some importance in asking how the fact of being women will affect our lives. What opportunities precisely have been given us and what withheld? What fate awaits our younger sisters, and what directions should they take? It is significant that books by women on women are in general animated in our day less by a wish to demand our rights than by an effort toward clarity and understanding. As we emerge from an era of excessive controversy, this book is offered as one attempt among others to confirm that statement.

But it is doubtless impossible to approach any human problem with a mind free from bias. The way in which questions are put, the points of view assumed, presuppose a relativity of interest; all characteristics imply values, and every objective description, so called, implies an ethical background. Rather than attempt to conceal principles more or less definitely implied, it is better to state them openly at the beginning. This will make it unnecessary to specify on every page in just what sense one uses such words as *superior, inferior, better, worse, progress, reaction,* and the like. If we survey some of the works on woman, we note that one of the points of view most frequently adopted is that of the public good, the general interest; and one always means by this the benefit of society as one wishes it to be maintained or established. For our part, we hold that the only public good is that which assures the private good of the citizens; we shall pass judgment on institutions according to their effectiveness in giving concrete opportunities to individuals. But we do not confuse the idea of private interest with that of happiness, although that is another common point of view. Are not women of the harem more happy than women voters? Is not the housekeeper happier than the working-woman? It is not too clear just what the word *happy* really means and still less what true values it may mask. There is no possibility of measuring the happiness of others, and it is always easy to describe as happy the situation in which one wishes to place them.

In particular those who are condemned to stagnation are often pronounced happy on the pretext that happiness consists in being at rest. This notion we reject, for our perspective is that of existentialist ethics. Every subject plays his part as such specifically through exploits or projects that serve as a mode of transcendence; he achieves liberty only through a continual reaching out toward other liberties. There is no justification for present existence other than its expansion into an indefinitely open future. Every time transcendence falls back into immanence, stagnation, there is a degradation of existence into the *"en-soi"*—the brutish life of subjection to given conditions—and of liberty into constraint and contingence. This downfall represents a moral fault if the subject consents to it; if it is inflicted upon him, it spells frustration and oppression. In both cases it is an absolute evil. Every individual concerned to justify his existence feels that his existence involves an undefined need to transcend himself, to engage in freely chosen projects.

Now, what peculiarly signalizes the situation of woman is that she—a free and autonomous being like all human creatures—nevertheless finds herself living in a world where men compel her to assume the status of the Other. They propose to stabilize her as object and to doom her to immanence since her transcendence is to be overshadowed and forever transcended by another ego (*conscience*) which is essential and sovereign. The drama of woman lies in this conflict between the fundamental aspirations of every subject (ego)—who always regards the self as the essential—and the compulsions of a situation in which she is the inessential. How can a human being in woman's situation attain fulfillment? What roads are open to her? Which are blocked? How can independence be recovered in a state of dependency? What circumstances limit woman's liberty and how can they be overcome? These are the fundamental questions on which I would fain throw some light. This means that I am interested in the fortunes of the individual as defined not in terms of happiness but in terms of liberty.

Quite evidently this problem would be without significance if we were to believe that woman's destiny is inevitably determined by physiological, psychological, or economic forces. Hence I shall discuss first of all the light in which woman is viewed by biology, psychoanalysis, and historical materialism. Next I shall try to show exactly how the concept of the "truly feminine" has been fashioned—why woman has been defined as the Other—and what have been the consequences from man's point of view. Then from woman's point of view I shall describe the world in which women must live; and thus we shall be able to envisage the difficulties in their way as, endeavoring to make their escape from the sphere hitherto assigned them, they aspire to full membership in the human race.

WILLARD VAN ORMAN QUINE
1908–

Willard Van Orman Quine was the youngest of the sons born to Robert Quine and Harriet Van Orman Quine of Akron, Ohio. His mother was a schoolteacher and his father a worker in heavy industry. As a child, Quine developed a lifelong fascination with travel and maps. On summer vacations, he would draw careful maps of nearby lakes and sell copies to local cabin owners. The young Quine also excelled in mathematics and languages. In 1926, he enrolled at Oberlin College, where he majored in mathematics and studied philosophy. His research led him to mathematical philosophy, logic, and the philosophy of Bertrand Russell. In Russell he found a kindred spirit—they shared a logical approach to philosophical problems and a religious skepticism.

Quine went to Harvard University for graduate studies in 1930. He married his college sweetheart, buried himself in studies with such noted philosophers as C.I. Lewis and Alfred North Whitehead, finished his course work, passed preliminary examinations, and received his master's degree—all in a year. The following year he completed a 290-page dissertation on logic and received his Ph.D. degree at age twenty-three. *A System of Logistic* (1934), a revision of this dissertation, became the first of his fifteen published books.

The year Quine received his doctorate, he was also awarded Harvard's Sheldon Traveling Fellowship. He took the title of the fellowship seriously, and in one year he and his wife visited twenty-seven countries. Quine met several members of the Vienna Circle and studied logic in Warsaw with the great Polish logicians Alfred Tarski, Stanisław Leśniewski, and Jan Łukasiewicz. At the end of the year, he was elected into Harvard's Society of Fellows, which gave him, among other emoluments, three years pay and no duties. Among his five colleagues as junior fellows was the promising young psychologist B.F. Skinner.

Quine taught at Harvard until 1942. During the Second World War, his skill in languages and his gift for logic were put to use translating and analyzing decoded messages from German submarines. In 1946, Quine returned to Harvard and teaching. Except for sabbaticals and visiting professorships (and traveling in over one hundred countries), Quine remained a professor at Harvard until his retirement in 1978. Quine still lives in Boston and uses an office at Harvard—when not traveling.

*   *   *

In his autobiography, Quine explains that he has always despised conceptual constraints and has "been at pains to blur the boundaries between natural science, mathematics, and philosophy." Nowhere is this impatience with divisions more apparent than in Quine's critique of the analytic-synthetic distinction.

Ever since Hume first distinguished between "relations of ideas" and "matters of fact," philosophers have divided all propositions into two categories: analytic and synthetic. Yet in his famous paper "Two Dogmas of Empiricism," reprinted here (complete), Quine argues on the basis of various tests of meaning, synonymity, definition, and semantics that such a division has never been clearly made and that there is no compelling reason for believing such a separation can be made.

For example, the foundational propositions of logic and mathematics have been held to be true by convention independent of any matters of fact. Thus the proposition (1) "No unmarried man is married" is true regardless of the various interpretations of "man" and "married." But there are also semantic propositions, such as (2) "No bachelor is married," which are claimed to be equally analytic. As Quine points out, it is common to believe that this latter (supposed) analytic proposition can be made into a truth of logic by "putting synonyms for synonyms; thus (2) can be turned into (1) by putting 'unmarried man' for its synonym 'bachelor'." But what is our criterion of synonymity and how is it any more clear than our criterion of "analyticity"? We could say that propositions (1) and (2) are synonymous if the term "bachelor" in (2) is *defined* as "unmarried man." But what is the basis for such a definition? Does analyticity depend on the empirical observations of a lexicographer or the authority of a dictionary? We could say that these propositions are synonymous if proposition (2) is "necessarily true." However, this would be begging the question; to say a proposition is "necessary" is to say it is analytic. Quine concludes that analyticity as a clearly distinguished notion is "an unempirical dogma of empiricists, a metaphysical article of faith."

Having critiqued the analytic-synthetic distinction, Quine next turns his attention to another empirical dogma: the verification theory of meaning and the reductionism that it presupposes. According to this theory of meaning, the meaning of any statement is the "method of empirically confirming or inferring it." But such a theory implies that each meaningful statement can be reduced to an equivalent statement that contains only references to immediate experience.

Logical positivist such as Ayer sought to develop such a reductionistic language. But according to Quine, Ayer and the others are relying on the nonexistent analytic-synthetic distinction to separate the "linguistic components" from the "factual components" in any individual statement. Furthermore, *no* statement, taken by itself, could be confirmed or discredited by sensory experience because there could always be a further experience that would overturn the original statement.

Quine concludes:

> The totality of our so-called knowledge or beliefs, from the most casual matters of geography and history to the profoundest laws of atomic physics or even of pure mathematics and logic, is a man-made fabric which impinges on experience only along the edges.

Individual experiences "along the edges" may be dismissed as errors or hallucinations if they disturb more central beliefs. But even our core beliefs of mathematics and logic are subject to possible revision. There is no final truth nor even a clear distinction between the truths of logic and the truths of experience, that is, between analytic and synthetic.

*   *   *

Alex Orenstein, *Willard Van Orman Quine* (Boston: Twayne, 1977) provides a good place to begin further study, whereas Roger F. Gibson, *The Philosophy of W.V. Quine: An Expository Essay* (Tampa: University Presses of Florida, 1982); George D. Romanas, *Quine and Analytic Philosophy* (Cambridge: MIT Press, 1983); Ilham Dilman, *Quine on Ontology, Necessity, and Experience: A Philosophical Critique* (Albany, NY: SUNY Press, 1984); and Christopher Hookway, *Quine: Language, Experience, and Reality* (Stanford, CA: Stanford University Press, 1988) have written critical investigations. For information on Quine's life, see his autobiography, *The Time of My Life: An Autobiography* (Cambridge: MIT Press, 1985). For collections of essays, see Donald Davidson and Jaakko Hintikka, eds., *Words and Objections: Essays on the Work of W.V. Quine* (Dordrecht, The Netherlands: D. Reidel, 1969); Robert W. Shahan and Chris Swoyer, eds., *Essays on the Philosophy of W.V. Quine* (Norman: University of Oklahoma Press, 1979); Robert Barrett and Roger Gibson, eds., *Perspectives on Quine* (Oxford: Basil Blackwell, 1993); Paolo Leonardi and Marlo Santambrogio, eds., *On Quine: New Essays* (Cambridge: Cambridge University Press, 1994); Robert L. Arrington and Johann Glock, eds., *Wittgenstein and Quine* (Oxford: Routledge, 1996); and, especially, Lewis Edwin Hahn and Paul Arthur Schilpp, eds., *The Philosophy of W.V. Quine* (La Salle, IL: Open Court, 1986), another volume in the Library of Living Philosophers Series, which includes Quine's responses to critics and a short version of his autobiography.

TWO DOGMAS OF EMPIRICISM

Modern empiricism has been conditioned in large part by two dogmas. One is a belief in some fundamental cleavage between truths which are *analytic,* or grounded in meanings independently of matters of fact, and truths which are *synthetic,* or grounded in fact. The other dogma is *reductionism:* the belief that each meaningful statement is equivalent to some logical construct upon terms which refer to immediate experience. Both dogmas, I shall argue, are ill-founded. One effect of abandoning them is, as we shall see, a blurring of the supposed boundary between speculative metaphysics and natural science. Another effect is a shift toward pragmatism.

1. Background for Analyticity

Kant's cleavage between analytic and synthetic truths was foreshadowed in Hume's distinction between relations of ideas and matters of fact, and in Leibniz's distinction between truths of reason and truths of fact. Leibniz spoke of the truths of reason as true in all possible worlds. Picturesqueness aside, this is to say that the truths of reason are those which could not possibly be false. In the same vein we hear analytic statements defined as statements whose denials are self-contradictory. But this definition has small explanatory value; for the notion of self-contradictoriness, in the quite broad sense needed for this definition of analyticity, stands in exactly the same need of clarification as does the notion of analyticity itself. The two notions are the two sides of a single dubious coin.

Kant conceived of an analytic statement as one that attributes to its subject no more than is already conceptually contained in the subject. This formulation has two shortcomings: it limits itself to statements of subject-predicate form, and it appeals to a notion of containment which is left at a metaphorical level. But Kant's intent, evident more from the use he makes of the notion of analyticity than from his definition of it, can be restated thus: a statement is analytic when it is true by virtue of meanings and independently of fact. Pursuing this line, let us examine the concept of *meaning* which is presupposed.

Meaning, let us remember, is not to be identified with naming. Frege's example of 'Evening Star' and 'Morning Star,' and Russell's of 'Scott' and 'the author of *Waverley,*' illustrate that terms can name the same thing but differ in meaning. The distinction between meaning and naming is no less important at the level of abstract terms. The terms '9' and 'the number of the planets' name one and the same abstract entity but presumably must be regarded as unlike in meaning; for astronomical observation was needed, and not mere reflection on meanings, to determine the sameness of the entity in question.

From Willard Van Orman Quine, *From a Logical Point of View,* Chapter 2, pp. 20–46. Cambridge: Harvard University Press, 1953. Copyright © 1953 by The President and Fellows of Harvard College. Reprinted by permission of Harvard University Press and *The Philosophical Review.*

The above examples consist of singular terms, concrete and abstract. With general terms, or predicates, the situation is somewhat different but parallel. Whereas a singular term purports to name an entity, abstract or concrete, a general term does not; but a general term is *true of* an entity, or of each of many, or of none. The class of all entities of which a general term is true is called the *extension* of the term. Now paralleling the contrast between the meaning of a singular term and the entity named, we must distinguish equally between the meaning of a general term and its extension. The general terms 'creature with a heart' and 'creature with kidneys,' for example, are perhaps alike in extension but unlike in meaning.

Confusion of meaning with extension, in the case of general terms, is less common than confusion of meaning with naming in the case of singular terms. It is indeed a commonplace in philosophy to oppose intension (or meaning) to extension, or, in a variant vocabulary, connotation to denotation.

The Aristotelian notion of essence was the forerunner, no doubt, of the modern notion of intension or meaning. For Aristotle it was essential in men to be rational, accidental to be two-legged. But there is an important difference between this attitude and the doctrine of meaning. From the latter point of view it may indeed be conceded (if only for the sake of argument) that rationality is involved in the meaning of the word 'man' while two-leggedness is not; but two-leggedness may at the same time be viewed as involved in the meaning of 'biped' while rationality is not. Thus from the point of view of the doctrine of meaning it makes no sense to say of the actual individual, who is at once a man and a biped, that his rationality is essential and his two-leggedness accidental or vice versa. Things had essences for Aristotle, but only linguistic forms have meanings. Meaning is what essence becomes when it is divorced from the object of reference and wedded to the word.

For the theory of meaning a conspicuous question is the nature of its objects: what sort of things are meanings? A felt need for meant entities may derive from an earlier failure to appreciate that meaning and reference are distinct. Once the theory of meaning is sharply separated from the theory of reference, it is a short step to recognizing as the primary business of the theory of meaning simply the synonymy of linguistic forms and the analyticity of statements; meanings themselves, as obscure intermediary entities, may well be abandoned.

The problem of analyticity then confronts us anew. Statements which are analytic by general philosophical acclaim are not, indeed, far to seek. They fall into two classes. Those of the first class, which may be called *logically true,* are typified by:

(1) No unmarried man is married.

The relevant feature of this example is that it not merely is true as it stands, but remains true under any and all reinterpretations of 'man' and 'married.' If we suppose a prior inventory of *logical* particles, comprising 'no,' 'un-,' 'not,' 'if,' 'then,' 'and,' etc., then in general a logical truth is a statement which is true and remains true under all reinterpretations of its components other than the logical particles.

But there is also a second class of analytic statements, typified by:

(2) No bachelor is married.

The characteristic of such a statement is that it can be turned into a logical truth by putting synonyms for synonyms; thus (2) can be turned into (1) by putting 'unmarried man' for its synonym 'bachelor.' We still lack a proper characterization of this second class of analytic statements, and therewith of analyticity generally, inasmuch as we have had in the above description to lean on a notion of "synonymy" which is no less in need of clarification than analyticity itself.

In recent years Carnap has tended to explain analyticity by appeal to what he calls state-descriptions. A state-description is any exhaustive assignment of truth values to the atomic, or noncompound, statements of the language. All other statements of the language are, Carnap assumes, built up of their component clauses by means of the familiar logical devices, in such a way that the truth value of any complex statement is fixed for each state-description by specifiable logical laws. A statement is then explained as analytic when it comes out true under every state description. This account is an adaptation of Leibniz's "true in all possible worlds." But note that this version of analyticity serves its purpose only if the atomic statements of the language are, unlike 'John is a bachelor' and 'John is married,' mutually independent. Otherwise there would be a state-description which assigned truth to 'John is a bachelor' and to 'John is married,' and consequently 'No bachelors are married' would turn out synthetic rather than analytic under the proposed criterion. Thus the criterion of analyticity in terms of state-descriptions serves only for languages devoid of extralogical synonym-pairs, such as 'bachelor' and 'unmarried man'—synonym-pairs of the type which give rise to the "second class" of analytic statements. The criterion in terms of state-descriptions is a reconstruction at best of logical truth, not of analyticity.

I do not mean to suggest that Carnap is under any illusions on this point. His simplified model language with its state-descriptions is aimed primarily not at the general problem of analyticity but at another purpose, the clarification of probability and induction. Our problem, however, is analyticity; and here the major difficulty lies not in the first class of analytic statements, the logical truths, but rather in the second class, which depends on the notion of synonymy.

2. DEFINITION

There are those who find it soothing to say that the analytic statements of the second class reduce to those of the first class, the logical truths, by *definition;* 'bachelor,' for example, is *defined* as 'unmarried man.' But how do we find that 'bachelor' is defined as 'unmarried man'? Who defined it thus, and when? Are we to appeal to the nearest dictionary, and accept the lexicographer's formulation as law? Clearly this would be to put the cart before the horse. The lexicographer is an empirical scientist, whose business is the recording of antecedent facts; and if he glosses 'bachelor' as 'unmarried man' it is because of his belief that there is a relation of synonymy between those forms, implicit in general or preferred usage prior to his own work. The notion of synonymy presupposed here has still to be clarified, presumably in terms relating to linguistic behavior. Certainly the "definition" which is the lexicographer's report of an observed synonymy cannot be taken as the ground of the synonymy.

Definition is not, indeed, an activity exclusively of philologists. Philosophers and scientists frequently have occasion to "define" a recondite term by paraphrasing it into terms of a more familiar vocabulary. But ordinarily such a definition, like the philologist's, is pure lexicography, affirming a relation of synonymy antecedent to the exposition in hand.

Just what it means to affirm synonymy, just what the interconnections may be which are necessary and sufficient in order that two linguistic forms be properly describable as synonymous, is far from clear; but, whatever these interconnections may be, ordinarily they are grounded in usage. Definitions reporting selected instances of synonymy come then as reports upon usage.

There is also, however, a variant type of definitional activity which does not limit itself to the reporting of preexisting synonymies. I have in mind what Carnap calls *explication*—an activity to which philosophers are given, and scientists also in their more philosophical moments. In explication the purpose is not merely to paraphrase the definiendum into an outright synonym, but actually to improve upon the definiendum by refining or supplementing its meaning. But even explication, though not merely reporting a preexisting synonymy between definiendum and definiens, does rest nevertheless on *other* preexisting synonymies. The matter may be viewed as follows. Any word worth explicating has some contexts which, as wholes, are clear and precise enough to be useful; and the purpose of explication is to preserve the usage of these favored contexts while sharpening the usage of other contexts. In order that a given definition be suitable for purposes of explication, therefore, what is required is not that the definiendum in its antecedent usage be synonymous with the definiens, but just that each of these favored contexts of the definiendum, taken as a whole in its antecedent usage, be synonymous with the corresponding context of the definiens.

Two alternative definientia may be equally appropriate for the purposes of a given task of explication and yet not be synonymous with each other; for they may serve interchangeably within the favored contexts but diverge elsewhere. By cleaving to one of these definientia rather than the other, a definition of explicative kind generates, by fiat, a relation of synonymy between definiendum and definiens which did not hold before. But such a definition still owes its explicative function, as seen, to preexisting synonymies.

There does, however, remain still an extreme sort of definition which does not hark back to prior synonymies at all: namely, the explicitly conventional introduction of novel notations for purposes of sheer abbreviation. Here the definiendum becomes synonymous with the definiens simply because it has been created expressly for the purpose of being synonymous with the definiens. Here we have a really transparent case of synonymy created by definition; would that all species of synonymy were as intelligible. For the rest, definition rests on synonymy rather than explaining it.

The word 'definition' has come to have a dangerously reassuring sound, owing no doubt to its frequent occurrence in logical and mathematical writings. We shall do well to digress now into a brief appraisal of the role of definition in formal work.

In logical and mathematical systems either of two mutually antagonistic types of economy may be striven for, and each has its peculiar practical utility. On the one hand we may seek economy of practical expression—ease and brevity in the statement of multifarious relations. This sort of economy calls usually for distinctive concise notations for a wealth of concepts. Second, however, and oppositely, we may seek economy in grammar and vocabulary; we may try to find a minimum of basic concepts such that, once a distinctive notation has been appropriated to each of them, it becomes possible to express any desired further concept by mere combination and iteration of our basic notations. This second sort of economy is impractical in one way, since a poverty in basic idioms tends to a necessary lengthening of discourse. But it is practical in another way: it greatly simplifies theoretical discourse *about* the language, through minimizing the terms and the forms of construction wherein the language consists.

Both sorts of economy, though prima facie incompatible, are valuable in their separate ways. The custom has consequently arisen of combining both sorts of economy by forging in effect two languages, the one a part of the other. The inclusive language, though redundant in grammar and vocabulary, is economical in message lengths, while the part, called primitive notation, is economical in grammar and vocabulary. Whole and part are correlated by rules of translation whereby each idiom not in primitive notation is equated to some complex built up of primitive notation. These rules of translation are the so-called *definitions* which appear in formalized systems. They are best viewed not as adjuncts to one language but as correlations between two languages, the one a part of the other.

But these correlations are not arbitrary. They are supposed to show how the primitive notations can accomplish all purposes, save brevity and convenience, of the redundant language. Hence the definiendum and its definiens may be expected, in each case, to be related in one or another of the three ways lately noted. The definiens may be a faithful paraphrase of the definiendum into the narrower notation, preserving a direct synonymy* as of antecedent usage; or the definiens may, in the spirit of explication, improve upon the antecedent usage of the definiendum; or finally, the definiendum may be a newly created notation, newly endowed with meaning here and now.

In formal and informal work alike, thus, we find that definition—except in the extreme case of the explicitly conventional introduction of new notations—hinges on prior relations of synonymy. Recognizing then that the notion of definition does not hold the key to synonymy and analyticity, let us look further into synonymy and say no more of definition.

3. INTERCHANGEABILITY

A natural suggestion, deserving close examination, is that the synonymy of two linguistic forms consists simply in their interchangeability in all contexts without change of truth value—interchangeability, in Leibniz's phrase, *salva veritate*. Note that synonyms so conceived need not even be free from vagueness, as long as the vaguenesses match.

But it is not quite true that the synonyms 'bachelor' and 'unmarried man' are everywhere interchangeable *salva veritate*. Truths which become false under substitution of 'unmarried man' for 'bachelor' are easily constructed with the help of 'bachelor of arts' or 'bachelor's buttons'; also with the help of quotation, thus:

'Bachelor' has less than ten letters.

Such counterinstances can, however, perhaps be set aside by treating the phrases 'bachelor of arts' and 'bachelor's buttons' and the quotation "bachelor" each as a single indivisible word and then stipulating that the interchangeability *salva veritate* which is to be the touchstone of synonymy is not supposed to apply to fragmentary occurrences inside of a word. This account of synonymy, supposing it acceptable on other counts, has indeed the drawback of appealing to a prior conception of "word" which can be counted on to present difficulties of formulation in its turn. Nevertheless some progress might be claimed in having reduced the problem of synonymy to a problem of wordhood. Let us pursue this line a bit, taking "word" for granted.

---

*According to an important variant sense of 'definition,' the relation preserved may be the weaker relation of mere agreement in reference. . . . But definition in this sense is better ignored in the present connection, being irrelevant to the question of synonymy.

The question remains whether interchangeability *salva veritate* (apart from oc-currences within words) is a strong enough condition for synonymy, or whether, on the contrary, some heteronymous expressions might be thus interchangeable. Now let us be clear that we are not concerned here with synonymy in the sense of complete iden-tity in psychological associations or poetic quality; indeed no two expressions are syn-onymous in such a sense. We are concerned only with what may be called *cognitive* synonymy. Just what this is cannot be said without successfully finishing the present study; but we know something about it from the need which arose for it in connection with analyticity in ¶1. The sort of synonymy needed there was merely such that any analytic statement could be turned into a logical truth by putting synonyms for syn-onyms. Turning the tables and assuming analyticity, indeed, we could explain cogni-tive synonymy of terms as follows (keeping to the familiar example): to say that 'bach-elor' and 'unmarried man' are cognitively synonymous is to say no more nor less than that the statement:

(3) All and only bachelors are unmarried men

is analytic.*

What we need is an account of cognitive synonymy not presupposing analytic-ity—if we are to explain analyticity conversely with help of cognitive synonymy as un-dertaken in ¶1. And indeed such an independent account of cognitive synonymy is at present up for consideration, namely, interchangeability *salva veritate* everywhere ex-cept within words. The question before us, to resume the thread at last, is whether such interchangeability is a sufficient condition for cognitive synonymy. We can quickly as-sure ourselves that it is, by examples of the following sort. The statement:

(4) Necessarily all and only bachelors are bachelors

is evidently true, even supposing 'necessarily' so narrowly construed as to be truly ap-plicable only to analytic statements. Then, if 'bachelor' and 'unmarried man' are inter-changeable *salva veritate,* the result:

(5) Necessarily all and only bachelors are unmarried men

of putting 'unmarried man' for an occurrence of 'bachelor' in (4) must, like (4), be true. But to say that (5) is true is to say that (3) is analytic, and hence that 'bachelor' and 'unmarried man' are cognitively synonymous.

Let us see what there is about the above argument that gives it its air of hocus-pocus. The condition of interchangeability *salva veritate* varies in its force with varia-tions in the richness of the language at hand. The above argument supposes we are working with a language rich enough to contain the adverb 'necessarily,' this adverb being so construed as to yield truth when and only when applied to an analytic state-ment. But can we condone a language which contains such an adverb? Does the adverb really make sense? To suppose that it does is to suppose that we have already made satisfactory sense of 'analytic.' Then what are we so hard at work on right now?

---

*This is cognitive synonymy in a primary, broad sense. Carnap and Lewis have suggested how, once this notion is at hand, a narrower sense of cognitive synonymy which is preferable for some purposes can in turn be derived. But this special ramification of concept-building lies aside from the present purposes and must not be confused with the broad sort of cognitive synonymy here concerned.

Our argument is not flatly circular, but something like it. It has the form, figuratively speaking, of a closed curve in space.

Interchangeability *salva veritate* is meaningless until relativized to a language whose extent is specified in relevant respects. Suppose now we consider a language containing just the following materials. There is an indefinitely large stock of one-place predicates (for example, '*F*' where '*Fx*' means that *x* is a man) and many-place predicates (for example, '*G*' where '*Gxy*' means that *x* loves *y*), mostly having to do with extralogical subject matter. The rest of the language is logical. The atomic sentences consist each of a predicate followed by one or more variables '*x*,' '*y*,' etc.; and the complex sentences are built up of the atomic ones by truth functions ('not,' 'and,' 'or,' etc.) and quantification. In effect such a language enjoys the benefits also of descriptions and indeed singular terms generally, these being contextually definable in known ways. Even abstract singular terms naming classes, classes of classes, etc., are contextually definable in case the assumed stock of predicates includes the two-place predicate of class membership. Such a language can be adequate to classical mathematics and indeed to scientific discourse generally, except in so far as the latter involves debatable devices such as contrary-to-fact conditionals or modal adverbs like 'necessarily.' Now a language of this type is extensional, in this sense: any two predicates which agree extensionally (that is, are true of the same objects) are interchangeable *salva veritate*.

In an extensional language, therefore, interchangeability *salva veritate* is no assurance of cognitive synonymy of the desired type. That 'bachelor' and 'unmarried man' are interchangeable *salva veritate* in an extensional language assures us of no more than that (3) is true. There is no assurance here that the extensional agreement of 'bachelor' and 'unmarried man' rests on meaning rather than merely on accidental matters of fact, as does the extensional agreement of 'creature with a heart' and 'creature with kidneys.'

For most purposes extensional agreement is the nearest approximation to synonymy we need care about. But the fact remains that extensional agreement falls far short of cognitive synonymy of the type required for explaining analyticity in the manner of ¶1. The type of cognitive synonymy required there is such as to equate the synonymy of 'bachelor' and 'unmarried man' with the analyticity of (3), not merely with the truth of (3).

So we must recognize that interchangeability *salva veritate,* if construed in relation to an extensional language, is not a sufficient condition of cognitive synonymy in the sense needed for deriving analyticity in the manner of ¶1. If a language contains an intensional adverb 'necessarily' in the sense lately noted, or other particles to the same effect, then interchangeability *salva veritate* in such a language does afford a sufficient condition of cognitive synonymy; but such a language is intelligible only in so far as the notion of analyticity is already understood in advance.

The effort to explain cognitive synonymy first, for the sake of deriving analyticity from it afterward as in ¶1, is perhaps the wrong approach. Instead we might try explaining analyticity somehow without appeal to cognitive synonymy. Afterward we could doubtless derive cognitive synonymy from analyticity satisfactorily enough if desired. We have seen that cognitive synonymy of 'bachelor' and 'unmarried man' can be explained as analyticity of (3). The same explanation works for any pair of one-place predicates, of course, and it can be extended in obvious fashion to many-place predicates. Other syntactical categories can also be accommodated in fairly parallel fashion. Singular terms may be said to be cognitively synonymous when the statement of identity formed by putting '=' between them is analytic. Statements may be said simply to be cognitively synonymous when their biconditional (the result of joining them by 'if and only if') is analytic.* If we care to lump all categories into a single formulation, at the expense of assuming again the notion of "word" which was appealed to early in this section, we can describe any two linguistic forms as cognitively synonymous when the two forms are interchangeable (apart from occurrences within "words") *salva* (no longer *veritate* but) *analyticitate*. Certain technical questions arise, indeed, over cases of ambiguity or homonymy; let us not pause for them, however, for we are already digressing. Let us rather turn our backs on the problem of synonymy and address ourselves anew to that of analyticity.

4. SEMANTICAL RULES

Analyticity at first seemed most naturally definable by appeal to a realm of meanings. On refinement, the appeal to meanings gave way to an appeal to synonymy or definition. But definition turned out to be a will-o'-the-wisp, and synonymy turned out to be best understood only by dint of a prior appeal to analyticity itself. So we are back at the problem of analyticity.

I do not know whether the statement 'Everything green is extended' is analytic. Now does my indecision over this example really betray an incomplete understanding, an incomplete grasp of the "meanings," of 'green' and 'extended'? I think not. The trouble is not with 'green' or 'extended,' but with 'analytic.'

It is often hinted that the difficulty in separating analytic statements from synthetic ones in ordinary language is due to the vagueness of ordinary language and that the distinction is clear when we have a precise artificial language with explicit "semantical rules." This, however, as I shall now attempt to show, is a confusion.

The notion of analyticity about which we are worrying is a purported relation between statements and languages: a statement S is said to be *analytic* for a language L, and the problem is to make sense of this relation generally, that is, for variable 'S' and 'L.' The gravity of this problem is not perceptibly less for artificial languages than for natural ones. The problem of making sense of the idiom 'S is analytic for L,' with variable 'S' and 'L,' retains its stubbornness even if we limit the range of the variable 'L' to artificial languages. Let me now try to make this point evident.

For artificial languages and semantical rules we look naturally to the writings of Carnap. His semantical rules take various forms, and to make my point I shall have to distinguish certain of the forms. Let us suppose, to begin with, an artificial language L_0 whose semantical rules have the form explicitly of a specification, by recursion or otherwise, of all the analytic statements of L_0. The rules tell us that such and such statements, and only those, are the analytic statements of L_0. Now here the difficulty is simply that the rules contain the word 'analytic,' which we do not understand! We understand what expressions the rules attribute analyticity to, but we do not understand what the rules attribute to those expressions. In short, before we can understand a rule which begins 'A statement S is analytic for language L_0 if and only if . . .,' we must understand the general relative term 'analytic for'; we must understand 'S is analytic for L' where 'S' and 'L' are variables.

Alternatively we may, indeed, view the so-called rule as a conventional definition of a new simple symbol 'analytic-for-L_0,' which might better be written untenden-

*The 'if and only if' itself is intended in the true functional sense.

tiously as 'K' so as not to seem to throw light on the interesting word 'analytic.' Obviously any number of classes K, M, N, etc. of statements of L_0 can be specified for various purposes or for no purpose; what does it mean to say that K, as against M, N, etc., is the class of the "analytic" statements of L_0?

By saying what statements are analytic for L_0 we explain 'analytic-for-L_0' but not 'analytic,' not 'analytic for.' We do not begin to explain the idiom 'S is analytic for L' with variable 'S' and 'L,' even if we are content to limit the range of 'L' to the realm of artificial languages.

Actually we do know enough about the intended significance of 'analytic' to know that analytic statements are supposed to be true. Let us then turn to a second form of semantical rule, which says not that such and such statements are analytic but simply that such and such statements are included among the truths. Such a rule is not subject to the criticism of containing the un-understood word 'analytic'; and we may grant for the sake of argument that there is no difficulty over the broader term 'true.' A semantical rule of this second type, a rule of truth, is not supposed to specify all the truths of the language; it merely stipulates, recursively or otherwise, a certain multitude of statements which, along with others unspecified, are to count as true. Such a rule may be conceded to be quite clear. Derivatively, afterward, analyticity can be demarcated thus: a statement is analytic if it is (not merely true but) true according to the semantical rule.

Still there is really no progress. Instead of appealing to an unexplained word 'analytic,' we are now appealing to an unexplained phrase 'semantical rule.' Not every true statement which says that the statements of some class are true can count as a semantical rule—otherwise *all* truths would be "analytic" in the sense of being true according to semantical rules. Semantical rules are distinguishable, apparently, only by the fact of appearing on a page under the heading 'Semantical Rules'; and this heading is itself then meaningless.

We can say indeed that a statement is *analytic-for-L_0* if and only if it is true according to such and such specifically appended "semantical rules," but then we find ourselves back at essentially the same case which was originally discussed: 'S is *analytic-for-L_0* if and only if. . . .' Once we seek to explain 'S is analytic for L' generally for variable 'L' (even allowing limitation of 'L' to artificial languages), the explanation 'true according to the semantical rules of L' is unavailing; for the relative term 'semantical rule of' is as much in need of clarification, at least, as 'analytic for.'

It may be instructive to compare the notion of semantical rule with that of postulate. Relative to a given set of postulates, it is easy to say what a postulate is: it is a member of the set. Relative to a given set of semantical rules, it is equally easy to say what a semantical rule is. But given simply a notation, mathematical or otherwise, and indeed as thoroughly understood a notation as you please in point of the translations or truth conditions of its statements, who can say which of its true statements rank as postulates? Obviously the question is meaningless—as meaningless as asking which points in Ohio are starting points. Any finite (or effectively specifiable infinite) selection of statements (preferably true ones, perhaps) is as much a set of postulates as any other. The word 'postulate' is significant only relative to an act of inquiry; we apply the word to a set of statements just in so far as we happen, for the year or the moment, to be thinking of those statements in relation to the statements which can be reached from them by some set of transformations to which we have seen fit to direct our attention. Now the notion of semantical rule is as sensible and meaningful as that of postulate, if conceived in a similarly relative spirit—relative, this time, to one or another particular enterprise of schooling unconversant persons in sufficient conditions for truth of statements of some natural or artificial language L. But from this point of view no one signalization of a subclass of the truths of L is intrinsically more a semantical rule than another; and, if 'analytic' means 'true by semantical rules,' no one truth of L is analytic to the exclusion of another.

It might conceivably be protested that an artificial language L (unlike a natural one) is a language in the ordinary sense *plus* a set of explicit semantical rules—the whole constituting, let us say, an ordered pair; and that the semantical rules of L then are specifiable simply as the second component of the pair L. But, by the same token and more simply, we might construe an artificial language L outright as an ordered pair whose second component is the class of its analytic statements; and then the analytic statements of L become specifiable simply as the statements in the second component of L. Or better still, we might just stop tugging at our bootstraps altogether.

Not all the explanations of analyticity known to Carnap and his readers have been covered explicitly in the above considerations, but the extension to other forms is not hard to see. Just one additional factor should be mentioned which sometimes enters: sometimes the semantical rules are in effect rules of translation into ordinary language, in which case the analytic statements of the artificial language are in effect recognized as such from the analyticity of their specified translations in ordinary language. Here certainly there can be no thought of an illumination of the problem of analyticity from the side of the artificial language.

From the point of view of the problem of analyticity the notion of an artificial language with semantical rules is a *feu follet par excellence*. Semantical rules determining the analytic statements of an artificial language are of interest only in so far as we already understand the notion of analyticity; they are of no help in gaining this understanding.

Appeal to hypothetical languages of an artificially simple kind could conceivably be useful in clarifying analyticity, if the mental or behavioral or cultural factors relevant to analyticity—whatever they may be—were somehow sketched into the simplified model. But a model which takes analyticity merely as an irreducible character is unlikely to throw light on the problem of explicating analyticity.

It is obvious that truth in general depends on both language and extralinguistic fact. The statement 'Brutus killed Caesar' would be false if the world had been different in certain ways, but it would also be false if the word 'killed' happened rather to have the sense of 'begat.' Thus one is tempted to suppose in general that the truth of a statement is somehow analyzable into a linguistic component and a factual component. Given this supposition, it next seems reasonable that in some statements the factual component should be null; and these are the analytic statements. But, for all its a priori reasonableness, a boundary between analytic and synthetic statements simply has not been drawn. That there is such a distinction to be drawn at all is an unempirical dogma of empiricists, a metaphysical article of faith.

5. THE VERIFICATION THEORY AND REDUCTIONISM

In the course of these somber reflections we have taken a dim view first of the notion of meaning, then of the notion of cognitive synonymy, and finally of the notion of analyticity. But what, it may be asked, of the verification theory of meaning? This phrase has established itself so firmly as a catchword of empiricism that we should be very unscientific indeed not to look beneath it for a possible key to the problem of meaning and the associated problems.

The verification theory of meaning, which has been conspicuous in the literature from Peirce onward, is that the meaning of a statement is the method of empirically confirming or infirming it. An analytic statement is that limiting case which is confirmed no matter what.

As urged in ¶1, we can as well pass over the question of meanings as entities and move straight to sameness of meaning, or synonymy. Then what the verification theory says is that statements are synonymous if and only if they are alike in point of method of empirical confirmation or infirmation.

This is an account of cognitive synonymy not of linguistic forms generally, but of statements.* However, from the concept of synonymy of statements we could derive the concept of synonymy for other linguistic forms, by considerations somewhat similar to those at the end of ¶3. Assuming the notion of "word," indeed, we could explain any two forms as synonymous when the putting of the one form for an occurrence of the other in any statement (apart from occurrences within "words") yields a synonymous statement. Finally, given the concept of synonymy thus for linguistic forms generally, we could define analyticity in terms of synonymy and logical truth as in ¶1. For that matter, we could define analyticity more simply in terms of just synonymy of statements together with logical truth; it is not necessary to appeal to synonymy of linguistic forms other than statements. For a statement may be described as analytic simply when it is synonymous with a logically true statement.

So, if the verification theory can be accepted as an adequate account of statement synonymy, the notion of analyticity is saved after all. However, let us reflect. Statement synonymy is said to be likeness of method of empirical confirmation or infirmation. Just what are these methods which are to be compared for likeness? What, in other words, is the nature of the relation between a statement and the experiences which contribute to or detract from its confirmation?

The most naive view of the relation is that it is one of direct report. This is *radical reductionism.* Every meaningful statement is held to be translatable into a statement (true or false) about immediate experience. Radical reductionism, in one form or another, well antedates the verification theory of meaning explicitly so called. Thus Locke and Hume held that every idea must either originate directly in sense experience or else be compounded of ideas thus originating; and taking a hint from Tooke we might rephrase this doctrine in semantical jargon by saying that a term, to be significant at all, must be either a name of a sense datum or a compound of such names or an abbreviation of such a compound. So stated, the doctrine remains ambiguous as between sense data as sensory events and sense data as sensory qualities; and it remains vague as to the admissible ways of compounding. Moreover, the doctrine is unnecessarily and intolerably restrictive in the term-by-term critique which it imposes. More reasonably, and without yet exceeding the limits of what I have called radical reductionism, we may take full statements as our significant units—thus demanding that our statements as wholes be translatable into sense-datum language, but not that they be translatable term by term.

This emendation would unquestionably have been welcome to Locke and Hume and Tooke, but historically it had to await an important reorientation in semantics—the reorientation whereby the primary vehicle of meaning came to be seen no longer in the

---

*The doctrine can indeed be formulated with terms rather than statements as the units. Thus Lewis describes the meaning of a term as "*a criterion in mind,* by reference to which one is able to apply or refuse to apply the expression in question in the case of presented, or imagined, things or situations."

term but in the statement. This reorientation, seen in Bentham and Frege, underlies Russell's concept of incomplete symbols defined in use; also it is implicit in the verification theory of meaning, since the objects of verification are statements.

Radical reductionism, conceived now with statements as units, set itself the task of specifying a sense-datum language and showing how to translate the rest of significant discourse, statement by statement, into it. Carnap embarked on this project in the *Aufbau*.

The language which Carnap adopted as his starting point was not a sense-datum language in the narrowest conceivable sense, for it included also the notations of logic, up through higher set theory. In effect it included the whole language of pure mathematics. The ontology implicit in it (that is, the range of values of its variables) embraced not only sensory events but classes, classes of classes, and so on. Empiricists there are who would boggle at such prodigality. Carnap's starting point is very parsimonious, however, in its extralogical or sensory part. In a series of constructions in which he exploits the resources of modern logic with much ingenuity, Carnap succeeds in defining a wide array of important additional sensory concepts which, but for his constructions, one would not have dreamed were definable on so slender a basis. He was the first empiricist who, not content with asserting the reducibility of science to terms of immediate experience, took serious steps toward carrying out the reduction.

If Carnap's starting point is satisfactory, still his constructions were, as he himself stressed, only a fragment of the full program. The construction of even the simplest statements about the physical world was left in a sketchy state. Carnap's suggestions on this subject were, despite their sketchiness, very suggestive. He explained spatio-temporal point-instants as quadruples of real numbers and envisaged assignment of sense qualities to point-instants according to certain canons. Roughly summarized, the plan was that qualities should be assigned to point-instants in such a way as to achieve the laziest world compatible with our experience. The principle of least action was to be our guide in constructing a world from experience.

Carnap did not seem to recognize, however, that his treatment of physical objects fell short of reduction not merely through sketchiness, but in principle. Statements of the form 'Quality q is at point-instant $x;y;z;t$' were, according to his canons, to be apportioned truth values in such a way as to maximize and minimize certain over-all features, and with growth of experience the truth values were to be progressively revised in the same spirit. I think this is a good schematization (deliberately oversimplified, to be sure) of what science really does; but it provides no indication, not even the sketchiest, of how a statement of the form 'Quality q is at $x;y;z;t$' could ever be translated into Carnap's initial language of sense data and logic. The connective 'is at' remains an added undefined connective; the canons counsel us in its use but not in its elimination.

Carnap seems to have appreciated this point afterward; for in his later writings he abandoned all notion of the translatability of statements about the physical world into statements about immediate experience. Reductionism in its radical form has long since ceased to figure in Carnap's philosophy.

But the dogma of reductionism has, in a subtler and more tenuous form, continued to influence the thought of empiricists. The notion lingers that to each statement, or each synthetic statement, there is associated a unique range of possible sensory events such that the occurrence of any of them would add to the likelihood of truth of the statement, and that there is associated also another unique range of possible sensory events whose occurrence would detract from that likelihood. This notion is of course implicit in the verification theory of meaning.

The dogma of reductionism survives in the supposition that each statement, taken in isolation from its fellows, can admit of confirmation or infirmation at all. My countersuggestion, issuing essentially from Carnap's doctrine of the physical world in the *Aufbau,* is that our statements about the external world face the tribunal of sense experience not individually but only as a corporate body.

The dogma of reductionism, even in its attenuated form, is intimately connected with the other dogma—that there is a cleavage between the analytic and the synthetic. We have found ourselves led, indeed, from the latter problem to the former through the verification theory of meaning. More directly, the one dogma clearly supports the other in this way: as long as it is taken to be significant in general to speak of the confirmation and infirmation of a statement, it seems significant to speak also of a limiting kind of statement which is vacuously confirmed, *ipso facto,* come what may; and such a statement is analytic.

The two dogmas are, indeed, at root identical. We lately reflected that in general the truth of statements does obviously depend both upon language and upon extralinguistic fact; and we noted that this obvious circumstance carries in its train, not logically but all too naturally, a feeling that the truth of a statement is somehow analyzable into a linguistic component and a factual component. The factual component must, if we are empiricists, boil down to a range of confirmatory experiences. In the extreme case where the linguistic component is all that matters, a true statement is analytic. But I hope we are now impressed with how stubbornly the distinction between analytic and synthetic has resisted any straightforward drawing. I am impressed also, apart from prefabricated examples of black and white balls in an urn, with how baffling the problem has always been of arriving at any explicit theory of the empirical confirmation of a synthetic statement. My present suggestion is that it is nonsense, and the root of much nonsense, to speak of a linguistic component and a factual component in the truth of any individual statement. Taken collectively, science has its double dependence upon language and experience; but this duality is not significantly traceable into the statements of science taken one by one.

The idea of defining a symbol in use was, as remarked, an advance over the impossible term-by-term empiricism of Locke and Hume. The statement, rather than the term, came with Bentham to be recognized as the unit accountable to an empiricist critique. But what I am now urging is that even in taking the statement as unit we have drawn our grid too finely. The unit of empirical significance is the whole of science.

6. EMPIRICISM WITHOUT THE DOGMAS

The totality of our so-called knowledge or beliefs, from the most casual matters of geography and history to the profoundest laws of atomic physics or even of pure mathematics and logic, is a man-made fabric which impinges on experience only along the edges. Or, to change the figure, total science is like a field of force whose boundary conditions are experience. A conflict with experience at the periphery occasions readjustments in the interior of the field. Truth values have to be redistributed over some of our statements. Reevaluation of some statements entails reevaluation of others, because of their logical interconnections—the logical laws being in turn simply certain further statements of the system, certain further elements of the field. Having reevaluated one statement we must reevaluate some others, which may be statements logically connected with the first or may be the statements of logical connections themselves. But the total field is so underdetermined by its boundary conditions, experience, that there is much latitude of choice as to what statements to reevaluate in the light of any single contrary experience. No particular experiences are linked with any particular statements in the interior of the field, except indirectly through considerations of equilibrium affecting the field as a whole.

If this view is right, it is misleading to speak of the empirical content of an individual statement—especially if it is a statement at all remote from the experiential periphery of the field. Furthermore it becomes folly to seek a boundary between synthetic statements, which hold contingently on experience, and analytic statements, which hold come what may. Any statement can be held true come what may, if we make drastic enough adjustments elsewhere in the system. Even a statement very close to the periphery can be held true in the face of recalcitrant experience by pleading hallucination or by amending certain statements of the kind called logical laws. Conversely, by the same token, no statement is immune to revision. Revision even of the logical law of the excluded middle has been proposed as a means of simplifying quantum mechanics; and what difference is there in principle between such a shift and the shift whereby Kepler superseded Ptolemy, or Einstein Newton, or Darwin Aristotle?

For vividness I have been speaking in terms of varying distances from a sensory periphery. Let me try now to clarify this notion without metaphor. Certain statements, though *about* physical objects and not sense experience, seem peculiarly germane to sense experience—and in a selective way: some statements to some experiences, others to others. Such statements, especially germane to particular experiences, I picture as near the periphery. But in this relation of "germaneness" I envisage nothing more than a loose association reflecting the relative likelihood, in practice, of our choosing one statement rather than another for revision in the event of recalcitrant experience. For example, we can imagine recalcitrant experiences to which we would surely be inclined to accommodate our system by reevaluating just the statement that there are brick houses on Elm Street, together with related statements on the same topic. We can imagine other recalcitrant experiences to which we would be inclined to accommodate our system by reevaluating just the statement that there are no centaurs, along with kindred statements. A recalcitrant experience can, I have urged, be accommodated by any of various alternative reevaluations in various alternative quarters of the total system; but, in the cases which we are now imagining, our natural tendency to disturb the total system as little as possible would lead us to focus our revisions upon these specific statements concerning brick houses or centaurs. These statements are felt, therefore, to have a sharper empirical reference than highly theoretical statements of physics or logic or ontology. The latter statements may be thought of as relatively centrally located within the total network, meaning merely that little preferential connection with any particular sense data obtrudes itself.

As an empiricist I continue to think of the conceptual scheme of science as a tool, ultimately, for predicting future experience in the light of past experience. Physical objects are conceptually imported into the situation as convenient intermediaries—not by definition in terms of experience, but simply as irreducible posits comparable, epistemologically, to the gods of Homer. For my part I do, qua lay physicist, believe in physical objects and not in Homer's gods; and I consider it a scientific error to believe otherwise. But in point of epistemological footing the physical objects and the gods differ only in degree and not in kind. Both sorts of entities enter our conception only as cultural posits. The myth of physical objects is epistemologically superior to most in that it has proved more efficacious than other myths as a device for working a manageable structure into the flux of experience.

Positing does not stop with macroscopic physical objects. Objects at the atomic level are posited to make the laws of macroscopic objects, and ultimately the laws of experience, simpler and more manageable; and we need not expect or demand full definition of atomic and subatomic entities in terms of macroscopic ones, any more than definition of macroscopic things in terms of sense data. Science is a continuation of common sense, and it continues the common-sense expedient of swelling ontology to simplify theory.

Physical objects, small and large, are not the only posits. Forces are another example; and indeed we are told nowadays that the boundary between energy and matter is obsolete. Moreover, the abstract entities which are the substance of mathematics—ultimately classes and classes of classes and so on up—are another posit in the same spirit. Epistemologically these are myths on the same footing with physical objects and gods, neither better nor worse except for differences in the degree to which they expedite our dealings with sense experiences.

The over-all algebra of rational and irrational numbers is underdetermined by the algebra of rational numbers, but is smoother and more convenient; and it includes the algebra of rational numbers as a jagged or gerrymandered part. Total science, mathematical and natural and human, is similarly but more extremely underdetermined by experience. The edge of the system must be kept squared with experience; the rest, with all its elaborate myths or fictions, has as its objective the simplicity of laws.

Ontological questions, under this view, are on a par with questions of natural science. Consider the question whether to countenance classes as entities. This, as I have argued elsewhere, is the question whether to quantify with respect to variables which take classes as values. Now Carnap has maintained that this is a question not of matters of fact but of choosing a convenient language form, a convenient conceptual scheme or framework for science. With this I agree, but only on the proviso that the same be conceded regarding scientific hypotheses generally. Carnap has recognized that he is able to preserve a double standard for ontological questions and scientific hypotheses only by assuming an absolute distinction between the analytic and the synthetic; and I need not say again that this is a distinction which I reject.

The issue over there being classes seems more a question of convenient conceptual scheme; the issue over there being centaurs, or brick houses on Elm Street, seems more a question of fact. But I have been urging that this difference is only one of degree, and that it turns upon our vaguely pragmatic inclination to adjust one strand of the fabric of science rather than another in accommodating some particular recalcitrant experience. Conservatism figures in such choices, and so does the quest for simplicity.

Carnap, Lewis, and others take a pragmatic stand on the question of choosing between language forms, scientific frameworks; but their pragmatism leaves off at the imagined boundary between the analytic and the synthetic. In repudiating such a boundary I espouse a more thorough pragmatism. Each man is given a scientific heritage plus a continuing barrage of sensory stimulation; and the considerations which guide him in warping his scientific heritage to fit his continuing sensory promptings are, where rational, pragmatic.

Maurice Merleau-Ponty
1908–1961

Jean-Jacques Maurice Merleau-Ponty was born in Rochefort-sur-Mer, a small town in southwestern France. He told his friend Jean-Paul Sartre that he enjoyed "an incomparable childhood." Though his father died in the First World War, Merleau-Ponty led a comfortable, bourgeois life with his mother, brother, and sister. When the family moved to Paris, Merleau-Ponty attended the Lycées Janson-de-Sailly and Louis-le-Grande, where he excelled academically. He enrolled at the École Normale Supérieure in 1926 where his scholarly superiority continued. Among his classmates at the renowned school were Jean-Paul Sartre and Simone de Beauvoir.

Following graduation from the École in 1930, Merleau-Ponty served briefly in the military. He then began teaching in a number of Lycées throughout France; during this period he had important encounters with Claude Lévi-Strauss, Jacques Lacan, and Catholic left-wing political groups. In 1935, he returned to teaching in Paris, where he heard historic lectures on Hegel given by Alexandre Kojève. These lectures and other influences moved Merleau-Ponty to reject Catholicism entirely and to turn to the phenomenology of Edmund Husserl.

With the outbreak of the Second World War in 1939, Merleau-Ponty was commissioned a second lieutenant and served on the General Staff of the Paris military district. After the surrender of French forces in June 1940, he joined the resistance group *Socialisme et liberté* ("Socialism and Liberty") and reestablished contact with his former classmate Sartre. This friendship proved to be productive as Sartre, Simone de Beauvoir, and Merleau-Ponty began the influential journal *Les Temps modernes* shortly after the Liberation in 1944. During the war

Merleau-Ponty wrote *The Structure of Behavior* (1942) and *Phenomenology of Perception* (1945), his major work.

After the war, Merleau-Ponty was awarded a doctorate for his two books and was called to the University of Lyon. In 1949, he returned to the Sorbonne in Paris to teach child psychology. Three years later, he was given the chair of philosophy at the Collège de France. The appointment to this highest post in French intellectual life scandalized three groups in particular: rightists, because of his existentialism; nationalists, because of his well-known respect for German thinkers (such as Husserl) and his sharp criticism of the French Descartes; and Catholics, because of his atheism. That same eventful year, Merleau-Ponty resigned as co-editor of *Les Temps modernes,* breaking with Sartre and de Beauvoir for political and philosophical reasons. Contrary to his former colleagues, Merleau-Ponty continued to support an increasingly harsh Soviet Union, going so far as to justify the judicious application of terror. *In Adventure of the Dialectic* (1955), Merleau-Ponty laid out his criticism of Sartre's politics and philosophy.

At the end of the 1950s, Merleau-Ponty began to change his mind about Soviet politics. As philosopher Barry Cooper explains, when the Soviet Gulag* was exposed, Merleau-Ponty concluded that "Marxism could serve only as a critical analytic or diagnostic instrument, useful in bringing to light the evils, stupidities, and contradictions of a capitalist industrial economy and a liberal political regime."** This political change facilitated a partial rapprochement with Sartre, a fresh questioning of Husserl, and an appreciation for the work of Martin Heidegger. Merleau-Ponty died suddenly in 1961, leaving philosophers to wonder at the next direction his always protean thought may have taken.

*   *   *

Merleau-Ponty's thought can best be characterized as a critique of Cartesian abstraction, a "disease" infecting virtually all Western philosophy. When Descartes explored the *Cogito,* the "I think," he discovered an abstract, disembodied subject. Descartes defined the subject as the self's *thoughts* of existing. He also understood the world in terms of the subject's *thoughts about* the world. As Merleau-Ponty explains in our selection from the *Phenomenology of Perception,* translated by Colin Smith, the "indubitability of the world" became the "indubitability of thought about the world":

> Descartes . . . detached the subject, or consciousness, by showing that I could not possibly apprehend anything as existing unless I first of all experienced myself as existing in the act of apprehending it.

According to Merleau-Ponty, subsequent thinkers criticized specifics in Descartes' philosophy without questioning the Cartesian primacy of the subject.

In opposition to these abstractions, Merleau-Ponty argues for the concrete, intentional, embodied character of lived experience. Borrowing the concept of

---

*Concentration camps for political prisoners.
**Barry Cooper, *Merleau-Ponty and Marxism: From Terror to Reform* (Toronto: University of Toronto Press, 1979), p. xiii.

Lebenswelt, or "life-world," from the later writings of Husserl,* Merleau-Ponty argues that we inhabit a "pregiven," prescientific world. Phenomenological reflection shows that we are "beings-in-the-world" prior to our conceptions about this world. Abstractions such as science are "second-order experiences" built on a concrete pregiven life-world. In fact, the entire subject-object dichotomy is secondary to a prior structure.

Further, as we examine our perceptual consciousness, we find that it is always consciousness *of* something beyond itself, and thus it is always intentional. Contrary to sense-datum theory, for example, our perceptual life is not a series of isolated sensations. Rather, each sensation has meaning only as part of a whole and is always directed toward something other than itself.

Finally, our lived experience as beings-in-the-world is always embodied. Contrary to Descartes, the body cannot be explained adequately as a "thing among things, . . . a collection of physico-chemical processes." Instead bodies are subjects, the location of habits, of our orientation toward the world. As Merleau-Ponty put it, "to be a body is to be tied to a certain world . . . our body is not primarily in space: it is of it." A study of the nervous system, for example, shows that the ability to perceive a particular quality cannot be assigned to a simple location. Rather, the body itself has intentional qualities, qualities that anticipate stimuli that will, in turn, reveal the world.

In attributing intentional characteristics to the *body,* Merleau-Ponty broke sharply from Sartre. Sartre had given intentionality to pure consciousness alone. Merleau-Ponty considered this much too abstract. Sartre also claimed that freedom is total, whereas Merleau-Ponty saw freedom limited by meaning. Social institutions and language convey meaning, for example, and so circumscribe freedom.

Immediately after his death, Merleau-Ponty's influence declined precipitously, as contemporary philosopher James Schmidt explains:

> Where Merleau-Ponty remained faithful to Husserl's call for a return to the "things themselves" and sought access, in the world of perception, to the "origin of truth," the most influential thinkers of the 1960s were suspicious of the entire vocabulary which spoke of origins, of returns, and even of truth . . . [Merleau-Ponty] came to suffer the cruellest of fates which can befall a French thinker: he became unfashionable.**

But fashions return. Merleau-Ponty's emphasis on the irreducible nature of perception, his attack on the subject-object dichotomy, and, especially, his groundbreaking work on the role of the body in perception are receiving new attention and have led some to hail him as the "first postmodernist." The suggested readings include recent appraisals of Merleau-Ponty's importance.

*   *   *

*See Edmund Husserl, *The Crisis of European Science and Transcendental Phenomenology: An Introduction to Phenomenological Philosophy,* Part III, A, §33 and §34, translated by David Carr (Evanston, IL: Northwestern University Press, 1970), reprinted in this volume, pp. 12–21.

**James Schmidt, *Maurice Merleau-Ponty: Between Phenomenology and Structuralism* (London: Macmillan, 1985), pp. 4–5.

General introductions to Merleau-Ponty's thought include Rémy C. Kwant, *The Phenomenological Philosophy of Merleau-Ponty* (Pittsburgh, PA: Duquesne University Press, 1963); Albert Rabil Jr., *Merleau-Ponty: Existentialist of the Social World* (New York: Columbia University Press, 1967); James Schmidt, *Maurice Merleau-Ponty: Between Phenomenology and Structuralism* (London: Macmillan, 1985); and the relevant section of Christopher McCann, *Four Phenomenological Philosophers: Husserl, Heidegger, Sartre, Merleau-Ponty* (London: Routledge, 1993). For a commentary on our selection, see Monika M. Langer, *Merleau-Ponty's Phenomenology of Perception: A Guide and Commentary* (Tallahassee, FL: Florida State University Press, 1989). Among the many studies of aspects of Merleau-Ponty's thought are Laurie Spurling, *Phenomenology and the Social World: The Philosophy of Merleau-Ponty and its Relation to the Social Sciences* (London: Routledge & Kegan Paul, 1977); Sonia Kruks, *The Political Philosophy of Merleau-Ponty* (Atlantic Highlands, NJ: Humanities Press, 1981); M.C. Dillon, *Merleau-Ponty's Ontology* (Bloomington: University of Indiana Press, 1988); Richard L. Lanigan, *Phenomenology of Communication: Merleau-Ponty's Thematics in Communicology and Semiology* (Pittsburgh, PA: Dusquesne University Press, 1988); Kerry H. Whitside, *Merleau-Ponty and the Foundation of an Existential Politics* (Princeton, NJ: Princeton University Press, 1988); and Jerry H. Gill, *Merleau-Ponty and Metaphor* (Atlantic Highlands, NJ: Humanities Press, 1991). Comparative studies include James Miller, *History and Human Existence: From Marx to Merleau-Ponty* (Berkeley: University of California Press, 1979); Barry Cooper, *Merleau-Ponty and Marxism: From Terror to Reform* (Toronto: University of Toronto Press, 1979); Nicholas F. Gier, *Wittgenstein and Phenomenology: A Comparative Study of the Later*

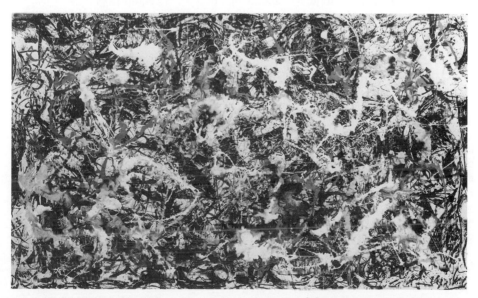

Convergence, 1952, by Jackson Pollock (1912–1956). Merleau-Ponty defined phenomenology as "a philosophy for which the world is always 'already there' before reflection begins as an inalienable presence." This description could also be applied to Pollock's intricate and complex paintings. *(Albright-Knox Art Gallery)*

Wittgenstein, Husserl, Heidegger, and Merleau-Ponty (Albany, NY: SUNY Press, 1981); Margaret Whitford, *Merleau-Ponty's Critique of Sartre's Philosophy* (Lexington, KY: French Forum, 1982); and Sandra B. Rosenthal and Patrick L. Bourgeois, *Mead and Merleau-Ponty: Toward a Common Vision* (Albany, NY: SUNY Press, 1991). For collections of essays, see John Sallis, ed., *Merleau-Ponty: Perception, Structure, Language* (Atlantic Highlands, NJ: Humanities Press, 1981); Galen A. Johnson and Michael B. Smith, eds., *Ontology and Alterity in Merleau-Ponty* (Evanston, IL: Northwestern University Press, 1990); and M.C. Dillon, ed., *Merleau-Ponty Vivant* (Albany, NY: SUNY Press, 1991).

WHAT IS PHENOMENOLOGY?

What is phenomenology? It may seem strange that this question has still to be asked half a century after the first works of Husserl. The fact remains that it has by no means been answered. Phenomenology is the study of essences; and according to it, all problems amount to finding definitions of essences: the essence of perception, or the essence of consciousness, for example. But phenomenology is also a philosophy which puts essences back into existence, and does not expect to arrive at an understanding of man and the world from any starting point other than that of their "facticity." It is a transcendental philosophy which places in abeyance the assertions arising out of the natural attitude, the better to understand them; but it is also a philosophy for which the world is always "already there" before reflection begins—as an inalienable presence; and all its efforts are concentrated upon re-achieving a direct and primitive contact with the world, and endowing that contact with a philosophical status. It is the search for a philosophy which shall be a "rigorous science," but it also offers an account of space, time and the world as we "live" them. It tries to give a direct description of our experience as it is, without taking account of its psychological origin and the causal explanations which the scientist, the historian, or the sociologist may be able to provide. Yet Husserl in his last works mentions a "genetic phenomenology," and even a "constructive phenomenology." One may try to do away with these contradictions by making a distinction between Husserl's and Heidegger's phenomenologies; yet the whole of *Sein und Zeit* springs from an indication given by Husserl and amounts to no more than an explicit account of the "*naturlicher Weltbegriff*" or the "*Lebenswelt*" which Husserl, towards the end of his life, identified as the central theme of phenomenology, with the result that the contradiction reappears in Husserl's own philosophy. The reader pressed for time will be inclined to give up the idea of covering a doctrine which says everything, and will wonder whether a philosophy which cannot define its scope deserves all the discussion which has gone on around it, and whether he is not faced rather by a myth or a fashion.

Maurice Merleau-Ponty, *Phenomenology of Perception,* translated by Colin Smith, Routledge & Kegan Paul Ltd., London, and The Humanities Press, New York, 1962, pp. vii–xxi. Reprinted by permission of the publishers.

Even if this were the case, there would still be a need to understand the prestige of the myth and the origin of the fashion, and the opinion of the responsible philosopher must be that *phenomenology can be practised and identified as a manner or style of thinking, that it existed as a movement before arriving at complete awareness of itself as a philosophy.* It has been long on the way, and its adherents have discovered it in every quarter, certainly in Hegel and Kierkegaard, but equally in Marx, Nietzsche and Freud. A purely linguistic examination of the texts in question would yield no proof; we find in texts only what we put into them, and if ever any kind of history has suggested the interpretations which should be put on it, it is the history of philosophy. We shall find in ourselves, and nowhere else, the unity and true meaning of phenomenology. It is less a question of counting up quotations than of determining and expressing in concrete form this *phenomenology for ourselves* which has given a number of present-day readers the impression, on reading Husserl or Heidegger, not so much of encountering a new philosophy as of recognizing what they had been waiting for. Phenomenology is accessible only through a phenomenological method. Let us, therefore, try systematically to bring together the celebrated phenomenological themes as they have grown spontaneously together in life. Perhaps we shall then understand why phenomenology has for so long remained at an initial stage, as a problem to be solved and a hope to be realized.

It is a matter of describing, not of explaining or analysing. Husserl's first directive to phenomenology, in its early stages, to be a "descriptive psychology," or to return to the "things themselves," is from the start a rejection of science. I am not the outcome or the meeting-point of numerous causal agencies which determine my bodily or psychological make-up. I cannot conceive myself as nothing but a bit of the world, a mere object of biological, psychological or sociological investigation. I cannot shut myself up within the realm of science. All my knowledge of the world, even my scientific knowledge, is gained from my own particular point of view, or from some experience of the world without which the symbols of science would be meaningless. The whole universe of science is built upon the world as directly experienced, and if we want to subject science itself to rigorous scrutiny and arrive at a precise assessment of its meaning and scope, we must begin by reawakening the basic experience of the world of which science is the second-order expression. Science has not and never will have, by its nature, the same significance *qua* form of being as the world which we perceive, for the simple reason that it is a rationale or explanation of that world. I am, not a "living creature" nor even a "man," nor again even "a consciousness" endowed with all the characteristics which zoology, social anatomy or inductive psychology recognize in these various products of the natural or historical process—I am the absolute source, my existence does not stem from my antecedents, from my physical and social environment; instead it moves out towards them and sustains them, for I alone bring into being for myself (and therefore into being in the only sense that the word can have for me) the tradition which I elect to carry on, or the horizon whose distance from me would be abolished—since that distance is not one of its properties—if I were not there to scan it with my gaze. Scientific points of view, according to which my existence is a moment of the world's, are always both naive and at the same time dishonest, because they take for granted, without explicitly mentioning it, the other point of view, namely that of consciousness, through which from the outset a world forms itself round me and begins to exist for me. To return to things themselves is to return to that world which precedes knowledge, of which knowledge always *speaks,* and in relation to which every scientific schematization is an abstract and derivative sign-language, as is geography in relation to the countryside in which we have learnt beforehand what a forest, a prairie or a river is.

    This move is absolutely distinct from the idealist return to consciousness, and the demand for a pure description excludes equally the procedure of analytical reflection on the one hand, and that of scientific explanation on the other. Descartes and particularly Kant detached the subject, or consciousness, by showing that I could not possibly apprehend anything as existing unless I first of all experienced myself as existing in the act of apprehending it. They presented consciousness, the absolute certainty of my existence for myself, as the condition of there being anything at all; and the act of relating as the basis of relatedness. It is true that the act of relating is nothing if divorced from the spectacle of the world in which relations are found; the unity of consciousness in Kant is achieved simultaneously with that of the world. And in Descartes methodical doubt does not deprive us of anything, since the whole world, at least in so far as we experience it, is reinstated in the *Cogito,* enjoying equal certainty, and simply labelled "thought about . . . ." But the relations between subject and world are not strictly bilateral: if they were, the certainty of the world would, in Descartes, be immediately given with that of the *Cogito,* and Kant would not have talked about his "Copernican revolution." Analytical reflection starts from our experience of the world and goes back to the subject as to a condition of possibility distinct from that experience, revealing the all-embracing synthesis as that without which there would be no world. To this extent it ceases to remain part of our experience and offers, in place of an account, a reconstruction. It is understandable, in view of this, that Husserl, having accused Kant of adopting a "faculty psychologism," should have urged, in place of a noetic analysis which bases the world on the synthesizing activity of the subject, his own *"noematic reflection"* which remains within the object and, instead of begetting it, brings to light its fundamental unity.

    The world is there before any possible analysis of mine, and it would be artificial to make it the outcome of a series of syntheses which link, in the first place sensations, then aspects of the object corresponding to different perspectives, when both are nothing but products of analysis, with no sort of prior reality. Analytical reflection believes that it can trace back the course followed by a prior constituting act and arrive, in the "inner man"—to use Saint Augustine's expression—at a constituting power which has always been identical with that inner self. Thus reflection itself is carried away and transplanted in an impregnable subjectivity, as yet untouched by being and time. But this is very ingenuous, or at least it is an incomplete form of reflection which loses sight of its own beginning. When I begin to reflect my reflection bears upon an unreflective experience; moreover my reflection cannot be unaware of itself as an event, and so it appears to itself in the light of a truly creative act, of a changed structure of consciousness, and yet it has to recognize, as having priority over its own operations, the world which is given to the subject, because the subject is given to himself. The real has to be described, not constructed or formed. Which means that I cannot put perception into the same category as the syntheses represented by judgements, acts or predications. My field of perception is constantly filled with a play of colours, noises and fleeting tactile sensations which I cannot relate precisely to the context of my clearly perceived world, yet which I nevertheless immediately "place" in the world, without ever confusing them with my daydreams. Equally constantly I weave dreams round things. I imagine people and things whose presence is not incompatible with the context, yet who are not in fact involved in it: they are ahead of reality, in the realm of the imaginary. If the reality of my perception were based solely on the intrinsic coherence of "representations," it ought to be for ever hesitant and, being wrapped up in my conjectures on probabilities, I ought to be ceaselessly taking apart misleading syntheses, and reinstating in reality stray phenomena which I had excluded in the first place.

But this does not happen. The real is a closely woven fabric. It does not await our judgement before incorporating the most surprising phenomena, or before rejecting the most plausible figments of our imagination. Perception is not a science of the world, it is not even an act, a deliberate taking up of a position; it is the background from which all acts stand out, and is presupposed by them. The world is not an object such that I have in my possession the law of its making; it is the natural setting of, and field for, all my thoughts and all my explicit perceptions. Truth does not "inhabit" only "the inner man," or more accurately, there is no inner man, man is in the world, and only in the world does he know himself. When I return to myself from an excursion into the realm of dogmatic common sense or of science, I find, not a source of intrinsic truth, but a subject destined to be in the world.

All of which reveals the true meaning of the famous phenomenological reduction. There is probably no question over which Husserl has spent more time—or to which he has more often returned, since the "problematic of reduction" occupies an important place in his unpublished work. For a long time, and even in recent texts, the reduction is presented as the return to a transcendental consciousness before which the world is spread out and completely transparent, quickened through and through by a series of apperceptions which it is the philosopher's task to reconstitute on the basis of their outcome. Thus my sensation of redness is *perceived as* the manifestation of a certain redness experienced, this in turn as the manifestation of a red surface, which is the manifestation of a piece of red cardboard, and this finally is the manifestation or outline of a red thing, namely this book. We are to understand, then, that it is the apprehension of a certain *hylè,* as indicating a phenomenon of a higher degree, the *Sinngebung,* or active meaning-giving operation which may be said to define consciousness, so that the world is nothing but "world-as-meaning," and the phenomenological reduction is idealistic, in the sense that there is here a transcendental idealism which treats the world as an indivisible unity of value shared by Peter and Paul, in which their perspectives blend. "Peter's consciousness" and "Paul's consciousness" are in communication, the perception of the world "by Peter" is not Peter's doing any more than its perception "by Paul" is Paul's doing; in each case it is the doing of pre-personal forms of consciousness, whose communication raises no problem, since it is demanded by the very definition of consciousness, meaning or truth. In so far as I am a consciousness, that is, in so far as something has meaning for me, I am neither here nor there, neither Peter nor Paul; I am in no way distinguishable from an "other" consciousness, since we are immediately in touch with the world and since the world is, by definition, unique, being the system in which all truths cohere. A logically consistent transcendental idealism rids the world of its opacity and its transcendence. The world is precisely that thing of which we form a representation, not as men or as empirical subjects, but in so far as we are all one light and participate in the One without destroying its unity. Analytical reflection knows nothing of the problem of other minds, or of that of the world, because it insists that with the first glimmer of consciousness there appears in me theoretically the power of reaching some universal truth, and that the other person, being equally without thisness, location or body, the Alter and the Ego are one and the same in the true world which is the unifier of minds. There is no difficulty in understanding how I can conceive the Other, because the I and consequently the Other are not conceived as part of the woven stuff of phenomena; they have validity rather than existence. There is nothing hidden behind these faces and gestures, no domain to which I have no access, merely a little shadow which owes its very existence to the light. For Husserl, on the contrary, it is well known that there is a problem of other people, and the *alter ego* is a paradox. If the other is truly for himself alone, beyond his being for me, and if we are for each other and not both for God, we must necessarily have some appearance for each other. He must and I must have an outer appearance, and there must be, besides the perspective of the For Oneself—my view of myself and the other's of himself—a perspective of For Others—my view of others and theirs of me. Of course, these two perspectives, in each one of us, cannot be simply juxtaposed, *for in that case it is not I that the other would see, nor he that I should see.* I must be the exterior that I present to others, and the body of the other must be the other himself. This paradox and the dialectic of the Ego and the Alter are possible only provided that the Ego and the Alter Ego are defined by their situation and are not freed from all inherence; that is provided that philosophy does not culminate in a return to the self, and that I discover by reflection not only my presence to myself, but also the possibility of an "outside spectator"; that is, again, provided that at the very moment when I experience my existence—at the ultimate extremity of reflection—I fall short of the ultimate density which would place me outside time, and that I discover within myself a kind of internal weakness standing in the way of my being totally individualized: a weakness which exposes me to the gaze of others as a man among men or at least as a consciousness among consciousnesses. Hitherto the *Cogito* depreciated the perception of others, teaching me as it did that the I is accessible only to itself, since it defined *me* as the thought which I have of myself, and which clearly I am alone in having, at least in this ultimate sense. For the "other" to be more than an empty word, it is necessary that my existence should never be reduced to my bare awareness of existing, but that it should take in also the awareness that *one* may have of it, and thus include my incarnation in some nature and the possibility, at least, of a historical situation. The *Cogito* must reveal me in a situation, and it is on this condition alone that transcendental subjectivity can, as Husserl puts it, *be* an intersubjectivity. As a meditating Ego, I can dearly distinguish from myself the world and things, since I certainly do not exist in the way in which things exist. I must even set aside from myself my body understood as a thing among things, as a collection of physico-chemical processes. But even if the *cogitatio,* which I thus discover, is without location in objective time and space, it is not without place in the phenomenological world. The world, which I distinguished from myself as the totality of things or of processes linked by causal relationships, I rediscover "in me" as the permanent horizon of all my *cogitationes* and as a dimension in relation to which I am constantly situating myself. The true *Cogito* does not define the subject's existence in terms of the thought he has of existing, and furthermore does not convert the indubitability of the world into the indubitability of thought about the world, nor finally does it replace the world itself by the world as meaning. On the contrary it recognizes my thought itself as an inalienable fact, and does away with any kind of idealism in revealing me as "being-in-the-world."

It is because we are through and through compounded of relationships with the world that for us the only way to become aware of the fact is to suspend the resultant activity, to refuse it our complicity (to look at it *ohne mitzumachen,* as Husserl often says), or yet again, to put it "out of play." Not because we reject the certainties of common sense and a natural attitude to things—they are, on the contrary, the constant theme of philosophy—but because, being the presupposed basis of any thought, they are taken for granted, and go unnoticed, and because in order to arouse them and bring them to view, we have to suspend for a moment our recognition of them. The best formulation of the reduction is probably that given by Eugen Fink, Husserl's assistant, when he spoke of "wonder" in the face of the world. Reflection does not withdraw from the world towards the unity of consciousness as the world's basis; it steps back to watch the forms of transcendence fly up like sparks from a fire; it slackens the intentional threads which attach us to the world and thus brings them to our notice; it alone is consciousness of the world because it reveals that world as strange and paradoxical. Husserl's transcendental is not Kant's and Husserl accuses Kant's philosophy of being "worldly," because it *makes use* of our relation to the world, which is the motive force of the transcendental deduction, and makes the world immanent in the subject, instead of *being filled with wonder* at it and conceiving the subject as a process of transcendence towards the world. All the misunderstandings with his interpreters, with the existentialist "dissidents" and finally with himself, have arisen from the fact that in order to see the world and grasp it as paradoxical, we must break with our familiar acceptance of it and, also, from the fact that from this break we can learn nothing but the unmotivated upsurge of the world. The most important lesson which the reduction teaches us is the impossibility of a complete reduction. This is why Husserl is constantly re-examining the possibility of the reduction. If we were absolute mind, the reduction would present no problem. But since, on the contrary, we are in the world, since indeed our reflections are carried out in the temporal flux on to which we are trying to seize (since they *sich einströmen,* as Husserl says), there is no thought which embraces all our thought. The philosopher, as the unpublished works declare, is a perpetual beginner, which means that he takes for granted nothing that men, learned or otherwise, believe they know. It means also that philosophy itself must not take itself for granted, in so far as it may have managed to say something true; that it is an ever-renewed experiment in making its own beginning; that it consists wholly in the description of this beginning, and finally, that radical reflection amounts to a consciousness of its own dependence on an unreflective life which is its initial situation, unchanging, given once and for all. Far from being, as has been thought, a procedure of idealistic philosophy, phenomenological reduction belongs to existential philosophy: Heidegger's "being-in-the-world" appears only against the background of the phenomenological reduction.

A misunderstanding of a similar kind confuses the notion of the "essences" in Husserl. Every reduction, says Husserl, as well as being transcendental is necessarily eidetic. That means that we cannot subject our perception of the world to philosophical scrutiny without ceasing to be identified with that act of positing the world, with that interest in it which delimits us, without drawing back from our commitment which is itself thus made to appear as a spectacle, without passing from the *fact* of our existence to its *nature,* from the *Dasein* to the *Wesen.* But it is clear that the essence is here not the end, but a means, that our effective involvement in the world is precisely what has to be understood and made amenable to conceptualization, for it is what polarizes all our conceptual particularizations. The need to proceed by way of essences does not mean that philosophy takes them as its object, but, on the contrary, that our existence is too tightly held in the world to be able to know itself as such at the moment of its involvement, and that it requires the field of ideality in order to become acquainted with and to prevail over its facticity. The Vienna Circle, as is well known, lays it down categorically that we can enter into relations only with meanings. For example, "consciousness" is not for the Vienna Circle identifiable with what we are. It is a complex meaning which has developed late in time, which should be handled with care, and only after the many meanings which have contributed, throughout the word's semantic development, to the formation of its present one have been made explicit. Logical positivism of this kind is the antithesis of Husserl's thought. Whatever the subtle changes of meaning which have ultimately brought us, as a linguistic acquisition, the word and concept of consciousness, we enjoy direct access to what it designates. For we have the experience of ourselves, of that consciousness which we are, and it is on the basis of this experience that all linguistic connotations are assessed, and precisely through it that language comes to have any meaning at all for us. "It is that as yet dumb experience . . . which we are concerned to lead to the pure expression of its own meaning." Husserl's essences are destined to bring back all the living relationships of experience, as the fisherman's net draws up from the depths of the ocean quivering fish and seaweed. Jean Waehl is therefore wrong in saying that "Husserl separates essences from existence." The separated essences are those of language. It is the office of language to cause essences to exist in a state of separation which is in fact merely apparent, since through language they still rest upon the ante-predicative life of consciousness. In the silence of primary consciousness can be seen appearing not only what words mean, but also what things mean: the core of primary meaning round which the acts of naming and expression take shape.

Seeking the essence of consciousness will therefore not consist in developing the *Wortbedeutung* of consciousness and escaping from existence into the universe of things said; it will consist in rediscovering my actual presence to myself, the fact of my consciousness which is in the last resort what the word and the concept of consciousness mean. Looking for the world's essence is not looking for what it is as an idea once it has been reduced to a theme of discourse; it is looking for what it is as a fact for us, before any thematization. Sensationalism "reduces" the world by noticing that after all we never experience anything but states of ourselves. Transcendental idealism too "reduces" the world since, in so far as it guarantees the world, it does so by regarding it as thought or consciousness of the world, and as the mere correlative of our knowledge, with the result that it becomes immanent in consciousness and the aseity of things is thereby done away with. The eidetic reduction is, on the other hand, the determination to bring the world to light as it is before any falling back on ourselves has occurred, it is the ambition to make reflection emulate the unreflective life of consciousness. I aim at and perceive a world. If I said, as do the sensationalists, that we have here only "states of consciousness," and if I tried to distinguish my perceptions from my dreams with the aid of "criteria," I should overlook the phenomenon of the world. For if I am able to talk about "dreams" and "reality," to bother my head about the distinction between imaginary and real, and cast doubt upon the "real," it is because this distinction is already made by me before any analysis; it is because I have an experience of the real as of the imaginary, and the problem then becomes one not of asking how critical thought can provide for itself secondary equivalents of this distinction, but of making explicit our primordial knowledge of the "real," of describing our perception of the world as that upon which our idea of truth is for ever based. We must not, therefore, wonder whether we really perceive a world, we must instead say: the world is what we perceive. In more general terms we must not wonder whether our self-evident truths are real truths, or whether, through some perversity inherent in our minds, that which is self-evident for us might not be illusory in relation to some truth in itself. For in so far as we talk about illusion, it is because we have identified illusions, and done so solely in the light of some perception which at the same time gave assurance of its own truth. It follows that doubt, or the fear of being mistaken, testifies as soon as it arises to our power of unmasking error, and that it could never finally tear us away from truth. We are in the realm of truth and it is "the experience of truth" which is self-evident. To seek the essence of perception is to declare that perception is, not presumed true, but defined as access to truth. So, if I now wanted, according to idealistic principles, to base this *de facto* self-evident truth, this irresistible belief, on some absolute self-evident truth, that is, on the absolute clarity which my thoughts have for me; if I tried to find in myself a creative thought which bodied forth the framework of the world or illumined it through and through, I should once more prove unfaithful to my experience of the world, and should be looking for what makes that experience possible instead of looking for what it is. The self-evidence of perception is not adequate thought or apodeictic self-evidence. The world is not what I think, but what I live through. I am open to the world, I have no doubt that I am in communication with it, but I do not possess it; it is inexhaustible. "There is a world," or rather: "There is the world"; I can never completely account for this ever-reiterated assertion in my life. This facticity of the world is what constitutes the *Weltlichkeit der Welt*, what causes the world to be the world; just as the facticity of the *cogito* is not an imperfection in itself, but rather what assures me of my existence. The eidetic method is the method of a phenomenological positivism which bases the possible on the real.

We can now consider the notion of intentionality, too often cited as the main discovery of phenomenology, whereas it is understandable only through the reduction. "All consciousness is consciousness of something"; there is nothing new in that. Kant showed, in the *Refutation of Idealism,* that inner perception is impossible without outer perception, that the world, as a collection of connected phenomena, is anticipated in the consciousness of my unity, and is the means whereby I come into being as a consciousness. What distinguishes intentionality from the Kantian relation to a possible object is that the unity of the world, before being posited by knowledge in a specific act of identification, is "lived" as ready-made or already there. Kant himself shows in the *Critique of Judgement* that there exists a unity of the imagination and the understanding and a unity of subjects *before the object,* and that, in experiencing the beautiful, for example, I am aware of a harmony between sensation and concept, between myself and others, which is itself without any concept. Here the subject is no longer the universal thinker of a system of objects rigorously interrelated, the positing power who subjects the manifold to the law of the understanding, in so far as he is to be able to put together a world—he discovers and enjoys his own nature as spontaneously in harmony with the law of the understanding. But if the subject has a nature, then the hidden art of the imagination must condition the categorial activity. It is no longer merely the aesthetic judgement, but knowledge too which rests upon this art, an art which forms the basis of the unity of consciousness and of consciousnesses.

Husserl takes up again the *Critique of Judgement* when he talks about a teleology of consciousness. It is not a matter of duplicating human consciousness with some absolute thought which, from outside, is imagined as assigning to it its aims. It is a question of recognizing consciousness itself as a project of the world, meant for a world which it neither embraces nor possesses, but towards which it is perpetually directed—and the world as this pre-objective individual whose imperious unity decrees what knowledge shall take as its goal. This is why Husserl distinguishes between intentionality of act, which is that of our judgements and of those occasions when we voluntarily take up a position—the only intentionality discussed in the *Critique of Pure Reason*—and operative intentionality [*fungierende Intentionalität*], or that which produces the natural and ante-predicative unity of the world and of our life, being apparent in our desires, our evaluations and in the landscape we see, more clearly than in objective knowledge, and furnishing the text which our knowledge tries to translate into precise language. Our relationship to the world, as it is untiringly enunciated within us, is not a thing which can be any further clarified by analysis; philosophy can only place it once more before our eyes and present it for our ratification.

Through this broadened notion of intentionality, phenomenological "comprehension" is distinguished from traditional "intellection," which is confined to "true and immutable natures," and so phenomenology can become a phenomenology of origins. Whether we are concerned with a thing perceived, a historical event or a doctrine, to "understand" is to take in the total intention—not only what these things are for representation (the "properties" of the thing perceived, the mass of "historical facts," the "ideas" introduced by the doctrine)—but the unique mode of existing expressed in the properties of the pebble, the glass or the piece of wax, in all the events of a revolution, in all the thoughts of a philosopher. It is a matter, in the case of each civilization, of finding the Idea in the Hegelian sense, that is, not a law of the physico-mathematical type, discoverable by objective thought, but that formula which sums up some unique manner of behaviour towards others, towards Nature, time and death: a certain way of patterning the world which the historian should be capable of seizing upon and making his own. These are the *dimensions* of history. In this context there is not a human word, not a gesture, even one which is the outcome of habit or absentmindedness, which has not some meaning. For example, I may have been under the impression that I lapsed into silence through weariness, or some minister may have thought he had uttered merely an appropriate platitude, yet my silence or his words immediately take on a significance, because my fatigue or his falling back upon a ready-made formula are not accidental, for they express a certain lack of interest, and hence some degree of adoption of a definite position in relation to the situation.

When an event is considered at close quarters, at the moment when it is lived through, everything seems subject to chance: one man's ambition, some lucky encounter, some local circumstance or other appears to have been decisive. But chance happenings offset each other, and facts in their multiplicity coalesce and show up a certain way of taking a stand in relation to the human situation, reveal in fact an *event* which has its definite outline and about which we can talk. Should the starting-point for the understanding of history be ideology, or politics, or religion, or economics? Should we try to understand a doctrine from its overt content, or from the psychological make-up and the biography of its author? We must seek an understanding from all these angles simultaneously, everything has meaning, and we shall find this same structure of being underlying all relationships. All these views are true provided that they are not isolated, that we delve deeply into history and reach the unique core of existential meaning which emerges in each perspective. It is true, as Marx says, that history does not walk on its head, but it is also true that it does not think with its feet. Or one should say rather that it is neither its "head" nor its "feet" that we have to worry about, but its body. All economic and psychological explanations of a doctrine are true, since the thinker never thinks from any starting-point but the one constituted by what he is. Reflection even on a doctrine will be complete only if it succeeds in linking up with the doctrine's history and the extraneous explanations of it, and in putting back the causes and meaning of the doctrine in an existential structure. There is, as Husserl says, a "genesis of meaning" [*Sinngenesis*], which alone, in the last resort, teaches us what the doctrine "means." Like understanding, criticism must be pursued at all levels, and naturally, it will be insufficient, for the refutation of a doctrine, to relate it to some accidental event in the author's life: its significance goes beyond, and there is no pure accident in existence or in co-existence, since both absorb random events and transmute them into the rational.

Finally, as it is indivisible in the present, history is equally so in its sequences. Considered in the light of its fundamental dimensions, all periods of history appear as manifestations of a single existence, or as episodes in a single drama—without our knowing whether it has an ending. Because we are in the world, we are *condemned to meaning,* and we cannot do or say anything without its acquiring a name in history.

Probably the chief gain from phenomenology is to have united extreme subjectivism and extreme objectivism in its notion of the world or of rationality. Rationality is precisely measured by the experiences in which it is disclosed. To say that there exists rationality is to say that perspectives blend, perceptions confirm each other, a meaning emerges. But it should not be set in a realm apart, transposed into absolute Spirit, or into a world in the realist sense. The phenomenological world is not pure being, but the sense which is revealed where the paths of my various experiences intersect, and also where my own and other people's intersect and engage each other like gears. It is thus inseparable from subjectivity and intersubjectivity, which find their unity when I either take up my past experiences in those of the present, or other people's in my own. For the first time the philosopher's thinking is sufficiently conscious not to anticipate itself and endow its own results with reified form in the world. The philosopher tries to conceive the world, others and himself and their interrelations. But the meditating Ego, the "impartial spectator" [*uninteressierter Zuschauer*] do not rediscover an already given rationality, they "establish themselves," and establish it, by an act of initiative which has no guarantee in being, its justification resting entirely on the effective power which it confers on us of taking our own history upon ourselves.

The phenomenological world is not the bringing to explicit expression of a preexisting being, but the laying down of being. Philosophy is not the reflection of a preexisting truth, but, like art, the act of bringing truth into being. One may well ask how this creation is *possible,* and if it does not recapture in things a pre-existing Reason. The answer is that the only pre-existent <*Logos*> is the world itself, and that the philosophy which brings it into visible existence does not begin by being *possible;* it is actual or real like the world of which it is a part, and no explanatory hypothesis is clearer than the act whereby we take up this unfinished world in an effort to complete and conceive it. Rationality is not a *problem.* There is behind it no unknown quantity which has to be determined by deduction, or, beginning with it, demonstrated inductively. We witness every minute the miracle of related experiences, and yet nobody knows better than we do how this miracle is worked, for we are ourselves this network of relationships. The world and reason are not problematical. We may say, if we wish, that they are mysterious, but their mystery defines them: there can be no question of dispelling it by some "solution," it is on the hither side of all solutions. True philosophy consists in relearning to look at the world, and in this sense a historical account can give meaning to the world quite as "deeply" as a philosophical treatise. We take our fate in our hands, we become responsible for our history through reflection, but equally by a decision on which we stake our life, and in both cases what is involved is a violent act which is validated by being performed.

Phenomenology, as a disclosure of the world, rests on itself, or rather provides its own foundation. All knowledge is sustained by a "ground" of postulates and finally by our communication with the world as primary embodiment of rationality. Philosophy, as radical reflection, dispenses in principle with this resource. As, however, it too is in history, it too exploits the world and constituted reason. It must therefore put to itself the question which it puts to all branches of knowledge, and so duplicate itself infinitely, being, as Husserl says, a dialogue or infinite meditation, and, in so far as it remains faithful to its intention, never knowing where it is going. The unfinished nature of phenomenology and the inchoative atmosphere which has surrounded it are not to be taken as a sign of failure, they were inevitable because phenomenology's task was to reveal the mystery of the world and of reason. If phenomenology was a movement before becoming a doctrine or a philosophical system, this was attributable neither to accident, nor to fraudulent intent. It is as painstaking as the works of Balzac, Proust, Valéry or Cézanne— by reason of the same kind of attentiveness and wonder, the same demand for awareness, the same will to seize the meaning of the world or of history as that meaning comes into being. In this way it merges into the general effort of modern thought.

J.L. AUSTIN
1911–1960

John Langshaw Austin was born in Lancaster, England, in 1911. One of five children, his father was an architect before serving in the First World War. After the war, Austin's father moved the family to St. Andrews, Scotland, taking an administrative position at St. Leonard's School. Austin remained in Scotland until he received a classics scholarship to Shrewsbury School at age thirteen.

After Shrewsbury, Austin received a scholarship in 1929 to Balliol College, Oxford, to study classics and philosophy. In 1933, he received a research fellowship at All Souls College. Two years later, he became a fellow and tutor at Magdalen College. Except for his service during the Second World War, Austin taught at Oxford the remainder of his short life.

Austin was extraordinarily successful as a teacher. His students were impressed by his patient and careful approach to philosophical problems. His colleagues eagerly solicited his opinions. His administrators appreciated his institutional responsibility. For example, as a faculty delegate to the Oxford University Press, he studied the business's operations and was acclaimed by the secretary of the press as "the best delegate I ever knew."

During the Second World War, Austin joined the British Intelligence Corps, became a section director, and in less than five years was promoted to Lt. Colonel. His preparation for D-Day was recognized after the war by French and American governments with medals. During the war, Austin married Jean Coutts and together they had four children.

When peace returned, Austin brought his problem-solving expertise to Oxford. For example, the innumerable logistical problems of D-Day had been solved by subdividing unwieldy masses into manageable chunks. Why couldn't the same be done in philosophy? Accordingly, Austin organized Saturday-morning workshops for solving philosophical problems. One of those who attended these meetings explained how the workshops functioned:

> A field of inquiry—for example, in one [academic] term the concept of a rule—was systematically divided into areas, and each area assigned to some one of those present for investigation ... Results were to be fairly formally reported, and records kept in writing.*

Although the sessions did not always produce the results Austin sought, this systematic approach influenced a generation of philosophers.

In 1952, Austin was elected to White's Chair of Moral Philosophy, one of only three philosophical professorships at Oxford. The honor was unusual because Austin had published only three papers—and no books. In fact, after a lifetime of work Austin published only seven articles.

Austin died young, at age forty-eight. At his death, Austin was at work on his only two books—*Sense and Sensibilia* and *How to Do Things with Words*—which were published posthumously. All Austin's other work was collected in *Philosophical Papers* (1961; revised in 1970 and 1979).

* * *

Austin did not really have a "philosophy." He had a method by which he approached philosophical problems. Austin believed that to investigate a particular area of philosophy fruitfully, one should discover its rules of language. To do this, one must carefully examine how ordinary language is used in the area. Austin believed ordinary language has distinctions formed from centuries of use that deserve careful attention. Austin did not in principle object to technical terms, nor did he believe that ordinary language was beyond improvement. But before introducing new, technical, or obscure language, one should study existing usage respectfully.

Using "ordinary language philosophy" (as it came to be called), Austin explored philosophical logic ("The Meaning of a Word," 1940), perception (*Sense and Sensibilia,* 1962), and free will ("A Plea for Excuses" and "Ifs and Cans," 1956). But he is best known for his work on the nature of language itself.

In his William James Lectures at Harvard, later published as *How to Do Things with Words* (1962), Austin invented speech act theory. In examining how language is used, Austin noticed that speech acts are not always descriptive and that there are more than just "constantive" (or true or false) assertions. In the selection given here, Austin identifies what he calls "performative" utterances. These sentences appear to be constantive, but in fact, they do not describe or report anything. Instead, uttering such a sentence "is, or is a part of, the doing of an action." Austin shows that the words "'I name this ship the Queen Elizabeth'— ... when smashing the bottle against the stem" is not describing anything. Rather, in saying the words the speaker is *doing* the action of naming.

As Austin explored speech acts and performative utterance, he came to the conclusion that there is an element of doing in *any* speech act. He distinguished

*G.J. Warnock, "John Langshaw Austin, A Biographical Sketch," in K.T. Fann, *Symposium on J.L. Austin* (New York: Humanities Press, 1969).

between the *locutionary element,* what one actually says, the *illocutionary element,* the action being performed by the utterance, and the *perlocutionary element,* the effect of the speech act. So, for example, if I say "What follows is our selection from Austin," the locutionary act is the reference to the words printed on the pages that follow; the illocutionary act is the act I perform by calling attention to the reading that follows; and the perlocutionary act would be the effect of this utterance—perhaps getting someone to read the material.

Austin's ordinary language philosophy, with its emphasis upon the careful analysis of language, has been influential in Anglo-American philosophy. His speech act theory, on the other hand, has been developed and expanded, especially by Continental philosophers. The reading from Derrida in this volume, for instance, begins with a quotation from Austin and treats speech act theory. Whenever he has been studied, Austin's carefulness has been admired and imitated.

*   *   *

For general introductions to Austin's philosophy, see Keith Graham, *J.L. Austin: A Critique of Ordinary Language Philosophy* (Atlantic Highlands, NJ: Humanities Press, 1977) and G.J. Warnock, *J.L. Austin* (London: Routledge, 1989). Mats Furberg, *Saying and Meaning: A Main Theme in J.L. Austin's Philosophy* (Oxford: Basil Blackwell, 1963) explores one area of Austin's thought. K.T. Fann, *Symposium on J.L. Austin* (New York: Humanities Press, 1969) provides a biographical sketch as well as essays grouped around central themes in Austin's work; Isaiah Berlin et al., *Essays on J.L. Austin* (Oxford: Oxford University Press, 1973) includes critical essays. John R. Searle, *Speech Acts: An Essay in the Philosophy of Language* (Cambridge: Cambridge University Press, 1969) and David Holdcroft, *Words and Deeds* (Oxford: Oxford University Press, 1978) are important books on speech act theory. Finally, Soshana Felman, *The Literary Speech Act: Don Juan with J.L. Austin, or Seduction in Two Languages,* translated by Catherine Porter (Ithaca, NY: Cornell University Press, 1983) is an unusual study of the speech act of promising.

HOW TO DO THINGS WITH WORDS
(in part)

LECTURE I

What I shall have to say here is neither difficult nor contentious; the only merit I should like to claim for it is that of being true, at least in parts. The phenomenon to be discussed is very widespread and obvious, and it cannot fail to have been already noticed, at least here and there, by others. Yet I have not found attention paid to it specifically.

J.L. Austin, *How to Do Things with Words* (Lectures 1 and 2), ed. by J.O. Urmson and Marina Sbisà (Cambridge, MA: Harvard University Press, 1962, 1975), pp. 1–24. © 1962, renewed 1975 by Harvard University Press. Reprinted by permission.

It was for too long the assumption of philosophers that the business of a "statement" can only be to "describe" some state of affairs, or to "state some fact," which it must do either truly or falsely. Grammarians, indeed, have regularly pointed out that not all "sentences" are (used in making) statements:* there are, traditionally, besides (grammarians') statements, also questions and exclamations, and sentences expressing commands or wishes or concessions. And doubtless philosophers have not intended to deny this, despite some loose use of "sentence" for "statement." Doubtless, too, both grammarians and philosophers have been aware that it is by no means easy to distinguish even questions, commands, and so on from statements by means of the few and jejune grammatical marks available, such as word order, mood, and the like: though perhaps it has not been usual to dwell on the difficulties which this fact obviously raises. For how do we decide which is which? What are the limits and definitions of each?

But now in recent years, many things which would once have been accepted without question as "statements" by both philosophers and grammarians have been scrutinized with new care. This scrutiny arose somewhat indirectly—at least in philosophy. First came the view, not always formulated without unfortunate dogmatism, that a statement (of fact) ought to be "verifiable," and this led to the view that many "statements" are only what may be called pseudo-statements. First and most obviously, many "statements" were shown to be, as Kant perhaps first argued systematically, strictly nonsense, despite an unexceptionable grammatical form: and the continual discovery of fresh types of nonsense, unsystematic though their classification and mysterious though their explanation is too often allowed to remain, has done on the whole nothing but good. Yet we, that is, even philosophers, set some limits to the amount of nonsense that we are prepared to admit we talk: so that it was natural to go on to ask, as a second stage, whether many apparent pseudo-statements really set out to be "statements" at all. It has come to be commonly held that many utterances which look like statements are either not intended at all, or only intended in part, to record or impart straightforward information about the facts: for example, "ethical propositions" are perhaps intended, solely or partly, to evince emotion or to prescribe conduct or to influence it in special ways. Here too Kant was among the pioneers. We very often also use utterances in ways beyond the scope at least of traditional grammar. It has come to be seen that many specially perplexing words embedded in apparently descriptive statements do not serve to indicate some specially odd additional feature in the reality reported, but to indicate (not to report) the circumstances in which the statement is made or reservations to which it is subject or the way in which it is to be taken and the like. To overlook these possibilities in the way once common is called the "descriptive" fallacy; but perhaps this is not a good name, as "descriptive" itself is special. Not all true or false statements are descriptions, and for this reason I prefer to use the word "Constative." Along these lines it has by now been shown piecemeal, or at least made to look likely, that many traditional philosophical perplexities have arisen through a mistake—the mistake of taking as straightforward statements of fact utterances which are *either* (in interesting non-grammatical ways) nonsensical *or else* intended as something quite different.

Whatever we may think of any particular one of these views and suggestions, and however much we may deplore the initial confusion into which philosophical doctrine and method have been plunged, it cannot be doubted that they are producing a

---

*It is, of course, not really correct that a sentence ever is a statement: rather, it is used in making a statement, and the statement itself is a "logical construction" out of the makings of statements.

revolution in philosophy. If anyone wishes to call it the greatest and most salutary in its history, this is not, if you come to think of it, a large claim. It is not surprising that beginnings have been piecemeal, with parti pris, and for extraneous aims; this is common with revolutions.

Preliminary Isolation of the Performative*

The type of utterance we are to consider here is not, of course, in general a type of nonsense; though misuse of it can, as we shall see, engender rather special varieties of "nonsense." Rather, it is one of our second class—the masqueraders. But it does not by any means necessarily masquerade as a statement of fact, descriptive or constative. Yet it does quite commonly do so, and that, oddly enough, when it assumes its most explicit form. Grammarians have not, I believe, seen through this "disguise," and philosophers only at best incidentally.** It will be convenient, therefore, to study it first in this misleading form, in order to bring out its characteristics by contrasting them with those of the statement of fact which it apes.

We shall take, then, for our first examples some utterances which can fall into no hitherto recognized *grammatical* category save that of "statement," which are not nonsense, and which contain none of those verbal danger signals which philosophers have by now detected or think they have detected (curious words like "good" or "all," suspect auxiliaries like "ought" or "can," and dubious constructions like the hypothetical): all will have, as it happens, humdrum verbs in the first person singular present indicative active.*** Utterances can be found, satisfying these conditions, yet such that

A. they do not "describe" or "report" or constate anything at all, are not "true or false"; and
B. the uttering of the sentence is, or is a part of, the doing of an action, which again would not *normally* be described as, or as "just," saying something.

This is far from being as paradoxical as it may sound or as I have meanly been trying to make it sound: indeed, the examples now to be given will be disappointing.
Examples:

(E. *a*) "I do (sc. take this woman to be my lawful wedded wife)"—as uttered in the course of the marriage ceremony.†
(E. *b*) "I name this ship the Queen Elizabeth"—as uttered when smashing the bottle against the stem.
(E. *c*) "I give and bequeath my watch to my brother"—as occurring in a will.
(E. *d*) "I bet you sixpence it will rain tomorrow."

*Everything said in these sections is provisional, and subject to revision in the light of later sections.
**Of all people, jurists should be best aware of the true state of affairs. Perhaps some now are. Yet they will succumb to their own timorous fiction, that a statement of "the law" is a statement of fact.
***Not without design: they are all "explicit" performatives, and of that prepotent class later called "exercitives."
†[Austin realized that the expression "I do" is not used in the marriage ceremony too late to correct his mistake. We have let it remain in the text as it is philosophically unimportant that it is a mistake—J.O.U.]

In these examples it seems clear that to utter the sentence (in, of course, the appropriate circumstances) is not to *describe* my doing of what I should be said in so uttering to be doing* or to state that I am doing it: it is to do it. None of the utterances cited is either true or false: I assert this as obvious and do not argue it. It needs argument no more than that "damn" is not true or false: it may be that the utterance "serves to inform you"—but that is quite different. To name the ship is to say (in the appropriate circumstances) the words "I name, &c." When I say, before the registrar or altar, &c., "I do," I am not reporting on a marriage: I am indulging in it.

What are we to call a sentence or an utterance of this type?** I propose to call it a performative sentence or a *performative utterance,* or, for short, "a performative." The term "performative" will be used in a variety of cognate ways and constructions, much as the term "imperative" is.*** The name is derived, of course, from "perform," the usual verb with the noun "action": it indicates that the issuing of the utterance is the performing of an action—it is not normally thought of as just saying something.

A number of other terms may suggest themselves, each of which would suitably cover this or that wider or narrower class of performatives: for example, many performatives are *contractual* ("I bet") or *declaratory* ("I declare war") utterances. But no term in current use that I know of is nearly wide enough to cover them all. One technical term that comes nearest to what we need is perhaps "operative," as it is used strictly by lawyers in referring to that part, i.e. those clauses, of an instrument which serves to effect the transaction (conveyance or what not) which is its main object, whereas the rest of the document merely "recites" the circumstances in which the transaction is to be effected.† But "operative" has other meanings, and indeed is often used nowadays to mean little more than "important." I have preferred a new word, to which, though its etymology is not irrelevant, we shall perhaps not be so ready to attach some preconceived meaning.

Can Saying Make it So?

Are we then to say things like this:

> "To marry is to say a few words," or
>   "Betting is simply saying something"?

Such a doctrine sounds odd or even flippant at first, but with sufficient safeguards it may become not odd at all.

A sound initial objection to them may be this; and it is not without some importance. In very many cases it is possible to perform an act of exactly the same kind

---

*Still less anything that I have already done or have yet to do.

**"Sentences" form a class of "utterances," which class is to be defined, so far as I am concerned, grammatically, though I doubt if the definition has yet been given satisfactorily. With performative utterances are contrasted, for example and essentially, "constative" utterances: to issue a constative utterance (i.e. to utter it with a historical reference) is to make a statement. To issue a performative utterance is, for example, to make a bet. See further below on "illocutions."

***Formerly I used "performatory": but "performative" is to be preferred as shorter, less ugly, more tractable, and more traditional in formation.

†I owe this observation to Professor H.L.A. Hart.

not by uttering words, whether written or spoken, but in some other way. For example, I may in some places effect marriage by cohabiting, or I may bet with a total-isator machine by putting a coin in a slot. We should then, perhaps, convert the propositions above, and put it that "to say a few certain words is to marry" or "to marry is, in some cases, simply to say a few words" or "simply to say a certain something is to bet."

But probably the real reason why such remarks sound dangerous lies in another obvious fact, to which we shall have to revert in detail later, which is this. The uttering of the words is, indeed, usually a, or even *the,* leading incident in the performance of the act (of betting or what not), the performance of which is also the object of the utterance, but it is far from being usually, even if it is ever, the sole thing necessary if the act is to be deemed to have been performed. Speaking generally, it is always necessary that the *circumstances* in which the words are uttered should be in some way, or ways, *appropriate,* and it is very commonly necessary that either the speaker himself or other persons should *also* perform certain *other* actions, whether "physical" or "mental" actions or even acts of uttering further words. Thus, for naming the ship, it is essential that I should be the person appointed to name her, for (Christian) marrying, it is essential that I should not be already married with a wife living, sane and undivorced, and so on: for a bet to have been made, it is generally necessary for the offer of the bet to have been accepted by a taker (who must have done something, such as to say "Done"), and it is hardly a gift if I *say* "I give it to you" but never hand it over.

So far, well and good. The action may be performed in ways other than by a performative utterance, and in any case the circumstances, including other actions, must be appropriate. But we may, in objecting, have something totally different, and this time quite mistaken, in mind, especially when we think of some of the more awe inspiring performatives such as "I promise to . . ." Surely the words must be spoken "seriously" so as to be taken "seriously"? This is, though vague, true enough in general—it is an important commonplace in discussing the purport of any utterance whatsoever. I must not be joking, for example, nor writing a poem. But we are apt to have a feeling that their being serious consists in their being uttered as (merely) the outward and visible sign, for convenience or other record or for information, of an inward and spiritual act: from which it is but a short step to go on to believe or to assume without realizing that for many purposes the outward utterance is a description, *true or false,* of the occurrence of the inward performance. The classic expression of this idea is to be found in the Hippolytus (I. 612), where *Hippolytus* says "my tongue swore to, but my heart (or mind or other backstage artiste) did not."* Thus "I promise to . . ." obliges me—puts on record my spiritual assumption of a spiritual shackle.

It is gratifying to observe in this very example how excess of profundity, or rather solemnity, at once paves the way for immodality. For one who says "promising is not merely a matter of uttering words! It is an inward and spiritual act!" is apt to appear as a solid moralist standing out against a generation of superficial theorizers: we see him as he sees himself, surveying the invisible depths of ethical space, with all the distinction of a specialist in the *sui generis.* Yet he provides Hippolytus with a let-out,

---

*But I do not mean to rule out all the offstage performers—the lights men, the stage manager, even the prompter. I am objecting only to certain officious understudies, who would duplicate the play.

the bigamist with an excuse for his "I do" and the welsher with a defence for his "I bet." Accuracy and morality alike are on the side of the plain saying that *our word is our bond.*

If we exclude such fictitious inward acts as this, can we suppose that any of the other things which certainly are normally required to accompany an utterance such as "I promise that . . ." or "I do (take this woman . . .)" are in fact described by it, and consequently do by their presence make it true or by their absence make it false? Well, taking the latter first, we shall next consider what we actually do say about the utterance concerned when one or another of its normal concomitants is *absent.* In no case do we say—that the utterance was false but rather that the utterance—or rather the *act,** e.g. the promise—was void, or given in bad faith, or not implemented, or the like. In the particular case of promising, as with many other performatives, it is appropriate that the person uttering the promise should have a certain intention, viz. here to keep his word: and perhaps of all concomitants this looks the most suitable to be that which "I promise" does describe or record. Do we not actually, when such intention is absent, speak of a "false" promise? Yet so to speak is *not* to say that the utterance "I promise that . . ." is false, in the sense that though he states that he does, he doesn't, or that though he describes he misdescribes-misreports. For he *does* promise: the promise here is not even void, though it is given *in bad faith.* His utterance is perhaps misleading, probably deceitful and doubtless wrong, but it is not a lie or a misstatement. At most we might make out a case for saying that it implies or insinuates a falsehood or a misstatement (to the effect that he does intend to do something): but that is a very different matter. Moreover, we do not speak of a false bet or a false christening; and that we *do* speak of a false promise need commit us no more than the fact that we speak of a false move. "False" is not necessarily used of statements only.

Lecture II

We were to consider, you will remember, some cases and senses (only some, Heaven help us!) in which to *say* something is to *do* something; or in which *by* saying or *in* saying something we are doing something. This topic is one development—there are many others—in the recent movement towards questioning an age-old assumption in philosophy—the assumption that to say something, at least in all cases worth considering, i.e. all cases considered, is always and simply to *state* something. This assumption is no doubt unconscious, no doubt is precipitate, but it is wholly natural in philosophy apparently. We must learn to run before we can walk. If we never made mistakes how should we correct them?

I began by drawing your attention, by way of example, to a few simple utterances of the kind known as performatorics or performatives. These have on the face of them the look—or at least the grammatical make-up—of "statements"; but nevertheless they are seen, when more closely inspected, to be, quite plainly, *not* utterances

---

*We deliberately avoid distinguishing these, precisely because the distinction is not in point.

which could be "true" or "false." Yet to be "true" or "false" is traditionally the characteristic mark of a statement. One of our examples was, for instance, the utterance "I do" (take this woman to be my lawful wedded wife), as uttered in the course of a marriage ceremony. Here we should say that in saying these words we are *doing* something—namely, marrying, rather than reporting something, namely *that* we are marrying. And the act of marrying, like, say, the act of betting, is at least *preferably* (though still not *accurately*) to be described as *saying certain words,* rather than as performing a different, inward and spiritual, action of which these words are merely the outward and audible sign. That this is so can perhaps hardly be *proved,* but it is, I should claim, a fact.

It is worthy of note that, as I am told, in the American law of evidence, a report of what someone else said is admitted as evidence if what he said is an utterance of our performative kind: because this is regarded as a report not so much of something he *said,* as which it would be hear-say and not admissible as evidence, but rather as something he *did,* an action of his. This coincides very well with our initial feelings about performatives.

So far then we have merely felt the firm ground of prejudice slide away beneath our feet. But now how, as philosophers, are we to proceed? One thing we might go on to do, of course, is to take it all back: another would be to bog, by logical stages, down. But all this must take time. Let us first at least concentrate attention on the little matter already mentioned in passing—this matter of "the appropriate circumstances." To bet is not, as I pointed out in passing, merely to utter the words "I bet, &c.": someone might do that all right, and yet we might still not agree that he had in fact, or at least entirely, succeeded in betting. To satisfy ourselves of this, we have only, for example, to announce our bet after the race is over. Besides the uttering of the words of the so called performative, a good many other things have as a general rule to be right and to go right if we are to be said to have happily brought off our action. What these are we may hope to discover by looking at and classifying types of case in which something goes wrong and the act—marrying, betting, bequeathing, christening, or what not—is therefore at least to some extent a failure: the utterance is then, we may say, not indeed false but in general *unhappy.* And for this reason we call the doctrine of *the things that can be and go wrong* on the occasion of such utterances, the doctrine of the infelicities.

Suppose we try first to state schematically—and I do not wish to claim any sort of finality for this scheme—some at least of the things which are necessary for the smooth or "happy" functioning of a performative (or at least of a highly developed explicit performative, such as we have hitherto been alone concerned with), and then give examples of infelicities and their effects. I fear, but at the same time of course hope, that these necessary conditions to be satisfied will strike you as obvious.

(A. 1) There must exist an accepted conventional procedure having a certain conventional effect, that procedure to include the uttering of certain words by certain persons in certain circumstances, and further,

(A. 2) the particular persons and circumstances in a given case must be appropriate for the invocation of the particular procedure invoked.

(B. 1) The procedure must be executed by all participants both correctly and

(B. 2) completely.

(Γ. 1) Where, as often, the procedure is designed for use by persons having certain thoughts or feelings, or for the inauguration of certain consequential conduct on the part of any participant, then a person participating in and so invoking the procedure must in fact have those thoughts or feelings, and the participants must intend so to conduct themselves,* and further

(Γ. 2) must actually so conduct themselves subsequently.

Now if we sin against any one (or more) of these six rules, our performative utterance will be (in one way or another) unhappy. But, of course, there are considerable differences between these "ways" of being unhappy—ways which are intended to be brought out by the letter numerals selected for each heading.

The first big distinction is between all the four rules A and B taken together, as opposed to the two rules Γ (hence the use of Roman as opposed to Greek letters). If we offend against any of the former rules (A's or B's)—that is if we, say, utter the formula incorrectly, or if, say, we are not in a position to do the act because we are, say, married already, or it is the purser and not the captain who is conducting the ceremony, then the act in question, e.g. marrying, is not successfully performed at all, does not come off, is not achieved. Whereas in the two Γ cases the act *is* achieved, although to achieve it in such circumstances, as when we are, say, insincere, is an abuse of the procedure. Thus, when I say "I promise" and have no intention of keeping it, I have promised but . . . We need names for referring to this general distinction, so we shall call in general those infelicities A. 1–B. 2 which are such that the act for the performing of which, and in the performing of which, the verbal formula in question is designed, is not achieved, by the name MISFIRES: and on the other hand we may christen those infelicities where the act is achieved ABUSES (do not stress the normal connotations of these names!). When the utterance is a misfire, the procedure which we purport to invoke is disallowed or is botched: and our act (marrying, &c.) is void or without effect, &c. We speak of our act as a purported act, or perhaps an attempt—or we use such an expression as "went through a form of marriage" by contrast with "married." On the other hand, in the G cases, we speak of our infelicitous act as "professed" or "hollow" rather than "purported" or "empty," and as not implemented, or not consummated, rather than as void or without effect. But let me hasten to add that these distinctions are not hard and fast, and more especially that such words as "purported" and "professed" will not bear very much stressing. Two final words about being void or without effect. This does not mean, of course, to say that we won't have done anything: lots of things will have been done—we shall most interestingly have committed the act of bigamy—but we shall not have done the purported act, viz. marrying. Because despite the name, you do not when bigamous marry twice. (In short, the algebra of marriage is BOOLEAN.) Further, "without effect" does not here mean "without consequences, results, effects."

Next, we must try to make clear the general distinction between the A cases and the B cases, among the misfires. In both of the cases labeled A there is *misinvocation* of a procedure—either because there *is,* speaking vaguely, no such procedure, or because the procedure in question cannot be made to apply in the way attempted. Hence infelicities of this kind A may be called *Misinvocations.* Among them, we may reasonably christen the second sort—where the procedure does exist all right but can't be applied as purported—*Misapplications.* But I have not succeeded in finding a good name for the other, former, class. By contrast with the A cases, the notion of the B cases is

*It will be explained later why the having of these thoughts, feelings, and intentions is not included as just one among the other "circumstances" already dealt with in (A).

rather that the procedure is all right, and it does apply all right, but we muff the execution of the ritual with more or less dire consequences: so B cases as opposed to A cases will be called *Misexecutions* as opposed to Misinvocations: the purported act is vitiated by a flaw or hitch in the conduct of the ceremony. The Class B. 1 is that of Flaws, the Class B. 2 that of Hitches.

We get then the following scheme:*

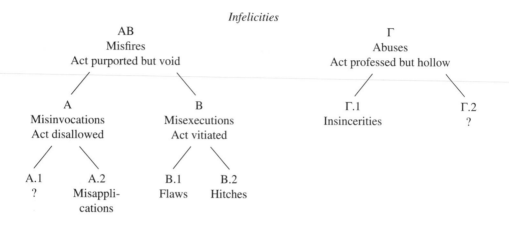

I expect some doubts will be entertained about A. 1 and G. 2; but we will postpone them for detailed consideration shortly.

But before going on to details, let me make some general remarks about these infelicities. We may ask:

(1) To what variety of "act" does the notion of infelicity apply?
(2) How complete is this classification of infelicity?
(3) Are these classes of infelicity mutually exclusive?

Let us take these questions in (that) order.
(1) How widespread is infelicity?

Well, it seems clear in the first place that, although it has excited us (or failed to excite us) in connexion with certain acts which are or are in part acts of *uttering words*, infelicity is an ill to which *all* acts are heir which have the general character of ritual or ceremonial, all *conventional* acts: not indeed that *every* ritual is liable to every form of infelicity (but then nor is every performative utterance). This is clear if only from the mere fact that many conventional acts, such as betting or conveyance of property, can be performed in non-verbal ways. The same sorts of rule must be observed in all such conventional procedures—we have only to omit the special reference to verbal utterance in our A. This much is obvious.

But, furthermore, it is worth pointing out—reminding you—how many of the "acts" which concern the jurist are or include the utterance of performatives, or at any

---

*[Austin from time to time used other names for the different infelicities. For interest some are here given: A. 1, Nonplays; A. 2, Misplays; B, Miscarriages; B. 1, Misexecutions; B. 2, Non-executions; G, Disrespects; G. I, Dissimulations; G. 2, Non-fulfilments, Disloyalties, Infractions, Indisciplines. Breaches. J.O.U.]

rate are or include the performance of some conventional procedures. And of course you will appreciate that in this way and that writers on jurisprudence have constantly shown themselves aware of the varieties of infelicity and even at times of the peculiarities of the performative utterance. Only the still widespread obsession that the utterances of the law, and utterances used in, say, "acts in the law," must somehow be statements true or false, has prevented many lawyers from getting this whole matter much straighter than we are likely to—and I would not even claim to know whether some of them have not already done so. Of more direct concern to us, however, is to realize that, by the same token, a great many of the acts which fall within the province of Ethics are *not,* as philosophers are too prone to assume, simply in the last resort *physical movements:* very many of them have the general character, in whole or part, of conventional or ritual acts, and are therefore, among other things, exposed to infelicity.

Lastly we may ask—and here I must let some of my cats on the table—does the notion of infelicity apply to utterances *which are statements?* So far we have produced the infelicity as characteristic of the *performative* utterance, which was "defined" (if we can call it so much) mainly by contrast with the supposedly familiar "statement." Yet I will content myself here with pointing out that one of the things that has been happening lately in philosophy is that close attention has been given even to "statements" which, though not false exactly nor yet "contradictory," are yet outrageous. For instance, statements which refer to something which does not exist as, for example, "The present King of France is bald." There might be a temptation to assimilate this to purporting to bequeath something which you do not own. Is there not a presupposition of existence in each? Is not a statement which refers to something which does not exist not so much false as void? And the more we consider a statement not as a sentence (or proposition) but as an act of speech (out of which the others are logical constructions) the more we are studying the whole thing as an act. Or again, there are obvious similarities between a lie and a false promise. We shall have to return to this matter later.

(2) Our second question was: How complete is this classification?

(i) Well, the first thing to remember is that, since in uttering our performatives we are undoubtedly in a sound enough sense "performing actions," then, as actions, these will be subject to certain whole dimensions of unsatisfactoriness to which all actions are subject but which are distinct—or distinguishable—from what we have chosen to discuss as infelicities. I mean that actions in general (not all) are liable, for example, to be done under duress, or by accident, or owing to this or that variety of mistake, say, or otherwise unintentionally. In many such cases we are certainly unwilling to say of some such act simply that it was done or that he did it. I am not going into the general doctrine here: in many such cases we may even say the act was "void" (or voidable for duress or undue influence) and so forth. Now I suppose some very general high-level doctrine might embrace both what we have called infelicities *and* these other "unhappy" features of the doing of actions—in our case actions containing a performative utterance—in a single doctrine: but we are not including this kind of unhappiness—we must just remember, though, that features of this sort can and do constantly obtrude into any particular case we are discussing. Features of this sort would normally come under the heading of "extenuating circumstances" or of "factors reducing or abrogating the agent's responsibility," and so on.

(ii) Secondly, as *utterances* our performatives are *also* heir to certain other kinds of ill which infect *all* utterances. And these likewise, though again they might be brought into a more general account, we are deliberately at present excluding. I mean, for example, the following: a performative utterance will, for example, be *in a peculiar way* hollow or void if said by an actor on the stage, or if introduced in a poem, or spoken in soliloquy. This applies in a similar manner to any and every utterance—a sea-change in special circumstances. Language in such circumstances is in special ways—intelligibly—used not seriously, but in ways *parasitic* upon its normal use— ways which fall under the doctrine of the *etiolations* of language. All this we are excluding from consideration. Our performative utterances, felicitous or not, are to be understood as issued in ordinary circumstances.

(iii) It is partly in order to keep this sort of consideration at least for the present out of it, that I have not here introduced a sort of "infelicity"—it might really be called such—arising out of "misunderstanding." It is obviously necessary that to have promised I must normally

    (A) have been *heard* by someone, perhaps the promisee;
    (B) have been understood by him as promising.

If one or another of these conditions is not satisfied, doubts arise as to whether I have really promised, and it might be held that my act was only attempted or was void. Special precautions are taken in law to avoid this and other infelicities, e.g. in the serving of writs or summonses. This particular very important consideration we shall have to return to later in another connexion.

(3) Are these cases of infelicity mutually exclusive? The answer to this is obvious.

    (*a*) No, in the sense that we can go wrong in two ways at once (we can insincerely promise a donkey to give it a carrot).
    (*b*) No, more importantly, in the sense that the ways of going wrong "shade into one another" and "overlap," and the decision between them is "arbitrary" in various ways.

Suppose, for example, I see a vessel on the stocks, walk up and smash the bottle hung at the stem, proclaim "I name this ship the *Mr. Stalin*" and for good measure kick away the chocks: but the trouble is, I was not the person chosen to name it (whether or not—an additional complication—*Mr. Stalin* was the destined name; perhaps in a way it is even more of a shame if it was). We can all agree

    (1) that the ship was not thereby named;*
    (2) that it is an infernal shame.

One could say that I "went through a form of" naming the vessel but that my "action" was "void" or "without effect," because I was not a proper person, had not the "capacity," to perform it: but one might also and alternatively say that, where there is not even a pretence of capacity or a colourable claim to it, then there is no accepted conventional procedure; it is a mockery, like a marriage with a monkey. Or again one could say that part of the procedure is getting oneself appointed. When the saint baptized the penguins, was this void because the procedure of baptizing is inappropriate to be applied to penguins, or because there is no accepted procedure of baptizing anything except humans? I do not think that these uncertainties matter in theory, though it is pleasant to investigate them and in practice convenient to be ready, as jurists are, with a terminology to cope with them.

---

*Naming babies is even more difficult; we might have the wrong name and the wrong cleric—that is, someone entitled to name babies but not intended to name this one.

DONALD DAVIDSON
1917–

Donald Herbert Davidson was born in Springfield, Massachusetts. He attended Harvard University, where he received his B.A. in 1939 and his M.A. in 1941. There, he met Quine, who was to be a major influence on his intellectual life. When the United States entered the Second World War, Davidson joined the Navy, serving from 1942 to 1945. After the war, Davidson returned to Harvard where he again studied with Quine. Writing a dissertation on Plato's *Philebus,* he completed his doctorate in 1949.

Davidson taught at a number of American universities, including Stanford (1951–1967), Princeton (1967–1970), Rockefeller (1970–1976), and the University of Chicago (1976–1981). Since 1981, Davidson has taught philosophy at the University of California, Berkeley.

* * *

Although he greatly admired his mentor, Davidson argued that Quine had not completely expunged Cartesianism from his thought. Davidson argued that Quine still believed that we construct the world as given to us by our senses. Such a belief assumes there is an organizing principle of mind or language that puts sense data into a conceptual scheme. But, Davidson argues, there is no such split between language and the world. Both are part of a *single* conceptual scheme. As he explains in his seminal article "The Method of Truth in Metaphysics" (1977), given here (complete), "in making manifest the large features of our language, we make manifest the large features of reality." To explore language, then, is another way to do metaphysics.

Much of Davidson's work is concerned with exploring language. Perhaps his most significant contribution has been in the field of "truth-conditional semantics." The German logician Gottlob Frege (1848–1925) had noted that the truth of a sentence depends on the semantic features of its parts. Accordingly, Frege developed an artificial language that clearly exposed truth-conditional semantics. Such a language was preferable to natural language, Frege claimed, because it was clearer in revealing structure. Davidson agrees with Frege's fundamental point that we must attend to semantic features in sentences to discern their truth. But where Frege was satisfied with a theory of truth for artificially constructed sentences, Davidson seeks a theory that encompasses "a reasonably powerful and significant part of a natural language." This includes a careful examination of the semantic features (verbs, nouns, etc.) in natural language. Much of Davidson's early writing focuses on developing such a theory of truth for messy, confusing, and inconsistent everyday language.

In more recent writings, Davidson has attacked traditional theories of language. In his essay "A Nice Derangement of Epitaphs" (1986), he claims "there is no such thing as a language, not if a language is anything like what many philosophers and linguists have supposed." If we consider a language to be a clearly defined structure, then it must be constituted by some clearly defined social structure. This social structure in turn must be identified by the conventions that govern it. But Davidson claims that communication does not really involve conventions, so there is no way that communication can be described as social practice. And as critic Bjørn Ramberg points out, "if [linguistic communication] is not a specifiable social practice, what content can we give to the notion of a language? None is Davidson's recent conclusion."*

Davidson finds the absence of a prior conceptual language scheme to be unifying, binding us together in intersubjectivity, and not an invitation to skepticism or relativism. To disagree with another, one must attribute some true beliefs to that other in order to attribute some other false ones. As Davidson put it in an interview, "agreement and disagreement depend upon mutual understanding . . . the wrong picture is that each of us has our own ideas and we develop language to find out whether we agree or disagree. It is not until communication springs up that we begin to have ideas."** Language, then, is not some "clearly defined shared structure which language-users acquire and then apply to cases." Prior to a shared picture of the world, before the intersubjective production of meanings, there are no ideas. Thought itself depends upon other people and the events we share in the world.

*   *   *

For a general overview of Davidson's thought, see Simon Evnine, *Donald Davidson* (Stanford, CA: Stanford University Press, 1991). Specialized studies include Bjørn T. Ramberg, *Donald Davidson's Philosophy of Language: An Introduction* (Oxford: Basil Blackwell, 1989) and J.E. Malpas, *Donald Davidson*

Donald Davidson's Philosophy of Language: An Introduction (Oxford: Basil Blackwell, 1989), p. 2.

**Giovanna Borradori, *The American Philosopher*, translated by Rosanna Crocitto (Chicago: University of Chicago Press, 1994), pp. 42–43.

and the Mirror of Meaning: Holism, Truth, Interpretation (Cambridge: Cambridge University Press, 1992). Frank B. Farrell, *Subjectivity, Realism, and Postmodernism—The Recovery of the World* (Cambridge: Cambridge University Press, 1994) puts Davidson in a larger context, which includes a comparison with Rorty. Collections of critical essays include Ernest LePore and Brian P. McLaughlin, eds., *Actions and Events: Perspectives on the Philosophy of Donald Davidson* (Oxford: Basil Blackwell, 1985); Bruce Vermazen and Merrill B. Hintikka, eds., *Essays on Davidson: Actions and Events* (Oxford: Clarendon Press, 1985); Ernest LePore, ed., *Truth and Interpretation: Perspectives on the Philosophy of Donald Davidson* (Oxford: Basil Blackwell, 1986); Johannes Brandl and Wolfgang L. Gombocz, eds., *The Mind of Donald Davidson* (Amsterdam: Rodopi, 1989); and Ralf Stoecker, ed., *Reflecting Davidson* (Berlin: Walter de Gruyter, 1993). The last book includes Davidson's response to each essay.

THE METHOD OF TRUTH
IN METAPHYSICS

In sharing a language, in whatever sense this is required for communication, we share a picture of the world that must, in its large features, be true. It follows that in making manifest the large features of our language, we make manifest the large features of reality. One way of pursuing metaphysics is therefore to study the general structure of our language. This is not, of course, the sole true method of metaphysics; there is no such. But it is one method, and it has been practiced by philosophers as widely separated by time or doctrine as Plato, Aristotle, Hume, Kant, Russell, Frege, Wittgenstein, Carnap, Quine, and Strawson. These philosophers have not, it goes without saying, agreed on what the large features of language are or on how they may best be studied and described; the metaphysical conclusions have in consequence been various.

The method I will describe and recommend is not new; every important feature of the method can be found in one philosopher or another, and the leading idea is implicit in much of the best work in philosophy of language. What is new is the explicit formulation of the approach, and the argument for its philosophical importance. I begin with the argument; then comes a description of the method; finally, some applications are sketched.

I. Why must our language—any language—incorporate or depend upon a largely correct, shared view of how things are? First consider why those who can understand one another's speech must share a view of the world, whether or not that view is correct. The reason is that we damage the intelligibility of our readings of the utterances

"The Method of Truth in Metaphysics" in *Midwest Studies in Philosophy,* II (1977), pp. 244–254. Copyright © University of Minnesota. Reprinted by permission of University of Minnesota Press. I am much indebted to Gilbert Harman, W.V. Quine, and John Wallace for comments on earlier versions of this paper. [Author's note.]

of others when our method of reading puts others into what we take to be broad error. We can make sense of differences all right, but only against a background of shared belief. What is shared does not in general call for comment; it is too dull, trite, or familiar to stand notice. But without a vast common ground, there is no place for disputants to have their quarrel. Of course, we can no more agree than disagree with someone else without much mutuality; but perhaps this is obvious.

Beliefs are identified and described only within a dense pattern of beliefs. I can believe a cloud is passing before the sun, but only because I believe there is a sun, that clouds are made of water vapor, that water can exist in liquid or gaseous form; and so on, without end. No particular list of further beliefs is required to give substance to my belief that a cloud is passing before the sun; but some appropriate set of related beliefs must be there. If I suppose that you believe a cloud is passing before the sun, I suppose you have the right sort of pattern of beliefs to support that one belief, and these beliefs I assume you to have must, to do their supporting work, be enough like my beliefs to justify the description of your belief as a belief that a cloud is passing before the sun. If I am right in attributing the belief to you, then you must have a pattern of beliefs much like mine. No wonder, then, I can interpret your words correctly only by interpreting so as to put us largely in agreement.

It may seem that the argument so far shows only that good interpretation breeds concurrence, while leaving quite open the question whether what is agreed upon is true. And certainly agreement, no matter how widespread, does not guarantee truth. This observation misses the point of the argument, however. The basic claim is that much community of belief is needed to provide a basis for communication or understanding; the extended claim should then be that objective error can occur only in a setting of largely true belief. Agreement does not make for truth, but much of what is agreed must be true if some of what is agreed is false.

Just as too much attributed error risks depriving the subject of his subject matter, so too much actual error robs a person of things to go wrong about. When we want to interpret, we work on one or another assumption about the general pattern of agreement. We suppose that much of what we take to be common is true, but we cannot, of course, assume we know where the truth lies. We cannot interpret on the basis of known truths, not because we know none, but because we do not always know which they are. We do not need to be omniscient to interpret, but there is nothing absurd in the idea of an omniscient interpreter; he attributes beliefs to others and interprets their speech on the basis of his own beliefs, just as the rest of us do. Since he does this as the rest of us do, he perforce finds as much agreement as is needed to make sense of his attributions and interpretations; and in this case, of course, what is agreed is by hypothesis true. But now it is plain why massive error about the world is simply unintelligible, for to suppose it intelligible is to suppose there could be an interpreter (the omniscient one) who correctly interpreted someone else as being massively mistaken, and this we have shown to be impossible.

II. Successful communication proves the existence of a shared, and largely true, view of the world. But what led us to demand the common view was the recognition that sentences held true—the linguistic representatives of belief—determine the meanings of the words they contain. Thus the common view shapes the shared language. This is why it is plausible to hold that by studying the most general aspects of language we will be studying the most general aspects of reality. It remains to say how these aspects may be identified and described.

Language is an instrument of communication because of its semantic dimension, the potentiality for truth or falsehood of its sentences, or better, of its utterances and inscriptions. The study of what sentences are true is in general the work of the various sciences; but the study of truth conditions is the province of semantics. What we must attend to in language, if we want to bring into relief general features of the world, is what it is in general for a sentence in the language to be true. The suggestion is that if the truth conditions of sentences are placed in the context of a comprehensive theory, the linguistic structure that emerges will reflect large features of reality.

The aim is a theory of truth for a reasonably powerful and significant part of a natural language. The scope of the theory—how much of the language is captured by the theory, and how convincingly—will be one factor on which the interest of any metaphysical results depends. The theory must show us how we can view each of a potential infinity of sentences as composed from a finite stock of semantically significant atoms (roughly, words) by means of a finite number of applications of a finite number of rules of composition. It must then give the truth conditions of each sentence (relative to the circumstances of its utterance) on the basis of its composition. The theory may thus be said to explain the conditions of truth of an utterance of a sentence on the basis of the roles of the words in the sentence.

Much here is owed to Frege. Frege saw the importance of giving an account of how the truth of a sentence depends on the semantic features of its parts, and he suggested how such an account could be given for impressive stretches of natural language. His method was one now familiar: he introduced a standardized notation whose syntax directly reflected the intended interpretation, and then urged that the new notation, as interpreted, had the same expressive power as important parts of natural language. Or rather, not quite the same expressive power, since Frege believed natural language was defective in some respects, and he regarded his new language as an improvement.

Frege was concerned with the semantic structure of sentences, and with semantic relations between sentences, in so far as these generated entailments. But he cannot be said to have conceived the idea of a comprehensive formal theory of truth for language as a whole. One consequence was a lack of interest in the semantic paradoxes. Another was an apparent willingness to accept an infinity of meanings (senses) and referents for every denoting phrase in the language.

Because Frege took the application of function to argument to be the sole mode of semantic combination, he was bound to treat sentences as a kind of name—the name of a truth value. Seen simply as an artful dodge on the way to characterizing the truth conditions of sentences, this device of Frege's is unexceptionable. But since sentences do not operate in language the way names do, Frege's approach undermines confidence that the ontology he needs to work his semantics has any direct connection with the ontology implicit in natural language. It is not clear, then, what one can learn about metaphysics from Frege's method. (I certainly do not mean by this that we can't learn about metaphysics from Frege's work; but to see how, arguments different from mine must be marshaled.)

Quine provided an essential ingredient for the project at hand by showing how a holistic approach to the problem of understanding a language supplies the needed empirical foundation. If metaphysical conclusions are to be drawn from a theory of truth in the way that I propose, the approach to language must be holistic. Quine himself does not see holism as having such direct metaphysical significance, however, and for a number of reasons. First, Quine has not made the theory of truth central either as a key to the ontology of a language or as a test of logical form. Second, like Frege, he views a satisfactorily regimented language as an improvement on natural language rather than as part of a theory about it. In one important respect, Quine seems even to go beyond Frege, for where Frege thinks his notation makes for better language, Quine thinks it also makes for better science. As a consequence, Quine ties his metaphysics to his canonical notation rather than to natural language; as he puts it, "The quest of a simplest, clearest overall pattern of canonical notation is not to be distinguished from a quest of ultimate categories, a limning of the most general traits of reality."*

The formal languages toward which I gravitate—first-order languages with standard logic—are those preferred by Quine. But our reasons for this choice diverge somewhat. Such languages please Quine because their logic is simple and the scientifically respectable parts of natural language can be translated into them; and with this I agree. But since I am interested not in improving on natural language but in understanding it, I view formal languages or canonical notations as devices for exploring the structure of natural language. We know how to give a theory of truth for the formal language; so if we also knew how to transform the sentences of a natural language systematically into sentences of the formal language, we would have a theory of truth for the natural language. From this point of view, standard formal languages are intermediate devices to assist us in treating natural languages as more complex formal languages.

Tarski's work on truth definitions for formalized languages serves as inspiration for the kind of theory of truth that is wanted for natural languages.** The method works by enumerating the semantic properties of the items in a finite vocabulary, and on this basis recursively characterizes truth for each of the infinity of sentences. Truth is reached from the basis by the intervention of a subtle and powerful concept (satisfaction) that relates both sentences and nonsentential expressions to objects in the world. An important feature of Tarski's approach is that a characterization of a truth predicate "x is true in L" is accepted only if it entails, for each sentence of the language L, a theorem of the form "x is true in L if and only if . . ." with "x" replaced by a description of the sentence and the dots replaced by a translation of the sentence into the language of the theory.

It is evident that these theorems, which we may call T-sentences, require a predicate that holds of just the true sentences of L. It is also plain, from the fact that the truth conditions for a sentence translate that sentence (i.e., what appears to the right of the "if and only if" in a T-sentence translates the sentence described on the left), that the theory shows how to characterize truth for any given sentence without appeal to conceptual resources not available in that sentence.

These remarks are only roughly correct. A theory of truth for a natural language must relativize the truth of a sentence to the circumstances of utterance, and when this is done the truth conditions given by a T-sentence will no longer translate the described sentence, nor will it be possible to avoid using concepts that are, perhaps, semantical, in giving the truth conditions of sentences with indexical elements. More important, the notion of translation, which can be made precise for artificial languages on which interpretations are imposed by fiat, has no precise or even clear application to natural languages.

For these and other reasons it is important to stress that a theory of truth for a natural language (as I conceive it) differs widely in both aim and interest from Tarski's truth definitions. Sharpness of application is lost, and with it most of what concerns

---

*W.V. Quine, *Word and Object* (Cambridge, MA: Harvard University Press, 1960), p. 161.
**A. Tarski, "The Concept of Truth in Formalized Languages," in *Logic, Semantics, Metamathematics* (Oxford, 1956).

mathematicians and logicians: consequences for consistency, for example. Tarski could take translation as syntactically specified and go on to define truth. But in application to a natural language it makes more sense to assume a partial understanding of truth and use the theory to throw light on meaning, interpretation, and translation.* Satisfaction of Tarski's Convention T remains a desideratum of a theory but is no longer available as a formal test.

What a theory of truth does for a natural language is reveal a structure. In treating each sentence as composed in accountable ways out of a finite number of truth-relevant words, it articulates this structure. When we study terms and sentences directly, not in the light of comprehensive theory, we must bring metaphysics to language; we assign roles to words and sentences in accord with the categories we independently posit on epistemological or metaphysical grounds. Operating in this way, philosophers ponder such questions as whether there must be entities, perhaps universals, that correspond to predicates, or nonexistent entities to correspond to nondenoting names or descriptions; or they argue that sentences do or do not correspond to facts or propositions.

A different light is shed on these matters when we look for a comprehensive theory of truth, for such a theory makes its own unavoidable demands.

III. Now let us consider some applications. We noticed that the requirement that the truth conditions of a sentence be given using only the conceptual resources of that sentence is not entirely clear where it can be met, nor everywhere applicable. The cases that invite exception are sentences that involve demonstratives, and here the cure of the difficulty is relatively simple.** These cases aside, the requirement, for all its obscurity, has what seem, and I think are, important implications.

Suppose we were to admit a rule like this as part of a theory of truth: "A sentence consisting of a singular term followed by a one-place predicate is true if and only if the object named by the singular term belongs to the class determined by the predicate."*** This rule offends the requirement, for if the rule were admitted, the T-sentence for "Socrates is wise" would be "'Socrates is wise' is true if and only if the object named by 'Socrates' belongs to the class determined by the predicate 'is wise,'" and here the statement of truth conditions involves two semantic concepts (naming and determining a class) not plausibly among the conceptual resources of "Socrates is wise."

It would be easy to get from the tendentious T-sentence just mentioned to the noncommittal and admissible "'Socrates is wise' is true if and only if Socrates is wise" if the theory also contained as postulates statements that the object named by "Socrates" is Socrates and that x belongs to the class determined by the predicate "is wise" if and only if x is wise. If enough such postulates are available to care for all proper names and primitive predicates, the results are clear. First, T-sentences free from unwanted semantic terms would be available for all the sentences involved; and the extra semantic terms would be unnecessary. For there would have to be a postulate for each name and predicate, and this there could be only if the list of names and primitive predicates were finite. But if the list were finite, there would be only a finite number of sentences consisting of a name and a one-place predicate, and nothing would stand in the way of giving the truth conditions for all such sentences straight off—the T-sentences themselves could serve as the axioms.

---

*For more on this, see my "Belief and the Basis of Meaning," *Synthese* 27 (1974): 309–323, and "Radical Interpretation," *Dialectica* 27 (1973): 313–328.

**See S. Weinstein, "Truth and Demonstratives," *Noûs* 8 (1974): 179–184.

***Compare R. Carnap, *Meaning and Necessity* (Chicago:University of Chicago Press, 1947), p. 5.

The example illustrates how keeping the vocabulary finite may allow the elimination of semantic concepts; it also shows how the demand for a satisfactory theory has ontological consequences. Here, the call for entities to correspond to predicates disappears when the theory is made to produce T-sentences without excess semantic baggage. Indeed in the case at hand the theory does not need to put expressions and objects into explicit correspondence at all, and so no ontology is involved; but this is because the supply of sentences whose truth conditions are to be given is finite.

Not that an infinity of sentences necessarily demands ontology. Given the finite supply of sentences with unstructured predicates that we have been imagining, it is easy to go on to infinity by adding one or more iterable devices for constructing sentences from sentences, such as negation, conjunction, or alternation. If ontology was not required to give the truth conditions for the simplest sentences, these devices will not call for more.

In general, however, semantically relevant structure is apt to demand ontology. Consider, for example, the view that quotations are to be treated as semantic atoms, on a par with proper names in lacking significant structure. Tarski says of this way of viewing quotations that it "seems to be the most natural one and completely in accordance with the customary way of using quotation marks."* He gives a model argument to show that quotation marks cannot be treated as an ordinary functional expression since a quotation does not name an entity that is a function of anything named by what the quotation marks enclose. About this Tarski is certainly right, but the moral of the lesson cannot be that quotations are like proper names—not, anyway, if a Tarski-style theory of truth can be given for a language containing quotations. For clearly there is an infinite number of quotations.

One idea for a possible solution can be extracted from Quine's remark that quotations may be replaced by spelling (much the same is said by Tarski). Spelling does have structure. It is a way of giving a semantically articulate description of an expression by the use—repeated if necessary—of a finite number of expressions: the concatenation sign, with associated parentheses, and (proper) names of the letters. Following this line, we should think of a quotation like "'cat'" as having a form more clearly given by "'c'⌢'a'⌢'t'," or, better still, by "(see)⌢(eh)⌢(tee)." This idea works, at least up to a point. But note the consequences. We no longer view the quotation "'cat'" as unstructured; rather we are treating it as an abbreviation of a sort for a complex description. Not, however, as an arbitrary abbreviation to be specified for the case at hand, but as a style of abbreviation that can be expanded mechanically into a description that shows structure more plainly. Indeed, talk of abbreviations is misleading; we may as well say this theory treats quotations as complex descriptions.

Another consequence is that in giving structure to quotations we have had to recognize in quotations repeatable and independent "words": names of the individual letters and of the concatenation sign. These "words" are, of course, finite in number—that was required—but they also reveal an ontological fact not apparent when quotations were viewed as unstructured names, a commitment to letters. We get a manageable theory when we explain molecules as made from atoms of a finite number of kinds; but we also get atoms.

A more stirring example of how postulating needed structure in language can bring ontology in its wake is provided by Frege's semantics for the oblique contexts created by sentences about propositional attitudes. In Frege's view, a sentence like

*"The Concept of Truth in Formalized Languages," p. 160.

"Daniel believes that there is a lion in the den" is dominated by the two-place predicate "believes" whose first place is filled by the singular term "Daniel" and whose second place is filled by a singular term that names a proposition or "sense." Taking this line requires us not only to treat sentences as singular terms but to find entities for them to name. And more is to come. For clearly an infinite number of sentences may occupy the spot after "Daniel believes that. . . ." So if we are to provide a truth definition, we must discover semantic structure in these singular terms: it must be shown how they can be treated as descriptions of propositions. To avoid the absurdities that would ensue if the singular terms in a sentence had their usual reference, Frege takes them as referring instead to intensional entities. Analogous changes must come over the semantic features of predicates, quantifiers, and sentential connectives. So far, a theory of truth of the sort we have been looking for can handle the situation, but only by treating each word of the language as ambiguous, having one interpretation in ordinary contexts and another after "believes that" and similar verbs. What is to the eye one word must, from the vantage point of this theory, be treated as two. Frege appreciated this, and held the ambiguity against natural language; Church, in the artificial languages of "A Formulation of the Logic of Sense and Denotation," eliminated the ambiguity by introducing distinct expressions, differing in subscript.*

Frege suggested that with each addition of a verb of propositional attitude before a referring expression that expression comes to refer to an entity of a higher semantical level. Thus every word and sentence is infinitely many-ways ambiguous; on Church's theory there will be an infinite basic vocabulary. In neither case is it possible to provide a theory of truth of the kind we want.

Frege was clear on the need, if we are to have a systematic theory, to view the truth value of each sentence as a function of the semantic roles of its parts or aspects—far clearer than anyone who went before, and clearer than most who followed. What Frege did not appreciate, as this last example brings out, was the additional restraints, in particular to a finite vocabulary, that flow from the demand for a comprehensive theory of truth. Frege brought semantics to a point where the demand was intelligible and even, perhaps, satisfiable; but it did not occur to him to formulate the demand.

Let us take a closer look at the bootstrap operation that enables us to bring latent structure to light by characterizing a truth predicate. Early steps may be illustrated by as simple a sentence as "Jack and Jill went up the hill"—under what conditions is this sentence true? The challenge lies in the presence in the sentence of an iterative device—conjunction. Clearly we can go on adding phrases like "and Mary" after the word "Jill" *ad libitum*. So any statement of truth conditions for this sentence must bear in mind the infinity of sentences, generated by the same device, that lie waiting for treatment. What is called for is a recursive clause in the truth theory that can be called into play as often as needed. The trick, as we all know, is to define truth for a basic, and finite, stock of simplest sentences, such as "Jack went up the hill" and "Jill went up the hill," and then make the truth conditions of "Jack and Jill went up the hill" a function of the truth of the two simple sentences. So we get

"Jack and Jill went up the hill" is true if and only if Jack went up the hill and Jill went up the hill.

*A. Church, "A Formulation of the Logic of Sense and Denotation," in *Structure, Method, and Meaning: Essays in Honor of H. M. Sheffer*, eds. Henle, Kallen, and Langer (New York, 1951).

as a consequence of a theory of truth. On the left a sentence of the vernacular, its structure transparent or not, is described; on the right of the "if and only if" a sentence of that same vernacular, but a part of the vernacular chosen for its ability to make explicit, through repeated applications of the same simple devices, the underlying semantic structure. If a theory of truth yields such a purified sentence for every sentence in the language, the portion of the total language used on the right may be considered a canonical notation. Indeed, with symbols substituted for some words, and grouping made plain by parentheses or some equivalent device, the part of the language used in stating truth conditions for all sentences may become indistinguishable from what is often called a formalized or artificial language. It would be a mistake, however, to suppose that it is essential to find such a canonical subdivision of the language. Since "and" may be written between sentences in English, we take the easy route of transforming "Jack and Jill went up the hill" into "Jack went up the hill and Jill went up the hill" and then giving the truth conditions of the latter in accord with a rule that says a conjunction of sentences is true if and only if each conjunct is. But suppose "and" never stood between sentences; its role as sentential connective would still be recognized by a rule saying that a sentence composed of a conjunctive subject ("Jack and Jill") and a predicate ("went up the hill") is true if and only if the sentence composed of the first conjoined subject and the predicate, and the sentence composed of the second conjoined subject and the predicate, are true. The rule required is less perspicuous and needs to be supplemented with others to do the work of the simple original rule. But the point remains: canonical notation is a convenience we can get along without if need be. It is good, but not necessary, to bring logical form to the surface.

Similarly, it would greatly ease the treatment of negation if we could plausibly transform all sentences containing negation into sentences, recognizably the same in truth value, in which the negating phrase always governed a sentence (as with, "it is not the case that"). But if this were not possible, negation would still be a sentential connective if the truth condition of a sentence like "Coal is not white" were given by adverting to the truth condition of "Coal is white." ("Coal is not white" is true if and only if "Coal is white" is not true.)

The issue of ontology is forced into the open only where the theory finds quantificational structure, and that is where the theory best accounts for the pattern of truth dependencies by systematically relating expressions to objects. It is striking how firmly the demand for theory puts to rest an ancient aporia: the question how to demonstrate the asymmetry, if any, of subject and predicate. As long as our attention is focused on single, simple sentences, we may wonder why an explanation of truth should involve predicates in ontology any less than singular terms. The class of wise objects, or the property of wisdom, offers itself as what might correspond to the predicate "wise" in "Socrates is wise" in much the same way Socrates corresponds to "Socrates." As pointed out above, no finite number of such sentences requires a theory of truth to bring ontology into the picture. Multiple generality, however—the admission of whatever, in natural language, is treated by theory as sentences with mixed quantification and predicates of any degree of complexity—totally changes the picture. With complex quantificational structure, the theory must match up expressions with objects. But there is no need, as long as the underlying logic is assumed to be first order, to introduce entities to correspond to predicates. Recognition of this fact will not, of course, settle the question whether there are such things as universals or classes. But it does demonstrate that there is a difference between singular term and predicate; for large stretches of language, anyway, variables, quantifiers, and singular terms must be construed as referential in function not so for predicates.

It is not always evident what the quantificational structure of a sentence in natural language is; what appear to be singular terms sometimes melt into something less ontic in implication when their logical relations with other sentences are studied, while the requirements of theory may suggest that a sentence plays a role that can be explained only by treating it as having a quantificational structure not apparent on the surface. Here is a familiar illustration.

What is the ontology of a sentence like:

"Jack fell down before Jack broke his crown"?

Jack and his crown seem to be the only candidates for entities that must exist if this sentence is to be true. And if, in place of "before," we had "and," this answer might satisfy us for the reason already explored: namely, that we can state, in a way that will work for endless similar cases, the truth conditions of the whole sentence "Jack fell down and Jack broke his crown" on the basis just of the truth of the component sentences, and we can hope to give the truth conditions for the components without more ontology than Jack and his crown. But "Jack fell down before Jack broke his crown" does not yield to this treatment, because "before" cannot be viewed as a truth-functional semantical connective: to see this, reflect that for the sentence to be true, both component sentences must be true, but this is not sufficient for its truth, since interchanging the components will make it false.

Frege showed us how to cope with the case: we can formulate the truth conditions for the sentence "Jack fell down before Jack broke his crown" as follows: it is true if and only if there exists a time t and there exists a time t' such that Jack fell down at t, Jack broke his crown at t', and t is before t'. So apparently we are committed to the existence of times if we accept any such sentence as true. And thinking of the holistic character of a truth definition, the discovery of hidden ontology in sentences containing "before" must carry over to other sentences: thus, "Jack fell down" is true if and only if there exists a time t such that Jack fell down at t.

Now for a more disturbing example. Consider first "Jack's fall caused the breaking of his crown." Here it is natural to take "Jack's fall" and the "breaking of his crown" as singular terms describing events, and "caused" as a two-place, or relational, predicate. But then, what is the semantic relation between such general terms as "fall" in "Jack's fall" or "the fall of Jack" and such verbs as "fell" in "Jack fell"? For that matter, how does "Jack's fall caused the breaking of his crown" differ, in its truth conditions, from "Jack fell, which caused it to be the case that Jack broke his crown," where the phrase "which caused it to be the case that" is, on the face of it, a sentential connective?

The correct theory of "caused" as I have argued at more length elsewhere, is parallel to Frege's theory for "before."* I suggest that "Jack fell down, which caused the breaking of his crown" is true if and only if there exist events e and f such that e is a fall Jack took, f is a breaking his crown suffered, and e caused f. According to this proposal, the predicate "is a fall," true of events, becomes primary, and contexts containing the verb are derived. Thus "Jack fell" is true if and only if there is a fall such that Jack took it. "Jack took a walk" is true if and only if there is a walk that he took, and so on. On this analysis, a noun phrase like "Jack's fall" becomes a genuine description, and what it describes is the one fall that Jack took.

*D. Davidson, "Causal Relations," *The Journal of Philosophy* 64 (1967): 691–703.

One consideration that may help reconcile us to an ontology of particular events is that we may then dispense with the abstract ontology of times we just now tentatively accepted, for events are as plausibly the relata of the before-relation as times. Another consideration is that by recognizing our commitment to an ontology of events we can see our way to a viable semantics of adverbs and adverbial modification. Without events there is the problem of explaining the logical relations between sentences like "Jones nicked his cheek while shaving with a razor in the bathroom on Saturday" and "Jones nicked his cheek in the bathroom" and "Jones nicked his cheek." It seems that some iterative device is at work; yet what, from a semantic point of view, can the device be? The books on logic do not say: they analyze these sentences to require relations with varying numbers of places depending on the number of adverbial modifications, but this leads to the unacceptable conclusion that there is an infinite basic vocabulary, and it fails to explain the obvious inferences. By interpreting these sentences as being about events, we can solve the problems. Then we can say that "Jones nicked his cheek in the bathroom on Saturday" is true if and only if there exists an event that is a nicking of his cheek by Jones, *and* that event took place in the bathroom, *and* it took place on Saturday. The iterative device is now obvious: it is the familiar collaboration of conjunction and quantification that enables us to deal with "Someone fell down and broke his crown."

This device works, but as we have seen, it takes an ontology to make it work: an ontology including people for "Someone fell down and broke his crown," an ontology of events (in addition) for "Jones nicked his cheek in the bathroom on Saturday." It is mildly ironic that in recent philosophy it has become a popular maneuver to try to avoid ontological problems by treating certain phrases as adverbial. One such suggestion is that we can abjure sense data if we render a sentence like "The mountain appears blue to Smith" as "The mountain appears bluely to Smith." Another similar idea is that we can do without an ontology of intensional objects by thinking of sentences about propositional attitudes as essentially adverbial: "Galileo said that the earth moves" would then come out, "Galileo spoke in a that-the-earth-moves-fashion." There is little chance, I think, that such adverbial clauses can be given a systematic semantical analysis without ontological entanglements.

There is a further, rather different, way in which a theory of truth may have metaphysical repercussions. In adjusting to the presence of demonstratives, and of demonstrative elements like tense, in a natural language, a theory of truth must treat truth as an attribute of utterances that depends (perhaps among other things) on the sentence uttered, the speaker, and the time. Alternatively, it may be possible to treat truth as a relation between speakers, sentences, and times. Thus an utterance of "I am five feet tall" is true if spoken at some times in the lives of most people, and true if spoken at any time during a considerable span in the lives of a few. "Your slip is showing" may be true when uttered by a speaker at a time when he faces west, though it might not have been true if he had faced north; and "Hilary climbed Everest" was for a long time false and is now forever true. Sentences without demonstrative elements cannot do the work of sentences with demonstrative elements; but if we are to have a theory of truth, we must be able to state, without the use of demonstratives, a rule that explains under what conditions sentences with demonstratives are true. Such rules will give the truth condition of sentences like "Hilary climbed Everest" only by quantifying over utterances, speakers, and times, or, perhaps, events.

If explicit appeal must be made to speakers and their circumstances in giving a theory of truth, then on the assumption that the general features of language reflect objective features of the world, we must conclude that an intelligible metaphysics will assign a central place to the idea of people (= speakers) with a location in public space and time.

It should be clear that "the method of truth" in metaphysics does not eliminate recourse to more standard, often essentially nonlinguistic, arguments or decisions. What it is possible to do in a theory of truth, for example, depends to a large extent on the logical resources the theory itself deploys, and the theory cannot decide this for us. Nor, as we have seen, does the method suggest what truths, beyond those it counts as logical, we must accept as a condition of mutual understanding. What a theory of truth does is describe the pattern truth must make among the sentences, without telling us where the pattern falls. So, for example, I argue that a very large number of our ordinary claims about the world cannot be true unless there are events. But a theory of truth, even if it took the form I propose, would not specify what events exist, nor even that any do. However, if I am right about the logical form of sentences concerning change, then unless there are events, there are no true sentences of very common kinds about change. And if there are no true sentences about change, there are no true sentences about objects that change. A metaphysician who is willing to suppose no sentences like "Vesuvius erupted in March 1944" or "Caesar crossed the Rubicon" are true will not be forced by a theory of truth to admit the existence of events or even, perhaps, of people or mountains. But if he accepts that many such sentences are true (whichever they may be), then it is obvious that he must accept the existence of people and volcanoes; and, if I am right, the existence of events like eruptions and crossings.

The merit of the method of truth is not that it settles such matters once and for all, or even that it settles them without further metaphysical reflection. But the method does serve to sharpen our sense of viable alternatives, and gives a comprehensive idea of the consequences of a decision. Metaphysics has generality as an aim; the method of truth expresses that demand by requiring a theory that touches all the bases. Thus the problems of metaphysics, while neither solved nor replaced, come to be seen as the problems of all good theory building. We want a theory that is simple and clear, with a logical apparatus that is understood and justified, and that accounts for the facts about how our language works. What those facts are may remain somewhat in dispute, as will certainly the wisdom of various tradeoffs as between simplicity and clarity. These questions will be, I do not doubt, the old questions of metaphysics in new dress. But the new dress is in many ways an attractive one.

MICHEL FOUCAULT
1926–1984

Michel Foucault resisted giving biographical details, claiming he "wrote to be invisible." Ironically, however, his life has been more visible than his writings for most people—several sensational biographies compete for attention (see the suggested readings).

Paul Michel Foucault was born in Poitiers, France, in 1926, the second child of Paul Foucault and Anne Malapert Foucault. Both parents were the children of doctors. Foucault's father was a successful surgeon and professor of anatomy at the local medical school. Foucault apparently came to hate his surgeon father, even dropping his father's Christian name, Paul, from his own name. As Foucault later related, the formative experiences of his childhood were not associated with family, but with the Second World War:

> I think that boys and girls of [my] generation had their childhood formed by [the events of the Second World War]. The menace of war was our background, our framework of existence.... Much more than the activities of family life, it was these events concerning the world which are the substance of our memory.... Maybe that is the reason why I am fascinated by history and the relationship between personal experience and those events of which we are a part.*

Despite the war around him, Foucault finished grade school successfully and, on a second try, gained admission to the prestigious École Normale Supérieure

---

*Michel Foucault, *Politics, Philosophy, Culture: Interviews and Other Writings, 1977–1984* (New York: Routledge, 1988), p. 7.

in Paris. Foucault's years studying philosophy there were not happy. He had trouble relating to his classmates, attempted suicide on several occasions, and seemed on the verge of madness. The doctor at the École said "these troubles resulted from an extreme difficulty in experiencing and accepting his homosexuality."* Although Foucault's École years were personally difficult, they were academically successful. He received, in turn, the *licence de philosophie* (1948), the *licence de psychologie* (1949), and the *agrégation de philosophie* (1952).

After graduation Foucault taught briefly at the University of Lille before becoming director of studies at the Maison Française in Uppsala, Sweden. Here he wrote his doctoral dissertation—later published in an abridged edition as *Madness and Civilization* (1961). Following brief teaching stints in Warsaw, Poland, and Hamburg, Germany, Foucault returned to France to chair the philosophy department at the University of Clermont-Ferrand. After *The Order of Things* (1966) made him famous, Foucault followed Daniel Defert, his lover, to Tunisia, until an offer to head the philosophy department at a new university in Vincennes drew him back to France in 1968. There he wrote *The Archeology of Knowledge* (1969). Two years later, he was elected Professor of the History of Systems of Thought at the Collège de France. From this position, Foucault periodically visited America, Canada, Japan, and Brazil, becoming an international celebrity. In 1976, Foucault completed three volumes of his *History of Sexuality*. Before he could complete the fourth volume, he died in 1984 of AIDS.

Throughout his life, Foucault was attracted to activities that pushed the envelope of cultural acceptability, oscillating often between radical positions. In the early-1950s, for example, he was a member of the French Communist Party, but he later took a strong anti-communist position. For a time in the early-1970s, he sided with the "Maoist" ultra-left. His next political passion was the Iranian Revolution. His consistent physical passion seems to have been the drug-and-gay bathhouse scene in San Francisco.

*   *   *

"Cultural defiance" describes Foucault's philosophy as well as his life. For most of his professional life, his thought was not only antimetaphysical, but also anti-Enlightenment and antihumanist. Perhaps the best way to discuss the history of his thought is by way of his own view of history.

Foucault held that history, rather than being linear, is marked by "ruptures." These ruptures create discontinuous epochs, which, like layers in an archeological dig, are not causally connected. The archaeology of Foucault's own thought can be divided into three layers, roughly correlating with the three decades of his work. The last layer is quite discontinuous from the first two, but all three reject evolutionary modes of thought.

The word "archaeology" was Foucault's key figure of speech in the 1960s. *The Birth of the Clinic* (1963), for example, is subtitled "An Archaeology of Medical Perception," and *The Order of Things* (1966) is subtitled "An Archaeology of the Human Sciences." Both books attack modern philosophy, which created "man" as both the subject and object of knowledge, and built thought (separate from empirical reality) on either *a priori* categories (Kant) or essentialized

*Didier Eribon, *Michel Foucault* (Cambridge, MA: Harvard University Press, 1991), p. 26.

consciousness (Husserl). Foucault, however, proclaims the "death of Man" merely molded by the "episteme," (structure of thought) that constitutes an era's "discursive practices." Foucault sees the Enlightenment *episteme* as turning the history of science into a teleology, in which progress is achieved only through rational exploration. But "rationality" itself is an artificial construct that situates discoveries of science in structures of belief rather than in individuals. In fact, contrary to Enlightenment ideals, there is no such thing as "disinterested truth," for knowledge is always created by power.

Many people misinterpret Foucault's use of "power" as comparable to Marxian "ideology." But Foucault came to regard Marxism as naive in its assumption of progress, and in its belief that there is an essential nature in humans, who need to be liberated from restrictive economic systems. For Foucault, power is located neither in human subjects nor in social institutions but is diffused throughout society. Indeterminate in character, with no origin, power is nevertheless generative of human thought and behavior. Foucault thus undermines human agency, ending his last work of the 1960s, *The Archaeology of Knowledge* (1969), with a philosophic extension of Nietzsche: "You may have killed God beneath the weight of all that you have said; but don't imagine that, with all that you are saying, you will make a man that will live longer than he."

Nietzsche's word "genealogy" became Foucault's key term in the 1970s. Foucault moved his analysis from operations of power on the mind to those that colonize the body. In so doing, he altered his focus from the changing constitution of knowledge to that of social practices and institutional systems. Human identity, or "subjectivity," is thus defined as "subjection" to structures and practices that normalize behavior. His most famous work from this decade, *Discipline and Punish* (1975), traces the genealogy of behavior toward criminals. He concludes that the humanist institutions of the nineteenth century, which sought to reform, were more despotic than earlier systems that tortured. Torture focused only on the body, whereas reform put the soul under the domination of cultural norms.

The first two phases of Foucault's work discussed "technologies of domination" over mind and body; his last phase explored "technologies of the self." He acknowledged, in contrast to his earlier work, the possibility of human agency— not through the discovery of self (which implies an essence independent of discourse) but through the reinvention of self. He advocates "micropolitics," in which small groups of people contest the discursive practices that dominate society. In contrast to the totalized vision of a Marxist revolution, then, Foucault encourages the proliferation of multiple voices, especially those previously silenced by the hegemonic system.

Although Foucault's work has its discontinuous epochs, there is still a genealogical relationship among his constructs. Throughout his career, he explored the discourses that define sickness versus health, deviancy versus normality, error versus truth. Foucault takes the side of those whose discourse has been shunned as unacceptable. As an advocate of pluralism, he discusses, in pluralistic ways, the modes of power that constitute society.

Yet throughout his writings, Foucault is aware of the irony of his own power as a speaker of "truth." In our selection, "What Is an Author?," translated by Josué V. Harari, Foucault tackles the issue of authorial authority. The word "author" usually refers to the individual who guarantees the unity and intention of a written work—a meaning-giver who is transcendent to the text. But, Foucault explains, "criticism and philosophy took note of the disappearance—or death—

of the author some time ago." Instead, Foucault examines the "author-function," exploring its characteristics, to find how it is used.

According to Foucault, as long as we are concerned with the author or the author-function, we will not focus on the text itself. For example, does the little biography of Foucault given here help you read the selection from Foucault that follows? Or does it cause you to focus on the author and not on the text itself? Instead of asking "What part of his deepest self did Foucault express in this discourse?," Foucault would have us look at the text itself and ask such questions as, "What are the modes of existence of this discourse? Where has it been used, how can it circulate, and who can appropriate it for himself?" But more fundamentally, Foucault would have us question the author-function itself and ask, "What difference does it make who is speaking?"

*   *   *

Foucault often used interviews as a way to explain his ideas, and these interviews provide a helpful route to further study: see Michel Foucault, *Politics, Philosophy, Culture: Interviews and Other Writings, 1977–1984* (New York: Routledge, 1988). For general overviews of Foucault's thought, see Mark Cousins and Athar Hussain, *Michel Foucault* (New York: St. Martin's Press, 1984); Barry Smart, *Michel Foucault* (Chichester, Sussex: Ellis Horwood, 1985); Gilles Deleuze, *Foucault,* translated by Seán Hand (Minneapolis: University of Minnesota Press, 1988); and David R. Shumway, *Michel Foucault* (Boston: Twayne, 1989). Didier Eribon, *Michel Foucault* (Cambridge, MA: Harvard University Press, 1991); James Miller, *The Passion of Michel Foucault* (New York: Simon & Schuster, 1993); and David Macey, *The Lives of Michel Foucault: A Biography* (New York: Pantheon, 1993) provide biographies. For comparative studies, see Allan Megill, *Prophets of Extremity: Nietzsche, Heidegger, Foucault, Derrida* (Berkeley: University of California Press, 1985); Roy Boyne, *Foucault and Derrida: The Other Side of Reason* (London: Unwin Hyman, 1990); Alex Honneth, *The Critique of Power: Reflective Stages in a Critical Social Theory,* translated by Kenneth Baynes (Cambridge, MA: MIT Press, 1991); Micheal Mahon, *Foucault's Nietzschean Genealogy: Truth, Power, and the Subject* (Albany, NY: SUNY Press, 1992); Honi Fern Haber, *Beyond Postmodern Politics: Lyotard, Rorty, Foucault* (New York: Routledge, 1994); and Michael Kelly, ed., *Critique and Power: Recasting the Foucault/Habermas Debate* (Cambridge, MA: MIT Press, 1994). For feminist readings of Foucault, see Jana Sawicki, *Disciplining Foucault: Feminism, Power, and the Body* (New York: Routledge, 1991); Caroline Ramazanoglu, ed., *Up Against Foucault: Explorations of Some Tensions Between Foucault and Feminism* (London: Routledge, 1993); and Susan J. Hekman, ed., *Feminist Interpretations of Michel Foucault* (College Park: Pennsylvania State University Press, 1996). Finally, for collections of critical essays, see David Hoy, ed., *Foucault: A Critical Reader* (Oxford: Basil Blackwell, 1986); Timothy J. Armstrong, ed. and trans., *Michel Foucault: Philosopher* (New York: Routledge, 1992); Gary Gutting, ed., *The Cambridge Companion to Foucault* (Cambridge: Cambridge University Press, 1994); and the multivolume Barry Smart, ed., *Michel Foucault: Critical Assessments* (Oxford: Routledge, 1994 & 1995).

WHAT IS AN AUTHOR?

The coming into being of the notion of "author" constitutes the privileged moment of *individualization* in the history of ideas, knowledge, literature, philosophy, and the sciences. Even today, when we reconstruct the history of a concept, literary genre, or school of philosophy, such categories seem relatively weak, secondary, and superimposed scansions in comparison with the solid and fundamental unit of the author and the work.

I shall not offer here a sociohistorical analysis of the author's persona. Certainly it would be worth examining how the author became individualized in a culture like ours, what status he has been given, at what moment studies of authenticity and attribution began, in what kind of system of valorization the author was involved, at what point we began to recount the lives of authors rather than of heroes, and how this fundamental category of "the-man-and-his-work criticism" began. For the moment, however, I want to deal solely with the relationship between text and author and with the manner in which the text points to this "figure" that, at least in appearance, is outside it and antecedes it.

Beckett nicely formulates the theme with which I would like to begin: "'What does it matter who is speaking,' someone said, 'what does it matter who is speaking.'" In this indifference appears one of the fundamental ethical principles of contemporary writing *[écriture]*. I say "ethical" because this indifference is not really a trait characterizing the manner in which one speaks and writes, but rather a kind of immanent rule, taken up over and over again, never fully applied, not designating writing as something completed, but dominating it as a practice. Since it is too familiar to require a lengthy analysis, this immanent rule can be adequately illustrated here by tracing two of its major themes.

First of all, we can say that today's writing has freed itself from the dimension of expression. Referring only to itself, but without being restricted to the confines of its interiority, writing is identified with its own unfolded exteriority. This means that it is an interplay of signs arranged less according to its signified content than according to the very nature of the signifier. Writing unfolds like a game *[jeu]* that invariably goes beyond its own rules and transgresses its limits. In writing, the point is not to manifest or exalt the act of writing, nor is it to pin a subject within language; it is, rather, a question of creating a space into which the writing subject constantly disappears.

The second theme, writing's relationship with death, is even more familiar. This link subverts an old tradition exemplified by the Greek epic, which was intended to perpetuate the immortality of the hero: if he was willing to die young, it was so that his life, consecrated and magnified by death, might pass into immortality; the narrative then redeemed this accepted death. In another way, the motivation, as well as the theme and the pretext of Arabian narratives—such as *The Thousand and One Nights*—was also the eluding of death: one spoke, telling stories into the early morning, in order to forestall death, to postpone the day of reckoning that would silence the narrator. Scheherazade's narrative is an effort, renewed each night, to keep death outside the circle of life.

Our culture has metamorphosed this idea of narrative, or writing, as something designed to ward off death. Writing has become linked to sacrifice, even to the sacrifice of life: it is now a voluntary effacement which does not need to be represented in books, since it is brought about in the writer's very existence. The work, which once had the duty of providing immortality, now possesses the right to kill, to be its author's murderer, as in the cases of Flaubert, Proust, and Kafka. That is not all, however: this relationship between writing and death is also manifested in the effacement of the writing subject's individual characteristics. Using all the contrivances that he sets up between himself and what he writes, the writing subject cancels out the signs of his particular individuality. As a result, the mark of the writer is reduced to nothing more than the singularity of his absence; he must assume the role of the dead man in the game of writing.

None of this is recent; criticism and philosophy took note of the disappearance—or death—of the author some time ago. But the consequences of their discovery of it have not been sufficiently examined, nor has its import been accurately measured. A certain number of notions that are intended to replace the privileged position of the author actually seem to preserve that privilege and suppress the real meaning of his disappearance. I shall examine two of these notions, both of great importance today.

The first is the idea of the work. It is a very familiar thesis that the task of criticism is not to bring out the work's relationships with the author, nor to reconstruct through the text a thought or experience, but rather to analyze the work through its structure, its architecture, its intrinsic form, and the play of its internal relationships. At this point, however, a problem arises: "What is a work? What is this curious unity which we designate as a work? Of what elements is it composed? Is it not what an author has written?" Difficulties appear immediately. If an individual were not an author, could we say that what he wrote, said, left behind in his papers, or what has been collected of his remarks, could be called a "work"? When Sade was not considered an author, what was the status of his papers? Were they simply rolls of paper onto which he ceaselessly uncoiled his fantasies during his imprisonment?

Even when an individual has been accepted as an author, we must still ask whether everything that he wrote, said, or left behind is part of his work. The problem is both theoretical and technical. When undertaking the publication of Nietzsche's works, for example, where should one stop? Surely everything must be published, but what is "everything"? Everything that Nietzsche himself published, certainly. And what about the rough drafts for his works? Obviously. The plans for his aphorisms? Yes. The deleted passages and the notes at the bottom of the page? Yes. What if, within a workbook filled with aphorisms, one finds a reference, the notation of a meeting or of an address, or a laundry list: Is it a work, or not? Why not? And so on, ad infinitum. How can one define a work amid the millions of traces left by someone after his death? A theory of the work does not exist, and the empirical task of those who naively undertake the editing of works often suffers in the absence of such a theory.

We could go even further: Does *The Thousand and One Nights* constitute a work? What about Clement of Alexandria's *Miscellanies* or Diogenes Laertius's *Lives?* A multitude of questions arises with regard to this notion of the work. Consequently, it is not enough to declare that we should do without the writer (the author) and study the work itself. The word work and the unity that it designates are probably as problematic as the status of the author's individuality.

Another notion which has hindered us from taking full measure of the author's disappearance, blurring and concealing the moment of this effacement and subtly preserving the author's existence, is the notion of writing *[écriture]*. When rigorously applied, this notion should allow us not only to circumvent references to the author, but also to situate his recent absence. The notion of writing, as currently employed, is concerned with neither the act of writing nor the indication—be it symptom or sign—of a meaning which someone might have wanted to express. We try, with great effort, to imagine the general condition of each text, the condition of both the space in which it is dispersed and the time in which it unfolds.

In current usage, however, the notion of writing seems to transpose the empirical characteristics of the author into a transcendental anonymity. We are content to efface the more visible marks of the author's empiricity by playing off, one against the other, two ways of characterizing writing, namely, the critical and the religious approaches. Giving writing a primal status seems to be a way of retranslating, in transcendental terms, both the theological affirmation of its sacred character and the critical affirmation of its creative character. To admit that writing is, because of the very history that it made possible, subject to the test of oblivion and repression, seems to represent, in transcendental terms, the religious principle of the hidden meaning (which requires interpretation) and the critical principle of implicit significations, silent determinations, and obscured contents (which gives rise to commentary). To imagine writing as absence seems to be a simple repetition, in transcendental terms, of both the religious principle of inalterable and yet never fulfilled tradition, and the aesthetic principle of the work's survival, its perpetuation beyond the author's death, and its enigmatic excess in relation to him.

This usage of the notion of writing runs the risk of maintaining the author's privileges under the protection of writing's a priori status: it keeps alive, in the gray light of neutralization, the interplay of those representations that formed a particular image of the author. The author's disappearance, which, since Mallarmé, has been a constantly recurring event, is subject to a series of transcendental barriers. There seems to be an important dividing line between those who believe that they can still locate today's discontinuities [ruptures] in the historico-transcendental tradition of the nineteenth century, and those who try to free themselves once and for all from that tradition.*

It is not enough, however, to repeat the empty affirmation that the author has disappeared. For the same reason, it is not enough to keep repeating (after Nietzsche) that God and man have died a common death. Instead, we must locate the space left empty by the author's disappearance, follow the distribution of gaps and breaches, and watch for the openings that this disappearance uncovers.

First, we need to clarify briefly the problems arising from the use of the author's name. What is an author's name? How does it function? Far from offering a solution, I shall only indicate some of the difficulties that it presents.

The author's name is a proper name, and therefore it raises the problems common to all proper names. (Here I refer to Searle's analyses, among others.**) Obviously, one cannot turn a proper name into a pure and simple reference. It has other than indicative functions: more than an indication, a gesture, a finger pointed at someone, it is the equivalent of a description. When one says "Aristotle," one employs a word that is the equivalent of one, or a series, of definite descriptions, such as "the author of the

*[For discussion of the notions of discontinuity and historical tradition see Foucault's *Les Mots et les choses* (Paris: Gallimard, 1966), translated as *The Order of Things* (New York: Pantheon, 1971).—Ed.]

**[John Searle, *Speech Acts: An Essay in the Philosophy of Language* (Cambridge: Cambridge University Press, 1969), pp. 162–174.—Ed.]

Analytics," "the founder of ontology," and so forth. One cannot stop there, however, because a proper name does not have just one signification. When we discover that Rimbaud did not write *La Chasse spirituelle,* we cannot pretend that the meaning of this proper name, or that of the author, has been altered. The proper name and the author's name are situated between the two poles of description and designation: they must have a certain link with what they name, but one that is neither entirely in the mode of designation nor in that of description; it must be a *specific* link. However— and it is here that the particular difficulties of the author's name arise—the links between the proper name and the individual named and between the author's name and what it names are not isomorphic and do not function in the same way. There are several differences.

If, for example, Pierre Dupont does not have blue eyes, or was not born in Paris, or is not a doctor, the name Pierre Dupont will still always refer to the same person; such things do not modify the link of designation. The problems raised by the author's name are much more complex, however. If I discover that Shakespeare was not born in the house that we visit today, this is a modification which, obviously, will not alter the functioning of the author's name. But if we proved that Shakespeare did not write those sonnets which pass for his, that would constitute a significant change and affect the manner in which the author's name functions. If we proved that Shakespeare wrote Bacon's *Organon* by showing that the same author wrote both the works of Bacon and those of Shakespeare, that would be a third type of change which would entirely modify the functioning of the author's name. The author's name is not, therefore, just a proper name like the rest.

Many other facts point out the paradoxical singularity of the author's name. To say that Pierre Dupont does not exist is not at all the same as saying that Homer or Hermes Trismegistus did not exist. In the first case, it means that no one has the name Pierre Dupont; in the second, it means that several people were mixed together under one name, or that the true author had none of the traits traditionally ascribed to the personae of Homer or Hermes. To say that X's real name is actually Jacques Durand instead of Pierre Dupont is not the same as saying that Stendhal's name was Henri Beyle. One could also question the meaning and functioning of propositions like "Bourbaki is so-and-so, so-and-so, etc." and "Victor Eremita, Climacus, Anticlimacus, Frater Taciturnus, Constantine Constantius, all of these are Kierkegaard."

These differences may result from the fact that an author's name is not simply an element in a discourse (capable of being either subject or object, of being replaced by a pronoun, and the like); it performs a certain role with regard to narrative discourse, assuring a classificatory function. Such a name permits one to group together a certain number of texts, define them, differentiate them from and contrast them to others. In addition, it establishes a relationship among the texts. Hermes Trismegistus did not exist, nor did Hippocrates—in the sense that Balzac existed—but the fact that several texts have been placed under the same name indicates that there has been established among them a relationship of homogeneity, filiation, authentication of some texts by the use of others, reciprocal explication, or concomitant utilization. The author's name serves to characterize a certain mode of being of discourse: the fact that the discourse has an author's name, that one can say "this was written by so-and-so" or "so-and-so is its author," shows that this discourse is not ordinary everyday speech that merely comes and goes, not something that is immediately consumable. On the contrary, it is a speech that must be received in a certain mode and that, in a given culture, must receive a certain status.

It would seem that the author's name, unlike other proper names, does not pass from the interior of a discourse to the real and exterior individual who produced it; instead, the name seems always to be present, marking off the edges of the text, revealing, or at least characterizing, its mode of being. The author's name manifests the appearance of a certain discursive set and indicates the status of this discourse within a society and a culture. It has no legal status, nor is it located in the fiction of the work; rather, it is located in the break that founds a certain discursive construct and its very particular mode of being. As a result, we could say that in a civilization like our own there are a certain number of discourses that are endowed with the "author function," while others are deprived of it. A private letter may well have a signer—it does not have an author; a contract may well have a guarantor—it does not have an author. An anonymous text posted on a wall probably has a writer—but not an author. The author function is therefore characteristic of the mode of existence, circulation, and functioning of certain discourses within a society.

Let us analyze this "author function" as we have just described it. In our culture, how does one characterize a discourse containing the author function? In what way is this discourse different from other discourses? If we limit our remarks to the author of a book or a text, we can isolate four different characteristics.

First of all, discourses are objects of appropriation. The form of ownership from which they spring is of a rather particular type, one that has been codified for many years. We should note that, historically, this type of ownership has always been subsequent to what one might call penal appropriation. Texts, books, and discourses really began to have authors (other than mythical, "sacralized" and "sacralizing" figures) to the extent that authors became subject to punishment, that is, to the extent that discourses could be transgressive. In our culture (and doubtless in many others), discourse was not originally a product, a thing, a kind of goods; it was essentially an act—an act placed in the bipolar field of the sacred and the profane, the licit and the illicit, the religious and the blasphemous. Historically, it was a gesture fraught with risks before becoming goods caught up in a circuit of ownership.

Once a system of ownership for texts came into being, once strict rules concerning author's rights, author-publisher relations, rights of reproduction, and related matters were enacted—at the end of the eighteenth and the beginning of the nineteenth century—the possibility of transgression attached to the act of writing took on, more and more, the form of an imperative peculiar to literature. It is as if the author, beginning with the moment at which he was placed in the system of property that characterizes our society, compensated for the status that he thus acquired by rediscovering the old bipolar field of discourse, systematically practicing transgression and thereby restoring danger to a writing which was now guaranteed the benefits of ownership.

The author function does not affect all discourses in a universal and constant way, however. This is its second characteristic. In our civilization, it has not always been the same types of texts which have required attribution to an author. There was a time when the texts that we today call "literary" (narratives, stories, epics, tragedies, comedies) were accepted, put into circulation, and valorized without any question about the identity of their author; their anonymity caused no difficulties since their ancientness, whether real or imagined, was regarded as a sufficient guarantee of their status. On the other hand, those texts that we now would call scientific—those dealing with cosmology and the heavens, medicine and illnesses, natural sciences and geography—were accepted in the Middle Ages, and accepted as "true," only when marked with the name of their author. "Hippocrates said," "Pliny recounts," were not really formulas of an argument based on authority; they were the markers inserted in discourses that were supposed to be received as statements of demonstrated truth.

A reversal occurred in the seventeenth or eighteenth century. Scientific discourses began to be received for themselves, in the anonymity of an established or always redemonstrable truth; their membership in a systematic ensemble, and not the reference to the individual who produced them, stood as their guarantee. The author function faded away, and the inventor's name served only to christen a theorem, proposition, particular effect, property, body, group of elements, or pathological syndrome. By the same token, literary discourses came to be accepted only when endowed with the author function. We now ask of each poetic or fictional text: From where does it come, who wrote it, when, under what circumstances, or beginning with what design? The meaning ascribed to it and the status or value accorded it depend on the manner in which we answer these questions. And if a text should be discovered in a state of anonymity—whether as a consequence of an accident or the author's explicit wish—the game becomes one of rediscovering the author. Since literary anonymity is not tolerable, we can accept it only in the guise of an enigma. As a result, the author function today plays an important role in our view of literary works. (These are obviously generalizations that would have to be refined insofar as recent critical practice is concerned.)

The third characteristic of this author function is that it does not develop spontaneously as the attribution of a discourse to an individual. It is, rather, the result of a complex operation which constructs a certain rational being that we call "author." Critics doubtless try to give this intelligible being a realistic status, by discerning, in the individual, a "deep" motive, a "creative" power, or a "design," the milieu in which writing originates. Nevertheless, these aspects of an individual which we designate as making him an author are only a projection, in more or less psychologizing terms, of the operations that we force texts to undergo, the connections that we make, the traits that we establish as pertinent, the continuities that we recognize, or the exclusions that we practice. All these operations vary according to periods and types of discourse. We do not construct a "philosophical author" as we do a "poet," just as, in the eighteenth century, one did not construct a novelist as we do today. Still, we can find through the ages certain constants in the rules of author construction.

It seems, for example, that the manner in which literary criticism once defined the author—or, rather, constructed the figure of the author beginning with existing texts and discourses—is directly derived from the manner in which Christian tradition authenticated (or rejected) the texts at its disposal. In order to "rediscover" an author in a work, modern criticism uses methods similar to those that Christian exegesis employed when trying to prove the value of a text by its author's saintliness. In *De viris illustribus,* Saint Jerome explains that homonymy is not sufficient to identify legitimately authors of more than one work: different individuals could have had the same name, or one man could have, illegitimately, borrowed another's patronymic. The name as an individual trademark is not enough when one works within a textual tradition.

How, then, can one attribute several discourses to one and the same author? How can one use the author function to determine if one is dealing with one or several individuals? Saint Jerome proposes four criteria: (1) if among several books attributed to an author one is inferior to the others, it must be withdrawn from the list of the author's works (the author is therefore defined as a constant level of value); (2) the same should be done if certain texts contradict the doctrine expounded in the author's other works (the author is thus defined as a field of conceptual or theoretical coherence); (3) one must also exclude works that are written in a different style, containing words and expressions not ordinarily found in the writer's production (the author is here conceived as a stylistic unity); (4) finally, passages quoting statements that were made or mentioning events that occurred after the author's death must be regarded as interpolated texts (the author is here seen as a historical figure at the crossroads of a certain number of events).

Modern literary criticism, even when—as is now customary—it is not concerned with questions of authentication, still defines the author the same way: the author provides the basis for explaining not only the presence of certain events in a work, but also their transformations, distortions, and diverse modifications (through his biography, the determination of his individual perspective, the analysis of his social position, and the revelation of his basic design). The author is also the principle of a certain unity of writing—all differences having to be resolved, at least in part, by the principles of evolution, maturation, or influence. The author also serves to neutralize the contradictions that may emerge in a series of texts: there must be—at a certain level of his thought or desire, of his consciousness or unconscious—a point where contradictions are resolved, where incompatible elements are at last tied together or organized around a fundamental or originating contradiction. Finally, the author is a particular source of expression that, in more or less completed forms, is manifested equally well, and with similar validity, in works, sketches, letters, fragments, and so on. Clearly, Saint Jerome's four criteria of authenticity (criteria which seem totally insufficient for today's exegetes) do define the four modalities according to which modern criticism brings the author function into play.

But the author function is not a pure and simple reconstruction made secondhand from a text given as passive material. The text always contains a certain number of signs referring to the author. These signs, well known to grammarians, are personal pronouns, adverbs of time and place, and verb conjugation. Such elements do not play the same role in discourses provided with the author function as in those lacking it. In the latter, such "shifters" refer to the real speaker and to the spatio-temporal coordinates of his discourse (although certain modifications can occur, as in the operation of relating discourses in the first person). In the former, however, their role is more complex and variable. Everyone knows that, in a novel narrated in the first person, neither the first-person pronoun nor the present indicative refers exactly either to the writer or to the moment in which he writes, but rather to an alter ego whose distance from the author varies, often changing in the course of the work. It would be just as wrong to equate the author with the real writer as to equate him with the fictitious speaker; the author function is carried out and operates in the scission itself, in this division and this distance.

One might object that this is a characteristic peculiar to novelistic or poetic discourse, a "game" in which only "quasi discourses" participate. In fact, however, all discourses endowed with the author function do possess this plurality of self. The self that speaks in the preface to a treatise on mathematics—and that indicates the circumstances of the treatise's composition—is identical neither in its position nor in its functioning to the self that speaks in the course of a demonstration, and that appears in the form of "I conclude" or "I suppose." In the first case, the "I" refers to an individual without an equivalent who, in a determined place and time, completed a certain task; in the second, the "I" indicates an instance and a level of demonstration which any individual could perform provided that he accepted the same system of symbols, play of axioms, and set of previous demonstrations. We could also, in the same treatise, locate a third self, one that speaks to tell the work's meaning, the obstacles encountered, the results obtained, and the remaining problems; this self is situated in the field of already existing or yet-to-appear mathematical discourses. The author function is not assumed by the first of these selves at the expense of the other two, which would then be nothing more than a fictitious splitting in two of the first one. On the contrary, in these discourses the author function operates so as to effect the dispersion of these three si-multaneous selves.

No doubt analysis could discover still more characteristic traits of the author function. I will limit myself to these four, however, because they seem both the most visible and the most important. They can be summarized as follows: (1) the author function is linked to the juridical and institutional system that encompasses, deter-mines, and articulates the universe of discourses; (2) it does not affect all discourses in the same way at all times and in all types of civilization; (3) it is not defined by the spontaneous attribution of a discourse to its producer, but rather by a series of specific and complex operations; (4) it does not refer purely and simply to a real individual, since it can give rise simultaneously to several selves, to several subjects positions that can be occupied by different classes of individuals.

Up to this point I have unjustifiably limited my subject. Certainly the author function in painting, music, and other arts should have been discussed, but even sup-posing that we remain within the world of discourse, as I want to do, I seem to have given the term "author" much too narrow a meaning. I have discussed the author only in the limited sense of a person to whom the production of a text, a book, or a work can be legitimately attributed. It is easy to see that in the sphere of discourse one can be the author of much more than a book—one can be the author of a theory, tradition, or dis-cipline in which other books and authors will in their turn find a place. These authors are in a position which we shall call "transdiscursive." This is a recurring phenome-non—certainly as old as our civilization. Homer, Aristotle, and the Church Fathers, as well as the first mathematicians and the originators of the Hippocratic tradition, all played this role.

Furthermore, in the course of the nineteenth century, there appeared in Europe another, more uncommon, kind of author, whom one should confuse with neither the "great" literary authors, nor the authors of religious texts, nor the founders of science. In a somewhat arbitrary way we shall call those who belong in this last group "founders of discursivity." They are unique in that they are not just the authors of their own works. They have produced something else: the possibilities and the rules for the formation of other texts. In this sense, they are very different, for example, from a nov-elist, who is, in fact, nothing more than the author of his own text. Freud is not just the author of *The Interpretation of Dreams* or *Jokes and Their Relation to the Uncon-scious;* Marx is not just the author of the *Communist Manifesto* or *Das Kapital:* they both have established an endless possibility of discourse.

Obviously, it is easy to object. One might say that it is not true that the author of a novel is only the author of his own text; in a sense, he also, provided that he acquires some "importance," governs and commands more than that. To take a very simple ex-ample, one could say that Ann Radcliffe not only wrote *The Castles of Athlin and Dun-bayne* and several other novels, but also made possible the appearance of the Gothic horror novel at the beginning of the nineteenth century; in that respect, her author func-tion exceeds her own work. But I think there is an answer to this objection. These founders of discursivity (I use Marx and Freud as examples, because I believe them to be both the first and the most important cases) make possible something altogether dif-ferent from what a novelist makes possible. Ann Radcliffe's texts opened the way for a certain number of resemblances and analogies which have their model or principle in her work. The latter contains characteristic signs, figures, relationships, and structures which could be reused by others. In other words, to say that Ann Radcliffe founded the Gothic horror novel means that in the nineteenth-century Gothic novel one will find, as in Ann Radcliffe's works, the theme of the heroine caught in the trap of her own innocence, the hidden castle, the character of the black, cursed hero devoted to making the world expiate the evil done to him, and all the rest of it.

On the other hand, when I speak of Marx or Freud as founders of discursivity, I mean that they made possible not only a certain number of analogies, but also (and equally important) a certain number of differences. They have created a possibility for something other than their discourse, yet something belonging to what they founded. To say that Freud founded psychoanalysis does not (simply) mean that we find the concept of the libido or the technique of dream analysis in the works of Karl Abraham or Melanie Klein; it means that Freud made possible a certain number of divergences—with respect to his own texts, concepts, and hypotheses—that all arise from the psychoanalytic discourse itself.

This would seem to present a new difficulty, however: is the above not true, after all, of any founder of a science, or of any author who has introduced some important transformation into a science? After all, Galileo made possible not only those discourses that repeated the laws that he had formulated, but also statements very different from what he himself had said. If Cuvier is the founder of biology or Saussure the founder of linguistics, it is not because they were imitated, nor because people have since taken up again the concept of organism or sign; it is because Cuvier made possible, to a certain extent, a theory of evolution diametrically opposed to his own fixism; it is because Saussure made possible a generative grammar radically different from his structural analyses. Superficially, then, the initiation of discursive practices appears similar to the founding of any scientific endeavor.

Still, there is a difference, and a notable one. In the case of a science, the act that founds it is on an equal footing with its future transformations; this act becomes in some respects part of the set of modifications that it makes possible. Of course, this belonging can take several forms. In the future development of a science, the founding act may appear as little more than a particular instance of a more general phenomenon which unveils itself in the process. It can also turn out to be marred by intuition and empirical bias; one must then reformulate it, making it the object of a certain number of supplementary theoretical operations which establish it more rigorously, etc. Finally, it can seem to be a hasty generalization which must be limited, and whose restricted domain of validity must be retraced. In other words, the founding act of a science can always be reintroduced within the machinery of those transformations that derive from it.

In contrast, the initiation of a discursive practice is heterogeneous to its subsequent transformations. To expand a type of discursivity, such as psychoanalysis as founded by Freud, is not to give it a formal generality that it would not have permitted at the outset, but rather to open it up to a certain number of possible applications. To limit psychoanalysis as a type of discursivity is, in reality, to try to isolate in the founding act an eventually restricted number of propositions or statements to which, alone, one grants a founding value, and in relation to which certain concepts or theories accepted by Freud might be considered as derived, secondary, and accessory. In addition, one does not declare certain propositions in the work of these founders to be false: instead, when trying to seize the act of founding, one sets aside those statements that are not pertinent, either because they are deemed inessential, or because they are considered "prehistoric" and derived from another type of discursivity. In other words, unlike the founding of a science, the initiation of a discursive practice does not participate in its later transformations.

As a result, one defines a proposition's theoretical validity in relation to the work of the founders—while, in the case of Galileo and Newton, it is in relation to what physics or cosmology is (in its intrinsic structure and "normativity") that one affirms the validity of any proposition that those men may have put forth. To phrase it very schematically: the work of initiators of discursivity is not situated in the space that science defines; rather, it is the science or the discursivity which refers back to their work as primary coordinates.

In this way we can understand the inevitable necessity, within these fields of discursivity, for a "return to the origin." This return, which is part of the discursive field itself, never stops modifying it. The return is not a historical supplement which would be added to the discursivity, or merely an ornament; on the contrary, it constitutes an effective and necessary task of transforming the discursive practice itself. Reexamination of Galileo's text may well change our knowledge of the history of mechanics, but it will never be able to change mechanics itself. On the other hand, reexamining Freud's texts modifies psychoanalysis itself, just as a reexamination of Marx's would modify Marxism.*

What I have just outlined regarding the initiation of discursive practices is, of course, very schematic; this is true, in particular, of the opposition that I have tried to draw between discursive initiation and scientific founding. It is not always easy to distinguish between the two; moreover, nothing proves that they are two mutually exclusive procedures. I have attempted the distinction for only one reason: to show that the author function, which is complex enough when one tries to situate it at the level of a book or a series of texts that carry a given signature, involves still more determining factors when one tries to analyze it in larger units, such as groups of works or entire disciplines.

To conclude, I would like to review the reasons why I attach a certain importance to what I have said.

First, there are theoretical reasons. On the one hand, an analysis in the direction that I have outlined might provide for an approach to a typology of discourse. It seems to me, at least at first glance, that such a typology cannot be constructed solely from the grammatical features, formal structures, and objects of discourse: more likely there exist properties or relationships peculiar to discourse (not reducible to the rules of grammar and logic), and one must use these to distinguish the major categories of discourse. The relationship (or nonrelationship) with an author, and the different forms this relationship takes, constitute—in a quite visible manner—one of these discursive properties.

On the other hand, I believe that one could find here an introduction to the historical analysis of discourse. Perhaps it is time to study discourses not only in terms of their expressive value or formal transformations, but according to their modes of existence. The modes of circulation, valorization, attribution, and appropriation of discourses vary with each culture and are modified within each. The manner in which

*[To define these returns more clearly, one must also emphasize that they tend to reinforce the enigmatic link between an author and his works. A text has an inaugurative value precisely because it is the work of a particular author, and our returns are conditioned by this knowledge. As in the case of Galileo, there is no possibility that the rediscovery of an unknown text by Newton or Cantor will modify classical cosmology or set theory as we know them (at best, such an exhumation might modify our historical knowledge of their genesis). On the other hand, the discovery of a text like Freud's "Project for a Scientific Psychology"—insofar as it is a text by Freud—always threatens to modify not the historical knowledge of psychoanalysis, but its theoretical field, even if only by shifting the accentuation or the center of gravity. Through such returns, which are part of their make-up, these discursive practices maintain a relationship with regard to their "fundamental" and indirect author unlike that which an ordinary text entertains with its immediate author.—Ed.]

they are articulated according to social relationships can be more readily understood, I believe, in the activity of the author function and in its modifications than in the themes or concepts that discourses set in motion.

It would seem that one could also, beginning with analyses of this type, reexamine the privileges of the subject. I realize that in undertaking the internal and architectonic analysis of a work (be it a literary text, philosophical system, or scientific work), in setting aside biographical and psychological references, one has already called back into question the absolute character and founding role of the subject. Still, perhaps one must return to this question, not in order to reestablish the theme of an originating subject, but to grasp the subject's points of insertion, modes of functioning, and system of dependencies. Doing so means overturning the traditional problem, no longer raising the questions "How can a free subject penetrate the substance of things and give it meaning? How can it activate the rules of a language from within and thus give rise to the designs which are properly its own?" Instead, these questions will be raised: "How, under what conditions, and in what forms can something like a subject appear in the order of discourse? What place can it occupy in each type of discourse, what functions can it assume, and by obeying what rules?" In short, it is a matter of depriving the subject (or its substitute) of its role as originator, and of analyzing the subject as a variable and complex function of discourse.

Second, there are reasons dealing with the "ideological" status of the author. The question then becomes: How can one reduce the great peril, the great danger with which fiction threatens our world? The answer is: one can reduce it with the author. The author allows a limitation of the cancerous and dangerous proliferation of significations within a world where one is thrifty not only with one's resources and riches, but also with one's discourses and their significations. The author is the principle of thrift in the proliferation of meaning. As a result, we must entirely reverse the traditional idea of the author. We are accustomed, as we have seen earlier, to saying that the author is the genial creator of a work in which he deposits, with infinite wealth and generosity, an inexhaustible world of significations. We are used to thinking that the author is so different from all other men, and so transcendent with regard to all languages that, as soon as he speaks, meaning begins to proliferate, to proliferate indefinitely.

The truth is quite the contrary: the author is not an indefinite source of significations which fill a work; the author does not precede the works; he is a certain functional principle by which, in our culture, one limits, excludes, and chooses; in short, by which one impedes the free circulation, the free manipulation, the free composition, decomposition, and recomposition of fiction. In fact, if we are accustomed to presenting the author as a genius, as a perpetual surging of invention, it is because, in reality, we make him function in exactly the opposite fashion. One can say that the author is an ideological product, since we represent him as the opposite of his historically real function. (When a historically given function is represented in a figure that inverts it, one has an ideological production.) The author is therefore the ideological figure by which one marks the manner in which we fear the proliferation of meaning.

In saying this, I seem to call for a form of culture in which fiction would not be limited by the figure of the author. It would be pure romanticism, however, to imagine a culture in which the fictive would operate in an absolutely free state, in which fiction would be put at the disposal of everyone and would develop without passing through something like a necessary or constraining figure. Although, since the eighteenth century, the author has played the role of the regulator of the fictive, a role quite characteristic of our era of industrial and bourgeois society, of individualism and private property; still, given the historical modifications that are taking place, it does not seem necessary that the author function remain constant in form, complexity, and even in existence. I think that, as our society changes, at the very moment when it is in the process of changing, the author function will disappear, and in such a manner that fiction and its polysemic texts will once again function according to another mode, but still with a system of constraint—one which will no longer be the author, but which will have to be determined or, perhaps, experienced.

All discourses, whatever their status, form, value, and whatever the treatment to which they will be subjected, would then develop in the anonymity of a murmur. We would no longer hear the questions that have been rehashed for so long: "Who really spoke? Is it really he and not someone else? With what authenticity or originality? And what part of his deepest self did he express in his discourse?" Instead, there would be other questions, like these: "What are the modes of existence of this discourse? Where has it been used, how can it circulate, and who can appropriate it for himself? What are the places in it where there is room for possible subjects? Who can assume these various subject functions?" And behind all these questions, we would hear hardly anything but the stirring of an indifference: "What difference does it make who is speaking?"

"TRUTH AND POWER"
(in part)

... The important thing here, I believe, is that truth isn't outside power, or lacking in power: contrary to a myth whose history and functions would repay further study, truth isn't the reward of free spirits, the child of protracted solitude, nor the privilege of those who have succeeded in liberating themselves. Truth is a thing of this world: it is produced only by virtue of multiple forms of constraint. And it induces regular effects of power. Each society has its regime of truth, its "general politics" of truth: that is, the types of discourse which it accepts and makes function as true; the mechanisms and instances which enable one to distinguish true and false statements, the means by which each is sanctioned; the techniques and procedures accorded value in the acquisition of truth; the status of those who are charged with saying what counts as true.

In societies like ours, the "political economy" of truth is characterised by five important traits. "Truth" is centred on the form of scientific discourse and the institutions which produce it; it is subject to constant economic and political incitement (the demand for truth, as much for economic production as for political power); it is the object, under diverse forms, of immense diffusion and consumption (circulating through apparatuses of education and information whose extent is relatively broad in the social body, not withstanding certain strict limitations); it is produced and transmitted under the control, dominant if not exclusive, of a few great political and economic apparatuses (university, army, writing, media); lastly, it is the issue of a whole political debate and social confrontation ("ideological" struggles).

It seems to me that what must now be taken into account in the intellectual is not the "bearer of universal values." Rather, it's the person occupying a specific position— but whose specificity is linked, in a society like ours, to the general functioning of an apparatus of truth. In other words, the intellectual has a three-fold specificity: that of his class position (whether as petty-bourgeois in the service of capitalism or "organic" intellectual of the proletariat); that of his conditions of life and work, linked to his condition as an intellectual (his field of research, his place in a laboratory, the political and economic demands to which he submits or against which he rebels, in the university, the hospital, etc.); lastly, the specificity of the politics of truth in our societies. And it's with this last factor that his position can take on a general significance and that his local, specific struggle can have effects and implications which are not simply professional or sectoral. The intellectual can operate and struggle at the general level of that regime of truth which is so essential to the structure and functioning of our society. There is a battle "for truth," or at least "around truth"—it being understood once again that by truth I do not mean "the ensemble of truths which are to be discovered and accepted," but rather "the ensemble of rules according to which the true and the false are separated and specific effects of power attached to the true," it being understood also that it's not a matter of a battle "on behalf" of the truth, but of a battle about the status of truth and the economic and political role it plays. It is necessary to think of the political problems of intellectuals not in terms of "science" and "ideology," but in terms of "truth" and "power." And thus the question of the professionalisation of intellectuals and the division between intellectual and manual labour can be envisaged in a new way.

All this must seem very confused and uncertain. Uncertain indeed, and what I am saying here is above all to be taken as a hypothesis. In order for it to be a little less confused, however, I would like to put forward a few "propositions"—not firm assertions, but simply suggestions to be further tested and evaluated.

"Truth" is to be understood as a system of ordered procedures for the production, regulation, distribution, circulation and operation of statements.

"Truth" is linked in a circular relation with systems of power which produce and sustain it, and to effects of power which it induces and which extend it. A regime of truth.

This regime is not merely ideological or superstructural; it was a condition of the formation and development of capitalism. And it's this same regime which, subject to certain modifications, operates in the socialist countries (I leave open here the question of China, about which I know little).

The essential political problem for the intellectual is not to criticise the ideological contents supposedly linked to science, or to ensure that his own scientific practice is accompanied by a correct ideology, but that of ascertaining the possibility of constituting a new politics of truth. The problem is not changing people's consciousnesses —or what's in their heads—but the political, economic, institutional regime of the production of truth.

It's not a matter of emancipating truth from every system of power (which would be a chimera, for truth is already power) but of detaching the power of truth from the forms of hegemony, social, economic and cultural, within which it operates at the present time.

The political question, to sum up, is not error, illusion, alienated consciousness or ideology; it is truth itself. Hence the importance of Nietzsche.

JACQUES DERRIDA
1930–

In the spirit of his celebrated dictum that "there is nothing outside the text," Jacques Derrida long resisted the publication of information about his life. For seventeen years (1962–1979) he even refused to have a personal photograph accompany his texts. However, his fame as the founder of what came to be called "deconstruction" led him to provide biographical "scraps."

Born in 1930 near Algiers, Jacques Derrida as a Jew was forced to leave school in 1942 until the Free French repealed Vichy racial laws. At nineteen, he moved to Paris to prepare for the École Normale Supérieure, where he subsequently studied and taught philosophy. Though his first published work (1962)—about Husserl's essay on geometry—won a philosophical prize, Derrida was not widely known until 1966. At a conference on France's new structuralism at Johns Hopkins University, Derrida gave a paper—"Structure, Sign, and Play in the Discourse of the Human Sciences"—that daringly exposed contradictions in the thought of structuralism's leading figure, Lévi-Strauss. Derrida's critique became one of the important building blocks in what came to be called "poststructuralism."

The following year, Derrida continued his critique, publishing no less than three books showing how structuralist positions refuted their own theses. The books—*Of Grammatology; Writing and Difference;* and *Speech and Phenomena* (as the titles were translated)—created a storm of philosophical debate in France. In these works, Derrida showed how his critique went beyond structuralism and attacked the enterprise of philosophy itself. "Deconstruction," as Derrida's approach in these works was now called, claimed that the very nature of a written text—of every traditional text and not just the structuralist's—undermines itself.

To "deconstruct" a text, then, is to dismantle inherent hierarchical systems of thought, to seek out unregarded details, to find the "margins" of the text, where there are new possibilities of interpretation.

In 1972, Derrida published three additional works, translated as *Dissemination, Margins of Philosophy,* and *Positions,* which continued to influence post-structuralism in the 1970s. As Derrida's fame grew, he accepted a visiting professorship first at Yale University, and then at the University of California in Irvine. In the 1980s, Derrida gave himself to political causes such as the abolition of apartheid. He also became actively interested in architecture, which he regarded as the last bastion of metaphysics. He helped architect Peter Eisenman design a garden in Paris that explores the relationship between center and periphery. Born on the periphery of colonial France, on the margin of Algiers, as a marginalized Jew, Derrida constantly examined the philosophical relation between margin and center (and often employed language that is only marginally understandable). All for a purpose.

*   *   *

Derrida believes that Western philosophy is built upon a "Metaphysics of Presence": upon, that is to say, the idea that there is an origin of knowledge from which "truth" can be made present. Philosophy has always seen itself as the arbiter of reason, the discipline that adjudicates what is and is not. Forms of writing other than philosophical discourse, such as poetic or literary writing, have been judged inferior, and removed from the truth. In *Of Grammatology,* Derrida calls this positing of a center that can situate certainty *logocentrism.* Philosophy thinks it can talk about "meaning" through a language unsullied by the imprecision of metaphors. *Au Contraire!* Philosophical discourse is not privileged in any way, and any attempt to explain what "meaning" *means* will self-destruct. Put more precisely, the signifiers of language systems cannot refer to a transcendental *signified* originating in the mind of the speaker because the "signified" is itself created by the conventional, and hence arbitrary, signifiers of language. Signifiers therefore merely refer to other signifiers (e.g., words refer only to other words). The "meaning" is always deferred and Presence is never actually present. Signifiers attain significance only in their differences from each other (the signifier "cat" is neither "cap" nor "car") or in what they define themselves against ("to be asleep" is understood in contrast to "to be awake").

To highlight the ambiguities of language, Derrida coined the word "*différance.*" In French, this word sounds no different from the French word "*differénce,*" which comes from the verb "*différer,*" meaning both "to differ" and "to defer." Whereas the definition of *différence* reminds us that signifiers defer meaning as they differ both from their referents and from each other, the written word *différance* calls attention in a striking way to the limitations of the spoken word. The spoken word can establish no aural distinction between *différence* and *différance.* Derrida thus questions the traditional privileging of speech over writing, which goes back at least as far as Plato. For example, in the *Phaedrus,* Plato had placed writing as one step further removed than speaking from Ideal Form. Derrida shows, however, that even as Plato sought to place speech closer to the source of meaning, he could not keep writing out of his system. At one point in the *Phaedrus,* Plato states that speech "is *written* in the soul of the listener" (emphasis added).

This is just one example of how Derrida repeatedly exposes the repressed figures of speech in even the most systematic of thinkers. According to Derrida, all systems of thought contain "traces" of that which they define themselves against. Thus, whereas many philosophers have thought literature merely sugarcoated philosophy, Derrida has reversed this hierarchy to say that the discourse of philosophy is merely literary medicine—an assumption that is hard for many to swallow. For Derrida, all writing is reduced (or elevated) to the same level, with no privileging of one genre as more "meaning-ful" than another. This may explain why deconstruction—with its close reading of texts to unearth language working against itself—made its greatest impact in literature, rather than in philosophy.

Our selection, "Signature, Event, Context," translated by Samuel Weber and Jeffrey Mehlman, exhibits these deconstructive themes. Derrida begins by deconstructing the signifier "communication," showing how context will not serve to clarify the meaning of this word. Next, he exposes the ways writing has been privileged over speech. Thirdly, he explores Austin's concept of a speech act, finding much with which to agree. But finally, he argues that Austin is still operating within the metaphysics of Presence, requiring a signature or some other continuing presence to secure the speech act.

Derrida concludes our selection by claiming that the inversion of the hierarchy—speech over writing, like that of philosophy over literature—is part of his deconstruction of binaries that have molded the tradition of Western metaphysics. Philosophy has continually worked with pairs in which the first term was seen as the origin or foundation for the second: truth/fiction, reality/appearance, thought/language, signified/signifier, center/margin, male/female, objective/subjective, essential/inessential. Derrida does not want merely to invert these polarities to create a new countersystem. Instead he "destabilizes" these pairings to show that any privileging of one term over the other is an arbitrary construction, usually politically motivated, which must be deconstructed. As he says, "Deconstruction does not consist in passing from one concept to another, but in overturning and displacing a conceptual order, as well as the nonconceptual order with which the conceptual order is articulated."

But what about Derrida's writings themselves—do they not represent a conceptual order, an attempt to communicate "meaning"? Derrida goes to great pains to avoid the systemization of his own thought, constantly inventing new terms to destabilize his readers' sense that they understand his "philosophy." In the meantime, although he works to expose the failures of language to make present meaning, he acknowledges that, since language is all we have, he must situate himself inside a system even as he is breaking it apart. He signals this paradox, or *aporia,* of language by borrowing a technique from Heidegger, who simultaneously included and deleted the word Being in his works by placing an X over it: B̶e̶i̶n̶g̶. Derrida crosses out certain metaphysically loaded words, putting them "under erasure." He asserts the inadequacy of a signifier like na̶t̶u̶re to have a definitive meaning, while also acknowledging that thought cannot operate without the term. Derrida demonstrates that his own writing—like everyone else's—is not innocent, that it cannot become a coherent theoretical system corresponding to reality. Derrida has therefore been called a nihilist. His defenders, however, call this accusation inaccurate. Derrida never denies the existence of an Absolute; he only asserts the impossibility of putting the Absolute into words.

*   *   *

For a general overview of Derrida, see Christopher Norris, *Derrida* (Cambridge, MA: Harvard University Press, 1987). Allan Megill, *Prophets of Extremity: Nietzsche, Heidegger, Foucault, Derrida* (Berkeley: University of California Press, 1985); Diane P. Michelfelder and Richard E. Palmer, eds., *Dialogue and Deconstruction: The Gadamer-Derrida Encounter* (Albany, NY: SUNY Press, 1989); Roy Boyne, *Foucault and Derrida: The Other Side of Reason* (London: Unwin Hyman, 1990); and Simon Critchley, *The Ethics of Deconstruction: Derrida & Levinas* (Oxford: Basil Blackwell, 1992) provide comparative studies. John D. Caputo, *The Prayers and Tears of Jacques Derrida: Religion without Religion* (Bloomington: Indiana University Press, 1997) is a recent specialized study. Gary A. Olson and Irene Gale, eds., *(Inter)view: Cross-Disciplinary Perspectives on Rhetoric and Literacy* (Carbondale: Southern Illinois University Press, 1991); Jacques Derrida, *Points. . . : Interview 1974–1994,* edited by Elisabeth Weber (Stanford, CA: Stanford University Press, 1995); and John Caputo, ed., *Deconstruction in a Nutshell: A Conversation with Jacques Derrida* (New York: Fordham University Press, 1997) include discussions with Derrida. For a treatment of the specific issues raised in our selection, see John R. Searle, *Expression and Meaning: Studies in the Theory of Speech Acts* (Cambridge: Cambridge University Press, 1979); Stanley Cavell, *Philosophical Passages: Wittgenstein, Emerson, Austin, Derrida* (Oxford: Blackwell, 1995); and Graham Ward, *Barth, Derrida and the Language of Theology* (Cambridge: Cambridge University Press, 1995). For a feminist reading of Derrida, see Ellen K. Feder, Mary C. Rawlinson, and Emily Zakin, eds., *Derrida and Feminism* (Oxford: Routledge, 1997). General collections of critical essays include John Sallis, ed., *Deconstruction and Philosophy: The Texts of Jacques Derrida* (Chicago: University of Chicago Press, 1987); David Wood, ed., *Derrida: A Critical Reader* (Oxford: Basil Blackwell, 1992); Harold Coward and Toby Foshay, eds., *Derrida and Negative Theology* (Albany, NY: SUNY Press, 1992); and Gary B. Madison, ed., *Working through Derrida* (Evanston, IL: Northwestern University Press, 1993). Finally, in Geoffrey Bennington and Jacques Derrida, *Jacques Derrida* (Chicago: University of Chicago Press, 1993), the top two-thirds of each page give Bennington's comment on Derrida's thought, whereas Derrida himself writes "in the margin" along the bottom of each page.

"SIGNATURE, EVENT, CONTEXT"

> "Still confining ourselves for simplicity
> to *spoken* utterance."
> —Austin, *How to Do Things with Words*

Is it certain that to the word *communication* corresponds a concept that is unique, univocal, rigorously controllable, and transmittable: in a word, communicable? Thus, in accordance with a strange figure of discourse, one must first of all ask oneself whether or not the word or signifier "communication" communicates a determinate content, an identifiable meaning, or a describable value. However, even to articulate and to propose this question I have had to anticipate the meaning of the word *communication:* I have been constrained to predetermine communication as a vehicle, a means of transport or transitional medium of a *meaning,* and moreover of a *unified* meaning. If *communication* possessed several meanings and if this plurality should prove to be irreducible, it would not be justifiable to define communication *a priori* as the transmission of a *meaning,* even supposing that we could agree on what each of these words (transmission, meaning, etc.) involved. And yet, we have no prior authorization for neglecting *communication* as a word, or for impoverishing its polysemic aspects; indeed, this word opens up a semantic domain that precisely does not limit itself to semantics, semiotics, and even less to linguistics. For one characteristic of the semantic field of the word communication is that it designates nonsemantic movements as well. Here, even a provisional recourse to ordinary language and to the equivocations of natural language instructs us that one can, for instance, *communicate a movement* or that a tremor *[ébranlement],* a shock, a displacement of force can be communicated—that is, propagated, transmitted. We also speak of different or remote places communicating with each other by means of a passage or opening. What takes place, in this sense, what is transmitted, communicated, does not involve phenomena of meaning or signification. In such cases we are dealing neither with a semantic or conceptual content, nor with a semiotic operation, and even less with a linguistic exchange.

We would not, however, assert that this non-semiotic meaning of the word *communication,* as it works in ordinary language, in one or more of the so-called natural languages, constitutes the *literal* or *primary [primitif]* meaning and that consequently the semantic, semiotic, or linguistic meaning corresponds to a derivation, extension, or reduction, a metaphoric displacement. We would not assert, as one might be tempted to do, that semio-linguistic communication acquired its title *more metaphorico,* by analogy with "physical" or "real" communication, inasmuch as it also serves as a passage, transporting and transmitting something, rendering it accessible. We will not assert this for the following reasons:

1. because the value of the notion of *literal meaning [sens propre]* appears more problematical than ever, and

2. because the value of displacement, of transport, etc., is precisely constitutive of the concept of metaphor with which one claims to comprehend the semantic dis-

Jacques Derrida, "Signature, Event, Context," translated by Samuel Weber and Jeffrey Mehlman, from *Glyph* 1, 1977. Reprinted by permission of the Johns Hopkins University Press.

placement that is brought about from communication as a non-semiolinguistic phenomenon to communication as a semio-linguistic phenomenon.

(Let me note parenthetically that this communication is going to concern, indeed already concerns, the problem of polysemy and of communication, of dissemination—which I shall oppose to polysemy—and of communication. In a moment a certain concept of writing cannot fail to arise that may transform itself and perhaps transform the problematic under consideration.)

It seems self-evident that the ambiguous field of the word "communication" can be massively reduced by the limits of what is called a context (and I give notice, again parenthetically, that this particular communication will be concerned with the problem of context and with the question of determining exactly how writing relates to context in general). For example, in a philosophic *colloquium* on philosophy in the *French language,* a conventional context—produced by a kind of consensus that is implicit but structurally vague—seems to prescribe that one propose "communications" concerning communication, communications in a discursive form, colloquial communications, oral communications destined to be listened to, and to engage or to pursue dialogues within the horizon of an intelligibility and truth that is meaningful, such that ultimately general agreement may, in principle, be attained. These communications are supposed to confine themselves to the element of a determinate, "natural" language, here designated as French, which commands certain very particular uses of the word communication. Above all, the object of such communications is supposed, by priority or by privilege, to organize itself around communication qua discourse, or in any case qua signification. Without exhausting all the implications and the entire structure of an "event" such as this one, an effort that would require extended preliminary analysis, the conditions that I have just recalled seem to be evident; and those who doubt it need only consult our program to be convinced.

But are the conditions *[les réquisits]* of a context ever absolutely determinable? This is, fundamentally, the most general question that I shall endeavor to elaborate. Is there a rigorous and scientific concept of *context?* Or does the notion of context not conceal, behind a certain confusion, philosophical presuppositions of a very determinate nature? Stating it in the most summary manner possible, I shall try to demonstrate why a context is never absolutely determinable, or rather, why its determination can never be entirely certain or saturated. This structural non-saturation would have a double effect:

1. it would mark the theoretical inadequacy of the *current concept of context* (linguistic or nonlinguistic), as it is accepted in numerous domains of research, including all the concepts with which it is systematically associated;

2. it would necessitate a certain generalization and a certain displacement of the concept of writing. This concept would no longer be comprehensible in terms of communication, at least in the limited sense of a transmission of meaning. Inversely, it is within the general domain of writing, defined in this way, that the effects of semantic communication can be determined as effects that are particular, secondary, inscribed, and supplementary.

Writing and Telecommunication

If we take the notion of writing in its currently accepted sense—one which should not—and that is essential—be considered innocent, primitive, or natural, it can only be seen as a *means of communication.* Indeed, one is compelled to regard it as an especially potent means of communication, *extending* enormously, if not infinitely, the domain of oral or gestural communication. This seems obvious, a matter of general agreement. I shall not describe all the *modes* of this extension in time and in space. I shall, however, pause for a moment to consider the import *[valeur]* of *extension* to which I have just referred. To say that writing extends the field and the powers of locutory or gestural communication presupposes, does it not, a sort of *homogeneous* space of communication? Of course the compass of voice or of gesture would encounter therein a factual limit, an empirical boundary of space and of time; while writing, in the same time and in the same space, would be capable of relaxing those limits and of opening the same *field* to a very much larger scope. The meaning or contents of the semantic message would thus be transmitted, *communicated,* by different *means,* by more powerful technical mediations, over a far greater distance, but still within a medium that remains fundamentally continuous and self-identical, a homogeneous element through which the unity and wholeness of meaning would not be affected in its essence. Any alteration would therefore be accidental.

The system of this interpretation (which is also, in a certain manner, *the* system of interpretation, or in any case of all hermeneutical interpretation), however currently accepted it may be, or inasmuch as it is current, like common sense, has been *represented* through the history of philosophy. I would even go so far as to say that it is the interpretation of writing that is peculiar and proper to philosophy. I shall limit myself to a single example, but I do not believe that a single counterexample can be found in the entire history of philosophy as such; I know of no analysis that contradicts, essentially, the one proposed by Condillac, under the direct influence of Warburton, in the *Essay on the Origin of Human Knowledge (Essai sur l'origine des connaissances humaines).* I have chosen this example because it contains an *explicit* reflection on the origin and function of the written text (this explicitness is not to be found in every philosophy, and the particular conditions both of its emergence and of its eclipse must be analyzed) which organizes itself here within a philosophical discourse that, in this case and throughout philosophy, presupposes the simplicity of the origin, the continuity of all derivation, of all production, of all analysis, and the homogeneity of all dimensions [ordres]. Analogy is a major concept in the thought of Condillac. I have also chosen this example because the analysis, "retracing" the origin and function of writing, is placed, in a rather uncritical manner, *under the authority of the category of communication.** If men write it is: (1) because they have to communicate; (2) because what they have to communicate is their "thought," their "ideas," their representations. Thought, as representation, precedes and governs communication, which transports the "idea," the signified content; (3) because men are *already* in a state that allows them to communicate their thought to themselves and to each other when, in a continuous manner, they invent the particular means of communication, writing. Here is a passage from chapter XIII of the Second Part ("On Language and Method"), First Section ("On the Origins and Progress of Language") (Writing is thus a modality of language and marks a continual progression in an essentially linguistic communication), paragraph XIII, "On Writing": "Men in a state of communicating their thoughts by means of sounds, felt the necessity of imagining new signs capable of perpetuating those thoughts and of making them known to persons who are *absent*" (I underscore this

---

*The Rousseauist theory of language and of writing is also introduced under the general title of *communication* ("On the diverse means of communicating our thoughts" is the title of the first chapter of the *Essay on the Origin of Languages).*

value of *absence,* which, if submitted to renewed questioning, will risk introducing a certain break in the homogeneity of the system). Once men are already in the state of "communicating their thoughts," and of doing it by means of sounds (which is, according to Condillac, a second step, when articulated language has come to "supplant" *[suppléer]* the language of action, which is the single and radical principle of all language), the birth and progress of writing will follow in a line that is direct, simple, and continuous. The history of writing will conform to a law of mechanical economy: to gain or save the most space and time possible by means of the most convenient abbreviation; hence writing will never have the slightest effect on either the structure or the contents of the meaning (the ideas) that it is supposed to transmit *[véhiculer].* The same content, formerly communicated by gestures and sounds, will henceforth be transmitted by writing, by successively different modes of notation, from pictographic writing to alphabetic writing, collaterally by the hieroglyphic writing of the Egyptians and the ideographic writing of the Chinese. Condillac continues:

> Thus, the imagination will represent to them only the very *same* images that they had already expressed through actions and words, and which had, from the very beginning, rendered language figural and metaphorical. *The most natural means* was thus to depict *[dessiner]* images of things. *To express the idea* of a man or of a horse, one represented the form of the one or of the other, and the first attempt at writing was nothing but a simple painting. (My emphasis—J.D.)

The representational character of the written communication—writing as picture, reproduction, imitation of its content—will be the invariant trait of all progress to come. The concept of *representation* is here indissociable from those of *communication* and of *expression* that I have emphasized in Condillac's text. Representation, of course, will become more complex, will develop supplementary ramifications and degrees; it will become the representation of a representation in various systems of writing, hieroglyphic, ideographic, or phonetic-alphabetical, but the representative structure which marks the first degree of expressive communication, the relation idea/sign, will never be either annulled or transformed. Describing the history of the types of writing, their continuous derivation from a common root that is never displaced and which establishes a sort of community of analogical participation among all the species of writing, Condillac concludes (in what is virtually a citation of Warburton, as is most of this chapter):

> Thus, the general history of writing proceeds by simple gradation from the state of painting to that of the letter; for letters are the final steps that are left to be taken after the Chinese marks which, on the one hand, participate in the nature of Egyptian hieroglyphics, and on the other, participate in that of letters just as the hieroglyphs participate both in Mexican paintings and Chinese characters. These characters are so close to our writing that an alphabet simply diminishes the inconvenience of their great number and is their succinct abbreviation.

Having thus confirmed the motif of economic reduction in its *homogeneous* and *mechanical* character, let us now return to the notion of *absence* that I underscored, in passing, in the text of Condillac. How is that notion determined there?

1. It is first of all the absence of the addressee. One writes in order to communicate something to those who are absent. The absence of the sender, of the receiver *[destinateur],* from the mark that he abandons, and which cuts itself off from him and continues to produce effects independently of his presence and of the present actuality

of his intentions *[vouloir-dire]*, indeed even after his death, his absence, which moreover belongs to the structure of all writing—and I shall add further on, of all language in general—this absence is not examined by Condillac.

2. The absence of which Condillac speaks is determined in the most classic manner as a continuous modification and progressive extenuation of presence. Representation regularly *supplants [supplée]* presence. However, articulating all the moments of experience insofar as it is involved in signification ("to supplant," *suppléer,* is one of the most decisive and most frequent operational concepts in Condillac's *Essay**), this operation of supplementation is not exhibited as a break in presence but rather as a continuous and homogeneous reparation and modification of presence in the representation.

I am not able to analyze, here, everything presupposed in Condillac's philosophy and elsewhere, by this concept of absence as the modification of presence. Let us note only that this concept governs another operational notion (for the sake of convenience I invoke the classical opposition between *operational* and *thematic*) which is no less decisive for the *Essay: tracing and retracing.* Like the concept of supplanting *[suppléance]*, the concept of trace would permit an interpretation quite different from Condillac's. According to him, tracing means "expressing," "representing," "recalling," "rendering present" ("Thus painting probably owes its origin to the necessity of tracing our thoughts in the manner described, and this necessity has doubtless contributed to preserving the language of action as that which is most readily depictable" ["On Writing," p. 128]). The sign comes into being at the same time as imagination and memory, the moment it is necessitated by the absence of the object from present perception *[la perception présente]* ("Memory, as we have seen, consists in nothing but the power of recalling the signs of our ideas, or the circumstances that accompanied them; and this power only takes place by virtue of the *analogy of the signs* [my emphasis—J.D.: this concept of analogy, which organizes the entire system of Condillac, provides the general guarantee of all the continuities and in particular that linking presence to absence] that we have chosen; and by the order that we have instituted among our ideas, the objects that we wish to retrace are bound up with several of our present needs." [1, 11 ch. iv, #39]). This holds true for all the orders of signs distinguished by Condillac (arbitrary, accidental, and even natural, distinctions that Condillac qualifies and, on certain points, even calls into question in his letters to Cramer). The philosophical operation that Condillac also calls "retracing" consists in reversing, by a process of analysis and continuous decomposition, the movement of genetic derivation that leads from simple sensation and present perception to the complex edifice of representation: from ordinary presence to the language of the most formal calculus *[calcul]*.

It would be easy to demonstrate that, fundamentally, this type of analysis of written signification neither begins nor ends with Condillac. If I call this analysis "ideological," I do so neither to oppose its notions to "scientific" concepts nor to appeal to the dogmatic—one might also say ideological—usage to which the term "ideology" is often put, while seldom subjecting either the various possibilities or the history of the word to serious consideration. If I define notions such as those of Condillac as "ideological" it is because, against the background *[sur le fond]* of a vast, powerful, and

---

*Language supplants action or perception: articulated language supplants the language of action: writing supplants articulated language, etc. [The word, *supplée,* used by Derrida and here by Rousseau, implies the double notion of supplanting, replacing, and also supplementing, bringing to completion, remedying—Trans.]

systematic philosophical tradition dominated by the prominence of the *idea (eidos, idea),* they delineate the field of reflection of the French "ideologues," who in the wake of Condillac elaborated a theory of the sign as representation of the idea which itself represented the object perceived. From that point on, communication is that which circulates a representation as an ideal content (meaning); and writing is a species of this general communication. A species: a communication admitting a relative specificity within a genre.

If we now ask ourselves what, in this analysis, is the essential predicate of this *specific difference,* we rediscover *absence.*

I offer here the following two propositions or hypotheses:

1. since every sign, whether in the "language of action" or in articulated language (before even the intervention of writing in the classical sense), presupposes a certain absence (to be determined), the absence within the particular field of writing will have to be of an original type if one intends to grant any specificity whatsoever to the written sign;

2. if perchance the predicate thus introduced to characterize the absence peculiar and proper to writing were to find itself no less appropriate to every species of sign and of communication, the consequence would be a general shift; writing would no longer be one species of communication, and all the concepts to whose generality writing had been subordinated (including the *concept* itself qua meaning, idea or grasp of meaning and of idea, the concept of communication, of the sign, etc.) would appear to be noncritical, ill-formed, or destined, rather, to insure the authority and the force of a certain historical discourse.

Let us attempt, then, while still continuing to take this classical discourse as our point of departure, to characterize the absence that seems to intervene in a specific manner in the functioning of writing.

A written sign is proffered in the absence of the receiver. How to style this absence? One could say that at the moment when I am writing, the receiver may be absent from my field of present perception. But is not this absence merely a distant presence, one which is delayed or which, in one form or another, is idealized in its representation? This does not seem to be the case, or at least this distance, divergence, delay, this deferral *[différance]* must be capable of being carried to a certain absoluteness of absence if the structure of writing, assuming that writing exists, is to constitute itself. It is at that point that the *différance* [difference and deferral, *trans.*] as writing could no longer (be) an (ontological) modification of presence. In order for my "written communication" to retain its function as writing, i.e., its readability, it must remain readable despite the absolute disappearance of any receiver, determined in general. My communication must be repeatable—iterable—in the absolute absence of the receiver or of any empirically determinable collectivity of receivers. Such iterability—(iter, again, probably comes from *itara, other* in Sanskrit, and everything that follows can be read as the working out of the logic that ties repetition to alterity) structures the mark of writing itself, no matter what particular type of writing is involved (whether pictographical, hieroglyphic, ideographic, phonetic, alphabetic, to cite the old categories). A writing that is not structurally readable—iterable—beyond the death of the addressee would not be writing. Although this would seem to be obvious, I do not want it accepted as such, and I shall examine the final objection that could be made to this proposition. Imagine a writing whose code would be so idiomatic as to be established and known, as secret cipher, by only two "subjects." Could we maintain that, following the death of the receiver, or even of both partners, the mark left by one of them is still writing? Yes, to the extent that, organized by a code, even an unknown and nonlinguistic one, it is constituted in its identity as a mark by its iterability, in the absence of such and such a person, and hence ultimately of every empirically determined "subject." This implies that there is no such thing as a code organon of iterability—which could be structurally secret. The possibility of repeating and thus of identifying the marks is implicit in every code, making it into a network *[une grille]* that is communicable, transmittable, decipherable, iterable for a third, and hence for every possible user in general. To be what it is, all writing must, therefore, be capable of functioning in the radical absence of every empirically determined receiver in general. And this absence is not a continuous modification of presence, it is a rupture in presence, the "death" or the possibility of the "death" of the receiver inscribed in the structure of the mark (I note in passing that this is the point where the value or the "effect" of transcendentality is linked necessarily to the possibility of writing and of "death" as analyzed). The perhaps paradoxical consequence of my here having recourse to iteration and to code: the disruption, in the last analysis, of the authority of the code as a finite system of rules; at the same time, the radical destruction of any context as the protocol of code. We will come to this in a moment.

What holds for the receiver holds also, for the same reasons, for the sender or the producer. To write is to produce a mark that will constitute a sort of machine which is productive in turn, and which my future disappearance will not, in principle, hinder in its functioning, offering things and itself to be read and to be rewritten. When I say "my future disappearance" *[disparition:* also, demise, *trans.],* it is in order to render this proposition more immediately acceptable. I ought to be able to say my disappearance, pure and simple, my nonpresence in general, for instance the nonpresence of my intention of saying something meaningful *[mon vouloir-dire, mon intention-designification],* of my wish to communicate, from the emission or production of the mark. For a writing to be a writing it must continue to "act" and to be readable even when what is called the author of the writing no longer answers for what he has written, for what he seems to have signed, be it because of a temporary absence, because he is dead or, more generally, because he has not employed his absolutely actual and present intention or attention, the plenitude of his desire to say what he means, in order to sustain what seems to be written "in his name." One could repeat at this point the analysis outlined above this time with regard to the addressee. The situation of the writer and of the underwriter *[du souscripteur:* the signatory, *trans.]* is, concerning the written text, basically the same as that of the reader. This essential drift *[dérive]* bearing on writing as an iterative structure, cut off from all absolute responsibility, from *consciousness* as the ultimate authority, orphaned and separated at birth from the assistance of its father, is precisely what Plato condemns in the *Phaedrus.* If Plato's gesture is, as I believe, the philosophical movement par excellence, one can measure what is at stake here.

Before elaborating more precisely the inevitable consequences of these nuclear traits of all writing—that is: (1) the break with the horizon of communication as communication of consciousnesses or of presences and as linguistical or semantic transport of the desire to mean what one says *[vouloir-dire];* (2) the disengagement of all writing from the semantic or hermeneutic horizons which, inasmuch as they are horizons of meaning, are riven *[crever]* by writing; (3) the necessity of disengaging from the concept of polysemics what I have elsewhere called *dissemination,* which is also the concept of writing; (4) the disqualification or the limiting of the concept of context, whether "real" or "linguistic," inasmuch as its rigorous theoretical determination as well as its empirical saturation is rendered impossible or insufficient by writing—I would like to demonstrate that the traits that can be recognized in the classical, narrowly defined concept of writing, are generalizable. They are valid not only for all orders of "signs" and for all languages in general but moreover, beyond semio-linguistic communication, for the entire field of what philosophy would call experience, even the experience of being: the above-mentioned "presence."

What are in effect the essential predicates in a minimal determination of the classical concept of writing?

1. A written sign, in the current meaning of this word, is a mark that subsists, one which does not exhaust itself in the moment of its inscription and which can give rise to an iteration in the absence and beyond the presence of the empirically determined subject who, in a given context, has emitted or produced it. This is what has enabled us, at least traditionally, to distinguish a "written" from an "oral" communication.

2. At the same time, a written sign carries with it a force that breaks with its context, that is, with the collectivity of presences organizing the moment of its inscription. This breaking force *[force de rupture]* is not an accidental predicate but the very structure of the written text. In the case of a so-called "real" context, what I have just asserted is all too evident. This allegedly real context includes a certain "present" of the inscription, the presence of the writer to what he has written, the entire environment and the horizon of his experience, and above all the intention, the wanting-to-say-what-he-means, which animates his inscription at a given moment. But the sign possesses the characteristic of being readable even if the moment of its production is irrevocably lost and even if I do not know what its alleged author-scriptor consciously intended to say at the moment he wrote it, i.e. abandoned it to its essential drift. As far as the internal semiotic context is concerned, the force of the rupture is no less important: by virtue of its essential iterability, a written syntagma can always be detached from the chain in which it is inserted or given without causing it to lose all possibility of functioning, if not all possibility of "communicating," precisely. One can perhaps come to recognize other possibilities in it by inscribing it *grafting* it onto other chains. No context can entirely enclose it. Nor any code, the code here being both the possibility and impossibility of writing, of its essential iterability (repetition alterity).

3. This force of rupture is tied to the spacing *[espacement]* that constitutes the written sign: spacing which separates it from other elements of the internal contextual chain (the always open possibility of its disengagement and graft), but also from all forms of present reference (whether past or future in the modified form of the present that is past or to come), objective or subjective. This spacing is not the simple negativity of a lacuna but rather the emergence of the mark. It does not remain, however, as the labor of the negative in the service of meaning, of the living concept, of the *telos,* supersedable and reducible in the *Aufhebung* of a dialectic.

Are these three predicates, together with the entire system they entail, limited, as is often believed, strictly to "written" communication in the narrow sense of this word? Are they not to be found in all language, in spoken language for instance, and ultimately in the totality of "experience" insofar as it is inseparable from this field of the mark, which is to say, from the network of effacement and of difference, of units of iterability, which are separable from their internal and external context and also from themselves, inasmuch as the very iterability which constituted their identity does not permit them ever to be a unity that is identical to itself?

Let us consider any element of spoken language, be it a small or large unit. The first condition of its functioning is its delineation with regard to a certain code; but I prefer not to become too involved here with this concept of code which does not seem very reliable to me; let us say that a certain self-identity of this element (mark, sign, etc.) is required to permit its recognition and repetition. Through empirical variations of tone, voice, etc., possibly of a certain accent, for example, we must be able to recog-

nize the identity, roughly speaking, of a signifying form. Why is this identity paradoxically the division or dissociation of itself, which will make of this phonic sign a
grapheme? Because this unity of the signifying form only constitutes itself by virtue of
its iterability, by the possibility of its being repeated in the absence not only of its "referent," which is self-evident, but in the absence of a determinate signified or of the intention of actual signification, as well as of all intention of present communication.
This structural possibility of being weaned from the referent or from the signified
(hence from communication and from its context) seems to me to make every mark, including those which are oral, a grapheme in general; which is to say, as we have seen,
the nonpresent *remainder [restance]* of a differential mark cut off from its putative
"production" or origin. And I shall even extend this law to all "experience" in general
if it is conceded that there is no experience consisting of pure presence but only of
chains of differential marks.

Let us dwell for a moment on this point and return to that absence of the referent
and even of the signified meaning, and hence of the correlative intention to signify.
The absence of referent is a possibility easily enough admitted today. This possibility
is not only an empirical eventuality. It constructs the mark; and the potential presence
of the referent at the moment it is designated does not modify in the slightest the structure of the mark, which implies that the mark can do without the referent. Husserl, in
his *Logical Investigations,* analyzed this possibility very rigorously, and in a two-fold
manner:

1. An utterance *[énoncé]* whose object is not impossible but only possible can
very well be made and understood without its real object (its referent) being present,
either to the person who produced the statement or to the one who receives it. If while
looking out the window, I say: "The sky is blue," this utterance will be intelligible (let
us say, provisionally if you like, communicable) even if the interlocutor does not see
the sky; even if I do not see it myself, if I see it badly, if I am mistaken or if I wish to
mislead my interlocutor. Not that this is always the case; but the structure of possibility
of this utterance includes the capability to be formed and to function as a reference that
is empty or cut off from its referent. Without this possibility, which is also that of iterability in general, "generable," and generative of all marks, there would be no utterance.

2. The absence of the signified. Husserl analyzes this as well. He judges it to be
always possible even if, according to the axiology and teleology that governs his
analysis, he judges this possibility to be inferior, dangerous, or "critical": it opens the
phenomenon of the crisis of meaning. This absence of meaning can take three forms:

A. I can manipulate symbols without animating them, in an active and actual
manner, with the attention and intention of signification (crisis of mathematical symbolism, according to Husserl). Husserl insists on the fact that this does not prevent the
sign from functioning: the crisis or the emptiness of mathematical meaning does not
limit its technical progress (the intervention of writing is decisive here, as Husserl himself remarks in *The Origin of Geometry*).

B. Certain utterances can have a meaning although they are deprived of *objective*
signification. "The circle is squared" is a proposition endowed with meaning. It has
sufficient meaning at least for me to judge it false or contradictory (*widersinnig* and
not *sinnlos,* Husserl says). I place this example under the category of the absence of the
signified, although in this case the tripartite division into signifier/signified/referent is
not adequate to a discussion of the Husserlian analysis. "Squared circle" marks the absence of a referent, certainly, as well as that of a certain signified, but not the absence
of meaning. In these two cases, the crisis of meaning (nonpresence in general, absence

as the absence of the referent—of the perception—or of the meaning—of the intention of actual signification) is still bound to the essential possibility of writing; and this crisis is not an accident, a factual and empirical anomaly of spoken language, it is also its positive possibility and its "internal" structure, in the form of a certain outside *[dehors]*.

C. Finally there is what Husserl calls *Sinnlosigkeit* or agrammaticality. For instance, "the green is either" or "abracadabra" *[le vert est ou;* the ambiguity of *ou* or *où* is noted below, *trans.].* In such cases Husserl considers that there is no language any more, or at least no "logical" language, no cognitive language such as Husserl construes in a teleological manner, no language accorded the possibility of the intuition of objects given in person and signified in *truth.* We are confronted here with a decisive difficulty. Before stopping to deal with it, I note a point that touches our discussion of communication, namely that the primary interest of the Husserlian analysis to which I am referring here (while precisely detaching it up to a certain point, from its context or its teleological and metaphysical horizon, an operation which itself ought to provoke us to ask how and why it is always possible), is its claim rigorously to dissociate (not without a certain degree of success) from every phenomenon of communication the analysis of the sign or the expression *(Ausdruck)* as signifying sign, the seeking to say something *(bedeutsames Zeichen).**

Let us return to the case of agrammatical *Sinnlosigkeit.* What interests Husserl in the *Logical Investigations* is the system of rules of a universal grammar, not from a linguistic point of view but from a logical and epistemological one. In an important note to the second edition,** he specifies that his concern is with a pure *logical* grammar, that is, with the universal conditions of possibility for a morphology of significations in their cognitive relation to a possible object, not with a pure grammar in *general,* considered from a psychological or linguistic point of view. Thus, it is solely in a context determined by a will to know, by an epistemic intention, by a conscious relation to the object as cognitive object within a horizon of truth, solely in this oriented contextual field is "the green is either" unacceptable. But as "the green is either" or "abracadabra" do not constitute their context by themselves, nothing prevents them from functioning in another context as signifying marks (or indices, as Husserl would say). Not only in contingent cases such as a translation from German into French, which would endow "the green is either" with grammaticality, since "either" *[oder]* becomes for the ear "where" *[où]* (a spatial mark). "Where has the green gone (of the lawn: the green is where)," "Where is the glass gone in which I wanted to give you something to drink?" *["Où est passé le verre dans lequel je voulais vous donner à boire?"]* But even "the

---

*"Up to now, we have considered expressions in their communicative function. This derives essentially from the fact that expressions operate as indexes. But a large role is also assigned to expressions in the life of the soul inasmuch as it is not engaged in a relation of communication. It is clear that this modification of the function does not affect what makes expressions expressions. They have, as before, their *Bedeutungen* and the same *Bedeutungen* as in collocution" *(Logical Investigations* I, ch. 1, #8). What I assert here implies the interpretation that I have offered of the Husserlian procedure on this point. I therefore refer the reader to *Speech and Phenomena (La voix et le phénomène).*

**"In the first edition I spoke of 'pure grammar,' a name that was conceived on the analogy of 'pure science of nature' in Kant, and expressly designated as such. But to the extent that it cannot be affirmed that the pure morphology of *Bedeutungen* englobes all grammatical *a prioris* in their universality, since for example relations of communication between psychic subjects, which are so important for grammar, entail their own *a prioris,* the expression of *pure logical grammar* deserves priority" *(LI* II, part 2, ch. iv).

green is either" itself still signifies an *example of agrammaticality*. And this is the possibility on which I want to insist: the possibility of disengagement and citational graft which belongs to the structure of every mark, spoken or written, and which constitutes every mark in writing before and outside of every horizon of semio-linguistic communication; in writing, which is to say in the possibility of its functioning being cut off, at a certain point, from its "original" desire-to-say-what-one-means *[vouloir-dire]* and from its participation in a saturable and constraining context. Every sign, linguistic or nonlinguistic, spoken or written (in the current sense of this opposition), in a small or large unit, can be cited, put between quotation marks; in so doing it can break with every given context, engendering an infinity of new contexts in a manner which is absolutely illimitable. This does not imply that the mark is valid outside of a context, but on the contrary that there are only contexts without any center or absolute anchoring *[ancrage]*. This citationality, this duplication or duplicity, this iterability of the mark is neither an accident nor an anomaly, it is that (normal/abnormal) without which a mark could not even have a function called "normal." What would a mark be that could not be cited? Or one whose origins would not get lost along the way?

PARASITES. ITER, OF WRITING: THAT IT PERHAPS DOES NOT EXIST

I now propose to elaborate a bit further this question with special attention to but in order, as well, to pass beyond—the problematic of the performative. It concerns us here for several reasons:

1. First of all, Austin, through his emphasis on an analysis of perlocution and above all of illocution, appears to consider speech acts only as acts of communication. The author of the introduction to the French edition of *How To Do Things With Words,* quoting Austin, notes as much: "It is by comparing constative utterances (i.e., classical 'assertions,' generally considered as true or false 'descriptions' of facts) with performative utterances (from the English 'performative,' i.e., allowing to accomplish something through speech itself) that Austin is led to consider every utterance worthy of the name (i.e., intended to communicate—thus excluding, for example, reflex-exclamations) as being primarily and above all a speech act produced in the total situation in which the interlocutors find themselves" (*How To Do Things With Words,* p. 147, G. Lane, Introduction to the French translation, p. 19).

2. This category of communication is relatively new. Austin's notions of illocution and perlocution do not designate the transference or passage of a thought-content, but, in some way, the communication of an original movement (to be defined within a *general theory of action*), an operation and the production of an effect. Communicating, in the case of the performative, if such a thing, in all rigor and in all purity, should exist (for the moment, I am working within that hypothesis and at that stage of the analysis), would be tantamount to communicating a force through the impetus *[impulsion]* of a mark.

3. As opposed to the classical assertion, to the constative utterance, the performative does not have its referent (but here that word is certainly no longer appropriate, and this precisely is the interest of the discovery) outside of itself or, in any event, before and in front of itself. It does not describe something that exists outside of language and prior to it. It produces or transforms a situation, it effects; and even if it can be said that a constative utterance also effectuates something and always transforms a situation, it cannot be maintained that that constitutes its internal structure, its manifest function or destination, as in the case of the performative.

4. Austin was obliged to free the analysis of the performative from the authority of the truth *value,* from the true/false opposition,* at least in its classical form, and to substitute for it at times the value of force, of difference of force (*illocutionary* or *perlocutionary* force). (In this line of thought, which is nothing less than Nietzschean, this in particular strikes me as moving in the direction of Nietzsche himself, who often acknowledged a certain affinity for a vein of English thought.)

For these four reasons, at least, it might seem that Austin has shattered the concept of communication as a purely semiotic, linguistic, or symbolic concept. The performative is a "communication" which is not limited strictly to the transference of a semantic content that is already constituted and dominated by an orientation toward truth (be it the *unveiling* of what is in its being or the *adequation-congruence* between a judicative utterance and the thing itself).

And yet—such at least is what I should like to attempt to indicate now—all the difficulties encountered by Austin in an analysis which is patient, open, aporetical, in constant transformation, often more fruitful in the acknowledgment of its impasses than in its positions, strike me as having a common root. Austin has not taken into account of what—in the structure of *locution* (thus before any illocutory or perlocutory determination)—already entails that system of predicates I call *graphematic in general* and consequently blurs *[brouille]* all the oppositions which follow, oppositions whose pertinence, purity, and rigor Austin has unsuccessfully attempted to establish.

In order to demonstrate this, I shall take for granted the fact that Austin's analyses at all times require a value of *context,* and even of a context exhaustively determined, in theory or teleologically; the long list of "infelicities" which in their variety may affect the performative event always comes back to an element in what Austin calls the total context.** One of those essential elements—and not one among others—remains, classically, consciousness, the conscious presence of the intention of the speaking subject in the totality of his speech act. As a result, performative communication becomes once more the communication of an intentional meaning,*** even if that meaning has no referent in the form of a thing or of a prior or exterior state of things. The conscious presence of speakers or receivers participating in the accomplishment of a performative, their conscious and intentional presence in the totality of the operation, implies teleologically that no *residue [reste]* escapes the present totalization. No residue, either in the definition of the requisite conventions, or in the internal and linguistic context, or in the grammatical form, or in the semantic determination of the words employed; no irreducible polysemy, that is, no "dissemination" escaping the horizon of the unity of meaning. I quote from the first two lectures of *How To Do Things With Words:*

> Speaking generally, it is always necessary that the *circumstances* in which the words are uttered should be in some way, or ways, *appropriate,* and it is very commonly necessary that either the speaker himself or other persons should *also* perform certain *other* actions, whether "physical" or "mental" actions or even acts of uttering further words. Thus, for

---

*Austin names the "two fetishes which I admit to an inclination to play Old Harry with, viz. (1) the true/false fetish, (2) the value/fact fetish" (p. 150).

**He says, for example, that "The total speech act in the total speech situation is the *only actual* phenomenon which, in the last resort, we are engaged in elucidating" (p. 147).

***Which occasionally requires Austin to reintroduce the criterion of truth in his description of performatives. Cf., for example, pp. 50–52 and pp. 89–90.

naming the ship, it is essential that I should be the person appointed to name her, for (Christian) marrying, it is essential that I should not be already married with a wife living, sane and undivorced, and so on; for a bet to have been made, it is generally necessary for the offer of the bet to have been accepted by a taker (who must have done something, such as to say "Done"), and it is hardly a gift if I *say* "I give it you" but never hand it over.

So far, well and good. (pp. 8–9 [reprinted p. 312 in this volume])

In the Second Lecture, after eliminating the grammatical criterion in his customary manner, Austin examines the possibility and the origin of failures or "infelicities" of performative utterance. He then defines the six indispensable—if not sufficient conditions of success. Through the values of "conventional procedure," "correctness," and "completeness," which occur in the definition, we necessarily find once more those of an exhaustively definable context, of a free consciousness present to the totality of the operation, and of absolutely meaningful speech *[vouloir-dire]* master of itself: the teleological jurisdiction of an entire field whose organizing center remains *intention.** Austin's procedure is rather remarkable and typical of that philosophical tradition with which he would like to have so few ties. It consists in recognizing that the possibility of the negative (in this case, of infelicities) is in fact a structural possibility, that failure is an essential risk of the operations under consideration; then, in a move which is almost *immediately simultaneous,* in the name of a kind of ideal regulation, it excludes that risk as accidental, exterior, one which teaches us nothing about the linguistic phenomenon being considered. This is all the more curious—and, strictly speaking, untenable—in view of Austin's ironic denunciation of the "fetishized" opposition: *value/fact.*

Thus, for example, concerning the conventionality without which there is no performative, Austin acknowledges that *all* conventional acts are exposed to failure: "it seems clear in the first place that, although it has excited us (or failed to excite us) in connexion with certain acts which are or are in part acts of *uttering words,* infelicity is an ill to which *all* acts are heir which have the general character of ritual or ceremonial, all *conventional* acts: not indeed that *every* ritual is liable to every form of infelicity (but then nor is every performative utterance)" (pp. 18–19, Austin's emphasis [reprinted p. 316 in this volume]).

In addition to the questions posed by a notion as historically sedimented as "convention," it should be noted at this point:

1. that Austin, at this juncture, appears to consider solely the conventionality constituting the *circumstance* of the utterance *[énoncé],* its contextual surroundings, and not a certain conventionality intrinsic to what constitutes the speech act *[locution]* itself, all that might be summarized rapidly under the problematical rubric of "the arbitrary nature of the sign," which extends, aggravates, and radicalizes the difficulty. "Ritual" is not a possible occurrence *[éventualité],* but rather, as iterability, a structural characteristic of every mark.

2. that the value of risk or exposure to infelicity, even though, as Austin recognizes, it can affect *a priori* the totality of conventional acts, is not interrogated as an essential predicate or as a *law.* Austin does not ponder the consequences issuing from the fact that a possibility—a possible risk—is *always* possible, and is in some sense a necessary possibility. Nor whether—once such a necessary possibility of infelicity is

*Pp. 10–15 [reprinted pp. 313–318 in this volume.]

recognized—infelicity still constitutes an accident. What is a success when the possibility of infelicity *[échec]* continues to constitute its structure?

The opposition success/failure *[échec]* in illocution and in perlocution thus seems quite insufficient and extremely secondary *[dérivée]*. It presupposes a general and systematic elaboration of the structure of locution that would avoid an endless alternation of essence and accident. Now it is highly significant that Austin rejects and defers that "general theory" on at least two occasions, specifically in the Second Lecture. I leave aside the first exclusion.

> I am not going into the general doctrine here: in many such cases we may even say the act was "void" (or voidable for duress or undue influence) and so forth. Now I suppose some very general high-level doctrine might embrace both what we have called infelicities *and* these other "unhappy" features of the doing of actions—in our case actions containing a performative utterance—in a single doctrine: but we are not including this kind of unhappiness—we must just remember, though, that features of this sort can and do constantly obtrude into any case we are discussing. Features of this sort would normally come under the heading of "extenuating circumstances" or of "factors reducing or abrogating the agent's responsibility," and so on. (p. 21, my emphasis [reprinted p. 317 in this volume])

The second case of this exclusion concerns our subject more directly. It involves precisely the possibility for every performative utterance (and *a priori* every other utterance) to be "quoted." Now Austin excludes this possibility (and the general theory which would account for it) with a kind of lateral insistence, all the more significant in its off-handedness. He insists on the fact that this possibility remains *abnormal,* parasitic, that it constitutes a kind of extenuation or agonized succumbing of language that we should strenuously distance ourselves from and resolutely ignore. And the concept of the "ordinary," thus of "ordinary language," to which he has recourse is clearly marked by this exclusion. As a result, the concept becomes all the more problematical, and before demonstrating as much, it would no doubt be best for me simply to read a paragraph from the Second Lecture:

> (ii) Secondly, as *utterances* our performances are *also* heir to certain other kinds of ill, which infect *all* utterances. And these likewise, though again they might be brought into a more general account, we are deliberately at present excluding. I mean, for example, the following: a performative utterance will, for example, be *in a peculiar way* hollow or void if said by an actor on the stage, or if introduced in a poem, or spoken in soliloquy. This applies in a similar manner to any and every utterance—a sea-change in special circumstances. Language in such circumstances is in special ways—intelligibly-used not *seriously* [my emphasis, J.D.], but in many ways *parasitic* upon its normal use—ways which fall under the doctrine of the *etiolations* of language. All this we are *excluding* from consideration. Our performative utterances, felicitous or not, are to be understood as issued in ordinary circumstances. (pp. 21–22 [reprinted pp. 317–318 in this volume].)

Austin thus excludes, along with what he calls a "sea-change," the "non-serious," "parasitism," "etiolation," "the non-ordinary" (along with the whole general theory which, if it succeeded in accounting for them, would no longer be governed by those oppositions), all of which he nevertheless recognizes as the possibility available to every act of utterance. It is as just such a "parasite" that writing has always been treated by the philosophical tradition, and the connection in this case is by no means coincidental.

Open Warfare, 1991, by Jeremy Gilbert-Rolfe. Derrida holds that the limits
or frame of a given piece defines an inside and an outside but also "permits,
and even encourages, a complicated movement or passage across it both
from inside-out and outside-in" (from David Carroll, *Paraesthetics:
Foucault, Lyotard, Derrida* (New York: Methuen, 1987), p 136). Gilbert-
Rolfe's painting exemplifies this deferral of meaning as its pattern suggests
a continuation beyond itself. *(Jeremy Gilbert-Rolfe)*

I would therefore pose the following question: is this general possibility necessarily one of a failure or trap into which language may *fall* or lose itself as in an abyss
situated outside of or in front of itself? What is the status of this *parasitism?* In other
words, does the quality of risk admitted by Austin surround language like a kind of
ditch or external place of perdition which speech *[la locution]* could never hope to
leave, but which it can escape by remaining "at home," by and in itself, in the shelter
of its essence or *telos?* Or, on the contrary, is this risk rather its internal and positive

condition of possibility? Is that outside its inside, the very force and law of its emergence? In this last case, what would be meant by an "ordinary" language defined by the exclusion of the very law of language? In excluding the general theory of this structural parasitism, does not Austin, who nevertheless claims to describe the facts and events of ordinary language, pass off as ordinary an ethical and teleological determination (the univocity of the utterance [énoncé]—that he acknowledges elsewhere [pp. 72–73] remains a philosophical "ideal"—the presence to self of a total context, the transparency of intentions, the presence of meaning [vouloir-dire] to the absolutely singular uniqueness of a speech act, etc.)?

For, ultimately, isn't it true that what Austin excludes as anomaly, exception, "nonserious,"* citation (on stage, in a poem, or a soliloquy) is the determined modification of a general citationality or rather, a general iterability—without which there would not even be a "successful" performative? So that—a paradoxical but unavoidable conclusion—a successful performative is necessarily an "impure" performative, to adopt the word advanced later on by Austin when he acknowledges that there is no "pure" performative.**

I take things up here from the perspective of positive possibility and not simply as instances of failure or infelicity: would a performative utterance be possible if a citational doubling [doublure] did not come to split and dissociate from itself the pure singularity of the event? I pose the question in this form in order to prevent an objection. For it might be said: you cannot claim to account for the so-called graphematic structure of locution merely on the basis of the occurrence of failures of the performative, however real those failures may be and however effective or general their possibility. You cannot deny that there are also performatives that succeed, and one has to account for them: meetings are called to order (Paul Ricoeur did as much yesterday); people say: "I pose a question"; they bet, challenge, christen ships, and sometimes even marry. It would seem that such events have occurred. And even if only one had taken place only once, we would still be obliged to account for it.

I'll answer: "Perhaps." We should first be clear on what constitutes the status of "occurrence" or the eventhood of an event that entails in its allegedly present and singular emergence the intervention of an utterance [énoncé] that in itself can be only repetitive or citational in its structure, or rather, since those two words may lead to confusion: iterable. I return then to a point that strikes me as fundamental and that now concerns the status of events in general, of events of speech or by speech, of the strange logic they entail and that often passes unseen.

Could a performative utterance succeed if its formulation did not repeat a "coded" or iterable utterance, or in other words, if the formula I pronounce in order to open a meeting, launch a ship or a marriage were not identifiable as conforming with an iterable model, if it were not then identifiable in some way as a "citation"? Not that citationality in this case is of the same sort as in a theatrical play, a philosophical reference, or the recitation of a poem. That is why there is a relative specificity, as Austin says, a "relative purity" of performatives. But this relative purity does not emerge in

---

*Austin often refers to the suspicious status of the "non-serious" (cf., for example, pp. 104, 121). This is fundamentally linked to what he says elsewhere about oratio obliqua (pp. 70–71) and mime.

**From this standpoint, one might question the fact, recognized by Austin, that "very commonly the same sentence is used on different occasions of utterance in both ways, performative and constative. The thing seems hopeless from the start, if we are to leave utterances as they stand and seek for a criterion." The graphematic root of citationality (iterability) is what creates this embarrassment and makes it impossible, as Austin says, "to lay down even a list of all possible criteria."

opposition to citationality or iterability, but in opposition to other kinds of iteration within a general iterability which constitutes a violation of the allegedly rigorous purity of every event of discourse or every *speech act*. Rather than oppose citation or iteration to the noniteration of an event, one ought to construct a differential typology of forms of iteration, assuming that such a project is tenable and can result in an exhaustive program, a question I hold in abeyance here. In such a typology, the category of intention will not disappear; it will have its place, but from that place it will no longer be able to govern the entire scene and system of utterances *[l'enonciation]*. Above all, at that point, we will be dealing with different kinds of marks or chains of iterable marks and not with an opposition between citational utterances, on the one hand, and singular and original event-utterances, on the other. The first consequence of this will be the following: given that structure of iteration, the intention animating the utterance will never be through and through present to itself and to its content. The iteration structuring it *a priori* introduces into it a dehiscence and a cleft *[brisure]* which are essential. The "non-serious," the *oratio obliqua* will no longer be able to be excluded, as Austin wished, from "ordinary" language. And if one maintains that such ordinary language, or the ordinary circumstances of language, excludes a general citationality or iterability, does that not mean that the "ordinariness" in question—the thing and the notion—shelter a lure, the teleological lure of consciousness (whose motivations, indestructible necessity, and systematic effects would be subject to analysis)? Above all, this essential absence of intending the actuality of utterance, this structural unconsciousness, if you like, prohibits any saturation of the context. In order for a context to be exhaustively determinable, in the sense required by Austin, conscious intention would at the very least have to be totally present and immediately transparent to itself and to others, since it is a determining center *[foyer]* of context. The concept of or the search for—the context thus seems to suffer at this point from the same theoretical and "interested" uncertainty as the concept of the "ordinary," from the same metaphysical origins: the ethical and teleological discourse of consciousness. A reading of the connotations, this time, of Austin's text, would confirm the reading of the descriptions; I have just indicated its principle.

   Différance, the irreducible absence of intention or attendance to the performative utterance, the most "event-ridden" utterance there is, is what authorizes me, taking account of the predicates just recalled, to posit the general graphematic structure of every "communication." By no means do I draw the conclusion that there is no relative specificity of effects of consciousness, or of effects of speech (as opposed to writing in the traditional sense), that there is no performative effect, no effect of ordinary language, no effect of presence or of discursive event (speech act). It is simply that those effects do not exclude what is generally opposed to them, term by term; on the contrary, they presuppose it, in an asymmetrical way, as the general space of their possibility.

SIGNATURES

That general space is first of all spacing as a disruption of presence in a mark, what I here call writing. That all the difficulties encountered by Austin intersect in the place where both writing and presence are in question is for me indicated in a passage such as that in Lecture V in which the divided instance of the juridic signature *[seing]* emerges.

Is it an accident if Austin is there obliged to note: "I must explain again that we are floundering here. To feel the firm ground of prejudice slipping away is exhilarating, but brings its revenges" (p. 61). Shortly before, an "impasse" had appeared, resulting from the search for "any *single simple* criterion of grammar and vocabulary" in distinguishing between performative or constative utterances. (I should say that it is this critique of linguisticism and of the authority of the code, a critique based on an analysis of language, that most interested and convinced me in Austin's undertaking.) He then attempts to justify, with nonlinguistic reasons, the preference he has shown in the analysis of performatives for the forms of the first person, the present indicative, the active voice. The justification, in the final instance, is the reference made therein to what Austin calls the *source* (p. 60)* of the utterance. This notion of *source*—and what is at stake in it is clear—frequently reappears in what follows and governs the entire analysis in the phase we are examining. Not only does Austin not doubt that the source of an oral utterance in the present indicative active is *present* to the utterance *[énonciation]* and its statement *[énoncé]* (I have attempted to explain why we had reasons not to believe so), but he does not even doubt that the equivalent of this tie to the source utterance is simply evident in and assured by a *signature:*

> Where there is *not,* in the verbal formula of the utterance, a reference to the person doing the uttering, and so the acting, by means of the pronoun "I" (or by his personal name), then in fact he will be "referred to" in one of two ways:
>
> (a) In verbal utterances, *by his being the person who does* the uttering—what we may call the utterance-*origin* which is used generally in any system of verbal reference-coordinates.
>
> (b) In written utterances (or "inscriptions"), *by his appending his signature* (this has to be done because, of course, written utterances are not tethered to their origin in the way spoken ones are). (pp. 60–61)

An analogous function is attributed by Austin to the formula "hereby" in official documents.

From this point of view, let us attempt to analyze signatures, their relation to the present and to the source. I shall consider it as an implication of the analysis that every predicate established will be equally valid for that oral "signature" constituted—or aspired to—by the presence of the "author" as a "person who utters," as a "source," to the production of the utterance.

By definition, a written signature implies the actual or empirical nonpresence of the signer. But, it will be claimed, the signature also marks and retains his having-been present in a past now or present *[maintenant]* which will remain a future *now* or present *[maintenant],* thus in a general *maintenant,* in the transcendental form of present-ness *[maintenance].* That general *maintenance* is in some way inscribed, pinpointed in the always evident and singular present punctuality of the form of the signature. Such is the enigmatic originality of every paraph. In order for the tethering to the source to occur, what must be retained is the absolute singularity of a signature-event and a signature-form: the pure reproducibility of a pure event.

*[Austin's term is "utterance origin"; Derrida's term (source) is hereafter translated as "source."—Trans.]

Is there such a thing? Does the absolute singularity of signature as event ever occur? Are there signatures?

Yes, of course, every day. Effects of signature are the most common thing in the world. But the condition of possibility of those effects is simultaneously, once again, the condition of their impossibility, of the impossibility of their rigorous purity. In order to function, that is, to be readable, a signature must have a repeatable, iterable, imitable form; it must be able to be detached from the present and singular intention of its production. It is its sameness which, by corrupting its identity and its singularity, divides its seal *[sceau]*. I have already indicated above the principle of this analysis.

To conclude this very *dry** discussion:

1. as writing, communication, if we retain that word, is not the means of transference of meaning, the exchange of intentions and meanings *[vouloir-dire]*, discourse and the "communication of consciousnesses." We are witnessing not an end of writing that would restore, in accord with McLuhan's ideological representation, a transparency or an immediacy to social relations; but rather the increasingly powerful historical expansion of a general writing, of which the system of speech, consciousness, meaning, presence, truth, etc., would be only an effect, and should be analyzed as such. It is the exposure of this effect that I have called elsewhere logocentrism;

2. the semantic horizon that habitually governs the notion of communication is exceeded or split by the intervention of writing, that is, by a dissemination irreducible to *polysemy*. Writing is read; it is not the site, "in the last instance," of a hermeneutic deciphering, the decoding of a meaning or truth;

3. despite the general displacement of the classical, "philosophical," occidental concept of writing, it seems necessary to retain, provisionally and strategically, the old name. This entails an entire logic of *paleonymics* that I cannot develop here.** Very schematically: an opposition of metaphysical concepts (e.g., speech/writing, presence/absence, etc.) is never the confrontation of two terms, but a hierarchy and the order of a subordination. Deconstruction cannot be restricted or immediately pass to a neutralization: it must, through a double gesture, a double science, a double writing— put into practice a reversal of the classical opposition *and* a general *displacement* of the system. It is on that condition alone that deconstruction will provide the means of *intervening* in the field of oppositions it criticizes and that is also a field of nondiscursive forces. Every concept, moreover, belongs to a systematic chain and constitutes in itself a system of predicates. There is no concept that is metaphysical in itself. There is a labor—metaphysical or not—performed on conceptual systems. Deconstruction does not consist in moving from one concept to another, but in reversing and displacing a conceptual order as well as the nonconceptual order with which it is articulated. For example, writing, as a classical concept, entails predicates that have been subordinated, excluded, or held in abeyance by forces and according to necessities to be analyzed. It is those predicates (I have recalled several of them) whose force of generality, generalization, and generativity is liberated, grafted onto a "new" concept of writing that corresponds as well to what has always *resisted* the prior organization of forces, always constituted the *residue* irreducible to the dominant force organizing the hierarchy that we may refer to, in brief, as logocentric. To leave to this new concept the old name of

---

*[The French word for dry here is sec which combines the initial letters of Derrida's three word title: Signature, Event, Context.]

**Cf. La dissémination and Positions.

writing is tantamount to maintaining the structure of the *graft,* the transition and indispensable adherence to an effective *intervention* in the constituted historical field. It is to give to everything at stake in the operations of deconstruction the chance and the force, the power of *communication.*

But this will have been understood, as a matter of course, especially in a philosophical colloquium: a disseminating operation removed from the presence (of being) according to all its modifications; writing, if there is any, perhaps communicates, but certainly does not exist. Or barely, hereby, in the form of the most improbable signature.

(*Remark:* the—written—text of this—oral—communication was to have been addressed to the *Association of French Speaking Societies of Philosophy* before the meeting. Such a missive therefore had to be signed. Which I did, and counterfeit here. Where? There. J.D.)

J. DERRIDA

RICHARD RORTY
1931–

Richard McKay Rorty was born in New York City to two writers—an interesting fact in light of Rorty's later philosophical attraction to literature. During Rorty's early childhood, his parents had worked closely with the American Communist Party, but with the party's increasing Stalinism they broke away in 1933. They were then attracted to the political philosophy of Stalin's rival, Leon Trotsky (1879–1940). The attraction was so deep that they sheltered one of Trotsky's secretaries after Stalin's agents assassinated Trotsky in Mexico in 1940. Rorty reflected on the effect of his parents' politics: "I grew up knowing that all decent people were, if not Trotskyites, at least socialists. . . . [By the age of] twelve I knew that the point of being human was to spend one's life fighting social injustice."*

As he developed his social conscience, Rorty also discovered his appetite for obscure, socially useless subjects, such as the study of wild orchids. As he embarked for the University of Chicago at fifteen, he sought a way to combine his often wild and disparate interests into a single vision. As he put it, "I wanted a way to be both an intellectual and spiritual snob and a friend of humanity—a nerdy recluse and a fighter for justice."** At the University of Chicago, Rorty found two possibilities for a life vision: Christianity and Platonism. Christianity seemed impossible for Rorty on a personal level, so he became a committed

---

*Richard Rorty, "Trotsky and the Wild Orchids," from Mark Edmundson, *Wild Orchids and Trotsky* (Harmondsworth, Middlesex: Penguin, 1993), pp. 34–35.
***Ibid.*, p. 36.

Platonist: "Platonism had all the advantages of religion, without requiring the humility that Christianity demanded, and of which I was apparently incapable."*

When he completed his B.A. and M.A. in philosophy at Chicago and moved to Yale for his Ph.D., Rorty began to doubt his Platonic vision. There seemed no neutral standpoint from which to determine if Platonism was a correct vision. How was one to avoid circularity in establishing the first principles by which a particular vision is supported? As Rorty explains,

> I gradually decided that the whole idea of holding reality and justice in a single vi-sion had been a mistake—that the pursuit of such a vision had been precisely what led Plato astray. More specifically, I decided that only religion—only a nonargu-mentative faith in a surrogate parent who, unlike any real parent, embodied love, power, and justice in equal manner—could do the trick Plato wanted done. Since I couldn't imagine becoming religious, and indeed had gotten more and more rau-cously secularist, I decided that the hope of achieving a single vision by becoming a philosopher had been a self-deceptive atheist's way out.**

After receiving his Ph.D. in 1956, Rorty was drafted and served two years in the U.S. Army. He taught at Wellesley College from 1958 to 1961 and then moved to Princeton University. For the next twenty years, he developed his "vi-sionless" philosophy. Building on the pragmatism of John Dewey, Rorty argued that instead of seeking objectivity, we should settle for "as much intersubjective agreement" as we can find. If philosophical truth cannot be Platonically objec-tive, at least it can have the pragmatic value of tolerance.

In 1982, Rorty moved to the University of Virginia, where he is Kenan Pro-fessor of Humanities. "Professor of Humanities" is an appropriate title, for in his recent work Rorty has moved from philosophy to literature and the arts as better means for serving humanity. As his thought has changed, so has his style, mov-ing increasingly from an argumentative to a narrative mode.

* * *

In *Philosophy and the Mirror of Nature* (1979), his most famous book, Rorty at-tacks another philosophical vision: mind as the "Mirror of Nature." Ever since Descartes, philosophers have examined the relation between the subjective mind and the objective world. As Rorty explains in our selection from Chapter 4, philosophers have looked for "privileged representations among those constitut-ing the Mirror"—that is, they have looked for the representations that most accu-rately reflect nature. Descartes understood these privileged, foundational repre-sentations to be "clear and distinct ideas" and thus sought to "clean up" the Mirror so that it would more accurately reflect "reality." Recently, analytic philosophers, such as Russell and Carnap, have claimed privilege for certain foundational assertions—certain kinds or uses of language.

Developing the work of Wittgenstein, Wilfred Sellars, and Quine, Rorty ar-gues that no "account of the nature of knowledge can rely on a theory of repre-sentations which stand in privileged relations to reality." Instead of providing in-sights into "reality," theoretical systems provide only descriptions of human

Ibid., p. 38.
**Ibid.*, p. 41.

behavior and so exhibit the values of a historical period. Epistemology no longer is the prestigious arbiter of meaning, offering nothing more to an understanding of knowledge and truth than common sense. As Rorty concludes,

> If we accept these criticisms, and therefore drop the notion of epistemology as the quest, initiated by Descartes, for those privileged items in the field of consciousness which are the touchstones of truth, we are in a position to ask whether there still remains something for epistemology to be. I want to urge that there does not.

In his later writings, *Consequences of Pragmatism* (1982) and *Contingency, Irony, and Solidarity* (1989), Rorty explores the implications of his dethroning of philosophy and suggests a return to Dewey's notion of social and political transformation. He displaces theory with practice, essence with function, the intrinsic with the contextual, and objectivity with solidarity. The question, says Rorty, is no longer the epistemological, "How do you know?," but the rhetorical, "Why do you find what you just said persuasive?"

According to Rorty, the vocabularies of social groups are contingent on time and place. Morality, then, "is a matter of what [Wilfred Sellars] calls 'we-intentions,' [so] that the core meaning of 'immoral action' is 'the sort of thing we don't do'."* Solidarity with a group's vocabulary supersedes ontological certainty as a basis for ethics. This does not mean that Rorty is a radical relativist; his pragmatism asserts that some vocabularies are better at eliminating cruelty than others. When disputes arise between groups and their "incommensurable" vocabularies, the best one group can do is show the other "how [that] other side looks from our own point of view," while at the same time imaginatively identifying with the other side's pain. It is the artist and the poet (not the moral philosopher) who can best elicit identification by creating vulnerable images of the "other" to which human beings can relate. Metaphor replaces logic as the language of change. Accordingly, Rorty's own goal is to persuade through metaphor and narrative, not philosophical argument.

*   *   *

For an introduction to Rorty's thought, see David L. Hall, *Richard Rorty: Prophet and Poet of the New Pragmatism* (Albany, NY: SUNY Press, 1994). Konstantin Kolenda, *Rorty's Humanistic Pragmatism: Philosophy Democratized* (Tampa: University of South Florida Press, 1990) and René Vincente Arcilla, *For the Love of Perfection: Richard Rorty and Liberal Education* (New York: Routledge, 1995) provide essentially positive studies of Rorty's work, whereas Roy Bhaskar, *Philosophy and the Idea of Freedom* (Oxford: Basil Blackwell, 1991); D. Vaden House, *Without God or His Doubles: Realism, Relativism, and Rorty* (Leiden, The Netherlands: E.J. Brill, 1994); Robert Heineman, *Authority and the Liberal Tradition: From Hobbes to Rorty*, 2nd edition (New Brunswick, NJ: Transaction, 1994); Frank B. Farrell, *Subjectivity, Realism, and Postmodernism: The Recovery of the World* (Cambridge: Cambridge University Press, 1994); Norman Geras, *Solidarity in the Conversation of Humankind: The Un-*

---

*Richard Rorty, *Contingency, Irony, and Solidarity* (Cambridge: Cambridge University Press, 1989), p. 59.

groundable Liberalism of Richard Rorty (London: Verso, 1995) offer critiques; Eric M. Gander, *The Last Conceptual Revolution: A Critique of Richard Rorty's Political Philosophy* (Albany, NY: SUNY Press, 1998); and Dianne Rothleder, *The Work of Friendship: Rorty, His Critics, and the Project of Solidarity* (Albany, NY: SUNY Press, 1999). Collections of essays include Alan Malachowski, ed., *Reading Rorty* (Oxford: Basil Blackwell, 1990); Lenore Langsdorf and Andrew R. Smith, eds., *Recovering Pragmatism's Voice: The Classical Tradition, Rorty, and the Philosophy of Communication* (Albany, NY: SUNY Press, 1995); and Herman J. Saatkamp, Jr., ed., *Rorty & Pragmatism: The Philosopher Responds to His Critics* (Nashville, TN: Vanderbilt University Press, 1995).

PHILOSOPHY AND THE MIRROR OF NATURE (in part)

CHAPTER 4: PRIVILEGED REPRESENTATIONS

1. APODICTIC TRUTH, PRIVILEGED REPRESENTATIONS, AND ANALYTIC PHILOSOPHY

At the end of the nineteenth century, philosophers were justifiably worried about the future of their discipline. On the one hand, the rise of empirical psychology had raised the question "What do we need to know about knowledge which psychology cannot tell us?"* Ever since Descartes's attempt to make the world safe for clear and distinct ideas and Kant's to make it safe for synthetic *a priori* truths, ontology had been dominated by epistemology. So the "naturalization" of epistemology by psychology suggested that a simple and relaxed physicalism might be the only sort of ontological view needed. On the other hand, the tradition of German idealism had declined—in England and America—into what has been well described as "a continuation of Protestantism by other means." The idealists purported to save the "spiritual values" which physicalism seemed to neglect by invoking Berkeleian arguments to get rid of material substance and Hegelian arguments to get rid of the individual ego (while resolutely ignoring Hegel's historicism). But few took these high-minded efforts seriously. The earnest reductionism of Bain and Mill and the equally earnest romanticism of Royce drove aesthetical ironists like James and Bradley, as well as social reformers like the young Dewey, to proclaim the unreality of traditional epistemological problems and solutions. They were provoked to radical criticisms of "truth as correspondence" and

---

*This question has echoed through our own century, in ways described in the following chapter. Psychology was born out of philosophy in the confused hope that we might get back behind Kant and recapture Lockean innocence. Ever since, psychologists have vainly protested their neglect by neo-Kantian philosophers (of both the analytic and the phenomenological sorts).

"knowledge as accuracy of representations," thus threatening the entire Kantian notion of philosophy as metacriticism of the special disciplines. Simultaneously, philosophers as various as Nietzsche, Bergson, and Dilthey were undermining some of the same Kantian presuppositions. For a time, it seemed as if philosophy might turn away once and for all from epistemology, from the quest for certainty, structure, and rigor, and from the attempt to constitute itself a tribunal of reason.

The spirit of playfulness which seemed about to enter philosophy around 1900 was, however, nipped in the bud. Just as mathematics had inspired Plato to invent "philosophical thinking," so serious-minded philosophers turned to mathematical logic for rescue from the exuberant satire of their critics. The paradigmatic figures in this attempt to recapture the mathematical spirit were Husserl and Russell. Husserl saw philosophy as trapped between "naturalism" and "historicism," neither of which offered the sort of "apodictic truths" which Kant had assured philosophers were their birthright.* Russell joined Husserl in denouncing the psychologism which had infected the philosophy of mathematics, and announced that logic was the essence of philosophy.** Driven by the need to find something to be apodictic about, Russell discovered "logical form" and Husserl discovered "essences," the "purely formal" aspects of the world which remained when the nonformal had been "bracketed." The discovery of these privileged representations began once again a quest for seriousness, purity, and rigor,*** a quest which lasted for some forty years. But, in the end, heretical followers of Husserl (Sartre and Heidegger) and heretical followers of Russell (Sellars and Quine) raised the same sorts of questions about the possibility of apodictic truth which Hegel had raised about Kant.

Phenomenology gradually became transformed into what Husserl despairingly called "mere anthropology,"† and "analytic" epistemology (i.e., "philosophy of sci-

---

*Cf. Edmund Husserl, "Philosophy as Rigorous Science," in *Phenomenology and the Crisis of Philosophy,* ed. and trans. Quentin Lauer (New York, 1965), p. 120. In this essay (published in 1910), Husserl analyzed both naturalism and historicism as forms of skepticism and relativism. See, for example, pp. 76–79, 122. He began his criticism of naturalism by repeating the attack on psychological conceptions of logic made in his *Logical Investigations.* (Cf. pp. 80ff. on naturalism's self-refutation through its reduction of norms to fact.)

**Bertrand Russell ended the chapter called "Logic as the Essence of Philosophy" in his *Our Knowledge of the External World* (London, 1914) with the following claims:

> The old logic put thought in fetters, while the new logic gives it wings. It has, in my opinion, introduced the same kind of advance into philosophy as Galileo introduced into physics, making it possible at last to see what kinds of problems may be capable of solution, and what kinds must be abandoned as beyond human powers. And where a solution appears possible, the new logic provides a method which enables us to obtain results that do not merely embody personal idiosyncrasies, but must command the assent of all who are competent to form an opinion.

For my present purposes, the standard charge (made, e.g., by Dummett and by Anscombe) that Russell confused the specifically semantical doctrines of Frege and Wittgenstein, which *did* spring from the new logic, with epistemological doctrines which did not, is irrelevant. The charge is fair enough, but without this very confusion the analytic movement either would not have got off the ground, or would have been quite a different thing. Only in the last two decades has a clear distinction between "linguistic philosophy" and "philosophy of language" begun to be made. See chapter six, section 1, for more on this distinction.

***See Russell, *Our Knowledge of the External World,* p. 61 (in the American edition [New York, 1924]), and Husserl, *Phenomenology,* pp. 110–111.

†See Herbert Spiegelberg, *The Phenomenological Movement,* 2d ed. (The Hague, 1965), 1, 275–283, and David Carr's "Translator's Introduction" to Edmund Husserl, *The Crisis of European Sciences and Transcendental Phenomenology* (Evanston, 1970), pp. xxv–xxxviii. See also Ryle's reaction to *Sein und Zeit,* exemplifying the kinship between Anglo-Saxon projects influenced by Russell and Husserl's original project: "It is my personal opinion that *qua* First Philosophy Phenomenology is at present heading for bankruptcy and disaster and will end either in self-ruinous Subjectivism or in a windy Mysticism" (*Mind,* 1929; cited by Spiegelberg, 1, 347). Ryle's prescient point was that the coming of "existential phenomenology" meant the end of phenomenology as "rigorous science."

ence") became increasingly historicist and decreasingly "logical" (as in Hanson, Kuhn, Harre, and Hesse). So, seventy years after Husserl's "Philosophy as Rigorous Science" and Russell's "Logic as the Essence of Philosophy," we are back with the same putative dangers which faced the authors of these manifestoes: if philosophy becomes too naturalistic, hard-nosed positive disciplines will nudge it aside; if it becomes too historicist, then intellectual history, literary criticism, and similar soft spots in "the humanities" will swallow it up.*

The full story of the splendors and the miseries of phenomenology and analytic philosophy is, obviously, far beyond the scope of this book. The story I want to tell in this chapter is merely how the notion of two sorts of representations—intuitions and concepts—fell into disrepute in the latter days of the analytic movement. I have been claiming that the Kantian picture of concepts and intuitions getting together to produce knowledge is needed to give sense to the idea of "theory of knowledge" as a specifically philosophical discipline, distinct from psychology. This is equivalent to saying that if we do not have the distinction between what is "given" and what is "added by the mind," or that between the "contingent" (because influenced by what is given) and the "necessary" (because entirely "within" the mind and under its control), then we will not know what would count as a "rational reconstruction" of our knowledge. We will not know what epistemology's goal or method could be. These two distinctions were attacked at intervals throughout the history of the analytic movement. Neurath had questioned Carnap's appeal to the given, for example, and doubts had often been expressed about Russell's notion of "knowledge by acquaintance" and Lewis's "expressive language." These doubts only came to a head, however, in the early 1950s, with the appearance of Wittgenstein's *Philosophical Investigations,* Austin's mockery of "the ontology of the sensible manifold," and Sellars's "Empiricism and the Philosophy of Mind." The distinction between the necessary and the contingent—revitalized by Russell and the Vienna Circle as the distinction between "true by virtue of meaning" and "true by virtue of experience"—had usually gone unchallenged, and had formed the least common denominator of "ideal language" and "ordinary language" analysis. However, also in the early fifties, Quine's "Two Dogmas of Empiricism" challenged this distinction, and with it the standard notion (common to Kant, Husserl, and Russell) that philosophy stood to empirical science as the study of structure to the study of content. Given Quine's doubts (buttressed by similar doubts in Wittgenstein's *Investigations*) about how to tell when we are responding to the compulsion of "language" rather than that of "experience," it became difficult to explain in what sense philosophy had a separate "formal" field of inquiry, and thus how its results might have the desired apodictic character. For these two challenges were challenges to the very idea of a "theory of knowledge," and thus to philosophy itself, conceived of as a discipline which centers around such a theory.

---

*I think that in England and America philosophy has already been displaced by literary criticism in its principal cultural function—as a source for youth's self-description of its own difference from the past. Cf. Harold Bloom, *A Map of Misreading* (New York, 1975), p. 39:

> The teacher of literature now in America, far more than the teacher of history or philosophy or religion, is condemned to teach the presentness of the past, because history, philosophy and religion have withdrawn as agents from the Scene of Instruction, leaving the bewildered teacher of literature at the altar, terrifiedly wondering whether he is to be sacrifice or priest.

This is roughly because of the Kantian and antihistoricist tenor of Anglo-Saxon philosophy. The cultural function of teachers of philosophy in countries where Hegel was not forgotten is quite different, and closer to the position of literary critics in America. See my "Professionalized Philosophy and Transcendentalist Culture," *Georgia Review* 30 (1976), 757–769.

In what follows, I shall confine myself to discussing two radical ways of criticizing the Kantian foundations of analytic philosophy—Sellars's behavioristic critique of "the whole framework of givenness" and Quine's behavioristic approach to the necessary-contingent distinction. I shall present both as forms of holism. As long as knowledge is conceived of as accurate representing—as the Mirror of Nature—Quine's and Sellars's holistic doctrines sound pointlessly paradoxical, because such accuracy requires a theory of privileged representations, ones which are automatically and intrinsically accurate. So the response to Sellars on givenness and Quine on analyticity is often that they have "gone too far"—that they have allowed holism to sweep them off their feet and away from common sense. In order to defend Sellars and Quine, I shall be arguing that their holism is a product of their commitment to the thesis that justification is not a matter of a special relation between ideas (or words) and objects, but of conversation, of social practice. Conversational justification, so to speak, is naturally holistic, whereas the notion of justification embedded in the epistemological tradition is reductive and atomistic. I shall try to show that Sellars and Quine invoke the same argument, one which bears equally against the given-versus-nongiven and the necessary-versus-contingent distinctions. The crucial premise of this argument is that we understand knowledge when we understand the social justification of belief, and thus have no need to view it as accuracy of representation.

Once conversation replaces confrontation, the notion of the mind as Mirror of Nature can be discarded. Then the notion of philosophy as the discipline which looks for privileged representations among those constituting the Mirror becomes unintelligible. A thoroughgoing holism has no place for the notion of philosophy as "conceptual," as "apodictic," as picking out the "foundations" of the rest of knowledge, as explaining which representations are "purely given" or "purely conceptual," as presenting a "canonical notation" rather than an empirical discovery, or as isolating "trans-framework heuristic categories." If we see knowledge as a matter of conversation and of social practice, rather than as an attempt to mirror nature, we will not be likely to envisage a metapractice which will be the critique of all possible forms of social practice. So holism produces, as Quine has argued in detail and Sellars has said in passing, a conception of philosophy which has nothing to do with the quest for certainty.

Neither Quine nor Sellars, however, has developed a new conception of philosophy in any detail. Quine, after arguing that there is no line between science and philosophy, tends to assume that he has thereby shown that science can replace philosophy. But it is not clear what task he is asking science to perform. Nor is it clear why natural science, rather than the arts, or politics, or religion, should take over the area left vacant. Further, Quine's conception of science is still curiously instrumentalist. It is based on a distinction between "stimuli" and "posits" which seems to lend aid and comfort to the old intuition-concept distinction. Yet Quine transcends both distinctions by granting that stimulations of sense organs are as much "posits" as anything else. It is as if Quine, having renounced the conceptual-empirical, analytic synthetic, and language-fact distinctions, were still not quite able to renounce that between the given and the postulated. Conversely, Sellars, having triumphed over the latter distinction, cannot quite renounce the former cluster. Despite courteous acknowledgment of Quine's triumph over analyticity, Sellars's writing is still permeated with the notion of "giving the analysis" of various terms or sentences, and with a tacit use of the distinction between the necessary and the contingent, the structural and the empirical, the philosophical and the scientific. Each of the two men tends to make continual, unofficial, tacit, heuristic use of the distinction which the other has transcended. It is as if analytic philosophy could not be written without at least *one* of the two great Kantian distinctions, and as if neither Quine nor Sellars were willing to cut the last links which bind them to Russell, Carnap, and "logic as the essence of philosophy."

Analytic philosophy *cannot,* I suspect, be written without one or the other of these distinctions. If there are no intuitions into which to resolve concepts (in the manner of the *Aufbau*) nor any internal relations among concepts to make possible "grammatical discoveries" (in the manner of "Oxford philosophy"), then indeed it is hard to imagine what an "analysis" might be. Wisely, few analytic philosophers any longer try to explain what it is to offer an analysis. Although there was a great deal of metaphilosophical literature in the 1930s and 1940s under the aegis of Russell and Carnap, and another spate of such literature in the 1950s which took the *Philosophical Investigations* and *The Concept of Mind* as paradigms,* there is now little attempt to bring "analytic philosophy" to self-consciousness by explaining how to tell a successful from an unsuccessful analysis. The present lack of metaphilosophical reflection within the analytic movement is, I think, symptomatic of the sociological fact that analytic philosophy is now, in several countries, the entrenched school of thought. Thus in these countries anything done by philosophers who employ a certain style, or mention certain topics, counts (*ex officiis suis,* so to speak) as continuing the work begun by Russell and Carnap. Once a radical movement takes over the establishment against which it revolted, there is less need for methodological self-consciousness, self-criticism, or a sense of location in dialectical space or historical time.

I do not think that there any longer exists anything identifiable as "analytic philosophy" except in some such stylistic or sociological way. But this is not a disparaging remark, as if some legitimate expectation had been disappointed. The analytic movement in philosophy (like any movement in any discipline) worked out the dialectical consequences of a set of assumptions, and now has little more to do. The sort of optimistic faith which Russell and Carnap shared with Kant—that philosophy, its essence and right method discovered at last, had finally been placed upon the secure path of a science—is not something to be mocked or deplored. Such optimism is possible only for men of high imagination and daring, the heroes of their times.

2. EPISTEMOLOGICAL BEHAVIORISM

The simplest way to describe the common features of Quine's and Sellars's attacks on logical empiricism is to say that both raise behaviorist questions about the epistemic privilege which logical empiricism claims for certain assertions, *qua* reports of privileged representations. Quine asks how an anthropologist is to discriminate the sentences to which natives invariably and wholeheartedly assent into contingent empirical platitudes on the one hand and necessary conceptual truths on the other. Sellars asks how the authority of first-person reports of, for example, how things appear to us, the pains from which we suffer, and the thoughts that drift before our minds differs from the authority of expert reports on, for example, mental stress, the mating behavior of birds, or the colors of physical objects. We can lump both questions together and simply ask, "How do our peers know which of our assertions to take our word for and which to look for further confirmation of?" It would seem enough for the natives to

---

*I attempted to summarize this literature, up through 1965, in the introduction to *The Linguistic Turn,* ed. Richard Rorty (Chicago, 1967).

know which sentences are unquestionably true, without knowing which are true "by virtue of language." It would seem enough for our peers to believe there to be no better way of finding out our inner states than from our reports, without their knowing what "lies behind" our making them. It would also seem enough for us to know that our peers have this acquiescent attitude. That alone seems sufficient for that inner certainty about our inner states which the tradition has explained by "immediate presence to consciousness," "sense of evidence," and other expressions of the assumption that reflections in the Mirror of Nature are intrinsically better known than nature itself. For Sellars, the certainty of "I have a pain" is a reflection of the fact that nobody cares to question it, not conversely. Just so, for Quine, the certainty of "All men are animals" and of "There have been some black dogs." Quine thinks that "meanings" drop out as wheels that are not part of the mechanism,* and Sellars thinks the same of "self-authenticating non-verbal episodes."** More broadly, if assertions are justified by society rather than by the character of the inner representations they express, then there is no point in attempting to isolate *privileged* representations.

Explaining rationality and epistemic authority by reference to what society lets us say, rather than the latter by the former, is the essence of what I shall call "epistemological behaviorism," an attitude common to Dewey and Wittgenstein. This sort of behaviorism can best be seen as a species of holism—but one which requires no idealist metaphysical underpinnings. It claims that if we understand the rules of a language-game, we understand all that there is to understand about why moves in that language-game are made (all, that is, save for the extra understanding obtained from inquiries nobody would call epistemological—into, for example, the history of the language, the structure of the brain, the evolution of the species, and the political or cultural ambiance of the players). If we are behaviorist in this sense, then it will not occur to us to invoke either of the traditional Kantian distinctions. But can we just go ahead and be behaviorist? Or, as Quine's and Sellars's critics suggest, doesn't behaviorism simply beg the question?*** Is there any reason to think that fundamental epistemic notions should be explicated in behavioral terms?

This last question comes down to: Can we treat the study of "the nature of human knowledge" just as the study of certain ways in which human beings interact, or does it require an ontological foundation (involving some specifically philosophical way of describing human beings)? Shall we take "S knows that p" (or "S knows noninferentially that p," or "S believes incorrigibly that p," or "S's knowledge that p is certain") as a remark about the status of S's reports among his peers, or shall we take it as a remark about the relation between subject and object, between nature and its mirror? The first alternative leads to a pragmatic view of truth and a therapeutic approach to ontology (in which philosophy can straighten out pointless quarrels between common sense and science, but not contribute any arguments of its own for the existence or inexistence of something). Thus for Quine, a necessary truth is just a statement such that nobody has given us any interesting alternatives which would lead us to question it. For Sellars, to say that a report of a passing thought is incorrigible is to say that nobody

*For an interpretation of Quine as attacking the explanatory utility of the "philosophical notion of meaning," see Gilbert Harman, "Quine on Meaning and Existence, I," *Review of Metaphysics* 21 (1967), 124, esp. 125, 135–141.

**Wilfrid Sellars, *Science, Perception and Reality* (London and New York, 1963), p. 167.

***For this sort of criticism of Quine's behaviorism, see H.P. Grice and P.F. Strawson, "In Defense of a Dogma," *Philosophical Review* 65 (1956), pp. 141–156. For such criticisms of Sellars, see Roderick Chisholm's criticisms of his claims about intentionality, in their correspondence printed in *Minnesota Studies in the Philosophy of Science* 2 (1958), pp. 521ff.

has yet suggested a good way of predicting and controlling human behavior which does not take sincere first-person contemporary reports of thoughts at face value. The second alternative leads to "ontological" explanations of the relations between minds and meanings, minds and immediate data of awareness, universals and particulars, thought and language, consciousness and brains, and so on. For philosophers like Chisholm and Bergmann, such explanations must be attempted if the realism of common sense is to be preserved. The aim of all such explanations is to make truth something more than what Dewey called "warranted assertability": more than what our peers will, *ceteris paribus,* let us get away with saying. Such explanations, when ontological, usually take the form of a redescription of the object of knowledge so as to "bridge the gap" between it and the knowing subject. To choose between these approaches is to choose between truth as "what it is good for us to believe" and truth as "contact with reality."

Thus the question of whether we can be behaviorist in our attitude toward knowledge is not a matter of the "adequacy" of behaviorist "analyses" of knowledge-claims or of mental states. Epistemological behaviorism (which might be called simply "pragmatism," were this term not a bit overladen) has nothing to do with Watson or with Ryle. Rather, it is the claim that philosophy will have no more to offer than common sense (supplemented by biology, history, etc.) about knowledge and truth. The question is not whether necessary and sufficient behavioral conditions for "S knows that p" can be offered; no one any longer dreams they can. Nor is the question whether such conditions can be offered for "S sees that p," or "It looks to S as if p," or "S is having the thought that p." To be behaviorist in the large sense in which Sellars and Quine are behaviorist is not to offer reductionist analyses, but to refuse to attempt a certain sort of explanation: the sort of explanation which not only interposes such a notion as "acquaintance with meanings" or "acquaintance with sensory appearances" between the impact of the environment on human beings and their reports about it, but uses such notions to explain the reliability of such reports.

But, once again, how are we to decide whether such notions are needed? It is tempting to answer on the basis of an antecedent decision about the nature of human beings—a decision on whether we need such notions as "mind," "stream of consciousness," and the like to describe them. But this would be the wrong answer. We can take the Sellars-Quine attitude toward knowledge while cheerfully "countenancing" raw feels, *a priori* concepts, innate ideas, sense-data, propositions, and anything else which a causal explanation of human behavior might find it helpful to postulate.* What we cannot do is to take knowledge of these "inner" or "abstract" entities as *premises* from which our knowledge of other entities is normally inferred, and without which the latter knowledge would be "ungrounded." The difference is between saying that to know a language is to be acquainted with the meanings of its terms, or that to see a table is to have a rectangular sense-impression, and explaining the *authority* of tokens of "All men are animals" or "That looks like a table" by virtue of the prior (internal, private, nonsocial) authority of a knowledge of meanings or of sense-impressions. Behaviorism in epistemology is a matter not of metaphysical parsimony, but of whether authority can attach to assertions by virtue of relations of "acquaintance" between persons and,

---

*I defend this claim when I discuss empirical psychology in chapter five [not included in this volume]. Sellars and Quine themselves, unfortunately, do not see the matter in this carefree way. . . . This criticism can be applied, *mutatis mutandis,* to Sellars's insistence on the claim that "the scientific image" excludes intentions; but Sellars's point is more subtle, and is involved with his Tractarian notion of picturing. . . .

for example, thoughts, impressions, universals, and propositions. The difference between the Quine-Sellars and the Chisholm-Bergmann outlooks on these matters is not the difference between lush and spare landscapes, but more like the difference between moral philosophers who think that rights and responsibilities are a matter of what society bestows and those who think that there is something inside a man which society "recognizes" when it makes its bestowal. The two schools of moral philosophy do not differ on the point that human beings have rights worth dying for. They differ rather about whether, once we have understood when and why these rights have been granted or denied, in the way in which social and intellectual historians understand this, there is more to understand. They differ, in short, about whether there are "ontological foundations for human rights," just as the Sellars-Quine approach differs from the empiricist and rationalist traditions about whether, once we understand (as historians of knowledge do) when and why various beliefs have been adopted or discarded, there is something called "the relation of knowledge to reality" left over to be understood.

This analogy with moral philosophy lets us focus the issue about behaviorism in epistemology yet again: the issue is not adequacy of explanation of fact, but rather whether a practice of justification can be given a "grounding" in fact. The question is not whether human knowledge in fact has "foundations," but whether it makes sense to suggest that it does—whether the idea of epistemic or moral authority having a "ground" in nature is a coherent one. For the pragmatist in morals, the claim that the customs of a given society are "grounded in human nature" is not one which he knows how to argue about. He is a pragmatist because he cannot see what it would be like for a custom to be so grounded. For the Quine-Sellars approach to epistemology, to say that truth and knowledge can only be judged by the standards of the inquirers of our own day is not to say that human knowledge is less noble or important, or more "cut off from the world," than we had thought. It is merely to say that nothing counts as justification unless by reference to what we already accept, and that there is no way to get outside our beliefs and our language so as to find some test other than coherence.

To say that the True and the Right are matters of social practice may seem to condemn us to a relativism which, all by itself, is a *reductio* of a behaviorist approach to either knowledge or morals. I shall take up this charge in discussing historicism, in chapters seven and eight. Here I shall simply remark that only the image of a discipline—philosophy—which will pick out a given set of scientific or moral views as more "rational" than the alternatives by appeal to something which forms a permanent neutral matrix for all inquiry and all history, makes it possible to think that such relativism must automatically rule out coherence theories of intellectual and practical justification. One reason why professional philosophers recoil from the claim that knowledge may not have foundations, or rights and duties an ontological ground, is that the kind of behaviorism which dispenses with foundations is in a fair way toward dispensing with philosophy. For the view that there is no permanent neutral matrix within which the dramas of inquiry and history are enacted has as a corollary that criticism of one's culture can only be piecemeal and partial—never "by reference to eternal standards." It threatens the neo-Kantian image of philosophy's relation to science and to culture. The urge to say that assertions and actions must not only cohere with other assertions and actions but "correspond" to something apart from what people are saying and doing has some claim to be called *the* philosophical urge. It is the urge which drove Plato to say that Socrates' words and deeds, failing as they did to cohere with current theory and practice, nonetheless corresponded to something which the Athenians could barely glimpse. The residual Platonism which Quine and Sellars are opposing is not the hypostatization of nonphysical entities, but the notion of "correspondence" with such entities as the touchstone by which to measure the worth of present practice.*

I am claiming, in short, that the Quine-Sellars attack on the Kantian notion of two sorts of representations—intuitions "given" to one faculty, and concepts (or meanings) "given" to another—is not the attempt to substitute one sort of account of human knowledge for another, but an attempt to get away from the notion of "an account of human knowledge." It amounts to a protest against an archetypal philosophical problem: the problem of how to reduce norms, rules, and justifications to facts, generalizations, and explanations.** For this reason, we will not find neutral metaphilosophical ground on which to argue the issues Quine and Sellars raise. For they are not offering an "account" to be tested for "adequacy" but pointing to the futility of offering an "account." To refuse, as both do, to justify assertions by appeal to behavioristically unverifiable episodes (in which the mind recognizes its own direct acquaintance with an instantiation of blueness or with the meaning of "blue") is just to say that justification must be holistic. If we are not to have a doctrine of "knowledge by acquaintance" which will give us a foundation, and if we do not simply deny that there is such a thing as justification, then we will claim with Sellars that "science is rational not because it has a foundation, but because it is a self-correcting enterprise which can put any claim in jeopardy, though not all at once."*** We will say with Quine that knowledge is not like an architectonic structure but like a field of force,† and that there are no assertions which are immune from revision. We will be holistic not because we have a taste for wholes, any more than we are behaviorist because of a distaste for "ghostly entities," but simply because justification has always *been* behavioristic and holistic. Only the professional philosopher has dreamed that it might be something else, for only he is frightened by the epistemological skeptic. A holistic approach to knowledge is not a matter of antifoundationalist polemic, but a distrust of the whole epistemological enterprise. A behavioristic approach to episodes of "direct awareness" is not a matter of antimentalistic polemic, but a distrust of the Platonic quest for that special sort of certainty associated with visual perception. The image of the Mirror of Nature—a mirror more easily and certainly seen than that which it mirrors—suggests, and is suggested by, the image of philosophy as such a quest.

If what I have been saying so far is sound, there is no way to argue for the views of Sellars and Quine except by replying to their critics. There is no neutral ground on

---

*Unfortunately, both men tend to substitute correspondence to physical entities, and specifically to the "basic entities" of physical science (elementary particles, or their successors). Sellars's (and Jay Rosenberg's) attempt to salvage *something* from the Platonic notion of knowledge as accuracy of picturing is criticized below (chapter six, section 5) [not included in this volume]. My own attitude is Strawson's (and Heidegger's): "The correspondence theory requires, not purification, but elimination." (P.F. Strawson, "Truth," reprinted in *Truth,* ed. George Pitcher [Englewood Cliffs, NJ, 1964], p. 32)—or, more mildly, it requires separation from epistemology and relegation to semantics. (See Robert Brandom, "Truth and Assertability," *Journal of Philosophy* 73 [1976], pp. 137–149.)

**Cf. Sellars's claim that "the idea that epistemic facts can be analyzed without remainder—even 'in principle'—into nonepistemic facts, whether phenomenal or behavioural, public or private, with no matter how lavish a sprinkling of subjunctives and hypotheticals is, I believe, a radical mistake—a mistake of a piece with the so-called 'naturalistic fallacy' in ethics" (*Science, Perception and Reality,* p. 131). I would argue that the importance of Sellars's approach to epistemology is that he sees the true and interesting irreducibility in the area not as between one sort of particular (mental, intentional) and another (physical) but as between descriptions on the one hand and norms, practices, and values on the other. . . .

***Sellars, *Science, Perception and Reality,* p. 170.

†W.V.O. Quine, *From a Logical Point of View* (Cambridge, MA: Harvard University Press, 1953), p. 42.

which to stand and show that they have overcome, respectively, "the given" and "the analytic" in a fair fight. The best we can do is to disentangle the pure form of their criticisms of the tradition from various extraneous issues which their critics (and, to some extent, Quine and Sellars themselves) have introduced, and thereby perhaps to mitigate the paradoxical air of their doctrines. In the next section, I shall take up Sellars's attack on the Myth of the Given, and try to disentangle it from the "unfair to babies" implications of the claim that there is no such thing as pre-linguistic awareness. Next, I shall take up Quine's attack on the distinction between language and fact and try to disentangle it from Quine's unhappy reductionist claims about the "indeterminacy" of translation and of the *Geisteswissenschaften.* When Sellars's and Quine's doctrines are purified, they appear as complementary expressions of a single claim: that no "account of the nature of knowledge" can rely on a theory of representations which stand in privileged relations to reality. The work of these two philosophers enables us to unravel, at long last, Locke's confusion between explanation and justification, and to make clear why an "account of the nature of knowledge" can be, at most, a description of human behavior.

* * *

5. Epistemological Behaviorism, Psychological Behaviorism, and Language

In the previous chapter I said that the epistemological tradition confused the causal process of acquiring knowledge with questions concerning its justification. In this chapter I have presented Sellars's criticism of the Myth of the Given and Quine's criticism of the notion of truth by virtue of meaning as two detailed developments of this more general criticism. If we accept these criticisms, and therefore drop the notion of epistemology as the quest, initiated by Descartes, for those privileged items in the field of consciousness which are the touchstones of truth, we are in a position to ask whether there still remains something for epistemology to be. I want to urge that there does not. To understand the matters which Descartes wanted to understand—the superiority of the New Science to Aristotle, the relations between this science and mathematics, common sense, theology, and morality—we need to turn outward rather than inward, toward the social context of justification rather than to the relations between inner representations. This attitude has been encouraged in recent decades by many philosophical developments, particularly those stemming from Wittgenstein's *Philosophical Investigations* and from Kuhn's *Structure of Scientific Revolutions.* Some of these developments will be canvassed in chapters seven and eight. Before doing so, however, I shall discuss two attempts to preserve something from the Cartesian tradition, attempts which may seem to shed some doubt on our ability simply to drop the image of the Mirror of Nature altogether.

The first of these attempts is the revolt against logical behaviorism in the philosophy of psychology, leading to the development of explanations of behavior in terms of inner representations without, necessarily, any linkup with the justification of beliefs and actions. I have already said that once explanation and justification are held apart there is no reason to object to explanation of the acquisition of knowledge in terms of representations, and that such explanations can be offered without resuscitating the traditional "mindbody problem." But I think that the defense of such explanations against

Ryle and Skinner can easily be distorted into a rehabilitation of the traditional seventeenth-century philosophical problematic, and thus I shall devote chapter five to a discussion of such defenses. My aim will be to disassociate empirical psychology from the remnants of epistemology by defending it against both Wittgensteinian criticisms and Chomskyan compliments.

The second attempt to preserve something from the Cartesian tradition which I shall discuss is the effort, within recent philosophy of language, to specify "how language hooks onto the world," thus creating an analogue of the Cartesian problem of how thought hooks onto the world. An attempt to use the notions of the reference of terms and the truth of sentences to aid in understanding the matters which troubled Descartes seems to me doomed to failure, but such a program is very tempting. Because language is a "public" Mirror of Nature, as thought is a "private" one, it seems that we should be able to reformulate a great many Cartesian and Kantian questions and answers in linguistic terms, and thereby rehabilitate a lot of standard philosophical issues (e.g., the choice between idealism and realism). I devote chapter six to various efforts at such rehabilitation, and argue that semantics should be kept as pure of epistemology as should psychology.

Once both the inner representations needed in psychological explanation and the word-world relations needed by semantics to produce a theory of meaning for natural languages are seen as irrelevant to issues of justification, we can see the abandonment of the search for privileged representations as the abandonment of the goal of a "theory of knowledge." The urge toward such a theory in the seventeenth century was a product of the change from one paradigm of understanding nature to another, as well as of the change from a religious to a secular culture. Philosophy as a discipline capable of giving us a "right method of seeking truth" depends upon finding some permanent neutral framework of all possible inquiry, an understanding of which will enable us to see, for example, why neither Aristotle nor Bellarmine was justified in believing what he believed. The mind as Mirror of Nature was the Cartesian tradition's response to the need for such a framework. If there are no privileged representations in this mirror, then it will no longer answer to the need for a touchstone for choice between justified and unjustified claims upon our belief. Unless some other such framework can be found, the abandonment of the image of the Mirror leads us to abandon the notion of philosophy as a discipline which adjudicates the claims of science and religion, mathematics and poetry, reason and sentiment, allocating an appropriate place to each. . . .

THE CONVERSATION CONTINUES: EMERGING CLASSICS SINCE 1980

◄○►

If philosophy can be called conversation, then the goal of our series, *Philosophic Classics,* has been to hear the major conversational partners in the history of that conversation. But who are the conversationalists today, and what are they saying? And which are the classics that will appear in third-millennium anthologies?

Only time will tell, of course, but there are themes one hears repeatedly in late twentieth-century philosophical circles. One is a questioning of the very process by which some voices dominate and others do not. Sometimes the questioning takes a specific form, such as asking why so many of the "classical" writers of the past spoke with a male voice. Thinkers such as Luce Irigaray question the structures that have privileged male "rationality." Sometimes the questioning asks the more general question, "What are the structures that allow *any* privileging of *any* dialogue?" Much of the recent work of Foucault, Derrida, and Rorty has been devoted to the archeology of these structures.

A second theme in recent philosophical conversation is the desire to make philosophy practical. Continuing Marx's point that the goal of philosophy is not to interpret the world but to change it, thinkers such as Jürgen Habermas have sought theories that bring social change. In arguing for practical social change, these philosophers have often brought the social sciences into the philosophical conversation.

A third theme is the need to move beyond the Enlightenment project of Descartes, Bacon, and the others. The old rationalist paradigm that the universe is orderly, knowable, and knowable best by human reason is under increasing criticism. Philosophers such as Hilary Putnam and Charles Taylor compete to find ways that philosophy can still speak with an Enlightenment accent.

In all these themes, one hears much conversation about the conversation itself. If there is any common conversation in the late-twentieth century, it is the nature of language. One hears Continental philosophers on the later Heidegger's adage that "language is the house of Being," and Anglo-American philosophers on the implications of the later Wittgenstein. The four selections given here take up the Great Tradition of philosophical history, apprize it, and then make their own contributions to the continuing conversation that is philosophy since the 1980s.

*   *   *

Several works noted in the introduction to this volume (p. xix) include discussions of recent philosophical work. Surveys that focus exclusively on recent philosophy include John Passmore, *Recent Philosophers* (La Salle, IL: Open Court, 1985); Hugh J. Silverman, ed., *Philosophy and Non-Philosophy since Merleau-Ponty* (London: Routledge, 1988); and John Lechte, *Fifty Key Contemporary Thinkers: From Structuralism to Postmodernity* (London: Routledge, 1994). Kenneth Baynes, et al., eds., *After Philosophy: End or Transformation* (Cambridge, MA: MIT Press, 1987) provides a collection of primary sources. For specific areas of recent philosophy, see John Rajchman and Cornel West, eds., *Post-Analytic Philosophy* (New York: Columbia University Press, 1985); Kai Nielsen, *After the Demise of the Tradition: Rorty, Critical Theory, and the Fate of Philosophy* (Boulder, CO: Westview Press, 1991); Raoul Mortley, *French Philosophers in Conversation: Levinas, Schneider, Serres, Irigaray, Le Doeuff, Derrida* (London: Routledge, 1991); Edmund Arens, *The Logic of Pragmatic Thinking: From Peirce to Habermas* (Atlantic Highlands, NJ: Humanities Press, 1994); and Frank B. Farrell, *Subjectivity, Realism, and Postmodernism: The Recovery of the World* (Cambridge: Cambridge University Press, 1994). Finally, Nancy Tuana, *Woman and the History of Philosophy* (New York: Paragon, 1992) is an interesting critique of the history of philosophy from a feminist perspective, whereas Cornel West, *Race Matters* (Boston: Beacon, 1993) is criticism from a multi-cultural perspective.

LUCE IRIGARAY
1930–

Luce Irigaray was born in Blanton, Belgium, in 1930 and attended the University of Louvain, the University of Paris, and the Paris Institute of Psychology. She was a member of the École Freudienne de Paris and a lecturer at the University of Paris at Vincennes. She is a practicing psychoanalyst and is currently Director of Research in Philosophy at the National Center for Scientific Research in Paris.

Irigaray's first work, translated as *The Language of Dementia* (1973), investigated the relationship between demented persons and language. She discovered that it makes more sense to say that words and phrases are spoken *through* demented persons rather than to say that they are the speakers. When she turned her attention to philosophy, she found that women, in general, were put in the same position as the demented she studied. The very language of philosophy is "phallocentric," she found, and language is constructed by and for men and their pleasure. Using *this* language, women are either reduced to silence or—what is much the same thing—are reduced to allowing men's words to be spoken through them. The language of philosophy erases women as women and forces them to see themselves through men's eyes. Even then, the dominant Freudian imagery sees women as incomplete, a lack, as human beings without penises. In short, as Margaret Whitford put it, Irigaray "fused a psychoanalytic attention to what is repressed by culture with a Derridean-inspired account of the repressions required by culture. In both cases, Irigaray argues, the feminine is excluded."

In our reading, "The Sex Which is Not One," translated by Claudia Reeder, Irigaray argues that "woman is traditionally use-value for man, exchange-value among men. Merchandise, then." As mere "merchandise," woman is excluded from being a complete subject to herself. She is understood—and understands herself—only as an object for men: "Woman is never anything more than the scene of more or less rival exchange between two men, even when they are competing for the possession of mother-earth." Furthermore, the foundational language that develops to describe sexual desire is the language of man. Irigaray explains that while man has one definitive sex organ, *"woman has sex organs just about everywhere."* Because the satisfaction of desire is not focused on a single object, woman cannot express desire in the terms developed by and for man, As Irigaray says,

> "She" is indefinitely other in herself. That is undoubtedly the reason she is called temperamental, incomprehensible, perturbed, capricious—not to mention her language in which "she" goes off in all directions and in which "he" is unable to discern the coherence of any meaning. Contradictory words seem a little crazy to the logic of reason, and inaudible for him who listens with ready-made grids, a code prepared in advance.

Since Irigaray's feminist critique has been one of the most radical critiques of philosophy, her writing has become increasingly influential. Yet a number of feminists have criticized Irigaray's apparent "essentialism." Mary Poovey, for example, writes, "Luce Irigaray . . . authorizes th[e] return to biology and essentialism in her creation of a myth of female desire and in [her] basing 'feminine' language on the physical properties of female genitalia."* Some feminists are worried that if a fixed nature is claimed for women, essentialism will bind women to their present oppressed position in society. Defenders reply either by saying that Irigaray is not an essentialist or that she may be an essentialist, depending on how the term is defined, but essentialism is not something for feminists to fear.

*   *   *

A good place to begin further study of Irigaray's work is Margaret Whitford, ed., *The Irigaray Reader* (Oxford: Basil Blackwell, 1991). For general overviews, see Elizabeth Grosz, *Sexual Subversion* (Sydney: Allen & Unwin, 1989) and Margaret Whitford, *Luce Irigaray: Philosophy in the Feminine* (New York: Routledge, 1991). For discussion of the place of Irigaray's thought in the larger context of feminism, see Drucilla Cornell, *Beyond Accommodation: Ethical Feminism, Deconstruction, and the Law* (New York: Routledge, 1991). Tina Chanter, *Ethics of Eros: Irigaray's Rewriting of the Philosophers* (New York: Routledge, 1995) explores the roots of Irigaray's thought in Hegel, Heidegger, De Beauvoir, Levinas, and Derrida while Patricia J. Huntington, *Ecstatic Subjects, Utopia, and Recognition: Kristeva, Heidegger, Irigaray* (Albany, NY: SUNY Press, 1998) uses Heideggerian models to explore Irigaray's work. For critical essays, see Carolyn Burke, Naomi Schor, and Margaret Whitford, eds., *Engaging with Irigaray* (New York: Columbia University Press, 1994).

---

*"Feminism and Deconstruction," *Feminist Studies* 14 (1) Spring, 1988 as quoted in Chanter, *Ethics of Eros,* p. 4.

THE SEX WHICH IS NOT ONE (in part)

Female sexuality has always been theorized within masculine parameters. Thus, the opposition "viril"* clitoral activity/"feminine" vaginal passivity which Freud— and many others—claims are alternative behaviors or steps in the process of becoming a sexually normal woman, seems prescribed more by the practice of masculine sexuality than by anything else. For the clitoris is thought of as a little penis which is pleasurable to masturbate, as long as the anxiety of castration does not exist (for the little boy), while the vagina derives its value from the "home" it offers the male penis when the now forbidden hand must find a substitute to take its place in giving pleasure.

According to these theorists, woman's erogenous zones are no more than a clitoris-sex, which cannot stand up in comparison with the valued phallic organ; or a hole-envelope, a sheath which surrounds and rubs the penis during coition; a nonsex organ or a masculine sex organ turned inside out in order to caress itself.

Woman and her pleasure are not mentioned in this conception of the sexual relationship. Her fate is one of "lack," "atrophy" (of her genitals), and "penis envy," since the penis is the only recognized sex organ of any worth. Therefore she tries to appropriate it for herself, by all the means at her disposal: by her somewhat servile love of the father-husband capable of giving it to her; by her desire of a penis-child, preferably male; by gaining access to those cultural values which are still "by right" reserved for males alone and are therefore always masculine, etc. Woman lives her desire only as an attempt to possess at long last the equivalent of the male sex organ.

All of that seems rather foreign to her pleasure however, unless she remains within the dominant phallic economy. Thus, for example, woman's autoeroticism is very different from man's. He needs an instrument in order to touch himself: his hand, woman's genitals, language—And this self-stimulation requires a minimum of activity. But a woman touches herself by and within herself directly, without mediation, and before any distinction between activity and passivity is possible. A woman "touches herself" constantly without anyone being able to forbid her to do so, for her sex is composed of two lips which embrace continually. Thus, within herself she is already two—but not divisible into ones—who stimulate each other.

This autoeroticism, which she needs in order not to risk the disappearance of her pleasure in the sex act, is interrupted by a violent intrusion: the brutal spreading of these two lips by a violating penis. If, in order to assure an articulation between auto-eroticism and heteroeroticism in coition (the encounter with the absolute other which always signifies death), the vagina must also, but not only, substitute for the little boy's hand, how can woman's autoeroticism possibly be perpetuated in the classic representation of sexuality? Will she not indeed be left the impossible choice between defensive virginity, fiercely turned back upon itself, or a body open for penetration, which no longer recognizes in its "hole" of a sex organ the pleasure of retouching itself? The almost exclusive, and ever so anxious, attention accorded the erection in Occidental sexuality proves to what extent the imaginary that commands it is foreign to everything female. For the most part, one finds in Occidental sexuality nothing more than impera-

*[Masculine]

Luce Irigaray, "The Sex Which is Not One," translated by Claudia Reeder, in *New French Feminisms*, eds. Elaine Marks and Isabelle de Courtivron (New York: Schoken, 1981), pp. 99–106. Reprinted by permission of Editions Minuet.

tives dictated by rivalry among males: the "strongest" being the one who "gets it up the most," who has the longest, thickest, hardest penis or indeed the one who "pisses the farthest" (cf. little boys' games). These imperatives can also be dictated by sado-masochist fantasies, which in turn are ordered by the relationship between man and mother: his desire to force open, to penetrate, to appropriate for himself the mystery of the stomach in which he was conceived, the secret of his conception, of his "origin." Desire-need, also, once again, to make blood flow in order to revive a very ancient—intrauterine, undoubtedly, but also prehistoric—relation to the maternal.

Woman, in this sexual imaginary, is only a more or less complacent facilitator for the working out of man's fantasies. It is possible, and even certain, that she experiences vicarious pleasure there, but this pleasure is above all a masochistic prostitution of her body to a desire that is not her own and that leaves her in her well-known state of dependency. Not knowing what she wants, ready for anything, even asking for more, if only he will "take" her as the "object" of *his* pleasure, she will not say what *she* wants. Moreover, she does not know, or no longer knows, what she wants. As Freud admits, the beginnings of the sexual life of the little girl are so "obscure," so "faded by the years," that one would have to dig very deep in order to find, behind the traces of this civilization, this history, the vestiges of a more archaic civilization which could give some indication as to what woman's sexuality is all about. This very ancient civilization undoubtedly would not have the same language, the same alphabet—desire most likely does not speak the same language as man's desire, and it probably has been covered over by the logic that has dominated the West since the Greeks.

In this logic, the prevalence of the gaze, discrimination of form, and individualization of form is particularly foreign to female eroticism. Woman finds pleasure more in touch than in sight and her entrance into a dominant scopic economy signifies, once again, her relegation to passivity: she will be the beautiful object. Although her body is in this way eroticized and solicited to a double movement between exhibition and pubic retreat in order to excite the instincts of the "subject," her sex organ represents the horror of having nothing to see. In this system of representation and desire, the vagina is a flaw, a hole in the representation's scoptophilic objective. It was admitted already in Greek statuary that this "nothing to be seen" must be excluded, rejected, from such a scene of representation. Woman's sexual organs are simply absent from this scene: they are masked and her "slit" is sewn up.

In addition, this sex organ which offers nothing to the view has no distinctive form of its own. Although woman finds pleasure precisely in this incompleteness of the form of her sex organ, which is why it retouches itself indefinitely, her pleasure is denied by a civilization that privileges phallomorphism. The value accorded to the only definable form excludes the form involved in female autoeroticism. The *one* of form, the individual sex, proper name, literal meaning—supersedes, by spreading apart and dividing, this touching of *at least two* (lips) which keeps woman in contact with herself, although it would be impossible to distinguish exactly what "parts" are touching each other.

Whence the mystery that she represents in a culture that claims to enumerate everything, cipher everything by units, inventory everything by individualities. *She is neither one nor two.* She cannot, strictly speaking, be determined either as one person or as two. She renders any definition inadequate. Moreover she has no "proper" name. And her sex organ, which is not *a* sex organ, is counted as *no* sex organ. It is the negative, the opposite, the reverse, the counterpart, of the only visible and morphologically designatable sex organ (even if it does pose a few problems in its passage from erection to detumescence): the penis.

But woman holds the secret of the "thickness" of this "form," its many-layered volume, its metamorphosis from smaller to larger and vice versa, and even the intervals at which this change takes place. Without even knowing it. When she is asked to maintain, to revive, man's desire, what this means in terms of the value of her own desire is neglected. Moreover, she is not aware of her desire, at least not explicitly. But the force and continuity of her desire are capable of nurturing all the "feminine" masquerades that are expected of her for a long time.

It is true that she still has the child, with whom her appetite for touching, for contact, is given free reign, unless this appetite is already lost, or alienated by the taboo placed upon touching in a largely obsessional civilization. In her relation to the child she finds compensatory pleasure for the frustrations she encounters all too often in sexual relations proper. Thus maternity supplants the deficiencies of repressed female sexuality. Is it possible that man and woman no longer even caress each other except indirectly through the mediation between them represented by the child? Preferably male. Man, identified with his son, rediscovers the pleasure of maternal coddling; woman retouches herself in fondling that part of her body: her baby-penis-clitoris.

What that entails for the amorous trio has been clearly spelled out. The Oedipal interdict seems, however, a rather artificial and imprecise law—even though it is the very means of perpetuating the authoritarian discourse of fathers—when it is decreed in a culture where sexual relations are impracticable, since the desire of man and the desire of woman are so foreign to each other. Each of them is forced to search for some common meeting ground by indirect means: either an archaic, sensory relation to the mother's body, or a current, active or passive prolongation of the law of the father. Their attempts are characterized by regressive emotional behavior and the exchange of words so far from the realm of the sexual that they are completely exiled from it. "Mother" and "father" dominate the couple's functioning, but only as social roles. The division of labor prevents them from making love. They produce or reproduce. Not knowing too well how to use their leisure. If indeed they have any, if moreover they want to have any leisure. For what can be done with leisure? What substitute for amorous invention can be created?

We could go on and on—but perhaps we should return to the repressed female imaginary? Thus woman does not have a sex. She has at least two of them, but they cannot be identified as ones. Indeed she has many more of them than that. Her sexuality, always at least double, is in fact *plural.* Plural as culture now wishes to be plural? Plural as the manner in which current texts are written, with very little knowledge of the censorship from which they arise? Indeed, woman's pleasure does not have to choose between clitoral activity and vaginal passivity, for example. The pleasure of the vaginal caress does not have to substitute itself for the pleasure of the clitoral caress. Both contribute irreplaceably to woman's pleasure but they are only two caresses among many to do so. Caressing the breasts, touching the vulva, opening the lips, gently stroking the posterior wall of the vagina, lightly massaging the cervix, etc., evoke a few of the most specifically female pleasures. They remain rather unfamiliar pleasures in the sexual difference as it is currently imagined, or rather as it is currently ignored: the other sex being only the indispensable complement of the only sex.

But *woman has sex organs just about everywhere.* She experiences pleasure almost everywhere. Even without speaking of the hysterization of her entire body, one can say that the geography of her pleasure is much more diversified, more multiple in its differences, more complex, more subtle, than is imagined—in an imaginary centered a bit too much on one and the same.

"She" is indefinitely other in herself. That is undoubtedly the reason she is called temperamental, incomprehensible, perturbed, capricious—not to mention her language in which "she" goes off in all directions and in which "he" is unable to discern the coherence of any meaning. Contradictory words seem a little crazy to the logic of reason, and inaudible for him who listens with ready-made grids, a code prepared in advance. In her statements—at least when she dares to speak out—woman retouches herself constantly. She just barely separates from herself some chatter, an exclamation, a half-secret, a sentence left in suspense—When she returns to it, it is only to set out again from another point of pleasure or pain. One must listen to her differently in order to hear an *"other meaning" which is constantly in the process of weaving itself, at the same time ceaselessly embracing words and yet casting them off to avoid becoming fixed, immobilized.* For when "she" says something, it is already no longer identical to what she means. Moreover, her statements are never identical to anything. Their distinguishing feature is one of contiguity. They touch (*upon*). And when they wander too far from this nearness, she stops and begins again from "zero": her body-sex organ.

It is therefore useless to trap women into giving an exact definition of what they mean, to make them repeat (themselves) so the meaning will be clear. They are already elsewhere than in this discursive machinery where you claim to take them by surprise. They have turned back within themselves, which does not mean the same thing as "within yourself." They do not experience the same interiority that you do and which perhaps you mistakenly presume they share. "Within themselves" means *in the privacy of this silent, multiple, diffuse tact.* If you ask them insistently what they are thinking about, they can only reply: nothing. Everything.

Thus they desire at the same time nothing and everything. It is always more and other than this *one*—of sex, for example—that you give them, that you attribute to them and which is often interpreted, and feared, as a sort of insatiable hunger, a voracity which will engulf you entirely. While in fact it is really a question of another economy which diverts the linearity of a project, undermines the target-object of a desire, explodes the polarization of desire on only one pleasure, and disconcerts fidelity to only one discourse.

Must the multiple nature of female desire and language be understood as the fragmentary, scattered remains of a raped or denied sexuality? This is not an easy question to answer. The rejection, the exclusion of a female imaginary undoubtedly places woman in a position where she can experience herself only fragmentarily as waste or as excess in the little structured margins of a dominant ideology, this mirror entrusted by the (masculine) "subject" with the task of reflecting and redoubling himself. The role of "femininity" is prescribed moreover by this masculine specula(riza)tion and corresponds only slightly to woman's desire, which is recuperated only secretly, in hiding, and in a disturbing and unpardonable manner.

But if the female imaginary happened to unfold, if it happened to come into play other than as pieces, scraps, deprived of their assemblage, would it present itself for all that as *a* universe? Would it indeed be volume rather than surface? No. Unless female imaginary is taken to mean, once again, the prerogative of the maternal over the female. This maternal would be phallic in nature however, closed in upon the jealous possession of its valuable product, and competing with man in his esteem for surplus. In this race for power, woman loses the uniqueness of her pleasure. By diminishing herself in volume, she renounces the pleasure derived from the nonsuture of her lips: she is a mother certainly, but she is a virgin mother. Mythology long ago assigned this role to her in which she is allowed a certain social power as long as she is reduced, with her own complicity, to sexual impotence.

Thus a woman's (re)discovery of herself can only signify the possibility of not sacrificing any of her pleasures to another, of not identifying with anyone in particular, of never being simply one. It is a sort of universe in expansion for which no limits could be fixed and which, for all that, would not be incoherency. Nor would it be the polymorphic perversion of the infant during which its erogenous zones await their consolidation under the primacy of the phallus.

Woman would always remain multiple, but she would be protected from dispersion because the other is a part of her, and is autoerotically familiar to her. That does not mean that she would appropriate the other for herself, that she would make it her property. Property and propriety are undoubtedly rather foreign to all that is female. At least sexually. Nearness, however, is not foreign to woman, a nearness so close that any identification of one or the other, and therefore any form of property, is impossible. Woman enjoys a closeness with the other that is *so near she cannot possess it, any more than she can possess herself.* She constantly trades herself for the other without any possible identification of either one of them. Woman's pleasure, which grows indefinitely from its passage in/through the other, poses a problem for any current economy in that all computations that attempt to account for woman's incalculable pleasure are irremediably destined to fail.

However, in order for woman to arrive at the point where she can enjoy her pleasure as a woman, a long detour by the analysis of the various systems of oppression which affect her is certainly necessary. By claiming to resort to pleasure alone as the solution to her problem, she runs the risk of missing the reconsideration of a social practice upon which *her* pleasure depends.

For woman is traditionally use-value for man, exchange-value among men. Merchandise, then. This makes her the guardian of matter whose price will be determined by "subjects": workers, tradesmen, consumers, according to the standard of their work and their need-desire. Women are marked phallically by their fathers, husbands, procurers. This stamp(ing) determines their value in sexual commerce. Woman is never anything more than the scene of more or less rival exchange between two men, even when they are competing for the possession of mother-earth.

How can this object of transaction assert a right to pleasure without extricating itself from the established commercial system? How can this merchandise relate to other goods on the market other than with aggressive jealousy? How can raw materials possess themselves without provoking in the consumer fear of the disappearance of his nourishing soil? How can this exchange in nothingness that can be defined in "proper" terms of woman's desire not seem to be pure enticement, folly, all too quickly covered over by a more sensible discourse and an apparently more tangible system of values?

A woman's evolution, however radical it might seek to be, would not suffice then to liberate woman's desire. Neither political theory nor political practice have yet resolved nor sufficiently taken into account this historical problem, although Marxism has announced its importance. But women are not, strictly speaking, a class and their dispersion in several classes makes their political struggle complex and their demands sometimes contradictory.

Their underdeveloped condition stemming from their submission by/to a culture which oppresses them, uses them, cashes in on them, still remains. Women reap no advantage from this situation except that of their quasimonopoly of masochistic pleasure, housework, and reproduction. The power of slaves? It is considerable since the master is not necessarily well served in matters of pleasure. Therefore, the inversion of the relationship, especially in sexual economy, does not seem to be an enviable objective.

But if women are to preserve their auto-eroticism, their homo-sexuality, and let it flourish, would not the renunciation of heterosexual pleasure simply be another form of this amputation of power that is traditionally associated with women? Would this renunciation not be a new incarceration, a new cloister that women would willingly build? Let women tacitly go on strike, avoid men long enough to learn to defend their desire notably by their speech, let them discover the love of other women protected from that imperious choice of men which puts them in a position of rival goods, let them forge a social status which demands recognition, let them earn their living in order to leave behind their condition of prostitute—These are certainly indispensable steps in their effort to escape their proletarization on the trade market. But, if their goal is to reverse the existing order—even if that were possible—history would simply repeat itself and return to phallocratism, where neither women's sex, their imaginary, nor their language can exist.

JÜRGEN HABERMAS
1929–

Jürgen Habermas grew up in Gummersbach, just east of Cologne, Germany. His father directed the small town's Chamber of Commerce—a difficult position after the Nazis came to power in 1933. Habermas later described his family's response to the Nazis as "bourgeois adaptation to a political environment with which one did not fully identify, but which one didn't seriously criticize either."* Habermas attended the Universities of Göttingen and Zürich, studying philosophy, history, psychology, and German literature. He received his doctorate in 1954 from the University of Bonn. After a brief period as a journalist, Habermas became a member of the "Frankfurt School." Centered in the Institute for Social Research, this group of philosophers, social scientists, and cultural critics seeks to continue the legacy of Karl Marx without the dogmatic excesses of Stalinist orthodoxy. Apart from brief periods at the University of Heidelberg and the Max Planck Institute in Starnberg, Habermas has remained in Frankfurt, where he is Professor of the History of Philosophy at the University of Frankfurt and the acknowledged intellectual leader of the Frankfurt School.

Habermas's goal, like Karl Marx's, has been not just to understand the world, but to change it. Building on the work of Max Horkheimer (1895–1973), Theodor Adorno (1903–1969), and other earlier members of the Frankfurt School, Habermas has designed a social theory for the self-emancipation of peoples. Using an approach called *critical theory,* Habermas combines philosophy

---

*Jürgen Habermas, *Autonomy and Solidarity,* p. 127, as quoted in William Outhwaite, *Habermas: A Critical Introduction* (Stanford, CA: Stanford University Press, 1994), p. 2.

and social science to develop a theory that is at once explanatory, normative, and practical.

In our selection from *The Philosophical Discourse of Modernity* (1987), Habermas outlines some basic features of his theory. He begins by exploring the contemporary critique of the modern, Enlightenment conception of reason. According to Habermas, the modern notion of reason is based on a "paradigm of self-consciousness" that claims the self as a "subject knowing and acting in isolation." Like the radical critics of modernity from Nietzsche to Foucault, Habermas believes this subject-centered paradigm is "exhausted." But Habermas also holds that its radical critics remain entangled in the very paradigm they critique. Heidegger and Foucault, for example, criticize any historical form of reason from the "perspective of the other" that the form excludes. But such a critique still requires that one be self-reflective and able to surpass one's historical situation. Such self-reflection is only possible, however, within a subject-centered paradigm. In short, Habermas concludes, this "supposedly radical critique of reason remains tied to the presuppositions of the philosophy of the subject from which it wanted to free itself."

In contrast, Habermas offers a new paradigm: "The paradigm of mutual understanding, that is, of the intersubjective relationship between individuals who are socialized through communication and [who] reciprocally recognize one another." This paradigm of understanding examines speech acts, or "communicative action," to understand the subject in community. Building on the work of J.L. Austin, Habermas identifies the three components of a speech act: the representation of a state of affairs, the establishment of interpersonal relationships, and the expression of one's own intention. Habermas then explores the implications of these linguistic functions for the theory of meaning, the theory of communications, and the concept of rationality itself. He concludes our selection by showing how the modern conception of instrumental reason is based on the paradigm of self-consciousness and, thus, on a misunderstanding of communicative action.

Throughout his work, Habermas argues that the problem with modernity is that it has not yet completed its course—or discourse. The goal for Habermas is not to overcome modernity but to complete its rational project. Contrary to post-structuralists and deconstructionists, Habermas contends, the "logocentrism" of Enlightenment thinking displays not an excess of rationality but a deficit. As one critic put it, "In the welter of recent counterenlightenment and postenlightenment theorizing, the work of Jürgen Habermas stands out for its unflinching defense of enlightenment rationality."*

*   *   *

A good place to begin further study of Habermas is William Outhwaite, *Habermas: A Critical Introduction* (Stanford, CA: Stanford University Press, 1994). Other general introductions to his thought include Thomas McCarthy, *The Critical Theory of Jürgen Habermas* (Cambridge, MA: MIT Press, 1978); *Jürgen Habermas, Autonomy and Solidarity: Interviews,* edited by Peter Dews (London: Verso, 1986); Stephen K. White, *The Recent Work of Jürgen Habermas* (Cambridge: Cambridge University Press, 1988); and Robert C. Holub, *Jürgen Haber-*

---

*Axel Honneth et al., eds., Cultural-Political Interventions in the Unfinished Project of Enlightenment, translated by Barbara Fultner (Cambridge, MA: MIT Press, 1992), p. ix.

mas: Critic in the Public Sphere (London: Routledge, 1991). M. Johanna Mee-han, ed., *Feminists Read Habermas: Gendering the Subject of Discourse* (London: Routledge, 1995); and Marie Fleming, *Emancipation and Illusion* (College Park: Pennsylvania State University Press, 1997) provide feminist critiques. Among the many comparative studies are Michael Kelly, ed., *Critique and Power: Recasting the Foucault/Habermas Debate* (Cambridge, MA: MIT Press, 1994); Steven Best, *The Politics of Historical Vision: Marx, Foucault, Habermas* (New York: Guilford, 1995); and Demetrius Teigas, *Knowledge and Hermeneutic Understanding: A Study of the Habermas-Gadamer Debate* (Lewisburg, PA: Bucknell University Press, 1995). For collections of essays, see Craig Calhoun, ed., *Habermas and the Public Sphere* (Cambridge, MA: MIT Press, 1992); Stephen K. White, ed., *The Cambridge Companion to Habermas* (Cambridge: Cambridge University Press, 1995); Maurizio Passerin d'Entrèves and Seyla Benhabib, eds., *Habermas and the Unfinished Project of Modernity* (Cambridge, MA: MIT Press, 1997); and Peter Dews, ed., *Habermas: A Critical Reader* (Oxford: Basil Blackwell, 1997).

For studies of critical theory, see David Held, *Introduction to Critical Theory: Horkheimer to Habermas* (London: Hutchinson, 1980); Raymond Geuss, *The Idea of a Critical Theory: Habermas & the Frankfurt School* (Cambridge: Cambridge University Press, 1981); Ian Craib, *Modern Social Theory: From Parsons to Habermas* (New York: St. Martin's Press, 1984); Martin J. Matuštík, *Postnational Identity: Critical Theory and Existential Philosophy in Habermas, Kierkegaard, and Havel* (New York: Guilford Press, 1993); Rolf Wiggerhaus, *The Franfurt School: Its History, Theories, and Political Significance,* translated by Michael Robertson (Cambridge, MA: MIT Press, 1994); and J.M. Bernstein, *Recovering Ethical Life: Jürgen Habermas and the Future of Critical Theory* (London: Routledge, 1995)

THE PHILOSOPHICAL DISCOURSE OF MODERNITY (in part)

LECTURE XI, "AN ALTERNATIVE WAY OUT OF THE PHILOSOPHY OF THE SUBJECT"

PART II

During the last decade, the radical critique of reason has become fashionable. A study by Hartmut and Gernot Böhme, who take up Foucault's idea of the rise of the modern form of knowledge in connection with the work and biography of Kant, is exemplary in theme and execution. In the style of a historiography of science expanded by

Jürgen Habermas, *The Philosophical Discourse of Modernity,* Lecture XI, Part II "An Alternative Way out of the Philosophy of the Subject" (Cambridge, MA: MIT Press, 1987), pp. 301–316. Reprinted by permission.

Collapse of the Berlin Wall, November 1989. With the collapse of the Soviet empire,
Marxism entered a new phase. Thinkers such as Jürgen Habermas have tried to continue
the legacy of Karl Marx without the dogmatic excesses of Stalinist Orthodoxy and its
results. (*Thomas Kienzzle, AP/Wide World Photos*)

cultural and social history, the authors take a look, so to speak, at what goes on behind
the back of the critique of pure and of practical reason. For example, they seek the real
motives for the critique of reason in the debate with the spiritual clairvoyant, Sweden-
borg, in whom Kant is supposed to have recognized his dark twin, his repressed counterimage.

They pursue these motives into the sphere of the personal, into the, as it were,
abstract conduct (turned away from everything sexual, bodily, and imaginative) of a
scholarly life marked by hypochondria, crotchetiness, and immobility. The authors
marshal before our eyes the "costs of reason" in terms of psychohistory. They undertake this cost/benefit accounting ingenuously with psychoanalytic arguments and document it with historical data, though without being able to specify the place at which
such arguments could claim any weight—if indeed the thesis they are concerned with
is supposed to make sense.

Kant had carried out his critique of reason from reason's own perspective, that is
to say, in the form of a rigorously argued self-limitation of reason. If, now, the production costs of this self-confining reason (which places anything metaphysical off limits)
are to be made clear, we require a horizon of reason reaching beyond this drawing of

boundaries in which the transcending discourse that adds up the bill can operate. This further radicalized critique of reason would have to postulate a more far-reaching and *comprehensive* reason. But the Böhme brothers do not intend to cast out the devil by Beelzebub; instead, with Foucault, they see in the transition from an exclusive reason (in the Kantian mold) to a comprehensive reason merely "the completion of the power-technique of exclusion by the power-technique of permeation."* If they were to be consistent, their own investigation of the other of reason would have to occupy a position utterly heterogeneous to reason—but what does consistency count for in a place that is a priori inaccessible to rational discourse? In this text, the paradoxes repeatedly played out since Nietzsche leave behind no recognizable traces of unrest. This method-ological enmity toward reason may have something to do with the type of historical in-nocence with which studies of this kind today move in the no-man's land between ar-gumentation, narration, and fiction. The New Critique of Reason suppresses that almost 200-year-old counterdiscourse inherent in modernity itself which I am trying to recall in these lectures.

The latter discourse set out from Kantian philosophy as an unconscious expres-sion of the modern age and pursued the goal of enlightening the Enlightenment about its own narrow-mindedness. The New Critique of Reason denies the continuity with this counterdiscourse, within which it nevertheless still stands: "No longer can it be a matter of completing the project of modernity (Habermas); it has to be a matter of re-vising it. Also, the Enlightenment has not remained incomplete, but unenlightened."** The intention of revising the Enlightenment with the very tools of the Enlightenment is, however, what united the critics of Kant from the start—Schiller with Schlegel, Fichte with the Tübingen seminarians. Further on we read: "Kant's philosophy was initiated as the enterprise of drawing boundaries. But nothing was said about the fact that drawing boundaries is a dynamic process, that reason retreated to firm ground and abandoned other areas, that drawing boundaries means self-inclusion and exclusion of others." At the start of our lectures, we saw how Hegel, along with Schelling and Hölderlin, saw as so many provocations the philosophy of reflection's achievements of delimitation—the opposition of faith and knowledge, of infinite and finite, the separa-tion of spirit and nature, of understanding and sensibility, of duty and inclination. We saw how they tracked the estrangement of an overblown subjective reason from inter-nal and external nature right into the "positivities" of the demolished *Sittlichkeit* of everyday political and private life. Indeed, Hegel saw the vanishing of the power of reconciliation from the life of mankind as the source of an objective need for philoso-phy. At any rate, he interpreted the boundaries drawn by subject-centered reason not as exclusions from but as dichotomies within reason, and ascribed to philosophy an ac-cess to the totality *that encompasses within itself* subjective reason and its other. Our authors' distrust is directed against this, when they continue: "Whatever reason is, however, remains unclear as long as its other is not thought along with it (in its irre-ducibility). For reason can be deceived about itself, take itself to be the whole (Hegel), or pretend to comprehend the totality."

This is just the objection that the Young Hegelians once made good against the master. They brought a suit against absolute reason in which the other of reason, what is always prior to it, was supposed to be rehabilitated in its own proper right. The con-cept of a *situated reason* issued from this process of desublimation; its relationship to

---

*H. Böhme and G. Böhme, *Das Andere der Vernunft* (Frankfurt, 1983), p. 326.
**Ibid.*, p. 11.

the historicity of time, to the facticity of external nature, to the decentered subjectivity of internal nature, and to the material character of society was defined neither by inclusion nor by exclusion, but by a praxis of projecting and developing essential powers that takes place under conditions "not themselves chosen." Society is portrayed as practices in which reason is embodied. This praxis takes place in the dimension of historical time; it mediates the inner nature of needful individuals with an external nature objectified by labor, within the horizon of a surrounding cosmic nature. This social practice is the place where a historically situated, bodily incarnated reason, confronted by external nature, is concretely mediated with its other. Whether this mediating practice is successful depends on its internal constitution, on the degrees of bifurcation and of reconciliation in the socially institutionalized context of life. What was called the system of egoism and divided ethical totality in Schiller and Hegel is transformed by Marx into a society split into social classes. Just as in Schiller and in the young Hegel, the social bond—that is, the community-forming and solidarity-building force of unalienated cooperation and living together—ultimately decides whether reason embodied in social practices is in touch with history and nature. It is the dichotomized society itself that exacts the repression of death, the leveling of historical consciousness, and the subjugation of both internal and external nature.

Within the context of the philosophy of history, the praxis philosophy of the young Marx has the significance of disconnecting Hegel's model of diremption from an *inclusive* concept of reason that incorporated even the other of reason in its totality. The reason of praxis philosophy is understood as finite; nevertheless it remains tied to a *comprehensive* reason—in the form of a critical social theory—insofar as it realizes that it could not identify the historical limits of subject-centered reason—as embodied in bourgeois social relations—without transcending them. Whoever fastens obstinately upon the model of exclusion has to be closed to this Hegelian insight, which, as is evident in Marx, can be had without paying the price of abolutizing the spirit. From such a restricted perspective, the Hegelian defect attending the birth of post-Hegelian theory is still also effective "where reason is criticized as instrumental, repressive, narrow: in Horkheimer and Adorno. Their critique still takes place in the name of a superior reason, namely, the comprehensive reason, to which the intention of totality is conceded, though it was always disputed when it came to real reason. There is no comprehensive reason. One should have learned from Freud or even from Nietzsche that reason does not exist apart from its other and that—functionally considered—it becomes necessary in virtue of this other."*

With this assertion, the Böhme brothers call to mind the place where Nietzsche, having recourse to the Romantic heritage, once set a totalizing critique of reason in opposition to an intrinsically dialectical Enlightenment. The dialectic of enlightenment would indeed only have played itself out if reason were robbed of any transcendent force and, in virtual impotence, remained confined, in the madness of its autonomy, to those boundaries that Kant had defined for understanding and for any state based on understanding: "That the subject of reason wants to owe no one and nothing outside itself is its ideal and its insanity at once."** Only if reason shows itself to be essentially narcissistic—an identifying, only seemingly universal power, bent upon self-assertion and particular self-aggrandizement, subjugating everything around it as an object—can the other of reason be thought for its part as a spontaneous, creative power that is at the

*Ibid., p. 18.
**Ibid., p. 19.

ground of Being, a power that is simultaneously vital and unperspicuous, that is no longer illuminated by any spark of reason. Only reason as reduced to the subjective faculty of understanding and purposive activity corresponds to the image of an *exclusive* reason that further uproots itself the more it strives triumphally for the heights, until, withered, it falls victim to the power of its concealed heterogeneous origin. The dynamism of self-destruction, in which the secret of the dialectic of enlightenment supposedly comes to light, can only function if reason cannot produce anything from itself except that naked power to which it actually hopes to provide an alternative, namely the unforced force of a better insight.

This move explains, moreover, the drastic leveling of Kant's architectonic of reason that results from the Nietzsche-inspired reading of Kant; it has to obliterate the connection of the critiques of pure and practical reason with the critique of judgment, so as to reduce the former to a theory of alienated, external nature and the latter to a theory of domination over internal nature.*

Whereas the *diremption model* of reason distinguishes solitary social practice as the locus of a historically situated reason in which the threads of outer nature, inner nature, and society converge, in the *exclusion model* of reason the space opened up by utopian thought gets completely filled in with an irreconcilable reason reduced to bare power. Here social practice only serves as the stage upon which disciplinary power finds ever new scenarios. It is haunted by a reason denied the power to gain access, without coercion, to what is prior to it. In its putative sovereignty, reason that has evaporated into subjectivity becomes the plaything of unmediated forces working upon it, as it were, mechanically—forces of the internal and external nature that have been excluded and rendered into objects.

The other of this self-inflated subjectivity is no longer the dirempted totality, which makes itself felt primarily in the avenging power of destroyed reciprocities and in the fateful causality of distorted communicative relationships, as well as through suffering from the disfigured totality of social life, from alienated inner and outer nature. In the model of exclusion, this complicated structure of a subjective reason that is socially divided and thereby torn away from nature is peculiarly de-differentiated: "The other of reason is nature, the human body, fantasy, desire, the feelings—or better: all this insofar as reason has not been able to appropriate it."** Thus, it is directly the vital forces of a split-off and repressed subjective nature, it is the sorts of phenomena rediscovered by Romanticism—dreams, fantasies, madness, orgiastic excitement, ecstacy—it is the aesthetic, body-centered experiences of a decentered subjectivity that function as the placeholders for the other of reason. To be sure, early Romanticism still wanted to establish art, in the form of a new mythology, as a public institution in the midst of social life; it wanted to elevate the excitement radiating from this into an equivalent for the unifying power of religion. Nietzsche was the first to transfer this

---

*Whereas Schiller and Hegel want to see the moral idea of self-legislation realized in an aesthetically reconciled society or in the totality of the context of ethical life, the Böhmes can see only the work of disciplinary power in moral autonomy:

> "If one wanted to envision the inner judicial process conducted in the name of the moral law with regard to maxims, one would have to recur to the Protestant examination of conscience, which displaced the model of the witch trial into the interiority of humans; or better still, go forward into the cool, hygienic interrogation rooms and the silent, elegant computer arsenals of the police gone scientific, whose ideal is the categorical imperative—the uninterrupted apprehension and control of everything particular and resistant, right into the interiority of the human being." (*Ibid.*, p. 349.)

**Ibid.*, p. 13.

potential for excitement into the beyond of modern society and of history overall. The modern origin of aesthetic experience heightened in an avant-garde fashion remains concealed.

The potential for excitement, stylized into the other of reason, becomes at once esoteric and pseudonymous; it comes up under different names—as Being, as the heterogeneous, as power. The cosmic nature of the metaphysicians and the God of the philosophers become blurred into an enchanting reminiscence, a moving remembrance on the part of the metaphysically and religiously isolated subject. The order from which this subject has emancipated himself—which is to say, internal and external nature in their unalienated form—appears now only in the past tense, as the archaic origin of metaphysics for Heidegger, as a turning point in the archeology of the human sciences for Foucault—and also, somewhat more fashionably, as follows: "Separated from the body, whose libidinous potencies could have supplied images of happiness, separated from a maternal nature, which embraced the archaic image of symbiotic wholeness and nurturing protection, separated from the feminine, mingling with which belonged to the primal images of happiness—the philosophy of a reason robbed of all images generated only a grandiose consciousness of the superiority in principle of the intelligible over nature and over the lowliness of the body and the woman. . . . Philosophy attributed to reason an omnipotence, infinity, and future perfection, whereas *the lost childlike relationship to nature* did not appear."*

Nonetheless, these recollections of origins by the modern subject serve as points of reference for responses to the question that the more consistent among Nietzsche's followers did not try to evade. As long as we speak in narrative form of the other of reason (whatever it might be called), and as long as this factor that is heterogeneous to discursive thought comes up in portrayals of the history of philosophy and science as a name without any further qualifications, the pose of innocence cannot make up for this underselling of the critique of reason inaugurated by Kant. In Heidegger and Foucault, subjective nature as the placeholder for the other has disappeared, because it can no longer be declared the other of reason once it is brought into scientific discourse as the individual or collective unconscious in the concepts of Freud or Jung, of Lacan or Lévi-Strauss. Whether in the form of meditative thought *[Andenken]* or of genealogy, Heidegger and Foucault want to initiate a *special discourse* that claims to operate *outside* the horizon of reason without being utterly irrational. To be sure, this merely shifts the paradox.

Reason is supposed to be criticizable in its historical forms from the perspective of the other that has been excluded from it; this requires, then, an ultimate act of self-reflection that surpasses itself, and indeed an act of reason for which the place of the *genitivus subjectivus* would have to be occupied by the other of reason. Subjectivity, as the relation-to-self of the knowing and acting subject, is represented in the bipolar relationship of self-reflection. This figure is retained, and yet subjectivity is supposed to appear only in the place reserved for the object. Heidegger and Foucault elaborate this paradox in a structurally similar way, inasmuch as they *generate* what is heterogeneous to reason by way of a self-exiling of reason, a banishing of reason from its own territory. This operation is understood as an unmasking reversal of the self-idolizing that subjectivity carries on and at the same time conceals from itself. In the process, it ascribes attributes to itself that it borrows from the shattered religious and metaphysical concepts of order. Conversely, the other they seek, which is heterogeneous to

Ibid., p. 23.

reason and still related to it as its heterogeneous factor, results from a radical finitizing of the absolute for which subjectivity had falsely substituted itself. As we have seen, Heidegger chooses time as the dimension of finitizing and conceives the other of reason as an anonymous, primordial power, set aflow temporally; Foucault chooses the dimension of spatial centering in the experience of one's own body and conceives the other of reason as the anonymous source of the empowerment of interactions tied to the body.

We have seen that this elaboration of the paradox by no means amounts to its solution; the paradox is withdrawn into the special status of extraordinary discourse. Just as meditative thought pertains to a mystified Being, genealogy pertains to power. Meditative thought is supposed to open up a privileged access to metaphysically buried truth; genealogy is supposed to take the place of the apparently degenerate human sciences. Whereas Heidegger remains reticent about the kind of privilege that is his—so that one is not sure of how the genre of his late philosophy could be judged in any sense—Foucault has carried out his work unpretentiously to the very last, in the awareness of being unable to dodge his methodological aporias.

PART III

The spatial metaphor of inclusive and exclusive reason reveals that the supposedly radical critique of reason remains tied to the presuppositions of the philosophy of the subject from which it wanted to free itself. Only a reason to which we ascribe a "power of the keys" could either include or exclude. Hence, inside and outside are linked with domination and subjugation; and the overcoming of reason-as-powerholder is linked with breaking open the prison gates and vouchsafing release into an indeterminate freedom. Thus, the other of reason remains the mirror image of reason in power. Surrender and letting-be remain as chained to the desire for control as the rebellion of counterpower does to the oppression of power. Those who would like to leave all paradigms behind along with the paradigm of the philosophy of consciousness, and go forth into the clearing of postmodernity, will just not be able to free themselves from the concepts of subject-centered reason and its impressively illustrated topography.

Since early Romanticism, limit experiences of an aesthetic and mystical kind have always been claimed for the purpose of a rapturous transcendence of the subject. The mystic is blinded by the light of the absolute and closes his eyes; aesthetic ecstasy finds expression in the stunning and dizzying effects of (the illuminating) shock. In both cases, the source of the experience of being shaken up evades any specification. In this indeterminacy, we can make out only the silhouette of the paradigm under attack—the outline of what has been deconstructed. In this constellation, which persists from Nietzsche to Heidegger and Foucault, there arises a readiness for excitement without any proper object; in its wake, subcultures are formed which simultaneously allay and keep alive their excitement in the face of future truths (of which they have been notified in an unspecified way) by means of cultic actions without any cultic object. This scurrilous game with religiously and aesthetically toned ecstasy finds an audience especially in circles of intellectuals who are prepared to make their *sacrificium intellectus* on the altar of their needs for orientation.

But here, too, a paradigm only loses its force when it is negated in a *determinate* manner by a *different* paradigm, that is, when it is devalued in an *insightful* way; it is certainly resistant to any simple invocation of the extinction of the subject. Even the furious labor of deconstruction has identifiable consequences only when the paradigm of self-consciousness, of the relation-to-self of a subject knowing and acting in isolation, is replaced by a different one—by the paradigm of mutual understanding, that is, of the intersubjective relationship between individuals who are socialized through communication and reciprocally recognize one another. Only then does the critique of the domineering thought of subject-centered reason emerge in a *determinate* form— namely, as a critique of Western "logocentrism," which is diagnosed not as an excess but as a deficit of rationality. Instead of overtrumping modernity, it takes up again the counterdiscourse inherent in modernity and leads it away from the battle lines between Hegel and Nietzsche, from which there is no exit. This critique renounces the high-flown originality of a return to archaic origins; it unleashes the subversive force of modern thought itself against the paradigm of the philosophy of consciousness that was installed in the period from Descartes to Kant.

The critique of the Western emphasis on logos inspired by Nietzsche proceeds in a destructive manner. It demonstrates that the embodied, speaking and acting subject is not master in its own house; it draws from this the conclusion that the subject positing itself in knowledge is in fact dependent upon something prior, anonymous, and transsubjective—be it the dispensation of Being, the accident of structure—formation, or the generative power of some discourse formation. The logos of an omnipotent subject thus appears as a misadventure of misguided specialization, which is as rich in consequences as it is wrongheaded. The hope awakened by such post-Nietzschean analyses has constantly the same quality of expectant indeterminacy. Once the defenses of subject-centered reason are razed, the logos, which for so long had held together an interiority protected by power, hollow within and aggressive without, will collapse into itself. It has to be delivered over to its other, whatever that may be.

A different, less dramatic, but step-by-step testable critique of the Western emphasis on logos starts from an attack on the abstractions surrounding logos itself, as free of language, as universalist, and as disembodied. It conceives of intersubjective understanding as the telos inscribed into communication in ordinary language, and of the logocentrism of Western thought, heightened by the philosophy of consciousness, as a systematic *foreshortening* and *distortion* of a potential always already operative in the communicative practice of everyday life, but only selectively exploited. As long as Occidental self-understanding views human beings as distinguished in their relationship to the world by their monopoly on encountering entities, knowing and dealing with objects, making true statements, and implementing plans, reason remains confined ontologically, epistemologically, or in terms of linguistic analysis to only one of its dimensions. The relationship of the human being to the world is cognitivistically reduced: Ontologically, the world is reduced to the world of entities as a whole (as the totality of objects that can be represented and of existing states of affairs); epistemologically, our relationship to that world is reduced to the capacity to know existing states of affairs or to bring them about in a purposive-rational fashion; semantically, it is reduced to fact-stating discourse in which assertoric sentences are used—and no validity claim is admitted besides propositional truth, which is available *in foro interno*.

Language philosophy—from Plato to Popper—has concentrated this logocentrism into the affirmation that the linguistic function of representing states of affairs is the sole human monopoly. Whereas human beings share the so-called appellative and expressive functions (Bühler) with animals, only the representative function is supposed to be constitutive of reason.* However, evidence from more recent ethology, especially experiments with the artificially induced acquisition of language by chimpanzees, teaches us that it is not the use of propositions per se, but only the *communicative use* of propositionally differentiated language that is proper to our socio-cultural form of life and is constitutive for the level of a genuinely social reproduction of life. In terms of language philosophy, the equiprimordiality and equal value of the three fundamental linguistic functions come into view as soon as we abandon the analytic level of the judgment or the sentence and expand our analysis to speech acts, precisely to the communicative use of sentences. Elementary speech acts display a structure in which three components are mutually combined: the propositional component for representing (or mentioning) states of affairs; the illocutionary component for taking up interpersonal relationships; and finally, the linguistic components that bring the intention of the speaker to expression. The clarification, in terms of speech-act theory, of the complex linguistic functions of representation, the establishment of interpersonal relationships, and the expression of one's own subjective experiences has far-reaching consequences for (a) the theory of meaning, (b) the ontological presuppositions of the theory of communication, and (c) the concept of rationality itself. Here I will only point out these consequences to the extent that they are directly relevant to (d) a *new orientation* for the critique of instrumental reason.

(a) Truth-condition semantics, as it has been developed from Frege to Dummett and Davidson, proceeds—as does the Husserlian theory of meaning—from the logocentric assumption that the truth reference of the assertoric sentence (and the indirect truth reference of intentional sentences related to the implementation of plans) offers a suitable point of departure for the explication of the linguistic accomplishment of mutual understanding generally. Thus, this theory arrives at the principle that we understand a sentence when we know the conditions under which it is true. (For understanding intentional and imperative sentences it requires a corresponding knowledge of "conditions for success.") The pragmatically expanded theory of meaning overcomes this fixation on the fact-mirroring function of language. Like truth-condition semantics, it affirms an internal connection between meaning and validity, but it does not reduce this to the validity proper to truth. Correlative to the three fundamental functions of language, each elementary speech act as a whole can be contested under three different aspects of validity. The hearer can reject the utterance of a speaker *in toto* by either disputing the truth of the proposition asserted in it (or of the existential presuppositions of its propositional content), or the *rightness* of the speech act in view of the normative context of the utterance (or the legitimacy of the presupposed context itself), or the truthfulness of the intention expressed by the speaker (that is, the agreement of what is meant with what is stated). Hence, the internal connection of meaning and validity holds for the *entire spectrum* of linguistic meanings—and not just for the meaning of expressions that can be expanded into assertoric sentences. It holds true not only for constative speech acts, but for any given speech act, that we understand its meaning when we know the conditions under which it can be accepted as valid.**

(b) If, however, not just constative but also regulative and expressive speech acts can be connected with validity claims and accepted as valid or rejected as invalid, the basic, ontological framework of the philosophy of consciousness (which has remained normative for linguistic philosophy as well, with exceptions such as Austin) proves to be too narrow. The "world" to which subjects can relate with their representations or

---

*Karl-Otto Apel, "Die Logosauszeichnung der menschlichen Sprache. Die philosophische Tragweite der Sprechakttheorie" (1984), manuscript.
**Ernst Tugendhat, Einführung in die sprachanalytische Philosophie (Frankfurt, 1976).\

propositions was hitherto conceived of as the totality of objects or existing states of affairs. The objective world is considered the correlative of all true assertoric sentences. But if normative rightness and subjective truthfulness are introduced as validity claims analogous to truth, "worlds" analogous to the world of facts have to be postulated for legitimately regulated interpersonal relationships and for attributable subjective experiences—a "world" not only for what is "objective," which appears to us in the attitude of the third person, but also one for what it normative, to which we feel obliged in the attitude of addresses, as well as one for what is subjective, which we either disclose or conceal to a public in the attitude of the first person. With any speech act, the speaker takes up a relation to something in the objective world, something in a common social world, and something in his own subjective world. The legacy of logocentrism is still noticeable in the terminological difficulty of expanding the ontological concept of "world" in this way.

The phenomenological concept (elaborated by Heidegger in particular) of a referential context, a lifeworld, that forms the unquestioned context for processes of mutual understanding—behind the backs of participants in interaction, so to speak—needs a corresponding expansion. Participants draw from this *lifeworld* not just consensual patterns of interpretation (the background knowledge from which propositional contents are fed), but also normatively reliable patterns of social relations (the tacitly presupposed solidarities on which illocutionary acts are based) and the competences acquired in socialization processes (the background of the speaker's intentions).

(c) "Rationality" refers in the first instance to the disposition of speaking and acting subjects to acquire and use fallible knowledge. As long as the basic concepts of the philosophy of consciousness lead us to understand knowledge exclusively as knowledge of something in the objective world, rationality is assessed by how the isolated subject orients himself to representational and propositional contents. Subject-centered reason finds its criteria in standards of truth and success that govern the relationships of knowing and purposively acting subjects to the world of possible objects or states of affairs. By contrast, as soon as we conceive of knowledge as communicatively mediated, rationality is assessed in terms of the capacity of responsible participants in interaction to orient themselves in relation to validity claims geared to intersubjective recognition. Communicative reason finds its criteria in the argumentative procedures for directly or indirectly redeeming claims to propositional truth, normative rightness, subjective truthfulness, and aesthetic harmony.*

Thus, a procedural concept of rationality can be worked out in terms of the interdependence of various forms of argumentation, that is to say, with the help of a pragmatic logic of argumentation. This concept is richer than that of purposive rationality, which is tailored to the cognitive-instrumental dimension, because it integrates the moral-practical as well as the aesthetic-expressive domains; it is an explicitation of the rational potential built into the validity basis of speech. This communicative rationality recalls older ideas of logos, inasmuch as it brings along with it the connotations of a noncoercively unifying, consensus-building force of a discourse in which the participants overcome their at first subjectively biased views in favor of a rationally motivated agreement. Communicative reason is expressed in a decentered understanding of the world.

---

*Albrecht Wellmer has shown that the harmony of a work of art—aesthetic truth as it is called—can by no means be reduced, without further ado, to authenticity or sincerity; see his "Truth, Semblance and Reconciliation," *Telos* 62(1984–1985):89–115.

(d) From this perspective, both cognitive-instrumental mastery of an objectivated nature (and society) and narcissistically overinflated autonomy (in the sense of purposively rational self-assertion) are derivative moments that have been rendered independent from the communicative structures of the lifeworld, that is, from the intersubjectivity of relationships of mutual understanding and relationships of reciprocal recognition. Subject-centered reason is the *product of division and usurpation,* indeed of a social process in the course of which a subordinated moment assumes the place of the whole, without having the power to assimilate the structure of the whole. Horkheimer and Adorno have, like Foucault, described this process of a self-overburdening and self-reifying subjectivity as a world-historical process. But both sides missed its deeper irony, which consists in the fact that the communicative potential of reason first had to be released in the patterns of modern lifeworlds before the unfettered imperatives of the economic and administrative subsystems could react back on the vulnerable practice of everyday life and could thereby promote the cognitive-instrumental dimension to domination over the suppressed moments of practical reason. The communicative potential of reason has been simultaneously developed and distorted in the course of capitalist modernization.

The paradoxical contemporaneity and interdependence of the two processes can only be grasped if the false alternative set up by Max Weber, with his opposition between substantive and formal rationality, is overcome. Its underlying assumption is that the disenchantment of religious-metaphysical world views robs rationality, along with the contents of tradition, of all substantive connotations and thereby strips it of its power to have a structure-forming influence on the lifeworld beyond the purposive-rational organization of means. As opposed to this, I would like to insist that, despite its purely procedural character as disburdened of all religious and metaphysical mortgages, communicative reason is directly implicated in social life-processes insofar as acts of mutual understanding take on the role of a mechanism for coordinating action. The network of communicative actions is nourished by resources of the lifeworld and is at the same time the *medium* by which concrete forms of life are reproduced.

Hence, the theory of communicative action can reconstruct Hegel's concept of the ethical context of life (independently of premises of the philosophy of consciousness). It disenchants the unfathomable causality of fate, which is distinguished from the destining of Being by reason of its *inexorable immanence.* Unlike the "from-time-immemorial" character of the happening of Being or of power, the pseudo-natural dynamics of impaired communicative life-contexts retains something of the character of a destining for which one is *"at fault" oneself*—though one can speak of "fault" here only in an intersubjective sense, that is, in the sense of an involuntary product of an entanglement that, however things stand with individual accountability, communicative agents would have to ascribe to communal responsibility. It is not by chance that suicides set loose a type of shock among those close to them, which allows even the most hardhearted to discover something of the *unavoidable communality* of such a fate.

HILARY PUTNAM
1926–

Hilary Putnam was born in Chicago. He received his B.A. from the University of Pennsylvania in 1948 and his Ph.D. from UCLA in 1951. He has taught at Northwestern, Princeton, and MIT. Since 1965, he has been at Harvard University, where he is Pearson Professor of Mathematical Logic. In 1976, Putnam became president of the American Philosophical Association and in 1980 president of the Association of Symbolic Logic. He is married to the American moral philosopher Ruth Anna Putnam, who teaches at Wellesley College in Massachusetts.

Putnam once said "Any philosophy that can be put in a nutshell belongs in one." Clearly this characterization does not apply to Putnam's own thought! His philosophical career began in analytical philosophy, dealing with logic. In the late-1950s and early-1960s, he worked extensively with philosophy of mind, developing the "functionalist" account of mental life, which claims that mentality is an "organization to function." For humans, this organization is called a computational, or "Turing," machine from the pioneer of computing theory, A.M. Turing (1912–1954). In short, according to Putnam, psychological states are essentially computations in the brain.

In the late-1960s, during the Vietnam War, Putnam underwent a profound crisis in relation to the student antiwar movement. He became the faculty advisor to the Harvard branch of the Students for a Democratic Society (SDS) and was actively involved in the Maoist Progressive Labor Party. Although he returned to traditional philosophical work after this period, he maintained his interest in the ethical and political implications of philosophy.

After the early-1970s (and his personal political crisis), Putnam's philosophical direction changed. He developed a "postanalytic" relation to philosophical problems, claiming "analytic philosophy has great accomplishments, to be sure; but those accomplishments are negative."* He has a breathtaking willingness to abandon previously held positions. "I no longer defend that theory" is a phrase heard often in Putnam. He rejected his earlier Turing-machine model of mental states and changed his view of the relation between reference and meaning. But the biggest change has been from what he now disparagingly calls "metaphysical realism" to a type of pragmatism.

In the first of his 1986 Carus lectures, "Is There Still Anything to Say about Reality and Truth?" from *The Many Faces of Realism,* Putnam explains his abandonment of metaphysical Realism. Using the careful analysis of his analytic background, Putnam explores the "Realism" that goes back to the seventeenth-century philosophers Descartes and Locke. "Realism with a capital 'R,'" claims that only scientific objects exist and that "much, if not all, of the common-sense world is mere 'projection'." This Realism claims, for instance, that the red sweater I see is "not red in the way I thought it was," but rather that it has some power to cause me to have "sense data." I cannot really make the common-sense claim that "there is a red sweater"; I can only say that there are certain sense data in my mind. What seem to be the "intrinsic properties" of the red sweater are really nothing more than "dispositions to affect us in certain ways . . . to produce certain sorts of 'states' in our brains and nervous systems," which we in turn project onto the thing "in itself."

As he explores these dispositions and projections, Putnam offers another realism: "internal" or "pragmatic" realism. This realism corresponds to our common-sense experience. It steers a middle course between extreme relativism and metaphysical Realism: it neither rejects transsubjective standards of rational justification nor claims a "God's-Eye point of view" over words and world. Putnam concludes our selection by explaining how this realism can be compatible with conceptual relativism without falling into extreme relativism.

*   *   *

For further reading in Putnam, see *Hilary Putnam, Words and Life,* edited by James Conant (Cambridge, MA: Harvard University Press, 1994). Giovanna Borradori, *The American Philosopher,* translated by Rosanna Crocitto (Chicago: University of Chicago Press, 1994) includes an interview with Putnam about his background and influences. George Boolos, ed., *Meaning and Method: Essays in Honor of Hilary Putnam* (Cambridge: Cambridge University Press, 1990) and Peter Clark and Bob Hale, eds., *Reading Putnam* (Oxford: Basil Blackwell, 1994) contain critical essays.

---

*"After Empiricism" in John Rajchman and Cornel West, eds., *Post-Analytic Philosophy* (New York: Columbia University Press, 1985), p. 28.

THE MANY FACES OF REALISM
(in part)

LECTURE I: IS THERE STILL ANYTHING TO SAY ABOUT REALITY AND TRUTH?

The man on the street, Eddington reminded us, visualizes a table as "solid"—that is, as *mostly* solid matter. But physics has discovered that the table is mostly empty space: that the distance between the particles is immense in relation to the radius of the electron or the nucleus of one of the atoms of which the table consists. One reaction to this state of affairs, the reaction of Wilfrid Sellars,* is to deny that there are tables at all as we ordinarily conceive them (although he chooses an ice cube rather than a table as his example). The commonsense conception of ordinary middle-sized material objects such as tables and ice cubes (the "manifest image") is simply *false* in Sellars's view (although not without at least some cognitive value—there are real objects that the "tables" and "ice cubes" of the manifest image "picture," according to Sellars, even if these real objects are not the layman's tables and ice cubes). I don't agree with this view of Sellars's, but I hope he will forgive me if I use it, or the phenomenon of its appearance on the philosophical scene, to highlight certain features of the philosophical debate about "realism."

First of all, this view illustrates the fact that Realism with a capital "R" doesn't always deliver what the innocent expect of it. If there is any appeal of Realism which is wholly legitimate it is the appeal to the commonsense feeling that *of course* there are tables and chairs, and any philosophy that tells us that there really aren't—that there are really only sense data, or only "texts," or whatever, is more than slightly crazy. In appealing to this commonsense feeling, Realism reminds me of the Seducer in the old-fashioned melodrama. In the melodramas of the 1890s the Seducer always promised various things to the Innocent Maiden which he failed to deliver when the time came. In this case the Realist (the evil Seducer) promises common sense (the Innocent Maiden) that he will rescue her from her enemies (Idealists, Kantians and NeoKantians, Pragmatists, and the fearsome self-described 'Irrealist' Nelson Goodman) who (the Realist says) want to deprive her of her good old ice cubes and chairs. Faced with this dreadful prospect, the fair Maiden naturally opts for the company of the commonsensical Realist. But when they have traveled together for a little while the "Scientific Realist" breaks the news that what the Maiden is going to get *isn't* her ice cubes and tables and chairs. In fact, all there really is—the Scientific Realist tells her over breakfast—is what "finished science" will say there is—whatever that may be. She is left with a promissory note for She Knows Not What, and the assurance that even if there *aren't* tables and chairs, still there are some *Dinge an sich* that her "manifest image" (or her "folk physics," as some Scientific Realists put it) "picture." Some will say that the lady has been had.

Science, Perception, and Reality (Atlantic Highlands, NJ: Humanities Press, 1963).

Thus, it is clear that the name "Realism" can be claimed by or given to at least two very different philosophical attitudes (and, in fact, to many). The philosopher who claims that only scientific objects "really exist" and that much, if not all, of the commonsense world is mere "projection" claims to be a "realist," but so does the philosopher who insists that there *really are* chairs and ice cubes (and some of these ice cubes really are *pink*), and these two attitudes, these two images of the world, can lead to and have led to many different programs for philosophy.

Husserl* traces the first line of thought, the line that denies that there "really are" commonsense objects, back to Galileo, and with good reason. The present Western world view depends, according to Husserl, on a new way of conceiving "external objects"—the way of mathematical physics. An external thing is conceived of as a congeries of particles (by atomists) or as some kind of extended disturbance (in the seventeenth century, a "vortex," and later a collection of "fields"). Either way, the table in front of me (or the object that I "picture as" a table) is described by "mathematical formulas," as Husserl says. And this, he points out, is what above all came into Western thinking with the Galilean revolution: the idea of the "external world" as something whose true description, whose description "in itself," consists of mathematical formulas.

It is important to this way of thinking that certain familiar properties of the table—its size and shape and location—are "real" properties, describable, for example, in the language of Descartes' analytic geometry. Other properties, however, the so-called "secondary" properties, of which *color* is a chief example, are *not* treated as real properties in the same sense. No "occurrent" (non dispositional) property of that swarm of molecules (or that space-time region) recognized in mathematical physics can be said to be what we all along called its *color.*

What about dispositional properties? It is often claimed that color is simply a function of *reflectancy,* that is, of the disposition of an object (or of the surface of an object) to selectively absorb certain wavelengths of incident light and reflect others. But this doesn't really do much for the reality of colors. Not only has recent research shown that this account is much too simple (because changes of reflectancy across edges turn out to play an important role in determining the colors we see), but reflectancy itself does not have one uniform physical explanation. A red star and a red apple and a reddish glass of colored water are red for quite different physical reasons. In fact, there may well be an infinite number of different physical conditions which could result in the disposition to reflect (or emit) red light and absorb light of other wavelengths. A dispositional property whose underlying non-dispositional "explanation" is so very non-uniform is simply incapable of being represented as a mathematical function of the dynamical variables. And these—the dynamical variables—are the parameters that this way of thinking treats as the "characteristics" of "external" objects.

Another problem** is that *hues* turn out to be much more subjective than we thought. In fact, any shade on the color chart in the green part of the spectrum will be classed as "standard green" by some subject—even if it lies at the extreme "yellow-green" end or the extreme "blue-green" end.

In sum, no "characteristic" recognized by this way of thinking—no "well-behaved function of the dynamical variables"—corresponds to such a familiar property of objects as *red* or *green.* The idea that there is a property all red objects have in

---

The Crisis of the European Sciences and Transcendental Phenomenology, translated by David Carr (Evanston, IL: Northwestern University Press, 1970).

**See C.L. Hardin's "Are 'Scientific' Objects Colored?" in *Mind,* XCIII, No. 22 (October 1964), 491–500.

common—the same in all cases—and another property all green objects have in common—the same in all cases—is a kind of illusion, on the view we have come more and more to take for granted since the age of Descartes and Locke.

However, Locke and Descartes did give us a sophisticated substitute for our prescientific notion of color; a substitute that has, perhaps, come to seem mere "post-scientific common sense" to most people. This substitute involves the idea of a sense datum (except that, in the seventeenth- and eighteenth-century vocabulary, sense data were referred to as "ideas" or "impressions"). The red sweater I see is not red in the way I thought it was (there is no "physical magnitude" which is its redness), but it does have a disposition (a Power, in the seventeenth- and eighteenth-century idiom) to affect me in a certain way—to cause me to have sense data. And these, the sense data, do truly have a simple, uniform, non-dispositional sort of "redness."

This is the famous picture, the dualistic picture of the physical world and its primary qualities, on the one hand, and the mind and its sense data, on the other, that philosophers have been wrangling over since the time of Galileo, as Husserl says. And it is Husserl's idea—as it was the idea of William James, who influenced Husserl—that this picture is disastrous.

But why should we regard it as disastrous? It was once shocking, to be sure, but as I have already said it is by now widely accepted as "post-scientific common sense." What is really wrong with this picture?

For one thing, *solidity* is in much the same boat as color. If objects do not have color as they "naively" seem to, no more do they have solidity as they "naively" seem to.* It is this that leads Sellars to say that such commonsense objects as ice cubes do not really exist at all. What is our conception of a typical commonsense object if not of something solid (or liquid) which exhibits certain colors? What there really are, in Sellars's scientific metaphysics, are objects of mathematical physics, on the one hand, and "raw feels," on the other. This is precisely the picture I have just described as 'disastrous'; it is the picture that denies precisely the common man's kind of realism, his realism about tables and chairs.

The reply to me (the reply a philosopher who accepts the post-Galilean picture will make) is obvious: "You are just nostalgic for an older and simpler world. This picture works; our acceptance of it is an 'inference to the best explanation.' We cannot regard it as an objection to a view that it does not preserve everything that laymen once falsely believed."

If it is an inference to the best explanation, it is a strange one, however. How does the familiar explanation of what happens when I "see something red" go? The light strikes the object (say, a sweater), and is reflected to my eye. There is an image on the retina (Berkeley knew about images on the retina, and so did Descartes, even if the wave aspect of light was not well understood until much later). There are resultant nerve impulses. (Descartes knew there was some kind of transmission along the nerves, even if he was wrong about its nature—and it is not clear we know its nature either, since there is again debate about the significance of chemical, as opposed to electrical, transmissions from neuron to neuron.) There are events in the brain, some of which we understand thanks to the work of Hubel and Wiesel, David Marr, and others. And then—this is the mysterious part—there is somehow a "sense datum" or a "raw feel." *This* is an *explanation?*

---

*The commonsense notion of "solidity" should not be confused with the physicist's notion of being in "the solid state." For example, a sand dune is in the "solid state" but is not solid in the ordinary sense of the term, while a bottle of milk may be solid, but most of its contents are not in the solid state.

An "explanation" that involves connections of a kind we do not understand at all ("nomological danglers," Herbert Feigl called them*) and concerning which we have not even the sketch of a theory is an explanation through something more obscure than the phenomenon to be explained. As has been pointed out by thinkers as different from one another as William James, Husserl, and John Austin, every single part of the sense datum story is supposition—theory—and theory of a most peculiar kind. Yet the epistemological role "sense data" are supposed to play by traditional philosophy required them to be what is "given," to be *what we are absolutely sure of independently of scientific theory.* The kind of scientific realism we have inherited from the seventeenth century has not lost all its prestige even yet, but it has saddled us with a disastrous picture of the world. It is high time we looked for a different picture.

INTRINSIC PROPERTIES: DISPOSITIONS

I want to suggest that the problem with the "Objectivist" picture of the world (to use Husserl's term for this kind of scientific realism) lies deeper than the postulation of "sense data"; sense data are, so to speak, the visible symptoms of a systemic disease, like the pock marks in the case of smallpox. The deep systemic root of the disease, I want to suggest, lies in the notion of an "intrinsic" property, a property something has "in itself," apart from any contribution made by language or the mind.

This notion, and the correlative notion of a property that is merely "appearance," or merely something we "project" onto the object, has proved extremely robust, judging by its appeal to different kinds of philosophers. In spite of their deep disagreements, all the strains of philosophy that accepted the seventeenth-century circle of problems—subjective idealists as well as dualists and materialists—accepted the distinction, even if they disagreed over its application. A subjective idealist would say that there are only sense data (or minds and sense data, in some versions), and that "red" is an intrinsic property of these objects, while persistence (being there even when we don't look) is something we "project"; a dualist or a materialist would say the "external" objects have persistence as an intrinsic property, but red is, in their case, something we "project." But all of these philosophers *have* the distinction. Even Kant, who expresses serious doubts about it in the first *Critique* (to the point of saying that the notion of a '*Ding an sich*' may be 'empty'), makes heavy use of it in the second *Critique*.

Putting aside the Berkeleyan view (that there aren't really any external objects at all) as an aberrant form of the seventeenth-century view, we may say that the remaining philosophers all accept the account of "redness" and "solidity" that I have been describing; these are not "intrinsic properties" of the external things we ascribe them to, but rather (in the case of external things) dispositions to affect us in certain ways—to produce certain sense data in us, or, the materialist philosophers would say, to produce certain sorts of "states" in our brains and nervous systems. The idea that these properties are "in" the things themselves, as intrinsic properties, is a spontaneous "projection."

The Achilles' Heel of this story is the notion of a disposition. To indicate the problems that arise—they have preoccupied many first-rate philosophical minds, start-

---

*"The 'Mental' and the 'Physical'," in *Minnesota Studies in the Philosophy of Science,* Vol. II: *Concepts, Theories and the Mind-Body Problem,* ed. by Feigl, Scriven, and Maxwell (Minneapolis: University of Minnesota Press, 1958), 370–497.

ing with Charles Peirce's—let me introduce a technical term (I shall not introduce much terminology in this lecture, I promise!). A disposition that something has to do something *no matter what,* I shall call a *strict disposition.* A disposition to do something under "normal conditions," I shall call an *"other things being equal" disposition.* Perhaps it would be wise to give examples.

The disposition of bodies with non-zero rest mass to travel at sub-light speeds is a strict disposition; it is physically impossible for a body with non-zero rest mass to travel at the speed of light. Of course, the notion of a "strict disposition" presupposes the notion of "physical necessity," as this example illustrates, but this is a notion I am allowing the "scientific realist," at least for the sake of argument. What of the disposition of sugar to dissolve in water?

This is not a strict disposition, since sugar which is placed in water which is already saturated with sugar (or even with other appropriate chemicals) will not dissolve. Is the disposition of sugar to dissolve in *chemically pure water,* then, a strict disposition?

This is also not a strict disposition; the first counterexample I shall mention comes from thermodynamics. Suppose I drop a sugar cube in water and the sugar cube dissolves. Consider sugar which is in water, but in such a way that while the situation is identical with the situation I just produced (the sugar is dissolved in the water) with respect to the position of each particle, and also with respect to the numerical value of the momentum of each particle, all the momentum vectors have the exactly opposite directions from the ones they now have. This is a famous example: what happens in the example is that the sugar, instead of staying dissolved, simply forms a sugar cube which spontaneously leaps out of the water! Since every normal state (every state in which sugar dissolves) can be paired with a state in which it "undissolves," we see that there are infinitely many physically possible conditions in which sugar "undissolves" instead of staying in solution. Of course, these are all states in which entropy decreases; but that is not impossible, only extremely improbable!

Shall we say, then, that sugar has a strict disposition to dissolve unless the condition is one in which an entropy decrease takes place? No, because if sugar is put in water and there is immediately a flash freeze, the sugar will not dissolve if the freezing takes place fast enough. . . .

The fact is that what we can say is that under *normal* conditions sugar will dissolve if placed in water. And there is no reason to think that all the various abnormal conditions (including bizarre quantum mechanical states, bizarre local fluctuations in the space-time, etc.) under which sugar would not dissolve if placed in water could be summed up in a closed formula in the language of fundamental physics.

This is exactly the problem we previously observed in connection with redness and solidity! If the "intrinsic" properties of "external" things are the ones that we can represent by formulas in the language of fundamental physics, by "suitable functions of the dynamical variables," then *solubility* is also not an "intrinsic" property of any external thing. And, similarly, neither is any "other things being equal" disposition. The Powers, to use the seventeenth-century language, have to be set over against, and carefully distinguished from, the properties the things have "in themselves."

INTRINSIC PROPERTIES: INTENTIONALITY

Well, what of it? Why should we not say that dispositions (or at least "other things being equal" dispositions, such as solubility) are also not "in the things themselves" but rather something we "project" onto those things? Philosophers who talk this way rarely if ever stop to say what *projection* itself is supposed to be. Where in the scheme does the ability of the mind to "project" anything onto anything come in?

Projection is thinking of something as having properties it does not have, but that we can imagine (perhaps because something else we are acquainted with really does have them), without being conscious that this is what we are doing. It is thus a species of *thought*—thought about something. Does the familiar "Objectivist" picture have anything to tell us about thought (or, as philosophers say, about "intentionality," that is, about *aboutness*)?

Descartes certainly intended that it should. His view was that there are two fundamental substances—mind and matter—not one, and, correspondingly there should be two fundamental sciences: physics and psychology. But we have ceased to think of mind as a separate "substance" at all. And a "fundamental science" of psychology which explains the nature of thought (including how thoughts can be true or false, warranted or unwarranted, about something or not about something) never did come into existence, contrary to Descartes' hopes. So to explain the features of the commonsense world, including color, solidity, causality—I include causality because the commonsense notion of "the cause" of something is a "projection" if dispositions are "projections"; it depends on the notion of "normal conditions" in exactly the same way—in terms of a mental operation called "projection" is to explain just about every feature of the commonsense world in terms of *thought*.

But wasn't that what idealists were accused of doing? This is the paradox that I pointed out at the beginning of this lecture. So far as the commonsense world is concerned (the world we experience ourselves as *living* in, which is why Husserl called it the *Lebenswelt*), the effect of what is called "realism" in philosophy is to deny objective reality, to make it all simply *thought*. It is the philosophers who in one way or another stand in the neo-Kantian tradition—James, Husserl, Wittgenstein—who claim that commonsense tables and chairs and sensations and electrons are *equally real,* and not the metaphysical realists.

Today, some metaphysical realists would say that we don't need a perfected science of psychology to account for thought and intentionality, because the problem is solved by some philosophical theory; while others claim that a perfected "cognitive science" based on the "computer model" will solve the problem for us in near or distant future. I obviously do not have time to examine these suggestions closely today, but I shall indicate briefly why I believe that none of them will withstand close inspection.

WHY INTENTIONALITY IS SO INTRACTABLE

The problem, in a nutshell, is that thought itself has come to be treated more and more as a "projection" by the philosophy that traces its pedigree to the seventeenth century. The reason is clear: we have not succeeded in giving the theory that thought is just a primitive property of a mysterious "substance," mind, any content. As Kant pointed out in the first *Critique,* we have no theory of this substance or its powers and no prospect of having one. If *unlike* the Kant of the first *Critique* (as I read the *Critique of Pure Reason*), we insist on sticking to the fundamental "Objectivist" assumptions, the only line we can then take is that *mental phenomena must be highly derived physical phenomena in some way,* as Diderot and Hobbes had already proposed. By the "fundamental Objectivist assumptions," I mean (1) the assumption that there is a clear distinction to be drawn between the properties things have "in themselves" and the properties which are "projected by us" and (2) the assumption that the fundamental science—in the singular, since only physics has that status today—tells us what properties things have "in themselves." (Even if we were to assume, with Wilfrid Sellars, that "raw feels"—fundamental sensuous qualities of experience—are not going to be reduced to physics, but are in some way going to be added to fundamental science in some future century, it would not affect the situation much; Sellars does not anticipate that *intentionality* will turn out to be something we have to add to physics in the same way, but rather supposes that a theory of the "use of words" is all that is needed to account for it.)

Modern Objectivism has simply become Materialism. And the central problem for Materialism is "explaining the emergence of mind." But if "explaining the emergence of mind" means solving Brentano's problem, that is, saying in *reductive* terms what "thinking there are a lot of cats in the neighborhood" *is,* and what "remembering where Paris is" *is,* etc., why should we now think *that's* possible? If reducing color or solidity or solubility to fundamental physics has proved impossible, why should this vastly more ambitious reduction program prove tractable?

Starting in the late 1950s, I myself proposed a program in the philosophy of mind that has become widely known under the name "Functionalism." The claim of my "Functionalism" was that thinking beings are *compositionally plastic*—that is, that there is no one physical state or event (i.e., no necessary and sufficient condition expressible by a finite formula in the language of first-order fundamental physics) for being even a *physically possible* (let alone "logically possible" or "metaphysically possible") occurrence of a thought with a given propositional content, or of a feeling of anger, or of a pain, etc. *A fortiori,* propositional attitudes, emotions, feelings, are *not identical* with brain states, or even with more broadly characterized physical states. When I advanced this claim, I pointed out that thinking of a being's mentality, affectivity, etc., as aspects of its *organization to function* allows one to recognize that all sorts of logically possible "systems" or beings could be conscious, exhibit mentality and affect, etc., in exactly the same sense without having the same matter (without even consisting of "matter" in the sense of elementary particles and electromagnetic fields at all). For beings of many different physical (and even "non-physical") constitutions could have the same functional organization. The thing we want insight into is the nature of human (and animal) functional organization, not the nature of a mysterious "substance," on the one hand, or merely additional physiological information on the other.

I also proposed a theory as to what our organization to function is, one I have now given up—this was the theory that our functional organization is that of a Turing machine. I have given this up because I believe that there are good arguments to show that mental states are not only compositionally plastic but also *computationally* plastic. What I mean by this is that physically possible creatures who believe that there are a lot of cats in the neighborhood, or whatever, may have an *indefinite number of different "programs."* The hypothesis that there is a necessary and sufficient condition for the presence of a given belief in computational (or computational *cum* physical) terms is unrealistic in just the way that the theory that there is a necessary and sufficient condition for the presence of a table in phenomenalistic terms is unrealistic. Such a condition would have to be infinitely long, and not constructed according to any effective rule, or even according to a non-effective prescription that we could state without using the very terms to be reduced. I do not believe that even all *humans* who have the same belief (in different cultures, or with different bodies of knowledge and different conceptual resources) have in common a physical *cum* computational feature which could be "identified with" that belief. The "intentional level" is simply not reducible to the "computational level" any more than it is to the "physical level."*

If this is right, then the Objectivist will have to conclude that intentionality too must be a mere "projection." But how can any philosopher think this suggestion has even the semblance of making sense? As we saw, the very notion of "projection" *pre-supposes* intentionality!

Strange to say, the idea that thought is a mere projection is being defended by a number of philosophers in the United States and England, in spite of its absurdity. The strength of the "Objectivist" tradition is so strong that some philosophers will abandon the deepest intuitions we have about ourselves-in-the-world, rather than ask (as Husserl and Wittgenstein did) whether the whole picture is not a mistake. Thus it is that in the closing decades of the twentieth century we have intelligent philosophers** claiming that intentionality itself is something we project by taking a "stance" to some parts of the world (as if "taking a stance" were not itself an intentional notion!), intelligent philosophers claiming that no one really has propositional attitudes (beliefs and desires), that "belief" and "desire" are just notions from a false theory called "folk psychology," and intelligent philosophers claiming there is no such property as "truth" and no such relation as reference, that "is true" is just a phrase we use to "raise the level of language." One of these—Richard Rorty—a thinker of great depth—sees that he is committed to rejecting the intuitions that underlay every kind of realism*** (and not just metaphysical realism), but most of these thinkers write as if they were *saving* realism (in its Materialist version) by abandoning intentionality! It's as if it were all right to say "I don't deny that there is an external world; I just deny that we *think* about it"! Come to think of it, this is the way Foucault wrote, too. The line between relativism *à la française* and Analytic Philosophy seems to be thinner than anglophone philosophers think! Amusingly enough, the dust-jacket of one of the latest attacks on "folk psychology"† bears an enthusiastic blurb in which a reviewer explains the importance of the book inside the dust-jacket by saying that most people *believe* that there are such things as beliefs!

"THE TRAIL OF THE HUMAN SERPENT IS OVER ALL"

If seventeenth-century Objectivism has led twentieth century philosophy into a blind alley, the solution is neither to fall into extreme relativism, as French philosophy has been doing, nor to deny our commonsense realism. There *are* tables and chairs and ice cubes. There are also electrons and space-time regions and prime numbers and people who are a menace to world peace and moments of beauty and transcendence and many other things. My old-fashioned story of the Seducer and the Innocent Maiden was meant as a double warning; a warning against giving up commonsense realism and, simultaneously, a warning against supposing that the seventeenth-century talk of "external world" and "sense impressions," "intrinsic properties," and "projections," etc., was

---

*This is argued in my *Representation and Reality* (Cambridge, MA: MIT Press, 1988).

**D.C. Dennett, *Content and Consciousness* (Atlantic Highlands, NJ: Humanities Press, 1969).

***Philosophy and the Mirror of Nature* (Princeton, NJ: Princeton University Press, 1979).

†Stephen Stich, *From Folk Psychology to Cognitive Science: The Case Against Belief* (Cambridge, MA: MIT Press, 1983).

in any way a Rescuer of our commonsense realism. Realism with a capital "R" is, sad to say, the foe, not the defender, of realism with a small "r."

If this is hard to see, it is because the task of overcoming the seventeenth-century world picture is only begun. I asked—as the title of this lecture—whether there is still anything to say, anything really new to say, about reality and truth. If 'new' means "absolutely unprecedented," I suspect the answer is "no." But if we allow that William James might have had something "new" to say—something new to us, not just new to his own time—or, at least, might have had a program for philosophy that is, in part, the right program, even if it has not been properly worked out yet (and may never be completely "worked out"); if we allow that Husserl and Wittgenstein and Austin may have shared something of the same program, even if they too, in their different ways, failed to state it properly; then there is still something new, something *unfinished and important* to say about reality and truth. And that is what I believe.

The key to working out the program of preserving commonsense realism while avoiding the absurdities and antinomies of metaphysical realism in all its familiar varieties (Brand X: Materialism; Brand Y: Subjective Idealism; Brand Z: Dualism. . . . . . .) is something I have called *internal realism.* (I should have called it pragmatic realism!) Internal realism is, at bottom, just the insistence that realism is not incompatible with conceptual relativity. One can be *both* a realist *and* a conceptual relativist. Realism (with a small "r") has already been introduced; as was said, it is a view that takes our familiar commonsense scheme, as well as our scientific and artistic and other schemes, at face value, without helping itself to the notion of the thing "in itself." But what is conceptual relativity?

Conceptual relativity sounds like "relativism," but has none of the "there is no truth to be found . . . 'true' is just a name for what a bunch of people can agree on" implications of "relativism." A simple example will illustrate what I mean. Consider "a world with three individuals" (Carnap often used examples like this when we were doing inductive logic together in the early 1950s), **x1, x2, x3.** How many *object*s are there in this world?

Well, I *said* "consider a world with just three individuals," didn't I? So mustn't there be three objects? Can there be non-abstract entities which are not "individuals"?

One possible answer is "no." We can identify "individual," "object," "particular," etc., and find no absurdity in a world with just three objects which are independent, unrelated "logical atoms." But there are perfectly good logical doctrines which lead to different results.

Suppose, for example, that like some Polish logicians, I believe that for every two particulars there is an object which is their sum. (This is the basic assumption of "mereology," the calculus of parts and wholes invented by Lezniewski.) If I ignore, for the moment, the so-called "null object," then I will find that the world of "three individuals" (as Carnap might have had it, at least when he was doing inductive logic) actually contains *seven* objects:

World 1	World 2
x1, x2, x3	x1, x2, x3, x1 1 x2, x1 + x3, x2 + x3, x1 + x2 + x3
(A world à la Carnap)	('Same' world à la Polish logician)

Some Polish logicians would also say that there is a "null object" which they count as a part of every object. If we accepted this suggestion, and added this individual (call it 0), then we would say that Carnap's world contains *eight* objects.

Now, the classic metaphysical realist way of dealing with such problems is well-known. It is to say that there is a single world (think of this as a piece of dough) which we can slice into pieces in different ways. But this "cookie cutter" metaphor founders on the question, "What are the 'parts' of this dough?" If the answer is that **0, x1, x2, x3, x1 + x2, x1 + x3, x2 + x3, x1 + x2 + x3** are all the different "pieces," then we have not a *neutral* description, but rather a *partisan* description—just the description of the Warsaw logician! And it is no accident that metaphysical realism cannot really recognize the phenomenon of conceptual relativity—for that phenomenon turns on the fact that *the logical primitives themselves, and in particular the notions of object and existence, have a multitude of different uses rather than one absolute "meaning."*

An example which is historically important, if more complex than the one just given, is the ancient dispute about the ontological status of the Euclidean plane. Imagine a Euclidean plane. Think of the points in the plane. Are these *parts* of the plane, as Leibniz thought? Or are they "mere limits," as Kant said?

If you say, in *this* case, that these are "two ways of slicing the same dough," then you must admit that what is a *part* of space, in one version of the facts, is an abstract entity (say, a set of convergent spheres—although there is not, of course, a *unique* way of construing points as limits) in the other version. But then you will have conceded that which entities are "abstract entities" and which are "concrete objects," at least, is version-relative. Metaphysical realists to this day continue to argue about whether points (space-time points, nowadays, rather than points in the plane or in three-dimensional space) are individuals or properties, particulars or mere limits, etc. My view is that God himself, if he consented to answer the question, "Do points really exist or are they mere limits?" would say "I don't know"; not because His omniscience is limited, but because there is a limit to how far questions make sense.

One last point before I leave these examples: *given* a version, the question, "How many objects are there?" has an answer, namely "three" in the case of the first version ("Carnap's World") and "seven" (or "eight") in the case of the second version ("The Polish Logician's World"). Once we make clear how we are using "object" (or "exist"), the question "How many objects exist?" has an answer that is not at all a matter of "convention." That is why I say that this sort of example does not support *radical* cultural relativism. Our concepts may be culturally relative, but it does not follow that the truth or falsity of everything we say using those concepts is simply "decided" by the culture. But the idea that there is an Archimedean point, or a use of "exist" inherent in the world itself, from which the question "How many objects *really* exist?" makes sense, is an illusion.

If this is right, then it may be possible to see how it can be that what is in one sense the "same" world (the two versions are deeply related) can be described as consisting of "tables and chairs" (and these described as colored, possessing dispositional properties, etc.) in one version *and* as consisting of space-time regions, particles and fields, etc., in other versions. To require that all of these must be reducible to a single version is to make the mistake of supposing that "Which are the real objects?" is a question that makes sense *independently of our choice of concepts.*

What I am saying is frankly programmatic. Let me close by briefly indicating where the program leads, and what I hope from it.

Many thinkers have argued that the traditional dichotomy between the world "in itself" and the concepts we use to think and talk about it must be given up. To mention only the most recent examples, Davidson has argued that the distinction between "scheme" and "content" cannot be drawn; Goodman has argued that the distinction between "world" and "versions" is untenable; and Quine has defended "ontological relativity." Like the great pragmatists, these thinkers have urged us to reject the spectator point of view in metaphysics and epistemology. Quine has urged us to accept the existence of abstract entities on the ground that these are indispensible in mathematics,* and of microparticles and space-time points on the ground that these are indispensible in physics; and what better justification is there for accepting an ontology than its indispensibility in our scientific practice? he asks. Goodman has urged us to take seriously the metaphors that artists use to restructure our worlds, on the ground that these are an indispensible way of understanding our experience. Davidson has rejected the idea that talk of propositional attitudes is "second class," on similar grounds. These thinkers have been somewhat hesitant to forthrightly extend the same approach to our moral images of ourselves and the world. Yet what can giving up the spectator view in philosophy mean if we don't extend the pragmatic approach to the most indispensible "versions" of ourselves and our world that we possess? Like William James (and like my teacher Morton White**), I propose to do exactly that. In the remaining lectures, I shall illustrate the standpoint of pragmatic realism in ethics by taking a look at some of our moral images, and particularly at the ones that underlie the central democratic value of *equality*. Although reality and truth are old, and to superficial appearances "dry," topics, I shall try to convince you in the course of these lectures that it is the persistence of obsolete assumptions about these "dry" topics that sabotages philosophical discussion about all the "exciting" topics, not to say the possibility of doing justice to the reality and mystery of our commonsense world.

---

*"On What There Is," reprinted in *From a Logical Point of View* (Cambridge, MA: Harvard University Press, 1953).

**White has advocated doing this early and late [*Toward Reunion in Philosophy* (Cambridge, MA: Harvard University Press, 1956); *What Is and What Ought to Be Done* (Oxford: Oxford University Press, 1981)].

CHARLES MARGRAVE TAYLOR
1931–

Charles Margrave Taylor has spent most of his life in his native Canada. After receiving his B.A. in 1952 from McGill University in Montreal, he went on to earn another B.A., and then his M.A. and Ph.D., from Oxford, where he was also a Fellow of All Souls' College. From 1976 to 1981, he was Chichele Professor of Social and Political Theory at the University of Oxford, and he has held a number of visiting professorships elsewhere. But he has always returned to McGill, where he has taught since 1961.

Taylor's interests have ranged widely, but his central focus remains "philosophical anthropology." In his first book, *The Explanation of Behaviour* (1964), an attack on behaviorism, Taylor carefully articulates a vision of human beings as "self-interpreting animals." What distinguishes us from other animals (or from computers), says Taylor, is not our behavior or calculative reason. Naturalistic explanations of the self—such as behaviorism, functionalism, or artificial-intelligence psychology—are inadequate. For example, *shame* cannot be explained in terms of behavior or an "objectively reasoning" self. Shame is a "subject referring" emotion that can exist only in a subject of experience. Emotions such as shame simply "do not fit into an objectivist's view of the world. [The objectivist's view] allows for an account of things in terms of objective properties, and then also perhaps for a subjective reaction to or view of things on the part of the subject. Emotions like shame do not fit into either slot."* The essential quality or center of the self cannot be understood by a mechanistic science:

---

*Charles Taylor, *Philosophical Papers,* Vol. 1 (Cambridge: Cambridge University Press, 1985), pp. 54–55.

"The center [of the self] is no longer the power to plan, but rather openness to certain matters of significance. This is now what is essential to personal agency."*

Among "matters of significance" essential to personal agency are language and human community. As subjective, self-defining beings, humans rely on the language they use in their historical settings, for humans are essentially social animals. "Atomistic" politics that "affirm the self-sufficiency of man alone"** and that overemphasize rights will usually fail to acknowledge human interconnectedness. But essential human identity is rooted in community.

In our selection "Overcoming Epistemology" (1987), Taylor applies his philosophical anthropology to the "epistemological viewpoint" so dominant in Western philosophy. He begins with an historical overview, examining the central tenets of modern epistemology. Whereas Rorty believes foundationalism is the heart of modern epistemology,*** Taylor believes the "representational model" is central. In this model, "knowledge is to be seen as correct representation of an independent reality." But, Taylor argues, this representational model is rooted in the same ideals as the behaviorism he had previously attacked. According to Taylor, modern epistemology is something that must be "overcome" so that we can "[come] to a better understanding of what we are as knowing agents—and hence also as language beings—and thereby [gain] insight into some of the crucial anthropological questions that underpin our moral and spiritual beliefs."

*   *   *

Charles Taylor, *Philosophical Papers,* two volumes (Cambridge: Cambridge University Press, 1985) includes a summary of Taylor's philosophical interests. The only secondary source at this time is James Tully, ed., *Philosophy in an Age of Pluralism: The Thought of Charles Taylor in Question* (Cambridge: Cambridge University Press, 1994), which includes critical essays and Taylor's responses. Especially interesting is an exchange with Richard Rorty on our selection.

"OVERCOMING EPISTEMOLOGY"

Epistemology, once the pride of modern philosophy, seems in a bad way these days. Fifty years ago, during the heyday of logical empiricism, which was not only a powerful movement in philosophy but also immensely influential in social science, it seemed

Ibid., p. 105.
**Ibid.*, Vol. 2, p. 189.
***See the selection from Rorty in this volume, pp. 376–386.

Charles Taylor, "Overcoming Epistemology," Kenneth Baynes, James Bohman, and Thomas McCarthy, eds., *After Philosophy: End or Transformation* (Cambridge, MA: MIT Press, 1987), pp. 464–485. Reprinted by permission. (English translations of German and French passages by Dr. F. Dale Brunner, unless otherwise noted.)

as though the very center of philosophy was its theory of knowledge. It seemed evident that that had to be philosophy's main contribution to a scientific culture. Science went ahead and gathered knowledge; philosophical reflection concerned the validity of knowledge claims. The preeminence of epistemology explains a phenomenon like Karl Popper. On the strength of his reputation as a theorist of scientific knowledge,* he could obtain a hearing for his intemperate views about famous philosophers of the tradition, which bore only a rather distant relation to the truth.** It is reminiscent of a parallel phenomenon in the arts, whereby the political opinions of a great performer or writer are often listened to with an attention and respect that their intrinsic worth hardly commands.

Of course, all this was only true of the Anglo-Saxon world. On the Continent the challenge to the epistemological tradition was already in full swing. Heidegger and Merleau-Ponty had a wide influence. It would be too simple to say that this skeptical stance has now spread to the English-speaking world. Rather it seems true to say that epistemology has come under more intensive critical scrutiny in *both* cultures. In France the generation of "structuralists" and "poststructuralists" was if anything even more alienated from this whole manner of thinking than Merleau-Ponty had been. In England and America the arguments of both generations of Continental thinkers have begun to have an impact. The publication of Richard Rorty's influential *Philosophy and the Mirror of Nature**** helped both to crystallize and to accelerate a trend toward the repudiation of the whole epistemological enterprise.

In some circles it seems to be rapidly becoming a new orthodoxy that the whole enterprise from Descartes, through Locke and Kant, and pursued by various nineteenth- and twentieth-century succession movements, was a mistake. Within this new agreement, however, what is becoming less and less clear is what exactly it means to overcome the epistemological standpoint or repudiate the enterprise. Just what exactly is one trying to deny?

Rorty's book seems to offer a clear and plausible answer. The heart of the old epistemology was the belief in a *foundational* enterprise.[†] What the positive sciences needed to complete them, on this view, was a rigorous discipline that could check the credentials of all truth claims. An alleged science could only be valid if its findings met this test; otherwise it rested on sand. Epistemology would ultimately make clear just what made knowledge claims valid, and what ultimate degree of validity they could lay claim to. (And, of course, one could come up with a rather pessimistic, skeptical answer to the latter question. Epistemology was not necessarily a rationalist enterprise. Indeed, its last great defenders were and are empiricists.)

In practice, of course, epistemologists took their cue from what they identified as the successful sciences of their day, all the way from Descartes's infatuation with mathematics to the contemporary vogue for reduction to physics. But the actual foundational science was not supposed itself to be dependent on any of the empirical sciences, and this obviously on pain of a circularity that would sacrifice its foundational character. Arguments about the source of valid knowledge claims were not supposed to be empirical.

If we follow this description, then it is clear what overcoming epistemology has to mean. It will mean abandoning foundationalism. On this view, Quine would figure

---

*K. Popper, *Logik der Forschung* (Vienna, 1935).
**C.f., e.g., *The Open Society and Its Enemies* (Princeton, NJ, 1950).
***Princeton, 1979.
†Rorty, chap. 3, p. 132.

among the prominent leaders of this new philosophical turn, since he proposes to "naturalize" epistemology, that is, deprive it of its a priori status and consider it as one science among others, one of many mutually interacting departments of our picture of the world.* And so Rorty does seem to consider him, albeit with some reservations.**

But there is a wider conception of the epistemological tradition, from whose viewpoint this last would be a rather grotesque judgment. This is the interpretation that focuses not so much on foundationalism as on the understanding of knowledge that made it possible. If I had to sum up this understanding in a single formula, it would be that knowledge is to be seen as correct representation of an independent reality. In its original form it saw knowledge as the inner depiction of an outer reality.***

The reason why some thinkers prefer to focus on this interpretation, rather than merely on the foundationalist ambitions that are ultimately (as Quine has shown) detachable from it, is that it is bound up with very influential and often not fully articulated notions about science and about the nature of human agency. Through these it connects with certain central moral and spiritual ideas of the modern age. If one's aim is, in challenging the primacy of epistemology, to challenge these latter as well, then one has to take it up in this wider—or deeper—focus, and not simply show the vanity of the foundational enterprise.

1. I'd like now to try to trace some of these connections. One of them is very evident: the link between this representational conception and the new, mechanistic science of the seventeenth century. This is, in fact, twofold. On one side, the mechanization of the world picture undermined the previously dominant understanding of knowledge and thus paved the way for the modern view. The most important traditional view was that of Aristotle, according to which when we come to know something, the mind ⟨nous⟩ becomes one with the object of thought.† Of course, this is not to say that they become materially the same thing; rather, the idea is that they are informed by the same ⟨eidos⟩.†† Here was a conception quite different from the representational model, even though some of the things Aristotle said could be construed as supporting this latter. The basic bent of Aristotle's model could much better be described as participational: being informed by the same ⟨eidos⟩, the mind participated in the being of the known object, rather than simply depicting it.

But this theory totally depends on the philosophy of forms. Once one no longer explains the way things are in terms of the species that inform them, this conception of knowledge is untenable and rapidly becomes close to unintelligible. We have great difficulty in understanding it today. The representational view can easily then appear as the only available alternative.

---

*"Epistemology Naturalized," in *Ontological Relativity and other Essays* (New York, 1969), pp. 69–90.

**Rorty, chap. 4, pp. 173ff [reprinted in this volume, pp. 376 ff].

***Cf. Descartes's statement in his letter to Gibieuf of 19 January 1642, where he declares himself "assured that I can have any knowledge of what is outside me, [that] by the mediation [of] key ideas that I have had in me." [Taylor gives this in French.] The notion that the modern epistemological tradition is basically dominated by this understanding of representation was pioneered by Heidegger in his *"Die Zeit des Weltbildes,"* ["The Time of the World Picture"] in *Holzwege* (Frankfurt, 1972), pp. 69–104; and the transition from the earlier view is brilliantly described by Foucault in the opening chapters of his *Les Mots et les choses* (Paris, 1966) [translated as *The Order of Things: An Archeology of the Human Sciences* (New York: Pantheon, 1971)].

†Cf., e.g., *De Anima* III, 430a20, also 431a1 and 431b20–23.

††Cf., e.g., *De Anima* III, 430a9 and 431b32.

This is the negative connection between mechanism and modern epistemology. The positive one obtrudes as soon as we attempt to explain our knowing activity itself in mechanistic terms. The key to this is obviously perception, and if we see this as another process in a mechanistic universe, we cannot but construe it as involving as a crucial component the passive reception of impressions from the external world. Knowledge then hangs on a certain relation holding between what is "out there" and certain inner states that this external reality causes in us. This construal, valid for Locke, applies just as much to the latest AI-inspired models of thinking. It is one of the mainsprings of the epistemological tradition.

The epistemological construal is, then, an understanding of knowledge that fits well with modern mechanistic science. This is one of its great strengths, and certainly this connection contributes to the present vogue of computer-based models of the mind. But that's not all this construal has going for it. It is in fact heavily overdetermined. For the representational view was also powered by the new ideals of science, and new conceptions of the excellences of thought, that arose at the same time.

This connection was central to Descartes's philosophy. It was one of his leading ideas that science, or real knowledge, does not just consist of a congruence between ideas in the mind and the reality outside. If the object of my musings happens to coincide with real events in the world, this doesn't give me *knowledge* of them. This congruence has to come about through a reliable method, generating well-founded confidence. Science requires certainty, and this can only be based on that undeniable clarity which Descartes called *évidence*. "Every science is a certain and evident knowledge,"* runs the opening sentence of the second of the *Rules for the Direction of the Mind.*

Now certainty is something that the mind has to generate for itself. It requires a reflexive turn, where instead of simply trusting the opinions one has acquired through one's upbringing, one examines their foundation, which is ultimately to be found in one's own mind. Of course, the theme that the sage has to turn away from merely current opinion and make a more rigorous examination that leads him to science, is a very old one, going back at least to Socrates and Plato. But what is different with Descartes is the reflexive nature of this turn. The seeker after science is not directed away from shifting and uncertain opinion toward the order of the unchanging, as with Plato, but rather within, to the contents of his own mind. These have to be carefully distinguished both from external reality and from their illusory localizations in the body, so that then the correct issue of science, that is, of certainty, can be posed—the issue of the correspondence of idea to reality, which Descartes raises and then disposes of through the supposition of the *malin génie* [evil genius] and the proof of his negation, the veracious God.

The confidence that underlies this whole operation is that certainty is something the thinker can generate for himself, by ordering his thoughts correctly—according to clear and distinct connections. This confidence is in a sense independent of the positive outcome of Descartes's argument to the existence of a veracious God, the guarantor of our science. The very fact of reflexive clarity is bound to improve our epistemic position, as long as knowledge is understood representationally. Even if we couldn't prove that the *malin génie* doesn't exist, Descartes would still be in a better position than the rest of us unreflecting minds, because he would have measured the full degree of uncertainty that hangs over all our beliefs about the world, and clearly separated off from these our undeniable belief in ourselves.

*[Taylor gives this text in French.]

Descartes is thus the originator of the modern notion that certainty is the child of reflexive clarity, or the examination of our own ideas in abstraction from what they "represent," which has exercised a powerful influence on Western culture, way beyond those who share his confidence in the power of argument to prove strong theses about external reality. Locke and Hume follow in the same path, although the latter goes about as far in the direction of skepticism as any modern has. Still, it remains true for Hume that we purge ourselves of our false confidence in our too-hasty extrapolations by focusing attention on their origin in our ideas. It is *there* that we see, for instance, that our beliefs in causation are based on nothing more than constant conjunction, that the self is nothing but a bundle of impressions, and so on.

This reflexive turn, which first took form in the seventeenth- and eighteenth-century "way of ideas," is of course indissolubly linked to modern representational epistemology. One might say it presupposes this construal of knowledge. If Plato or Aristotle were right, the road to certainty couldn't be inward—indeed, the very notion of certainty would be different: defined more in terms of the kinds of being that admit of it, rather than by the ordering of our thoughts. But I believe that there is also a motivational connection in the *other* direction: the ideal of self-given certainty is a strong incentive to construe knowledge in such a way that our thought about the real can be distinguished from its objects and examined on its own. And this incentive has long outlived the original way of ideas. Even in an age when we no longer want to talk of Lockean "ideas" or of "sense data," where the representational view is reconstrued in terms of linguistic representations or bodily states (and these are perhaps not genuine alternatives), there is still a strong draw toward distinguishing and mapping the formal operations of our thinking. In certain circles it would seem that an almost boundless confidence is placed in the defining of formal relations as a way of achieving clarity and certainty about our thinking, be it in the (mis)application of rational choice theory to ethical problems or in the great popularity of computer models of the mind, which I referred to earlier.

This latter is an excellent example of what I called above the "over-determination" of the epistemological construal. The plausibility of the computer as a model of thinking comes partly from the fact that it is a machine, hence living "proof" that materialism can accommodate explanations in terms of intelligent performance; but partly too from the widespread faith that our intelligent performances are ultimately to be understood in terms of formal operations. The computer, it can be said, is a "syntactic engine."* A great controversy rages over precisely this point. The most perspicuous critics of the runaway enthusiasm with the computer model, such as Hubert Dreyfus,** tirelessly point out how implausible it is to understand certain of our intelligent performances in terms of a formal calculus, including our most common everyday ones, such as making our way around our rooms, streets, and gardens, picking up and manipulating the objects we use, and so on. But the great difficulties that computer simulations have encountered in this area don't seem to have dimmed the enthusiasm of real believers in this model. It is as though they had been vouchsafed some certain revelation a priori that it *must* all be done by formal calculi. Now this "revelation," I submit,

---

*Daniel Dennett coined the term "semantic engine" to describe the computer in "Three Kinds of Intentional Psychology," in R.A. Healey, ed., *Reduction, Time and Reality* (Cambridge, 1981). But it can, of course, only deserve this description because its functioning first of all matches certain formal operations, which are then understood as *interpreted* in some way. Cf. the discussion in John Haugeland's "Semantic Engines," the introduction to a volume he edited, entitled *Mind Design* (Cambridge, MA, 1981).

***What Computers Can't Do*, second ed. (New York, 1979).

comes from the depths of our modern culture and the epistemological model that is anchored in it, whose strength is based not just on its affinity to mechanistic science but also on its congruence to the powerful ideal of reflexive, self-given certainty.

For this has to be understood as something like a moral ideal. The power of this ideal can be sensed in the following passage from Husserl's *Cartesian Meditations*, all the more significant in that Husserl had already broken with some of the main theses of the epistemological tradition. Husserl asks in the first meditation whether the *"Trostlosigkeit"* ["despair"; "hopelessness"] of our present philosophical predicament doesn't spring from our having abandoned Descartes's original "spirit of radical philosophical self-responsibility." And he continues:

> Should the supposedly exaggerated demand for a finally possible [and] disengaged philosophy of presuppositionlessness [or impartiality] not, on the contrary, belong rather to a philosophy that in the deepest sense shapes itself in real autonomy out of finally self-produced evidences and, so, is thereby absolutely self-responsible?*

This ideal of "self-responsibility" is foundational to modern culture. It emerges not only in our picture of the growth of modern science as the fruit of the heroism of the great scientist, standing out against the opinion of his age on the basis of his own self-responsible certainty—Copernicus, Galileo (he wobbled a bit before the Holy Office, but who can blame him?), Darwin, Freud. It is also closely linked to the modern ideal of freedom as self-autonomy, as the passage from Husserl implies. To be free in our modern sense is to be self-responsible, to rely on one's own judgment, to find one's purpose in oneself.

And so the epistemological tradition is also intricated in a certain notion of freedom, and the dignity attaching to us in virtue of this. The theory of knowledge partly draws its strength from this connection. But also reciprocally, the ideal of freedom has drawn strength from its sensed connection with the construal of knowledge seemingly favored by modern science. From this point of view it has been fateful that this notion of freedom has been interpreted as involving certain key theses about the nature of the human agent; we might call them anthropological beliefs. Whether these are in fact inseparable from the modern aspiration to autonomy is an open question, and a very important one, to which I will return briefly below. But the three connected notions that I would like to mention here are in fact historically closely connected with the epistemological construal.

The first is the picture of the subject as ideally disengaged, that is, as free and rational to the extent that he has fully distinguished himself from his natural and social worlds, so that his identity is no longer to be defined in terms of what lies outside him in these worlds. The second, which flows from this, is a punctual view of the self, ideally ready qua free and rational to treat these worlds—and even some of the features of his own character—instrumentally, as subject to change and reordering in order the better to secure the welfare of himself and other like subjects. The third is the social consequence of the first two: an atomistic construal of society as constituted by, or ultimately to be explained in terms of, individual purposes.

The first notion emerges originally in classical dualism, where the subject withdraws even from his own body, which he is able to look on as an object; but it continues beyond the demise of this dualism in the contemporary demand for a neutral,

---

Cartesianische Meditationen (The Hague, 1950), p. 47. [Taylor gives this text in German.]

objectifying science of human life and action. The second originates in the ideals of the government and reform of the self that have such an important place in the seventeenth century and of which Locke develops an influential version;* it continues today in the tremendous force that instrumental reason and engineering models have in our social policy, medicine, psychiatry, politics, and so on. The third first takes shape in seventeenth-century social contract theories, but continues not only in their contemporary successors but also in many of the assumptions of contemporary liberalism and mainstream social science.

One does not need to unpack these ideas any further to see that the epistemological tradition is connected with some of the most important moral and spiritual ideas of our civilization—and also with some of the most controversial and questionable. To challenge these is sooner or later to run up against the force of this tradition, which stands with them in a complex relation of mutual support. Overcoming or criticizing these ideas involves coming to grips with epistemology. But this means taking it in what I identified as its broad focus, the whole representational construal of knowledge, not just as the faith in foundationalism.

2. When we turn to the famous, now classic critiques of epistemology, we find that they have, in fact, mostly been attuned to this interpenetration of the scientific and the moral. Hegel, in his celebrated attack on this tradition in the introduction to the *Phenomenology of Spirit,* speaks of a "fear of error" that "reveals itself rather as fear of the truth,"** and he goes on to show how this stance is bound up with a certain aspiration to individuality and separatedness, refusing what he sees as the "truth" of subject-object identity. Heidegger notoriously treats the rise of the modern epistemological standpoint as a stage in the development of a stance of domination to the world, which culminates in contemporary technological society. Merleau-Ponty draws more explicitly political connections and clarifies the alternative notion of freedom that arises from the critique of empiricism and intellectualism.*** The moral consequences of the devastating critique of epistemology in the later Wittgenstein are, naturally, less evident. Wittgenstein was strongly averse to making this kind of thing explicit. But those who have followed him have shown a certain affinity for the critique of disengagement, instrumental reason, and atomism.

It is safe to say that all these critics were largely motivated by a dislike of the moral and spiritual consequences of epistemology and by a strong affinity for some alternative. Indeed, the connection between the scientific and the moral is generally made more evident in their work than in that of mainstream supporters of the epistemological standpoint. But an important feature of all these critiques is that they establish a new moral outlook *through* overturning the modern conception of knowledge. They do not just register their dissidence from the anthropological beliefs associated with this conception, but show the foundations of these beliefs to be unsound, based as they are in an untenable construal of knowledge.

All four of the authors I have mentioned—whom I take to be the most important and influential critics of epistemology, the founders of the most influential forms of critique—offer new construals of knowledge. Moreover, in spite of the great differences, all four share a common basic form of argument, which finds its origins in Kant, and which one might call "the argument from transcendental conditions."

---

*Cf. the penetrating analysis of James Tully, in his "Governing Conduct," in E. Leites, ed., *Conscience and Casuistry in Early Modern Europe* (Cambridge, 1986).
**Miller translation (Oxford, 1977), p. 47.
***Cf. *La Phenomenologie de la perception* (Paris, 1945), part 3, chap. 3.

By this I mean something like the following: We argue the inadequacy of the epistemological construal, and the necessity of a new conception, from what we show to be the indispensable conditions of there being anything like experience or awareness of the world in the first place. Just how to characterize this latter reality, whose conditions we are defining, can itself be a problem, of course. Kant speaks of it simply as "experience"; but Heidegger, with his concern to get beyond subjectivistic formulations, ends up talking about the "clearing" *[Lichtung]*. Where the Kantian expression focuses on the mind of the subject and the conditions of his having what we can call experience, the Heideggerian formulation points us rather toward another facet of this same phenomenon, the fact that anything *appears,* or comes to light at all. This of course requires that there be a being *to* whom it appears, *for* whom it is an object; it requires a knower, in some sense. But the *Lichtung* formulation focuses us rather on the fact (which we are meant to come to perceive as astonishing) that the knower-known complex is at all, rather than taking the knower for granted as "subject" and examining what makes it possible for him to have knowledge or experience of a world.*

For all this extremely important shift in the center of gravity of what we take as the starting point, there is a continuity between Kant and Heidegger, Wittgenstein, or Merleau-Ponty. They start from the intuition that this central phenomenon of experience, or the clearing, is not made intelligible on the epistemological construal, in either its empiricist or rationalist variants. These offer an account of the stages of the knower that consists of an ultimately incoherent amalgam of two features: (*a*) these states (the ideas) are self-enclosed, in the sense that they can be accurately identified and described in abstraction from the "outside" world (this is, of course, essential to the whole rationalist thrust of reflexive testing of the grounds of knowledge); and (*b*) they nevertheless point toward and represent things in that outside world.

The incoherence of this combination may be hidden from us by the existence of things that seem to have *a,* such as certain sensations, and even of states that seem to combine *a* and *b,* such as stable illusions. But what clearly emerges out of the whole argument of the last couple of centuries is that the condition of states of ourselves having *b* is that they cannot satisfy *a.* This already began to be evident with classical empiricism in its uncertain shuffling between two definitions of the "idea" or "impression": on one reading, it was simply a content of the mind, an inner quasi-object; it called for an object-description; on another, it had to be a *claim* about how things stood; it could only be captured in a *that*-clause.

Feature *b* is what later came to be called in the Brentano-Husserl tradition "intentionality"; our ideas are essentially "of" or "about" something. Here is another way of characterizing a central condition of experience or the clearing. What Kant calls "transcendental" conditions are conditions of intentionality, and the lines of argument that descend from Kant can be seen as exploring what these have to be.**

---

*It is in terms of this notion of the clearing, I believe, that one has to interpret Heidegger's famous invocation of the Leibnizian question: *"Warum ist überhaupt Seiendes und nicht vielmehr Nichts?"* ["Why is there Being at all and not, rather, nothing?"] *Einführung in die Metaphysik* (Tubingen, 1966), p. 1.

**In a sense, this question becomes an inevitable one in the modern age. As long as the Platonic or Aristotelian construals were dominant, the question couldn't arise. The universe itself was shaped by *eidē,* which were in a sense self-revealing. The clearing, to use Heidegger's word, was grounded in the nature of the beings known. Once this answer no longer becomes available, the question, What are the bases of intentionality? is ready to be asked. It takes an insensitivity, which is largely generated and legitimated by the epistemological tradition, to avoid raising it.

Kant already showed that the atomistic understanding of knowledge that Hume espoused was untenable in the light of these conditions. If our states were to count as experience of an objective reality, they had to be bound together to form a coherent whole, or bound together by rules, as Kant conceived it. However much this formulation may be challenged, the incoherence of the Humean picture, which made the basis of all knowledge the reception of raw, atomic, uninterpreted data, was brilliantly demonstrated. How did Kant show this? He established in fact an argument form that has been used by his successors ever since. It can be seen as a kind of appeal to intuition. In the case of this particular refutation of Hume (which is, I believe, the main theme of the Transcendental Deduction in the first edition of the *Critique of Pure Reason*), he makes us aware, first, that we wouldn't have what we recognize as experience at all unless it were construable as of an object (I take this as a kind of proto-thesis of intentionality), and second, that their being of an object entails a certain relatedness among our "representations." Without this, Kant says, "it would be possible for appearances to crowd in upon the soul, and yet to be such as would never allow of experience." Our perceptions "would not then belong to any experience, consequently would be without an object, merely a blind play of representations, less even than a dream."*

I think this kind of appeal to intuition is better understood as an appeal to what I want to call our "agent's knowledge." As those effectively engaged in the activities of getting to perceive and know the world, we are capable of identifying certain conditions without which our activity would fall apart into incoherence. The philosophical achievement is to define the issues properly. Once this is done, as Kant does so brilliantly in relation to Humean empiricism, we find there is only one rational answer. Plainly we couldn't have experience of the world at all if we had to start with a swirl of uninterpreted data. Indeed, these wouldn't even be "data," because even this minimal description depends on our distinguishing what is "given" by some objective source from what we merely supply ourselves.**

Now the four authors I have mentioned push this argument form farther, and explore conditions of intentionality that require a more fundamental break with the epistemological tradition. And in particular, they push it far enough to undermine the anthropological beliefs I described in the previous section: beliefs in the disengaged subject, the punctual self, and described atomism.

The arguments of Heidegger and Merleau-Ponty put paid to the first. Heidegger, for instance, shows—especially in his celebrated analysis of being-in-the-world—that the condition of our forming disengaged representations of reality is that we be already engaged in coping with our world, dealing with the things in it, at grips with them.*** Disengaged description is one special possibility, realizable only intermittently, of a being (which Heidegger calls *Dasein*) who is always "in" the world in another way, as an agent engaged in realizing a certain form of life. That is what we are about "first and mostly" (*zunächst und zumeist*).

The tremendous contribution of Heidegger, like that of Kant, consists in having focused the issue properly. Once this is done, we cannot deny the picture that emerges.

---

*Critique of Pure Reason, A111, 112.

**I have discussed this argument form at greater length in "The Validity of Transcendental Arguments" in the *Proceedings of the Aristotelian Society* 79 (1978–1979), pp. 151–165.

***Being and Time, division I, chaps. 2 and 3A.

It becomes evident that even in our theoretical stance to the world we are agents. Even to find out about the world and formulate disinterested pictures, we have to come to grips with it, experiment, set ourselves to observe, control conditions. But in all this, which forms the indispensable basis of theory, we are engaged as agents coping with things. It is clear that we couldn't form disinterested representations any other way.

But once one takes this point, then the entire epistemological position is undermined. Obviously foundationalism goes, since our representations of things—the kinds of objects we pick out as whole, enduring entities, for instance—are grounded in the way we deal with these things. These dealings are largely inarticulate, and the project of articulating them fully is an essentially incoherent one, just because any articulative project would itself rely on a background or horizon of nonexplicit engagement with the world.

But the argument here cuts deeper. Foundationalism is undermined, because you can't go on digging under our ordinary representations to uncover further, more basic representations. What you get underlying our representations of the world—the kinds of things we formulate, for instance, in declarative sentences—is not further representations but rather a certain grasp of the world that we have as agents in it. This shows the whole epistemological construal of knowledge to be mistaken. It doesn't just consist of inner pictures of outer reality, but grounds in something quite other. And in this "foundation" the crucial move of the epistemological construal, distinguishing states of the subject—our "ideas"—from features of the external world, can't be effected. We can draw a neat line between my *picture* of an object and that object, but not between my *dealing* with the object and that object. It may make sense to ask one to focus on what one *believes* about something, say a football, even in the absence of that thing; but when it comes to *playing* football, the corresponding suggestion would be absurd. The actions involved in the game cannot be done without the object; they include the object. Take it away and we have something quite different—people miming a match on the stage, perhaps. The notion that our understanding of the world is grounded in our dealings with it is equivalent to the thesis that this understanding is not ultimately based on representations at all, in the sense of depictions that are separately identifiable from what they are of.*

Heidegger's reflections take us entirely outside the epistemological construal. Our reflections on the conditions of intentionality show that these include our being "first and mostly" agents in the world. But then this also ruins the conception of the agent as one whose ideal could be total disengagement. This turns out to be an impossibility, one that it would be destructive to attempt. We cannot turn the background from which we think into an object for us. The task of reason has to be conceived quite differently: as that of articulating this background, "disclosing" what it involves. This may open the way to detaching ourselves from or altering part of what has constituted it—may, indeed, make such alteration irresistible; but only through our unquestioning reliance on the rest.

---

*Of course, a proponent of a computer-based model of human performance would contest this latter claim and try to explain our skilled performances on the football field in terms of some computation on hits of informational input, which have the same role as the representations of the classical theory. But this would be in fact to challenge the grounding of our understanding in our dealings with things. It is to say rather that this order of grounding is merely apparent, merely how things look in experience, whereas the real order is the reverse: skilled performance is based on computation over explicit representations—albeit on an unconscious level. This can't be ruled out by an a priori argument, of course; but its implausibility has been well shown in H. Dreyfus, *What Computers Can't Do.*

And just as the notion of the agent underpinning the ideal of disengagement is rendered impossible, so is the punctual notion of the self. Heidegger and Merleau-Ponty both show how the inescapability of the background involves an understanding of the depth of the agent, but they do so by exploring the conditions of intentionality in complementary directions. Heidegger shows how *Dasein*'s world is defined by the related purposes of a certain way of life shared with others. Merleau-Ponty shows how our agency is essentially embodied and how this lived body is the locus of directions of action and desire that we never fully grasp or control by personal decision.

This critique also puts in question the third anthropological belief I singled out above, that in atomism. I have just mentioned how Heidegger's notion of *Dasein*'s way of life is essentially that of a collectivity. A general feature of all the paradigm-setting critiques I am discussing here is that they strongly reject this third view and show rather the priority of society as the locus of the individual's identity. But crucially this point is made through an exploration of the role of language. The new theory of language that arises at the end of the eighteenth century, most notably in the work of Herder and Humboldt, not only gives a new account of how language is essential to human thought, but also places the capacity to speak not simply in the individual but primarily in the speech community.* This totally upsets the outlook of the mainstream epistemological tradition. Now arguments to this effect have formed part of the refutation of the atomism that has proceeded via an overturning of standard modern epistemology.

Important examples of arguments of this kind are Hegel's in the first chapter of the *Phenomenology of Spirit,* against the position that he defines as "sensible certainty," where he shows both the indispensability of language and its holistic character;** and Wittgenstein's famous demonstrations of the uselessness of private ostensive definitions, by making plain the crucial role played by language in identifying the object and the impossibility of a purely private language.*** Both of these are, I believe, excellent examples of arguments that explore the conditions of intentionality and show their conclusions to be inescapable.

It is evident that these arguments give us a quite different notion of what it is to overcome epistemology from those that merely eschew foundationalism. We can measure the full gulf by comparing any of the four—Heidegger, perhaps, or Merleau-Ponty—with the Quine of "Epistemology Naturalized." It is plain that the essential elements of the epistemological construal have remained standing in Quine, and not surprisingly therefore the central anthropological beliefs of the tradition. Disengagement emerges in his "taste for desert landscapes,"† the punctual self in his behaviorism;†† and atomism seems to inform Quine's particular brand of political conservatism. In face of differences of this magnitude, a question arises concerning what it means exactly to "overcome epistemology."

---

*I have discussed this at greater length in "Language and Human Nature" and "Theories of Meaning," both to be found in my *Human Agency and Language: Philosophical Papers,* Vol. I (Cambridge, 1985).

**Cf. my discussion in "The Opening Arguments of the Phenomenology" in Alasdair MacIntyre, ed., *Hegel: A Collection of Critical Essays* (Notre Dame, 1976).

***Cf. the *Philosophical Investigations* (New York, 1958), 1. 28ff., 1. 258ff.

†Cf. *From a Logical Point of View* (New York, 1955), p. 4.

††Cf. for instance, *Word and Object* (Cambridge, MA, 1960).

3. A picture has been emerging in the previous sections of what this ought to be—a tendentious one, I freely admit. This accepts the wider or deeper definition of the task: overcoming the distorted anthropological beliefs through a critique and correction of the construal of knowledge that is interwoven with them and has done so much to give them undeserved credit. Otherwise put: through a clarification of the conditions of intentionality, coming to a better understanding of what we are as knowing agents—and hence also as language beings—and thereby gaining insight into some of the crucial anthropological questions that underpin our moral and spiritual beliefs.

For all its radical break with the tradition, this kind of philosophy would in one respect be in continuity with it. It would be carrying further the demand for self-clarity about our nature as knowing agents, by adopting a better and more critically defensible notion of what this entails. Instead of searching for an impossible foundational justification of knowledge or hoping to achieve total reflexive clarity about the bases of our beliefs, we would now conceive this self-understanding as awareness about the limits and conditions of our knowing, an awareness that would help us to overcome the illusions of disengagement and atomic individuality that are constantly being generated by a civilization founded on mobility and instrumental reason.

We could understand this as carrying the project of modern reason, even of "self-responsible" reason, farther by giving it a new meaning. This is how Husserl, for instance, conceived the critical project in his last great lectures on the "crisis of the European sciences," given in Vienna in 1935. Husserl thinks of us as struggling to realize a fundamental task, that of the *"europäischen Geist"* ["European spirit"], whose goal is to achieve the fullness of reflexive clarity. We should see ourselves as *"Funktionäre der neuzeitlichen philosophischen Menschheit"* ["functionaries of the modern philosophical humanity"]. The *"Urstiftung"* ["primal establishment"] of the European tradition points to an *"Endstiftung"* ["final establishment"], and only in this latter is the goal we have been pursuing (*"Urstiftung"*) fully revealed:

> Only through [the final establishment] can the unified directedness of all philosophies and philosophers open up. From here elucidation can be attained which enables us to understand past thinkers in a way that they could never have understood themselves.*

Husserl's hope here sounds ridiculously overstated; and this may have something to do with his having failed to push through his critique of foundationalism to the very end. This overstatement has played an important role, as we will see below, in casting discredit on the task as I have outlined it. But if we purge Husserl's formulation of the prospect of a "final foundation" where absolute apodicticity would at last be won, if we concentrate merely on the gain for reason in coming to understand what is illusory in the modern epistemological project and in articulating the insights about us that flow from this, then the claim to have taken the modern project of reason a little farther, and to have understood our forbears a little better than they understood themselves, isn't so unbelievable.

---

*Cf. *Die Krisis der europäischen Wissenschaften und die transzendentalen Phänomenologie*, Felix Meiner (Hamburg, 1977), sect. 15, pp. 78, 80. [Taylor gives this text in German. The translation given here comes from The Crisis of European Science and Transcendental Phenomenology: An Introduction to Phenomenological Philosophy, translated by David Carr (Evanston, IL: Northwestern University Press, 1970), p. 73.]

What reflection in this direction would entail is already fairly well known. It involves, first, conceiving reason differently, as including—alongside the familiar forms of the Enlightenment—a new department, whose excellence consists in our being able to articulate the background of our lives perspicuously. We can use the word "disclosure" for this, following Heidegger. And along with this goes a conception of critical reasoning, of especial relevance for moral thinking, that focuses on the nature of transitions in our thought, of which "immanent critique" is only the best-known example.*

In moral thought, what emerges from this critique is a rejection of moralities based purely on instrumental reason, viz., utilitarianism; and also critical distance from those that are based on a punctual notion of the self, such as the various derivations of Kant. The critique of Rawls's theory by Michael Sandel, in the name of a less "thin" theory of the agent, is an excellent example of this.** In social theory, the result is a rejection of atomist theories, of reductive causal theories (such as "vulgar" Marxism or sociobiology), and of theories that cannot accommodate intersubjective meaning.*** Social science is seen as being closer to historiography of a certain kind. In politics, the anti-atomist thrust of the critique makes it hostile to certain forms of contemporary conservatism, but also to radical doctrines of nonsituated freedom.† I believe there is a natural affinity between this critique, with its stress on situated freedom and the roots of our identity in community, on the one hand, and the civic humanist tradition on the other, as the works of a number of writers, from Humboldt to Arendt, testify.††

It might seem from the above as though everything should run on smoothly, toward a set of anthropological conclusions with a certain moral-political hue. But in fact all this is hotly contested, not just by those who wish to defend the epistemological tradition, which would be well understandable, but by those who also consider themselves its critics. Foremost among these are a range of thinkers who have defined themselves in relation to a certain reading of Nietzsche. The most interesting and considerable of them, in my opinion, is Michel Foucault. In keeping with the themes of this paper, we can perhaps get most directly to the basis of their dissent if we go to the moral or spiritual outlook they wish to defend. In the case of Foucault this became relatively clear at the end of his life. He rejected the conception of the punctual self, which could take an instrumental stance toward its life and character—this is indeed what arises out of the practices and "truths" of the disciplinary society, which he painted in such repellent colors (whatever protestations of neutrality accompanied the depiction). But he could not accept the rival notion of a deep or authentic self that arises out of the critical traditions of Hegel and, in another way, Heidegger or Merleau-Ponty. This seemed to him another prison. He rejected both of these in favor of a Nietzschean notion of the self as potentially self-making, the self as a work of art, a central conception of an "aesthetics of existence."§

Something analogous, but on a much more frivolous level, seems to animate some of the "poststructuralist" thinkers—Derrida, for instance. Paradoxically, for all

---

*I have tried to characterize this further in my "Explanation and Practical Reason" (forthcoming).

**Michael Sandel, Liberalism and the Limits of Justice (Cambridge, 1982).

***I have explored this in my "Interpretation and the Sciences of Man," reprinted in my Philosophy and the Human Sciences: Philosophical Papers, Vol. 2 (Cambridge, 1985).

†I have discussed this in my Hegel and Modern Society (Cambridge, 1979), chap. 3.

††Cf. the latter's The Human Condition (Chicago, 1958). I have tried to deal with some of the issues connected with this understanding of politics and modern society in "Legitimation Crisis?" in my Philosophy and the Human Sciences: Philosophical Papers, Vol. 2.

§Cf. the interview published as an appendix in the second edition of Herbert Dreyfus and Paul Rabinow, Michel Foucault: Beyond Structuralism and Hermeneutics (Chicago, 1983).

the talk of the "end of subjectivity," one of the strong attractions of this kind of position is precisely the license it offers to subjectivity, unfettered by anything in the nature of a correct interpretation or an irrecusable meaning of either life or text, to effect its own transformations, to invent meaning. Self-making is again primary.

Nietzsche's insights into the way in which our language imposes order on our world, into theory as a kind of violence, was hence crucial to all views of this kind. It offers an alternative to the kind of possible critique of epistemology in which we discover something deeper and more valid about ourselves in carrying it through—the kind I have been describing. Instead it attacks the very aspiration to truth, as this is usually understood. All epistemic orders are imposed, and the epistemological construal is just another one of those orders. It has no claim to ultimate correctness, not because it has been shown inadequate by an exploration of the conditions of intentionality, but just because all such claims are bogus. They mistake an act of power for a revelation of truth. Husserl's "*Urstiftung*" takes on a quite different and more sinister air.

It is clear that this is the critique of epistemology that is most compatible with the spiritual stance of self-making. It makes the will primary in a radical way: while the critique through the conditions of intentionality purports to show us more of what we really are like—to show us, as it were, something of our deep or authentic nature as selves. So those who take the Nietzschean road are naturally very critical of the understanding of critique as *gain* in reason. They would rather deny that reason can have anything to do here with our choices of what to be.

This is not to say that they propose the end of epistemology as a quite radical break. Just as the critique through conditions of intentionality represents a kind of continuity-through-transformation in the tradition of self-critical reason, so the Nietzschean refusal represents a continuity-through-transformation of another facet of the modern identity—the primacy of the will. This played an important role in the rise of modern science and its associated epistemological standpoint; in a sense a voluntaristic anthropology, with its roots in a voluntaristic theology, prepared the ground over centuries for the seventeenth century revolution, most notably in the form of Nominalism. It is a crucial point of division among moderns, what we think of this primacy of the will. This is one of the issues at stake between these two conceptions of what it means to overcome the epistemological tradition.

Although this represents perhaps the most dramatic opposition among critics of epistemology, it is far from exhausting the field. Jürgen Habermas, for instance, has staked out a position equivalent to neither. Against the neo-Nietzscheans, he wants strongly to defend the tradition of critical reason, but he has his own grounds for distrusting Heideggerian disclosure and wants instead to hold on to a formal understanding of reason, and in consequence a procedural ethic, although purged of the monological errors of earlier variants. He has drawn heavily on the critique of epistemology in the four main authors mentioned above, but fears for the fate of a truly universal and critical ethic should one go all the way with this critique.*

How does one adjudicate this kind of dispute? How does one decide what it really means to overcome epistemology? I cannot hope to decide the issue here, only to

---

*I have discussed the motives and limitations of this kind of procedural ethic in my "Sprache und Gesellschaft" in A. Honneth and H. Joas, eds., *Kommunikatives Handeln: Beiträge zur Habermas' Theorie des kommunikativen Handelns* (Frankfurt, 1986); and in "Justice after Virtue" in M. Benedikt and R. Berger, eds., *Kritische Methode und Zukurzft der Anthropologie* (Vienna, 1985), pp. 23–48.

make a claim as to how it must be settled. In order to define this better, I want to return to the most dramatic dispute, that between the neo-Nietzscheans and the defenders of critical reason.

It seems to me that, whoever is ultimately right, the dispute has to be fought on the terrain of the latter. The Nietzschean position too stands and falls with a certain construal of knowledge: that it is relative to various ultimately imposed "regimes of truth," to use Foucault's expression. This has to show itself to be a superior construal to that which emerges from the exploration of the conditions of intentionality. Does it?

Certainly the Nietzschean conception has brought important insights: no construal is quite innocent, something is always suppressed; and what is more, some interlocutors are always advantaged relative to others, for any language. But the issue is whether this settles the matter of truth between construals. Does this mean that there can be no talk of epistemic gain in passing from one construal to another? That there is such a gain is the claim of those exploring the conditions of intentionality. This claim doesn't stand and fall with a naive, angelic conception of philosophical construals as utterly uninvolved with power. Where is the argument that will show the more radical Nietzschean claim to be true and the thesis of critical reason untenable?

I regret to say that one hears very little serious argument in this domain. Neo-Nietzscheans seem to think that they are dispensed from it since it is already evident, or alternatively, that they are debarred from engaging in it on pain of compromising their position. Derrida and his followers seem to belong to the first category. The main weight of argument is carried here by an utterly caricatural view of the alternative as involving a belief in a kind of total self-transparent clarity, which would make even Hegel blush. The rhetoric deployed around this has the effect of obscuring the possibility that there might be a third alternative to the two rather dotty ones on offer; and as long as you go along with this, the Derridian one seems to win as the least mad, albeit by a hair.

Others try to argue on behalf of Foucault that he couldn't enter the argument concerning construals of knowledge without already abandoning his Nietzschean position, that there is nothing to *argue* between them.* True enough, but then the issue whether there is something to argue itself demands some kind of support. Something can surely be said about that. Indeed, lots *has* been said, by Nietzsche for instance, and some also by Foucault—in talking for instance of "regimes of truth"; the question is, whether it is really persuasive or involves a lot of slippery slides and evasion.**

In short, the arguments for not arguing seriously are uniformly bad. And in fact, Foucault did on one occasion make a serious attempt to engage with the exploration of the conditions of intentionality, and that was in the latter part of *Les Mots et les choses,* where he talks about the invention of Man and the "transcendental-empirical double."*** This was admittedly prior to his last, much more centrally Nietzschean phase, but it can be seen as preparing the ground for this, as indeed Dreyfus and Rabinow see it.†

The arguments here seem to me much more to build on the Heideggerian and Merleau-Pontyan critique against Kant than to be a challenge to this critique. And the

---

*These points are well made by William Connolly in a debate with me about Foucault. See his "Taylor, Foucault and Otherness," *Political Theory* 13, no. 3 (August 1985), pp. 365–376.

**Cf. Connolly, "Taylor, Foucault and Otherness."

***Les Mots et les choses (Paris, 1966), chap. 9.

†Herbert Dreyfus and Paul Rabinow, *Michel Foucault: Beyond Structuralism and Hermeneutics* (Chicago, 1982), chap. 2.

arguments, if valid, would have the consequence that nothing coherent could be said at all about the conditions of intentionality. I can't see how this could fail to undercut the Nietzschean view as well. In *Les Mols et les choses,* Foucault takes refuge in a species of structuralism, which is meant to avoid this question altogether. But he abandons this soon afterwards; and we are left uncertain where this argument is meant to take us. In general among neo-Nietzscheans, however, an atmosphere reigns in which this issue is felt as already settled. We are exhorted by Lyotard not to take metanarratives seriously any more, but the argument for this seems to rely on something of a caricature.*

  If I am right, the issue is far from settled. And yet at stake in this struggle over the corpse of epistemology are some of the most important spiritual issues of our time. The question, what it is to overcome epistemology, turns out to be of more than just historical interest.

  La Condition postmoderne (Paris, 1979), p. 7 [translated as *The Postmodern Condition: A Report on Knowledge* (Minneapolis: University of Minnesota Press, 1984)]. The "postmodern," according to Lyotard, is characterized by *"l'incrédulité à l'égard des métarécits"* ["incredulity in regard to the metastory"].